Computer Architecture and Organization

McGraw-Hill Series in Computer Organization and Architecture

McGraw-Hill Series in Computer Engineering

SENIOR CONSULTING EDITORS

Stephen W. Director, University of Michigan, Ann Arbor

C.L. Liu, University of Illinois, Urbana-Champaign

Bartee: *Computer Architecture and Logic Design*

Bose, Liang: *Neural Network Fundamentals with Graphs, Algorithms, and Applications*

Chang and Sze: *ULSI Technology*

De Micheli: *Synthesis and Optimization of Digital Circuits*

Feldman and Retter: *Computer Architecture: A Designer's Text Based on a Generic RISC*

Hamacher, Vranesic, and Zaky: *Computer Organization*

Hayes: *Computer Architecture and Organization*

Horvath: *Introduction to Microprocessors Using the MC6809 or the MC68000*

Hwang: *Advanced Computer Architecture: Parallelism, Scalability, Programmability*

Hwang: *Scalable Parallel and Cluster Computing: Architecture and Programming*

Kang and Leblebici: *CMOS Digital Integrated Circuits: Analysis and Design*

Kohavi: *Switching and Finite Automata Theory*

Krishna and Shin: *Real-Time Systems*

Lawrence-Mauch: *Real-Time Microcomputer System Design: An Introduction*

Levine: *Vision in Man and Machine*

Navabi: *VHDL: Analysis and Modeling of Digital Systems*

Peatman: *Design with Microcontrollers*

Peatman: *Digital Hardware Design*

Rosen: *Discrete Mathematics and Its Applications*

Ross: *Fuzzy Logic with Engineering Applications*

Sandige: *Modern Digital Design*

Sarrafzadeh and Wong: *An Introduction to VLSI Physical Design*

Schalkoff: *Artificial Neural Networks*

Stadler: *Analytical Robotics and Mechatronics*

Sze: *VLSI Technology*

Taub: *Digital Circuits and Microprocessors*

Wear, Pinkert, Wear, and Lane: *Computers: An Introduction to Hardware and Software Design*

Computer Architecture and Organization

THIRD EDITION

John P. Hayes
University of Michigan

WCB
McGraw-Hill

Boston   Burr Ridge, IL   Dubuque, IA   Madison, WI   New York   San Francisco   St. Louis
Bangkok   Bogotá   Caracas   Lisbon   London   Madrid
Mexico City   Milan   New Delhi   Seoul   Singapore   Sydney   Taipei   Toronto

WCB
McGraw-Hill

WCB/McGraw-Hill
A Division of the McGraw-Hill Companies

COMPUTER ARCHITECTURE AND ORGANIZATION

This book is printed on acid-free paper.

1 2 3 4 5 6 7 8 9 0 DOC/DOC 9 0 9 8 7

ISBN 0-07-027355-3

Vice president and editorial director: *Kevin T. Kane*
Publisher: *Tom Casson*
Sponsoring editor: *Lynn Cox*
Developmental editor: *Bradley Kosirog*
Marketing manager: *John T. Wannemacher*
Project manager: *Pat Frederickson*
Production supervisor: *Madelyn Underwood*
Designer: *Michael Warrell*
Compositor: *Publication Services, Inc.*
Typeface: *10/12 Times Roman*
Printer: *R. R. Donnelley & Sons Company*

Library of Congress Cataloging-in-Publication Data

Hayes, John P. (John Patrick) (date)
    Computer architecture and organization / John P. Hayes. -- 3rd ed.
        p.   cm. -- (Electrical and computer engineering)
    Includes bibliographical references and index.
    ISBN 0-07-027355-3
    1. Computer architecture.   2. Electronic digital computers--Design and construction.   I. Title.   II. Series: McGraw-Hill series in electrical and computer engineering.
    QA76.9.A73H39   1998
    621.39'2--dc21   97-45598
http://www.mhhe.com

ABOUT THE AUTHOR

JOHN P. HAYES is a professor in the electrical engineering and computer science department at the University of Michigan, where he was the founding director of the Advanced Computer Architecture Laboratory. He teaches and conducts research in the areas of computer architecture; computer-aided design, verification, and testing; VLSI design; and fault-tolerant systems. Dr. Hayes is the author of two patents, more than 150 technical papers, and five books, including *Layout Minimization for CMOS Cells* (Kluwer, 1992, coauthored with R. L. Maziasz) and *Introduction to Digital Logic Design* (Addison-Wesley, 1993). He has served as editor of various journals, including the *IEEE Transactions on Parallel and Distributed Systems* and the *Journal of Electronic Testing,* and was technical program chairman of the 1991 International Computer Architecture Symposium, Toronto.

Dr. Hayes received his undergraduate degree from the National University of Ireland, Dublin, and his M.S. and Ph.D. degrees in electrical engineering from the University of Illinois, Urbana-Champaign. Prior to joining the University of Michigan, he was a faculty member at the University of Southern California. Dr. Hayes has also held visiting positions at various academic and industrial organizations, including Stanford University, McGill University, Université de Montréal, and Logic-Vision Inc. He is a fellow of the Institute of Electrical and Electronics Engineers and a member of the Association for Computing Machinery and Sigma Xi.

To My Father
Patrick J. Hayes
(1910–1968)
In Memoriam

CONTENTS

PREFACE

This book is about the design of computers; it covers both their overall design, or architecture, and their internal details, or organization. It aims to provide a comprehensive and self-contained view of computer design at an introductory level, primarily from a hardware viewpoint. The third edition of *Computer Architecture and Organization* is intended as a text for computer science, computer engineering, and electrical engineering courses at the undergraduate or beginning graduate levels; it should also be useful for self-study. This text assumes little in the way of prerequisites beyond some familiarity with computer programming, binary numbers, and digital logic. Like the previous editions, the book focuses on basic principles but has been thoroughly updated and has substantially more coverage of performance-related issues.

The book is divided into seven chapters. Chapter 1 discusses the nature and limitations of computation. This chapter surveys the historical evolution of computer design to introduce and motivate the key ideas encountered later. Chapter 2 deals with computer design methodology and examines the two major computer design levels, the register (or register transfer) and processor levels, in detail. It also reviews gate-level logic design and discusses computer-aided design (CAD) and performance evaluation methods. Chapter 3 describes the central processing unit (CPU), or microprocessor that lies at the heart of every computer, focusing on instruction set design and data representation. The next two chapters address CPU design issues: Chapter 4 covers the data-processing part, or datapath, of a processor, while Chapter 5 deals with control-unit design. The principles of arithmetic-logic unit (ALU) design for both fixed-point and floating-point operations are covered in Chapter 4. Both hardwired and microprogrammed control are examined in Chapter 5, along with the design of pipelined and superscalar processors. Chapter 6 deals with a computer's memory subsystem; the chapter discusses the principal memory technologies and their characteristics from a hierarchical viewpoint, with emphasis on cache memories. Finally, Chapter 7 addresses the overall organization of a computer system, including inter- and intrasystem communication, input-output (IO) systems, and parallel processing to achieve very high performance and reliability. Various representative computer systems, such as von Neumann's classic IAS computer, the ARM RISC microprocessor, the Intel Pentium, the Motorola PowerPC, the MIPS RX000, and the Tandem NonStop fault-tolerant multiprocessor, appear as examples throughout the book.

The book has been in use for many years at universities around the world. It contains more than sufficient material for a typical one-semester (15 week) course, allowing the instructor some leeway in choosing the topics to emphasize. Much of the background material in Chapter 1 and the first part of Chapter 2 can be left as a reading assignment, or omitted if the students are suitably prepared. The more advanced material in Chapter 7 can be covered briefly or skipped if desired without loss of continuity. The Instructor's Manual contains some representative course outlines.

This edition updates the contents of the previous edition and responds to the suggestions of its users while retaining the book's time-proven emphasis on basic concepts. The third edition is somewhat shorter than its predecessors, and the material is more accessible to readers who are less familiar with computers. Every section has been rewritten to reflect the dramatic changes that have occurred in the computer industry over the last decade. The main structural changes are the reorganization of the two old chapters on processor design and control design into three chapters: the new Chapters 3, 4, and 5; and the consolidation of the two old chapters on system organization and parallel processing in the new Chapter 7. The treatment of performance-related topics such as pipeline control, cache design, and superscalar architecture has been expanded. Topics that receive less space in this edition include gate-level design, microprogramming, operating systems, and vector processing. The third edition also includes many new examples (case studies) and end-of-chapter problems. There are now more than 300 problems, about 80 percent of which are new to this edition. Course instructors can obtain an Instructor's Manual, which contains solutions to all the problems, directly from the publisher.

The specific changes made in the third edition are as follows: The historical material in Chapter 1 has been streamlined and brought up to date. Gate-level design has been de-emphasized in Chapter 2, while the discussion of performance evaluation has been expanded. A new section on programmable logic devices (PLDs) has been added, and the role of computer-aided design (CAD) has been stressed. The old third chapter (on processor design) has been split into Chapter 3, "Processor Basics," and Chapter 4, "Datapath Design." Chapter 3 contains an expanded treatment of RISC and CISC CPUs and their instruction sets. It introduces the ARM and MIPS RX000 microprocessor series as major examples; the Motorola 680X0 series continues to be used as an example, however. The material on computer arithmetic and ALU design now appears in Chapter 4. The old chapter on control design, which is now Chapter 5, has been completely revised with a more practical treatment of hardwired control and a briefer treatment of microprogramming. A new section on pipeline control includes some material from the old Chapter 7, as well as new material on superscalar processing. Chapter 6 presents an updated treatment of the old fifth chapter on memory organization. Chapter 6 continues to present a systematic, hierarchical view of computer memories but has a greatly expanded treatment of cache memories. Chapter 7, "System Organization," merges material from the old sixth and seventh chapters. The sections on operating systems and parallel processing have been shortened and modernized.

The material for this book has been developed primarily for courses on computer architecture and organization that I have taught over the years, initially at the University of Southern California and later at the University of Michigan. I am grateful to my colleagues and students at these and other schools for their many helpful comments and suggestions.

As always, I owe a special thanks to my wife Terrie for proofreading assistance, as well as her never-failing support and love.

John P. Hayes

CHAPTER 1

Computing and Computers

This chapter provides a broad overview of digital computers while introducing many of the concepts that are covered in depth later. It first examines the nature and limitations of the computing process. Then it briefly traces the historical development of computing machines and ends with a discussion of contemporary VLSI-based computer systems.

1.1
THE NATURE OF COMPUTING

Throughout history humans have relied mainly on their brains to perform calculations; in other words, they were the computers [Boyer 1989]. As civilization advanced, a variety of computing tools were invented that aided, but did not replace, manual computation. The earliest peoples used their fingers, pebbles, or tally sticks for counting purposes. The Latin words *digitus* meaning "finger" and *calculus* meaning "pebble" have given us *digital* and *calculate* and indicate the ancient origins of these computing concepts.

Two early computational aids that were widely used until quite recently are the abacus and the slide rule, both of which are illustrated in Figure 1.1. The abacus has columns of pebblelike beads mounted on rods. The beads are moved by hand to positions that represent numbers. Manipulating the beads according to certain simple rules enables people to count, add, and perform the other basic operations of arithmetic. The slide rule, on the other hand, represents numbers by lengths marked on rulerlike scales that can be moved relative to one another. By adding a length a on a fixed scale to a length b on a second, sliding scale, their combined length $c = a + b$ can be read off the fixed scale. The slide rule's main scales are logarithmic, so that the process of adding two lengths on these scales effectively multiplies two

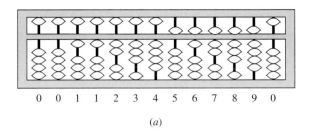

(a)

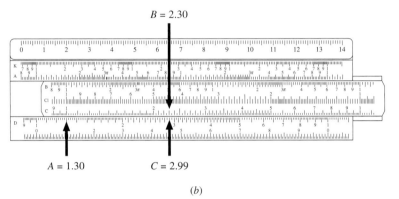

(b)

Figure 1.1
(a) Japanese abacus (*soroban*) displaying the number 0011234567890;
(b) slide rule illustrating the multiplication $1.30 \times 2.30 = 2.99$.

numbers.[1] Slide rules are marked with various other scales that allow an experienced user to evaluate complicated expressions such as $2.15 \times 17.9^{-50} \sin \pi$ in several steps.

As the size and complexity of the calculations being carried out increases, two serious limitations of manual computation become apparent.

- The speed at which a human computer can work is limited. A typical elementary operation such as addition or multiplication takes several seconds or minutes. Problems requiring billions of such operations could never be solved manually in a reasonable period of time or at reasonable cost. Fortunately, modern computers routinely tackle and quickly solve such problems.
- Humans are notoriously prone to error, so long calculations done by hand are unreliable unless elaborate precautions are taken to eliminate mistakes. Most sources of human error (distraction, fatigue, and the like) do not affect machines, so they can provide results that are, within broad limits, free from error.

The English computer pioneer Charles Babbage (1792–1871) often cited the following example to justify construction of his first automatic computing

---

[1]Logarithms are defined by the relation $10^a = A$, where $a = \log_{10} A$. A length marked A on a log scale is proportional to $\log_{10} A = a$. When we add two lengths marked A and B on a slide rule, we are actually adding $a = \log_{10} A$ and $b = \log_{10} B$. Therefore, the result c represents $\log_{10} A + \log_{10} B$. Now $10^a \times 10^b = 10^{a+b}$ implies $c = \log_{10} A + \log_{10} B = \log_{10}(A \times B)$, so if we read c from the first scale, we will obtain the number whose log is c, that is, $A \times B$.

machine, the Difference Engine [Morrison and Morrison 1961]. In 1794 the French
government began a project to compute entirely by hand an enormous set of mathematical tables. Among the many required tables were the logs of the numbers from 1 to 200,000 calculated to 19 decimal places. The entire project took two years to complete and employed about 100 people. The mathematical abilities of most of these human computers were limited to addition and subtraction, and they performed their calculations using pen and paper. A few skilled mathematicians provided the instructions. To minimize errors, each number was calculated independently by two human calculators. The final set of tables occupied 17 large volumes. The log table alone contained about 8 million digits.

1.1.1 The Elements of Computers

Every computer, human or artificial, contains the following components: a processor able to interpret and execute programs; a memory for storing the programs and the data they process; and input-output equipment for transferring information between the computer and the outside world.

The brain versus the computer. Consider the actions involved in a manual calculation using pencil and paper—for example, filling out an income tax return. The purpose of the paper is *information storage*. The information stored can include a list of instructions—more formally called a *program, algorithm,* or *procedure*—to be followed in carrying out the calculation, as well as the numbers or *data* to be used. During the calculation intermediate results and ultimately the final results are recorded on the paper. The data processing takes place in the human brain, which serves as the *(central) processor*. The brain performs two distinct functions: a *control* function that interprets the instructions and ensures that they are performed in the proper sequence and an *execution* function that performs specific steps such as addition, subtraction, multiplication, and division. A pocket calculator often serves as an aid to the brain. Figure 1.2*a* illustrates this view of human computation.

A computer has several key components that roughly correspond to those just mentioned; see Figure 1.2*b*. The *main memory* corresponds to the paper used in the manual calculation. Its purpose is to store instructions and data. The computer's brain is its *central processing unit* (CPU). It contains a *program control unit* (also known as an instruction unit) whose function is to fetch instructions from memory and interpret them. An *arithmetic-logic unit* (ALU), which is part of the CPU's data-processing or execution unit, carries out the instructions. The ALU is so called because many instructions specify either arithmetic (numerical) operations or various forms of nonnumerical operations that loosely correspond to logical reasoning or decision making.

There are important similarities and differences between human beings and artificial computers in the way in which they represent information. In both cases information is usually in *digital* or discrete form. This is contrasted with *analog* or continuous information as used, for example, in the slide rule of Figure 1.1*b*. Distance is a continuous quantity, and on a slide-rule scale it represents, or serves as an analog for, a continuous sequence of numbers. The problem is that such analog quantities have very limited accuracy. The numbers on a slide rule, for example,

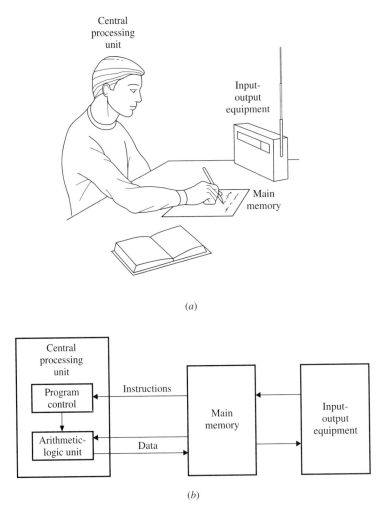

(a)

(b)

Figure 1.2
Main components of (a) human computation and (b) machine computation.

cannot be read to more than three decimal places. On the other hand, a digital device can easily handle a large number of digits. Even the simple abacus of Figure 1.1a can display a number—admittedly just one—to 13 places of accuracy. This advantage of digital data representation over analog is also seen in the higher fidelity of the sound recorded on a compact disc (CD), a digital device, compared to an old-fashioned record (LP), which is an analog device.

Humans employ languages with a wide range of digital symbols, and they usually represent numbers in decimal (base 10) form. It is not practical to build computers to handle symbolic or decimal data directly. Instead, computers process data in binary form, that is, using the two symbols 0 and 1 called *bits* (binary digits). Computers are built from electronic switches that have two natural states: off (0) and on (1). Hence the internal "language" of computers comprises forbidding-looking strings of bits such as 10010011 11011001. To provide communication

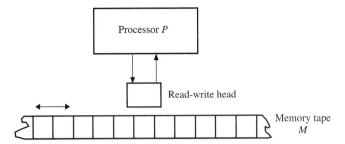

Figure 1.3
A Turing machine.

between a computer and its human users, a means of translating information between human and machine (binary) formats is necessary. The *input-output equipment* shown in Figure 1.2b performs this task.

An abstract computer. We are interested in the computational abilities of general-purpose digital computers. One might raise the following question at the outset: Are there any computations that a "reasonable" computer can never perform? Three notions of reasonableness are widely accepted.

- The computer should not store the answers to all possible problems.
- The computer should only be required to solve problems for which a solution procedure or program can be given.
- The computer should process information at a finite speed.

A reasonable computer can therefore solve a particular problem only if it is supplied with a program that can generate the answer in a finite amount of time.

In the 1930s the English mathematician Alan M. Turing (1912–54) introduced an abstract model of a computer that satisfies all the foregoing criteria [Barwise and Etchemendy 1993]. This model, now called a *Turing machine*, has the structure shown in Figure 1.3. As we noted earlier two essential elements of any computer are a memory and a processor. The memory of a Turing machine is a tape M which resembles that of a tape recorder. Unlike the tape recorder, however, the Turing machine's tape is of unbounded length and is divided lengthwise into squares. Each square can be blank, or it can contain one of a small set of symbols. The Turing machine's processor P is a simple device with a small number of internal configurations or *states*. It is linked to M by a *read-write head* that can read the contents of one square Q and write a new symbol into Q to replace the old one in a single time step. Instead of writing on the tape, the processor can also just read the current symbol and move the tape one square to the left or right of the current square Q.

We can view the Turing machine as having a set of instructions that we will write in the compact, four-part format

$$S_h \quad T_i \quad O_j \quad S_k$$

This instruction is interpreted in the following way: If the present state of the processor P is S_h and the symbol it reads on the square of M under the read-write head is T_i, then perform the action (such as write a new symbol or move the tape) specified by O_j and change the state of P to S_k. Another way of expressing this instruction, which is more in tune with the style of a modern computer programming language, is

if *oldstate* $= S_h$ **and** *input* $= T_i$ **then** *output* $= O_j$ **and** *newstate* $= S_k$;

The output operation indicated by O_j can be any one of the following:

1. $O_j = T_j$, meaning write the symbol T_j on the tape to replace the symbol T_i.
2. $O_j = R$, meaning move the tape so that the read-write head is over the square to the right of the current square. (The tape is moved one square to the left.)
3. $O_j = L$, meaning move the tape so that the read-write head is over the square to the left of the current square. (The tape is moved one square to the right.)
4. $O_j = H$, meaning halt the computation.

The foregoing apparently restricted form of instruction, with just a few different symbols to write on M and a few different states for P, turns out to be sufficient to define programs that can perform all reasonable computations. To determine the value of $Z = F(X)$ via a Turing machine, where F is some function of interest, we proceed as follows: The input data X is placed in a suitably coded form on an otherwise blank tape M. The processor P is supplied with a program that specifies a sequence of steps that are designed to compute F. The Turing machine is then started and executes instruction after instruction, moving the tape M and writing intermediate results on it. Eventually, the Turing machine should halt, and the final result Z should be found on the tape.

EXAMPLE 1.1 A TURING MACHINE TO ADD TWO UNARY NUMBERS. Any natural number n, that is, a positive integer selected from the set we usually write as 0, 1, 2, 3, 4, 5,..., can be written in the *unary* form consisting of a sequence of n 1s. For example, 5 can be written as 11111 and 13 as 1111111111111. When we record numbers using tally or check marks only, we are using a unary notation. (Surprisingly, unary numbers still have a small place in computer design [Poppelbaum et al. 1985].)

We will now show how to program a Turing machine to compute the sum of two unary numbers n_1 and n_2. The tape symbols needed are 1 and b, where b denotes a blank. We start with a blank tape (one containing b in every square) and write the two input numbers in the following format:

$$\ldots b\,b\,\underline{b}\,1\,1\,\ldots\,1\,b\,1\,1\,1\,\ldots\,1\,b\,b\,b\,\ldots$$

$$\underbrace{}_{n_1}\quad\underbrace{}_{n_2}$$

We position the read-write head over the blank square (underlined above) to the left of the left-most 1. Our Turing machine then computes $n_1 + n_2$ by the simple expedient of finding the single blank that separates n_1 and n_2 and replacing it with 1. The machine then finds and deletes the left-most 1 of n_1. The resulting pattern of 1s and bs

$$\ldots b\,b\,\underline{b}\,b\,1\,1\,\ldots\,1\,1\,1\,1\,1\,\ldots\,1\,b\,b\,b\,\ldots$$

$$\underbrace{}_{n_1 + n_2}$$

appearing on the tape is the required answer in the same unary format as the input data. The behavior of a seven-instruction Turing machine that implements this procedure is given with explanatory comments in Figure 1.4. Observe that although the tape M can have an arbitrarily large number of states, the processor P has only the four states S_0, S_1, S_2, and S_3.

Instruction				Comment
S_0	b	R	S_1	Move read-write head one square to right.
S_1	1	R	S_1	Move read-write head rightward across n_1.
S_1	b	1	S_2	Replace blank between n_1 and n_2 by 1.
S_2	1	L	S_2	Move read-write head leftward across n_1.
S_2	b	R	S_3	Blank square reached; move one square to right.
S_3	1	b	S_3	Replace left-most 1 by blank.
S_3	b	H	S_3	Halt; the result $n_1 + n_2$ is now on the tape.

Figure 1.4
Turing machine program to add two unary numbers.

One of Turing's most remarkable achievements was to prove that a *universal* Turing machine (not unlike the above unary adding machine) can by itself perform *every* reasonable computation. A universal Turing machine is essentially a simulator of Turing machines. If given a description of some particular Turing machine *TM*—a program description like that of Figure 1.4 will do—the universal machine simulates all the operations performed by *TM*. A universal Turing machine needs only t different tape symbols and s different processor states, where $ts < 30$, implying that it can have a very small instruction set. Nevertheless, such a machine can perform any reasonable computation. It can therefore do anything that any real computer can do and so serves as an abstract model of the modern general-purpose computer. The universal Turing machine also captures a little of the flavor of reduced instruction set computers (RISCs), which, despite having relatively few instruction types, are among the most powerful computing machines available today.

1.1.2 Limitations of Computers

We turn next to the question of what problems computers can and cannot solve, either in principle or in practice [Barwise and Etchemendy 1993; Cormen and Leiserson 1990; Garey and Johnson 1979].

Unsolvable problems. Problems exist that no Turing machine and therefore no practical computer can solve. There are well-defined problems, some quite famous, for which no solutions or solution procedures are known. An example from pure mathematics is *Goldbach's conjecture,* formulated by the mathematician Christian Goldbach (1690–1764), which states that every even integer greater than 2 is the sum of exactly two prime numbers. For instance, $8 = 3 + 5$ and $108 = 37 + 71$. Goldbach's conjecture has been tested for an enormous number of even integers and is true in all test cases. Nevertheless, it is not yet known if the conjecture is true for *every* even integer, nor is any reasonable procedure known to determine whether the conjecture is true. The number of even integers is infinite, so a complete or exhaustive examination of all even integers and their prime factors is not feasible.

Goldbach's conjecture is an example of an unsolved problem that may eventually be solved—we just don't have a suitable solution procedure yet. Turing machines have proven another class of problems to be unsolvable, so there is no hope of ever solving them; such problems are said to be *undecidable*. An example of an undecidable problem is to determine if an arbitrary polynomial equation of the form

$$a_0 + a_1x + a_2x^2 + \cdots + a_{n-1}x^{n-1} + a_nx^n = b$$

has a solution consisting entirely of integers. This problem may be answerable for specific equations, but a general procedure or program can never be constructed that can analyze *any* possible polynomial equation and decide if it has an integer solution.

Turing identified an undecidable problem that involves the basic nature of Turing machines. Does a procedure exist to determine if an arbitrary Turing machine with arbitrary input data will ever halt once it has been set in motion? Turing proved that the answer is no, so the *Turing machine halting problem* as this particular problem is called, is also undecidable. This result has some practical implications. A common and costly error made by inexperienced computer programmers is to write programs that contain infinite loops and therefore fail to halt under certain input conditions. It would be useful to have a debugging program that could determine whether any given program contains an infinite loop. The undecidability of the Turing machine halting problem implies that no such infinite-loop-detecting tool can ever be realized.

The Turing machine model of a computer has one unrealistic, if not unreasonable, aspect: The length of the tape memory, and hence the total number of states in the Turing machine, is infinite. Real computers have a finite amount of memory and are therefore referred to as *finite-state machines*. Therefore, Turing machines can perform some computations that, in principle, finite-state machines cannot perform. For example, a finite-state machine cannot multiply two arbitrarily large numbers because it eventually runs out of the states needed to compute the product. The number of states of a typical computer is enormous, so this finiteness limitation has little significance. A typical general-purpose computer has billions of states and can quickly multiply numbers of any practical length.

Intractable problems. Real (finite-state) computers can solve most computational problems to an acceptable degree of accuracy. The question then becomes: Can a computer of reasonable size and cost solve a given problem in a reasonable amount of time? If so, the problem is said to be *tractable*; otherwise, it is *intractable*. Whether a given problem is tractable depends on several factors: the nature of the problem itself, the solution method or program used, and the computing speed or *performance* of the computer available to solve it. Figure 1.5 gives an indication of the speed of modern computers. It shows how the number of basic operations, such as the addition of two numbers, that a CPU can perform has been evolving with advances in computer hardware.

Example 1.2 illustrates the impact of the solution method on problem difficulty.

EXAMPLE 1.2 FINDING AN EULER CIRCUIT IN A GRAPH. A well-known problem associated with the Swiss mathematician Leonhard Euler (1707–1783) is the following: Given a set of connected paths such as the aisles in an exhibition hall (Figure 1.6*a*), is it possible to make a tour of the hall so that one walks along every aisle exactly once and ends up at the starting point? The problem can be represented abstractly by means of a *graph*, as shown in Figure 1.6*b*. Each aisle is modeled by a

Component technology	Date	Number of basic operations per second
Electromechanical: relays	1940	10
Electronic: vacuum tubes (valves)	1945	10^3
Electronic: transistors	1950	10^4
Small-scale integrated circuits	1960	10^5
Medium-scale integrated circuits	1980	10^6
Very large-scale integrated circuits	2000	10^9

Figure 1.5
Influence of hardware technology on computing speed.

line called an *edge*, and the junction of two or more aisles by a point called a *node*. The graph of Figure 1.6b has five nodes A, B, C, D, and E and eight edges a, b, c, d, e, f, g, and h. Restated in graph terms, the walking-tour problem becomes that of finding a closed path around the graph that contains every edge exactly once; such a path is known as an *Euler circuit*. We consider two possible ways to determine whether a graph contains an Euler circuit.

A "brute force" or exhaustive approach is to generate a list of the possible orderings or *permutations* of the edges of the graph. Each permutation then corresponds to a potential tour of the exhibition hall. The list of permutations can be written in the form

$$abcdefgh, \ acbdefgh, \ adbcefgh, \ aebcdfgh, \ afbcdegh, \ ... \qquad (1.1)$$

We can search the permutation list and check each entry to see if it specifies an Euler circuit. Clearly, the list is huge, and most of its entries do not represent Euler circuits. For example, the first permutation *abcdefgh* does not represent an Euler circuit, because while it is possible to go from *a* to *b* and from *b* to *c*, it is not possible to go directly from *c* to *d*. A tour starting at node A that traverses *a, b,* and *c* must continue along *g*, at which point *f* or *h* may be followed. The permutation *abcgfdhe* appearing

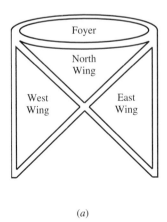

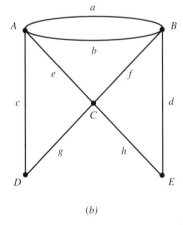

(a)　　　　　　　　　　　(b)

Figure 1.6
(a) Plan of the aisles in an exhibition hall and (b) the corresponding graph model.

somewhere down the list represents a circuit of the desired kind, as can be quickly verified. Thus we conclude that the graph of Figure 1.6b does indeed contain an Euler circuit.

The main drawback of this brute-force method is the length the permutation list; the time needed to generate, store, and check it is enormous. Most of the list's entries do not represent Euler circuits, but in the worst case, we might have to search the entire list to find an Euler circuit or prove that none exists. The number of possible permutations of the eight edges in our example is 8!, which denotes eight factorial. Therefore

$$8! = 8 \times 7 \times 6 \times 5 \times 4 \times 3 \times 2 \times 1 = 40,320$$

is the length of list (1.1). When q, the number of edges present, is large, the size of the permutation list $q!$ is approximated by

$$\sqrt{2\pi q}\left(\frac{q}{e}\right)^q$$

which shows that the size of the brute-force procedure in terms of storage requirements and computing speed increases exponentially with q. If q were 80 instead of 8, then we would have $q! = 80! \approx 7.16 \times 10^{118}$. This huge number exceeds the estimated number (10^{10}) of neurons in the human brain. A very fast computer capable of processing a trillion (10^{12}) permutations per second would spend 2.27×10^{99} years dealing with 80! permutations. We can therefore conclude with some confidence that the problem of finding an Euler circuit is intractable via the brute-force approach.

An alternative but very tractable solution procedure for the same problem depends on Euler's discovery that a graph has the desired circuit if and only if every node is the junction of an even number of edges. Intuitively, this result follows from the fact that every edge used to enter a node must be paired with an edge used to exit the node. Now the task of determining whether a graph contains an Euler cycle reduces to checking each node in turn and counting the edges that it connects. In the example of Figure 1.6b, nodes A, B, C, D, and E form the junctions of 4, 4, 4, 2, and 2 edges, respectively. It follows immediately that the graph has an Euler circuit. While the brute-force method requires a computation time and a storage capacity that grow exponentially with the number of edges q, the second method has a computational complexity that is proportional to q. The second method can easily solve problems with 80 or more edges.

Because the problem of finding an Euler circuit has an efficient and practical solution procedure, as shown in Example 1.2, we regard the problem itself as inherently tractable. We usually regard a problem as intractable if all its known solution methods grow exponentially with the size of the problem. Many problems, some of great practical importance, are inherently intractable in this way. Only small versions of such intractable problems can be solved in practice, where smallness is measured by some problem-dependent parameter such as the number of input variables present.

An example of an intractable problem related to Example 1.2 is the *traveling salesman problem*. Here the goal is also to make a tour, this time by car or plane through a given set of n cities, and eventually return to the starting point. The distance between each pair of cities is known, and the problem is to determine a tour that minimizes the total distance traveled. Again it is convenient to use a graph model with nodes denoting cities and edges denoting intercity highways with distances marked on them—the graph is tantamount to a roadmap. The best solution procedures known for this problem, although better than the brute-force approach of listing all possible tours through the n cities, are exponential in n. Quite a few practical problems are closely related to the traveling salesman problem: The scheduling of airline flights, the routing of wires in an electronic circuit, and the sequencing of steps in a factory assembly line are examples. Such difficult computing problems are a major motivation for the design and construction of bigger and faster computers.

An intractable problem can be solved exactly in a reasonable amount of time only when its size n is below some maximum value n_{MAX}. The value of n_{MAX} depends both on the problem itself and on the speed of the computers available to solve it. It might be expected that computer speeds could be increased to make n_{MAX} any desired value. We now present arguments to indicate that this is highly unlikely.

Speed limitations. An algorithm A has *time complexity* of order $f(n)$, denoted $O(f(n))$, if the number of basic operations—the precise nature of these operations is not important—A uses to solve a problem of size n is at most $cf(n)$, where $f(n)$ is some function of n and c is a constant. The function $f(n)$ therefore indicates the rate at which the computing time that A needs to obtain a solution grows with the problem size n.

To gauge the impact of computing speed on the size n_{MAX} of the largest solvable problem, we consider four algorithms A_1, A_2, A_3, and A_4 of varying degrees of difficulty. Let the time complexities of A_1, A_2, A_3, and A_4 be $O(n)$, $O(n^2)$, $O(n^{100})$, and $O(2^n)$, respectively. Because A_4 has a time complexity that is exponential in n, it is the only obviously intractable procedure. Suppose that all four algorithms are programmed on a computer M having a speed of S basic operations per second. Let n_i denote the size of the largest problem that algorithm A_i can solve in a fixed time period of T seconds. Let n_i' denote the size of the largest problem that the same algorithm A_i can solve in T seconds on a new computer M' that is 100 times faster than M; the speed of M' is therefore $100S$ operations per second. M' could be implemented by a different and faster hardware technology than M. It could also—at least in principle—be implemented by a "supercomputer" consisting of 100 copies of M all working in parallel on the same problem, a technique referred to as *parallel processing*.

Figure 1.7 shows the values of n_i' relative to n_i for the four algorithms. In the case of the intractable algorithm A_4, the increase in the size of the largest problem that can be handled on moving from M to M' is insignificant. This is also true for A_3, even though it does not fall within the strict definition of intractability. To increase the size of the maximum problem that A_3 and A_4 can solve in the given

Algorithm	Time complexity	Maximum problem size	
		Computer M	Computer M'
A_1	$O(n)$	n_1	$n_1' = 100n_1$
A_2	$O(n^2)$	n_2	$n_2' = 10n_2$
A_3	$O(n^{100})$	n_3	$n_3' = 1.047n_3$
A_4	$O(2^n)$	n_4	$n_4' = n_4 + 6.644$

Figure 1.7
Effect of computer speedup by 100 on four algorithms.

time period by a factor of 100, we would need computers with speeds of $10^{200}S$ and $10^{30n4}S$, respectively. It is reasonable to expect that problems of these magnitudes can *never* be solved by the given algorithms on realistic computers.

Because so many important problems are intractable, we often devise approximate or inexact methods to solve them. Two major techniques follow.

1. We replace the intractable problem Q with a tractable problem Q' whose solution approximates that of Q.
2. We examine a relatively small set of possible solutions to Q using reasonable, intuitive, and often poorly understood selection criteria and take the "best" of these as the solution to Q. Methods that are designed to produce acceptable, if not optimal, answers using a reasonable amount of computing time are sometimes called *heuristic* procedures.

To illustrate the heuristic approach, consider again the traveling salesman problem. The salesman must visit n cities and return to his starting point. All intercity distances are specified, and the objective of the problem is to find a tour that minimizes the total distance traveled by the salesman. We can represent the problem on a graph similar to that of Figure 1.6*b*, whose nodes denote cities and whose edges denote intercity links. A brute-force approach of the kind discussed in Example 1.2, which involves listing all $n!$ possible tours and their distances, is intractable, and no obviously tractable method to obtain a minimum-distance tour is known.

Real traveling salesmen often use the following simple heuristic: Go to the previously unvisited city that is closest to the current city and return to the start in the final leg of the tour. Hence for each of the n legs, the only computation needed is to compare the distances between the current city and each of at most $n - 1$ other cities. The city that is the shortest distance away (if there are several such cities, select any one of them) is visited next. Because this heuristic makes decisions that are optimal on a local basis only, it will not always find an overall optimum. Nevertheless, for most practical problems this heuristic provides a solution of minimum or near-minimum length, but there is no guarantee that it will do so in any particular case.

Computers are continually being applied to new problems whose computational requirements far exceed those of older problems. For example, the processing of high-quality speech and visual images for multimedia applications can require speeds measured in trillions of basic operations per second. To meet the ever-increasing demand for high-performance computation, we need better algorithms and heuristics, as well as faster computers. Although computers continue to increase in speed because of advances in hardware technology, the rate of increase (see Figure 1.5) has not kept pace with demand. As a result, we still need to find new ways to improve the performance of computers at reasonable cost—which is the basic rationale for the study of computer architecture and organization.

1.2
THE EVOLUTION OF COMPUTERS

Calculating machines capable of performing the elementary operations of arithmetic (addition, subtraction, multiplication, and division) appeared in the 16th century, and perhaps earlier [Randell 1982; Augarten 1984]. These were clever mechanical devices constructed from gears, levers, and the like. The French philosopher Blaise Pascal (1623–62) invented an early and influential mechanical calculator that could add and subtract decimal numbers. Decimal numerals were engraved on counter wheels much like those in a car's odometer. Pascal's main technical innovation was a ratchet device for automatically transferring a carry from a digit d_i to the digit d_{i+1} on its left whenever d_i passed from 9 to 0. In Germany, Gottfried Leibniz (1646–1716) extended Pascal's design to one that could also perform multiplication and division. Mechanical computing devices such as these remained academic curiosities until the 19th century, when the commercial production of mechanical four-function calculators began.

1.2.1 The Mechanical Era

Various attempts were made to build general-purpose programmable computers from the same mechanical devices used in calculators. This technology posed some daunting problems, and they were not satisfactorily solved until the introduction of electronic computing techniques in the mid-20th century.

Babbage's Difference Engine. In the 19th century Charles Babbage designed the first computers to perform multistep operations automatically, that is, without a human intervening in every step [Morrison and Morrison 1961]. Again the technologies were entirely mechanical. Babbage's first computing machine, which he called the Difference Engine, was intended to compute and print mathematical tables automatically, thereby avoiding the many errors occurring in tables that are computed and typeset by hand. The Difference Engine performed only one arithmetic operation: addition. However, the *method of (finite) differences* embodied in the Difference Engine can calculate many complex and useful functions by means of addition alone.

EXAMPLE 1.3 COMPUTING x^2 BY THE METHOD OF DIFFERENCES. Consider the task of calculating a table of the squares $y_j = x_j^2$, for $x_j = 1, 2, 3, \ldots$ using the method of differences. To understand the underlying concept, suppose we already have the list of squares given in Figure 1.8a. Subtract each square $y_j = x_j^2$ from the next value $y_{j+1} = (x_j + 1)^2$ in the list. The result $(x_j + 1)^2 - x_j^2 = 2x_j + 1$ is called the first difference of y and is denoted by $\Delta^1 y_j$; the corresponding list of values in Figure 1.8a is 3, 5, 7, ... If we subtract two consecutive first-difference values, we obtain $2(x_j + 1) + 1 - (2x_j + 1) = 2$, which is the second difference $\Delta^2 y_j$ of y. Note that the second difference is constant for all j.

The Difference Engine evaluates x^2 by taking the constant second difference $\Delta^2 y_j$ and adding it to the first difference $\Delta^1 y_j$. The result is

$$\Delta^1 y_{j+1} = \Delta^1 y_j + \Delta^2 y_j \tag{1.2}$$

which is the next value of the first difference. At the same time, the engine calculates

$$y_{j+1} = y_j + \Delta^1 y_j \tag{1.3}$$

which is the next value of x^2. By repeatedly executing the two addition steps (1.2) and (1.3), the Difference Engine can generate any desired sequence of consecutive squares. It must be "primed" by manually inserting the initial values $y_1 = 1$, $\Delta^1 y_1 = 3$,

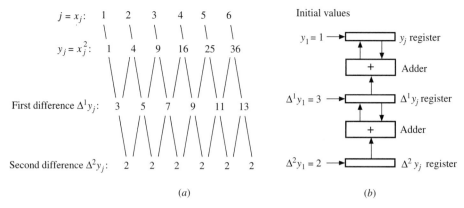

Figure 1.8
Computing x^2 by the method of differences: (a) a representative computation and
(b) the corresponding Difference Engine configuration.

and $\Delta^2 y_1 = 2$ for $j = 1$, which appear at the left end of the corresponding lists in Figure 1.8a. Then the Difference Engine computes $\Delta^1 y_2 = 3 + 2 = 5$ according to (1.2) and $y_2 = 1 + 3 = 4$ according to (1.3). It never has to recompute $\Delta^2 y_j$, which remains unchanged at 2 for all j. Once the values for $j = 2$ are known, the Difference Engine can calculate $\Delta^1 y_3$ and y_3, and so on indefinitely. At the end of the computation illustrated in Figure 1.8a, we have $y_6 = 36$, $\Delta^1 y_6 = 13$, and $\Delta^2 y_6 = 2$. One more iteration yields $\Delta^1 y_7 = 13 + 2 = 15$ and $y_7 = 36 + 13 = 49$, which is, of course, 7^2.

Figure 1.8b outlines the essential features of a small Difference Engine that executes the foregoing procedure. It contains several *registers;* these are memory devices, each of which stores a single number. Here we need three registers to store the three numbers y_j, $\Delta^1 y_j$, and $\Delta^2 y_j$. The engine employs a pair of processing units called *adders* to perform the addition steps specified by (1.2) and (1.3). Each adder takes the contents of two registers, calculates their sum, and returns it to one of the registers so that the sum becomes that register's new contents. The arrows in Figure 1.8b indicate the manner in which information flows through the Difference Engine during operation.

We can easily show that the *n*th difference of x^n is always a constant, from which it follows the *n*th difference of any *n*th-order polynomial of the form

$$y(x) = a_0 + a_1 x + a_2 x^2 + \cdots + a_{n-1} x^{n-1} + a_n x^n \tag{1.4}$$

is also a constant K. A Difference Engine can therefore calculate $y(x)$ by evaluating a set of n difference equations of the form

$$\Delta^i y_j = \Delta^i y_{j-1} + \Delta^{i+1} y_{j-1}$$

where $0 \le i \le n - 1$, $\Delta^0 y_j = y_j$, and $\Delta^n y_j = K$. Many useful functions encountered in science and engineering are expressible as polynomials like (1.4) and therefore can be evaluated by the method of differences. The trigonometric sine function, for instance, can be written as

$$\sin x = x - \frac{x^3}{3!} + \frac{x^5}{5!} - \frac{x^7}{7!} + \frac{x^9}{9!} - \frac{x^{11}}{11!} + \cdots \tag{1.5}$$

The first k terms of (1.5) form a $(2k - 1)$th-order polynomial that approximates $\sin x$. A higher-order polynomial will produce more accurate results.

Babbage constructed a small portion of his first Difference Engine in 1832, which served as a demonstration prototype. He later designed an improved version (Difference Engine No. 2), which was to handle seventh-order polynomials and have 31 decimal digits of accuracy. Like some of his modern successors, Babbage conceived his computers on a grand scale that strained the limits of the technology—and funds—available to build them. He never completed Difference Engine No. 2, mainly because of the difficulty of fabricating its 4000 or so high-precision mechanical parts. The complexity of this 3-ton machine can be appreciated from Figure 1.9, which is based on one of Babbage's own drawings. The vertical "figure-wheel columns" constitute the registers for storing 31-digit numbers, while the adders are implemented by the rack-and-lever mechanism underneath. It was not until 1991 that a working version of Difference Engine No. 2 was actually constructed (at a cost of around $500,000) by the Science Museum in London to celebrate the bicentennial of Babbage's birth [Swade 1993].

The Analytical Engine. Another reason for Babbage's failure to complete his Difference Engine was that he conceived of a much more powerful computing machine that he called the Analytical Engine. This machine is considered to be the first general-purpose programmable computer ever designed.

The overall organization of the Analytical Engine is outlined in Figure 1.10. It contains in rudimentary form many of the basic features found in all subsequent computers—compare Figure 1.10 to Figure 1.2. The main components of the

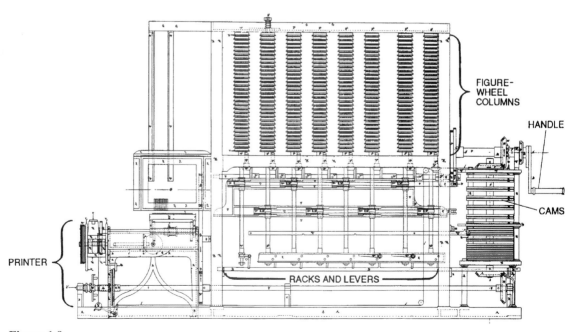

Figure 1.9
Diagram by Babbage of Difference Engine No. 2 [Courtesy of the National Science Museum/Science & Society Picture Library].

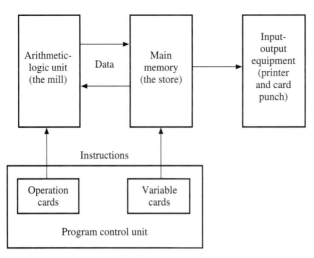

Figure 1.10
Structure of Babbage's Analytical Engine.

Analytical Engine are a memory called the *store* and an ALU called the *mill*; the latter was designed to perform the four basic arithmetic operations. To control the operation of the machine, Babbage proposed to use punched cards of a type developed earlier for controlling the Jacquard loom. A program for the Analytical Engine was composed of two sequences of punched cards: *operation cards* used to select the operation to be performed by the mill, and *variable cards* to specify the locations in the store from which inputs were to be taken or results sent. An action such as $a \times b = c$ would be specified by an instruction consisting of an operation card denoting multiply and variable cards specifying the store locations assigned to *a, b,* and *c*. Babbage intended the results to be printed on paper or punched on cards.

One of Babbage's key innovations was a mechanism to enable a program to alter the sequence of its operations automatically. In modern terms he conceived of conditional-branch or **if–then–else** instructions. They were to be implemented by testing the sign of a computed number; one course of action was taken if the sign were positive, another if negative. Babbage also designed a device to advance or reverse the flow of punched cards to permit branching to any desired instruction within a program. This type of conditional branching distinguishes the Analytical Engine from the Difference Engine: a program for the latter could only execute a fixed set of instructions in a fixed order. Conditional branching is the source of much of the power of the Analytical Engine and subsequent computers; it is the feature that makes them truly general purpose.

Again Babbage proposed to build the Analytical Engine on a grand scale using the same mechanical technology as his Difference Engines. The store, for instance, was to have a capacity of a thousand 50-digit numbers. He estimated that the addition of two numbers would take a second, and multiplication, a minute. Babbage spent much of the latter half of his life refining the design of the Analytical Engine, but only a small part of it was ever constructed.

Later developments. Many improvements were made to the design of four-function mechanical calculators in the 19th century, which led to their widespread use. The Comptometer, designed by the American Dorr E. Felt (1862–1930) in 1885, was one of the earliest calculators to use depressible keys for entering data and commands; it also printed its results on paper. A later innovation was the use of electric motors to drive the mechanical components, thus making calculators "electromechanical" and greatly increasing their speed. Another important development was the use of punched cards to sort and tabulate large amounts of data. The punched-card tabulating machine was invented by Herman Hollerith (1860–1929) and used to process the data collected in the 1880 United States census. In 1896 Hollerith formed a company to manufacture his electromechanical equipment. This company subsequently merged with several others and in 1924 was renamed the International Business Machines Corp. (IBM).

No significant attempts to build general-purpose, program-controlled computers were made after Babbage's death until the 1930s [Randell 1982]. In Germany, Konrad Zuse built a small mechanical computer, the Z1, in 1938, apparently unaware of Babbage's work. Unlike previous computers, the Z1 used binary, instead of decimal, arithmetic. A subsequent Zuse machine, the Z3, which was completed in 1941, is believed to have been the first operational general-purpose computer. Zuse's work was interrupted by the Second World War and had little influence on the subsequent development of computers. Of great influence, however, was a general-purpose electromechanical computer proposed in 1937 by Howard Aiken (1900–73), a physicist at Harvard University. Aiken arranged to have IBM construct this computer according to his basic design. Work began on Aiken's Automatic Sequence Controlled Calculator, later called the Harvard Mark I, in 1939; it became operational in 1944. Like Babbage's machines, the Mark I employed decimal counter wheels for its main memory. It could store seventy-two 23-digit numbers. The computer was controlled by a punched paper tape, which combined the functions of Babbage's operation and variable cards. Although less ambitious than the Analytical Engine, the Mark I was in many ways the realization of Babbage's dream.

1.2.2 Electronic Computers

A mechanical computer has two serious drawbacks: Its computing speed is limited by the inertia of its moving parts, and the transmission of digital information by mechanical means is quite unreliable. In an electronic computer, on the other hand, the "moving parts" are electrons, which can be transmitted and processed reliably at speeds approaching that of light (300,000 km/s). Electronic devices such as the vacuum tube or electronic valve, which was developed in the early 1900s, permit the processing and storage of digital signals at speeds far exceeding those of any mechanical device.

The first generation. The earliest attempt to construct an electronic computer using vacuum tubes appears to have been made in the late 1930s by John V. Atanasoff (1903–95) at Iowa State University [Randell 1982]. This special-purpose machine was intended for solving linear equations, but it was never completed. The first widely known general-purpose electronic computer was the Electronic Numerical Integrator and Calculator (ENIAC) that John W. Mauchly (1907–80) and J.

Presper Eckert (1919–95) built at the University of Pennsylvania. Like Babbage's Difference Engine, a motivation for the ENIAC was the need to construct mathematical tables automatically—this time ballistic tables for the U.S. Army. Work on the ENIAC began in 1943 and was completed in 1946. It was an enormous machine weighing about 30 tons and containing more than 18,000 vacuum tubes. It was also substantially faster than any previous computer. While the Harvard Mark I required about 3 s to perform a 10-digit multiplication, the ENIAC required only 3 ms.

The ENIAC had a set of electronic memory units called accumulators with a combined capacity of twenty 10-digit decimal numbers. Each digit was stored in a 10-bit ring counter, where the binary pattern 1000000000 denoted the decimal digit 0, 0100000000 denoted 1, 0010000000 denoted 2, and so on. The ring counter was the electronic equivalent of the decimal counter wheel of earlier mechanical calculators. Like counter wheels, the ENIAC's accumulators combined the function of storage with addition and subtraction. Additional units performed multiplication, division, and the extraction of square roots. The ENIAC was programmed by the cumbersome process of plugging and unplugging cables and by manually setting a master programming unit to specify multistep operations. Results were punched on cards or printed on an electric typewriter. In computing ability, the ENIAC is roughly comparable to a modern pocket calculator!

Like the Analytical Engine, the Harvard Mark I and the ENIAC stored their programs and data in separate memories. Entering or altering the programs was a tedious task. The idea of storing programs and their data in the same high-speed memory—the *stored-program* concept—is attributed to the ENIAC's designers, notably the Hungarian-born mathematician John von Neumann (1903–57) who was a consultant to the ENIAC project. The concept was first published in a 1945 proposal by von Neumann for a new computer, the Electronic Discrete Variable Computer (EDVAC). Besides facilitating the programming process, the stored-program concept enables a program to modify its own instructions. (Such self-modifying programs have undesirable aspects, however, and are rarely used.)

The EDVAC differed from most of its predecessors in that it stored and processed numbers in true binary or base 2 form. To minimize hardware costs, data was processed serially, or bit by bit. The EDVAC had two kinds of memory: a fast main memory with a capacity of 1024 or 1K words (numbers or instructions) and a slower secondary memory with a capacity of 20K words. Prior to their execution, a set of instructions forming a program was placed in the EDVAC's main memory. The instructions were then transferred one at a time from the main memory to the CPU for execution. Each instruction had a well-defined structure of the form

$$A_1 \quad A_2 \quad A_3 \quad A_4 \quad OP \qquad\qquad (1.6)$$

meaning: Perform the operation OP (addition, multiplication, etc.) on the contents of main memory locations or "addresses" A_1 and A_2 and then place the result in memory location A_3. The fourth address A_4 specifies the location of the next instruction to be executed. A variant of this instruction format implements conditional branching, where the next instruction address is either A_3 or A_4, depending on the relative sizes of the numbers stored in A_1 and A_2. Yet another instruction type specifies input-output operations that transfer words between main memory and secondary memory or between secondary memory and a printer. The EDVAC became operational in 1951.

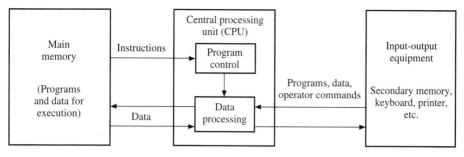

Figure 1.11
Organization of a first-generation computer.

In 1947 von Neumann and his colleagues began to design a new stored-program electronic computer, now referred to as the IAS computer, at the Institute for Advanced Studies in Princeton. Like the EDVAC, it had the general structure depicted in Figure 1.11, with a CPU for executing instructions, a main memory for storing active programs, a secondary memory for backup storage, and miscellaneous input-output equipment. Unlike the EDVAC, however, the IAS machine was designed to process all bits of a binary number simultaneously or in parallel. Several reports describing the IAS computer were published [Burks, Goldstine, and von Neumann 1946] and had far-reaching influence. In its overall design the IAS is quite modern, and it can be regarded as the prototype of most subsequent general-purpose computers. Because of its pervasive influence, we will examine the IAS computer in more detail below.

In the late 1940s and 1950s, the number of vacuum-tube computers grew rapidly. We usually refer to computers of this period as *first generation,* reflecting a somewhat narrow view of computer history [Randell 1982]. Besides those mentioned already, important early computers included the Whirlwind I constructed at the Massachusetts Institute of Technology and a series of machines designed at Manchester University [Siewiorek, Bell, and Newell 1982]. In 1947 Eckert and Mauchly formed Eckert-Mauchly Corp. to manufacture computers commercially. Their first successful product was the Universal Automatic Computer (UNIVAC) delivered in 1951. IBM, which had earlier constructed the Harvard Mark I, introduced its first electronic stored-program computer, the 701, in 1953. Besides their use of vacuum tubes in the CPU, first-generation computers experimented with various technologies for main and secondary memory. The Whirlwind introduced the ferrite-core memory in which a bit of information was stored in magnetic form on a tiny ring of magnetic material. Ferrite cores remained the principal technology for main memories until the 1970s.

The earliest computers had their instructions written in a binary code known as *machine language* that could be executed directly. An instruction in machine language meaning "add the contents of two memory locations" might take the form

$$00111011000000001001100100000111$$

Machine-language programs are extremely difficult for humans to write and so are very error-prone. A substantial improvement is obtained by allowing operations and operand addresses to be expressed in an easily understood symbolic form such as

$$\text{ADD} \quad \text{X1, X2}$$

This symbolic format, which is referred to as an *assembly language,* came into use in the 1950s, as computer programs were growing in size and complexity. An assembly language requires a special "system" program (an assembler) to translate it into machine language before it can be executed. First-generation computers were supplied with almost no system software; often little more than an assembler was available to the user. Moreover, assembly and machine languages varied widely from computer to computer so first-generation software was far from portable.

The IAS computer. It is instructive to examine the design of the Princeton IAS computer. Because of the size and high cost of the CPU's electronic hardware, the designers made every effort to keep the CPU, and therefore its instruction set, small and simple. Cost also heavily influenced the design of the memory subsystem. Because fast memories were expensive, the size of the main memory (initially 1K words but expandable to 4K) was less than most users would have wished. Consequently, a larger (16K words) but cheaper secondary memory based on an electromechanical magnetic drum technology was provided for bulk storage. Essentially similar cost-performance considerations remain central to computer design today, despite vast changes over the years in the available technologies and their actual costs.

The basic unit of information in the IAS computer is a 40-bit *word,* which is the standard packet of information stored in a memory location or transferred in one step between the CPU and the main memory M. Each location in M can be used to store either a single 40-bit number or else a pair of 20-bit instructions. The IAS's number format is *fixed-point,* meaning that it contains an implicit binary point in some fixed position. Numbers are usually treated as signed binary fractions lying between –1 and +1, but they can also be interpreted as integers. Examples of the IAS's binary number format are

$$01101000000\ 0000000000\ 0000000000\ 0000000000 = +.8125$$

$$10011000000\ 0000000000\ 0000000000\ 0000000000 = -0.8125$$

Numbers that lie outside the range ±1 must be suitably scaled for processing by IAS.

An IAS instruction consists of an 8-bit *opcode* (operation code) OP followed by a 12-bit *address* A that identifies one of up to $2^{12} = 4K$ 40-bit words stored in M. The IAS computer thus has a *one-address* instruction format, which we represent symbolically as

$$\text{OP} \quad \text{A}$$

This format may appear very restrictive compared with the EDVAC's four-address instruction format (1.6). The IAS's shorter format clearly saves memory space. The fact that it does not restrict the machine's computational capabilities follows from two key aspects of the IAS's design that have been incorporated into all later computers:

1. The CPU contains a small set of high-speed storage devices called *registers,* which serve as implicit storage locations for operands and results. For example,

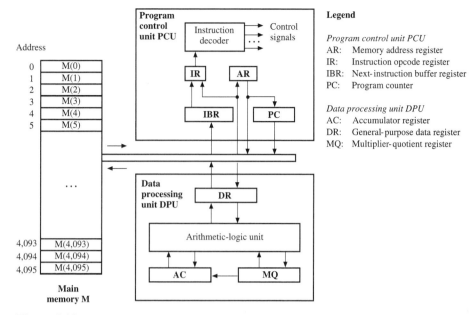

Figure 1.12
Organization of the CPU and main memory of the IAS computer.

an instruction of the form

$$\text{ADD} \quad X \tag{1.7}$$

fetches the contents of the memory location X from main memory and adds it to the contents of a CPU register known as the accumulator register AC. The resulting sum is then placed in AC. Hence X and AC play the role of the three memory addresses A_1, A_2, and A_3 appearing in (1.6).

2. A program's instructions are stored in M in approximately the sequence in which they are executed. Hence the address of the next instruction word is usually that of the current instruction plus one. Therefore, the EDVAC's next-instruction address A_4 can be replaced by a CPU register (the program counter PC), which stores the address of the current instruction word and is incremented by one when the CPU needs a new instruction word. Branch instructions are provided to permit the instruction execution sequence to be varied.

Figure 1.12 gives a programmer's perspective of the IAS, using modern notation and terminology. One of the two main parts of the CPU is responsible for fetching instructions from main memory and interpreting them; this part is variously known as the *program control unit (PCU)* or the *I-unit* (instruction unit). The second major part of the CPU is responsible for executing instructions and is known as the *data processing unit (DPU)*, the *datapath*, or the *E-unit* (execution unit).

The major components of the PCU are the *instruction register IR*, which stores the opcode that is currently being executed, and the *program counter PC*, which automatically stores and keeps track of the address of the next instruction to be fetched. The PCU has circuits to interpret opcodes and to issue control signals to the DPU, M, and other circuits involved in executing instructions. The PCU can modify the instruction execution sequence when required to do so by branch instructions. There is also a 12-bit *address register* AR in the PCU that holds the address of a data operand to be fetched from or sent to main memory. Because the IAS has the unusual feature of fetching two instructions at a time from M, it contains a second register, the *instruction buffer register* (IBR), for holding a second instruction.

The main components of the DPU are the ALU, which contains the circuits that perform addition, multiplication, etc., as required by the possible opcodes, and several *data registers* to store data words temporarily during program execution. The IAS has two general-purpose 40-bit data registers: AC (accumulator) and DR (data register). It also has a third, special-purpose data register MQ (multiplier-quotient) intended for use by multiply and divide instructions.

Main memory M is a 4096 word or 4096×40-bit array of storage cells. Each storage location in M is associated with a unique 12-bit number called its *address*, which the CPU uses to refer to that location. To read data from a particular memory location, the CPU must have its address X (which it can store in PC or AR). The CPU accomplishes the read operation by sending the address X to M accompanied by control signals that specify "read." M responds by transferring a copy of M(X), the word stored at address X, to the CPU, where it is loaded into DR. In a similar way the CPU writes new data into main memory by sending to M the destination address X, a data word D to be stored, and control signals that specify "write."

Instruction set. The IAS machine had around 30 types of instructions. These were chosen to provide a balance between application needs—the machine's focus was on numerical computation for scientific applications—and computer hardware costs as they existed at the time. To represent instructions, we will use a notation called a *hardware description language* (HDL) or *register-transfer language* (RTL) that approximates the assembly language used to prepare programs for the computer; the designers of the IAS computer also used such a descriptive language [Burks, Goldstine, and von Neumann 1946]. The HDL introduced here and used throughout this book is largely self-explanatory. Storage locations in M or the CPU are referred to by acronym. The transfer of information is denoted by the assignment symbol :=, which suggests the left-going arrow ←. Hence, AC := MQ means transfer (copy) the contents of register MQ to register AC without altering the contents of MQ. Elements of main memory M are denoted by appending to M an address in parentheses. For example, M(X) denotes the 40-bit memory word with address X, while M(X,0:19) denotes the half-word consisting of bits 0 through 19 of M(X).

Figure 1.13 illustrates our descriptive notation for a simple three-instruction IAS program that adds two numbers. The numbers to be added are stored in the main memory locations with addresses 100 and 101; their sum is placed in memory location 102. Note the role played by the accumulator AC as an intermediate source and destination of data.

The set of instructions defined for the IAS computer is given in Figure 1.14 [Burks, Goldstine, and von Neumann 1946], omitting only those intended for

Instruction	Comment
AC := M(100)	Load the contents of memory location 100 into the accumulator.
AC := AC + M(101)	Add the contents of memory location 101 to the accumulator.
M(102) := AC	Store the contents of the accumulator in memory location 102.

Figure 1.13
An IAS program to add two numbers stored in main memory.

input-output operations. We have divided them into three categories: data-transfer, data-processing, and program-control instructions. Observe that some instructions have all their operands in CPU registers; others have one operand in memory location M(X). The data-processing instructions do most of the "real" work; all the others play supporting roles. Because only one memory address X can be specified at a time, multioperand instructions such as add and multiply must use CPU registers to store some of their operands. Consequently, it is necessary to precede or follow a typical data-processing instruction by data-transfer instructions that load input operands into CPU registers or transfer results from the CPU to memory. This requirement is illustrated by the add operation in Figure 1.13, where two data-transfer instructions and one add instruction are needed to accomplish a single addition operation. Hence the IAS like many of its successors contains quite a few data-transfer instructions whose purpose is to shuttle information unchanged (except possibly in sign) between CPU registers and memory. The IAS's data-processing instructions perform all the basic operations of arithmetic on signed 40-bit numbers. The IAS can also perform nonnumerical operations, but with some difficulty, because it treats all its operands as numbers.

The group of instructions called program-control or branch instructions determine the sequence in which instructions are executed. Recall that the program counter PC specifies the address of the next instruction to be executed. Instructions are normally executed in a fixed order determined by incrementing the program counter PC. The program-control instructions are designed to change this order. The IAS has two unconditional branch instructions (also called "jump" or "go to" instructions), which load part of X into PC and cause the next instruction to be taken from the left half or right half of M(X). The two conditional branch instructions permit a program branch to occur if and only if AC contains a nonnegative number. These instructions allow the results of a computation to alter the instruction execution sequence and so are of great importance.

The last two instructions listed in Figure 1.14 are "address-modify" instructions that permit 12-bit addresses to be computed in the CPU and then inserted directly into instructions stored in M. Address-modify instructions allow a program to alter itself, enabling, for example, the same data-processing instruction to refer to different operands at different times. Modifying programs during their execution is now considered obsolete and undesirable, but it was an important feature of early computers like IAS.

Instruction execution. The IAS fetches and executes instructions in several steps that form an *instruction cycle*. Since two instructions are packed into a 40-bit

Instruction type	Instruction	Description
Data transfer	AC := MQ	Transfer contents of register MQ to register AC.
	AC := M(X)	Transfer contents of memory location X to AC.
	M(X) := AC	Transfer contents of AC to memory location X.
	MQ := M(X)	Transfer M(X) to MQ.
	AC := −M(X)	Transfer minus M(X) to AC.
	AC := $\lvert M(X) \rvert$	Transfer absolute value of M(X) to AC.
	AC := −$\lvert M(X) \rvert$	Transfer minus $\lvert M(X) \rvert$ to AC.
Data processing	AC := AC + M(X)	Add M(X) to AC putting the result in AC.
	AC := AC + $\lvert M(X) \rvert$	Add absolute value of M(X) to AC.
	AC := AC − M(X)	Subtract M(X) from AC.
	AC := AC − $\lvert M(X) \rvert$	Subtract $\lvert M(X) \rvert$ from AC.
	AC.MQ := MQ × M(X)	Multiply MQ by M(X) putting the double-word product in AC and MQ.
	MQ.AC := AC ÷ M(X)	Divide AC by M(X) putting the quotient in AC and the remainder in MQ.
	AC := AC × 2	Multiply AC by two (1-bit left shift).
	AC := AC ÷ 2	Divide AC by two (1-bit right shift).
Program control	**go to** M(X, O:19)	Take next instruction from left half of M(X)
	go to M(X, 20:39)	Take next instruction from right half of M(X).
	if AC ≥ 0 **then** **go to** M(X, 0:19)	If AC contains a nonnegative number, then take next instruction from left half of M(X).
	if AC ≥ 0 **then** **go to** M(X, 20:39)	If AC contains a nonnegative number, then take next instruction from right half of M(X).
	M(X, 8:19) := AC (28:39)	Replace left instruction address field in M(X) by 12 right-most bits of AC.
	M(X, 28:39) := AC(28:39)	Replace right instruction address field in M(X) by 12 right-most bits of AC.

Figure 1.14
Instruction set of the IAS computer.

word, the IAS fetches two instructions in each instruction cycle. One instruction has its opcode placed in the instruction register IR and its address field (if any) placed in the address register AR. The other instruction is transferred to the IBR register for possible later execution. Whenever the next instruction needed by the CPU is not in IBR, the program counter PC is incremented to generate the next instruction address.

Once the desired instruction has been loaded into the CPU, its execution phase begins. The PCU decodes the instruction's opcode, and the PCU's subsequent actions depend on the opcode's bit pattern. Typically, these actions involve one or two register-transfer (micro) operations of the form $S := f(S_1, S_2, \ldots, S_k)$, where the

S_i's are the locations of operands and f is a data-transfer or arithmetic operation. For example, the add instruction AC := AC + M(X) is executed by the following two register-transfer operations:

$$DR := M(AR);$$

$$AC := AC + DR$$

First, the contents of the memory location M(AR) specified by the address register AR are transferred to the data register DR. Then the contents of DR and the accumulator AC are added via the DPU's arithmetic-logic unit, and the result is placed in AC. The unconditional branch instruction **go to** M(X,0:19) has an address field containing some address X; after fetching this instruction, X is placed in AR. This instruction is then executed via the single register-transfer operation PC := AR, which makes PC point to the desired next instruction stored in the half-word M(X,0:19).

EXAMPLE 1.4 AN IAS PROGRAM TO PERFORM VECTOR ADDITION. Let A = A(1), A(2), ..., A(1000) and B = B(1), B(2), ..., B(1000) be two vectors, that is, one-dimensional arrays, of numbers to be added. The desired vector sum C = A + B is defined by

C(1), C(2), ..., C(1000) = A(1) + B(1), A(2) +B(2), ..., A(1000) + B(1000)

For simplicity we will assume that the numbers processed by the IAS, including the vector elements A(I), B(I), and C(I) are 40-bit integers, and that the input vectors are prestored in the IAS's main memory M. We need to perform the add operation

$$C(I) := A(I) + B(I)$$

1000 times, specifically for I = 1, 2, ..., 1000. Using the operations available in the IAS instruction set, the basic addition step above can be realized by the following three-instruction sequence (compare Figure 1.13):

$$AC := A(I)$$
$$AC := AC + B(I) \tag{1.8}$$
$$C(I) := AC$$

Clearly, a program with 1000 copies of these three instructions, each with a different index I, would implement the vector addition. However, such a program, besides being very inconvenient to write, would not fit in M along with the three vectors A, B, and C. We need some type of loop or iterative program that contains one copy of (1.8) but can modify the index I to step through all elements of the vectors.

Figure 1.15 shows such a program. The vectors A, B, and C are assumed to be stored sequentially, beginning at locations 1001, 2001, and 3001, respectively. The symbol to the left of each instruction in Figure 1.15 is its location in M. For instance, 2L (2R) denotes the left (right) half of M(2). The first location M(0) is used to store a counting variable N and is initially set to 999. N is systematically decremented by one after each addition step; when it reaches –1, the program halts. The conditional branch instruction in 5R performs this termination test. The three instructions in locations 3L, 3R, and 4L are the key ones that implement (1.8). The address-modify instructions in 8L, 9L, and 10L decrement the address parts of the three instructions in 3L, 3R, and

Location	Instruction or data	Comment
0	999	Constant (count N).
1	1	Constant.
2	1000	Constant.
3L	AC := M(2000)	Load A(I) into AC.
3R	AC := AC + M(3000)	Compute A(I) + B(I).
4L	M(4000) := AC	Store sum C(I).
4R	AC := M(0)	Load count N into AC.
5L	AC := AC − M(1)	Decrement count N by one.
5R	**if** AC ≥ 0 **then go to** M(6, 20:39)	Test N and branch to 6R if nonnegative.
6L	**go to** M(6, 0:19)	Halt.
6R	M(0) := AC	Update count N.
7L	AC := AC + M(1)	Increment AC by one.
7R	AC := AC + M(2)	Modify address in 3L.
8L	M(3, 8:19) := AC(28:39)	
8R	AC := AC + M(2)	Modify address in 3R.
9L	M(3, 28:39) := AC(28:39)	
9R	AC := AC + M(2)	Modify address in 4L.
10L	M(4, 8:19) := AC(28:39)	
10R	**go to** M(3, 0:19)	Branch to 3L.

Figure 1.15
An IAS program for vector addition.

4L, respectively. Thus the program continuously modifies itself during execution. Figure 1.15 shows the program before execution commences. At the end of the computation, the first three instructions will have changed to the following:

$$3L \quad AC := M(1001)$$

$$3R \quad AC := AC + M(2001)$$

$$4L \quad M(3001) := AC$$

Critique. In the years that have elapsed since the IAS computer was completed, numerous improvements in computer design have appeared. Hindsight enables us to point out some of the IAS's shortcomings.

1. The program self-modification process illustrated in the preceding example for decrementing the index I is inefficient. In general, writing and debugging a program whose instructions change themselves is difficult and error-prone. Further, before every execution of the program, the original version must be reloaded into M. Later computers employ special instruction types and registers for index control, which eliminates the need for address-modify instructions.

2. The small amount of storage space in the CPU results in a great deal of unproductive data-transfer traffic between the CPU and main memory M; it also adds to program length. Later computers have more CPU registers and a special memory called a *cache* that acts as a buffer between the CPU registers and M.

3. No facilities were provided for structuring programs. For example, the IAS has no procedure call or return instructions to link different programs.
4. The instruction set is biased toward numerical computation. Programs for nonnumerical tasks such as text processing were difficult to write and executed slowly.
5. Input-output (IO) instructions were considered of minor importance—in fact, they are not mentioned in Burks, Goldstine, and von Neumann [1946] beyond noting that they are necessary. IAS had two basic and rather inefficient IO instruction types [Estrin 1953]. The input instruction INPUT(X, N) transferred N words from an input device to the CPU and then to N consecutive main memory locations, starting at address X. The OUTPUT(X, N) instruction transferred N consecutive words from the memory region with starting address X to an output device.

1.2.3 The Later Generations

In spite of their design deficiencies and the limitations on size and speed imposed by early electronic technology, the IAS and other first-generation computers introduced many features that are central to later computers: the use of a CPU with a small set of registers, a separate main memory for instruction and data storage, and an instruction set with a limited range of operations and addressing capabilities. Indeed the term *von Neumann computer* has become synonymous with a computer of conventional design.

The second generation. Computer hardware and software evolved rapidly after the introduction of the first commercial computers around 1950. The vacuum tube quickly gave way to the transistor, which was invented at Bell Laboratories in 1947, and a second generation of computers based on transistors superseded the first generation of vacuum tube–based machines. Like a vacuum tube, a transistor serves as a high-speed electronic switch for binary signals, but it is smaller, cheaper, sturdier, and requires much less power than a vacuum tube. Similar progress occurred in the field of memory technology, with ferrite cores becoming the dominant technology for main memories until superseded by all-transistor memories in the 1970s. Magnetic disks became the principal technology for secondary memories, a position that they continue to hold.

Besides better electronic circuits, the second generation, which spans the decade 1954–64, introduced some important changes in the design of CPUs and their instruction sets. The IAS computer still served as the basic model, but more registers were added to the CPU to facilitate data and address manipulation. For example, index registers were introduced to store an index variable I of the kind appearing in the statement

$$C(I) := A(I) + B(I) \tag{1.9}$$

Index registers make it possible to have *indexed* instructions, which increment or decrement a designated index I before (or after) they execute their main operation. Consequently, repeated execution of an indexed operation like (1.9) allows it to step automatically through a large array of data. The index value I is stored in a CPU register and not in the program, so the program itself does not change during execution. Another innovation was the introduction of two program-control instructions, now referred to as *call* and *return*, to facilitate the linking of programs; see also Example 1.5.

"Scientific" computers of the second generation, such as the IBM 7094 which appeared in 1962, introduced floating-point number formats and supporting instructions to facilitate numerical processing. Floating point is a type of scientific notation where a number such as 0.0000000709 is denoted by 7.09×10^{-8}. A *floating-point number* consists of a pair of fixed-point numbers, a mantissa M and an exponent E, and has the value $M \times B^{-E}$. In the preceding example $M = 7.09$, $E = -8$, and $B = 10$. In their computer representation M and E are encoded in binary and embedded in a word of suitable size; the base B is implicit. Floating-point numbers eliminate the need for number scaling; floating-point numbers are automatically scaled as they are processed. The hardware needed to implement floating-point arithmetic instructions directly is relatively expensive. Consequently, many computers (then and now) rely on software subroutines to implement floating-point operations via fixed-point arithmetic.

Input-output operations. Computer designers soon realized that IO operations, that is, the transfer of information to and from peripheral devices like printers and secondary memory, can severely degrade overall computer performance if done inefficiently. Most IO transfers have main memory as their final source or destination and involve the transfer of large blocks of information, for instance, moving a program from secondary to main memory for execution. Such a transfer can take place via the CPU, as in the following fragment of a hypothetical IO program:

Location	Instruction	Comment
LOOP	AC := D(I)	Input word from IO device D into AC.
	M(I) := AC	Output word from AC to main memory.
	I := I + 1	Increment index I.
	if I ≤ MAX **go to** LOOP	Test for end of loop.

Clearly, the IO operation ties up the CPU with a trivial data-transfer task. Moreover, many IO devices transfer data at low speeds compared to that of the CPU because of their inherent reliance on electromechanical rather than electronic technology. Thus the CPU is idle most of the time when executing an IO program directed at a relatively slow device such as a printer. To eliminate this bottleneck, computers such as the IBM 7094 introduced *input-output processors (IOPs)*, or *channels* in IBM parlance, which are special-purpose processing units designed exclusively to control IO operations. They do so by executing IO programs (see preceding sample), but channeling the data through registers in the IO processor, rather than through the CPU. Hence IO data transfers can take place independently of the CPU, permitting the CPU to execute user programs while IO operations are taking place.

Programming languages. An important development of the mid-1950s was the introduction of "high level" programming languages, which are far easier to use than assembly languages because they permit programs to be written in a form much closer to a computer user's problem specification. A high-level language is intended to be usable on many different computers. A special program called a *compiler* translates a user program from the high-level language in which it is written into the machine language of the particular computer on which the program is to be executed.

The first successful high-level programming language was FORTRAN (from FORmula TRANslation), developed by an IBM group under the direction of John Backus from 1954 to 1957. FORTRAN permits the specification of numerical algorithms in a form approximating normal algebraic notation. For example, the vector addition task in Figure 1.16 can be expressed by the following two-line program in the original version of FORTRAN:

$$DO \; 5 \; I = 1, 1000$$

$$5 \quad C(I) = A(I) + B(I)$$

FORTRAN has continued to be widely used for scientific programming and, like natural languages, it has changed over the years. The version of FORTRAN known as FORTRAN90 introduced in 1990 replaces the preceding DO loop with the single vector statement

$$C(1:1000) = A(1:1000) + B(1:1000) \tag{1.10}$$

High-level languages were also developed in the 1950s for business applications. These are characterized by instructions that resemble English statements and operate on textual as well as numerical data. One of the earliest such languages was Common Business Oriented Language (COBOL), which was defined in 1959 by a group representing computer users and manufacturers and sponsored by the U.S. Department of Defense. Like FORTRAN, COBOL has continued (in various revised forms) to be among the most widely used programming languages. FORTRAN and COBOL are the forerunners of other important high-level languages, including Basic, Pascal, C, and Java, the latter dating from the mid-1990s.

EXAMPLE 1.5 A NONSTANDARD ARCHITECTURE: STACK COMPUTERS. Although most computers follow the von Neumann model, a few alternatives were explored quite early in the electronic era. In the stack organization illustrated in Figure 1.16a a stack memory replaces the accumulator and other CPU registers used for temporary data storage. A *stack* resembles the array of contiguous storage locations found in main memory, but it has a very different mode of access. Stack locations have no external addresses; all read and write operations refer to one end of the stack called the *top of the stack* TOS. A *push* operation writes a word into the next unused location TOS + 1 and causes this location to become the new TOS. A *pop* operation reads the word stored in the current TOS and causes the location TOS − 1 below TOS to become the new TOS. Hence TOS serves as a dynamic entry point to the stack, which expands and contracts in response to push and pop operations, respectively. The region above the stack (shaded in Figure 1.16a) is unused, but it is available for future use. Among

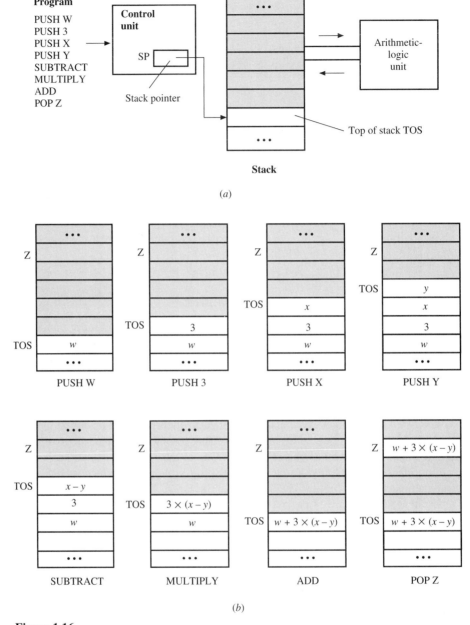

Figure 1.16
(*a*) Essentials of a stack processor; (*b*) stack states during the execution of
$z := w + 3 \times (x - y)$.

the earliest stack computers was the Burroughs B5000, first delivered in 1963
[Siewiorek, Bell, and Newell 1982]; a recent example is the Sun picoJava microprocessor designed for fast execution of compiled Java code [O'Connor and Tremblay
1997].

In a stack machine an instruction's operands are stored at the top of the stack, so
data-processing instructions do not need to contain addresses as they do in a conven-

tional, von Neumann computer. The add operation $x + y$ is specified for a stack machine by the following sequence of three instructions:

$$\text{PUSH } x$$

$$\text{PUSH } y$$

$$\text{ADD}$$

The first PUSH instruction loads x into TOS. Execution of PUSH y causes x's location to become TOS $-$ 1 and places y in the new TOS immediately above x. To execute ADD, the top two words of the stack are popped into the ALU where they are added, and the sum is pushed back into the stack. Hence in the preceding program fragment, ADD computes $x + y$, which replaces x and y at the top of the stack. The electronic circuits that carry out these actions can be complicated, but they are hidden from the programmer. A key component is a register called the *stack pointer* SP which stores the internal address of TOS, and automatically adjusts the TOS for every push and pop operation. A program counter PC keeps track of instruction addresses in the usual manner.

A stack computer evaluates arithmetic and other expressions using a format known as *Polish notation*, named after the Polish logician Jan Lukasiewicz (1878–1956). Instead of placing an operator between its operands as in $x + y$, the operator is placed to the right of its operands as in $x\ y\ +$. A more complex expression such as $z := w + 3 \times (x - y)$ becomes

$$z\ w\ 3\ x\ y\ -\ \times\ +\ := \tag{1.11}$$

in Polish notation, and the expression is evaluated from left to right. Note that Polish notation eliminates the need for parentheses. The Polish expression (1.11) leads directly to the eight-instruction stack program shown in Figure 1.16a. The step-by-step execution of this code fragment is illustrated in Figure 1.16b. Here it is assumed that w, x, y, z represent the values of operands stored at the memory addresses W, X, Y, and Z, respectively.

Stack computers such as the B5000 employ a main memory M to store programs and data in much the same way as a conventional computer. For cost reasons, the CPU contains only a small stack—a two-word stack in the B5000 case—implemented by high-speed registers. However, the stack expands automatically into M by treating some main memory locations as if they were stack registers and coupling them with those in the CPU. While stack processors can evaluate complex expressions such as (1.11) efficiently, they are generally slower than von Neumann machines, especially when executing vector operations such as (1.10). Large stack computers were successfully marketed for many years, notably by Burroughs Corp. However, the stack concept eventually became widely used in only two specialized applications:

1. Pocket calculators sometimes employ a stack organization to take advantage of the conciseness of Polish notation when entering data and commands manually via a keypad.
2. Stacks are included in most conventional computers to implement subroutine call and return instructions. In its basic form, a call-subroutine instruction takes the form CALL SUB. It first saves the current contents of PC—the calling routine's return address—by pushing it into a stack region of M that is under the control of a stack pointer SP. Then SUB, the start address of the subroutine being called, is loaded into PC, and its execution begins. Control is returned to the calling program when the subroutine executes a RETURN instruction, whose function is to pop the return address from the top of the stack and load it back into PC.

System management. In the early days, all programs or jobs were run separately, and the computer had to be halted and prepared manually for each new program to be executed. With the improvements in IO equipment and programming methodology that came with the second-generation machines, it became feasible to prepare a batch of jobs in advance, store them on magnetic tape, and then have the computer process the jobs in one continuous sequence, placing the results on another magnetic tape. This mode of system management is termed *batch processing*. Batch processing requires the use of a supervisory program called a *batch monitor*, which is permanently resident in main memory. A batch monitor is a rudimentary version of an *operating system*, a system program (as opposed to a user or application program) designed to manage a computer's resources efficiently and provide a set of common services to its users.

Later operating systems were designed to enable a single CPU to process a set of independent user programs concurrently, a technique called *multiprogramming*. It recognizes that a typical program alternates between program execution when it requires use of the CPU, and IO operations when it requires use of an IOP. Multiprogramming is accomplished by the CPU temporarily suspending execution of its current program, beginning execution of a second program, and returning to the first program later. Whenever possible, a suspended program is assigned an IOP, which performs any needed IO functions. Consequently, multiprogramming attempts to keep a CPU (usually viewed as the computer's most precious resource) and any available IOPs busy by overlapping CPU and IO operations. Multiprogrammed computers that process many user programs concurrently and support users at interactive terminals or workstations are sometimes called *time-sharing* systems.

The third generation. This generation is traditionally associated with the introduction of integrated circuits (ICs), which first appeared commercially in 1961, to replace the discrete electronic circuits used in second-generation computers. The transistor continued as the basic switching device, but ICs allowed large numbers of transistors and associated components to be combined on a tiny piece of semiconductor material, usually silicon. IC technology initiated a long-term trend in computer design toward smaller size, higher speed, and lower hardware cost.

Perhaps the most significant event of the third-generation period (which began around 1965) was recognition of the need to standardize computers in order to allow software to be developed and used more efficiently. By the mid-1960s a few dozen manufacturers of computers around the world were each producing machines that were incompatible with those of other manufacturers. The cost of writing and maintaining programs for a particular computer—the software cost—began to exceed that of the computer's hardware. At the same time many big users of computers, such as banks and insurance companies, were creating huge amounts of application software on which their business operations were becoming very dependent. Switching to a different computer and making one's old software obsolete was thus an increasingly unattractive proposition.

Influenced by these considerations, IBM developed (at a cost of about $5 billion) what was to be the most influential third-generation computer, the System/360, which it announced in 1964 and delivered the following year; see Figure 1.17. System/360 was actually a series of computers distinguished by model numbers

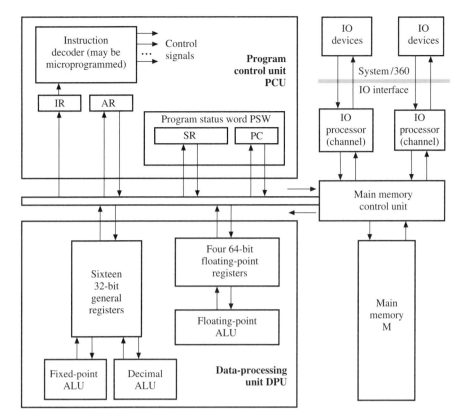

Figure 1.17
Structure of the IBM System/360.

and intended to cover a wide range of computing performance [Siewiorek, Bell, and Newell 1982; Prasad 1989]. The various System/360 models were designed to be *software compatible* with one another, meaning that all models in the series shared a common instruction set. Programs written for one model could be run without modification on any other; only the execution time, memory usage, and the like would change. Software compatibility enabled computer owners to upgrade their systems without having to rewrite large amounts of software. The System/360 models also used a common operating system, OS/360, and the manufacturer supplied specialized software to support such widely used applications as transaction processing and database management. In addition, the System/360 models had many hardware characteristics in common, including the same interface for attaching IO devices.

While the System/360 standardized much of IBM's own product line, it also became a de facto standard for large computers, now referred to as *mainframe* computers, produced by other manufacturers. The long list of makers of System/360-compatible machines includes such companies as Amdahl in the United States and Hitachi in Japan. The System/360 series was also remarkably long-lived. It evolved into various newer mainframe computer series introduced by IBM over the years, all of which maintained software compatibility with the original System/

360; for example, the System/370 introduced in 1970, the 4300 introduced in 1979, and the System/390 introduced in 1990.

The System/360 added only modestly to the basic principles of the von Neumann computer, but it established a number of widely followed conventions and design styles. It had about 200 distinct instruction types (opcodes) with many addressing modes and data types, including fixed-point and floating-point numbers of various sizes. It replaced the small and unstructured set of data registers (AC, MQ, etc.) found in earlier computers with a set of 16 identical general-purpose registers, all individually addressable. This is called the *general-register organization*. The System/360 had separate arithmetic-logic units for processing various data types; the fixed-point ALU was used for address computations including indexing. The 8-bit unit *byte* was defined as the smallest unit of information for data transmission and storage purposes. The System/360 also made 32 bits (4 bytes) the main CPU word size, so that 32 bits and "word" have become synonymous in the context of large computers.

The CPU had two major control states: a *supervisor state* for use by the operating system and a *user state* for executing application programs. Certain program-control instructions were "privileged" in that they could be executed only when the CPU was in supervisor state. These and other special control states gave rise to the concept of a *program status word* (PSW) which was stored in a special CPU register, now generally referred to as a *status register* (SR). The SR register encapsulated the key information used by the CPU to record exceptional conditions such as CPU-detected errors (an instruction attempting to divide by zero, for example), hardware faults detected by error-checking circuits, and urgent service requests or *interrupts* generated by IO devices.

Architecture versus implementation. With the advent of the third generation, a distinction between a computer's overall design and its implementation details became apparent. As defined by System/360's designers [Prasad 1989], the *architecture* of a computer is its structure and behavior as seen by a programmer working at the assembly-language level. The architecture includes the computer's instruction set, data formats, and addressing modes, as well as the general design of its CPU, main memory, and IO subsystems. The architecture therefore defines a conceptual model of a computer at a particular level of abstraction. A computer's *implementation*, on the other hand, refers to the logical and physical design techniques used to realize the architecture in any specific instance. The term *computer organization* also refers to the logical aspects of the implementation, but the boundary between the terms *architecture* and *organization* is vague.

Hence we can say that the models of the IBM System/360 series have a common architecture but different implementations. These differences reflect the existence of physical circuit technologies with different cost/performance ratios for constructing processing circuits and memories. To achieve instruction-set compatibility across many models, the System/360 also used an implementation technique called *microprogramming*. Originally proposed in the early 1950s by Maurice V. Wilkes at Cambridge University, microprogramming allows a CPU's program control unit PCU to be designed in a systematic and flexible way [Wilkes and Stringer 1953]. Low-level control sequences known as *microprograms* are placed in a special control memory in the PCU so that an instruction from the CPU's main instruction set is executed by invoking and executing the corresponding micropro-gram. A CPU with no floating-point arithmetic circuits can execute floating-point instructions (albeit slowly) if microprograms are written to perform the desired floating-point operations by means of fixed-point arithmetic circuits. Micropro-gramming allowed the smaller System/360 models to implement the full System/360 instruction set with less hardware than the larger, faster models, some of which were not microprogrammed.

Other developments. The System/360 was typical of commercial computers aimed at both business and scientific applications. Efforts were also directed by various manufacturers towards the design of extremely powerful (and expensive) scientific computers, loosely termed *supercomputers*. Control Data Corp., for instance, produced a series of commercially successful supercomputers beginning with the CDC 6660 in 1964, and continuing into the 1980s with the subsequent CYBER series. These early supercomputers experimented with various types of parallel processing to improve their performance. One such technique called *pipe-lining* involves overlapping the execution of instructions from the same program within a specially designed CPU. Another technique, which allows instructions from different programs to be executed simultaneously, employs a computer with more than one CPU; such a computer is called a *multiprocessor*.

A contrasting development of this period was the mass production of small, low-cost computers called *minicomputers*. Their origins can be traced to the LINC (Laboratory Instrument Computer) developed at MIT in the early 1960s [Siewiorek, Bell, and Newell 1982]. This machine influenced the design of the PDP (Programmed Data Processor) series of small computers introduced by Dig-ital Equipment Corp. (Digital) in 1965, which did much to establish the mini-computer market. Minicomputers are characterized by short word size—CPU word sizes of 8 and 16 bits were typical—limited hardware and software facili-ties, and small physical size. Most important, their low cost made them suitable for many new applications, such as the industrial process control where a com-puter is permanently assigned to one particular application. The Digital VAX series of minicomputers introduced in 1978 brought general-purpose computing to many small organizations that could not afford the high cost of a mainframe computer.

1.3
THE VLSI ERA

Since the 1960s the dominant technology for manufacturing computer logic and memory circuits has been the integrated circuit or IC. This technology has evolved steadily from ICs containing just a few transistors to those containing thousands or millions of transistors; the latter case is termed *very large-scale integration* or VLSI. The impact of VLSI on computer design and application has been profound. VLSI allows manufacturers to fabricate a CPU, main memory, or even all the elec-tronic circuits of a computer, on a single IC that can be mass-produced at very low cost. This has resulted in new classes of machines ranging from portable personal computers to supercomputers that contain thousands of CPUs.

(a)   (b)   (c)

Figure 1.18
Some representative IC packages: (a) 32-pin small-outline J-lead (SOJ); (b) 132-pin plastic
quad flatpack (PQFP); (c) 84-pin pin-grid array (PGA). [Courtesy of Sharp Electronics
Corp.]

1.3.1 Integrated Circuits

The integrated circuit was invented in 1959 at Texas Instruments and Fairchild
Corporations [Braun and McDonald 1982]. It quickly became the basic building
block for computers of the third and subsequent generations. (The designation of
computers by generation largely fell into disuse after the third generation.) An IC is
an electronic circuit composed mainly of transistors that is manufactured in a tiny
rectangle or *chip* of semiconductor material. The IC is mounted into a protective
plastic or ceramic package, which provides electrical connection points called *pins*
or *leads* that allow the IC to be connected to other ICs, to input-output devices like
a keypad or screen, or to a power supply. Figure 1.18 depicts several representative
IC packages. Typical chip dimensions are 10×10 mm, while a package like that of
Figure 1.18b is approximately $30 \times 30 \times 4$ mm. The IC package is often considerably bigger than the chip it contains because of the space taken by the pins. The
PGA package of Figure 1.18c has an array of pins (as many as 300 or more) pro-
jecting from its underside. A *multichip module* is a package containing several IC
chips attached to a substrate that provides mechanical support, as well as electrical
connections between the chips. Packaged ICs are often mounted on a *printed circuit board* that serves to support and interconnect the ICs. A contemporary computer consists of a set of ICs, a set of IO devices, and a power supply. The number
of ICs can range from one IC to several thousand, depending on the computer's
size and the IC types it uses.

   IC density. An integrated circuit is roughly characterized by its *density,*
defined as the number of transistors contained in the chip. As manufacturing techniques improved over the years, the size of the transistors in an IC and their interconnecting wires shrank, eventually reaching dimensions below a micron or 1 μm.
(By comparison, the width of a human hair is about 75 μm.) Consequently, IC densities have increased steadily, while chip size has varied very little.

   The earliest ICs—the first commercial IC appeared in 1961—contained fewer
than 100 transistors and employed *small-scale integration* or SSI. The terms
medium-scale, large-scale, and *very-large-scale integration* (MSI, LSI and VLSI,

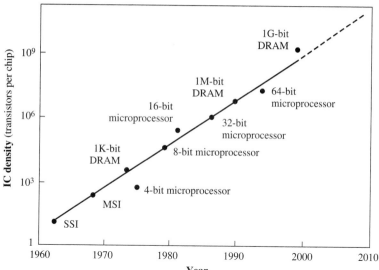

Figure 1.19
Evolution of the density of commercial ICs.

respectively) are applied to ICs containing hundreds, thousands, and millions of transistors, respectively. The boundaries between these IC classes are loose, and VLSI often serves as a catchall term for very dense circuits. Because their manufacture is highly automated—it resembles a printing process—ICs can be manufactured in high volume at low cost per circuit. Indeed, except for the latest and densest circuits, the cost of an IC has stayed fairly constant over the years, implying that newer generations of ICs deliver far greater value (measured by computing performance or storage capacity) per unit cost than their predecessors did.

Figure 1.19 shows the evolution of IC density as measured by two of the densest chip types: the dynamic random-access memory (DRAM), a basic component of main memories, and the single-chip CPU or *microprocessor*. Around 1970 it became possible to manufacture all the electronic circuits for a pocket calculator on a single IC chip. This development was quickly followed by single-chip DRAMs and microprocessors. As Figure 1.19 shows, the capacity of the largest available DRAM chip was $1K = 2^{10}$ bits in 1970 and has been growing steadily since then, reaching $1M = 2^{20}$ bits around 1985. A similar growth has occurred in the complexity of microprocessors. The first microprocessor, Intel's 4004, which was introduced in 1971, was designed to process 4-bit words. The Japanese calculator manufacturer Busicom commissioned the 4004 microprocessor, but after Busicom's early demise, Intel successfully marketed the 4004 as a programmable controller to replace standard, nonprogrammable logic circuits. As IC technology improved and chip density increased, the complexity and performance of one-chip microprocessors increased steadily, as reflected in the increase in CPU word size to 8 and then 16 bits by the mid-1980s. By 1990 manufacturers could fabricate the entire CPU of a System/360-class computer, along with part of its main memory, on a single IC. The combination of a CPU, memory, and IO circuits in one IC (or a small number of ICs) is called a *microcomputer*.

IC families. Within IC technology several subtechnologies exist that are distinguished by the transistor and circuit types they employ. Two of the most important of these technologies are bipolar and unipolar; the latter is normally referred to as MOS (metal-oxide-semiconductor) after its physical structure. Both bipolar and MOS circuits have transistors as their basic elements. They differ, however, in the polarities of the electric charges associated with the primary carriers of electrical signals within their transistors. *Bipolar circuits* use both negative carriers (electrons) and positive carriers (holes). *MOS circuits,* on the other hand, use only one type of charge carrier: positive in the case of P-type MOS (PMOS) and negative in the case of N-type MOS (NMOS). Various bipolar and MOS IC circuit types or *IC families* have been developed that provide trade-offs among density, operating speed, power consumption, and manufacturing cost. An MOS family that efficiently combines PMOS and NMOS transistors in the same IC is *complementary MOS* or *CMOS*. This technology came into widespread use in the 1980s and has been the technology of choice for microprocessors and other VLSI ICs since then because of its combination of high density, high speed, and very low power consumption [Weste and Eshragian 1992].

EXAMPLE 1.6 A ZERO-DETECTION CIRCUIT EMPLOYING CMOS TECHNOLOGY. To illustrate the role of transistors in computing, we examine a small CMOS circuit whose function is to detect when a 4-bit word $x_0 x_1 x_2 x_3$ becomes zero. The circuit's output z should be 1 when $x_0 x_1 x_2 x_3 = 0000$; it should be 0 for the other 15 combinations of input values. Zero detection is quite a common operation in data processing. For example, it is used to determine when a program loop terminates, as in the **if** statement (location 5R) appearing in the IAS program of Figure 1.15.

Figure 1.20 shows a particular implementation ZD of zero detection using a representative CMOS subfamily known as *static CMOS*. The circuit is shown in standard symbolic form in Figure 1.20a. It consists of equal numbers of PMOS transistors denoted $S_1{:}S_7$ and NMOS transistors denoted $S_8{:}S_{14}$. Each transistor acts as an on-off switch with three terminals, where the center terminal c controls the switch's state. When turned on, a signal propagation path is created between the transistor's upper and lower terminals; when turned off, that path is broken. An NMOS transistor is turned on by applying 1 to its control terminal c; it is turned off by applying 0 to c. A PMOS transistor, on the other hand, is turned on by $c = 0$ and turned off by $c = 1$.

Each set of input signals applied to ZD causes some transistors to switch on and others to switch off, which creates various signal paths through the circuit. In Figure 1.20 the constant signals 0 and 1 are applied at various points in ZD. (These signals are derived from ZD's electrical power supply.) The 0/1 signals "flow" through the circuit along the paths created by the transistors and determine various internal signal values, as well as the value applied to the main output line z. Figure 1.20b shows the signals and signal transmission paths produced by $x_0 x_1 x_2 x_3 = 0001$. The first input signal $x_0 = 0$ is applied to PMOS transistor S_1 and NMOS transistor S_8; hence S_1 is turned on and S_8 is turned off. Similarly, $x_1 = 0$ turns S_2 on and S_9 off. A path is created through S_1 and S_2, which applies 1 to the internal line y_1, as shown by the left-most heavy arrow in Figure 1.20b. In the same way the remaining input combinations make $y_2 = 0$ and $y_3 = 1$. The latter signal is applied to the two right-most transistors turning S_7 off and S_{14} on, which creates a path from the zero source to the primary output line via S_{14}, so $z = 0$ as required.

If we change input x_3 from 1 to 0 in Figure 1.20b, the following chain of events occurs: S_4 turns on and S_{11} turns off, changing y_2 to 1. Then S_{13} turns on and S_6 turns off, making $y_3 = 0$. Finally, the new value of y_3 turns S_7 on and S_{14} off, so z becomes 1.

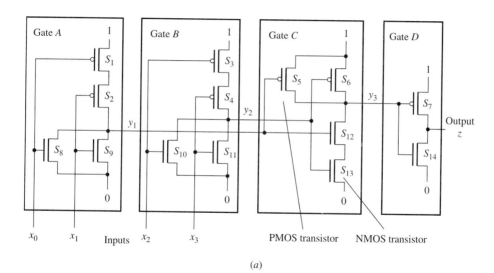

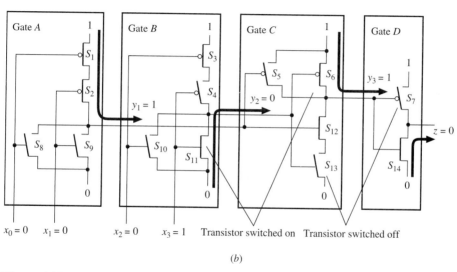

Figure 1.20
(a) CMOS circuit *ZD* for zero detection; (b) state of *ZD* with input combination
$x_0x_1x_2x_3 = 0001$ making $z = 0$.

Hence the zero input combination $x_0x_1x_2x_3 = 0000$ makes $z = 1$ as required. It can readily be verified that no other input combination does this.

A transistor circuit like that of Figure 1.20 models the behavior of a digital circuit at a low level of abstraction called the *switch level*. Because many of the ICs of interest contain huge numbers of transistors, it is rarely practical to analyze their computing functions at the switch level. Instead, we move to higher abstraction levels, two of which are illustrated in Figure 1.21. At the *gate* or *logic* level illustrated by Figure 1.21a, we represent certain common subcircuits by symbolic

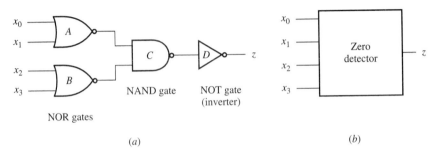

(a)   (b)

Figure 1.21
The zero-detection circuit of Figure 1.20 modeled at (a) the gate level and (b) the register level of abstraction.

components called (logic) *gates*. This particular logic circuit comprises four gates A, B, C, and D of three different types as indicated; note that each gate type has a distinct graphic symbol. In moving from the switch level, we collapse a multi-transistor circuit into a single gate and discard all its internal details. A key advantage of the logic level is that it is *technology independent,* so it can be used equally well to describe the behavior of any IC family. In dealing with computer design, we also use an even higher level of abstraction known as the *register* or *register-transfer* level. It treats the entire zero-detection circuit as a primitive or indivisible component, as in Figure 1.21b. The register level is the level at which we describe the internal workings of a CPU or other processor as, for example, in Figures 1.2 and 1.17. Observe that the primitive components (represented by boxes) in these diagrams include registers, ALUs, and the like. When we treat an entire CPU, memory, or computer as a primitive component, we have moved to the highest level of abstraction, which is called the *processor* or *system* level.

1.3.2 Processor Architecture

By 1980 computers were classified into three main types: mainframe computers, minicomputers, and microcomputers. The term *mainframe* was applied to the traditional "large" computer system, often containing thousands of ICs and costing millions of dollars. It typically served as the central computing facility for an organization such as a university, a factory, or a bank. Mainframes were then room-sized machines placed in special computer centers and not directly accessible to the average user. The minicomputer was a smaller (desk size) and slower version of the mainframe, but its relatively low cost (hundreds of thousands of dollars) made it suitable as a "departmental" computer to be shared by a group of users—in a small business, for example. The microcomputer was even smaller, slower, and cheaper (a few thousand dollars), packing all the electronics of a computer into a handful of ICs, including microprocessor (CPU), memory, and IO chips.

Personal computers. Microcomputer technology gave rise to a new class of general-purpose machines called *personal computers* (PCs), which are intended for a single user. These small, inexpensive computers are designed to sit on an office desk or fold into a compact form to be carried. The more powerful desktop computers intended for scientific computing are referred to as *workstations*. A typical

PC has the von Neumann organization, with a microprocessor, a multimegabyte main memory, and an assortment of IO devices: a keyboard, a video monitor or screen, a magnetic or optical disk drive unit for high-capacity secondary memory, and interface circuits for connecting the PC to printers and to other computers. Personal computers have proliferated to the point that, in the more developed societies, they are present in most offices and many homes. Two of the main applications of PCs are word processing, where personal computers have assumed and greatly expanded all the functions of the typewriter, and data-processing tasks like financial record keeping. They are also used for entertainment, education, and increasingly, communication with other computers via the World Wide Web.

Personal computers were introduced in the mid-1970s by a small electronics kit maker, MITS Inc. [Augarten 1984]. The MITS Altair computer was built around the Intel 8008, an early 8-bit microprocessor, and cost only $395 in kit form. The most successful personal computer family was the IBM PC series introduced in 1981. Following the precedent set by earlier IBM computers, it quickly become the de facto standard for this class of machine. A new factor also aided the standardization process—namely, IBM's decision to give the PC what came to be called an *open architecture*, by making its design specifications available to other manufacturers of computer hardware and software. As a result, the IBM PC became very popular, and many versions of it—the so-called *PC clones*—were produced by others, including startup companies that made the manufacture of low-cost PC clones their main business. The PC's open architecture also provided an incentive for the development of a vast amount of application-specific software from many sources. Indeed a new software industry emerged aimed at the mass-production of low-cost, self-contained programs aimed at specific applications of the IBM PC and a few other widely used computer families.

The IBM PC series is based on Intel Corp.'s 80X86 family of microprocessors, which began with the 8086 microprocessor introduced in 1978 and was followed by the 80286 (1983), the 80386 (1986), the 80486 (1989), and the Pentium[2] (1993) [Albert and Avnon 1993]; the Pentium II appeared in 1997. The IBM PC series is also distinguished by its use of the MS/DOS operating system and the Windows graphical user interface, both developed by Microsoft Corp. Another popular personal computer series is Apple Computer's Macintosh, introduced in 1984 and built around the Motorola 680X0 microprocessor family, whose evolution from the 68000 microprocessor (1979) parallels that of the 80X86/Pentium [Farrell 1984]. In 1994 the Macintosh CPU was changed to a new microprocessor known as the PowerPC.

Figure 1.22 shows the organization of a typical personal computer from the mid-1990s. Its legacy from earlier von Neumann computers is apparent—compare Figure 1.22 to Figure 1.17. At the core of this computer is a single-chip microprocessor such as the Pentium or PowerPC. As we will see, the microprocessor's internal (micro) architecture usually contains a number of speedup features not found in its predecessors. A system bus connects the microprocessor to a main memory based on semiconductor DRAM technology and to an IO subsystem. A separate IO bus, such as the industry standard PCI (peripheral component interconnect) "local"

---

[2]A legal ruling that microprocessor names that are numbers cannot have trademark protection, resulted in the 80486 being followed by a microprocessor called the Pentium rather than the 80586.

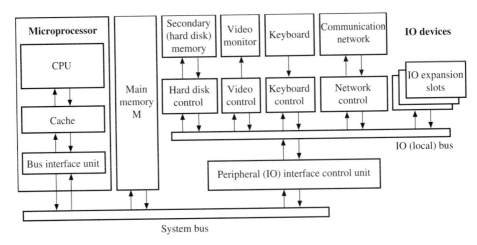

Figure 1.22
A typical personal computer system.

bus, connects directly to the IO devices and their individual controllers. The IO bus is linked to the system bus, to which the microprocessor and memory are attached via a special bus-to-bus control unit sometimes referred to as a *bridge*. The IO devices of a personal computer include the traditional keyboard, a CRT-based or flat-panel video monitor, and disk drive units for the hard and flexible (floppy) disk storage devices that constitute secondary memory. More recent additions to the IO device repertoire include drive units for CD-ROMs (compact disc read-only memories), which have extremely high capacity and allow sound and video images to be stored and retrieved efficiently. Other common audiovisual IO devices in personal computers are microphones, loudspeakers, video scanners, and the like, which are referred to as *multimedia* equipment.

Performance considerations. As processor hardware became much less expensive in the 1970s, thanks mainly to advances in VLSI technology (Figure 1.19), computer designers increased the use of complex, multistep instructions. This reduces N, the total number of instructions that must be executed for a given task, since a single complex instruction can replace several simpler ones. For example, a multiply instruction can replace a multiinstruction subroutine that implements multiplication by repeated execution of add instructions. Reducing N in this way tends to reduce overall program execution time T, as well as the time that the CPU spends fetching instructions and their operands from memory. The same advances in VLSI made it possible to add new features to old microprocessors, such as new instructions, data types, instruction sets, and addressing modes, while retaining the ability to execute programs written for the older machines.

The Intel 80X86/Pentium series illustrates the trend toward more complex instruction sets. The 1978-vintage 8086 microprocessor chip, which contained a mere 20,000 transistors, was designed to process 16-bit data words and had no instructions for operating on floating-point numbers [Morse et al. 1978]. Twenty-five years later, its direct descendant, the Pentium, contained over 3 million transistors, processed 32-bit and 64-bit words directly, and executed a comprehensive set of floating-point instructions [Albert and Avnon 1993]. The Pentium accumulated most of the architectural features of its various predecessors in order to enable it to execute, with little or no modification, programs written for earlier 80X86-series machines. Reflecting these characteristics, the 80X86, 680X0, and most older computer series have been called *complex instruction set computers* (CISCs).[3]

By the 1980s it became apparent that complex instructions have certain disadvantages and that execution of even a small percentage of such instructions can sometimes *reduce* a computer's overall performance. To illustrate this condition, suppose that a particular microprocessor has only fast, simple instructions, each of which requires k time units, to execute. Thus the microprocessor can execute 100 instructions in $100k$ time units. Now suppose that 5 percent of the instructions are slow, complex instructions requiring $21k$ time units each. To execute an average set of 100 instructions therefore requires $(5 \times 21 + 95)k = 200k$ time units, assuming no other factors are involved. Consequently, the 5 percent of complex instructions can, as in this particular example, double the overall program execution time.

Thus while complex instructions reduce program size, this technology does not necessarily translate into faster program execution. Moreover, complex instructions require relatively complex processing circuits, which tend to put CISCs in the largest and most expensive IC category. These drawbacks were first recognized by John Cocke and his colleagues at IBM in the mid-1970s, who developed an experimental computer called 801 that aimed to achieve very fast overall performance via a streamlined instruction set that could be executed extremely fast [Cocke and Markstein 1990]. The 801 and subsequent machines with a similar design philosophy have been called *reduced instruction set computers* (RISCs). A number of commercially successful RISC microprocessors were introduced in the 1980s, including the IBM RISC System/6000 and SPARC, an "open" microprocessor developed by Sun Microsystems and based on RISC research at the University of California, Berkeley [Patterson 1985]. Many of the speedup features of RISC machines have found their way into other new computers, including such CISC microprocessors as the Pentium. Indeed, the term *RISC* is often used to refer to *any* computer with an instruction set and an associated CPU organization designed for very high performance; the actual size of the instruction set is relatively unimportant.

A computer's performance is also strongly affected by other factors besides its instruction set, especially the time required to move instructions and data between the CPU and main memory M and, to a lesser extent, the time required to move information between M and IO devices. It typically takes the CPU about five times longer to obtain a word from M than from one of its internal registers. This difference in speed has existed since the first electronic computers, despite strenuous efforts by circuit designers to develop memory devices and processor–memory interface circuits that are fast enough to keep up with the fastest microprocessors. Indeed the CPU–M speed disparity has become such a feature of standard (von Neumann) computers that is sometimes referred to as the *von Neumann bottleneck*. RISC computers usually limit access to main memory to a few load and store instructions; other instructions, including all data-processing and program-control instructions, must have their operands in CPU registers. This so-

---

[3]The public became aware of CISC complexity when a design flaw affecting the floating-point division instruction of the Pentium was discovered in 1994. The cost to Intel of this bug, including the replacement cost of Pentium chips already installed in PCs, was about $475 million.

called *load-store architecture* is intended to reduce the impact of the von Neumann bottleneck by reducing the total number of the memory accesses made by the CPU.

Performance measures. A rough indication of CPU speed is the number of "basic" operations that it can perform per unit of time. A typical basic operation is the fixed-point addition of the contents of two registers R1 and R2, as in the symbolic instruction

$$R1 := R1 + R2$$

Such operations are timed by a regular stream of signals (ticks or beats) issued by a central timing signal, the system *clock*. The speed of the clock is its frequency f measured in millions of ticks per second; the units for this are megahertz (MHz). Each tick of the clock triggers a basic operation; hence the time required to execute the operation is $1/f$ microseconds (μs). This value is called the *clock cycle* or *clock period* T_{clock}. For example, a computer clocked at 250 MHz can perform one basic operation in the clock period $T_{clock} = 1/250 = 0.004$ μs. Complicated operations such as division or operations on floating-point numbers can require more than one clock cycle to complete their execution.

Generally speaking, smaller electronic devices operate faster than larger ones, so the increase in IC chip density discussed above has been accompanied by a steady, but less dramatic, increase in clock speed. For example, from 1981 to 1995 microprocessor clock speeds increased from about 10 MHz to 100 MHz. Clock speeds of 1 gigahertz (1 GHz or 1000 MHz) and beyond are feasible using faster versions of current CMOS technology. It might therefore seem possible to achieve any desired processor speed simply by increasing the CPU clock frequency. However, the rate at which clock frequency is increasing due to IC technology improvements is relatively slow and may be approaching limits determined by the speed of light, power dissipation, and similar physical considerations. Extremely fast circuits also tend to be very expensive to manufacture.

The CPU's processing of an instruction involves several steps, each of which requires at least one clock cycle:

1. Fetch the instruction from main memory M.
2. Decode the instruction's opcode.
3. Load (read) from M any operands needed unless they are already in CPU registers.
4. Execute the instruction via a register-to-register operation using an appropriate functional unit of the CPU, such as a fixed-point adder.
5. Store (write) the results in M unless they are to be retained in CPU registers.

The fastest instructions have all their operands in CPU registers and can be executed by the CPU in a single clock cycle, so steps 1 to 3 all take one clock cycle. The slowest instructions require multiple memory accesses and multiple register-to-register operations to complete their execution. Consequently, measures of instruction execution performance are based on average figures, which are usually determined experimentally by measuring the run times of representative or *benchmark programs*. The more representative the programs are, that is, the more accurately they reflect real applications, the better the performance figures they provide.

Suppose that execution of a particular benchmark program or set (suite) of such programs Q on a given CPU takes T seconds and involves the execution of a total of N machine (object) instructions. Here N is the actual number of instructions executed, including repeated executions of the same instruction; it is not the number of instructions appearing in Q. As far as the typical computer user is concerned, the key performance goal is to minimize the total *program execution time T*. While T can be determined accurately only by measurement of Q's run time in actual or simulated execution, we can relate T to some basic parameters of the computer's architecture and implementation. One such parameter is the (average) number of *instructions executed per second*, which we denote by *IPS*. Clearly, $T = N/IPS$ s. Another common measure of the performance of a CPU is the average number of *cycles per instruction* or *CPI* needed to execute Q. Now $CPI = (f \times 10^6)/IPS$, where f is the CPU's clock frequency in MHz. Hence, the program execution time T is given by

$$T = \frac{N \times CPI}{f \times 10^6} \quad \text{s} \tag{1.12}$$

It is also common to measure CPU performance in terms of *millions of instructions executed per second*, denoted *MIPS*, where $MIPS = IPS \times 10^6$. Clearly $MIPS = f/CPI$.

Equation (1.12) indicates how the three separate factors software, architecture, and hardware technology jointly determine a computer's performance.

1. *Software*: The efficiency with which the programs are written and compiled into object code influences N, the number of instructions executed. Other factors being equal, reducing N tends to reduce the overall execution time T.
2. *Architecture*: The efficiency with which individual instructions are processed directly affects CPI, the number of cycles per instruction executed. Reducing CPI also tends to reduce T.
3. *Hardware*: The raw speed of the processor circuits determines f, the clock frequency. Increasing f tends to reduce T.

In general, the complex instruction sets of CISC processors aim to reduce N at the expense of CPI, whereas RISC processors aim to reduce CPI at the expense of N. Advances in VLSI technology affecting all types of computers tend to increase f.

Speedup techniques. A number of speed-enhancing features have been incorporated into the design of computers in recent years [Hwang 1993]; they are summarized in Figure 1.23. These methods were defined as far back as the 1960s and 1970s for use in mainframe computers. A *cache* is a memory unit placed between the CPU and main memory M and used to store instructions, data, or both. It has much smaller storage capacity than M, but it can be accessed (read from or written into) more rapidly and is often placed (at least partly) on the same chip as the CPU. The cache's effect is to reduce the average time required to access an instruction or data word, typically to just a single clock cycle. Special hardware and software techniques support the complex flow of information among M, the cache, and the registers of the CPU.

Another important speedup technique known as *pipelining* allows the processing of several instructions to be partially overlapped. Pipelining is most easily done

Feature	Objective	Description
Cache memory	To provide the CPU with faster access to instructions and data.	A cache is a memory unit inserted between the CPU and main memory M. It is faster than M but has less storage capacity.
Pipelined processing	To increase performance by allowing the processing of several instructions to be partially overlapped.	The CPU is constructed from independent subunits (stages), which can hold several instructions in different stages of execution.
Superscalar processing	To increase performance by allowing several instructions to be processed in parallel (full overlapping).	Multiple (pipelined) units are provided for instruction processing. Instructions can be issued simultaneously to each unit.

Figure 1.23
Some important speedup features of modern computers.

for a sequence of instructions of the same or similar types that employ a single E-unit, such as a floating-point processor. However, all the common steps involved in instruction processing by the CPU can be pipelined: instruction fetching (IF), instruction decoding (ID), operand loading (OL), execution (EX), and operand storing (OS). A pipelined system is often compared to an assembly line on which many products are in various stages of manufacture at the same time. In a nonpipelined CPU, instructions are executed in strict sequence, as depicted in Figure 1.24a. Pipelining permits the situation shown in Figure 1.24b, where each major step of

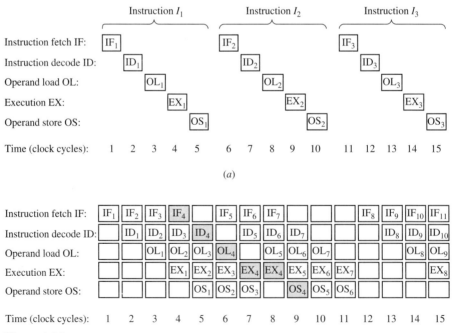

Figure 1.24
Instruction processing: (a) sequential or nonpipelined and (b) pipelined.

instruction processing is assigned to, and handled independently by, a separate sub-unit (stage) of the CPU pipeline. In this example, up to five instructions can be overlapped, provided the necessary pipeline stages are available. Note that performance-reducing delays occur, as in the case of instruction I_4 (shaded), which must use the EX stage for two consecutive cycles. A similar problem occurs in the case of branch instructions like I_7 in Figure 1.24b, where the outcome of I_7's EX step must be known before the location of the next instruction (I_8) to be processed can be identified.

A microprocessor's effective *MIPS* rate can also be increased by replicating various instruction-processing circuits so that several instructions can be in the same processing phase at the same time. This makes it possible to start the processing of, or *issue*, two or more instructions simultaneously or in parallel; in other words, the instructions can be completely overlapped. CPUs with this capability are said to be *superscalar*. (Note that two instructions in the same pipeline must be issued sequentially rather than in parallel.) For example, if the logic needed for the IF, ID, OL, EX, and OS steps is duplicated (with or without pipelining), then two instructions can be issued simultaneously. However, if the instructions are not independent, for example, if they share the same operands or one takes as input a result computed by the other, then delays not unlike those illustrated in Figure 1.24b can occur. Pipelining and superscalar design are both instances of *instruction-level parallelism*. The logic circuits needed to deal with parallelism of this kind add considerable complexity to the CPU's program control and execution units.

EXAMPLE 1.7 THE POWERPC MICROPROCESSOR SERIES [MOTOROLA 1993]. In the early 1990s Apple, IBM, and Motorola jointly developed the PowerPC. It is a family of single-chip microprocessors, including the 601, 603, and other models, which share a common architecture derived from the POWER architecture used in IBM's RISC System/6000 [Diefendorf, Oehler, and Hochsprung 1994; Weiss and Smith 1994]. Although it is also designated a RISC, the PowerPC has a large number of instructions—more than 200 distinct types, in fact—and its design is far from simple. Nevertheless, it exhibits the following features that are typical of contemporary RISC-style designs:

1. Instructions have a fixed length (32 bits or one word) and employ just a few opcode formats and addressing modes.
2. Only load and store instructions can access main memory; all other instructions must have their operands in CPU registers. This load/store architecture reduces the time devoted to accessing memory. This time is further reduced by the use of one or more levels of cache memory.
3. Instruction processing is heavily pipelined. For example, the PowerPC has an E-unit for integer (fixed-point) operations that has the four pipeline stages: fetch, decode, execute, and write results. Hence if an E-unit's pipeline can be kept full, a new result emerges from it every clock cycle, thus achieving the ideal performance level of one fully executed instruction per clock cycle.
4. The CPU contains several E-units—the number depends on the model—which allow it to issue several instructions simultaneously and puts the PowerPC in the superscalar category.

The organization shown in Figure 1.25 is typical of the early PowerPC models, such as the 601 and 603, which have three E-units: an integer execution unit, a floating-point unit, and a branch processing unit, allowing up to three instructions to be

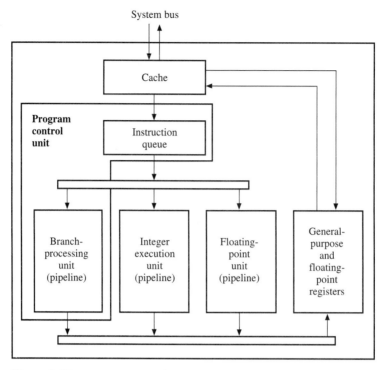

Figure 1.25
Overall organization of the PowerPC.

issued in the same clock cycle. The integer unit executes all fixed-point numerical and logic operations, including those associated with load-store instructions. Although part of the CPU's program control unit, the branch processing unit is considered an E-unit for branch instructions. Each PowerPC chip also contains a cache memory, whose size and organization vary with the model. For example, the PowerPC 603, which was introduced in 1995 and is aimed at low-power applications like laptop computers, has a 16 KB cache, half of which stores data while the other half stores instructions. A hint of the complexity of the 603 can be seen from Figure 1.26. It contains 1.6 million transistors in an IC chip of area 7.4×11.5 mm (in its earliest versions) and consumes less than 3 watts of power.

To illustrate the PowerPC's instruction set, consider the vector addition discussed earlier and expressed by the FORTRAN90 statement

$$C(1:1000) = A(1:1000) + B(1:1000)$$

Assume that each vector consists of 1000 double-precision (64-bit), floating-point numbers. An assembly-language program for the PowerPC that carries out this vector operation appears in Figure 1.27. (We have slightly simplified the language syntax here.) The last five instructions form the program's main loop and are executed 1000 times. The key data-processing instruction in this loop has the opcode fadd, and performs a double-precision, floating-point addition. All fadd's operands are in 64-bit floating-point registers, of which the PowerPC has 32, denoted fr0:fr31 here. The program communicates with memory via the instructions lw (load word), lfdu (load floating-point double-precision with update), and stfdu (store floating-point double-precision with update); these are just a few of the PowerPC's many types of load-store

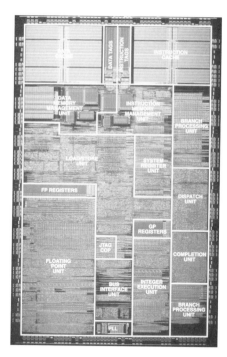

Figure 1.26
Photomicrograph of the PowerPC 603 microprocessor chip. [Courtesy of Motorola Inc.]

instructions. The PowerPC has 32 general-purpose registers r0:r31, several of which
serve as memory address registers in our program. The update option, indicated by the
u suffix on lfdu and stfdu invokes a kind of automatic indexing, which causes the contents of the memory address register to be initially incremented. For example, the
instruction

$$\text{lfdu} \quad \text{fr1, 1(r5)}$$

invokes the following two operations: increment the address register r5 and then load
the data register fr1. In other words

$$r5 := r5 + 1; \; fr1 := mem(r5); \tag{1.13}$$

Location	Instruction		Comment
	mtspr	CTR, #1000	Move vector length N = 1000 to special register CTR.
	lw	r5, #A	Load start address of vector A into general register r5.
	lw	r6, #B	Load start address of vector B into general register r6.
	lw	r7, #C	Load start address of vector C into general register r7.
LOOP	lfdu	fr1, 1(r5)	Load A(i + 1) into floating-point register fr1; update r5.
	lfdu	fr2, 1(r6)	Load B(i + 1) into floating-point register fr2; update r6.
	fadd	fr1, fr2, fr1	Perform floating-point addition fr1 := fr1 + fr2.
	stfdu	fr1, 1(r7)	Store fr1 as C(i + 1); update r7.
	bne	LOOP	Decrement CTR, then branch to LOOP if CTR $\neq$ 0.

Figure 1.27
A PowerPC program for vector addition.

The memory data denoted by mem(r5) in (1.13) is normally in the PowerPC's cache memory which, at any time, mimics a portion of the main memory M that is in active use. Thus if the current memory address defined by r5 is assigned to the cache, the data required by lfdu is fetched from the cache, rather than from M, where a "master" copy of the same data resides. Similarly, the store instruction stfdu writes its data into a cache location, although (eventually) the corresponding data in M must be updated. Should mem(r7) not be currently assigned to the cache, the PowerPC's elaborate memory access control automatically transfers data between M and the cache to assign the relevant portion of the processor's address space to the cache. The last instruction bne (branch if not equal) appearing in Figure 1.27 is a powerful conditional branch instruction. First bne automatically decrements the "special" register called CTR (counter) and tests it for zero. If CTR $\neq 0$, then the next instruction executed is the one stored in location LOOP. When CTR reaches zero, the vector addition terminates and the instruction following bne is executed. Observe that the five-instruction program loop typically resides in the cache for the duration of the program's execution.

As Figure 1.25 indicates, the Power PC has three (more in some models) separate E-units for executing integer, floating-point, and branch instructions. This superscalar design allows up to three separate instructions to be dispatched (issued) for execution in every clock cycle. Moreover, these E-units are pipelined to varying degrees, so that an active E-unit can contain several consecutive instructions in various stages of execution. Hence, for our vector addition task, we would expect to find the CPU concurrently executing several operations of the form

$$C(j) := A(j) + B(j), C(j+1) := A(j+1) + B(j+1), C(j+2) := A(j+2) + B(j+2), \ldots$$

The concurrency achieved, and therefore the execution time of the program, depend on various implementation details and cannot be determined from inspection of the program code alone.

The vector addition programs for the IAS (Figure 1.15) and the PowerPC (Figure 1.27) reflect the evolution of computer architecture over a 50-year period. The two programs are fundamentally similar in that each program is designed to loop N times through the three basic steps: load data from M, add data in CPU registers, and store results in M. The computers share the same basic features of the von Neumann architecture. However, the IAS machine has far fewer data types, a much weaker instruction set (especially in the area of program control), and essentially no instruction-level parallelism. The IAS lacks floating-point data formats and instructions, so a much more complicated IAS program would be required to handle double-precision, floating-point numbers comparable to those assumed in Figure 1.27. The IAS also lacks the following features of the PowerPC's instruction set: indexed addressing modes; conditional branch instructions that can decrement and test a variable; and powerful arithmetic instructions such as multiply, divide, and multiply-and-add. Note also the vast differences in physical size, performance, and cost between the IAS and PowerPC.

1.3.3 System Architecture

We next review the overall organization of contemporary computer systems, including those formed by linking computers together into large networks.

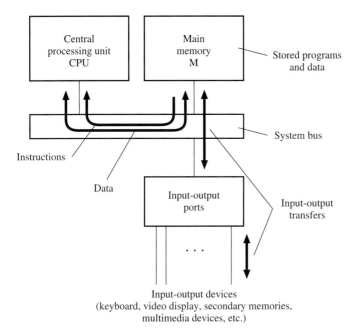

Figure 1.28
Overview of computer system operation.

Basic organization. A stand-alone computer system, which is most commonly seen as a desktop machine (a PC or workstation) intended for a single user, has the basic organization illustrated by Figure 1.28; see also Figure 1.22. This organization has changed little from that found in earlier generations, despite the massive improvements in implementation technologies that have occurred in recent years. The computer's main hardware components continue to be a CPU, a main memory, and an IO subsystem, which communicate with one another over a system bus. Its main software component is an operating system that performs most system management functions.

The key hardware element is a single-chip microprocessor, embodying a modern version of the von Neumann architecture. The microprocessor serves as the computer's CPU and is responsible for fetching, decoding, and executing instructions. Data and instructions are typically composed of 32-bit words, which constitute the basic information units processed by the computer. The CPU is characterized by an instruction set containing up to 200 or so instruction types, which perform data transfer, data processing, and program control operations that have changed little over the years. The CPU may be augmented by on-chip or off-chip *coprocessors* that implement such specialized functions as managing the graphical user interface (GUI).

The role of the computer's main or primary memory M is to store programs and data as they are being processed by the CPU. M is a random-access memory (RAM) comprising a linear store of items (usually 8-bit bytes), each of which is assigned a unique address that permits the CPU to read or change (write) its contents via load or store instructions, respectively. M is backed up by a much larger but slower secondary memory, typically implemented by hard disks employing magnetic or optical storage technology and forming part of the IO subsystem. As in the PowerPC (Figure 1.25), an intermediate memory called a cache may also be inserted between the CPU and M. Thus we find a hierarchy of memory devices composed of the CPU's registers, the cache, the main memory, and the secondary memory. This complex structure results from the fact that the fastest memory devices are also the most costly. The memory hierarchy is intended to provide the CPU with fast access to large amounts of data at a fairly low cost.

The purpose of the IO system is to enable a user to communicate with the computer. IO devices are attached to the host computer by means of IO *ports*, whose function is to control data transfers between IO devices and main memory. Active programs communicate with IO ports in much the same way as they communicate with M. An IO device is assigned a set of memory-like addresses, which allow input and output instructions to be implemented in essentially the same way as load and store instructions, respectively. However, the CPU usually takes much longer to access a word stored in the IO system than to access a word stored in M—most IO operations are quite slow.

The traditional input and output devices are a keyboard and screen (provided by a CRT or a flat-panel display), respectively, which are convenient for handling textual information. Adding a pointing device like a mouse makes a display screen into an input device, permitting communication between the user and the computer via graphical images. Special software, such as the Windows interface found in personal computers, supports GUIs. Audio interfaces for speech generation and recognition extend the computer into a multimedia system. A major component of most IO systems is a set of secondary memory devices that provide bulk storage of programs and data. Rapid transfer of information between primary and secondary memories is often a key factor in a system's overall performance.

Microcontrollers. Their small size and low cost have made it feasible to use miniature general-purpose computers, referred to as *microcontrollers,* for tasks that previously employed either special-purpose control circuits or had no control logic at all, for example, controlling a home washing machine or the ignition system of a car. Programs stored in a read-only memory (ROM) that forms a part of the main memory tailor a microcontroller to a particular application. The microcontroller is built into, or *embedded* in, the controlled device, often in a way that is invisible to the end user. Hence an embedded microcontroller that has been programmed to handle the application in question can replace application-specific control circuits, often at substantial cost savings. Furthermore, by bringing the power of a computer to bear on relatively mundane applications, manufacturers can readily introduce many new features to improve flexibility, performance, or ease of use. As a result, most computers in operation today are microcontrollers in embedded systems.

Figure 1.29 shows one of the first applications of a microcontroller: a point-of-sale (POS) terminal that has replaced cash registers in retail stores. The microcontroller has a conventional computer organization built around a system bus to which are attached a microprocessor (the CPU), one or more ROM chips for program storage, and one or more RAM chips for data and working storage. All IO devices are also connected to the system bus using IO ports with standard interfaces. The IO devices in a typical POS terminal are a keyboard, a receipt printer, a visual display, a product-code scanner, and a credit-card reader. The latter is used

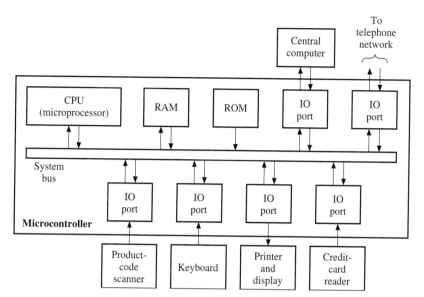

Figure 1.29
A microcontroller-based point-of-sale terminal.

for credit authorization and requires a connection to the telephone system. The final component is a link to a central computer used to provide pricing information, perform inventory control, and so forth.

Computer networks. The computer in Figure 1.29 is linked directly to a central computer and indirectly to a potentially huge number of computers via the telephone network. The linking of computers to form networks of various types has become an increasingly important feature of modern computing; see Figure 1.30. A

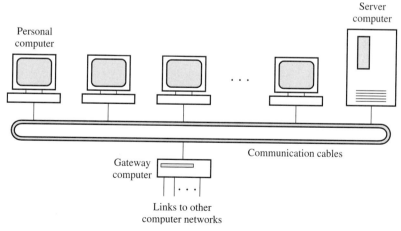

Figure 1.30
A local-area computer network.

computer in an office or industrial environment is typically linked to other computers in the same organization via communication links that can be thought of as an extension to the system bus. The linked computers then form a small, closed computer network known as a *local-area network* (LAN) or *intranet*. The physical links between the computers can be built in various ways, including electrical cables, optical fibers, and radio (wireless) links. Special IO programs (communication software) enable the computers on the network to exchange information and access common computing resources called *servers*.

Computer networks have several advantages over the large, centralized (mainframe) computers that they have come to replace. The individual user has direct access to a computer (his or her personal computer) that can quickly and conveniently handle many routine computing tasks. Users can also access computing facilities that they need less frequently, for example a high-performance supercomputer or costly IO equipment, via the computer network. Many widely dispersed users can share such specialized equipment via the network, thus lowering its cost to individual users. Furthermore, a computer network provides useful new services such as electronic mail, remote library services, and on-line shopping.

Several LANs can be linked together by various means including the telephone networks, which increasingly are designed to accommodate digital data transmission, including video data, as well as the traditional (digitized) voice communication. In Figure 1.30, one computer serves as a *gateway* device that manages communication between the LAN and other computer networks. A collection of linked LANs forms a large computer network that can be worldwide in scope. In the early 1990s a network of this sort known as the *Internet* emerged, which because of its huge size and global reach—an estimated 16 million server sites in 180 countries with 72 million users in 1997—has had a profound impact on the way people compute and communicate.

The Internet had its origins in a computer network called the ARPANET sponsored by the Advanced Research Projects Agency of the U.S. Department of Defense around 1970. This experimental network was originally designed to connect research institutions in the United States via leased lines; Figure 1.31 shows the structure of the ARPANET at an early stage in its evolution (1972) when it linked 26 research organizations in the United States. The ARPANET pioneered an information-transmission technique called *packet switching,* which divides both long and short messages into *packets of* fixed length that can be transmitted independently from source to destination via variable numbers of intermediate nodes. Each node contains a server that is responsible for sorting the packets from the various messages and forwarding them to the appropriate next destinations. Different packages can be sent by different routes determined by the network traffic conditions. At the final destination, a message is reassembled from its constituent packets. The communication software designed for the ARPANET and known as *TCP/IP* (*Transmission Control Protocol/Internet Protocol*) defines the communication standards for the Internet.

In the early years the Internet was used almost exclusively to transfer text files such as electronic mail (e-mail) messages. This situation changed fundamentally in 1989 when scientists at CERN (Centre Européen pour la Recherche Nucléaire) in Geneva overlaid on TCP/IP a new, high-level protocol called *http* (*hypertext transport protocol*) and an associated programming language *html* (*hypertext markup*

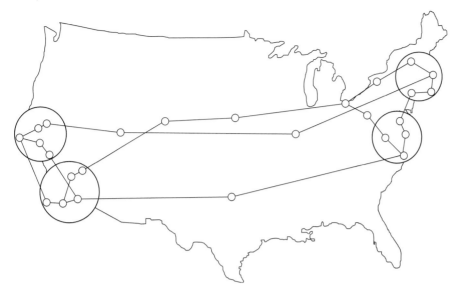

Figure 1.31
The ARPANET in 1972.

language) to permit the linking of diverse file types—text, still pictures, movies, sound, etc.—in an simple way. This combination enabled users to create multimedia files easily and transmit them rapidly over the Internet. For example, using html, a text file can be tagged with commands that tell a computer where to find and insert visual images into the text file; the required image files can be located anywhere on the Internet. The human end user can access the information from a remote host via a simple point-and-click operation on a PC or workstation. The result is an enormously rich collection of easily accessible data that has come to be known as the *World Wide Web*.

Parallel processing. So-called supercomputers capable of executing many instructions in parallel have existed since the 1950s. Early commercial supercomputers relied heavily on pipeline processing and had a single CPU organized around one or more multistage pipelines. This organization allows several instructions to be in process simultaneously in each pipeline, resulting in a potential increase in performance of a factor of n per n-stage pipeline. The Cray-1 supercomputer, first marketed by Cray Research Inc. in 1976, contained 12 pipeline processors for arithmetic-logic operations, several of which could operate in parallel [Russell 1978]. The Cray-1 could execute up to 160 million operations such as floating-point addition per second. Computers of this type have been most successfully applied to scientific computations involving large amounts of vector and matrix calculations; consequently they are sometimes called *vector processors*. The degree of parallelism n possible with a pipeline is small, typically less than 10. As the PowerPC demonstrates (Example 1.7), pipeline processing of instructions is now a standard feature of microprocessors. Indeed, single-chip microprocessors reached the Cray-1's level of performance in scientific computation in the mid-1990s.

An alternative approach to parallel processing with the potential of achieving unlimited degrees of parallelism is to use many independent processors operating in unison. For example, a network of computers can be programmed to work concurrently on different parts of the same task. Such a *loosely coupled* or *distributed* system is useful for computing tasks that can easily be partitioned into independent subtasks, with infrequent communication of results among the subtasks. However, many large-scale scientific computations permit a task to be partitioned into subtasks but require frequent and rapid exchange of results between the subtasks. The time required for such exchanges—they are essentially slow IO transfers—limits the usefulness of a computer network as a supercomputer. To address the interprocessor communication problem, computers have been built that employ *n* separate CPUs that are tightly coupled, both physically and logically. Processors in these machines can access one another's data rapidly and are called *multiprocessors*. The task of writing parallel programs and optimizing compilers for multiprocessors is far less well understood than the corresponding problem for a single (pipelined or nonpipelined) processor. Nevertheless, machines of this type have been studied for many years, and in the 1980s powerful multiprocessors employing many low-cost microprocessors as their CPUs began to be manufactured commercially, mainly as scientific computers.

Two types of multiprocessors are shared-memory and distributed-memory machines. In *shared-memory* machines all the processors have access to a common main memory through which they communicate to share programs and data. In *distributed-memory* machines each processor has only a private or local main memory and communicates with other processors by sending them messages through an IO subsystem linking the processors. In each case a key issue is to design processor-to-memory or processor-to-processor interconnection networks that are of high-speed and reasonable cost. For small multiprocessors containing up to 30 or so processors, a fast bus can serve as an interconnection network. In effect, the basic organization of Figure 1.30 is used with multiple CPUs attached to a high-speed system bus. To construct *massively parallel* multiprocessors, that is, computers with hundreds or thousands of CPUs, various specialized interconnection networks have been developed, which we will examine in Chapter 7. Massively parallel multiprocessors are difficult to program and cannot run conventional (uniprocessor) programs efficiently. As a result, these machines have so far had a limited impact on the commercial computer marketplace.

1.4
SUMMARY

Humans have struggled with difficult computations since ancient times. Some of these problems are inherently unsolvable—they cannot be solved even in principle by a Turing machine, which is a simple, abstract, but completely general digital computer. Some theoretically solvable problems are intractable in that they cannot be solved within a reasonable amount of time by practical computers. However, given a suitable algorithm or solution method as well as a computer of sufficient power, many important problems can be satisfactorily solved. Designing practical computers that provide the highest possible performance at acceptable cost is the basic job of the computer architect.

The design of computing machines has evolved over a long period of time. Charles Babbage conceived the concept of a general-purpose, program-controlled computer in the mid-19th century. Such a machine was not completed until the 1940s, however, when the first electronic computers were successfully constructed. Since then, progress has been dramatic, mainly driven by advances in computer hardware technology.

John von Neumann and others defined the basic organization of the modern computer. It comprises the following major components: a CPU responsible for fetching and executing instructions; a main memory used for instruction and data storage; and a set of input-output devices, such as user terminals, printers, and secondary memory devices. Three main instruction types are found in every computer: data-transfer, data-processing, and program-control instructions. The instruction set and the way the instructions are processed define the power of a computer. The computer is typically programmed in a high-level language such as C++ or Java, which is automatically compiled into executable code (object programs) built from its instruction set.

Integrated circuit technology has had a profound impact on computer design via the single-chip microprocessor and the high-capacity RAM chip. IC technology has enabled manufacturers to build very small, low-cost computers for general use (personal computers and workstations) as well as for special applications (embedded microcontrollers). IC technology has also been the driving force in the proliferation of large-scale computer networks—the Internet, for example—and high-performance multiprocessors.

As the computer industry has matured, a few computer series have tended to become de facto architectural standards, notably IBM's System/360 mainframe family introduced in the 1960s and its PC personal computer family introduced in the 1980s. Recent computer families are distinguished by powerful RISC-style instruction sets and such performance-enhancing features as pipelining, instruction-level parallelism, and cache memories. Continuing advances in hardware and software technology, such as the introduction of multimedia computing and the World Wide Web, suggest that major advances in computer design will continue into the foreseeable future.

1.5
PROBLEMS

1.1. To what extent does each of the following items play the role of processor and/or memory when used in numerical computations: an abacus; a slide rule; an electronic pocket calculator?

1.2. Consider the Turing machine program of Figure 1.4, which adds two unary numbers n_1 and n_2. A unary zero is represented by one or more blanks, which is an undesirable feature of the unary system. Determine how the given Turing machine behaves (a) if $n_1 = n_2 = 0$, that is, the initial tape is entirely blank; and (b) if $n_1 \neq 0$ but $n_2 = 0$. In each case specify the final contents of the tape.

1.3. Design a a Turing machine that subtracts a unary number n_2 from another unary number $n_1 > n_2$. Assume that n_1, n_2, and the result $n_1 - n_2$ are stored in the formats described in Example 1.1. That is, the tape initially contains only n_1 and n_2 separated by a blank, while the final tape should contain only $n_1 - n_2$. Describe your machine by a program listing with comments, following the style used in Figure 1.4.

1.4. Construct a Turing machine program *Count_up* in the style of Figure 1.4 that increments an arbitrary binary number by one. For example, if the number 10011 denoting 19 is initially on an otherwise blank tape, *Count_up* should replace it with 10100 denoting 20. Assume that the read-write head starts and ends on the blank square immediately to the left of the number on the tape. Describe your machine by a program listing with comments, following the style used in Figure 1.4. [*Hint:* Fewer than 20 instructions employing fewer than 10 states suffice for this problem.]

1.5. The number of possible sequences of moves (distinct games) in chess has been estimated at around 10^{120}. Is developing a surefire winning strategy for chess therefore an unsolvable problem?

1.6. Determine whether each of the following computational tasks is unsolvable, undecidable, or intractable. Explain your reasoning. (*a*) Determining the minimum amount of wire needed to connect any set of n points (wiring terminals) that are in specified but arbitrary positions on a rectangular circuit board. Assume that at most two wires may be attached to each terminal. (*b*) Solving the preceding wiring problem when the n points and the wires that connect them are constrained to lie on the periphery of the board; that is, the wire segments connecting the n points must lie on a fixed rectangle.

1.7. Most word-processing computer programs contain a spelling checker. An obvious brute-force method to check the spelling of a word W is to search the entire on-line dictionary from beginning to end and compare W to every entry in the dictionary. Outline a faster method to check spelling and compare its time complexity to that of the brute-force method.

1.8. Consider the four algorithms listed in Figure 1.7. With the given data, calculate the maximum problem size that each algorithm can handle on a computer M' that is 10,000 times faster than M. Repeat the calculation for a computer M'' that is 1,000,000 times faster than M.

1.9. The brute-force technique illustrated by the Euler-circuit algorithm in Example 1.2, which involves the enumeration and examination of all possible cases, is applicable to many computing problems. To make the method tractable, problem-specific techniques are used to reduce the number of cases that need to be considered. For example, the eight-edge graph of Figure 1.6*b* can be simplified by replacing the edge-pair *cg* with a single edge because any Euler circuit that contains *c* must also contain *g*, and vice versa. Similarly, the pair *dh* can be replaced by a single edge. The problem then reduces to checking for an Euler circuit in a six-edge graph. For the same problem, suggest another method that can sometimes substantially reduce the number of cases that must considered, illustrating it with a different graph example.

1.10. Consider the heuristic method to solve the traveling salesman problem discussed briefly in section 1.1.2. Construct a specific problem involving at most five cities, for which the total distance d_{heur} traveled in the heuristic solution is not the minimum distance d_{min}. Conclude from your example (or from other considerations) that the heuristic solution can be made arbitrarily bad, that is, "worst case" problems can be contrived in which $d_{heur} - d_{min}$ can be made arbitrarily large.

1.11. Consider the computation of x^2 by the method of differences covered in Example 1.3. Suppose we want to determine x^2 for $x = 0.5, 1.0, 1.5, 2.0, 2.5, 3.0$, that is, at intervals of 0.5. Explain how to modify the method of Example 1.3 to accomplish this task.

1.12. Use the method of differences embodied in Babbage's Difference Engine to compute x^3 for integer values of x from 1 to 10.

1.13. Use the method of differences to compute x^5, for integer values of x from 1 to 8. What is the smallest value of i for which the ith difference of x^5 is a constant? What is the value of that constant?

1.14. Consider the problem of computing a table of the natural logarithms of the integers from 1 to 200,000 to 19 decimal places, a task carried out manually in 1795. Select any modern commercially available computer system with which you are familiar and estimate the total time it would require to compute and print this table. Define all the parameters used in your estimation.

1.15. Discuss the advantages and disadvantages of storing programs and data in the same memory (the stored program concept). Under what circumstances is it desirable to store programs and data in separate memories?

1.16. Computers with separate program and data memories implemented in RAMs and ROMs, respectively, are sometimes called *Harvard-class* machines after the Harvard Mark 1 computer. Computers with a single (RAM) memory for program and data storage are then called *Princeton-class* after the IAS computer. Most currently installed computers belong to one of these classes. Which one? Explain why the class you selected is the most widely used.

1.17. Write a program using the IAS computer's instruction set (Figure 1.14) to compute x^2 by means of the method of finite differences described in Example 1.3. For simplicity, assume that the numbers being processed are 40-bit integers and that the only data-processing instructions you may use are the IAS's add and subtract instructions. The results $x^2, (x + 1)^2, (x + 2)^2, \ldots, (x + k - 1)^2$, should be stored in k consecutive memory locations with starting address 3001.

1.18. A vector of 10 nonnegative numbers is stored in consecutive locations beginning in location 100 in the memory of the IAS computer. Using the instruction set of Figure 1.14, write a program that computes the address of the largest number in this array. If several locations contain the largest number, specify the smallest address.

1.19. The designers of the IAS decided not to implement a square root instruction (ENIAC had one), citing the fact that $y = x^{1/2}$ can be computed iteratively—and very efficiently—via the following formula known in ancient Babylon:

$$y_{j+1} = (y_j + x/y_j)/2$$

Here $j = 1, 2, 3, \ldots$, and y_0 is an initial approximation to $x^{1/2}$. Assuming that IAS processes real (floating-point) numbers directly, construct a program in the style of Figure 1.15 to calculate the square root of a given positive number x according to this formula.

1.20. Early computer literature describes the IAS and other first-generation computers as "parallel," unlike some of their predecessors. In what sense was the IAS a parallel computer? What forms of parallelism do modern computers have that are lacking in the IAS?

1.21. The IAS had no call or return instructions designed for transferring control between programs. (*a*) Describe how call and return can be programmed using the IAS's original instruction set. (*b*) What feature would you suggest adding to the IAS to support call and return operations?

1.22. Construct both a Polish expression and a stack program of the kind given in Figure 1.16*a* to evaluate the following expression:

$$f := (4 \times (a^2 + b + c) - d)/(e + f \times g) \qquad (1.14)$$

1.23. From the data presented in Figure 1.19, estimate how long it takes, on average, for the density of leading-edge ICs to double. This doubling rate, which has remained remarkably constant over the years, is referred to as *Moore's law,* after Gordon E. Moore, a cofounder of Intel Corp., who formulated it in the 1960s.

1.24. Using the circuit of Figure 1.20 as an illustration, discuss and justify the following general properties of CMOS circuits: (*a*) Power consumption is very low and most of it occurs when the circuit is changing state (switching). (*b*) The logic signals 0 and 1 correspond to electrical voltage levels. (*c*) The subcircuits that constitute logic gates draw their power directly from the global power supply rather than from the external (primary) input signals; hence the gates perform signal amplification.

1.25. The CMOS zero-detection circuit of Figures 1.20 and 1.21 can be implemented as a single four-input logic gate. Identify the gate in question and redesign the circuit in the more compact single-gate form.

1.26. Design a CMOS ones-detection circuit in the multigate style of Figure 1.20. It should produce the output $z = 1$ if and only if $x_0 x_1 x_2 x_3 = 1111$. Give both a transistor (switch-level) circuit and a gate-level circuit for your design.

1.27. Discuss the impact of developments in computer hardware technology on the evolution of each of the following: (*a*) the logical complexity of the smallest replaceable components; (*b*) the operating speed of the smallest replaceable components; and (*c*) the formats used for data and instruction representation.

1.28. Define the terms *software compatibility* and *hardware compatibility.* What role have they played in the evolution of computers?

1.29. Identify and briefly describe three distinct ways in which parallelism can be introduced into the microarchitecture of a computer in order to increase its overall instruction execution speed.

1.30. Compare and contrast the IAS and PowerPC processors in terms of the complexity of writing assembly-language programs for them. Use the vector addition programs of Figures 1.15 and 1.27 to illustrate your answer.

1.31. A popular microprocessor of the 1970s was the Intel 8085, a direct ancestor of the 80X86/Pentium series, which has the structure shown in Figure 1.32. The data word size in the CPU and M is 8 bits, while the address size is 16 bits. Because the 8085's IC package has only 40 pins, the lines AD for transmitting addresses and data between the CPU and M are shared (multiplexed) as indicated. AD is used to attach IO devices as well as M to the 8085; there is also a separate serial (two line) IO port. The 8085 has about 70 different instruction types. Its most complex arithmetic instructions are addition and subtraction of 8-bit fixed-point (binary and decimal) numbers. There are six 8-bit registers designated B, C, D, E, H, and L, which, with the accumulator A, form a general-purpose CPU register file. The register-pairs BC, DE, and HL serve as 16-bit address registers. A program counter PC maintains the address of the next instruction byte required from M in the usual manner. The 8085 also has stack pointer SP that points to the top of a user-defined stack area in M. (*a*) What is the maximum capacity

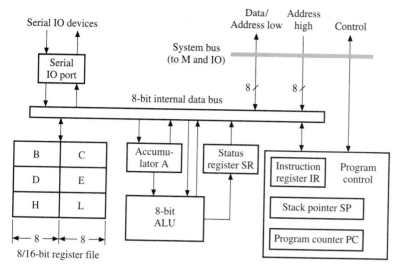

Figure 1.32
Structure of the Intel 8085 microprocessor.

Location	Instruction		Comment
ADDEC:	LXI	D, NUM1 + 16	Initialize address: DE := NUM1 + 16.
	LXI	H, NUM2 + 16	Initialize address: HL := NUM2 + 16.
	MVI	C, 16	Initialize count: C := 16.
	LDAX	D	Load data: D := M(DE).
LOOP:	ADC	M	A := A + CY + M(HL). Update CY flag.
	DAA		Convert sum in A to decimal.
	MOV	M,A	Store data: M(HL) := A.
	DCX	D	Decrement address: DE := DE − 1.
	DCX	H	Decrement address: HL := HL − 1.
	DCR	C	Decrement count: C := C − 1. Update Z flag.
	JNZ	LOOP	Jump to LOOP if Z ≠ 1.

Figure 1.33
An 8085 program to add two 32-digit decimal integers.

of the 8085's main memory? (*b*) What is the size of PC? (*c*) What is the purpose of SP? (*d*) Identify three common features of more recent microprocessors that the 8085 lacks.

1.32. Consider the Intel 8085 described in the preceding problem. A taste of its software can be found in Figure 1.33, which lists a program ADDEC written in 8085 assembly language that performs the addition of two long (*n* digit) decimal numbers NUM1 and NUM2. The numbers are added two digits (8 bits) at a time using the instructions ADC (add with carry) and DAA (decimal adjust accumulator). ADC takes a byte from M and, treating it as an 8-bit binary number, adds it and a carry bit CY to the contents of the A register. DAA then changes the binary sum in A to binary-coded decimal form. This calculation uses several flag bits of the status register SR: the carry flag CY, which is set to 1 (0) whenever the 9th bit resulting from an 8-bit addition is 1 (0); and the zero flag Z, which is set to 1 (0) when the result of an arithmetic instruction such as add or decrement is 0 (non-0). (*a*) From the information given here, determine the size n of the numbers being added and the (symbolic) location in M where the sum NUM1 + NUM2 is stored. (*b*) Ignoring the size of the 8085's instruction set, would you classify it as CISC or RISC? Justify your answers.

1.33. The performance of a 100 MHz microprocessor P is measured by executing 10,000,000 instructions of benchmark code, which is found to take 0.25 s. What are the values of *CPI* and *MIPS* for this performance experiment? Is P likely to be superscalar?

1.34. Suppose that a single-chip microprocessor P operating at a clock frequency of 50 MHz is replaced by a new model P', which has the same architecture as P but has a clock frequency of 75 MHz. (*a*) If P has a performance rating of p MIPS for a particular benchmark program Q, what is the corresponding MIPS rating p' for P'? (*b*) P takes 250 s to execute Q in a particular personal computer system C. On replacing P by P' in C, the execution time of Q drops only to 220 s. Suggest a possible reason for this disappointing performance improvement.

1.35. (*a*) What are the usual definitions of the terms *CISC* and *RISC*? Identify two key architectural features that distinguish recent RISC and CISC machines. (*b*) When developing the RISC/6000, the direct predecessor of the PowerPC, IBM viewed the word *RISC* to mean "reduced instruction set *cycles*." Explain why this meaning might be more appropriate for the PowerPC than the usual one.

1.6
REFERENCES

1. Albert, D. and D. Avnon. "Architecture of the Pentium Microprocessor." *IEEE Micro,* vol. 13 (June 1993) pp. 11–21.
2. Augarten, S. *Bit by Bit: An Illustrated History of Computers.* New York: Ticknor and Fields, 1984.
3. Barwise, J. and J. Etchemendy. *Turing's World 3.0: An Introduction to Computability Theory.* Stanford, CA: CSLI Publications, 1993.
4. Boyer, C. B. *A History of Mathematics.* 2nd ed. New York: Wiley, 1989.
5. Braun, E. and S. MacDonald. *Revolution in Miniature. The History and Impact of Semiconductor Electronics.* 2nd ed. Cambridge, England: Cambridge University Press, 1982.
6. Burks, A. W., H. H. Goldstine, and J. von Neumann. "Preliminary Discussion of the Logical Design of an Electronic Computing Instrument." Report prepared for U.S. Army Ordnance Department, 1946. (Reprinted in Ref. 26, vol. 5, pp. 34–79.)
7. Cocke, J. and V. Markstein. "The Evolution of RISC Technology at IBM." *IBM Journal of Research and Development,* vol. 34 (January 1990) pp. 4–11.
8. Cormen, T. H., C. E. Leiserson, and R. L. Rivest. *Introduction to Algorithms.* MIT Press, Cambridge, MA, and McGraw-Hill, New York, 1990.
9. Diefendorf, K., R. Oehler, and R. Hochsprung. "Evolution of the PowerPC Architecture." *IEEE Micro,* vol. 14 (April 1994) pp. 34–49.
10. Estrin, G. "The Electronic Computer at the Institute for Advanced Studies." *Mathematical Tables and Other Aids to Computation,* vol. 7 (April 1953) pp. 108–14.
11. Farrell, J. J. "The Advancing Technology of Motorola's Microprocessors and Microcomputers." *IEEE Micro,* vol. 4 (October 1984) pp. 55–63.

12. Garey, M. R. and D. S. Johnson. *Computers and Intractability.* San Francisco: W. H. Freeman, 1979.
13. Goldstine, H. H. and J. von Neumann. "Planning and Coding Problems for an Electronic Computing Instrument." Part II, vols. 1 to 3. Three reports prepared for U.S. Army Ordnance Department, 1947–1948. (Reprinted in Ref. 26, vol. 5, pp. 80–235.)
14. Hwang, K. *Advanced Computer Architecture.* New York: McGraw-Hill, 1993.
15. Morrison, P. and E. Morrison (eds.). *Charles Babbage and His Calculating Engines.* New York: Dover, 1961.
16. Morse, S. P. et al. "Intel Microprocessors: 8008 to 8086." Santa Clara, CA: Intel, 1978. (Reprinted in Ref. 24, pp. 615–46.)
17. Motorola Inc. *PowerPC 601 RISC Microprocessor User's Manual.* Phoenix, AZ, 1993. (Also published by IBM Microelectronics, Essex Junction, VT, 1993).
18. O'Connor, J. M. and M. Tremblay. "picoJava-I: The Java Virtual Machine in Hardware." *IEEE Micro,* vol. 17 (March/April 1997) pp. 45–53.
19. Patterson, D. "Reduced Instruction Set Computers." *Communications of the ACM,* vol. 28, (January 1985) pp. 8–21.
20. Poppelbaum, W. J. et al. "Unary Processing." *Advances in Computers,* vol. 26, ed. M. Yovits. New York: Academic Press, 1985, pp. 47–92.
21. Prasad, N. S. *IBM Mainframes: Architecture and Design.* New York: McGraw-Hill, 1989.
22. Randell, B. (ed.) *The Origins of Digital Computers: Selected Papers.* 3rd ed. Berlin: Springer-Verlag, 1982.
23. Russell, R. M. "The CRAY-1 Computer System." *Communications of the ACM,* vol. 21 (January 1978), pp. 63–78. (Reprinted in Ref. 24, pp. 743–52.)
24. Siewiorek, D. P., C. G. Bell, and A. Newell. *Computer Structures: Readings and Examples.* New York: McGraw-Hill, 1982.
25. Swade, D. D. "Redeeming Charles Babbage's Mechanical Computer." *Scientific American,* vol. 268 (February 1993) pp. 86–91.
26. von Neumann, J. *Collected Works,* ed. A. Taub, 6 vols. New York: Pergamon, 1963.
27. Weiss, S. and J. E. Smith. *Power and PowerPC.* San Francisco, CA: Morgan Kaufmann, 1994.
28. Weste, N. and K. Eshragian. *Principles of CMOS VLSI Design.* 2nd ed. Reading, MA: Addison-Wesley, 1992.
29. Wilkes, M. V. and J. B. Stringer. "Microprogramming and the Design of Control Circuits in an Electronic Digital Computer." *Proc. Cambridge Phil. Soc.,* pt. 2, vol. 49 (April 1953) pp. 230–38. (Reprinted in Ref. 24, pp. 158–63.)

CHAPTER 2

Design Methodology

.

This chapter views the design process for digital systems at three basic levels of abstraction: the gate, the register, and the processor levels. It discusses the nature of the design process, examines design at the register and processor levels in detail, and briefly introduces computer-aided design (CAD) and analysis methods.

2.1
SYSTEM DESIGN

A computer is an example of a *system,* which is defined informally as a collection—often a large and complex one—of objects called *components,* that are connected to form a coherent entity with a specific function or purpose. The function of the system is determined by the functions of its components and how the components are connected. We are interested in information-processing systems whose function is to map a set A of input information items (a program and its data, for example) into output information B (the results computed by the program acting on the data). The mapping can be expressed formally by a mathematical function f from A to B. If f maps element a of A onto element b of B, we write $b = f(a)$ or $b :=$ $f(a)$. We also restrict membership of A and B to digital or discrete quantities, whose values are defined only at discrete points of time.

2.1.1 System Representation

A useful way of modeling a system is a graph. A (directed) *graph* consists of a set of objects $V = \{v_1, v_2, v_3, \ldots, v_n\}$ called *nodes* or *vertices* and a set of edges E whose members are (ordered) pairs of nodes taken from the set $\{(v_1, v_2),$ $(v_1, v_3), \ldots, (v_{n-1}, v_n)\}$ of all such pairs. The edge $e = (v_i, v_j)$ joins or connects node v_i to node v_j. A graph is often defined by a diagram in which nodes are represented by circles, dots, or other symbols and edges are represented by lines; this diagram is synonymous with the graph. The ordering implied by the notation (v_i, v_j) may be indicated in the diagram by an arrowhead pointing from v_i to v_j as, for instance, in Figure 2.1.

The systems of interest comprise two classes of objects: a set of information-processing components C and a set of lines S that carry information signals between components. In modeling the system by a graph G, we associate C with the nodes of G and S with the edges of G; the resulting graph is often called a *block diagram*. This name comes from the fact that it is convenient to draw each node (component) as a block or box in which its name and/or its function can be written. Thus the various diagrams of computer structures presented in Chapter 1—Figure 1.29, for instance—are block diagrams. Figure 2.2 shows a block diagram representing a small gate-level logic circuit called an *EXCLUSIVE-OR* or *modulo-2 adder*. This circuit has the same general form as the more abstract graph of Figure 2.1.

Structure versus behavior. Two central properties of any system are its structure and behavior; these very general concepts are often confused. We define the *structure* of a system as the abstract graph consisting of its block diagram with no functional information. Thus Figure 2.1 shows the structure of the small system of Figure 2.2. A structural description merely names components and defines their interconnection. A behavioral description, on the other hand, enables one to determine for any given input signal a to the system, the corresponding output $f(a)$. We define the function f to be the *behavior* of the system. The behavior f may be represented in many different ways. Figure 2.3 shows one kind of behavioral description for the logic circuit of Figure 2.2. This tabulation of all possible combinations of input-output values is called a *truth table*. Another description of the same EXCLUSIVE-OR behavior can be written in terms of mathematical equations as follows, noting that $f(a) = f(x_1, x_2)$:

$$f(0,0) = 0$$
$$f(0,1) = 1$$
$$f(1,0) = 1$$
$$f(1,1) = 0$$

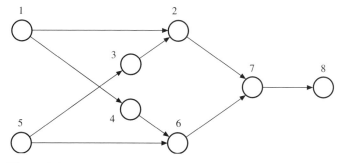

Figure 2.1
A graph with eight nodes and nine edges.

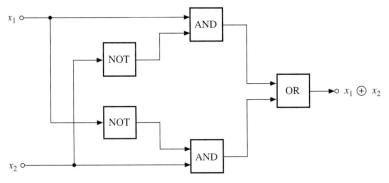

Figure 2.2
A block diagram representing an EXCLUSIVE-OR logic circuit.

The structural and behavioral descriptions embodied in Figures 2.1 and 2.3 are independent; neither can be derived from the other. The block diagram of Figure 2.2 serves as both a structural and behavioral description for the logic circuit in question, since from it we can derive Figures 2.1 and 2.3.

In general, a block diagram conveys structure rather than behavior. For example, some of the block diagrams of computers in Chapter 1 identify blocks as being arithmetic-logic units or memory circuits. Such functional descriptions do not completely describe the behavior of the components in question; therefore, we cannot deduce the behavior of the system as a whole from the block diagram. If we need a more precise description of system behavior, we generally supply a separate narrative text, or a more formal description such as a truth table or a list of equations.

Hardware description languages. As we have seen, we can fully describe a system's structure and behavior by means of a block diagram—the term *schematic diagram* is also used—in which we identify the functions of the components. We can convey the same detailed information by means of a *hardware description language* (HDL), a format that resembles (and is usually derived from) a high-level programming language such as Ada or C. The construction of such description languages can be traced back at least as far as Babbage [Morrison and Morrison 1961]. Babbage's notation, of which he was very proud, centered around the use of special symbols such as $\rightarrow$ to represent the movement of mechanical components. In modern times Claude E. Shannon [Shannon 1938] introduced Boolean algebra

Input a		Output
x_1	x_2	$f(a)$
0	0	0
0	1	1
1	0	1
1	1	0

Figure 2.3
Truth table for the EXCLUSIVE-OR function.

as a concise and rigorous descriptive method for logic circuits. Beginning in the 1950s, academic and industrial researchers developed many ad hoc HDLs. These eventually evolved into a few widely used languages, notably VHDL and Verilog,[1] which were standardized in the 1980s and 90s [Smith 1996; Thomas and Moorby 1996].

Hardware description languages such as VHDL have several advantages. They can provide precise, technology-independent descriptions of digital circuits at various levels of abstraction, primarily the gate and register levels. Consequently, they are widely used for documentation purposes. Like programming languages, HDLs can be processed by computers and so are suitable for use with computer-aided design (CAD) programs which, as discussed later, play an important role in the design process. For example, an HDL description of a processor P can be employed to simulate the behavior of P before all the details of its design have been specified. On the negative side, HDL descriptions are often long and verbose; they lack the intuitive appeal and rapid insights that circuit diagrams and less formal descriptive methods provide.

EXAMPLE 2.1 VHDL DESCRIPTION OF A HALF ADDER. To illustrate the use of HDLs, we give in Figure 2.4*a* a VHDL description of a simple logic component known as a *half adder*. Its purpose is to add two 1-bit binary numbers x and y to form a 2-bit result consisting of a sum bit *sum* and a carry bit *carry*. For example, if $x = y = 1$, the half adder should produce *carry* = 1, *sum* = 0, corresponding to the binary number 10, that is, two.

A VHDL description has two main parts: an **entity** part and an **architecture** part. The **entity** part is a formal statement of the system's structure at the highest level, that is, as a single component. It describes the system's *interface,* which is the "face" presented to external devices but says nothing about the system's behavior or its internal structure. In this example the **entity** statement gives the half adder's formal name *half_adder* and the names assigned to its input-output (IO) signals; IO signals are referred to in VHDL by their connection terminals or *ports.* Inputs and outputs are

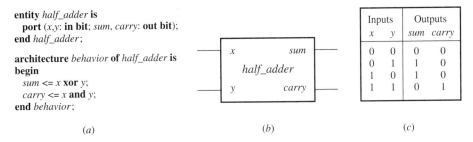

```
entity half_adder is
   port (x,y: in bit; sum, carry: out bit);
end half_adder;

architecture behavior of half_adder is
begin
   sum <= x xor y;
   carry <= x and y;
end behavior;
```

	Inputs		Outputs	
	x	y	*sum*	*carry*
	0	0	0	0
	0	1	1	0
	1	0	1	0
	1	1	0	1

(*a*)   (*b*)   (*c*)

Figure 2.4
Half adder: (*a*) behavioral VHDL description; (*b*) block symbol; and (*c*) truth table.

---

[1]VHDL was sponsored by the U.S. Department of Defense. Its name stands for VHSIC hardware description language, where VHSIC (very high-speed integrated circuits) is the acronym of another Department of Defense research program. VHDL is based on the programming language Ada, while Verilog, whose origins are industrial, is based on the C language. Both HDLs are now embodied in formal standards sponsored by the Institute of Electrical and Electronics Engineers (IEEE).

distinguished by the keywords **in** and **out**, respectively. The size of each IO port, meaning the number of signals associated with it, is specified here as 1 bit by the keyword **bit**. Thus we can conclude from the **entity** part of Figure 2.4a that *half_adder* has two 1-bit inputs, named x and y, and two 1-bit outputs, named *sum* and *carry*. Figure 2.4b presents the same information in graphical form. It is customary in such diagrams to put inputs on the left and outputs on the right, eliminating the need for arrowheads to indicate the direction of signal flow.

The **architecture** part of a VHDL description specifies behavior and/or internal structure. Figure 2.4a defines the half adder's behavior only; we are assuming for the moment that it is a primitive module or "black box," whose internal structure is either not known or not of interest. The functions of the half adder's two outputs *sum* and *carry* are specified by two Boolean functions **xor** and **and**, which are built into VHDL; that is, they are predefined functions. In VHDL **xor** stands for the EXCLUSIVE-OR function, which we have encountered already—it is defined in Figure 2.3. The AND function denoted by **and** is another basic logic function, which may be defined as follows: $AND(x,y) = 1$ if and only if $x = 1$ and $y = 1$. Note that VHDL expresses $AND(x,y)$ in the equivalent "infix" format x **and** y. An alternative description of the behavior of *half_adder* appears in Figure 2.4c in the form of a truth table.

Figure 2.4a illustrates a few of the many notational conventions of VHDL, which collectively make the language quite complex. The symbol <= is called *signal assignment* and indicates that the value of the expression on the right of <= is assigned to the signal on the left. Hence

$$carry <= x \textbf{ and } y \tag{2.1}$$

means that the signal *carry* is the AND function of x and y. This notation is equivalent to writing $carry = AND(x, y)$ in ordinary mathematical notation. The other features of Figure 2.4a such as the use of **begin-end** to bracket related items represent minor syntactical details borrowed from programming languages.

VHDL is a rich language that can say the same thing in several ways. For example, we might replace (2.1) by

if $xy = {'}11{'}$ **then** *carry* <= 1 **else** *carry* <= 0;

VHDL can also convey timing or performance information in various ways. For example, to indicate that it takes 5 ns for the *carry* signal to change in response to a change in its input signals x and y, we can rewrite statement (2.1) as

$carry <= x$ **and** y **after** 5 ns;

If the half adder's internal structure is of interest, we can specify it by means of a structural **architecture** description, as shown in Figure 2.5a. The same structure is defined by the block diagram of Figure 2.5b. Again inputs are assumed to be on the left and outputs on the right. Two internal component types are identified and are described by VHDL **component** statements that have much the same form as **entity**. They name the component types (*xor_circuit* and *nand_gate* in the example) and specify the names and types of the components' IO signals. Internal signals (lines or buses) created by connections between the components are specified by a **signal** statement, in this case a 1-bit internal signal named *alpha*. Finally, all the copies of each component used in the circuit are individually named and their IO connections are specified. This is accomplished by the part of the **architecture** description in Figure 2.5a bracketed by **begin-end**, which may be thought of as a (wiring) network specification or *netlist*. There is one copy named XOR of *xor_circuit* and two copies of *nand_gate* named NAND1 and NAND2. The second line in this netlist

NAND1: *nand_gate* **port map** ($d => x, e => y, f => alpha$);

```
entity half_adder is
  port (x,y: in bit; sum, carry: out bit);
end half_adder;

architecture structure of half_adder is
  component xor_circuit port (a,b: in bit; c: out bit); end component;
  component nand_gate port (d,e: in bit; f: out bit); end component;
  signal alpha: bit;
begin
  XOR: xor_circuit port map (a => x, b => y, c => sum);
  NAND1: nand_gate port map (d => x, e => y, f => alpha);
  NAND2: nand_gate port map (d => alpha, e => alpha, f => carry);
end structure;
```

(a)

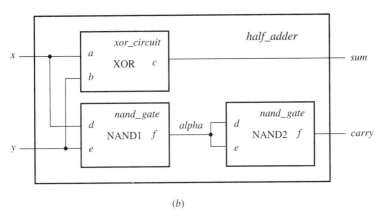

(b)

Figure 2.5
Half adder: (a) structural VHDL description; (b) block diagram.

states that *half_adder* has a component called NAND1, which is of type *nand_gate* and has its *d*, *e*, and *f* ports (terminals) mapped (connected) to the signals *x*, *y*, and *alpha*, respectively.

2.1.2 Design Process

Given a system's structure, the task of determining its function or behavior is termed *analysis*. The converse problem of determining a system structure that exhibits a given behavior is *design* or *synthesis*.

Design problem. We can now state in broad terms the problem facing the computer designer or, indeed, any system designer.

Given a desired range of behavior and a set of available components, determine a structure (design) formed from these components that achieves the desired behavior with acceptable cost and performance.

While assuring the correctness of the new design's behavior is the overriding goal of the design process, other typical requirements are to minimize cost as measured by the cost of manufacture and to maximize performance as measured by the speed of operation. There are some other performance- and cost-related constraints to satisfy such as high reliability, low power consumption, and compatibility with existing systems. These multiple objectives interact in poorly understood ways that depend on the complexity and novelty of the design.

Despite careful attention to detail and the assistance of CAD tools, the initial versions of a new system often fail to meet some design objective, sometimes in subtle and hard-to-detect ways. This failure can be attributed to incomplete specifications for the design (some mode of behavior was overlooked), errors made by human designers or their CAD tools (which are also ultimately due to human error), and unanticipated interactions between structure, performance, and cost. For example, increasing a system's speed to a desired level can make the cost unacceptably high.

The complexity of computer systems is such that the design problem must be broken down into smaller, easier tasks involving various classes of components. These smaller problems can then be solved independently by different designers or design teams. Each major design step is often implemented via the multistep or iterative process depicted by a flowchart in Figure 2.6. An initial design is created, perhaps in ad hoc fashion, by adapting an existing design of a similar system. The result is then evaluated to see if it meets the relevant design objectives. If not, the design is revised and the result reevaluated. Many iterations through the redesign and evaluation steps of Figure 2.6 may be necessary to obtain a satisfactory design.

Computer-aided design. The emergence of powerful and inexpensive desktop computers with good graphics interfaces provides designers with a range of programs to support their design tasks. CAD tools are used to automate, at least in

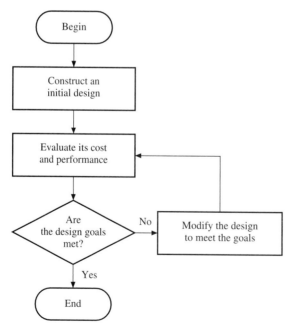

Figure 2.6
Flowchart of an iterative
design process.

part, the more tedious design and evaluation steps and contribute in three important ways to the overall design process.

- CAD *editors* or *translators* convert design data into forms such as HDL descriptions or schematic diagrams, which humans, computers, or both can efficiently process.
- *Simulators* create computer models of a new design, which can mimic the design's behavior and help designers determine how well the design meets various performance and cost goals.
- *Synthesizers* automate the design process itself by deriving structures that implement all or part of some design step.

Editing is the easiest of these three tasks, and synthesis the most difficult. Some synthesis methods incorporate exact or *optimal* algorithms which, even if easy to program into CAD tools, often demand excessive amounts of computing resources. Many synthesis approaches are therefore based on trial-and-error methods and experience with earlier designs. These computationally efficient but inexact methods are called *heuristics* and form the basis of most practical CAD tools.

Design levels. The design of a complex system such as a computer is carried out at several levels of abstraction. Three such levels are generally recognized in computer design, although they are referred to by various different names in the literature:

- The *processor* level, also called the *architecture, behavior,* or *system* level.
- The *register* level, also called the *register-transfer level (RTL).*
- The *gate* level, also called the *logic* level.

As Figure 2.7 indicates we are naming each level for a key component treated as primitive or indivisible at that level of abstraction. The processor level corresponds to a user's or manager's view of a computer. The register level is approximately the level of detail seen by a programmer. The gate level is primarily the concern of the hardware designer. These three design levels also correspond roughly to the major subdivisions of integrated-circuit technology into VLSI, MSI, and SSI components. The boundaries between the levels are far from clear-cut, and it is common to encounter descriptions that mix components from more than one level.

Level	Components	IC density	Information units	Time units
Gate	Logic gates, flip-flops.	SSI	Bits	10^{-12} to 10^{-9} s
Register	Registers, counters, combinational circuits, small sequential circuits.	MSI	Words	10^{-9} to 10^{-6} s
Processor	CPUs, memories, IO devices.	VLSI	Blocks of words	10^{-3} to 10^{3} s

Figure 2.7
The major computer design levels.

A few basic component types from each design level are listed in Figure 2.7. The logic gates recognized as primitive at the gate level include AND, OR, NAND, NOR, and NOT gates. Consequently, the EXCLUSIVE-OR circuit of Figure 2.2 is an example of a gate-level circuit composed of five gates. The component marked XOR in Figure 2.5b performs the EXCLUSIVE-OR function and so can be thought of as a more abstract or higher-level view of the circuit of Figure 2.2, in which all internal structure has been abstracted away. Similarly, the half-adder block of Figure 2.4b represents a higher-level view of the three-component circuit of Figure 2.5b. We consider a half adder to be a register-level component. We might regard the circuit of Figure 2.5b as being at the register level also, but because NAND is another gate type and XOR is sometimes treated as a gate, this circuit can also be viewed as gate level.

Figure 2.7 indicates some further differences between the design levels. The units of information being processed increase in complexity as one goes from the gate to the processor level. At the gate level individual bits (0s and 1s) are processed. At the register level information is organized into multibit words or vectors, usually of a small number of standard types. Such words represent numbers, instructions, and the like. At the processor level the units of information are blocks of words, for example, a program or a data set. Another important difference lies in the time required for an elementary operation; successive levels can differ by several orders of magnitude in this parameter. At the gate level the time required to switch the output of a gate between 0 and 1 (the gate delay) serves as the time unit and typically is a nanosecond (ns) or less. A clock cycle of, say, 10 ns, is a commonly used unit of time at the register level. The time unit at the processor level might be a program's execution time, a quantity that can vary widely.

System hierarchy. It is customary to refer to a design level as high or low; the more complex the components, the higher the level. In this book we are primarily concerned with the two highest levels listed in Figure 2.7, the processor and register levels, which embrace what is generally regarded as computer architecture. The ordering of the levels suggested by the terms high and low is, in fact, quite strong. A component in any level L_i is equivalent to a (sub) system of components taken from the level L_{i-1} beneath it. This relationship is illustrated in Figure 2.8. Formally speaking, there is a one-to-one mapping h_i between components in L_i and disjoint subsystems in level L_{i-1}; a system with levels of this type is called a *hierarchical system.* Thus in Figure 2.8 the subsystem composed of blocks 1, 3, and 4 in the low-level description maps onto block A in the high-level description. Figures 2.4b and 2.5b show two hierarchical descriptions of a half-adder circuit.

Complex systems, both natural and artificial, tend to have a well-defined hierarchical organization. A profound explanation of this phenomenon has been given by Herbert A. Simon [Simon 1962]. The components of a hierarchical system at each level are self-contained and stable entities. The evolution of systems from simple to complex organizations is greatly helped by the existence of stable intermediate structures. Hierarchical organization also has important implications in the design of computer systems. It is perhaps most natural to proceed from higher to lower design levels because this sequence corresponds to a progression of successively greater levels of detail. Thus if a complex system is to be designed using small-scale ICs or a single IC composed of standard cells, the design process might consist of the following three steps.

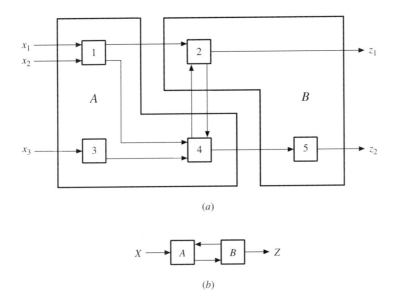

(a)

$X \longrightarrow \boxed{A} \longrightarrow \boxed{B} \longrightarrow Z$

(b)

Figure 2.8
Two descriptions of a hierarchical system: (*a*) low level; (*b*) high level.

1. Specify the processor-level structure of the system.
2. Specify the register-level structure of each component type identified in step 1.
3. Specify the gate-level structure of each component type identified in step 2.

This design approach is termed *top down;* it is extensively used in both hardware and software design. If the foregoing system is to be designed using medium-scale ICs or standard cells, then the third step, gate-level design, is no longer needed.

As might be expected, the design problems arising at each level are quite different. Only in the case of gate-level design is there a substantial theoretical basis (Boolean algebra). The register and processor levels are of most interest in computer design, but unfortunately, design at these levels is largely an art that depends on the designers' skill and experience. In the following sections we examine design at the register and processor levels in detail, beginning with the better-understood register level. We assume that the reader is familiar with binary numbers and with gate-level design concepts [Armstrong and Gray 1993; Hayes 1993; Hachtel and Somenzi 1996], which we review in the next section.

2.1.3 The Gate Level

Gate-level (logic) design is concerned with processing binary variables whose possible values are restricted to the bits (binary digits) 0 and 1. The design components are logic gates, which are simple, memoryless processing elements, and flip-flops, which are bit-storage devices.

Combinational logic. A *combinational function,* also referred to as a *logic* or a *Boolean* function, is a mapping from the set of 2^n input combinations of n binary variables onto the output values 0 and 1. Such a function is denoted by $z(x_1, x_2,...,$

x_n) or simply by z. The function z can be defined by a truth table, which specifies for every input combination $(x_1, x_2, \ldots, x_n)$ the corresponding value of $z(x_1, x_2, \ldots, x_n)$. Figure 2.9a shows the truth table for a pair of three-variable functions, $s_0(x_0, y_0, c_{-1})$ and $c_0(x_0, y_0, c_{-1})$, which are the sum and carry outputs, respectively, of a logic circuit called a *full adder*. This useful logic circuit computes the numerical sum of its three input bits using binary (base 2) arithmetic:

$$c_0 s_0 = x_0 \, \textbf{\textit{plus}} \, y_0 \, \textbf{\textit{plus}} \, c_{-1} \tag{2.2}$$

For example, the last row of the truth table of Figure 2.9a expresses the fact that the sum of three 1s is $c_0 s_0 = 11_2$, that is, the base-2 representation of the number three. When discussing logic circuits, we will normally reserve the plus symbol (+) for the logical OR operation, and write out *plus* for numerical addition. We will also use a subscript to identify the number base when it is not clear from the context; for example, twelve is denoted by 12_{10} in decimal and by 1100_2 in binary.

A combinational function z can be realized in many different ways by combinational circuits built from the standard gate types, which include AND, OR,

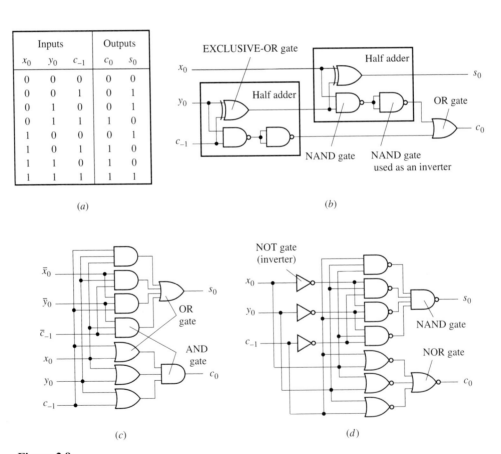

Inputs			Outputs	
x_0	y_0	c_{-1}	c_0	s_0
0	0	0	0	0
0	0	1	0	1
0	1	0	0	1
0	1	1	1	0
1	0	0	0	1
1	0	1	1	0
1	1	0	1	0
1	1	1	1	1

(a)

(b)

(c)

(d)

Figure 2.9
Full adder: (a) truth table; (b) realization using half adders; (c) realization using AND and OR gates; (d) realization using NAND, NOR, and NOT gates.

EXCLUSIVE-OR, NOT (inverter), NAND, and NOR. The functions performed by AND, OR, EXCLUSIVE-OR, and NOT gates are denoted by logic expressions of the form x_1x_2, $x_1 + x_2$, $x_1 \oplus x_2$, and $\bar{x}_1$, respectively, and are defined as follows:

> AND: $x_1x_2 = 1$ if and only if x_1 and x_2 are both 1.
> OR: $x_1 + x_2 = 1$ if and only if x_1 or x_2 or both are 1.
> EXCLUSIVE-OR: $x_1 \oplus x_2 = 1$ if and only if x_1 or x_2 but not both are 1.
> NOT: $\bar{x}_1 = 1$ if and only if $x_1 = 0$.

The function performed by a NOT gate is known as *inversion*. The NAND or NOR functions are obtained by inverting AND and OR, respectively. NAND is denoted by $\overline{x_1x_2}$ and NOR by $\overline{x_1 + x_2}$. The preceding definitions (except that of NOT) can be extended to gates with any number of inputs k, but practical considerations limit k, which is called the gate's *fan-in*, to a maximum value of 10 or so. Note that the NOT gate or inverter can be regarded as a one-input version of NAND or NOR.

A set G of gate types is said to be (*functionally*) *complete* if any logic function can be realized by a circuit that contains gates from G only. Examples of complete sets of gates are {AND, OR, NOT}, {AND, NOT}, {NAND}, and {NOR}. NANDs and NORs are particularly important in logic design because they are easily manufactured using most IC technologies and are the only standard gate types that are functionally complete by themselves. With any complete set of logic operations, the set of all logic functions of up to n variables forms a *Boolean algebra,* named after George Boole (1815–1864), a contemporary of Babbage's [Brown 1990]. Boolean algebra allows the function realized by a combinational circuit to be described in a form that resembles the circuit's structure. It is similar to ordinary (numerical) algebra in many respects, and both numerical and Boolean algebra are embedded in the syntax of a typical HDL.

Figure 2.9*b* shows a possible gate-level realization of a full adder that employs two copies of the half adder defined in Figures 2.4 and 2.5 along with a single OR gate. Here we use standard, distinctively shaped symbols for the various gate types instead of the generic box symbols of Figure 2.5*b*. Observe that the two NANDs in each half adder, one of which is used as an inverter, can be replaced by a single, functionally equivalent AND gate. This equivalence is seen from the fact that the inversions associated with the two NANDs cancel; in algebraic terms, $\overline{\overline{ab}} = ab$.

Two alternative gate-level designs for the full adder appear in Figures 2.9*c* and 2.9*d*. The AND-OR circuit of Figure 2.9*c* is defined by the logic (Boolean) equations

$$s_0 = x_0 y_0 c_{-1} + \bar{x}_0 y_0 \bar{c}_{-1} + \bar{x}_0 \bar{y}_0 c_{-1} + x_0 \bar{y}_0 \bar{c}_{-1} \tag{2.3}$$

$$c_0 = (x_0 + c_{-1})(x_0 + y_0)(y_0 + c_{-1}) \tag{2.4}$$

whose structure also corresponds closely to that of the circuit. By analogy with ordinary algebra, (2.3) and (2.4) are referred to as *sum-of-products* (*SOP*) and *product-of-sums* (*POS*) expressions, respectively. The circuit of Figure 2.9*c* is called a *two-level* or depth-two logic circuit because there are only two gates, one AND and one OR, along each path from this adder's external or primary inputs x_0, y_0, c_{-1} to its primary outputs s_0, c_0, assuming each primary input variable is available in both true and inverted (complemented) form. The number of logic levels is defined by the number of gates along the circuit's longest IO path. Because each gate imposes some delay (typically 1 ns or so) on every signal that propagates through it, the fewer the logic levels, the faster the circuit.

The half-adder-based circuit of Figure 2.9b has IO paths containing up to four gates and so is considered to have four levels of logic. If all gates have the same propagation delay, then the two-level adder (Figure 2.9c) is twice as fast as the four-level design (Figure 2.9b). However, the two-level adder has more gates and so has a higher hardware cost. A basic task in logic design is to synthesize a gate-level circuit realization of a given set of combinational functions that achieves a satisfactory balance between hardware cost as measured by the number of gates, and operating speed as measured by the number of logic levels used. Often the types of gates that may be used are restricted by IC technology considerations, for example, to NAND gates with five or fewer inputs per gate. The design of Figure 2.9d, which has essentially the same structure as that of Figure 2.9c, uses NAND and NOR gates instead of ANDs and ORs. In this particular case the primary inputs are provided in true (noninverted) form x_0, y_0, c_{-1} only; hence inverters are introduced to generate the inverted inputs $\bar{x}_0$, $\bar{y}_0$, $\bar{c}_{-1}$.

Computer-aided synthesis tools are available to design circuits like those of Figure 2.9 automatically. The input to such a *logic synthesizer* is a specification of the desired function, such as a truth table like Figure 2.9a, or a set of logic equations like (2.3) or (2.4); these are often embedded in a behavioral HDL description. Also given to the synthesizer are such design constraints as the gate types to use and restrictions on the circuit's interconnection structure. One such restriction is an upper bound on the number of inputs (fan-in) of a gate G. Another is an upper bound on the number of inputs of other gates to which G's output line may connect; this is called the (maximum) *fan-out* of G. The output of the synthesizer is a structural description of a logic circuit that implements the desired function and meets the specified constraints as closely as possible.

Exact methods for designing two-level circuits like that of Figure 2.9c (or Figure 2.9d with its inverters removed) using the minimum number of gates have long been known. They are computationally complex, however—gate minimization falls into the class of intractable problems discussed in section 1.1.2—so they are only practical for designing small circuits. However, practical heuristic methods for synthesizing two-level and multilevel logic circuits that are often nearly optimal are known and implemented in CAD programs (see Example 2.2). Once a good design of a useful function is known, it can be placed in a library for future use. A full adder, for instance, can be used to build a multibit, multilevel adder, as shown in Figure 2.10a.[2] This circuit adds two 4-bit numbers $X = (x_3, x_2, x_1, x_0)$ and $Y = (y_3, y_2, y_1, y_0)$ and computes their sum $S = (s_3, s_2, s_1, s_0)$; it also accepts an input carry signal c_{-1} and produces an output carry c_3. A multibit adder is treated as a primitive component at the register level, as shown Figure 2.10b, at which point its internal structure or logic design may no longer be of interest.

Flip-flops. By adding memory to a combinational circuit in the form of 1-bit storage elements called flip-flops, we obtain a sequential logic circuit. Flip-flops rely on an external clock signal CK to synchronize the times at which they respond

---

[2]This design, which is known as a *ripple-carry adder,* and other types of binary adders are examined in detail in Chapter 4.

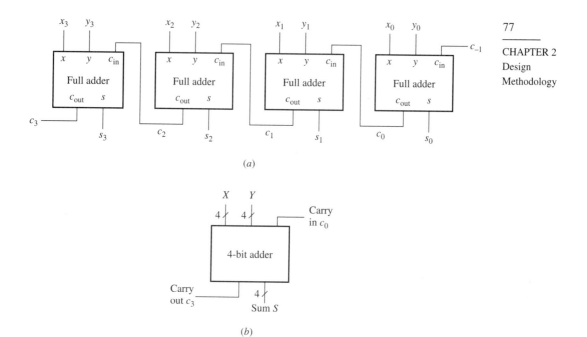

Figure 2.10
Four-bit ripple-carry: (*a*) logic structure; (*b*) high-level symbol.

to changes on their input data lines. They are also designed to be unaffected by transient signal changes (noise) produced by the combinational logic that feeds them. An efficient way to meet these requirements is *edge triggering,* which confines the flip-flop's state changes to a narrow window of time around one edge (the 0-to-1 or 1-to-0 transition point) of *CK*.

Figure 2.11 summarizes the behavior of the most common kind of flip-flop, an edge-triggered *D* (*delay*) *flip-flop.* (Another well-known flip-flop type, the JK flip-flop, is discussed in problem 2.11.) The output signal *y* constitutes the stored data or *state* of the flip-flop. The D flip-flop reads in the data value on its *D* line when the 0-to-1 triggering edge of clock signal *CK* arrives; this *D* value becomes the new value of *y*. The triangular symbol on the clock's input port in Figure 2.11*a* specifies edge triggering; its omission indicates *level triggering,* in which case the flip-flop (then usually referred to as a *latch*) responds to all changes in signal value on *D*. Since there is just one triggering edge in each clock cycle, there can be just one change in *y* per clock cycle. Hence we can view the edge-triggered flip-flop as traversing a sequence of discrete state values $y(i)$, one for every clock cycle i.

The input data line *D* can be varied independently and so can go through several changes in any clock cycle i. However, only the data value $D(i)$ present just before the arrival of the triggering edge of *CK* determines the next state $y(i + 1)$. To change the flip-flop's state, the *D* signal must be held steady for a minimum period known as the *setup time* T_{setup} before the flip-flop is triggered. For example, in Figure 2.11*c*, which shows a sample of the D flip-flop's behavior, we have $D(1) = 1$ and $y(1) = 0$ in clock cycle 1. At the start of the next clock cycle, *y* changes to 1 in response to $D(1) = 1$, making $y(2) = 1$. In clock cycle 3, *y* changes

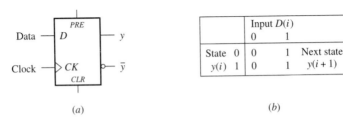

(a)

(b)

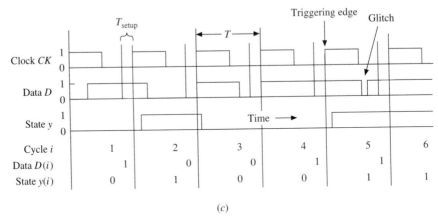

(c)

Figure 2.11
D flip-flop: (*a*) graphic symbol; (*b*) state table; (*c*) timing diagram.

back to 0, making $y(3) = 0$. Even though $D = 1$ for most of clock cycle 3, $D(3) = 0$ during the critical setup phase of cycle 3, thus ensuring that $y(4) = 0$. Observe that the spurious pulse or *glitch* affecting D in cycle 5 has no effect on y. Hence edge-triggered flip-flops have the very useful property of filtering out noise signals appearing at their inputs.

When a flip-flop is first switched on, its state y is uncertain unless it is explicitly brought to a known initial state. It is therefore desirable to be able to initialize (reset) the flip-flop asynchronously, that is, independently of the clock signal CK, at the start of operation. To this end, a flip-flop can have one or two *asynchronous* control inputs, CLR (clear) and PRE (preset), as shown in Figure 2.11*a*. Each is designed to respond to a brief input pulse that forces y to 0 in the case of CLR or to 1 in the case of PRE.

In normal *synchronous* operation with a clock that is matched to the timing characteristics of its flip-flops, we can be sure that one well-defined change of state takes place in a sequential circuit during each clock cycle. We do not have to worry about the exact times at which signals change within the clock cycle. We can therefore consider the actions of a flip-flop, and hence of any sequential circuit employing it, to occur at a discrete sequence of points of time $i = 1, 2, 3, \ldots$ In effect, the clock quantizes time into discrete, technology-independent time steps, each of which represents a clock cycle. We can then describe a D flip-flop's next-state behavior by the following *characteristic equation:*

$$y(i + 1) = D(i) \tag{2.5}$$

which simply says that y takes the value of D delayed by one clock cycle, hence the D flip-flop's name.

Figure 2.11b shows another convenient way to represent the flip-flop's next-state behavior. This *state table* tabulates the possible values of the next state $y(i + 1)$ for every possible combination of the present input $D(i)$ and the present state $y(i)$. It is not customary (or necessary) to include clock-signal values explicitly in characteristic equations or state tables. The clock is considered to be the implicit generator of time steps and so is always present in the background. Asynchronous inputs are also omitted as they are associated only with initialization.

Sequential circuits. A sequential circuit consists of a combinational circuit and a set of flip-flops. The combinational logic forms the computational or data-processing part of the circuit. The flip-flops store information on the circuit's past behavior; this stored information defines the circuit's *internal state Y*. If the primary inputs are X and the primary outputs are Z, then Z is a function of both X and Y, denoted $Z(X,Y)$. It is usual to supply a sequential circuit with a precisely controlled clock signal that determines the times at which the flip-flops change state; the resulting circuit is said to be *clocked* or *synchronous*. Each tick (cycle or period) of the clock permits a single change in the circuit's state Y as discussed above; it can also trigger changes in the primary output Z. Reflecting the importance of state behavior, the term *finite-state machine* (FSM) is often applied to a sequential circuit.

The behavior of a sequential circuit can be specified by a state table that includes the possible values of its primary outputs and its internal states. Figure 2.12a shows the state table of a small but useful sequential circuit, a serial adder, which is intended to add two unsigned binary numbers X_1 and X_2 of arbitrary length, producing their sum $Z = X_1$ *plus* X_2. The numbers are supplied serially, that is, bit by bit, and the result is also produced serially. In contrast, the combinational

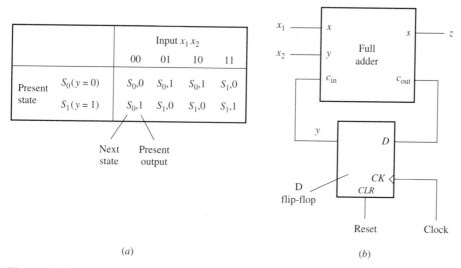

Figure 2.12
(a) State table; (b) logic circuit for a serial adder.

adder of Figure 2.10 is a "parallel" adder, which, ignoring its internal-signal propagation delays, adds all bits of the input numbers simultaneously. In one clock cycle i, the serial adder receives 2 input bits $x_1(i)$ and $x_2(i)$ and computes 1 bit $z(i)$ of Z. It also computes a carry signal $c(i)$ that affects the addition in the next clock cycle. Thus the output computed in clock cycle i is

$$c(i)z(i) = x_1(i) \textit{ plus } x_2(i) \textit{ plus } c(i-1) \tag{2.6}$$

where $c(i-1)$ must be determined from the adder's present state $S(i)$. Observe that (2.6) is equivalent to the expression (2.2) for the full-adder function defined earlier. It follows that two possible internal states exist: S_0, meaning that the previous carry signal $c(i-1) = 0$, and S_1, meaning that $c(i-1) = 1$. These considerations lead to the two-state state table of Figure 2.12a. An entry in row $S(i)$ and column $x_1(i)x_2(i)$ of the state table has the format $S(i+1), z(i)$, where $S(i+1)$ is the next internal state that the circuit must have when the present state is $S(i)$ and the present primary input combination is $x_1(i)x_2(i)$; $z(i)$ is the corresponding primary output signal that must be generated.

Because the serial adder has only two internal states, its memory consists of a single flip-flop storing a state variable y. There are only two possible ways to assign 0s and 1s to y. We select the "natural" state assignment that has $y = 0$ for S_0 and $y = 1$ for S_1, since this equates $y(i)$ with the stored carry signal $c(i-1)$. Assume that we use an edge-triggered D flip-flop (Figure 2.11) to store y. The combinational logic C then must generate two signals: the primary output $z(i)$ and a secondary output signal $D(i)$ that is applied to the D flip-flop's data input. The flip-flop's behavior is defined by its characteristic equation (2.5); that is, $y(i+1) = D(i)$. Hence we have

$$D(i) = c(i)$$

It follows from the above discussion that C can be implemented directly by a full-adder circuit such as that of Figure 2.9b, whose sum output is z and whose carry output is D; see Figure 2.12b. Before entering two new numbers to be added, it is necessary to reset the serial adder to the S_0 state. The easiest way to do so is to apply a reset pulse to the flip-flop's asynchronous clear (CLR) input.

Example 2.2 involves a similar, but more complex sequential circuit and demonstrates the use of CAD tools in its design.

EXAMPLE 2.2 DESIGN OF A 4-BIT-STREAM SERIAL ADDER. Consider another type of serial adder that adds four number streams instead of the two handled by a conventional serial adder (Figure 2.12). The new adder has four primary input lines x_1, x_2, x_3, x_4 and a single primary output z. To determine the circuit's state behavior—often the most difficult part of the design process—we first identify the information to be stored. As in the standard serial adder case, the circuit must remember carry information computed in earlier clock cycles. The current 2-bit sum $SUM(i) = c(i)z(i)$ is given by

$$SUM(i) = x_1(i) \textit{ plus } x_2(i) \textit{ plus } x_3(i) \textit{ plus } x_4(i) \textit{ plus } c(i-1)$$

where $c(i-1)$ is the carry computed in the preceding clock cycle. If $c(i-1)$ is 0 and each $x_j(i) = 1$, then $SUM(i) = 1 \textit{ plus } 1 \textit{ plus } 1 \textit{ plus } 1 \textit{ plus } 0 = 4 = 100_2$, so $c(i) = 10_2$. With $c(i-1) = 10_2$, $SUM(i)$ becomes $6 = 110_2$, making $c(i) = 11_2$. Finally, $c(i-1) = 11_2$ makes $SUM(i) = 111_2$ and $c(i) = 11_2$, which is the maximum possible value of c. The carry data to be stored is a binary number ranging from 00_2 to 11_2, which implies that the adder needs four states and two flip-flops. We will denote the four states by S_0, S_1, S_2, S_3, where S_i represents a stored carry of (decimal) value i.

Figure 2.13a shows the adder's state table, which has four rows and 16 columns. For present state $S(i)$ and input combination j, the next-state/output entry S_k, z is obtained by adding i_2 and the 4 input bits that determine j to form $SUM(i) = (k_2 k_1 k_0)_2$. It follows that $k = (k_2 k_1)_2$ and $z = k_0$. For example, with present state S_2 and present input 7, $SUM(i) = 0$ *plus* 1 *plus* 1 *plus* 1 *plus* $10_2 = 101_2$, so $z = 1$ and $k = 10_2 = 2$, making S_2 the next-state. Following this pattern, it is straightforward to construct the adder's state table. With D flip-flops, the next-state values $y_1(i + 1) y_2(i + 1)$ coincide with the flip-flops' data input values $D_1(i)D_2(i)$. The adder thus has the general structure shown in Figure 2.13b.

A truth table for the combinational logic C appears in Figure 2.13c. It is derived directly from Figure 2.13a with the states assigned the four bit patterns of $y_1 y_2$ as follows: $S_0 = 00$, $S_1 = 01$, $S_2 = 10$, and $S_3 = 11$. Suppose we want to design C as a two-level

		Present inputs $x_1 x_2 x_3 x_4$ (decimal)														
		0	1	2	3	4	5	6	7	8	9	10	11	12	13	14	15
	S_0	$S_0,0$	$S_0,1$	$S_0,1$	$S_1,0$	$S_0,1$	$S_1,0$	$S_1,0$	$S_1,1$	$S_0,1$	$S_1,0$	$S_1,0$	$S_1,1$	$S_1,0$	$S_1,1$	$S_1,1$	$S_2,0$
Present	S_1	$S_0,1$	$S_1,0$	$S_1,0$	$S_1,1$	$S_1,0$	$S_1,1$	$S_1,1$	$S_2,0$	$S_1,0$	$S_1,1$	$S_1,1$	$S_2,0$	$S_1,1$	$S_2,0$	$S_2,0$	$S_2,1$
state	S_2	$S_1,0$	$S_1,1$	$S_1,1$	$S_2,0$	$S_1,1$	$S_2,0$	$S_2,0$	$S_2,1$	$S_1,1$	$S_2,0$	$S_2,0$	$S_2,1$	$S_2,0$	$S_2,1$	$S_2,1$	$S_3,0$
	S_3	$S_1,1$	$S_2,0$	$S_2,0$	$S_2,1$	$S_2,0$	$S_2,1$	$S_2,1$	$S_3,0$	$S_2,0$	$S_2,1$	$S_2,1$	$S_3,0$	$S_2,1$	$S_3,0$	$S_3,0$	$S_3,1$

(a)

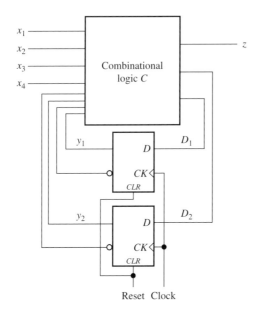

(b)

	Present inputs $x_1 x_2 x_3 x_4$	Present state $y_1 \quad y_2$	Secondary outputs $D_1 \quad D_2$	Primary output z
0	0 0 0 0	0 0	0 0	0
1	0 0 0 0	0 1	0 0	1
2	0 0 0 0	1 0	0 1	0
3	0 0 0 0	1 1	0 1	1
4	0 0 0 1	0 0	0 0	1
5	0 0 0 1	0 1	0 1	0
6	0 0 0 1	1 0	0 1	1
7	0 0 0 1	1 1	1 0	0
8	0 0 1 0	0 0	0 0	1
	. . .		. . .	
59	1 1 1 0	1 1	1 1	0
60	1 1 1 1	0 0	1 0	0
61	1 1 1 1	0 1	1 0	1
62	1 1 1 1	1 0	1 1	0
63	1 1 1 1	1 1	1 1	1

(c)

Figure 2.13
Four-bit-stream serial adder: (a) state table; (b) overall structure; (c) truth table for C.

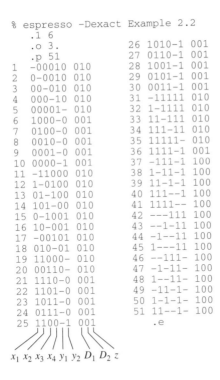

```
% espresso -Dexact Example 2.2
.i 6
.o 3.
.p 51
1   -00010 010        26 1010-1 001
2   0-0010 010        27 0110-1 001
3   00-010 010        28 1001-1 001
4   000-10 010        29 0101-1 001
5   00001- 010        30 0011-1 001
6   1000-0 001        31 -11111 010
7   0100-0 001        32 1-1111 010
8   0010-0 001        33 11-111 010
9   0001-0 001        34 111-11 010
10  0000-1 001        35 11111- 010
11  -11000 010        36 1111-1 001
12  1-0100 010        37 -111-1 100
13  01-100 010        38 1-11-1 100
14  101-00 010        39 11-1-1 100
15  0-1001 010        40 111--1 100
16  10-001 010        41 1111-- 100
17  -00101 010        42 ---111 100
18  010-01 010        43 --1-11 100
19  11000- 010        44 -1--11 100
20  00110- 010        45 1---11 100
21  1110-0 001        46 --111- 100
22  1101-0 001        47 -1-11- 100
23  1011-0 001        48 1--11- 100
24  0111-0 001        49 -11-1- 100
25  1100-1 001        50 1-1-1- 100
                      51 11--1- 100
                      .e
```

$x_1\ x_2\ x_3\ x_4\ y_1\ y_2\ D_1\ D_2\ z$

Figure 2.14
Minimal two-level (SOP) design for C computed by *ESPRESSO*.

circuit like that of Figure 2.9c, using the minimum number of gates. Manual minimization methods [Hayes 1993] are painfully slow in this case without computer aid. We have therefore used a logic synthesis program called *Espresso* [Brayton et al. 1984; Hachtel and Somenzi 1996] to obtain a two-level SOP design. To instruct *Espresso* to compute the minimum-cost SOP design on a UNIX-based computer requires issuing a command like

         `%espresso seradd4`

where `seradd4` is a file containing the truth table of Figure 2.13c or an equivalent description of C. *Espresso* responds with the table of Figure 2.14, which specifies an SOP design containing the fewest product terms (these are in a minimal form called prime implicants [Hayes 1993]), in this case, 51. For example, row 26, which has the format

$$x_1x_2x_3x_4y_1y_2 \quad D_1D_2z = 1010\text{-}1 \quad 001$$

states that output z (but not the outputs D_1 or D_2) has $x_1\bar{x}_2x_3\bar{x}_4y_2$ as one of its chosen product terms. The dash in 1010-1 indicates a literal, in this case y_1, that is not included in the term in question. Similarly, row 51 (11--1- 100) states that $x_1x_2y_1$ is a term of D_1. We conclude from Figure 2.14 that an SOP realization of C for the four-stream adder has 51 product terms, none of which happen to be shared among the output functions. This conclusion implies a two-level circuit containing the equivalent of at least 54 gates (51 ANDs and three ORs), some—especially the OR gates—with very high fan-in, which makes this type of two-level design expensive and impractical for many IC technologies. Example 2.6 in section 2.2.3 shows an alternative approach that leads to a lower-cost, multilevel design for this adder.

Minimizing the number of gates in a sequential circuit is difficult because it is affected by the flip-flop types, the state assignment, and, of course, the way in which the combinational subcircuit C is designed. Other design techniques exist to simplify the design process at the expense of using more logic elements. It is impractical to deal with complete binary descriptions like state tables if they contain more than, say, a dozen states. Consequently, large, sequential circuits are designed by heuristic techniques whose implementations use reasonable but nonminimal amounts of hardware [Hayes 1993; Hachtel and Somenzi 1996]. These circuits are often best designed at the more abstract register level rather than the gate level.

2.2
THE REGISTER LEVEL

At the register or register-transfer level, related information bits are grouped into ordered sets called *words* or *vectors*. The primitive components are small combinational or sequential circuits intended to process or store words.

2.2.1 Register-Level Components

Register-level circuits are composed of word-oriented devices, the more important of which are listed in Figure 2.15. The key sequential component, which gives this level of abstraction its name, is a (parallel) *register,* a storage device for words. Other common sequential elements are shift registers and counters. A number of standard combinational components exist, ranging from general-purpose devices, such as word gates, to more specialized circuits, such as decoders and adders.

Type	Component	Functions
Combinational	Word gates.	Logical (Boolean) operations.
	Multiplexers.	Data routing; general combinational functions.
	Decoders and encoders.	Code checking and conversion.
	Adders.	Addition and subtraction.
	Arithmetic-logic units.	Numerical and logical operations.
	Programmable logic devices.	General combinational functions.
Sequential	(Parallel) registers.	Information storage.
	Shift registers.	Information storage; serial-parallel conversion.
	Counters.	Control/timing signal generation.
	Programmable logic devices.	General sequential functions.

Figure 2.15
The major component types at the register level.

Register-level components are linked to form circuits by means of word-carrying groups of lines, referred to as *buses.*

Types. The component types of Figure 2.15 are generally useful in register-level design; they are available as MSI parts in various IC series and as standard cells in VLSI design libraries. However, they cannot be identified a priori based on some property analogous to the functional completeness of gate-level operations. For example, we will show that multiplexers can realize any combinational function. This completeness property is incidental to the main application of multiplexers, which is signal selection or path switching.

There are no universally accepted graphic symbols for register-level components. They are usually represented in circuit diagrams by blocks containing an abbreviated description of their behavior, as in Figure 2.16. A single signal line in a diagram can represent a bus transmitting $m > 1$ bits of information in parallel; m is indicated explicitly by placing a slash (/) in the line and writing m next to it (see Figure 2.16). A components's IO lines are often separated into data and control lines. An m-bit bus may be given a name that identifies the bus's role, for example, the type of data transmitted over a data bus. A control line's name indicates the operation determined by the line in its *active, enabled,* or *asserted* state. Unless otherwise indicated, the active state of a bus occurs when its lines assume the logical 1 value. A small circle representing inversion is placed at an input or output port of a block to indicate that the corresponding lines are active in the 0 state and inactive in the 1 state. Alternatively, the name of a signal whose active value is 0 includes an overbar.

The input control lines associated with a multifunction block fall into two broad categories: *select* lines, which specify one of several possible operations that the unit is to perform, and *enable* lines, which specify the time or condition for a selected operation to be performed. Thus in Figure 2.16, to perform some operation F_1, first set the select line F to a bit pattern denoting F_1 and then activate the edge-triggered enable line E by applying a 0-to-1 edge signal. Enable lines are often connected to clock sources. The output control signals, if any, indicate when or how the unit completes its processing. Figure 2.16 indicates termination by $\bar{S} = 0$. The arrowheads are omitted when we can infer signal direction from the circuit structure or signal names.

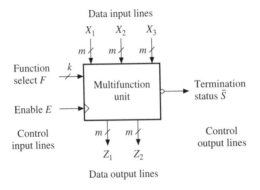

Figure 2.16
Generic block representation of a register-level component.

Operations. Gate-level logic design is concerned with combinational functions whose signal values are from the two-valued set $B = \{0,1\}$ and form a Boolean algebra. We can extend these functions to functions whose values are taken from B^m, the set of 2^m m-bit words, rather than from B. Let $z(x_1, x_2, \ldots, x_n)$ be any two-valued combinational function. Let $X_1, X_2, \ldots, X_n$ denote m-bit binary words having the form $X_i = (x_{i,1}, x_{i,2}, \ldots, x_{i,m})$ for $i = 1, 2, \ldots, n$. We define the *word operation z* as follows:

$$z(X_1, X_2, \ldots, X_n) = [z(x_{1,1}, x_{2,1}, \ldots, x_{n,1}), z(x_{1,2}, x_{2,2}, \ldots, x_{n,2}), \ldots, z(x_{1,m}, x_{2,m}, \ldots, x_{n,m})] \quad (2.7)$$

This definition simply generalizes the usual Boolean operations, AND, NAND, and so forth, from 1-bit to m-bit words. If z is the OR function, for instance, we have

$$X_1 + X_2 + \cdots + X_n = (x_{1,1} + x_{2,1} + \cdots + x_{n,1}, x_{1,2} + x_{2,2} + \cdots + x_{n,2},$$
$$\ldots, x_{1,m} + x_{2,m} + \cdots + x_{n,m})$$

which applies OR bitwise to the corresponding bits of n m-bit words.

The set of all $2^{2^{mn}}$ combinational functions defined on n m-bit words forms a Boolean algebra with respect to the word operations for AND, OR, and NOT. This generalization of Boolean algebra to multibit words is analogous to the extension of the ordinary algebra from single numbers (scalars) to vectors. Pursuing this analogy, we can treat bits as scalars and words as vectors, and obtain more complex logical operations, such as

$$yX = (yx_1, yx_2, \ldots, yx_m)$$

$$y + X = (y + x_1, y + x_2, \ldots, y + x_m) \quad (2.8)$$

Word-based logical operations of this type are useful in some aspects of register-level design. However, they do not by themselves provide an adequate design theory for several reasons.

• The operations performed by some basic register-level components are numerical rather than logical; they are not easily incorporated into a Boolean framework.
• Many of the logical operations associated with register-level components are complex and do not have the properties of the gates—interchangeability of inputs, for example—that simplify gate-level design.
• Although a system often has a standard word length w based on the width of some important buses or registers, some buses carry signals with a different number of bits. For example, the outcome of a test on a set S of w-bit words (does S have property P?) is 1 bit rather than w. The lack of a uniform word size for all signals makes it difficult to define a useful algebra to describe operations on these signals.

Lacking an adequate general theory, register-level design is tackled mainly with heuristic and intuitive methods.

We next introduce the major combinational and sequential components used in design at the register level. (Refer to Figure 2.15).

Word gates. Let $X = (x_1, x_2, \ldots, x_m)$ and $Y = (y_1, y_2, \ldots, y_m)$ be two m-bit binary words. As noted already, it is useful to perform gate operations bitwise on X and Y to obtain another m-bit word $Z = (z_1, z_2, \ldots, z_m)$. We coin the term *word-gate operations* for logical functions of this type. In general, if f is any logic operator, we write $Z = f(X, Y)$ if $z_i = f(x_i, y_i)$ for $i = 1, 2, \ldots, m$. For example, $Z = \overline{XY}$ denotes the m-bit NAND operation defined by

$$Z = (z_1, z_2, \ldots, z_m) = (\overline{x_1 y_1}, \overline{x_2 y_2}, \ldots, \overline{x_m y_m})$$

This generalized NAND is realized by the gate-level circuit in Figure 2.17a. It is represented in register-level diagrams by the two-input NAND symbol of Figure 2.17b, which is an example of a *word gate*. It is also useful to represent scalar-vector operations by a single gate symbol. For example, the operation $y + X$ defined by (2.8) and realized by the circuit of Figure 2.18a can be represented by the register-level gate symbol of Figure 2.18b.

Word gates are universal in that they suffice to implement any logic circuit; moreover, word-gate circuits can be analyzed using Boolean algebra. In practice, however, the usefulness of word gates is severely limited by the relative simplicity of the operations they perform and by the variability in word size found at the register level.

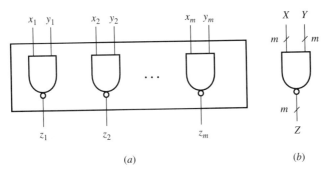

(a) (b)

Figure 2.17
Two-input, m-bit NAND word gate: (a) logic diagram and (b) symbol.

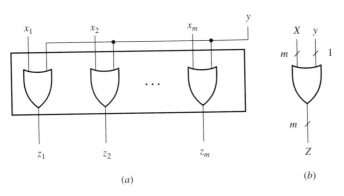

(a) (b)

Figure 2.18
OR word gate implementing $y + X$: (a) logic diagram; (b) symbol.

Multiplexers. A *multiplexer* is a device intended to route data from one of several sources to a common destination; the source is specified by applying appropriate control (select) signals to the multiplexer. If the maximum number of data sources is k and each IO data line carries m bits, the multiplexer is referred to as a *k-input* (or *k-way*), *m-bit multiplexer*. It is convenient to make $k = 2^p$, so that data source selection is determined by an encoded pattern or *address* of p bits. The 2^p addresses then cover the range $00...0, 00...1, ..., 11...1 = 2^p - 1$. A multiplexer is easily denoted by a suitably labeled version of the generic block symbol of Figure 2.16; the tapered block symbol shown in Figure 2.19, where the narrow end indicates the data output side, is also common.

Let $a_i = 1$ when we want to select the m-bit input data bus $X_i = (x_{i,0}, x_{i,1}, ..., x_{i,m-1})$ of the multiplexer of Figure 2.19. Then $a_i = 1$ when we apply the word corresponding to the binary number i to the select bus S. The binary variable a_i denotes the selection of input data bus X_i—a_i is not a physical signal. The data word on X_i is then transferred to Z when $e = 1$. The operation of the 2^p-input m-bit multiplexer is therefore defined by m sum-of-product Boolean equations of the form

$$z_j = (x_{0,j}a_0 + x_{1,j}a_1 + \cdots + x_{2^p-1,j}a_{2^p-1})e \qquad \text{for } j = 0, 1, ..., m - 1 \qquad (2.9)$$

or by the single word-based equation

$$Z = (X_0a_0 + X_1a_1 + \cdots + X_{2^p-1}a_{2^p-1})e$$

Figure 2.20 shows a typical gate-level realization of a two-input, 4-bit multiplexer.

Several k-input multiplexers can be used to route more than k data paths by connecting them in the treelike fashion shown in Figure 2.21. A q-level tree circuit of this type forms a k^q-input multiplexer. A distinct select line is associated with every level of the tree and is connected to all multiplexers in that level. Thus each level performs a partial selection of the data line X_i to be connected to the output Z.

Multiplexers as function generators. Multiplexers have the interesting property that they can compute any combinational function and so form a type of universal logic generator. Specifically, a 2^n-input, 1-bit multiplexer *MUX* can generate any n-variable function $z(v_0, v_1, ..., v_{n-1})$. This is accomplished by applying the n input variables $v_0, v_1, ..., v_{n-1}$ to the n select lines $s_0, s_1, ..., s_{n-1}$ of *MUX*, and 2^n function-specific constant values (0 or 1) to *MUX*'s 2^n input data lines $x_0, x_1, ...,$

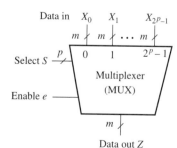

Figure 2.19
A 2^p-input, m-bit multiplexer.

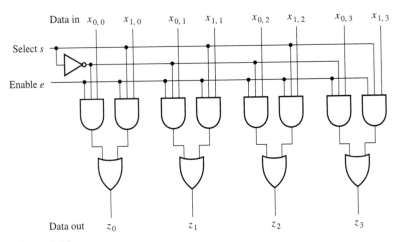

Figure 2.20
Realization of a two-input, 4-bit multiplexer.

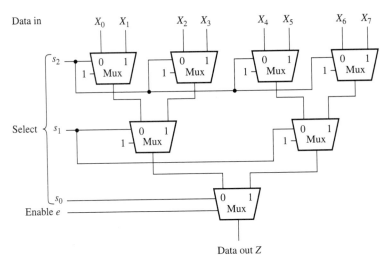

Figure 2.21
An eight-input multiplexer constructed from two-input multiplexers.

x_{2^n-1}. The output of MUX is then

$$z = \left(x_0 a_0 + x_1 a_1 + \cdots + x_{2^n-1} a_{2^n-1}\right)e \qquad (2.10)$$

as defined by (2.9), where again a_i denotes the selection of input data bus x_i. Clearly, a_i corresponds to the ith row in z's truth table with respect to the input variables $v_0, v_1, \ldots, v_{n-1}$. With $e = 1$, setting $x_i = 1$ (0) if row i of the truth table for z is 1 (0) makes (2.10) into a sum-of-products expression for z. Hence by connecting each input data line to the appropriate logic value 0 or 1, we can realize any of the 2^{2^n} possible logic functions of n variables.

EXAMPLE 2.3 USING A MULTIPLEXER TO IMPLEMENT A FULL ADDER. As we saw in section 2.1, a full adder is a three-input, two-output circuit that adds 3 bits x_0, y_0, and c_{-1} (the carry in) to obtain a 2-bit result consisting of s_0 (the sum bit) and c_0 (the carry out). It is the basic component of a serial adder (Figure 2.12) and has various gate-level realizations such as those of Figure 2.9. A multiplexer MUX_1 with $m = 2$ and $n = 2^p = 8$, that is, an eight-input, 2-bit multiplexer, can implement the full adder, as shown in Figure 2.22b. The adder's input variables are applied to the three select lines, not as might be expected, to the multiplexer's data input buses. Instead constant values 0 or 1 are applied to the data inputs as indicated. Each pattern i of $x_0 y_0 c_{-1}$ selects a specific input data bus X_i and routes its 2-bit word to the output bus $z = s_0 c_0$. Observe how this procedure effectively maps the truth table for s_0 and c_0 (Figure 2.22a) directly onto MUX_1's input data lines.

If one input variable of the full adder, say c_{-1}, is available in both true and complemented form, we can implement the adder with the smaller, four-input, 2-bit multiplexer MUX_2 shown in Figure 2.22c. The two inputs x_0, y_0 are applied to MUX_2's select lines as before, but we apply one of c_{-1}, $\bar{c}_{-1}$, 0, or 1 to each line $x_{i,j}$ of data bus X_i. Now $x_{i,j}$ must realize two rows of the form $x_0 y_0 0$ and $x_0 y_0 1$ in the adder's truth table. If, for example, these rows have the same fixed value α for the output (s_0 or c_0) of interest, then we apply α to $x_{i,j}$. If the rows have different values, then either c_{-1} or $\bar{c}_{-1}$ is applied

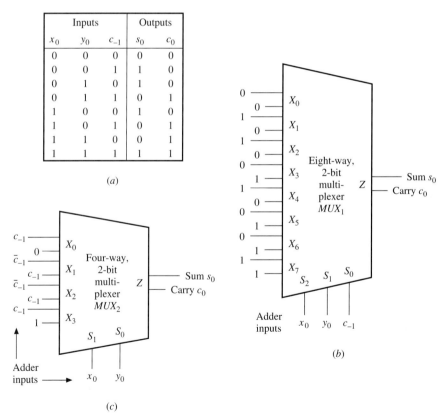

Inputs			Outputs	
x_0	y_0	c_{-1}	s_0	c_0
0	0	0	0	0
0	0	1	1	0
0	1	0	1	0
0	1	1	0	1
1	0	0	1	0
1	0	1	0	1
1	1	0	0	1
1	1	1	1	1

(a)

(b)

(c)

Figure 2.22
Multiplexer-based full adder: (a) truth table; (b) first version; (c) second version.

to $x_{i,j}$, as appropriate. We see from this example that a 2^n-input, m-bit multiplexer can realize any $(n + 1)$-variable, m-output logic function.

Decoders. A 1-out-of-2^n or $1/2^n$ *decoder* is a combinational circuit with n input lines X and 2^n output lines Z such that each of the 2^n possible input combinations A_i applied to X activates a corresponding output line z_i. Figure 2.23 shows a 1/4 decoder. Several $1/2^n$ decoders can be used to decode more than n lines by connecting them in a tree configuration analogous to the multiplexer tree of Figure 2.21. The main application of decoders is address decoding, where A_i is interpreted as an address that selects a specific output line z_i or some circuit attached to z_i. For example, decoders are used in RAMs to select storage cells to be read from or written into.

Another common application of decoders is that of routing data from a common source to one of several destinations. A circuit of this kind is called a *demultiplexer,* since it is, in effect, the inverse of a multiplexer. In this application the control input e (enable) of the decoder is viewed as a 1-bit data source to be routed to one of 2^n destinations, as determined by the address applied to the decoder. Thus a $1/2^n$ decoder is also a 2^n-output, 1-bit demultiplexer. A k-output, m-bit demultiplexer can be readily constructed from a network of decoders. Figure 2.24 shows a four-output, 2-bit demultiplexer that employs two 1/4 decoders of the type in Figure 2.23.

Encoders. An *encoder* is a circuit intended to generate the address or index of an active input line; it is therefore the inverse of a decoder. Most encoders have 2^k input data lines and k output data lines. For example, when $k = 3$, entering a data

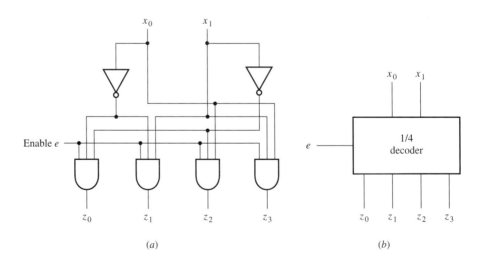

(a)

(b)

Figure 2.23
A 1/4 decoder: (*a*) logic diagram; (*b*) symbol.

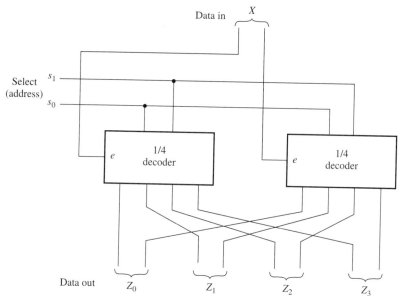

Data in X

Select s_1
(address)
s_0

e | 1/4 decoder

e | 1/4 decoder

Data out Z_0 Z_1 Z_2 Z_3

Figure 2.24
A four-output, 2-bit demultiplexer.

pattern such as $x_0 x_1 x_2 x_3 x_4 x_5 x_6 x_7 = 00000010$ into an eight-input encoder should produce the response $z_2 z_1 z_0 = 110$, denoting the number 6, and indicating that $x_6 = 1$. Additional (control) outputs are necessary to distinguish the input x_0 active and no input active states. Moreover, it is also necessary to assign priorities to the input lines and design the encoder so that the output address is always that of the active input line with the highest priority. A circuit of this type is called a *priority encoder;* see Figure 2.25. A fixed priority is assigned to each input line such that x_i has higher priority than x_j if $i > j$. We leave the logic design of this priority encoder as an exercise (problem 2.22).

Arithmetic elements. A few fairly simple arithmetic functions, notably addition and subtraction of fixed-point numbers, can be implemented by combinational register-level components. Most forms of fixed-point multiplication and division and essentially all floating-point operations are too complex to be realized by single components at this design level. However, adders and subtracters for fixed-point binary numbers are basic register-level components from which we can derive a variety of other arithmetic circuits, as we will see later. Figure 2.26a shows a component that adds two 4-bit data words and an input carry bit; it is called a 4-bit adder. (A full adder is sometimes called a 1-bit adder.) The adder's carry-in and carry-out lines allow several copies of this component to be chained together to add numbers of arbitrary size; note, however, that the addition time increases with the number size. (See Chapter 4 for coverage of the design of adders and more-complex arithmetic circuits). Another useful arithmetic component is a *magnitude comparator,* whose function is to compare the magnitudes of two binary numbers. Figure 2.26b shows the overall structure of a 4-bit comparator.

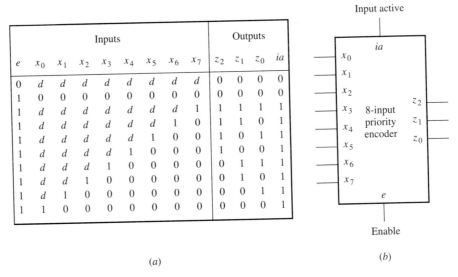

Inputs									Outputs			
e	x_0	x_1	x_2	x_3	x_4	x_5	x_6	x_7	z_2	z_1	z_0	ia
0	d	d	d	d	d	d	d	d	0	0	0	0
1	0	0	0	0	0	0	0	0	0	0	0	0
1	d	d	d	d	d	d	d	1	1	1	1	1
1	d	d	d	d	d	d	1	0	1	1	0	1
1	d	d	d	d	d	1	0	0	1	0	1	1
1	d	d	d	d	1	0	0	0	1	0	0	1
1	d	d	d	1	0	0	0	0	0	1	1	1
1	d	d	1	0	0	0	0	0	0	1	0	1
1	d	1	0	0	0	0	0	0	0	0	1	1
1	1	0	0	0	0	0	0	0	0	0	0	1

(a)

(b)

Figure 2.25
An 8-input priority encoder: (a) truth table; (b) symbol.

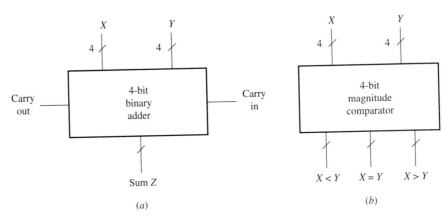

Figure 2.26
Symbols for (a) a 4-bit parallel adder; (b) a 4-bit magnitude comparator.

Magnitude comparators are relatively complex circuits requiring either many gates or many logic levels.

EXAMPLE 2.4 DESIGN OF A 4-BIT MAGNITUDE COMPARATOR. Consider the internal design of the magnitude comparator depicted in Figure 2.26b. It has eight input lines, implying that its truth table has $2^8 = 256$ rows. The comparator is quite difficult to design at the gate level. Furthermore, a two-level (SOP or POS) realization is impractical because of the many gates involved, as well as their large fan-in.

We can design a magnitude comparator for two n-bit numbers X and Y efficiently at the register level by noting that $X > Y$ is equivalent to

$$X - Y > 0 \qquad (2.11)$$

Now Y can be computed by the subtraction step $(2^n - 1) - \bar{Y}$, where $\bar{Y}$ is the bitwise complement of Y and $2^n - 1$ is a sequence of n 1s. For example, if $n = 4$ and $Y = 1001$ (9), then $\bar{Y} = 0110$ (6), $2^4 - 1 = 1111$ (15), and $Y = 1111 - 0110 = 1001$. Hence inequality (2.11) can be replaced by $X - (2^n - 1 - \bar{Y}) > 0$, implying

$$X + \bar{Y} > 2^n - 1 = 11\ldots1 \tag{2.12}$$

Now suppose we add X and $\bar{Y}$ using an adder such as that of Figure 2.26a. If the inequality of (2.12) is satisfied, then the adder's carry-out signal c_{out} will be 1, because $X + \bar{Y}$ will exceed the largest n-bit number $2^n - 1$. In the preceding example with $X = 1100$ (12) and $Y = 1001$ (9), we have $X + Y = 1100 + 0110 = 10010$ (18), for which the output carry is 1. We can therefore perform the original magnitude test $X > Y$ as follows:

1. Compute $\bar{Y}$ from Y using an n-bit word inverter.
2. Add X and $\bar{Y}$ via an n-bit adder and use the output-carry signal c_{out} as the primary output. If $c_{out} = 1$, then $X > Y$; if $c_{out} = 0$, then $X \leq Y$.

Figure 2.27 shows a direct realization of the above scheme to implement $z_3 = (X > Y)$ for the 4-bit case. By switching X and Y, we can generate $z_1 = (X < Y)$ in exactly the same manner. We do not need the sum outputs of the two adder modules; hence we can discard them and their associated circuits, thereby reducing the adders to carry-generation circuits.

We have yet to compute the "equals" output denoted $z_2 = (X = Y)$. This calculation requires comparing each bit X_i of X to the corresponding bit Y_i of Y, which can be done by an EXCLUSIVE-NOR gate that produces $\overline{X_i \oplus Y_i}$. Now $z_2 = 1$ when $\overline{X_i \oplus Y_i} = 1$ for all i; that is,

$$z_2 = \left(\overline{X_{n-1} \oplus Y_{n-1}}\right)\left(\overline{X_{n-2} \oplus Y_{n-2}}\right)\cdots\left(\overline{X_0 \oplus Y_0}\right) \tag{2.13}$$

Figure 2.27 also gives a 4-bit implementation of (2.13) using EXCLUSIVE-NOR and AND word gates. Practical magnitude comparators such as the 74X85 [Texas Instruments 1988] use a similar design that incorporates a fast carry-generation technique (carry lookahead).

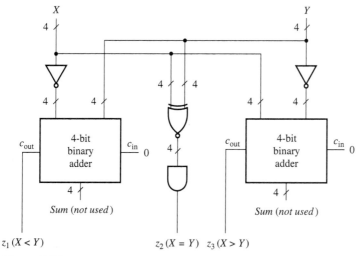

$z_1 (X < Y)$

$z_2 (X = Y)\quad z_3 (X > Y)$

Figure 2.27
Register-level design of a 4-bit magnitude comparator.

We turn now to the main sequential components used at the register level.

Registers. An m-bit register is an ordered set of m flip-flops designed to store an m-bit word $(z_0, z_1, ..., z_{m-1})$. Each bit of the word is stored in a separate flip-flop, but the flip-flops have common control lines (clock, clear, and so on). Registers can be constructed from various flip-flop types. Figure 2.28a shows a 4-bit register constructed from four D flip-flops, and Figure 2.28b shows a suitable graphic symbol for it. The register and its output signal (which denotes the register's state) are frequently assigned the same name.

The register Z of Figure 2.28 reads in the data word X each time it is clocked. Therefore, to maintain the contents or state of Z at a constant value, it is necessary to apply that value continuously to Z's input bus. Often we want to load a new value of X into Z in a particular clock cycle and subsequently change X without changing Z. To this end, we introduce a control line *LOAD*, which should cause the register to read in (load) the current value of X when it is clocked and *LOAD* has been set to 1. When *LOAD* = 0, the state of Z should not change when the register is clocked; it should retain the last value loaded into it. To add this load feature to register Z of Figure 2.28, we insert a two-input, 4-bit multiplexer *MUX* into its input data bus as shown in Figure 2.29a. The new control line *LOAD* is connected

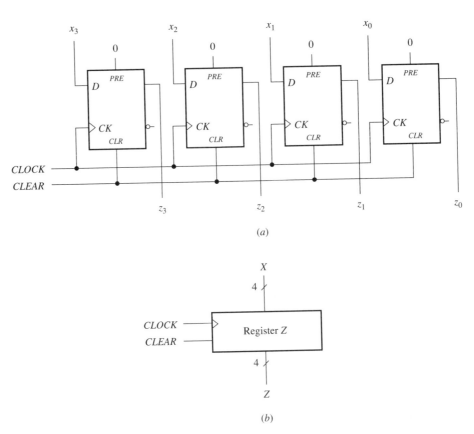

Figure 2.28
A 4-bit D register with parallel IO: (*a*) logic diagram; (*b*) symbol.

to *MUX*'s select line *s*. *MUX*'s data input lines are connected to *X* and to the register output *Z* so that the circuit behaves as follows in each clock cycle. If $LOAD = 1$, then *X* is loaded into the register from the input bus; that is, $Z := X$. If $LOAD = 0$, then the old value of *Z* is loaded back into the register; that is, $Z := Z$.

Registers like those of Figures 2.28 and 2.29 are designed so that external data can be transferred to or from all its flip-flops simultaneously; this mode of operation is called *parallel input-output*. In some computer-design situations it is useful to transfer (shift) the contents of a register in and out 1 bit at a time. A register designed for such operations is a *shift register*. A right-shift operation changes the register's state as described by the following register-transfer statement:

$$(x, z_{m-1}, z_{m-2}, \ldots, z_1) := (z_{m-1}, z_{m-2}, \ldots, z_1, z_0)$$

A left shift performs the similar transformation:

$$(z_{m-2}, z_{m-3}, \ldots, z_0, x) := (z_{m-1}, z_{m-2}, \ldots, z_1, z_0)$$

In each case a bit of stored data is lost from one end of the shift register, while a new data bit *x* is brought in at the other end. In its simplest form, an *m*-bit shift register consists of *m* flip-flops each of which is connected to its left or right neighbor. Data can be entered 1 bit at a time at one end of the register and can be removed (read) 1 bit at a time from the other end; this process is called *serial input-output*. Figure 2.30 shows a 4-bit shift register built from D flip-flops. A right shift is accomplished by activating the *SHIFT* enable line connected to the clock input *CK* of each flip-flop. In addition to the serial data lines, *m* input or output lines are often provided to permit parallel data transfers to or from the shift register. Additional control lines are required to select the serial or parallel input modes. A further refinement is to permit both left- and right-shift operations.

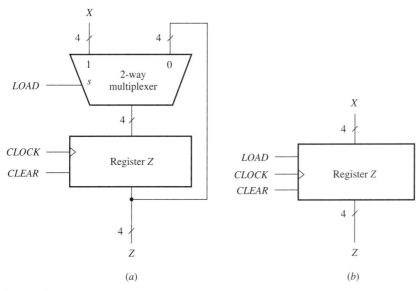

(a)   (b)

Figure 2.29
A 4-bit D register with parallel load: (*a*) logic diagram; (*b*) symbol.

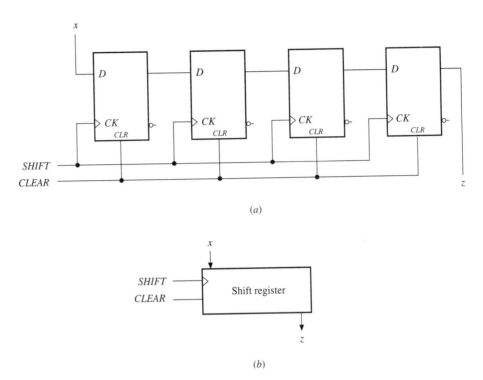

Figure 2.30
A 4-bit, right-shift register: (*a*) logic diagram; (*b*) symbol.

Shift registers are useful design components in a number of applications, including storage of serial data and serial-to-parallel or parallel-to-serial data conversion. They can also be used to perform certain arithmetic operations on binary numbers, because left- (right-) shifting corresponds to multiplication (division) by two. The instruction sets of most computers include shift operations.

Counters. A counter is a sequential circuit designed to cycle through a predetermined sequence of k distinct states $S_0, S_1, \ldots, S_{k-1}$ in response to signals (1-pulses) on an input line. The k states represent k consecutive numbers, so the state transitions can be described by the statement

$$S_{i+1} := S_i \textbf{ plus } 1 \quad (\text{modulo } k)$$

Each 1-input increments the state by one; the circuit can therefore be viewed as counting the input 1s. Counters come in many different varieties depending on the number codes used, the modulus k, and the timing mode (synchronous or asynchronous).

Figure 2.31 shows a counter designed to count 1-pulses applied to its *COUNT ENABLE* input line. The counting is modulo-2^n; that is, the counter's modulus $k = 2^n$, and it has 2^n states $S_0, S_1, \ldots, S_{2^n-1}$. The output is an n-bit binary number $COUNT = S_i$, and the count sequence is either up or down, as determined by the control line *DOWN*. In the up-counting mode ($DOWN = 0$), the counter's behavior is

$$S_{i+1} := S_i \textbf{ plus } 1 \quad (\text{modulo } 2^n)$$

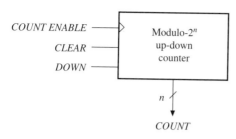

Figure 2.31
A modulo-2^n up-down counter.

whereas in the down-counting mode ($DOWN = 1$), the behavior becomes

$$S_{i+1} := S_i \textbf{ minus } 1 \quad (\text{modulo } 2^n)$$

In some counters modulus-select control lines can alter the modulus; such counters are termed programmable.

Counters have several applications in computer design. They can store the state of a control unit, as in a program counter. Incrementing a counter provides an efficient means of generating a sequence of control states. Counters can also generate timing signals and introduce precise delays into a system.

Buses. A bus is a set of lines (wires) designed to transfer all bits of a word from a specified source to a specified destination on the same or a different IC; the source and destination are typically registers. A bus can be unidirectional, that is, capable of transmitting data in one direction only, or it can be bidirectional. Although buses perform no logical function, a significant cost is associated with them, since they require logic circuits to control access to them and, when used over longer distances, signal amplification circuits (drivers and receivers). The pin requirements and gate density of an IC increase rapidly with the number of external buses connected to it. If these buses are long, the cost of the wires or cables used must also be taken into account.

To reduce costs, buses are often shared, especially when they connect many devices. A *shared* bus is one that can connect one of several sources to one of several destinations. Bus sharing reduces the number of connecting lines but requires more complex bus-control mechanisms. Although shared buses are relatively cheap, they do not permit simultaneous transfers between different pairs of devices, which is possible with unshared or *dedicated* buses. Bus structures are explored further in Chapter 7.

2.2.2 Programmable Logic Devices

Next we examine a class of components called *programmable logic devices* or PLDs, a term applied to ICs containing many gates or other general-purpose cells whose interconnections can be configured or "programmed" to implement any desired combinational or sequential function [Alford 1989]. PLDs are relatively easy to design and inexpensive to manufacture. They constitute a key technology for building application-specific integrated circuits (ASICs). Two techniques are used to program PLDs: *mask programming,* which requires a few special steps in the IC chip-manufacturing process, and *field programming,* which is done by designers or end users "in the field" via small, low-cost programming units. Some field-programmable PLDs are erasable, implying that the same IC can be reprogrammed many times. This technology is especially convenient when developing and debugging a prototype design for a new product.

Programmable arrays. The connections leading to and from logic elements in a PLD contain transistor switches that can be programmed to be permanently switched on or switched off. These switches are laid out in two-dimensional arrays so that large gates can be implemented with minimum IC area. The programmable logic gates of a PLD array are represented abstractly in Figure 2.32b, with × denoting a programmable connection or *crosspoint* in a gate's input line. The absence of an × means that the corresponding connection has been programmed to the off (disconnected) state.

The gate structures of Figure 2.32b can be combined in various ways to implement logic functions. The *programmable logic array* (PLA) shown in Figure 2.33 is intended to realize a set of combinational logic functions in minimal SOP form. It consists of an array of AND gates (the AND plane), which realize a set of product terms (prime implicants), and a set of OR gates (the OR plane), which form various logical sums of the product terms. The inputs to the AND gates are programmable and include all the input variables and their complements. Hence it is possible to program any desired product term into any row of the PLA. For example, the top row of the PLA in Figure 2.33 is programmed to generate the term $\bar{x}_2\bar{x}_3\bar{x}_4 y_1 \bar{y}_2$, which is used in computing the output D_2; the last row is programmed to generate $x_1 x_2 y_1$ for output D_1. The inputs to the OR gates are also programmable, so each output column can include any subset of the product terms produced by the rows. The PLA in Figure 2.33 realizes the combinational part C of the 4-bit-stream adder specified in Figure 2.13. The AND plane generates the 51 six-variable product terms according to the SOP design given in Figure 2.14.

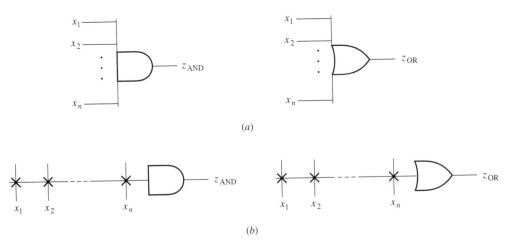

Figure 2.32
AND and OR gates: (*a*) normal notation; (*b*) PLD notation.

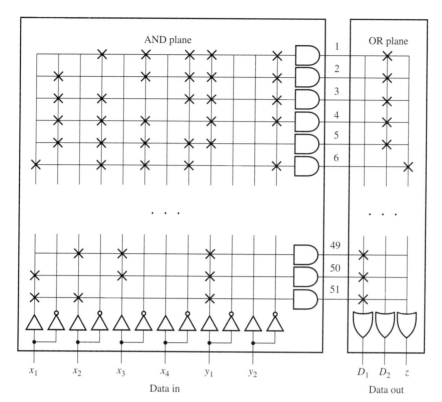

Figure 2.33
PLA implementing the combinational part C of the adder of Figure 2.13.

Closely related to a PLA is a *read-only memory* (ROM) that generates all 2^n possible n-variable product terms (minterms) in its AND plane. This enables each output column of the OR plane to realize any desired function of n or fewer variables in sum-of-minterms form. Unlike a PLA, the AND plane is fixed; the programming that determines the functions generated by a ROM is confined to the OR plane. A small ROM with three input variables, $2^3 = 8$ rows, and two output columns is shown in Figure 2.34b. It has been programmed to realize the full-adder function defined by Figure 2.34a—compare the multiplexer realizations of the full adder appearing in Figure 2.22. Note the use of dots to denote the fixed connections in the AND plane. This particular ROM can be programmed to realize any two of the 256 Boolean functions of three or fewer variables. Field-programmable ROMs are known as *PROMs* (programmable ROMs).

PLAs and ROMs are universal function generators capable of realizing a set of logic functions that depend on some maximum number of variables. They are two-level logic circuits in which the lines can have large fan-out and the gates (especially the output gates) can have large fan-in. High fan-in and fan-out tends to make these circuits' propagation delays quite high, however. A ROM is a memory device only in the sense that its OR plane "stores" the 2^n data words that have been programmed into it. A stored word is read out each time the ROM receives a new input combination or *address*. The AND plane therefore serves as a 1-out-of-2^n address decoder.

Inputs			Outputs	
x_0	y_0	c_{-1}	s_0	c_0
0	0	0	0	0
0	0	1	1	0
0	1	0	1	0
0	1	1	0	1
1	0	0	1	0
1	0	1	0	1
1	1	0	0	1
1	1	1	1	1

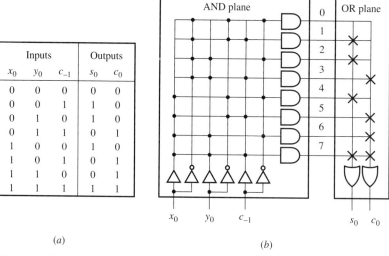

(a)   (b)

Figure 2.34
ROM implementation of a full adder: (*a*) truth table; (*b*) ROM array.

Comparing Figures 2.34*a* and 2.34*b*, we see that a ROM effectively stores the entire truth table of the functions it generates. Consequently, the effort needed to design a ROM is trivial. The process of reading the stored information from a ROM is referred to as *table lookup*. Read-only memories are suitable for implementing circuits whose IO functions are difficult to specify in logical terms; some code conversion and arithmetic circuits are of this type. The usefulness of ROMs is limited by the fact that their size doubles with each new primary input variable. Unlike a ROM, a PLA stores a condensed (minimized) form of the truth table and so generally occupies much less chip area than an equivalent ROM.

Many variants of the preceding PLD types exist [Alford 1989]. *Registered PLAs* have flip-flops attached via programmable connections to the outputs of the OR plane, allowing a single IC to implement medium-sized sequential circuits. *Programmable array logic* (PAL) circuits have an AND plane that is programmable, but an OR plane with fixed connections designed to link each output line to a fixed set of AND rows, typically about eight rows. Such a PAL output can realize only a two-level expression containing at most eight terms. A PAL's advantages are ease of use in some applications, as well as higher speed because output fan-out is restricted.

Field-programmable gate arrays. This important class of PLDs was introduced in the mid-1980s. A *field-programmable gate array* (FPGA) is a two-dimensional array of general-purpose logic circuits, called *cells* or *logic blocks*, whose functions are programmable; the cells are linked to one another by programmable buses. The cell types are not restricted to gates. They are small multifunction circuits capable of realizing all Boolean functions of a few variables; a cell may also contain one or two flip-flops. Like all field-programmable devices, FPGAs are suitable for implementing prototype designs and for small-scale manufacture.

FPGAs can store the program that determines the circuit to be implemented in a RAM or PROM on the FPGA chip. The pattern of the data in this *configuration* memory *CM* determines the cells' functions and their interconnection wiring. Each bit of *CM* controls a transistor switch in the target circuit that can select some cell function or make (break) some connection. By replacing the contents of *CM*, designers can make design changes or correct design errors. This type of FPGA can be reprogrammed repeatedly, which significantly reduces development and manufacturing costs. Some FPGAs employ fuses or antifuses as switches, which means that each FPGA IC can be programmed only once. These one-time programmable FPGAs have other advantages, however, such as higher density, and smaller or more predictable delays.

Two types of logic cells found in FPGAs are those based on multiplexers and those based on PROM table-lookup memories. Figure 2.35*a* shows a cell type (the C-module) employed by Actel Corp.'s ACT series of multiplexer-based FPGAs [Greene, Hamdy, and Beal 1993; Actel 1994]. This cell is a four-input, 1-bit multiplexer with an AND and OR gate added. A variant called the S-module has a D flip-flop connected to the primary output; there are also special cells attached to the FPGA's IO pins. An ACT FPGA contains a large array (many thousands) of such cells organized in rows separated by horizontal wiring channels as illustrated in Figure 2.35*b*. Vertical wire segments are attached to each cell's IO terminals. These wires enable connections to be established between the cells and the wiring channels by means of one-time-programmable antifuses positioned where the horizontal and vertical wires cross. In addition, long vertical wires run across the entire array to carry primary IO signals, power (logical 1), and ground (logical 0).

Our discussion of multiplexers as function generators implies that the FPGA cell of Figure 2.35*a* can generate any Boolean function of up to three variables if the inputs are supplied in both true and complemented form. This cell can also generate various useful functions of more than three variables due to the presence

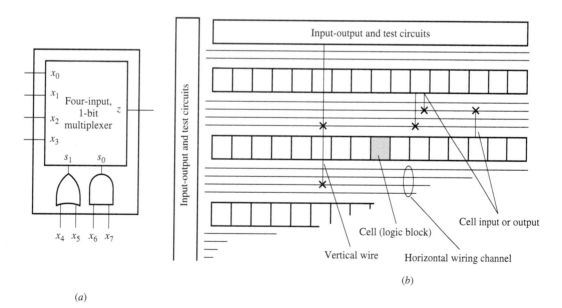

(a)

(b)

Figure 2.35
Actel ACT-series FPGA: (*a*) basic cell (C-module); (*b*) chip architecture.

of the two extra gates. Figures 2.36a, 2.36b, and 2.36c show how this cell implements a functionally complete set of logic gates. Observe how the cell's AND and OR gates help to realize four-input AND and OR functions. Figure 2.36d shows how the same, basically combinational cell implements an edge-triggered D flip-flop.

EXAMPLE 2.5 FPGA IMPLEMENTATION OF A SERIAL ADDER. We will use the Actel C-module of Figure 2.35a to realize the serial adder of Figure 2.12. The target circuit contains a combinational part C, which is a full adder defined by the equations

$$z = x_1 \oplus x_2 \oplus y$$

$$c = x_1 x_2 + x_1 y + x_2 y \qquad (2.14)$$

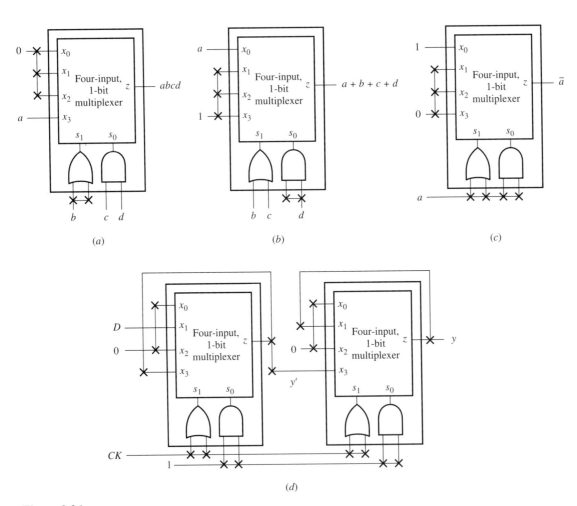

(a)

(b)

(c)

(d)

Figure 2.36
FPGA cell of Figure 2.35a programmed to realize: (a) a four-input AND gate; (b) a four-input OR gate; (c) an inverter; (d) a D flip-flop.

Here z is the sum bit and c is the carry bit. A single D flip-flop stores the value of c produced in each clock cycle and applies it to C as y in the next clock cycle. We will assume that if the complements of any of the input variables x_1, x_2, or y are needed, they must be generated explicitly in the FPGA. We will also try to use as few cells as possible in the target circuit.

Figure 2.36d shows that two cells are required for the D flip-flop, assuming that we don't need the complement of y. It's not immediately clear how many cells are needed to produce the sum and carry. A little experimentation shows that the carry function does indeed have a one-cell realization; see Figure 2.37. Observe that Equation (2.14) can be rewritten as

$$c = y(x_1 + x_2) + x_1 x_2$$

which suggests the way we use the Actel cell's AND and OR gates. No amount of experimentation yields a one-cell realization of the sum function. The multiplexer realization of the full adder we gave earlier (Figure 2.22c) requires the data inputs to be supplied to the sum part in both true and complemented form. We will therefore devote a third cell to generating $\bar{y}$ so we can realize z in the manner of Figure 2.22c.

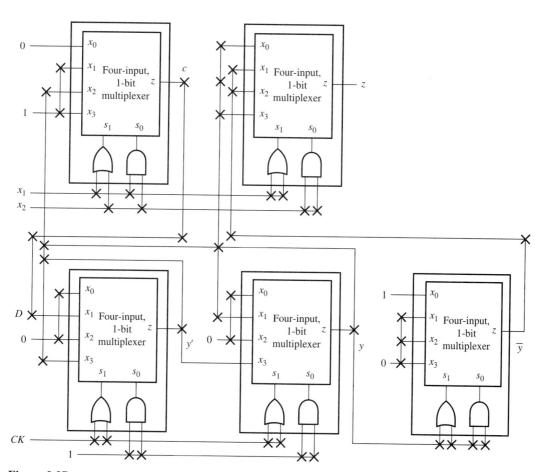

Figure 2.37
FPGA implementation of a serial adder.

The resulting design given in Figure 2.37 for the serial adder employs a total of five cells.

FPGAs are very well suited to computer-aided design and manufacture; the process of mapping a new design into one or more FPGA chips can be almost entirely automated. It requires first translating or "compiling" the design specification—a schematic diagram or an HDL description, for example—into a logic (gate and flip-flop) model. Specialized place-and-route CAD software is then employed to assign the logic elements to cells, to determine the switch settings needed to set each cell's function, and to establish the intercell connections. Finally, the design is physically transferred to one or more copies of the FPGA chip via an appropriate programming unit, a process that has been aptly described as "desktop manufacturing."

2.2.3 Register-Level Design

A register-level system consists of a set of registers linked by combinational data-transfer and data-processing circuits. A block diagram can define its structure, and the set of operations it performs on data words can define its behavior. Each operation is typically implemented by one or more elementary register-transfer steps of the form

$$cond: Z := f(X_1, X_2, \ldots, X_k); \tag{2.15}$$

where f is a function to be performed or an instruction to be executed in one clock cycle. Here $X_1, X_2, \ldots, X_k$ and Z denote data words or the registers that store them. The prefix $cond$ denotes a control condition that must be satisfied ($cond = 1$) for the indicated operation to take place. Statement (2.15) is read as follows: when $cond$ holds, compute the (combinational) function f on $X_1, X_2, \ldots, X_k$ and assign the resulting value to Z.

Data and control. A simple register-level system like that of Figure 2.38a performs a single action, in this case, the add operation $Z := A + B$. Figure 2.38b shows a more complicated system that can perform several different operations. Such a *multifunction* system is generally partitioned into a data-processing part, called a *datapath,* and a controlling part, the *control unit,* which is responsible for selecting and controlling the actions of the datapath. In the example in Figure 2.38b, control unit CU selects the operation (add, shift, and so on) for the ALU to perform in each clock cycle. It also determines the input operands to apply to the ALU and the destination of its results. It is easy to see that this circuit has the connection paths necessary to perform the following data-processing operations, as well as many others.

$$Z := A + B;$$

$$B := A - B;$$

Less obvious operations that can be performed are the simple data transfer $Z := B$, which is implemented as $Z := 0 + B$; the clear operation $B := 0$, which is implemented as $B := B - B$; and the negation operation $B := 0 - B$. A few double opera-

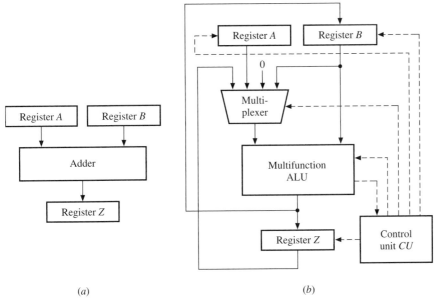

(a)   *(b)*

Figure 2.38
(a) Single-function circuit performing $Z := A + B$; *(b)* a multifunction circuit.

tions can also be performed in one clock cycle, for example,

$$B := Z + B, Z := Z + B;$$

Each of the foregoing operations requires *CU* to send specific control signals, indicated by dashed lines in Figure 2.38*b*, to various places in the datapath. For instance, to execute the subtraction $Z := A - B$, the controller *CU* must send select signals to the ALU to select its subtract function; it must send select signals to the multiplexer that connects register *A* to the ALU's left port; and it must send a "load data" control signal to the output register *Z*.

An example of a large multifunction system is a computer's CPU. Its control unit, which is responsible for the interpretation of instructions, is called the program control unit or I-unit. The CPU's datapath is also called the E-unit. Further datapath/control subdivisions are possible in complex systems, yielding a hierarchy of levels of control. In relatively simple machines such as that of Figure 2.38*b*, the control unit can be a special-purpose hard-wired sequential circuit designed using standard gate-level techniques. In more complex cases, both the datapath and control units may have to be treated at the register level.

A description language. HDLs, which were introduced in section 2.1.1, provide both behavioral and structural descriptions at the register level. A full-fledged HDL like VHDL is very complex, however, so we will use a much smaller HDL that suffices for our purposes and is largely self-explanatory. An essential element of all HDLs, including ours, is a *state assignment* or *register-transfer statement*, which has the general form of (2.15), and specifies a conditional state transition that takes place in a single clock cycle. An alternative notation for (2.15) is

$$\textbf{if } cond = 1 \textbf{ then } Z := f(X_1, X_2, \ldots, X_k);$$

There is often a close correspondence between the elements of an HDL description and hardware components and signals in the system being described. For example, the statement $Z := A + B$ describes the circuit of Figure 2.38a. In this interpretation, + represents the adder. The input connections to the adder from registers A and B are inferred from the fact that A and B are the arguments of +, while the output connection from the adder to register Z is inferred from $Z :=$. An exact correspondence between hardware structures and HDL constructs can be hard to specify without considerable verbosity. To keep our HDL concise, we use it primarily for behavioral descriptions and supplement it with block diagrams to describe structure.

Figure 2.39 illustrates the use of our HDL to describe the behavior of a complete system at the register level. This 8-bit multiplication circuit, named *multiplier8*, computes the product $Z = Y \times X$, where the numbers are 8-bit binary fractions in sign-magnitude form. (The actual design of this multiplier, which implements a binary version of "long" multiplication based on repeated addition and shifting, is examined later in Example 2.7.) Two 8-bit buses *INBUS* and *OUT-BUS* form *multiplier8*'s input and output ports, respectively, and link it to the outside world. The circuit contains three 8-bit data registers A, M, and Q, as well as a 3-bit control register *COUNT* that counts the number of add-and-shift steps to decide when multiplication is complete. The A and Q registers can be merged into a single 16-bit shift register denoted $A.Q$. The operands X (the multiplier) and Y (the multiplicand) are initially transferred from *INBUS* into the Q and M registers, respectively. The product is computed by multiplying Y by 1 bit of X at a time and adding the result to A. After each addition step, the contents of $A.Q$ are shifted 1 bit to the right so that the next multiplier bit required is always in $Q[7]$, the right-most bit in the Q register. (Consequently, the multiplier Y is eventually shifted out of Q and lost.) After seven iterations to multiply the magnitude parts of X and Y, the sign of the product is computed and placed in the left-most position of A, that is, in $A[0]$.

multiplier8	(**in:** *INBUS*; **out:** *OUTBUS*);
	register $A[0:7]$, $M[0:7]$, $Q[0:7]$, $COUNT[0:2]$;
	bus $INBUS[0:7]$, $OUTBUS[0:7]$;
BEGIN:	$A := 0$, $COUNT := 0$, $M := INBUS$;
	$Q := INBUS$;
ADD:	$A[0:7] := A[1:7] + M[1:7] \times Q[7]$;
SHIFT:	$A[0] := 0$, $A[1:7].Q := A.Q[0:6]$,
TEST:	$COUNT := COUNT + 1$;
	if $COUNT \neq 7$ **then go to** *ADD*,
FINISH:	$A[0] := M[0]$ **xor** $Q[7]$, $Q[7] := 0$;
OUTPUT:	$OUTBUS := Q$;
	$OUTBUS := A$;
end *multiplier8*;	

Figure 2.39
Formal language description of an 8-bit binary multiplier.

The final product ends up in $A.Q$, from which it is transferred 8 bits at a time to OUTBUS.

The description of the multiplier consists mostly of register-transfer operations. The registers are defined by the initial **register** statement, which gives their names, their sizes, and the order in which their bits are indexed. For example,

$$\textbf{register } M[0{:}7];$$

means that M is a register composed of eight flip-flops individually identified as $M[i]$, where i runs from 0 to 7 from left to right. Equivalently, we could write

$$M = M[0].M[1].M[2].M[3].M[4].M[5].M[6].M[7];$$

Buses are used in much the same way as registers and are defined similarly. Register-transfer operations that take place simultaneously, that is, during the same clock cycle, are separated by commas, while a semicolon separates sets of operations that must occur in successive clock cycles. Thus the statement

$$A := 0, \ COUNT := 0, \ M := INBUS;$$

appearing on the line labeled BEGIN in Figure 2.39, specifies three distinct actions to take place in the same clock period: clear the A register (transfer the all-0 operand to it), clear the COUNT register, and transfer the data on INBUS to register M. Note that a register can be read from and written into in the same clock cycle, as happens to Q in the statement

$$A[0] := M(0) \ \textbf{\textit{xor}} \ Q[7], \ Q[7] := 0;$$

The order in which a list of statements terminating in semicolons are written is the sequence in which the actions they define should occur. Deviations from this sequence are specified by control statements and by the use of statement labels. We use the **if … then** control statement to make an action sequence depend on some circuit condition. For example, the conditional branch statement

$$\textbf{if } COUNT \neq 7 \textbf{ then go to } ADD, \tag{2.16}$$

in Figure 2.39 means the following: Test the state of the 3-bit COUNT register. If COUNT is not equal to 7, that is, 111_2, then the next action to be taken is specified by the statement labeled ADD. If $COUNT = 7$, then the next action is specified by the statement FINISH.

Design techniques. The design problem for register-level systems is as follows. Given a set of operations to be executed, design a circuit using a specified set of register-level components that implement the desired functions while satisfying certain cost and performance criteria. As noted already, it is difficult to impose useful mathematical structures on register-level behavior or structure corresponding to, say, Boolean algebra and the two-level constraint in gate-level design. Lacking such mathematical tools, register-level design methods tend to be heuristic and depend heavily on the designer's expertise. We can, however, state the following general approach to the design problem.

1. Define the desired behavior by a set of sequences of register-transfer operations, such that each operation can be implemented directly using the available design components. This constitutes an *algorithm AL* to be executed.

2. Analyze *AL* to determine the types of components and the number of each type required for the datapath *DP*.
3. Construct a block diagram for *DP* using the components identified in step 2. Make the connections between the components so that all data paths implied by *AL* are present and the given performance-cost constraints are met.
4. Analyze *AL* and *DP* to identify the control signals needed. Introduce into *DP* the logic or *control points* necessary to apply these signals.
5. Design a control unit *CU* for *DP* that meets all the requirements of *AL*.
6. Verify, typically by computer simulation, that the final design operates correctly and meets all performance-cost goals.

Algorithm design (step 1) involves a creative design process analogous to writing a computer program and depends heavily on the skill and experience of the designer. The identification of the data-processing components in step 2 is straightforward, but complications arise when the possibility of sharing components exists. For example,

$$c: \quad A := A + B, C := C + D;$$

defines two addition operations. Since these additions do not involve the same operands, they can be done in parallel if two independent adders are provided. However, costs can be lowered by sharing a single adder and performing the two additions sequentially, thus:

$$c(t_0): \quad A := A + B;$$

$$c(t_0 + 1): \quad C := C + D;$$

This example illustrates a fundamental cost-performance trade-off. The identification of the parallelism inherent in a multistep algorithm can be exceedingly difficult.

A typical datapath unit *DP* has a regular and relatively simple structure designed for processing data of some fixed word size *w*. Its main components are registers, buses, and combinational circuits, all oriented toward *w*-bit words. The design of *DP* (step 3 above) requires defining an interconnection structure that links the components needed by the various parts of *AL*. The specification and design of the control unit *CU* (steps 4 and 5) is a relatively independent process. Unlike *DP*, the control unit often has a small number of states that interact in an irregular fashion, making it suitable for gate-level, sequential circuit design (section 2.1.3). Specialized methods such as microprogramming are used to design large control units, a topic we consider in Chapter 5.

Design verification (step 6) plays a crucial role in the development process because mistakes, often of a subtle kind, are unavoidable in the design of a complex system. Simulation via CAD tools is used to identify and correct functional errors before the new design is committed to hardware. CAD tools are also used to predict or measure the system's operating speed. If a particular design does not meet some specification —an algorithm step is executed too slowly, or component costs are exceeded—it is necessary to return, sometimes repeatedly, to steps 1 through 5 and modify *AL*, *DP*, or *CU*.

We now present two examples of sequential circuits designed at the register level. The first revisits the 4-bit-stream adder, whose behavior and gate-level design are covered in Example 2.2. It illustrates some advantages of a high-level, functional approach to design, as well as the important design technique of pipelining.

EXAMPLE 2.6 DESIGN OF A PIPELINED 4-BIT-STREAM SERIAL ADDER. Consider again the design of a circuit to add four unsigned binary numbers presented serially (least significant bits first) to produce their arithmetic sum, also in serial form. This adder has four input lines x_1, x_2, x_3, x_4 and a single output line z. Our first, gate-level design (Example 2.2) started with the construction of a (4×16)-entry state table (Figure 2.13a), and culminated in a circuit (Figure 2.13b) containing two D flip-flops and a large (eight-input, three-output) combinational circuit.

This time we will start with the observation that we can add the four bit streams in pairs using a basic register-level component, the serial adder (Figure 2.12). We can add streams x_1 and x_2 using one serial adder SA_1 and, at the same time, add streams x_3 and x_4 using a second serial adder SA_2. The outputs of SA_1 and SA_2 are then combined by a third serial adder SA_3 to obtain the desired output z. This process leads to the circuit $4ADD_1$ in Figure 2.40a, which contains three D flip-flops and three full adders. Because the full adders are relatively simple—several representative logic realizations appear in Figure 2.9—$4ADD_1$ contains far fewer gates than the design of Figure 2.13.

SA_3's combinational logic (a full adder) receives signals directly from the corresponding full adders in SA_1 and SA_2. Hence $4ADD_1$ has more levels of combinational logic than a simple serial adder. Consequently, for $4ADD_1$ to operate properly, it must be clocked at a frequency $f' < f$, where f is the maximum permissible frequency of a serial adder. We can, however, operate the 4-bit-stream adder at the higher frequency f, if we insert a pair of flip-flops as buffers between $SA_1:SA_2$ and SA_3, as illustrated in Figure 2.40b. Now the inputs to SA_3 in clock cycle i consist only of the signals computed by SA_1 and SA_2 in cycle $i - 1$ and stored in the buffer flip-flops of the new design $4ADD_2$. This, however, means that each result bit produced by $4ADD_2$ is delayed by one clock cycle. It might therefore be thought that $4ADD_2$ is significantly slower than $4ADD_1$. This is not the case, however, because in both circuits *a new final result bit z is generated in every clock cycle.* Although it takes two clock cycles to calculate each sum bit, $4ADD_2$ overlaps the computation of two successive sum bits so that, once it is in full operation, it also produces one result bit per cycle. Breaking a computation into a sequence of simpler subcomputations that can be overlapped is called *pipelining* and is an important technique in computer design.

In the final circuit $4ADD_3$ (Figure 2.40c), we have introduced a flip-flop to store the output z of SA_3; we have also regrouped the internal (carry) flip-flops of the serial adders to make them part of the buffer registers—recall that their role is to store carry bits generated in clock cycle $i - 1$ and used in clock cycle i. $4ADD_3$ has a circuit structure called a *pipeline.* It is composed of two *stages,* each of which consists of some combinational logic followed by a buffer register. Suppose the first four data bits enter stage 1 at time (clock cycle) 1. Their partial sum bits z_1 and z_2 are computed and passed on to stage 2. The first result bit $z = z_1$ ***plus*** z_2 is then computed by stage 2 during clock cycle 2. At the same time a second set of four data bits can be entered into and processed by stage 1. In clock cycle 3, the result sum is computed by stage 2 while stage 1 handles a third set of input data, and so on. Clearly if a steady stream of data enters the pipeline, then a new result bit emerges every clock cycle, beginning with clock cycle 2.

Modern computers often employ pipelines of this sort for complex arithmetic operations such as floating-point addition, as we will see in Chapter 4. They also process instructions by means of a special multifunction pipeline composed of as many as a dozen stages (Chapter 5).

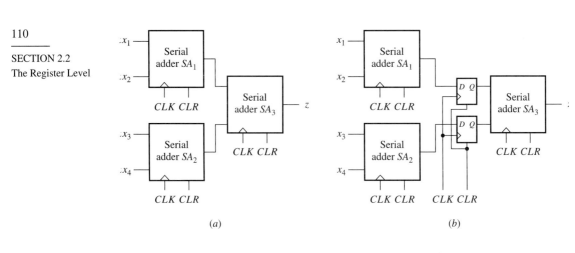

(a)   (b)

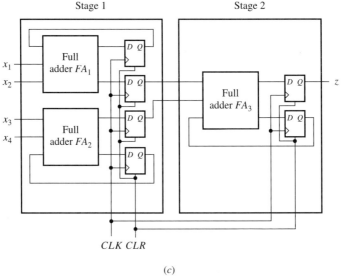

(c)

Figure 2.40
Four-bit-stream serial adder: (a) basic design $4ADD_1$; (b) buffered design $4ADD_2$; (c) two-stage pipeline design $4ADD_3$.

Next we examine a bigger register-level design problem, a sequential circuit that multiplies two binary numbers. This circuit is too complex to design at the gate level; it also has well-defined data-processing and control parts.

EXAMPLE 2.7 DESIGN OF A FIXED-POINT BINARY MULTIPLIER. Fixed-point multiplication is often implemented in computers by a binary version of the manual multiplication algorithm for decimal numbers based on repeated addition and shifting. Consider the task of multiplying two 8-bit binary fractions $X = x_0x_1x_2x_3x_4x_5x_6x_7$ and $Y = y_0y_1y_2y_3y_4y_5y_6y_7$ to form the product $P = X \times Y$. Each number is assumed to be in sign-magnitude form, where the left-most bit (with subscript 0) of the number denotes its sign: 0 for positive and 1 for negative. The remaining seven bits represent the number's magnitude. Note that for fractions, it is convenient to index the numbers from left to right, so that bit x_i has weight 2^{-i}. Hence when $x_0 = 0$, $X = x_0x_1x_2x_3x_4x_5x_6x_7$ denotes

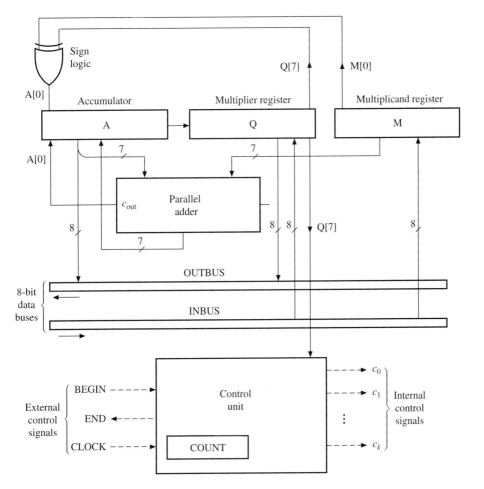

Figure 2.41
Block diagram of an 8-bit binary multiplier *multiplier8*.

the positive number N given by

$$N = x_1 2^{-1} + x_2 2^{-2} + x_3 2^{-3} + x_4 2^{-4} + x_5 2^{-5} + x_6 2^{-6} + x_7 2^{-7}$$

When $x_0 = 1$, X denotes $-N$.

The multiplication algorithm that we will implement first multiplies the magnitude parts X_M and Y_M of X and Y thus:

$$P_M := X_M \times Y_M \tag{2.17}$$

where $P_M = p_1 p_2 \dots p_{14}$ is the magnitude of the product P. It computes the sign p_0 of P via the simple operation $p_0 := x_0 \textbf{ xor } y_0$. The final result $P = p_0 p_1 p_2 \dots p_{14}$ is 15 bits long. The magnitude multiplication (2.17) is clearly the central design problem. The unsigned product P_M is computed in seven add-and-shift steps defined as follows:

$$P_i := P_i + x_{7-i} \times Y_M; \tag{2.18}$$

$$P_{i+1} := 2^{-1} P_i; \tag{2.19}$$

Step	Action	Accumulator A	Register Q
0	Initialize registers	00000000	10110011 = multiplier X
1		01010101	= multiplicand $M = Y$
	Add M to A	01010101	10110011
	Shift $A.Q$	00101010	11011001
2		01010101	
	Add M to A	01111111	11011001
	Shift $A.Q$	00111111	11101100
3		00000000	
	Add 0 to A	00111111	11101100
	Shift $A.Q$	00011111	11110110
4		00000000	
	Add 0 to A	00011111	11110110
	Shift $A.Q$	00001111	11111011
5		01010101	
	Add M to A	01100100	11111011
	Shift $A.Q$	00110010	01111101
6		01010101	
	Add M to A	10000111	01111101
	Shift $A.Q$	01000011	10111110
7		00000000	
	Add 0 to A	01000011	10111110
	Shift $A.Q$	00100001	11011111
8	Put sign of P in $A[0]$ and set $Q[7]$ to 0	10100001	11011110 = product P

Figure 2.42
Illustration of the binary multiplication algorithm.

where $P_0 = 0$, $P_7 = P_M$, and i goes from 1 to 7. The quantities $P_0, P_1, \ldots, P_7$ are referred to as *partial products*. When the current multiplier bit x_{7-i} is 1, (2.18) becomes $P_i := P_i + Y_M$; when $x_{7-i} = 0$, (2.18) becomes $P_i := P_i + 0$. Hence step (2.18) requires adding either the multiplicand Y_M or 0 to the current partial product P_i. The factor 2^{-1} in (2.19) indicates that P_i is right-shifted by 1 bit after each addition; this factor is equivalent to division by 2. Note that each add-and-shift step appends 1 bit to the partial product, which therefore grows from 7 to 15 bits (including the sign bit p_0) over the course of the multiplication.

With these preliminaries, we can now specify the main components needed for *multiplier8*. Two 8-bit registers, conventionally denoted Q (for multiplier-*q*uotient) and M (for *m*ultiplicand), are required to store X and Y, respectively. A double-length, 16-bit register A (for *a*ccumulator) stores the P_i's; this standard length is more convenient than the actual 15-bit maximum size of P. A 7-bit combinational adder is used for the addition specified by (2.18) (The serial adder of Figure 2.12 could also be used, but it would be about seven times slower.) The adder must have its output and one input connected to A, while its other input must be switched between M and zero. The 1-bit right-shift function (2.19) can be conveniently obtained by constructing A from a right-shift register with parallel IO.

As specified by (2.18), addition is controlled by bit x_{7-i}, which is stored in the Q register. The multiplier's control unit must be able to scan the contents of Q from right to left in the course of the multiplication. If Q is a right-shift register, then x_{7-i} can always be obtained from Q's right-most flip-flop $Q[7]$ by right-shifting Q before the next x_{7-i} is needed. Consequently, X_M is gradually reduced from 7 to 0 bits while P_i is expanding from 7 to 14 bits, also by right-shifting. Hence we can combine A and Q into a single 16-bit, right-shift register, the left half of which is A while the right half is Q. The multiplier is completed by the inclusion of external data buses *INBUS* and *OUT-BUS* and a control unit, which contains a 3-bit iteration counter named *COUNT*. The resulting circuit has the structure depicted in Figure 2.41. A complete HDL description of the multiplication algorithm developed above appears in Figure 2.39.

At the core of our design is the adder and the $A.Q$ register that implement (2.18) and (2.19), respectively. The output-carry signal c_{OUT} of the adder is the most significant bit of an 8-bit sum and so is connected to the data input of $A[0]$. The counter *COUNT* is incremented and tested at the end of each add-shift step to determine if the add-shift phase should terminate. When *COUNT* is found to contain 7, P_M occupies bits 1:14 of the register-pair $A.Q$; that is, bits $A[1:7].Q[0:6]$. The sign bit p_0 is then computed from x_0 and y_0, which are stored in $Q[7]$ and $M[0]$, respectively, and p_0 is placed in $A[0]$. At the same time 0 is written into $Q[7]$ to expand the final product from 15 to 16 bits. Figure 2.42 shows the complete step-by-step multiplication process for two sample fractions $X = 10110011$ and $Y = 01010101$. The sign bit $x_0 = 1$ of X (indicating that it is a negative number) is marked by an underline. The data in $A.Q$ to the left of x_0 is the current partial product P_i.

The control unit of Figure 2.41 is designed by first identifying from the formal description (Figure 2.39) all the control signals and control points needed to implement the specified register-transfer operations. Figure 2.43 lists a possible set of control

Control signal	Operation controlled
c_0	Clear accumulator A (reset to 0).
c_1	Clear counter *COUNT* (reset to 0).
c_2	Load $A[0]$.
c_3	Load multiplicand register M from *INBUS*.
c_4	Load multiplier register Q from *INBUS*.
c_5	Load main adder outputs into $A[1:7]$.
c_6	Select M or 0 to apply to right input of adder.
c_7	Right-shift $A.Q$.
c_8	Increment counter *COUNT*.
c_9	Select *COUT* or $M[0]$ **xor** $Q[7]$ to load into $A[0]$.
c_{10}	Clear $Q[7]$.
c_{11}	Transfer contents of A to *OUTBUS*.
c_{12}	Transfer contents of Q to *OUTBUS*.

Figure 2.43
Control signals for *multiplier8*.

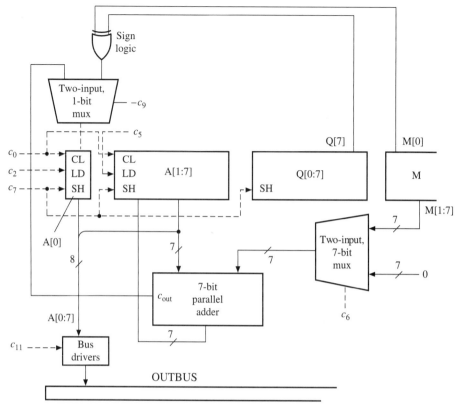

Figure 2.44
Implementation of some control points of *multiplier8*.

signals for the multiplier. In some cases several control signals implement a particular operation. For instance, the add operation employs c_6 to select the adder's right input operand, c_9 to select c_{OUT} for loading into $A[0]$, and c_2 and c_5 to actually load the 8-bit sum into $A[0:7]$. The number of distinguished control signals will vary with the details of the logic used to implement the control unit. Figure 2.44 shows a straightforward implementation of the control logic associated with the accumulator and adder subcircuits using the control signals defined in Figure 2.43.

2.3
THE PROCESSOR LEVEL

The processor or system level is the highest in the computer design hierarchy. It is concerned with the storage and processing of blocks of information such as programs and data files. The components at this level are complex, usually sequential, circuits that are based on VLSI technology. Processor-level design is very much a heuristic process, as there is little design theory at this level of abstraction.

2.3.1 Processor-Level Components

The component types recognized at the processor level fall into four main groups: processors, memories, IO devices, and interconnection networks; see Figure 2.45. In this section we give only a brief summary of the characteristics of processor-level components; they are examined individually and in much greater depth in later chapters.

Central processing unit. We define a CPU to be a general-purpose, instruction-set processor that has overall responsibility for program interpretation and execution in a computer system. The qualifier *general-purpose* distinguishes CPUs from other, more specialized processors, such as IO processors (IOPs), whose functions are restricted. An instruction-set processor is characterized by the fact that it operates on word-organized instructions and data, which the processor obtains from an external memory that also stores results computed by the processor. Most contemporary CPUs are microprocessors, implying that their physical implementation is a single VLSI chip.

Figure 2.46 shows the essential internal organization of a CPU at the register level. The CPU contains the logic needed to execute its particular instruction set and is divided into datapath and control units. The control part (the I-unit) generates the addresses of instructions and data stored in external memory. In this particular system a cache memory is interposed between the main memory M and the CPU. The cache is a fast buffer memory designed to hold an active portion of the system's address space; it is often placed, wholly or in part, on the same IC as the CPU. Each memory request generated by the CPU is first directed to the cache. If the required information is not currently assigned to the cache, the request is redirected to M and the cache is automatically updated from M. The I-unit fetches instructions from the cache or M and decodes them to derive the control signals needed for their execution. The CPU's datapath (E-unit) has the arithmetic-logic circuits that execute most instructions; it also has a set of registers for temporary data storage. The CPU manages a system bus, which is the main communication link among the CPU-cache subsystem, main memory, and the IO devices.

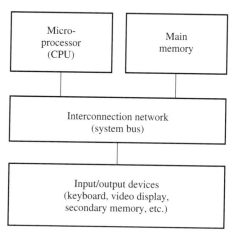

Figure 2.45
Major components of a computer system.

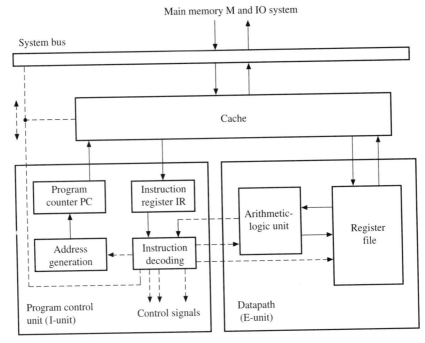

Figure 2.46
Internal organization of a CPU and cache memory.

The CPU is a synchronous sequential circuit whose clock period is the computer's basic unit of time. In one clock cycle the CPU can perform a register-transfer operation, such as fetching an instruction word from M via the system bus and loading it into the instruction register IR. This operation can be expressed formally by

$$IR := M(PC);$$

where PC is the program counter the CPU uses to hold the expected address of the next instruction word. Once in the I-unit, an instruction is decoded to determine the actions needed for its execution; for example, perform an arithmetic operation on data words stored in CPU registers. The I-unit then issues the sequence of control signals that enables execution of the instruction in question. The entire process of fetching, decoding, and executing an instruction constitutes the CPU's *instruction cycle*.

Memories. CPUs and other instruction-set processors operate in conjunction with external memories that store the programs and data required by the processors. Numerous memory technologies exist, and they vary greatly in cost and performance. The cost of a memory device generally increases rapidly with its speed of operation. The memory part of a computer can be divided into several major subsystems:

1. Main memory M, consisting of relatively fast storage ICs connected directly to, and controlled by, the CPU.

2. Secondary memory, consisting of less expensive devices that have very high storage capacity. These devices often involve mechanical motion and so are much slower than M. They are generally connected indirectly (via M) to the CPU and form part of the computer's IO system.

3. Many computers have a third type of memory called a cache, which is positioned between the CPU and main memory. The cache is intended to further reduce the average time taken by the CPU to access the memory system. Some or all of the cache may be integrated on the same IC chip as the CPU itself.

Main memory M is a word-organized addressable *random-access memory* (RAM). The term *random access* stems from the fact that the access time for every location in M is the same. Random access is contrasted with *serial access,* where memory access times vary with the location being accessed. Serial access memories are slower and less expensive than RAMs; most secondary-memory devices use some form of serial access. Because of their lower operating speeds and serial-access mode, the manner in which the stored information is organized in secondary memories is more complex than the simple word organization of main memory. Caches also use random access or an even faster memory-accessing method called associative or content addressing. Memory technologies and the organization of stored information are covered in Chapter 6.

IO devices. Input-output devices are the means by which a computer communicates with the outside world. A primary function of IO devices is to act as data transducers, that is, to convert information from one physical representation to another. Unlike processors, IO devices do not alter the information content or meaning of the data on which they act. Since data is transferred and processed within a computer system in the form of digital electrical signals, input (output) devices transform other forms of information to (from) digital electrical signals. Figure 2.47 lists some widely used IO devices and the information media they involve. Many of these devices use electromechanical technologies; hence their speed of operation is slow compared with processor and main-memory speeds. Although the CPU can take direct control of an IO device it is often under the immediate control of a special-purpose processor or control unit that directs the flow of information between the IO device and main memory. The design of IO systems is considered in Chapter 7.

Interconnection networks. Processor-level components communicate by word-oriented buses. In systems with many components, communication may be controlled by a subsystem called an *interconnection network;* terms such as *switching network, communications controller,* and *bus controller* are also used in this context. The function of the interconnection network is to establish dynamic communication paths among the components via the buses under its control. For cost reasons, these paths are usually shared. Only two communicating devices can access and use a shared bus at any time, so contention results when several system components request use of the bus. The interconnection network resolves such contention by selecting one of the requesting devices on some priority basis and connecting it to the bus. The interconnection network may place the other requesting devices in a queue.

IO device	Type		Medium to/from which IO device transforms digital electrical signals
	Input	Output	
Analog-digital converter	x		Analog (continuous) electrical signals
CD-ROM drive	x		Characters (and coded images) on optical disk
Document scanner/reader	x		Images on paper
Dot-matrix display panel		x	Images on screen
Keyboard/keypad	x		Characters on keyboard
Laser printer		x	Images on paper
Loudspeaker		x	Spoken words and sounds
Magnetic-disk drive	x	x	Characters (and coded images) on magnetic disk
Magnetic-tape drive	x	x	Characters (and coded images) on magnetic tape
Microphone	x		Spoken words and sounds
Mouse/touchpad	x		Spatial position on pad

Figure 2.47
Some representative IO devices.

Simultaneous requests for access to some unit or bus result from the fact that communication between processor-level components is generally asynchronous in that the components cannot be synchronized directly by a common clock signal. This synchronization problem can be attributed to several causes.

- A high degree of independence exists among the components. For example, CPUs and IOPs execute different types of programs and interact relatively infrequently and at unpredictable times.
- Component operating speeds vary over a wide range. CPUs operate from 1 to 10 times faster than main-memory devices, while main-memory speeds can be many orders of magnitude faster than IO-device speeds.
- The physical distance separating the components can be too large to permit synchronous transmission of information between them.

Bus control is one of the functions of a processor such as a CPU or an IOP. An IOP controls a common IO bus to which many IO devices are connected. The IOP is responsible for selecting a device to be connected to the IO bus and from there to main memory. It also acts as a buffer between the relatively slow IO devices and the relatively fast main memory. Larger systems have special processors whose sole function is to supervise data transfers over shared buses.

2.3.2 Processor-Level Design

Processor-level design is less amenable to formal analysis than is design at the register level. This is due in part to the difficulty of giving a precise description of the desired system behavior. To say that the computer should execute efficiently all programs supplied to it is of little help to the designer. The common approach to design at this level is to take a *prototype design* of known performance and modify it where necessary to accommodate new technologies or meet new performance requirements. The performance specifications usually take the following form:

- The computer should be capable of executing a instructions of type b per second.
- The computer should be able to support c memory or IO devices of type d.
- The computer should be compatible with computers of type e.
- The total cost of the system should not exceed f.

Even when a new computer is closely based on a known design, it may not be possible to predict its performance accurately. This is due to our lack of understanding of the relation between the structure of a computer and its performance. Performance evaluation must generally be done experimentally during the design process, either by computer simulation or by measurement of the performance of a copy of the machine under working conditions. Reflecting its limited theoretical basis, only a small amount of useful performance evaluation can be done via mathematical analysis [Kant 1992].

Prototype structures. We view the design process as involving two major steps: First select a prototype design and adapt it to satisfy the given performance constraints. Then determine the performance of the proposed system. If unsatisfactory, modify the design and repeat this step; continue until an acceptable design is obtained. This conservative approach to computer design has been widely followed and accounts in part for the relatively slow evolution of computer architecture. It is rare to find a successful computer structure that deviates substantially from the norm. The need to remain compatible with existing hardware and software standards also influences the adherence to proven designs. Computer owners are understandably reluctant to spend money retraining users and programmers, or replacing well-tested software.

The systems of interest here are general-purpose computers, which differ from one another primarily in the number of components used and their autonomy. The variety of interconnection or communication structures used is fairly small. We will represent these structures by means of block diagrams that are basically graphs (section 2.1.1). Figure 2.48 shows the structure that applies to first-generation computers and many small, modern microprocessor-based systems. The addition of special-purpose IO processors typical of the second and subsequent generations is

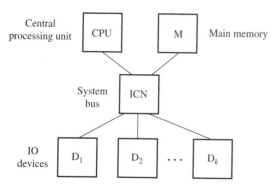

Figure 2.48
Basic computer structure.

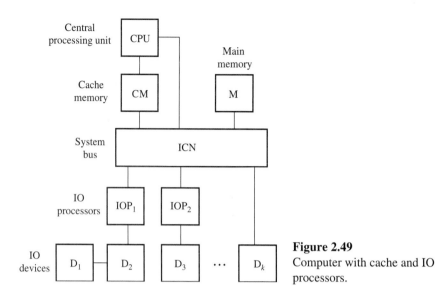

Figure 2.49
Computer with cache and IO processors.

shown in Figure 2.49. Here ICN denotes an interconnection (switching) network that controls memory-processor communication. Figure 2.50 shows a prototype structure employing two CPUs; it is therefore a multiprocessor. The uniprocessor systems of Figures 2.48 and 2.49 are special cases of this structure. Even more complex structures such as computer networks can be obtained by linking several copies of the foregoing prototype structures.

Performance measurement. Many performance figures for computers are derived from the characteristics of its CPU. As observed in section 1.3.2, CPU

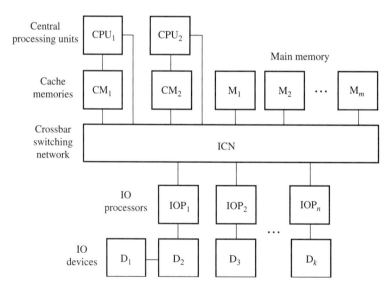

Figure 2.50
Computer with multiple CPUs and main memory banks.

speed can be measured easily, but roughly, by its clock frequency f in megahertz. Other, and usually better, performance indicators are *MIPS*, which is the average instruction execution speed in millions of instructions per second, and *CPI*, which is the average number of CPU clock cycles required per instruction. As discussed in section 1.3.2, these performance measures are related to the average time T in microseconds (μs) required to execute N instructions by the formula

$$T = \frac{N \times CPI}{f} \quad \mu s$$

Hence the average time t_E to execute an instruction is

$$t_E = T/N = CPI/f \quad \mu s$$

While f depends mainly on the IC technology used to implement the CPU, *CPI* depends primarily on the system architecture.

We can get another perspective on t_E by considering the distribution of instructions of different types and speeds in typical program workloads. Let $I_1, I_2, \ldots, I_n$ be a set of representative instruction types. Let t_i denote the average execution time (μs) of an instruction of type I_i and let p_i denote the occurrence probability of type-I_i instructions in representative object code. Then the average instruction execution time t_E is given by

$$t_E = \sum_{i=1}^{n} p_i t_i \quad \mu s \tag{2.20}$$

The t_i figures can be obtained fairly easily from the CPU specifications, but accurate p_i data must usually be obtained by experiment.

The set of instruction types selected for (2.20) and their occurrence probabilities define an *instruction mix*. Numerous instruction mixes have been published that represent various computers and their workloads [Siewiorek, Bell, and Newell 1982]. Figure 2.51 gives some recent data collected for two representative

	Probability of occurrence	
Instruction type	**Program A** (commercial)	**Program B** (scientific)
Memory load	0.24	0.29
Memory store	0.12	0.15
Fixed-point operations	0.27	0.15
Floating-point operations	0.00	0.19
Branch	0.17	0.10
Other	0.20	0.12

Figure 2.51
Representative instruction-mix data.
Source: McGrory, Carlton, and Askins 1992.

programs running on computers employing the Hewlett-Packard PA-RISC architecture under the UNIX operating system [McGrory, Carlton, and Askins 1992]. The execution probabilities are derived from counting the number of times an instruction of each type is executed while running each program; instructions from both the application program and the supporting system code are included in this count. Program A is a program TPC-A designed to represent commercial on-line transaction processing. Program B is a scientific program FEM that performs finite-element modeling. In each case, memory-access instructions (load and store) account for more than a third of all the instructions executed. The computation-intensive scientific program makes heavy use of floating-point instructions, whereas the commercial program employs fixed-point instructions only. Conditional and unconditional branch instructions account for 1 in 6 instructions in program A and for 1 in 10 instructions in program B. Other published instruction mixes suggest that as many as 1 in 4 instructions can be of the branch type.

A few performance parameters are based on other system components, especially memory. Main memory and cache size in megabytes (MB) can provide a rough indication of system capacity. A memory parameter related to computing speed is *bandwidth*, defined as the maximum rate in millions of bits per second (Mb/s) at which information can be transferred to or from a memory unit. Memory bandwidth affects CPU performance because the latter's processing speed is ultimately limited by the rate at which it can fetch instructions and data from its cache or main memory.

Perhaps the most satisfactory measure of computer performance is the cost of executing a set of representative programs on the target system. This cost can be the total execution time *T*, including contributions from the CPU, caches, main memory, and other system components. A set of actual programs that are representative of a particular computing environment can be used for performance evaluation. Such programs are called *benchmarks* and are run by the user on a copy (actual or simulated) of the computer being evaluated [Price 1989]. It is also useful to devise artificial or *synthetic benchmark* programs, whose sole purpose is to obtain data for performance evaluation. The program TPC-A providing the data for program A in Figure 2.51 is an example of a synthetic benchmark.

EXAMPLE 2.8 PERFORMANCE COMPARISON OF SEVERAL COMPUTERS
[MCLELLAN 1993]. Figure 2.52 presents some published data on the performance of three machines manufactured by Digital Equipment Corp. in the early 1990s, based on various versions of its 64-bit Alpha microprocessor. The SPEC (Standard Performance Evaluation Cooperative) ratings are derived from a set of benchmark programs that computer companies use to compare their products. The SPECint92 and SPECfp92 parameters indicate instruction execution speed relative to a standardized 1-MIPS computer (a 1978-vintage Digital VAX 11/780 minicomputer) when executing benchmark programs involving integer (fixed point) and floating-point operations, respectively. Hence the SPEC figures approximate MIPS measurements for two major classes of application programs like those of Figure 2.51. The remaining data in Figure 2.52 are relative performance figures for executing some other well-known benchmark programs, most aimed at scientific computing.

Data of this sort are better suited to measuring relative rather than absolute performance. For example, suppose we wish to compare the performance of the Digital 3000 and 10000 machines listed in Figure 2.52. The ratio of their SPECint92 MIPS numbers is 104.3/63.8 = 1.65. The corresponding ratios for the other five benchmarks range

Performance measure	DEC 3000 Model 400	DEC 4000 Model 610	DEC 10000 Model 610
CPU clock frequency (MHz)	133	160	200
Cache size (MB)	0.5	1	4
SPECint92	63.8	81.2	104.3
SPECfp92	112.2	143.1	200.4
Linpack 1000×1000	90	114	155
Perfect BM suite	18.1	22.9	28.6
Cernlib	16.9	21.0	26.0
Livermore loops	18.7	22.9	28.1

Figure 2.52
Performance comparison of three computers based on the Digital Alpha
processor.
Source: McLellan 1993.

from 1.50 to 1.79, suggesting that the Digital 10000 is about two-thirds faster than the
Digital 3000. Note also that the ratio of their clock frequencies is 200/133 = 1.50.

Queueing models. In order to give a flavor of analytic performance modeling,
we outline an approach based on queueing theory. The origins of this branch of
applied probability theory are usually traced to the analysis of congestion in telephone systems made by the Danish engineer A. K. Erlang (1878–1929) in 1909.
Our treatment is quite informal; the interested reader is referred to [Allen 1980;
Robertazzi 1994] for further details.

The queueing model that we will consider is the single-queue, single-server
case depicted in Figure 2.53; this is known as the *M/M/1 model* for historical reasons. It represents a "server" such as a CPU or a computer with a set of tasks (programs) to be executed. The tasks are activated or arrive at random times and are
queued in memory until they can be processed or "serviced" by the CPU on a first-
come first-served basis. The key parameters of the model are the rate at which
tasks requiring service arrive and the rate at which the tasks are serviced, both measured in tasks/s. The mean or average arrival and service rates are conventionally
denoted by λ (lambda) and μ (mu), respectively. The actual arrival and service
rates vary randomly around these mean values and are represented by probability

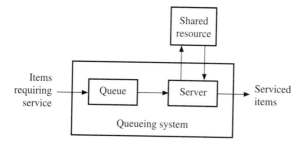

Figure 2.53 Simple queueing
model of a computer.

distributions. The latter are chosen to approximate the actual behavior of the system being modeled; how well they do so must be determined by observation and measurement.

The symbol ρ (rho) denotes λ/μ and represents the *mean utilization* of the server, that is, the fraction of time it is busy, on average. For example, if an average of two tasks arrive per second ($\lambda = 2$) and the server can process them at an average rate of eight tasks per second ($\mu = 8$), then $\rho = 2/8 = 0.25$.

The arrival of tasks at the system is a random process characterized by the *interarrival time distribution* $p_I(t)$ defined as the probability that at least one task arrives during a period of length t. The M/M/1 case assumes a *Poisson* arrival process—named after the French mathematician Siméon-Denis Poisson (1781–1840)—for which the probability distribution is

$$p_I(t) = 1 - e^{-\lambda t}$$

This exponential distribution has $p_I(t) = 0$ when $t = 0$. As t increases, $p_I(t)$ increases steadily toward 1 at a rate determined by λ. Exponential distributions characterize the randomness of many queueing models quite well. They are also mathematically tractable and lead to simple formulas for various performance-related quantities of interest. It is therefore usual to model the behavior of the server (the service process) by an exponential distribution also. Let $p_S(t)$ be the probability that the service required by a task is completed by the CPU in time t or less after its removal from the queue. Then the service process is characterized by

$$p_S(t) = 1 - e^{-\mu t}$$

Various performance parameters can characterize the steady-state performance of the single-server queueing system under the foregoing assumptions.

- The utilization $\rho = \lambda/\mu$ of the server, that is, the average fraction of time it is busy.
- The average number of tasks queued in the system, including tasks waiting for service and those actually being served. The parameter is called the *mean queue length* and is denoted by l_Q. It can be shown [Robertazzi 1994] that

$$l_Q = \rho/(1 - \rho) \tag{2.21}$$

- The average time that arriving tasks spend in the system, both waiting for service and being served, which is called the *mean waiting time* t_Q. The quantities t_Q and l_Q are related directly as follows. An average task X passing through the system under steady-state conditions should encounter the same number of waiting tasks l_Q when it enters the system as it leaves behind when it departs from the system after being serviced. The number left behind is λt_Q, which is the number of tasks that enter the system at rate λ during the period t_Q when X is present. Hence we conclude that $l_Q = \lambda t_Q$; in other words,

$$t_Q = l_Q/\lambda \tag{2.22}$$

Equation (2.22) is called *Little's equation*. It is valid for all types of queueing systems, not just the M/M/1 model. Combining (2.21) and (2.22), we get

$$t_Q = 1/(\mu - \lambda) \tag{2.23}$$

The quantities l_Q and t_Q refer to tasks that are either waiting for access to the server or are actually being served. The mean number of tasks waiting in the queue excluding those being served is denoted by l_W, while t_W denotes the mean time spent waiting in the queue, excluding service time. (The subscript W stands for "waiting.") The mean utilization of the server in an M/M/1 system, that is, the mean number of tasks being serviced, is λ/μ; hence subtracting this from l_Q yields l_W:

$$l_W = l_Q - \rho = \frac{\lambda^2}{\mu(\mu - \lambda)} \tag{2.24}$$

Similarly

$$t_W = t_Q - 1/\mu = \frac{\lambda}{\mu(\mu - \lambda)} \tag{2.25}$$

where $1/\mu$ is the mean time it takes to service a task. Comparing (2.24) and (2.25) we see that $t_W = l_W/\lambda$; therefore, Little's equation holds for both the Q and the W subscripts.

To illustrate the use of the foregoing formulas, consider a server computer that is processing jobs in a way that can be approximated by the M/M/1 model. Arriving jobs are queued in main memory until they are fully executed in one step by the CPU, which therefore is the server. New jobs arrive at an average rate of 10 per minute, and the computer is, on the average, idle 25 percent of the time. We ask two questions: What is the average time T that each job spends in the computer? What is the average number of jobs N in main memory that are waiting to begin execution? To answer, we assume that steady-state conditions prevail, from which it follows that T is t_Q, and N is l_W. Since the system is busy 75 percent of the time, $\rho = \lambda/\mu = 0.75$. We are given that $\lambda = 10$ jobs/min; hence the service rate μ is 40/3 jobs/min. Substituting into (2.23) yields $T = t_Q = 1/(40/3 - 10) = 0.3$ min. From Little's equation, $N = l_Q = \lambda t_Q = 3$; hence by (2.25), $l_W = 3 - 0.75 = 2.25$ jobs.

EXAMPLE 2.9 ANALYSIS OF SHARED COMPUTER USAGE [ALLEN 1980]. A small company has a computer system with a single terminal that is shared by its engineering staff. An average of 10 engineers use the terminal during an eight-hour work day, and each user occupies the terminal for an average of 30 minutes, mostly for simple and routine calculations. The company manager feels that the computer is underutilized, since the system is idle an average of three hours a day. The users, however, complain that it is *overutilized*, since they typically wait an hour or more to gain access to the terminal; they want the manager to purchase new terminals and add them to the system. We will now attempt to analyze this apparent contradiction using basic queueing theory.

Assume that the computer and its users are adequately represented by an M/M/1 queueing system. Since there are 10 users per eight hours on average, we set $\lambda = 10/8$ users/hour = 0.0208 users/min. The system is busy an average of five out of eight hours; hence the utilization $\rho = 5/8$, implying that $\mu = 1/30 = 0.0333$. Substituting these values for λ and μ into (2.25) yields $t_W = 50$ min, which confirms the users' estimate of their average waiting time for terminal access.

The manager is now convinced that the company needs additional terminals and agrees to buy enough to reduce t_W from 50 to 10 min. The question then arises: How many new terminals should he buy? We can approach this problem by representing each terminal and its users by an independent M/M/1 queueing system. Let m be the minimum number of terminals needed to make $t_W < 10$ or, equivalently, $t_Q < 40$. The arriving users are assumed to divide evenly into m queues, one for each terminal. The arrival rate λ^* per terminal is taken to be $\lambda/m = 0.0208/m$ users/min. If, as indicated above, the computer's CPU is lightly utilized, then a few additional terminals should not affect the response time experienced at a terminal; hence we assume that each terminal's mean service rate is $\mu^* = \mu = 0.0333$ users/min. To meet the desired performance goal, we require

$$t^*_Q = 1/(\mu^* - \lambda^*) = 1/(\mu - \lambda/m) < 40$$

from which it follows that $m > 2.5$. Hence three terminals are needed, so two new terminals should be acquired. This result is pessimistic, since the users are unlikely to form three separate queues for three terminals or to maintain the independence of the queues by not jumping from one queue to another whose terminal has become available. Nevertheless, this simple analysis gives the useful result that m should be 2 or 3.

2.4
SUMMARY

The central problem facing the digital system designer is to a devise a structure (a circuit, network, or system) from given components that exhibits a specified behavior or performs a specified range of operations at minimum cost. Various methods exist for describing structure and behavior, including block diagrams (for structure), truth and state tables (for behavior), and HDLs (for behavior and structure). Computer systems can be viewed at several levels of abstraction, where each level is determined by its primitive components and information units. Three levels have been presented here: the gate, register, and processor levels, whose components process bits, words, and blocks of words, respectively. Design at all levels is a complex process and depends heavily on CAD tools.

The gate level employs logic gates as components and has a well-developed theory based on Boolean algebra. A combinational circuit implements logic or Boolean functions of the form $z(x_1, x_2, ..., x_n)$, where z and the x_i's assume the values 0 and 1. The circuit can be constructed from any functionally complete set of gate types such as {AND, OR, NOT} or {NAND}. Every logic function can be realized by a two-level circuit that can be obtained using exact or heuristic minimization techniques. Sequential circuits implement logic functions that depend on time; unlike combinational circuits, sequential circuits have memory. They are built from gates and 1-bit storage elements (flip-flops) that store the circuit's state and are synchronized by means of clock signals.

Register-level components include combinational devices such as word gates, multiplexers, decoders, and adders, as well as sequential devices such as (parallel) registers, shift registers, and counters. Various general-purpose programmable elements also exist, including PLAs, ROMs, and FPGAs. Little formal theory exists for the design and analysis of register-level circuits. They are often described by HDLs whose fundamental construct is the register-transfer statement

$$cond: Z := F_i(X_1, X_2, ..., X_k);$$

denoting the conditional transfer of data from registers $X_1, X_2, \ldots, X_k$ to register Z via a combinational processing circuit F_i. Register-level circuits often consist of a datapath unit and a control unit. The first step in register-level design is to construct a formal (HDL) description of the desired behavior from which the components and connections for the datapath unit can be determined. The logic signals needed to control the datapath are then identified. Finally, a control unit is designed that generates these control signals.

The components recognized at the processor level are CPUs and other processors, memories, IO devices, and interconnection networks. The behavior of processor-level systems is complex and is often specified in approximate terms using average or worst-case behavior. Processor-level design is heavily based on the use of prototype structures. A prototype design is selected and modified to meet the given performance specifications. The actual performance of the system is then evaluated, and the design is further modified until a satisfactory result is achieved. Typical performance measures are millions of instructions executed per second (MIPS) and clock cycles per instruction (CPI). A few analytical methods for performance evaluation exist—notably queueing theory—but their usefulness is limited. Instead, experimental approaches using computer-based simulation or performance measurements on an actual system are used extensively.

2.5
PROBLEMS

2.1. Explain the difference between structure and behavior in the digital system context. Illustrate your answer by giving (*a*) a purely structural description and (*b*) a purely behavioral description of a half-subtracter circuit that computes the 1-bit difference $d = x - y$ and also generates a borrow signal b whenever $x < y$.

2.2. (*a*) Following the example of Figure 2.4, construct a behavioral VHDL description of the full-adder circuit of Figure 2.9*b*. (*b*) Following Figure 2.5, construct a structural VHDL description of the full adder.

2.3. Construct both structural and behavioral descriptions in VHDL of the EXCLUSIVE-OR circuit appearing in Figure 2.2.

2.4. Figure 2.54 describes a half adder in the widely used Verilog HDL. The Verilog symbols for the logic operations AND, OR, EXCLUSIVE-OR, and NOT are &, |, ^, and ~, respectively. (*a*) Is this description behavioral or structural? (*b*) Construct a similar description in Verilog for a full adder.

module *half_adder* (x_0, y_0, s_0, c_0);

  Input x_0, y_0; **output** s_0, c_0;

   assign $s_0 = x_0 \wedge y_0$;

   assign $c_0 = x_0 \,\&\, y_0$;

endmodule

Figure 2.54
Verilog description of a half adder.

Inputs			Outputs	
x_i	y_i	b_{i-1}	d_i	b_i
0	0	0	0	0
0	0	1	1	1
0	1	0	1	1
0	1	1	0	1
1	0	0	1	0
1	0	1	0	0
1	1	0	0	0
1	1	1	1	1

Figure 2.55
Truth table of a full subtracter.

2.5. Assign each of the following components to one of the three major design levels—processor, register, or gate—and justify your answers. (*a*) A multiplier of two *n*-bit numbers N_1 and N_2. (*b*) An *identity* circuit that outputs a 1 if all its *n* inputs (which represent a number *N*) are the same; it outputs a 0 otherwise. (*c*) A *negation* circuit that converts *N* to –*N*. (*d*) A *first-in first-out* (FIFO) memory, that stores a sequence of numbers in the order received; it also outputs the numbers in the same order.

2.6. Certain very small-scale ICs contain a single two-input gate. The ICs are manufactured in three varieties—NAND, OR, and EXCLUSIVE-OR—as indicated by a printed label on the IC's package. By mistake, a batch of all three varieties is manufactured without their labels. (*a*) Devise an efficient test that a technician can apply to any IC from this batch to determine which gate type it contains. (*b*) Suppose the batch of unlabeled ICs contains NOR gates, as well as NAND, OR, and EXCLUSIVE-OR. Devise an efficient testing procedure to determine each IC's gate type.

2.7. Construct a logic circuit implementing the 1-bit (full) subtracter defined in Figure 2.55 using as few gates as you can.

2.8. (*a*) Obtain an efficient all-NAND realization for the following four-variable Boolean function:

$$f_1(a,b,c,d) = a(b + \bar{c})d + \bar{a}(b + d)(b + c)(c + d) + \bar{b}\,\bar{c}\,\bar{d}$$

(*b*) Construct an efficient all-NOR design for $f_1(a,b,c,d)$.

2.9. Design a two-level combinational circuit in the sum-of-products style that computes the 3-bit sum of two 2-bit binary numbers. The circuit is to be implemented using AND and OR gates.

2.10. Consider the D flip-flop of Figure 2.11. (*a*) Explain why the glitch does not affect the flip-flop's state *y*. (*b*) This flip-flop is said to be *positive edge-triggered* because it triggers on the positive (rising or 0 to 1) edge of the clock *CK*. A *negative edge-triggered* flip-flop triggers on the negative (falling or 1 to 0) edge of *CK*, which is indicated by placing an inversion bubble at the *CK* input like that at the $\bar{y}$ output. Redraw the *y* part of Figure 2.11 for a negative edge-triggered flip-flop.

2.11. Figure 2.56 defines a 1-bit storage device called a *JK flip-flop*. It has the same edge-triggered clocking as the D flip-flop of Figure 2.11 but has two data inputs instead of one. The *J* input is activated to store a 1 in the flip-flop; that is, *JK* = 10 sets *y* =

	Inputs JK				
	00	01	10	11	
State 0	0	0	1	1	Next state
$y(i)$ 1	1	0	1	0	$y(i+1)$

(a)   (b)

Figure 2.56
JK flip-flop: (a) graphic symbol; (b) state table.

1. Similarly, the K input is activated to store a 0 in the flip-flop; that is, $JK = 01$ re-sets y to 0. The input combination $JK = 00$ leaves the state unchanged, while $JK = 11$ always changes, or toggles, the state. (a) What is the characteristic equation for a JK flip-flop, analogous to (2.5)? (b) Show how to build a JK flip-flop from a D flip-flop and a few NAND gates.

2.12. Derive a state table for a synchronous sequential circuit that acts as a serial incre-menter. An unsigned number N of arbitrary length is entered serially on input line x, causing the circuit to output serially the number $N + 1$ on its output line z. Give the intuitive meaning of each state and identify the reset state.

2.13. An alternative to a state table for representing the behavior of a sequential circuit SC is a *state diagram* or *state transition graph*, whose nodes denote states $\{S_1, S_2, ..., S_p\}$ and whose edges, which are indicated by arrows, denote transitions between states. A transition arrow from S_i to S_j is labeled X_u/Z_v if, when SC is in state S_i and input X_u is applied, the (present) output Z_v is produced and SC's next state is S_j. (a) Construct a state table equivalent to the state diagram for SC appear-ing in Figure 2.57. (b) How many flip-flops are needed to implement SC?

2.14. Design the sequential circuit SC whose behavior is defined in Figure 2.57 using D flip-flops and NAND gates. SC has a single primary input line and a single primary output line. Your answer should include a complete logic diagram for SC. Use as few gates and flip-flops as you can in your design.

2.15. Implement the sequential circuit SC specified in the preceding problem, this time using JK flip-flops (see problem 2.11) and NOR gates. Derive a logic diagram for SC and use as few gates and flip-flops as you can.

2.16. Design a serial subtracter analogous to the serial adder. The subtracter's inputs are two unsigned binary numbers n_1 and n_2; the output is the difference $n_1 - n_2$. Construct

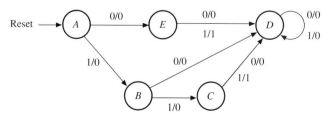

Figure 2.57
State diagram for a sequential circuit SC.

a state table, an excitation table, and a logic circuit that uses JK flip-flops and NOR gates only.

2.17. Design a sequential circuit that multiplies an unsigned binary number N of arbitrary length by 3. N is entered serially via input line x with its least significant bit first. The result representing $3N$ emerges serially from the circuit's output line z. Construct a state table for your circuit and give a complete logic circuit that uses D flip-flops and NAND gates only.

2.18. An important property of gates is functional completeness, which ensures that a complete gate set is adequate for all types of digital computation. (*a*) It has been asserted that functional completeness is irrelevant at the register level when dealing with components such as multiplexers, decoders, and PLDs. Explain concisely why this is so. (*b*) Suggest a logical property of sets of such components that might be substituted for completeness as an indication of the components' general usefulness in digital design. Give a brief argument supporting your position.

2.19. Redraw the gate-level multiplexer circuit of Figure 2.20 at the register level using word gates. Use as few such gates as you can and mark all bus sizes. Observe that a signal such as e that fans out to m lines can be considered to create an m-bit bus carrying the m-bit word $E = (e,e,...,e)$.

2.20. Figure 2.55 gives the truth table for a full subtracter, which computes the difference $x_i - y_i - b_{i-1}$, where b_{i-1} denotes the borrow-in bit. The subtracter's outputs are b_i, d_i, where b_i denotes the borrow-out bit. Show how to use (*a*) an eight-input multiplexer and (*b*) a four-input multiplexer to realize the full subtracter.

2.21. Show how to design a 1/16 decoder using the 1/4 decoder of Figure 2.23*b* as your sole building block.

2.22. Describe how to implement the priority encoder of Figure 2.25 by (*a*) a two-level AND-OR circuit and (*b*) a multiplexer of suitable size. Demonstrate that one design is much less costly than the other and derive a logic diagram for the less expensive design.

2.23. Design a 16-bit priority encoder using two copies of an 8-bit priority encoder. You may use a few additional gates of any standard types in your design, if needed.

2.24. A magnitude-comparator circuit compares two unsigned numbers X and Y and produces three outputs z_1, z_2, and z_3, which indicate $X = Y$, $X > Y$, and $X < Y$, respectively. (*a*) Show how to implement a magnitude comparator for 2-bit numbers using a single 16-input, 3-bit multiplexer of appropriate size. (*b*) Show how to implement the same comparator using an eight-input, 2-bit multiplexer and a few (not more than five) two-input NOR gates.

2.25. Commercial magnitude comparators such as the 74X85 have three control inputs confusingly labeled $X = Y$, $X > Y$, and $X < Y$, like the comparator's output lines. These inputs permit an array of k copies of a 4-bit magnitude comparator to be expanded to form a $4k$-bit magnitude comparator as shown in Figure 2.58. Modify the 4-bit magnitude comparator of Figure 2.27 to add the three new control inputs and explain briefly how they work. [*Hint*: The unused carry input lines denoted c_{in} in Figure 2.27 play a central role in the modification.]

2.26. Show how to connect n half adders (Figure 2.5) to form an n-bit combinational incrementer whose function is to add one (modulo 2^n) to an n-bit number X. For example, if $X = 10100111$, the incrementer should output $Z = 10101000$; if $X = 11111111$, it should output $Z = 00000000$.

2.27. Show how the register circuit of Figure 2.29 can be simplified by using the *LOAD* line to enable and disable the register's clock signal *CLOCK*. Explain clearly why this *gated-clocking* technique is often considered a violation of good design practice.

2.28. A useful operation related to shifting is called *rotation*. Left rotation of an *m*-bit register is defined by the register-transfer statement

$$(z_{m-2}, z_{m-3}, \ldots, z_0, z_{m-1}) := (z_{m-1}, z_{m-2}, \ldots, z_1, z_0) \qquad (2.26)$$

(*a*) Give an assignment statement similar to (2.26) that defines right rotation. Show how the 4-bit right-shift register *SR* of Figure 2.30 can easily be made to implement right rotation. (*b*) Using as few additional components and control lines as possible, show how to extend *SR* to implement *both* right shifting and right rotation.

2.29. Design an 8-bit counter using only the following component types: 4-bit D-type registers, half adders, full adders, and two-input NAND gates. The counter's inputs are a *CLEAR* signal that resets it to the all-0 state and a *COUNT* signal whose 0-to-1 (positive) edge causes the current count to be incremented by one. Use as few components as you can, assuming for simplicity that each component type has the same cost.

2.30. Assuming that input variables are available in true form only, show how to make the Actel FPGA cell of Figure 2.35*a* realize two-input versions of the NAND, NOR, and EXLCLUSIVE-OR functions.

2.31. (*a*) Assuming that input variables are available in true form only, what is the fan-in of the largest NAND gate that can be implemented with a single Actel FPGA cell (Figure 2.35*a*)? (*b*) What is the largest NAND if both true and complemented inputs are available and we allow some or all of the inputs to the NAND to be inverted?

2.32. Show how to implement the full subtracter defined in Figure 2.55 using as few copies as you can of the Actel C-module. Again assume that the input variables are supplied in true form only.

2.33. Figure 2.59 shows the Actel FPGA S-module, which adds a D flip-flop to the output of the C-module discussed in the text. Show how to use one copy of this cell to implement the edge-triggered JK flip-flop defined in problem 2.11, assuming only the true output *y* is needed and that either one of the flip-flop's *J* or *K* inputs can be complemented.

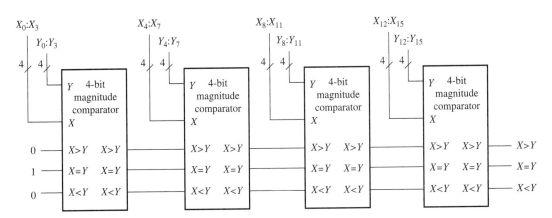

Figure 2.58
Expansion of a 4-bit magnitude comparator to form a 16-bit comparator.

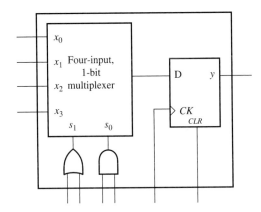

Figure 2.59
S-module from the Actel FPGA series.

2.34. Reconsider the FPGA implementation of the serial adder given in Figure 2.37. Suppose that it can now be implemented using two cell types: the original Actel C-module and the more recent sequential S-module defined in Figure 2.59. Construct a new version of the adder in the style of Figure 2.37 using as few modules as you can.

2.35. The 4-bit-stream serial adder $4ADD_1$ of Figure 2.40a contains three flip-flops, one in each serial adder, so it can have up to eight internal states. However, according to the analysis in Example 2.2, only four states are needed for 4-bit-stream serial addition. Does this imply that one flip-flop can be removed from $4ADD_1$ and, if so, which one? Explain your reasoning clearly.

2.36. Consider the operation of the serial adder pipeline $4ADD_3$ shown in Figure 2.40c. It is reset to the all-0 state in clock cycle 0, and the following data is entered into the pipeline at the indicated times:

Clock cycle:	0	1	2	3	4	5	6	7	8
x_1:	0	1	0	1	1	0	0	0	0
x_2:	0	1	1	1	1	0	0	0	0
x_3:	0	0	0	1	1	0	0	0	0
x_4:	0	1	1	1	0	0	0	0	0
z:									

Determine the value of z for each clock cycle in the above table.

2.37. Suppose that the pipelined serial adder of Figure 2.40c is reset in clock cycle 0. The least significant bits of four serial numbers (integers) N_1, N_2, N_3, N_4 to be added are applied to the adder in clock cycle 1, and four new data bits are applied in each subsequent clock cycle. If each number consists of thirty-two 1-bits and therefore represents $2^{32} - 1$, in what clock cycle will the most significant bit of the sum $N_1 + N_2 + N_3 + N_4$ be loaded into the output z flip-flop?

2.38. Construct a pipelined adder in the style of Figure 2.40c that can add six instead of four separate bit streams.

2.39. Design at the register level a modulo-16 binary counter *CNTR*. The counter has two function control input lines: *LOAD,* which loads the counter with an initial value from a 4-bit external bus *BUS,* and *COUNT,* which increments the counter by one. The available component types (use as many of each as you need) for building *CNTR* are the 4-bit D register of Figure 2.28; the 4-bit adder of Figure 2.26a; the two-input, 4-bit multiplexer of Figure 2.20; and the two-input, *m*-bit NAND word gate of Figure 2.17 with *m* = 1,2, and 4.

2.40. Consider the counter described in the preceding problem. Suppose that there is another control input *DOWN* which, when set to 1, causes the counter to count down (decrement) instead of up. When *DOWN* = 0, *CNTR* behaves like an up-counter, as in the original design. In each case a suitable pulse applied to the *COUNT* line increments or decrements the counter. Using the same set of register-level component types, design this modulo-16 up-down counter.

2.41. Figure 2.60 is an HDL description of an algorithm for multiplication in low-speed digital systems. It is implemented by three up-down counters *CQ, CM,* and *CP* which store the multiplier, multiplicand, and product, respectively, and the product *P* is formed by incrementing the counter *CP* a total of *P* times. Although this multiplication method is slow, it requires a simple logic circuit and can easily accommodate complicated number codes. Suppose that the numbers to be multiplied are four-digit integers in sign-magnitude BCD code. For example, the number −1709 is represented by the bit sequence 1 0001 0111 0000 1001. *CQ, CM,* and *CP* are to be constructed from modulo-10 up-down counters with parallel input-output capability. Carry out the logic design of this multiplier at the register level.

2.42. Devise a counting algorithm similar to that of Figure 2.60 to perform integer division on unsigned four-digit BCD integers. The inputs are a dividend *Y* and a divisor *X*; the outputs are a quotient *Q* and a remainder *R*, which must satisfy the following equation:

$$Y = Q \times X + R, \quad \text{with } 0 \le R < X$$

	multiplierbc(IOBUS[16:0]);
	register *Q*[15:0], *CQ*[15:0], *CM*[15:0], *CP*[31:0], *QS, MS*;
BEGIN:	*Q* := *IOBUS*[15:0], *QS* := *IOBUS*[16];
	CM := *IOBUS*[15:0], *MS* := *IOBUS*[16], *CQ* := *Q, CP* := 0;
TEST1:	**if** *CM* := 0 **or** *CQ* = 0 **then go to** *DONE,*
ADD:	*CQ* := *CQ* - 1, *CP* := *CP* + 1
TEST2:	**if** *CQ* ≠ 0 **then go to** *ADD,*
SUB:	*CM* := *CM* - 1, *CQ* := *Q*;
TEST3:	**if** *CM* ≠ 0 **then go to** *ADD,*
DONE:	*IOBUS*[16] := *QS* **xor** *MS, IOBUS*[15:0] := *CP*[31:16];
	IOBUS[15:0] := *CP*[15:0];

Figure 2.60

A multiplication algorithm using counters.

Describe your algorithm formally by means of our HDL. Carry out the register-level logic design of a machine that performs division on four-digit BCD integers using the counting approach.

2.43. (*a*) Name the various types or levels of memory found in a typical computer. Why is more than one memory type needed? (*b*) Identify all the places in a computer where instructions are stored at various times. (*c*) Explain why secondary-memory units such as hard-disk drives are part of the IO system, whereas main memory is not.

2.44. Let P be a processor that operates at a clock frequency of 100 MHz. Suppose, further, that advances in VLSI technology allow P to be replaced by a new CPU P' whose architecture and organization are identical to those of P, but whose clock rate is 125 MHz. How does replacing P by P' in the execution of a set of benchmark programs Q affect (*a*) the value of its *CPI* and (*b*) the total CPU time required to execute Q?

2.45. A possible measure of the performance of a CPU P that employs instruction-level parallelism is the average number of *instructions per cycle* or *IPC* needed to execute a benchmark program set Q. Suppose that a total of N instructions are executed in the processing of Q by P. Further suppose that P has a clock cycle time of T_{clock}, and T is the total CPU time required for P to execute Q. Obtain an expression for *IPC* in terms of N, T, and T_{clock}.

2.46. Consider the instruction mixes appearing in Figure 2.51. Suppose that the system's clock frequency is 100 MHz, and all instructions except floating-point instructions have an average execution time of 10 ns. (*a*) What is the average execution time of floating-point instructions, if the overall average execution time per instruction for program B is 18.1 ns? (*b*) What is the *CPI* for program B?

2.47. Suppose that the instructions listed in Figure 2.51 have the following average execution characteristics: load, store, and floating-point instructions require four clock cycles each; fixed-point instructions require two clock cycles; all others require one clock cycle. If both programs involve the execution of 2.5 million instructions, which of the two completes execution sooner?

2.48. The MIPS performance measure is often considered useful only when used to compare members of the one processor family from the same manufacturer, as in Figure 2.52. Give some reasons why this is generally true. (Misuse of this measure has led to the suggestion that MIPS really means "meaningless information from pushy salesmen!")

2.49. What happens in a single-server queue like that of Figure 2.53 if $\lambda > \mu$?

2.50. Suppose that CPU behavior in a multiprogramming system can be analyzed using the M/M/1 queueing model. Programs are sent to the CPU for execution at a mean rate of eight programs per minute and are executed on a first-come first-served basis. The average program requires six seconds of CPU execution time. (*a*) What is the mean time between program arrivals at the CPU? (*b*) What is the mean number of programs waiting for CPU execution to be completed? (*c*) What is the mean time a program must wait for its execution to be completed?

2.51. Suppose that people arrive at a public telephone booth at an average rate of 10 per hour. The lengths of the calls made from the booth are found to have a negative exponential distribution with a mean length of 2.5 minutes. (*a*) What is the probability that someone arriving at the telephone booth will find it occupied? (*b*) The telephone company will install a second booth if a customer must wait an average of

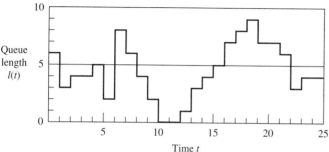

Figure 2.61
Observed queue lengths in a single-server queueing system.

four minutes or more to gain access to the first telephone. By how much must the flow of customers to the first telephone increase in order for the telephone company to install the second phone?

2.52. A certain computer system executes a stream of tasks in a manner that can be accurately modeled by an M/M/1 queueing system. The computer is busy 75 percent of the time, and the average job spends four minutes in the computer. (*a*) How many jobs are in the computer on average? (*b*) What is the maximum rate at which jobs may arrive at the system before it becomes overloaded? State clearly your definition of overloaded.

2.53. Figure 2.61 shows the queue lengths observed in a single-server queueing system over a "typical" operating period of 25 time units. Each value of $l(t)$ represents the observed queue length, including the item being served, at time t. Stating your assumptions, answer the following questions about this system. (*a*) What is the mean queue length l_Q? (*b*) What is the mean utilization of the server?

2.54. This problem involves manual simulation of a computer system that is executing a stream of jobs. The jobs arrive randomly, are queued until selected for execution, and depart immediately after execution is completed. The arrival and execution times for a particular job stream are given by the following table:

Job number	1	2	3	4	5	6	7	8	9	10	11	12
Arrival time:	9:00	9:05	9:08	9:09	9:16	9:21	9:24	9:26	9:32	9:39	9:40	9:43 AM
Execution time (min):	2	5	8	1	6	5	8	2	4	1	3	7
Departure time:												
System response time (min):												

Assuming that jobs are executed on a first-come first-served basis, find the mean response time t_Q of the system by completing the above table. What is the computer's utilization factor ρ from 9:00 AM until the last job departs?

2.55. Consider the computer job stream in the preceding problem. Suppose the FCFS queueing discipline is replaced by *shortest job first* (SJF), in which the next job selected for execution is the one in the queue with the shortest execution time. (Assume that all execution times are known in advance.) Using the data given above, determine the system utilization ρ and mean response time t_Q with SJF replacing FCFS. Provide a brief intuitive explanation for the difference (or lack of difference) in the values of ρ and t_Q obtained with the two methods.

2.6
REFERENCES

1. Actel Corp. *FPGA Data Book and Design Guide.* Sunnyvale, CA, 1994.
2. Alford, R. C. *Programmable Logic Designer's Guide.* Indianapolis: Howard W. Sams, 1989.
3. Allen, A. O. "Queueing Models of Computer Systems." *IEEE Computer,* vol. 13, (April 1980) pp. 13–24.
4. Armstrong, J. R. and F. G. Gray. *Structured Logic Design with VHDL.* Englewood Cliffs, NJ: Prentice-Hall, 1993.
5. Brayton, R. K. et al. *Logic Minimization Algorithms for VLSI Synthesis.* Boston: Kluwer, 1984.
6. Brown, F. M. *Boolean Reasoning.* Boston: Kluwer, 1990.
7. Greene, J., E. Hamdy, and S. Beal. "Antifuse Field Programmable Gate Arrays." *Proceedings of the IEEE,* vol. 81 (July 1993) pp. 1042–56. [Reprinted in Ref. 1, pp. 4-29 to 4-43].
8. Hachtel, G. D. and F. Somenzi. *Logic Synthesis and Verification Algorithms.* Boston: Kluwer, 1996.
9. Hayes, J. P. *Introduction to Digital Logic Design.* Reading, MA: Addison-Wesley, 1993.
10. Kant, K. *Introduction to Computer System Performance Evaluation.* New York: McGraw-Hill, 1992.
11. McGrory, J. J., A. Carlton, and B. J. Askins. "Transaction Processing Performance on PA-RISC Commercial Unix Systems." *Digest of Papers: COMPCON Spring 1992,* San Francisco, February 1992, pp. 199–206.
12. McLellan, E. "The Alpha AXP Architecture and 21064 Processor." *IEEE Micro,* vol. 13 (June 1993) pp. 36–47.
13. Morrison, P. and E. Morrison, eds. *Charles Babbage and His Calculating Engines.* New York: Dover, 1961.
14. Navabi, Z. *VHDL Modeling and Analysis of Digital Systems.* New York: McGraw-Hill, 1993.
15. Price, W. J. "Benchmark Tutorial." *IEEE Micro,* vol. 9 (October 1989) pp. 28–43.
16. Robertazzi, T. G. *Computer Networks and Systems: Queueing Theory and Performance Evaluation.* 2nd ed. New York: Springer-Verlag, 1994.
17. Shannon, C. E.: "A Symbolic Analysis of Relay and Switching Circuits." *Trans. AIEE,* vol. 57 (1938) pp. 713–23. [Reprinted in N. J. A. Sloane and A. D. Wyner, eds. *Claude Elwood Shannon Collected Papers.* New York: IEEE Press, 1993, pp. 471–95.]
18. Siewiorek, D. P., C. G. Bell, and A. Newell. *Computer Structures: Readings and Examples.* New York: McGraw-Hill, 1982.
19. Simon, H. A. "The Architecture of Complexity." *Proc. Amer. Phil. Soc.,* vol. 106 (December 1962) pp. 467–82. [Reprinted with revisions in H. A. Simon. *The Sciences of the Artificial.* 3rd ed. Cambridge, MA: MIT Press, 1996, pp. 183–216.]
20. Smith, D. J. *HDL Chip Design.* Madison, AL: Doone Publications, 1996.
21. Texas Instruments. *TTL Logic Data Book.* Dallas, 1988.
22. Thomas, D. E. and P. R. Moorby. *The Verilog Hardware Description Language.* 3rd ed. Boston: Kluwer, 1996.

CHAPTER 3

Processor Basics

This chapter considers the overall design of instruction-set processors as exemplified by the central processing unit (CPU) of a computer. The fundamentals of CPU organization and operation are examined, along with the selection and formats of instruction and data types. Various representative microprocessors of both the RISC and CISC types are presented and discussed.

3.1
CPU ORGANIZATION

We begin by considering the organization of the central processor (microprocessor) of a computer and the methods used to represent the information it is intended to process.

3.1.1 Fundamentals

The primary function of the CPU and other instruction-set processors is to execute sequences of instructions, that is, programs, which are stored in an external main memory. Program execution is therefore carried out as follows:

1. The CPU transfers instructions and, when necessary, their input data (operands) from main memory to registers in the CPU.
2. The CPU executes the instructions in their stored sequence except when the execution sequence is explicitly altered by a branch instruction.
3. When necessary, the CPU transfers output data (results) from the CPU registers to main memory.

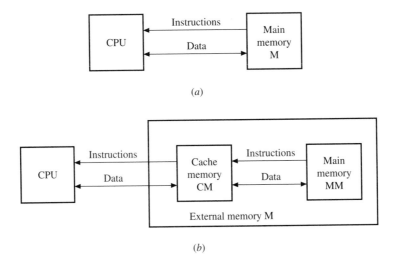

(a)

(b)

Figure 3.1
Processor-memory communication: (a) without a cache and (b) with a cache.

Consequently, streams of instructions and data flow between the external memory and the set of registers that forms the CPU's internal memory. The efficient management of these instruction and data streams is a basic function of the CPU.

External communication. If, as in Figure 3.1a, no cache memory is present, the CPU communicates directly with the main memory M, which is typically a high-capacity multichip random-access memory (RAM). The CPU is significantly faster than M; that is, it can read from or write to the CPU's registers perhaps 5 to 10 times faster than it can read from or write to M. VLSI technology, especially the single-chip microprocessor, has tended to increase the processor/main-memory speed disparity.

To remedy this situation, many computers have a cache memory CM positioned between the CPU and main memory. The cache CM is smaller and faster than main memory and may reside, wholly or in part, on the same chip as the CPU. It typically permits the CPU to perform a memory load or store operation in a single clock cycle, whereas a memory access that bypasses the cache and is handled by main memory takes many clock cycles. The cache is designed to be transparent to the CPU's instructions, which "see" the cache and main memory as forming a single, seamless memory space consisting of 2^m addressable storage locations M(0), M(1), ..., M(2^m-1). In this chapter we will take this viewpoint and use M to refer to the *external memory*, whether or not a cache is present. A specific memory location in M with address *adr* is referred to as M(*adr*) or simply as *adr*. When necessary, we will use MM to distinguish the main memory from the cache memory CM, as in Figure 3.1b. The structure of caches and their interactions with main memory are further studied in Chapter 6.

The CPU communicates with IO devices in much the same way as it communicates with external memory. The IO devices are associated with addressable registers called *IO ports* to which the CPU can store a word (an output operation) or from which it can load a word (an input operation). In some computers there are no IO instructions per se; all IO data transfers are implemented by memory-referencing instructions, an approach called *memory-mapped IO*. This approach requires that memory locations and IO ports share the same set of addresses, so an address bit pattern that is assigned to memory cannot also be assigned to an IO port, and vice versa. Other computers employ IO instructions that are distinct from memory-referencing instructions. These instructions produce control signals to which IO ports, but not memory locations, respond. This second approach is sometimes called *IO-mapped IO*.

User and supervisor modes. The programs executed by a general-purpose computer fall into two broad groups: user programs and supervisor programs. A *user* or *application program* handles a specific application, such as word processing, of interest to the computer's users. A *supervisor program*, on the other hand, manages various routine aspects of the computer system on behalf of its users; it is typically part of the computer's operating system. Examples of supervisory functions are controlling a graphics interface and transferring data between secondary and main memory. In normal operation the CPU continually switches back and forth between user and supervisor programs. For example, while executing a user program, the need often arises for information that is available only on some hard disk unit in the computer's IO system. This condition causes the supervisor to temporarily suspend execution of the user program, execute a routine that initiates the required IO data-transfer operation, and then resume execution of the user program.

It is generally useful to design a CPU so that it can receive requests for supervisor services directly from secondary memory units and other IO devices. Such a request is called an *interrupt*. In the event of an interrupt, the CPU suspends execution of the program that it is currently executing and transfers to an appropriate interrupt-handling program. As interrupts, particularly from IO devices, require a rapid response from the CPU, it checks frequently for the presence of interrupt requests.

CPU operation. The flowchart in Figure 3.2 summarizes the main functions of a CPU. The sequence of operations performed by the CPU in processing an instruction constitutes an *instruction cycle*. While the details of the instruction cycle vary with the type of instruction, all instructions require two major steps: a *fetch step* during which a new instruction is read from the external memory M and an *execute step* during which the operations specified by the instruction are executed. A check for pending interrupt requests is also usually included in the instruction cycle, as shown in Figure 3.2.

The actions of the CPU during an instruction cycle are defined by a sequence of microoperations, each of which typically involves a register-transfer operation. The time required for the shortest well-defined CPU microoperation is the *CPU cycle time* or *clock period* T_{clock} and is a basic unit of time for measuring CPU actions. Recall that f, the CPU's clock frequency (in MHz) is related to T_{clock} (in μs) by $T_{\text{clock}} = 1/f$. As we will see, the number of CPU cycles required to process an instruction varies with the instruction type and the extent to which the processing of individual instructions can be overlapped. For the moment we will assume that each instruction is fetched from M in one CPU clock cycle (this is usually true when M is a cache) and can be executed in another CPU cycle.

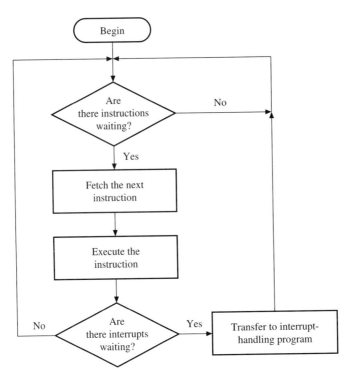

Figure 3.2
Overview of CPU behavior.

Accumulator-based CPU. Despite the improvements in IC technology over the years, CPU design continues to be based on the premise that the CPU should be as fast as the available technology and overall design requirements allow. Since cost generally increases with circuit complexity, the number of components in the CPU must be kept relatively small. The CPU organization proposed by von Neumann and his colleagues for the IAS computer (section 1.2.2) is the basis for most subsequent designs. It comprises a small set of registers and the circuits needed to execute a functionally complete set of instructions. In many early designs, one of the CPU registers, the *accumulator,*[1] played a central role, being used to store an input or output operand (result) in the execution of many instructions.

Figure 3.3 shows at the register level the essential structure of a small accumulator-oriented CPU. This organization is typical of first-generation computers (compare Figure 1.12) and low-cost microcontrollers. Assume for simplicity that instructions and data have some fixed word size n bits and that instructions can be adequately expressed by means of register-transfer operations in our HDL. Instructions are fetched by the program control unit PCU, whose main register is the pro-

---

[1]The term *accumulator* originally meant a device that combined the functions of number storage and addition. Any quantity transferred to an accumulator was automatically added to its previous contents. *Accumulator* is still often used in this restricted sense.

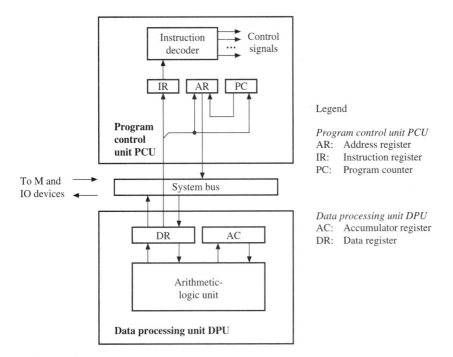

Figure 3.3
A small accumulator-based CPU.

gram counter PC. They are executed in the data processing unit DPU, which contains an n-bit arithmetic-logic unit (ALU) and two data registers AC and DR. Most instructions perform operations of the form

$$X1 := f_i(X1, X2)$$

where X1 and X2 denote a CPU register (AC, DR, or PC) or an external memory location M(*adr*). The operations f_i performed by the ALU are limited to fixed-point (integer) addition and subtraction, shifting, and logical (word-gate) operations.

Some instructions have an operand in an external memory location M(*adr*), and must therefore include the address part *adr*. Memory addresses are stored in two address registers in the PCU: the program counter PC, which stores instruction addresses only, and the general-purpose (data) address register AR. An instruction *I* that refers to a data word in M contains two parts, an opcode *op* and a memory address *adr*, and may be written as *I* = *op.adr*. Each instruction cycle begins with the instruction fetch operation

$$\text{IR.AR} := \text{M}(PC); \tag{3.1}$$

which transfers the instruction word *I* from M to the CPU. The opcode *op* is loaded into the PCU's instruction register IR, and the address *adr* is loaded into address register AR. Hence (3.1) is equivalent to

$$\text{IR} := op, \text{AR} := adr;$$

Instructions that do not reference M do not use AR; their opcode part specifies the CPU registers to use, as well as the operation f_i to be carried out. Once it has placed the opcode of I in IR, the CPU proceeds to decode and execute it. Note that, at this point, the CPU can increment PC in order to obtain the address of the next instruction.

The two essential memory-addressing instructions are called load and store. The *load* instruction for our sample CPU is

$$AC := M(adr);$$

which transfers a word from the memory location with address *adr* to the accumulator. It is often written in assembly-language programs as LD *adr*. The corresponding *store* instruction is

$$M(adr) := AC;$$

which transfers a word from AC to M and may be written as ST *adr*. Note how the accumulator AC serves as an implicit source or destination register for data words.

Programming considerations. Data-processing operations normally require up to three operands. For example, the addition

$$Z := X + Y \tag{3.2}$$

has three distinct operands X, Y, and Z. The accumulator-based CPU of Figure 3.3 supports only *single-address* instructions, that is, instructions with one explicit memory address. However, AC and DR can serve as *implicit* operand locations so that multioperand operations can be implemented by executing several instructions in sequence. For example, a program to implement (3.2), assuming that X, Y, and Z all refer to data words in M, can take the following form:

HDL format	Assembly-language format	Narrative format (comment)
AC := M(X);	LD X	Load X from M into accumulator AC.
DR := AC;	MOV DR, AC	Move contents of AC to DR.
AC := M(Y);	LD Y	Load Y into accumulator AC.
AC := AC + DR;	ADD	Add DR to AC.
M(Z) := AC;	ST Z	Store contents of AC in M.

The preceding program fragment uses only the load and store instructions to access memory, a feature called *load/store architecture*. It is common (but as we will see, not always desirable) to allow other instructions to specify operands in memory. A CPU like that of Figure 3.3 can be designed to implement memory-referencing instructions of the form

$$AC := f_i(AC, M(adr))$$

whose execution requires two steps: one to move M(*adr*) to or from DR and one to perform the designated operation f_i. With an add instruction of this form, we can reduce the foregoing program from five to three instructions.

HDL Format	Assembly-language format	Narrative format (comment)
AC := M(*X*);	LD *X*	Load *X* from M into accumulator AC.
AC := AC + M(*Y*);	ADD *Y*	Load *Y* into DR and add to AC.
M(*Z*) := AC;	ST *Z*	Store contents of AC in M.

The memory-referencing ADD *Y* instruction can be expected to take longer to execute than the original ADD instruction that references only CPU registers. Memory references also complicate the instruction-decoding logic in the PCU. However, overall execution time should be reduced because we have eliminated an LD and a MOV instruction completely. As we will see later, the cost-performance impact of replacing a simple instruction with a more complex one has subtle implications that lie at the heart of the RISC–CISC debate.

Instruction set. Figure 3.4 gives a possible instruction set for our simple accumulator-based CPU, assuming a load/store architecture. These 10 instructions have the flavor of the instruction sets of some recent RISC machines, which demonstrate that small instruction sets can be both complete and efficient. We are, however, ignoring some important practical implementation issues in the interest of simplicity. We have not, for instance, specified the precise instruction or data formats to be used, and we do not consider such problems as numerical overflow—this condition occurs when an arithmetic instruction produces a result that is too big to fit in its destination register.

Type	Instruction	HDL format	Assembly-language format	Narrative format (comment)
Data transfer	Load	AC := M(*X*)	LD X	Load *X* from M into AC.
	Store	M(*X*) := AC	ST X	Store contents of AC in M as *X*.
	Move register	DR := AC	MOV DR, AC	Copy contents of AC to DR.
	Move register	AC := DR	MOV AC, DR	Copy contents of DR to AC.
Data processing	Add	AC := AC + DR	ADD	Add DR to AC.
	Subtract	AC := AC − DR	SUB	Subtract DR from AC.
	And	AC := AC *and* DR	AND	And bitwise DR to AC.
	Not	AC := *not* AC	NOT	Complement contents of AC
Program control	Branch	PC := M(*adr*)	BRA adr	Jump to instruction with address *adr*.
	Branch zero	**if** AC = 0 **then** PC := M(*adr*)	BZ adr	Jump to instruction *adr* if AC = 0.

Figure 3.4
Instruction set for the CPU of Figure 3.3.

The load and store instructions obviously suffice for transferring data between the CPU and main memory. We know from Boolean algebra that the AND and NOT operations are functionally complete, implying that the instruction set enables any logical operation to be programmed. We also know that addition and subtraction suffice for implementing most arithmetic operations. Consider, for example, the arithmetic operation negation, for which many CPUs have a single instruction of the type AC := −AC. We can easily implement negation by a three-instruction sequence as follows:

HDL format	Assembly-language format	Narrative format (comment)
DR := AC;	MOV DR, AC	Copy contents X of AC to DR.
AC := AC − DR;	SUB	Compute AC = $X − X$ = 0.
AC := AC − DR;	SUB	Compute AC = $0 − X = −X$.

Figure 3.4 also gives a small set of program control instructions: an unconditional branch instruction BRA and a conditional branch-on-zero instruction BZ that tests the contents of AC. Observe that these instructions load a new address into the program counter PC, thus altering the instruction execution sequence. The BZ instruction allows more powerful program control operations such as procedure call and return to be implemented; it also facilitates complex operations such as multiplication, as we demonstrate in Example 3.1.

EXAMPLE 3.1 A MULTIPLICATION PROGRAM. Suppose we want to use the tiny instruction set of Figure 3.4 to program the multiplication operation

$$AC := AC \times N$$

where the multiplicand is the initial contents of the accumulator AC and the multiplier N is a variable stored in memory. We will assume that the multiplier and multiplicand are both unsigned numbers and that they are sufficiently small that the product will fit in a single word. We can construct the desired program along the following lines. We will execute the basic ADD instruction N times to implement $AC \times N$ in the form AC + AC + ... + AC. We will treat the memory location storing N as a count register and, after each addition step, decrement it by one until it reaches zero. We will test for $N = 0$ by means of the BZ instruction, and so we will have to transfer N to AC in order to perform this test. We will also have to use some memory locations as temporary registers for storing intermediate results and some other quantities, such as the initial value Y of AC. In particular, we will use memory locations *one*, *mult*, *ac*, and *prod* to store the constant 1, N, Y, and the partial product P, respectively. Here *one*, *mult*, *ac*, and *prod* are symbolic names for certain memory addresses that we have arbitrarily assigned. They are translated into numerical memory addresses by an assembler program prior to execution.

An assembly-language program implementing this plan appears in Figure 3.5. Its main body (lines 5 to 17) is traversed N times in the course of a multiplication. At the end the result P is in memory location *prod*. The first two instructions (lines 5 and 6) of the program check the value of N by reading it into AC and testing it with the BZ instruction. If the initial value of N is zero, the program exits immediately with the correct result $P = 0$. If N is nonzero, the instructions in lines 7 to 11 load it from *mult* into AC, subtract one from it, and then return the new, decremented value of N to *mult*. The

Line	Location	Instruction or data	Comment
0	*one*	00 ... 001	The constant one.
1	*mult*	N	The multiplier.
2	*ac*	00 ... 000	Location for initial value Y of AC.
3	*prod*	00 ... 000	Location for (partial) product P.
4		ST *ac*	Save initial value Y of AC.
5	*loop*	LD *mult*	Load N into AC to test for termination.
6		BZ *exit*	Exit if N = 0; otherwise continue.
7		LD *one*	Load 1 into AC.
8		MOV DR, AC	Move 1 from AC to DR.
9		LD *mult*	Load N into AC to decrement it.
10		SUB	Subtract 1 from N.
11		ST *mult*	Store decremented N.
12		LD *ac*	Load initial value Y of AC.
13		MOV DR, AC	Move Y from AC to DR.
14		LD *prod*	Load current partial product P.
15		ADD	Add Y to P.
16		ST *prod*	Store the new partial product P.
17		BRA *loop*	Branch to *loop*.
18	*exit*	. . .	

Figure 3.5

A program for the multiplication operation $AC := AC \times N$.

main step of adding Y to the accumulating partial product, that is, $P := P + Y$, is implemented in straightforward fashion by lines 12 to 16 of the program. Finally, a return is made to *loop* via the unconditional branch BRA (line 17).

This program uses most of the available instruction types and illustrates several weaknesses of an accumulator-based CPU. Because there are only a few data registers in the CPU, a considerable amount of time is spent shuttling the same information back and forth between the CPU and memory. Indeed, most of the instructions in this program are of the data-transfer type (ST, LD, and MOV), which do bookkeeping for the few instructions that actually compute the product P. It would both shorten the program and speed up its execution if we could store the quantities 1, N, Y, and P in their own CPU registers, as they are repeatedly required by the CPU.

Program execution. We now examine the execution process for the multiplication program of Figure 3.5. Of course, the program must be translated into executable object code prior to execution, but we can treat the assembly-language program as a symbolic representation of the object code. Recall that we are assuming that every instruction is one word long and can be fetched from M in a single CPU clock cycle. We further assume that every instruction is also executed in a single clock cycle. Hence each instruction requires two CPU clock cycles—one to fetch the instruction from M and one to execute it. At the end of

Clock cycle	Instruction cycle	PC	AR	PCU actions	DPU actions
1	ST *ac*	1004		IR.AR := M(PC), PC := PC + 1	
2			1002		M(AR) := AC
3	LD *mult*	1005		IR.AR := M(PC), PC := PC + 1	
4			1001		AC := M(AR)
5	BZ *exit*	1006		IR.AR := M(PC), PC := PC + 1	
6			1001	Test A; no further action if A ≠ 0	None
7	LD *one*	1007		IR.AR := M(PC), PC := PC + 1	
8			1000		AC := M(AR)
9	MOV DR, AC	1008		IR.AR := M(PC), PC := PC + 1	
10			*dddd*		DR := AC
11	LD *mult*	1009		IR.AR := M(PC), PC := PC + 1	
12			1001		AC := M(AR)
13	SUB	1010		IR.AR := M(PC), PC := PC + 1	
14			*dddd*		AC := AC − DR
15	ST *mult*	1011		IR.AR := M(PC), PC := PC + 1	
16			1001		M(AR) := AC
17	LD *ac*	1012		IR.AR := M(PC), PC := PC + 1	
18			1002		AC := M(AR)
19	MOV DR, AC	1013		IR.AR := M(PC), PC := PC + 1	
20			*dddd*		DR := AC
21	LD *prod*	1014		IR.AR := M(PC), PC := PC + 1	
22			1003		AC := M(AR)
23	ADD	1015		IR.AR := M(PC), PC := PC + 1	
24			*dddd*		AC := AC + DR
25	ST *prod*	1016		IR.AR := M(PC), PC := PC + 1	
26			1003		M(AR) := AC
27	BRA *loop*	1017		IR.AR := M(PC), PC := PC + 1	
28			1005	PC := AR	None
29	LD *mult*	1005		IR.AR := M(PC), PC := PC + 1	
30			1001		AC := M(AR)
31	BZ *exit*	1006		IR.AR := M(PC), PC := PC + 1	
32			1018	Test A: PC := AR if A = 0	None
33		1018		. . .	

Figure 3.6
Cycle-by-cycle execution trace of the multiplication program of Figure 3.5.

the fetch step, the PCU decodes the instruction's opcode to determine what operation to perform during the execution stage. It can also increment PC in preparation for the next instruction fetch. Recall that an edge-triggered register can be both read from and written into in the same clock cycle so that the new data is ready for use at the beginning of the next clock cycle. Hence every fetch cycle includes the following pair of register-transfer operations:

$$\text{IR.AR} := M(PC), \, PC := PC + 1 \qquad (3.3)$$

The subsequent execution cycle depends on the instruction opcode placed in IR.

Figure 3.6 depicts all the main actions taken by the CPU, including the memory addresses it generates, during execution of the program of Figure 3.5. Data of this type is referred to as an *execution trace* and is often obtained by simulation of the target CPU. (In effect, Figure 3.6 is a hand simulation of the multiplication program.) Execution traces are useful for analyzing program behavior and execution speed. In this example the program's data and instructions have been assigned to a consecutive sequence of memory locations 1000, 1001, 1002, . . . , where 1001 is the location named *one* in Figure 3.5. The first executable instruction is ST *ac*, which is in location 1004, so execution begins when PC is set to 1004. Observe how the contents of the program counter PC are incremented steadily until a branch instruction is encountered, at which point the branch address contained in the branch instruction may replace the incremented contents of PC.

3.1.2 Additional Features

Next we examine some more advanced features of CPUs and look at representative commercial microprocessors of the RISC and CISC types.

Architecture extensions. There are many ways in which the basic design of Figure 3.3 can be improved. Most recent CPUs contain the following extensions, which significantly improve their performance and ease of programming.

* *Multipurpose register set for storing data and addresses*: These replace the accumulator AC and the auxiliary registers DR and AR of our basic CPU. The resulting CPU is sometimes said to have the *general register organization* exemplified by the third-generation IBM System/360-370 (Figure 1.17), which has 32 such registers. The set of general registers is now usually referred to as a *register file*.
* *Additional data, instruction, and address types*: Most CPUs have instructions to handle data and addresses with several different word sizes and formats. Although some microprocessors have only add and subtract instructions in the arithmetic category, relatively little extra circuitry is required for (fixed-point) multiply and divide instructions, which simplify many programming tasks. Call and return instructions also simplify program design.
* *Register to indicate computation status*: A *status register* (also called a *condition code* or *flag* register) indicates infrequent or *exceptional conditions* resulting from the instruction execution. Examples are the appearance of an all-zero result or an invalid instruction like divide by zero. A status register can also indicate the user and supervisor states. Conditional branch instructions can test the status register, which simplifies the programming of conditional actions.

• *Program control stack*: Various special registers and instructions facilitate the transfer of control among programs due to procedure calling or external interrupts. Many CPUs use a flexible scheme for program-control transfer, which employs part of the external memory M as a push-down stack (see also Example 1.5). The stack memory is intended for saving key information about an interrupted program via push operations so that the saved information can be retrieved later via pop operations. A CPU address register called a *stack pointer* automatically keeps track of the stack's entry point.

Figure 3.7 shows the organization of a processor with the foregoing features. It has a register file in the DPU for data and/or address storage. The ALU obtains most of its operands from the register file and also stores most of its results there. A status register monitors the output of the ALU and other key points. The principal special-purpose address registers are the program counter and the stack pointer. Special circuits are included for address computation, although the main ALU can also be used for this purpose. The control circuits in the PCU derive their inputs from the instruction register, which stores the opcode of the current instruction, and

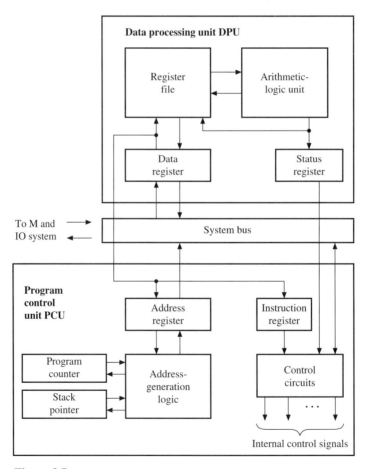

Figure 3.7
A typical CPU with the general register organization.

the status register. Communication with the outside world is via a system bus that transmits address, data, and control information among the CPU, M, and the IO system. Various nonprogrammable "buffer" registers serve as temporary storage points between the system bus and the CPU.

Pipelining. As discussed in Chapter 1, modern CPUs employ a variety of speedup techniques, including cache memories, and several forms of instruction-level parallelism. Such parallelism may be present in the internal organization of the DPU or in the overlapping of the operations carried out by the DPU and PCU. These features add to the CPU's complexity and will be explored in depth later in this book.

The considerable potential for parallel processing at the instruction level is evident even in the simple CPU of Figure 3.3. We see from the execution trace of Figure 3.6 that the main PCU and DPU activities take place in different clock cycles. If these activities do not share a resource such as the system bus, they can be carried out at the same time. In other words, while the current instruction is being executed in the DPU, the next instruction can be fetched by the PCU. For example, the three-instruction negation routine we gave earlier to change AC to –AC would be executed as follows in the style of Figure 3.6:

Clock cycle	Instruction cycle	PC	PCU actions	DPU actions
1	MOV DR, AC	2000	IR.AR := M(PC), PC := PC + 1	
2		2001		DR := AC
3	SUB	2001	IR.AR := M(PC), PC := PC + 1	
4		2002		AC := AC – DR
5	SUB	2002	IR.AR := M(PC), PC := PC + 1	
6		2003		AC := AC – DR

By merging the execution part of each instruction cycle with the fetch part of the following instruction cycle, we can reduce the overall execution time from six clock cycles to four, as shown below. (We use subscripts to distinguish the first and second SUB instructions.)

Clock cycle	Instruction cycle	PC	PCU actions	DPU actions
1	MOV	2000	IR.AR := M(PC), PC := PC + 1	
2	MOV/SUB$_1$	2001	IR.AR := M(PC), PC := PC + 1	DR := AC
3	SUB$_1$/SUB$_2$	2002	IR.AR := M(PC), PC := PC + 1	AC := AC – DR
4	SUB$_2$	2003		AC := AC – DR

This overlapping of instruction fetching and execution is an example of *instruction pipelining*, which is an important speedup feature of RISC processors. Figure 3.8 illustrates graphically the type of *two-stage* pipelining discussed above. Each instruction can be thought of as passing through two consecutive stages of

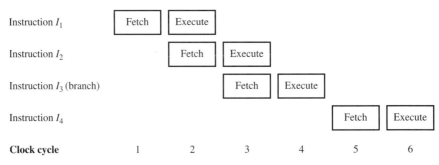

Instruction I_1	Fetch	Execute				
Instruction I_2		Fetch	Execute			
Instruction I_3 (branch)			Fetch	Execute		
Instruction I_4					Fetch	Execute
Clock cycle	1	2	3	4	5	6

Figure 3.8
Overlapping instructions in a two-stage instruction pipeline.

processing: a fetch stage implemented mainly by the PCU and an execution stage implemented mainly by the DPU. Hence two instructions can be processed simultaneously in every CPU clock cycle, with one completing its fetch phase and the other completing its execute phase. A two-stage pipeline can therefore double the CPU's performance from one instruction every two clock cycles to one instruction every clock cycle.

A problem arises when a branch instruction is encountered, such as the BRA *loop* instruction stored in address (line) 17 of the multiplication program (Figure 3.5). Immediately before this instruction is fetched in some clock cycle i the program counter PC stores the address 17. PC is then incremented to 18 in preparation for clock cycle $i + 1$. Clearly in clock cycle $i + 1$, the CPU should *not* fetch the instruction stored at address 18—that instruction is not even in the multiplication program. In clock cycle $i + 1$, BRA is executed, which causes *loop* = 5 to be loaded into PC, implying that the next instruction should be taken from location 5. The fetching of this instruction can't begin until cycle $i + 2$, however, as illustrated in Figure 3.8 with $i = 4$. It follows that we cannot overlap the branch instruction and the instruction that follows it (I_3 and I_4 in the case of Figure 3.8).

Thus we see that branch instructions reduce the efficiency of instruction pipelining, although we will see later that steps can be taken to reduce this problem. We will also see that instruction processing is usually broken into more than two stages to increase the level of the parallelism attainable.

EXAMPLE 3.2 THE ARM6 MICROPROCESSOR [VAN SOMEREN AND ATACK 1994]. We now examine in some detail the architecture of a microprocessor family that embodies the RISC design philosophy in a relatively direct and elegant form. The ARM has its origins in the Acorn RISC Machine, a microprocessor developed in the United Kingdom in the 1980s to serve as the CPU of a personal computer. Subsequently, the family name was changed—without changing its acronym, however—to Advanced RISC Machine. The ARM family is primarily aimed at low-cost, low-power applications such as portable computers and games. For example, the Newton, a handheld "personal digital assistant" introduced by Apple Corp. in 1993 employs the ARM6 microprocessor, whose main features are described below.

The ARM6 is a 32-bit processor in that both its data words and its address words are 32 bits (4 bytes) long. It has a load/store architecture, so only its load and store instructions can address external memory M. As in most computers since the IBM System/360, main memory is organized as an array of individually addressable bytes. Thus the maximum memory size of an ARM6 computer is 2^{32} bytes, also referred to as 4 gigabytes (4G bytes). The ARM6 employs an instruction pipeline to meet the goal of one instruction executed per CPU clock cycle. Note that it shares all these features with a more powerful (and more expensive) RISC microprocessor, the PowerPC (Example 1.7). The ARM6's instruction set is much smaller than the PowerPC's, however—it has no floating-point instructions, for example.

The internal organization of the ARM's CPU is shown in Figure 3.9. It has a 32-bit ALU and a file of 32-bit general-purpose registers. To permit direct interaction between data and control registers, the ARM has the unusual feature of placing its PC and status registers in the register file; conceptually, we will continue to view these registers as part of the PCU. There are several modes of operation, including the normal user and supervisor modes, and four special modes associated with interrupt handling. In user mode the register file appears to contain sixteen 32-bit registers designated R0:R15, where R15 is also the program counter PC, as well as a current program status register designated CPSR. (Additional registers, which we will not discuss here, are used when the CPU is in other operating modes; they are "invisible" in user mode.) The ALU is designed to perform basic arithmetic operations on 32-bit integers. It employs combinational logic for addition and subtraction and a sequential shift-and-add method similar to that described in Example 2.7 for multiplication. A combinational shift circuit is attached to the ALU to support multiplication and other operations. A separate address-incrementer circuit implements address-manipulation operations such as PC := PC + 1 independently of the ALU. Access to external memory M (a cache or main memory) is straightforward. The address of the desired location in M is placed in the PCU's address register. In the case of a store instruction, the data to be stored is also placed in the DPU's write data register. A load instruction causes a data word to be fetched from memory and placed in the read data register. Several internal buses transfer data efficiently among the DPU's registers and data processing circuits.

All ARM6 instructions are 32 bits long, and they have a variety of formats and addressing modes. There are about 25 main instruction types, which are listed in Figure 3.10. (We have omitted block move and coprocessor instructions.) This number is deceptively small, however, as instructions have options that substantially increase the number of operations they can perform. Most instructions can be applied either to 32-bit operands (words) or to 8-bit operands (bytes). Operands and addresses are usually stored in registers that can be referred to by short, 4-bit names, allowing a single ARM6 instruction to specify as many as four operands. The available address space is shared between memory and IO devices (memory-mapped IO). Consequently, the load/store instructions used for CPU-memory transfers are also used for IO operations.

Any instruction can be conditionally executed, meaning that execution may or may not occur depending on the value of designated status bits (flags) in the CPSR. The status flags are set by a previous instruction and include a negative flag N (the previous result R computed by the ALU was a negative number), a zero flag Z (R was zero), a carry flag C (R generated an output carry), and an overflow flag V (R generated a sign overflow). Hence every ARM6 instruction is effectively combined with a conditional branch instruction. The basic unconditional move instruction MOV R0, R1 can have any of 15 conditions attached to it to determine if it is to be executed (see problem 3.8). Some examples:

MOVCC R0, R1   ; If flag C = 0, then R0 := R1

MOVCS R0, R1   ; If flag C = 1, then R0 := R1

MOVHI R0, R1   ; If flag C = 1 and flag Z = 0, then R0 := R1

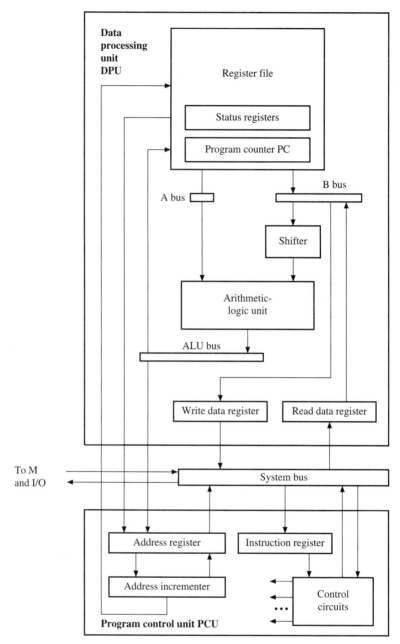

Figure 3.9
Overall organization of the ARM6.

An ARM6 instruction can also include a shift or rotation operation that is applied to one of its operands. For instance:

$$\text{MOV} \quad \text{R0, R1, LSL \#2} \qquad ; \text{R0} := \text{R1} \times 4 \qquad (3.4)$$

means logically left shift (LSL) the contents of R1 by 2 bits and move the result to RO. This shift is tantamount to multiplying R1 by four before the move.

The opcode suffix S specifies whether or not an instruction affects the status flags. If S is present, appropriate flags are changed; otherwise, the flags are not affected. For example, the ARM6's move instructions affect the N, Z, and C flags, so appending S

Type	Instruction	HDL format	Assembly-language format	Narrative format (comment)
Data transfer	Move register	R3 := R9	MOV R3,R9	Copy contents of register R9 to register R3.
	Move register	R0 := 12	MOV R0,#12	Copy operand (decimal number 12) to register R0.
	Move inverted	R7 := $\overline{\text{R0}}$	MVN R7,R0	Copy bitwise inverted contents of R0 to R7
	Load	R5 := M(adr)	LDR R5, adr	Load R5 with contents of memory location adr.
	Store	M(adr) := R8	STR R8,adr	Store contents of R8 in memory location adr.
Data processing	Add	R3 := R5 + 25	ADD R3,R5,#25	Add 25 to R5; place sum in R3.
	Add with carry	R3 := R5 + R6 + C	ADC R3,R5,R6	Add R6 and carry bit C to R5; place sum in R3.
	Subtract	R3 := R5 − 9	SUB R3,R5,#9	Subtract 9 from R5; place difference in R3.
	Subtract with carry	R3 := R5 − 9 − C	SBC R3,R5,#9	Subtract 9 and borrow bit from R5; place difference in R3.
	Reverse subtract	R3 := 9 − R5	RSB R3,R5,#9	Subtract R5 from 9; place difference in R3.
	Reverse subtract with carry	R3 := 9 − R5 − C	RSC R3,R5,#9	Subtract R5 and borrow bit from 9; place difference in R3.
	Multiply	R1 := R3 × R2	MUL R1,R2,R3	Multiply R3 by R2; place result in R1.
	Multiply and add	R1 := (R3 × R2) + R4	MLA R1,R2,R3,R4	Multiply R3 by R2; add R4; place result in R1.
	And	R4 := R11 *and* 25_{16}	AND R4,R11,0x25	Bitwise AND R11 and 25_{16}; place result in R4.
	Or	R4 := R11 *or* 25_{16}	ORR R4,R11,0x25	Bitwise OR R11 and 25_{16}; place result in R4.
	Exclusive-or	R4 := R11 *xor* 25_{16}	EOR R4,R11,0x25	Bitwise XOR R11 and 25_{16}; place result in R4.
	Bit clear	R4 := R11 ∧ $\overline{25}_{16}$	BIC R4,R11,#25	Bitwise invert 25; AND it to R11; place result in R4.
Program control	Branch	PC := PC + *adr*	B *adr*	Jump to designated instruction.
	Branch and link	R14 := PC, PC := PC + *adr*	BL *adr*	Save old PC in "link" register R14; then jump to designated instruction.
	Software interrupt		SWI	Enter supervisor mode.
	Compare	Flags := R1 − 14	CMP r1,#14	Subtract 14 from R1 and set flags.
	Compare inverted	Flags := R1 + 14	CMN r1,#14	Add 14 to R1 and set flags.
	Logical compare	Flags := R1 *xor* 14	TEQ r1,#14	XOR 14 to R1 and set flags.
	Compare inverted	Flags := R1 *or* 14	TST r1,#14	AND 14 to R1 and set flags.

Figure 3.10
Core instruction set of the ARM6.

to, say, MOVCS, yields MOVCSS, which checks the moved data item D. It sets N = 1 (0) if D_{31} = 1 (0), it sets Z = 1 (0) if D is zero (nonzero), and it sets C to the shifter's output value.

Like other RISCs, the ARM6 has an instruction pipeline that permits the various stages of instruction processing to be overlapped. The pipeline has three stages: fetch, decode, and execute; in effect, the ARM6 breaks the first stage of the two-stage pipeline of Figure 3.8 in two. This structure permits the CPU to check every instruction's condition code in stage 2 to determine whether the instruction should be executed in stage 3. Some instructions such as multiply require more than one cycle for execution, but most require only one. Note that inclusion of an operand shift in an instruction as in (3.4) does not require an additional cycle, thanks to the fast (combinational) shifter.

A CISC machine. We turn next to a widely used CPU family, the Motorola 680X0 family, which was introduced in 1979 with the 68000 microprocessor. This example of an older CISC architecture is more streamlined and "RISC-like" than other CISCs. Later members of the family such as the 68060 [Circello et al. 1995] have speedup features such as instruction pipelining, floating-point execution units, and superscalar instruction issue. We examine an intermediate member of the series, the 68020, a 32-bit machine whose design broadly resembles that of a third-generation mainframe computer [Motorola 1989].

The 68020 is a one-chip microprocessor introduced in 1985 to serve as the CPU of a general-purpose computer such as a personal computer or workstation. Figure 3.11 outlines the organization of the 68020. It is designed to handle 32-bit words (termed *long* words in 680X0 literature) efficiently, but instructions are also provided to handle operands of 1, 8, 16, and 64 bits. As in the ARM6, memory addresses are 32 bits long, permitting a total of 2^{32} different memory locations, each storing 1 byte. Memory-mapped IO is also used in the 680X0 series. The data-processing unit has a register file containing sixteen 32-bit registers, half of which are data registers designated D0:D7 and half are address registers designated A0:A7. The ALU can execute a large set of fixed-point (but not floating-point) instructions. Instruction interpretation and other control functions of the CPU are implemented by a microprogrammed control unit.

The 68020 has about 70 distinct instruction types (or around 200 if all opcode variants are distinguished), which are summarized in Figure 3.12. A given instruction such as MOVE can be defined with several different types of operands, and the operands can be addressed in various ways. For example, the following move-register instruction written in 680X0 assembly-language format

$$\text{MOVE.L} \quad \text{D1, A6} \qquad (3.5)$$

causes the entire contents (a long word as indicated by the opcode suffix .L) of data register D1 to be copied to address register A6. In other words, (3.5) implements the register transfer A6 := D1. If .L is replaced by .B, then the resulting instruction

$$\text{MOVE.B} \quad \text{D1, A6}$$

causes only the byte stored in the low-order position (bits 0:7) of D1 to be copied to the corresponding part of A6.

Besides the *direct addressing* mode illustrated by the preceding example, the 68020 has several other addressing modes that give the programmer considerable

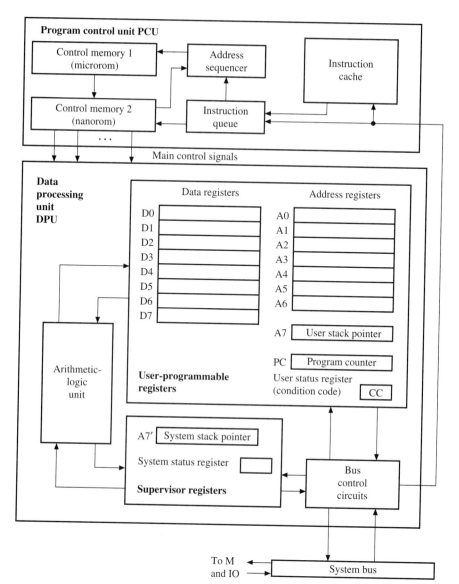

Figure 3.11
Organization of the 68020.

flexibility in accessing data. Most instructions can address memory as well as CPU registers. For example, if (3.5) is replaced by

$$\text{MOVE.L} \quad \text{D1, (A6)} \tag{3.6}$$

the resulting operation is M(A6) := D1, that is, a store operation with A6 serving as the memory-address register. This is an instance of *indirect addressing*. Note that while (3.5) takes 4 clock cycles to execute, (3.6) takes 12 cycles because of the time required to access external memory. The 68020's data-processing instructions can also access M directly, so the 68020 does *not* have the load/store architecture

Type	Opcode	Description
Data transfer	EXG	Exchange (swap) contents of two registers.
	MOVE	Move (copy) data unchanged from source to destination in CPU or M.
	MOVEA	Copy data to address register.
	MOVEC	Copy data to or from control register (privileged instruction).
	MOVEM	Copy multiple data items to or from specified list of registers.
	MOVEP	Copy data between register and alternate bytes of memory.
	MOVEQ	Copy "quick" (8-bit) immediate data to register.
	MOVES	Copy data using address space specified by a control register (privileged instruction).
	SWAP	Swap left and right halves of register.
Data processing	ABCD	Add decimal (BCD) numbers with carry (extend) flag.
	ADD	Add binary (twos-complement) numbers.
	ADDA	Add to address register (unsigned binary addition).
	ADDI	Add immediate binary operand.
	ADDQ	Add "quick" (3-bit) immediate binary operand.
	ADDX	Add binary with carry (extension) flag.
	ANDx	Bitwise logical AND (x = I denotes immediate operand).
	ASx	Arithmetic left (x = L) or right (x = R) shift with extension.
	CLR	Clear operand by resetting all bits to 0.
	DIVx	Divide signed (x = S) or unsigned (x = U) binary numbers.
	EORx	Bitwise logical EXCLUSIVE OR (x = I denotes immediate operand).
	EXT	Extend the sign bit of subword to fill register.
	LSx	Logical (simple) left (x = L) or right (x = R) shift.
	MULx	Multiply signed (x = S) or unsigned (x = U) binary numbers.
	NBCD	Negate decimal number (subtract with carry from zero).
	NEG	Negate binary number (subtract from zero).
	NEGX	Negate binary number (subtract with carry from zero).
	NOT	Bitwise logical complement.
	ORx	Bitwise logical OR (x = I denotes immediate operand).
	PACK*	Convert number from unpacked to packed BCD format.
	ROx	Rotate (circular shift) left (x = L) or right (x = R).
	ROXx	Rotate left (x = L) or right (x = R) including the X (extend) flag.
	SBCD	Subtract decimal (BCD) numbers.
	SUB	Subtract binary (twos-complement) numbers.
	SUBA	Subtract from address register (unsigned binary subtraction).
	SUBI	Subtract immediate binary operand.
	SUBQ	Subtract "quick" (3-bit) immediate binary operand.
	SUBX	Subtract binary with borrow (extend) flag.
	UNPK*	Convert number from packed to unpacked BCD format.

Figure 3.12
Instruction set of the 68020.

characteristic of a RISC. For example:

$$\text{ADD} \quad (A0), D0$$

specifies the memory-to-register add operation $D0 := M(A0) + D0$.

EXAMPLE 3.3 680X0 PROGRAM FOR VECTOR ADDITION. Figure 3.13 gives an example of 680X0 assembly-language code that illustrates several of its basic instruction types and addressing methods. This program adds two 1000-element vectors A and B to produce a third vector C. Each vector is assumed to be a decimal

Type	Opcode	Description
Program control	B*cc*	Branch relative to PC if specified condition code *cc* is set.
	B*xxx*	Test, modify, and/or transfer (depending on *xxx*) a specified bit; set Z flag to indicate old bit value.
	BF*xxx**	Test, modify, and/or transfer (depending on *xxx*) a specified bit field; set flags to indicate old bit-field value.
	BKPT*	Execute a breakpoint trap (used for debugging).
	BRA	Branch unconditionally relative to PC.
	BSR	Call (branch to) subroutine at address relative to PC; save old PC in stack.
	CALLM*	Call subroutine (program module) saving specified control information in stack.
	CAS*x**	Compare specified operands and update register.
	CHK*x*	Check register against specified values (address bounds); trap if bounds are exceeded.
	CMP*x*	Compare two operand values; set flags based on result; *x* indicates operand type.
	DB*cc*	Loop instruction: Test condition *cc* and perform no operation if condition is met; otherwise, decrement specified register and branch to specified address.
	ILLEGAL*	Perform trap operation corresponding to an illegal opcode.
	JMP	Branch unconditionally to specified (nonrelative) address.
	JSR	Call (jump to) subroutine at specified (nonrelative) address; save old PC in stack.
	LEA	Compute effective address and load into address register.
	LINK	Allocate local data and parameter region in the stack.
	NOP	No operation (except increment PC); instruction execution continues.
	PEA	Compute effective address and push into stack.
	RTD	Return from subroutine and deallocate stack parameter region.
	RTE	Return from exception (privileged instruction).
	RTM*	Return and restore control (module state) information.
	RTR	Return and restore condition codes.
	RTS	Return from subroutine.
	S*cc*	Set operand to 1s (0s) if condition code *cc* is true (false).
	STOP	Load status register and halt (privileged instruction).
	TRAP	Begin exception processing at specified address.
	TRAP*cc*	If condition *cc* is true, then begin exception processing.
	TST	Test an operand by comparing it to zero and setting flags.
	UNLK	Deallocate local data and parameter area in the stack.
External synchronization	cp*xxx**	If condition holds, then branch with external coprocessor as specified by *xxx*.
	RESET	Reset or restart external device (privileged instruction).
	TAS	Test operand and set one of its bits to 1 using an indivisible memory-access cycle.

*Instruction not in the original 68000 instruction set.

Figure 3.12
(continued).

number composed of 1000 two-digit bytes. Each vector is stored in a fixed block of main memory whose location is known. For example, vector A is stored in memory locations 1001,1002,1003, ...,1999,2000.

The desired addition is accomplished by executing the ABCD (add using the BCD number format) instruction 1000 times. The address registers A0, A1, and A2 are used as pointers to the current 1-byte operands, and they are initialized to the required starting values using the first three MOVE instructions. These instructions use immediate addressing denoted by the prefix # to specify instruction fields that contain actual address values, while a register name such as A0 indicates that the desired operand is

Location	Instruction		Comment
	MOVE.L	#2001, A0	Load address 2001 into register A0 (pointer to vector A).
	MOVE.L	#3001, A1	Load address 3001 into register A1 (pointer to vector B).
	MOVE.L	#4001, A2	Load address 4001 into register A2 (pointer to vector C).
START	ABCD	–(A0), –(A1)	Decrement contents of A0 and A1 by 1, then add M(A0) to M(A1) using 1-byte decimal addition.
	MOVE.B	(A1), –(A2)	Decrement A2 and then store the 1-byte sum M(A1) in location M(A2) of vector C.
TEST	CMPA	#1001, A0	Compare 1001 to address in A0. If equal, set the Z flag (condition code) to 1; otherwise, reset Z to 0.
	BNE	START	Branch to START if Z is not equal to 1.

Figure 3.13
680X0 assembly-language program for vector addition.

the contents of the named register—this is direct addressing. The ABCD and MOVE.B (move byte) instructions use indirect addressing, indicated by parentheses. In this case the data specified by (A0) is the content of the memory location whose address is stored in A0, that is, the data in M(A0). Finally the minus prefix in the operand –(A0) means that A0 is decremented by one before it is used to access main memory, a mode of addressing called *autoindexing*.

The program of Figure 3.13 loads three starting addresses into the selected address registers. Since the ABCD and MOVE.B instructions begin by automatically decrementing these registers, their initial values are made one bigger than the biggest address assigned to the corresponding vector. The ABCD instruction performs the following set of operations:

$$A0 := A0 - 1, A1 := A1 - 1; M(A1) := M(A1) + M(A0); \text{ set flags}$$

which are relatively slow because of the memory access required. The MOVE.B instruction implements the memory-to-memory move operation with autoindexing

$$A2 := A2 - 1; M(A2) := M(A1); \text{ set flags}$$

The compare-address instruction CMPA checks for program termination by comparing the current address in A0 to 1001, the lowest address assigned to vector A. It actually subtracts its first operand (1001 in this case) from its second and sets the status flags (condition code) based on the result. Hence if A0 > 1001, then A0 – 1001 > 0 and CMPA sets the zero flag Z to 0, indicating a nonzero result. (It also sets various other flags not used by this program). When A0 finally reaches 1001, A0 – 1001 = 0, so CMPA sets Z to 1. Now the last instruction BNE, which stands for branch if not equal to zero, is a conditional branch instruction whose operation is described by

if $Z \neq 1$ **then** PC := START

It therefore transfers execution back to the ABCD instruction in location START as long as A0 >1001. When A0 finally reaches 1001, Z becomes 1, and PC is incremented normally to exit from the program.

It is interesting to compare this 680X0 program with the similar programs given earlier for the IAS (Figure 1.15) and PowerPC (Figure 1.27) computers.

Coprocessors. The built-in instruction repertoire of the 68020 includes fixed-point multiplication and division and stack-based instructions for transferring control between programs. Hardware-implemented floating-point instructions are not available directly; however, they are provided indirectly by means of an auxiliary IC, the 68881 floating-point coprocessor. (The ARM6 also has provisions for external coprocessors.) In general, a *coprocessor P* is a specialized instruction execution unit that can be coupled to a microprocessor so that instructions to be executed by *P* can be included in programs fetched by the microprocessor. Thus the coprocessor serves as an extension to the microprocessor and forms part of the CPU as indicated in Figure 3.14.

The 68881 (and the similar but faster 68882) contains a set of eight 80-bit registers for storing floating-point numbers of various formats, including 32- and 64-bit numbers conforming to the standard IEEE 754 format (presented later). Additional control registers in the 68881 allow it to communicate with the 68020. A set of coprocessor instructions are defined for the 68020; they contain command fields specifying floating-point operations that the 68881 can execute. When the 68020 fetches and decodes such an instruction, it transfers the command portion to the coprocessor, which then executes it. Further exchanges take place between the main processor and the coprocessor until the coprocessor completes execution of its current operation, at which point the 68020 proceeds to its next instruction. The commands executed by the 68881 include the basic

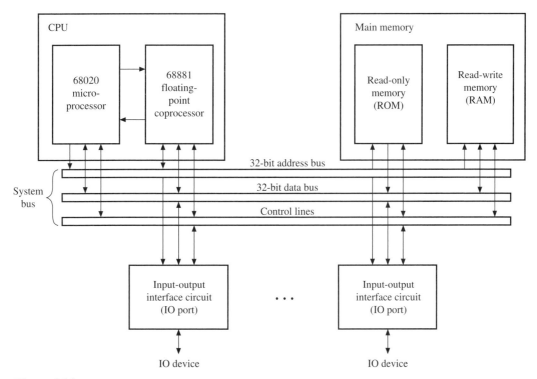

Figure 3.14
68020-based microcomputer with floating-point coprocessor.

arithmetic operations (add, subtract, multiply, and divide), square root, loga-rithms, and trigonometric functions. Other types of coprocessors may be attached to the 68020 in similar fashion. Later members of the 680X0 family take advantage of advances in VLSI to integrate a floating-point (co)processor into the CPU chip.

Other design features. Like the IBM System/360-370 and the ARM6, the CPU has a supervisor state intended for operating system use and a user state for appli-cation programs. As Figures 3.11 and 3.12 indicate, certain "privileged" control registers and instructions can be used only in the supervisor state. User and super-visory programs are thus clearly separated—for example, they employ different stack pointers—thereby improving system security. 680X0-based computers are also designed to allow easy implementation of *virtual memory*, whereby the oper-ating system makes the main memory appear larger to user programs than it really is. Hardware support for virtual memory is provided by the 68851 memory man-agement unit (MMU), another 680X0 coprocessor.

Provided they meet certain independence conditions, up to three 68020 instruc-tions can be processed simultaneously in pipeline fashion. This pipelining is com-plicated by the fact that instruction lengths and execution times vary, a problem that RISCs try to eliminate. Another speedup feature found in the 68020 is a small instruction-only cache (I-cache). The 68020 prefetches instructions from main memory while the system bus is idle; the instructions can subsequently be read much more quickly from the on-chip cache than from the off-chip main memory. An unusual feature of the 68020 noted in Figure 3.11 is its use of two levels of microprogramming to implement the CPU's control logic. For the manufacturer, this feature increases design flexibility while reducing IC area compared with con-ventional (one-level) microprogrammed control.

3.2
DATA REPRESENTATION

The basic items of information handled by a computer are instructions and data. We now examine the methods used to represent such information, focusing on the formats for numerical data.

3.2.1 Basic Formats

Figure 3.15 shows the fundamental division of information into instructions (oper-ation or control words) and data (operands). Data can be further subdivided into numerical and nonnumerical. In view of the importance of numerical computation, computer designs have paid a great deal of attention to the representation of num-bers. Two main number formats have evolved: fixed-point and floating-point. The binary fixed-point format takes the form $b_A b_B b_C ... b_K$, where each b_i is 0 or 1 and a binary point is present in some fixed but implicit position. A floating-point num-ber, on the other hand, consists of a pair of fixed-point numbers $M,E,$ which denote the number $M \times B^E$, where B is a predetermined base. The many formats used to encode fixed-point and floating-point numbers will be examined later in

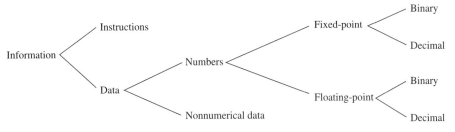

Figure 3.15
The basic information types.

the chapter. Nonnumerical data usually take the form of variable-length character strings encoded in one of several standard codes, such as ASCII (American Standards Committee on Information Exchange) code.

Word length. Information is represented in a digital computer by means of binary words, where a *word* is a unit of information of some fixed length n. An n-bit word allows up to 2^n different items to be represented. For example, with $n = 4$, we can encode the 10 decimal digits as follows:

$$0 = 0000 \quad 1 = 0001 \quad 2 = 0010 \quad 3 = 0011 \quad 4 = 0100$$
$$5 = 0101 \quad 6 = 0110 \quad 7 = 0111 \quad 8 = 1000 \quad 9 = 1001 \tag{3.7}$$

To encode alphanumeric symbols or *characters,* 8-bit words called *bytes* are commonly used. As well as being able to encode all the standard keyboard symbols, a byte allows efficient representation of decimal numbers that are encoded in binary according to (3.7). A byte can store two decimal digits with no wasted space. Most computers have the 8-bit byte as the smallest addressable unit of information in their main memories. The CPU also has a standard word size for the data it processes. Word size is typically a multiple of 8, common CPU word sizes being 8, 16, 32, and 64 bits.

No single word length is suitable for representing every kind of information encountered in a typical computer. Even within a single domain such as a computer's instruction set, we often find several different word sizes. For example, instructions such as load and store that reference memory need long address fields. Instructions whose operands are all in the CPU need not contain memory addresses and so can be shorter. The precision of a number word is determined by its length; it is common therefore to have numbers of various sizes. Figure 3.16 gives a sampling of data sizes used by the Motorola 680X0. As here, the term *word* is often restricted to mean a 32-bit (4 byte) word. (680X0 literature refers to 32-bit words with the nonstandard term *long word*.) Fixed-point numbers come in lengths of 1, 2, 4, or more bytes. Floating-point numbers also come in several lengths, the shortest (single precision) number being one word (32 bits) long.

The circuits of a CPU must be carefully designed to permit various information formats to coexist smoothly. For example, if instruction length varies, as is the case in many CISC microprocessors, the program control unit must be designed to determine an instruction's length from its opcode and to fetch a variable number of instruction bytes from memory. It must also increment the program counter by a

Bits	Name	Illustration	Typical uses
1	Bit		Status flag. Logic variable.
8	Byte		Smallest addressable memory item. Binary-coded decimal digit pair.
16	Halfword		Short fixed-point number. Short address (offset). Short instruction.
32	Word		Fixed- or floating-point number. Memory address. Instruction.
64	Double word		Long instruction. Double-precision floating-point number.

Figure 3.16
Some information formats of the Motorola 680X0 microprocessor series.

variable amount to obtain the address of the next consecutive instruction. Thus while the ARM6 has instructions of length 4 bytes only, the 68020's instructions range in length from 2 to 10 bytes.

Instruction sets commonly have features to make it easy to apply instructions to nonstandard-length operands. An example is the add-with-carry (ADC) instruction and its counterpart subtract with carry, which enable add and subtract instructions to apply to long fixed-point numbers by adding them in short segments and propagating carries from segment to segment. Suppose, for example, that we want to add two unsigned 64-bit (double word) binary integers A and B using the ARM6 instruction set (Figure 3.10), which is designed to add 32-bit words. Let A be placed in registers R0 and R1, with the right (least significant) half of A in R0. Similarly, let B be placed in registers R2 and R3, with its right half in R2. We first apply the ADD instruction with inputs R0 and R2 and place the resulting sum in R4. We also instruct ADD to activate the status flags, which requires an S suffix to the ARM6 opcode, changing it to ADDS. (In most other computers the flags are set automatically by all data-processing instructions.) ADDS results in the carry flag C assuming the value of the carry-out bit produced by the addition R0 + R2. Then we apply the ADC (add with carry) instruction with inputs R1 and R3 to compute the sum R1 + R3. In the following ARM6 code, the final sum $A + B$ is placed in R4 and R5.

HDL format	ARM6 assembly-language format	Narrative format (comment)
C.R4 := R0 + R2	ADDS R4,R0,R2	Add right words and store carry signal C.
R5 : = R1 + R3 + C	ADC R5,R1,R3	Add left words plus C.

Storage order. A small but important aspect of data representation is the way in which the bits of a word are indexed. We will usually follow the convention illustrated in Figure 3.17, where the right-most bit is assigned the index 0 and the bits are labeled in increasing order from right to left. The advantage of this convention is that when the word is interpreted as an unsigned binary integer, the low-order indexes correspond to the numerically less significant bits and the high-order indexes correspond to the numerically more significant bits. Similarly, we label the

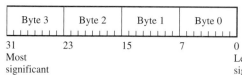

31   23   15   7   0
Most   Least
significant   significant
bit   bit

Figure 3.17
Indexing convention for the bits
and bytes of a word.

bytes of a word from right to left, with index 0 assigned to the numerically least significant byte. Figure 3.17 therefore shows the format used to store a 4-byte word in a one-word register.

Since words are stored as individually addressable bytes in memory M, a question arises as to the storage order in M of the bytes within each word. Suppose that a sequence $W_0, W_1, \ldots, W_m$ of m 4-byte number words is to be stored. Suppose further that we write W_i as $B_{i,3}, B_{i,2}, B_{i,1}, B_{i,0}$, where as in Figure 3.17, we place the least significant byte $B_{i,0}$ on the right and assign it the lowest index 0. Now the entire sequence can be rewritten as

$$W_0, W_1, \ldots, W_m = B_{0,3}, B_{0,2}, B_{0,1}, B_{0,0}, B_{1,3}, B_{1,2}, B_{1,1}, B_{1,0}, \ldots, \\ B_{m,3}, B_{m,2}, B_{m,1}, B_{m,0} \tag{3.8}$$

Suppose we store these $4(m + 1)$ bytes in M using the "natural" order defined by (3.8); that is, we assign a sequence of increasing memory addresses

$$adr_0, \; adr_1, \; adr_2, \; adr_3, \; \ldots, \; adr_{4m+2}, \; adr_{4m+3}$$

to the bytes as listed in (3.8). This storage sequence, which is illustrated in Figure 3.18a, is a byte-storage convention called *big-endian*.[2] It is so named because the most significant (biggest) byte $B_{i,3}$ of word W_i is assigned the lowest address and the least significant byte $B_{i,0}$ is assigned the highest address. In other words, the big-endian scheme assigns the highest address to byte 0. The alternative byte-storage scheme called *little-endian* assigns the lowest address to byte 0. This corresponds to

$$W_0, W_1, \ldots, W_m = B_{0,0}, B_{0,1}, B_{0,2}, B_{0,3}, B_{1,0}, B_{1,1}, B_{1,2}, B_{1,3}, \ldots, B_{m,0}, B_{m,1}, B_{m,2}, B_{m,3}$$

and is illustrated by Figure 3.18b.

Interestingly, computer manufacturers have never agreed on this issue, so both the big-endian and little-endian conventions are in widespread use. For example, the Motorola 680X0 uses the big-endian method, whereas the Intel 80X86 series is little-endian. Some computers including the ARM family can switch between the two endian conventions.

Tags. In the von Neumann computer, instruction and data words are stored together in main memory and are indistinguishable from one another—this is the classic "stored program" concept. An item plucked at random from memory cannot be identified as an instruction or data. Different data types such as fixed-point and floating-point numbers also cannot be distinguished by inspection. A word's type is determined by the way a processor interprets it. In principle, the same word can be treated as an instruction and data at different times, for example, the word X in

---

[2]The allusion is to an argument appearing in *Gulliver's Travels* on whether an egg should be opened at its big or little end [Cohen 1981].

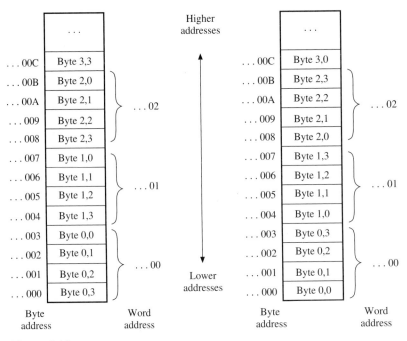

Figure 3.18
Basic byte storage methods: (*a*) big-endian and (*b*) little-endian.

the instruction sequence

$$X := X + Y;$$

go to X;

It is the programmer's (and compiler's) responsibility to ensure that data are not interpreted as instructions, and vice versa. A reason for this deliberate indistinguishability of data and instructions can be seen in the design of the IAS computer (section 1.2.2). The IAS's address-modify instructions alter stored instructions in main memory. The ability to modify instructions in this way—in effect, treating them as data—is useful when processing indexed variables, as illustrated in Example 1.4. However, this type of instruction modification in memory became obsolete with the introduction of address-indexing hardware.

A few computer designers have argued that the major information types should be assigned formats that identify them [Feustel 1973; Myers 1982]. This can be done by associating with each information word a group of bits, called a *tag*, that identifies the word's type. The tag may be considered as a physical implementation of the **type** declaration found in some high-level programming languages. One of the earliest machines to use tags was the 1960s-vintage Burroughs B6500/7500 series, which employed a 3-bit tag field in every word so that eight word types could be distinguished. The 52-bit word format of the B6500/7500 and the interpretation of its tag appear in Figure 3.19.

Tagging simplifies instruction specification. In conventional, nontagged computers, an instruction's opcode must explicitly or implicitly specify the type of data on which it operates. The PCU must know the operand types in order to route them

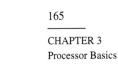

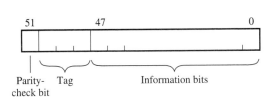

Tag	Interpretation
000	Single-precision number.
001	Indirect reference word.
010	Double-precision number.
011	Segment descriptor.
100	Step-index control word.
101	Data descriptor.
110	Uninitialized operand.
111	Instruction.

Figure 3.19
Tagged-word format of the Burroughs B6500/7500 series.

to the proper arithmetic circuits and registers. It is therefore necessary to provide distinct instructions for each data type; for example, add binary word, add binary half-word, add BCD word, add floating-point word, and add floating-point double word. If, on the other hand, tags distinguish the operand types, then a single ADD opcode suffices for all cases. The processor merely has to inspect an operand's tag to determine its type. Furthermore, tag inspection permits the hardware to check for software errors, such as an attempt to add operands whose types are incompatible. Tags have a serious cost disadvantage, however. They increase memory size and add to the system hardware costs without increasing computing performance. This fact has severely restricted the use of tagged architectures.

Error detection and correction. Various factors like manufacturing defects and environmental effects cause errors in computation. Such errors frequently appear when information is being transmitted between two relatively distant points within a computer or is being stored in a memory unit. "Noise" in the communication link can corrupt a bit x that is being sent from A to B so that B receives $\bar{x}$ instead of x. To guard against errors of this type, the information can be encoded so that special logic circuits can detect, and possibly even correct, the errors.

A general way to detect or correct errors is to append special check bits to every word. One popular technique employs a single check bit c_0 called a *parity bit*. The parity bit is appended to an n-bit word $X = (x_0, x_1, \ldots, x_{n-1})$ to form the $(n + 1)$-bit word $X^* = (x_0, x_1, \ldots, x_{n-1}, c_0)$; see Figure 3.19. Bit c_0 is assigned the value 0 or 1 that makes the number of ones in X^* even, in the case of *even-parity* codes, or odd, in the case of *odd-parity* codes. In the even-parity case, c_0 is defined by the logic equation

$$c_0 = x_0 \oplus x_1 \oplus \ldots \oplus x_{n-1} \qquad (3.9)$$

where $\oplus$ denotes EXCLUSIVE-OR, while in the odd-parity case

$$\bar{c}_0 = x_0 \oplus x_1 \oplus \ldots \oplus x_{n-1}$$

Suppose that the information X is to be transmitted from A to B. The value of c_0 is generated at the source point A using, say, (3.9), and X^* is sent to B. Let B receive the word $X' = (x'_0, x'_1, \ldots, x'_{n-1}, c'_0)$. B then determines the parity of the received word by recomputing the parity bit according to (3.9) thus:

$$c^*_0 = x'_0 \oplus x'_1 \oplus \ldots \oplus x'_{n-1}$$

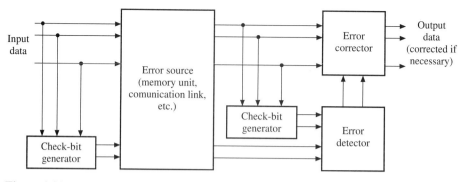

Figure 3.20
Error detection and correction logic.

The received parity bit c'_0 and the reconstituted parity bit c^*_0 are then compared. If $c'_0 \neq c^*_0$, the received information contains an error. In particular, if exactly 1 bit of X^* has been inverted during the transmission process (a single-bit error), then $c'_0 \neq c^*_0$. If $c'_0 = c^*_0$, it can be concluded that no single-bit error occurred, but the possibility of multiple-bit errors is not ruled out. For example, if a 0 changes to 1 and a 1 changes to 0 (a double error), then the parity of X' is the same as that of X^* and the error will go undetected. The parity bit c_0 therefore provides *single-error detection*. It does not detect all multiple errors, much less provide any information about the location of the erroneous bits.

The parity-checking concept can be extended to the detection of multiple errors or to the location of single or multiple errors. These goals are achieved by providing additional parity bits, each of which checks the parity of some subset of the bits in the word X^*. By appropriately overlapping these subsets, the correctness of every bit can be determined. Suppose, for instance, that we can deduce from the parity checks the identity of the bit x_i responsible for a single-bit error. It is then a simple matter to introduce logic circuits to replace x_i by $\bar{x}_i$, thus providing *single-error correction*. Let c be the number of check bits required to achieve single-error correction with n-bit data words. Clearly the check bits have 2^c patterns that must distinguish between $n + c$ possible error locations and the single error-free case. Hence c must satisfy the inequality

$$2^c \geq n + c + 1 \tag{3.10}$$

For $n = 16$, (3.10) implies that $c \geq 5$, while for $n = 32$ we have $c \geq 6$. A variety of practical single-error-correcting parity-check codes meet the lower bound on c implied by (3.10) [Siewiorek and Swarz 1992]. Some of these codes can also detect double errors and so are called *single-error-correcting double-error-detecting* (SECDED) codes. As the main memories of computers have increased in storage capacity and decreased in physical size, they have become more prone to transient failures that are often correctable via SECDED codes. Figure 3.20 shows the structure of a typical error detection and correction scheme used with a computer's main memory.

3.2.2 Fixed-Point Numbers

In selecting a number representation to be used in a computer, the following factors should be taken into account:

- The number types to be represented; for example, integers or real numbers.
- The range of values (number magnitudes) likely to be encountered.
- The precision of the numbers, which refers to the maximum accuracy of the representation.
- The cost of the hardware required to store and process the numbers.

The two principal number formats are fixed-point and floating-point. Fixed-point formats allow a limited range of values and have relatively simple hardware requirements. Floating-point numbers, on the other hand, allow a much larger range of values but require either costly processing hardware or lengthy software implementations.

Binary numbers. The fixed-point format is derived directly from the ordinary (decimal) representation of a number as a sequence of digits separated by a decimal point. The digits to the left of the decimal point represent an integer; the digits to the right represent a fraction. This is *positional notation* in which each digit has a fixed *weight* according to its position relative to the decimal point. If $i > 1$, the ith digit to the left (right) of the decimal point has weight 10^{i-1} (10^{-i}). Thus the five-digit decimal number 192.73 is equivalent to

$$1 \times 10^2 + 9 \times 10^1 + 2 \times 10^0 + 7 \times 10^{-1} + 3 \times 10^{-2}$$

More generally, we can assign weights of the form r^i, where r is the *base* or *radix* of the number system, to each digit.

The most fundamental number representation used in computers employs a base-two positional notation. A binary word of the form

$$b_N \ldots b_3 b_2 b_1 b_0 \, . \, b_{-1} b_{-2} b_{-3} b_{-4} \ldots b_M \tag{3.11}$$

represents the number

$$\sum_{i=M}^{N} b_i 2^i$$

When unclear from the context, the base r being used will be indicated by appending r as a subscript to the number. Thus 1010_2 denotes the binary equivalent of the decimal number 10_{10}, whereas 10_2 denotes 2_{10}. The format of (3.11) is an example of a fixed-point binary number and is used to denote unsigned numbers. Several distinct methods used for representing signed (positive and negative) numbers are discussed below.

Suppose that an n-bit word is to contain a signed binary number. One bit is reserved to represent the sign of the number, while the remaining bits indicate its magnitude. To permit uniform processing of all n bits, the sign is placed in the left-most position, and 0 and 1 are used to denote plus and minus, respectively. This leads to the format

$$x_{n-1}x_{n-2}x_{n-3} \cdots x_2x_1x_0 \qquad (3.12)$$

Sign   Magnitude

The precision allowed by this format is $n - 1$ bits, which is equivalent to $(n - 1)$ $\log_2 10$ decimal digits. The binary point is not explicitly represented; instead, it is implicitly assigned to some fixed location in the word. The binary point's position is not very important from the point of view of design. In many situations the numbers being processed are integers, so the binary point is assumed to lie immediately to the right of the least significant bit x_0. Monetary quantities are often expressed as integers; for instance, \$54.30 might be expressed as 5430 cents. Using an n-bit integer format, we can represent all integers N with magnitude $|N|$ in the range $0 \leq |N| \leq 2^n - 1$. The other most widely used fixed-point format treats (3.12) as a fraction with the binary point lying between x_{n-1} and x_{n-2}. The fraction format denotes numbers with magnitudes in the range $0 \leq |N| \leq 1 - 2^{-n}$.

Signed numbers. Suppose that both positive and negative binary numbers are to be represented by an n-bit word $X = x_{n-1}x_{n-2}x_{n-3}\ldots x_2x_1x_0$. The standard format for positive numbers is given by (3.12) with a sign bit of 0 on the left and the magnitude to the right in the usual positional notation. This means that each magnitude bit x_i, $0 \leq i \leq n - 2$, has a fixed weight of the form 2^{k+i}, where k depends on the position of the binary point. A natural way to represent negative numbers is to employ the same positional notation for the magnitude and simply change the sign bit x_{n-1} to 1 to indicate minus. Thus with $n = 8$, $+75 = 01001011$, while $-75 = 11001011$. This number code is called *sign magnitude*. Note that humans normally use decimal versions of sign-magnitude code. Nevertheless, operations like subtraction are costly to implement by logic circuits when sign-magnitude codes are used. However, multiplication and division of sign-magnitude numbers is almost as easy as the corresponding operation for unsigned numbers, as Example 2.7 (section 2.3.3) shows.

Several number codes have been devised that use the same representation for positive numbers as the sign-magnitude code but represent negative numbers in different ways. For example, in the *ones-complement* code, $-X$ is denoted by $\bar{X}$, the bitwise logical complement of X. In this code we again have $+75 = 01001011$, but now $-75 = 10110100$. In the *twos-complement* code, $-X$ is formed by adding 1 to the least significant bit of $\bar{X}$ and ignoring any carry bit generated from the most significant (sign) position. If $X = x_{n-1}x_{n-2}\ldots x_0$ is an n-bit binary fraction, $-X$ can be expressed as follows:

$$-X = \bar{x}_{n-1} . \bar{x}_{n-2}\bar{x}_{n-3} \cdots \bar{x}_1\bar{x}_0 + 0.00 \ldots 01 \quad \text{(modulo 2)} \qquad (3.13)$$

Implicit binary point   Implicit binary point

where the use of modulo-2 addition corresponds to ignoring carries from the sign position. If X is an integer, then (3.13) becomes

$$-X = \bar{x}_{n-1}\bar{x}_{n-2}\bar{x}_{n-3} \cdots \bar{x}_1\bar{x}_0 . + 000 \ldots 01. \quad \text{(modulo } 2^n) \qquad (3.14)$$

Implicit binary point   Implicit binary point

For example, in twos-complement code $+75 = 01001011$ and $-75 = 10110101$. Note that in both complement codes x_{n-1} retains its role as the sign bit, but the remaining bits no longer form a simple positional code when the number is negative.

The primary advantage of the complement codes is that subtraction can be performed by logical complementation and addition only. Consider the twos-complement code. To subtract X from Y, just add $-X$ to Y, where $-X$ is obtained by logical complementation and addition of a 1 bit, as in (3.13) and (3.14). As we will see later, the sign bits do not require special treatment; consequently, twos-complement addition and subtraction can be implemented by a simple adder designed for unsigned numbers. Multiplication and division are more difficult to implement if twos-complement code is used instead of sign magnitude. The addition of ones-complement numbers is complicated by the fact that a carry bit from the most significant magnitude bit x_{n-2} must be added to the least significant bit position x_0. Otherwise ones-complement codes are quite similar to twos-complement codes and so will not be considered further.

Figure 3.21 illustrates how integers are represented using all three codes when $n = 4$. These codes are all referred to as *binary* codes to distinguish them from the so-called decimal codes discussed below. Observe that in all cases, 0000 represents zero. Only in the case of twos-complement code, however, is the nega-

Decimal representation	Binary code		
	Sign magnitude	Ones complement	Twos complement
+7	0111	0111	0111
+6	0110	0110	0110
+5	0101	0101	0101
+4	0100	0100	0100
+3	0011	0011	0011
+2	0010	0010	0010
+1	0001	0001	0001
+0	0000	0000	0000
−0	1000	1111	0000
−1	1001	1110	1111
−2	1010	1101	1110
−3	1011	1100	1101
−4	1100	1011	1100
−5	1101	1010	1011
−6	1110	1001	1010
−7	1111	1000	1001

Figure 3.21
Comparison of three 4-bit codes for signed binary numbers.

tive (numerical complement) of 0000 also 0000. This unique representation of zero is a significant advantage, for example, in implementing instructions like BNE in Figure 3.13 that test for zero. Consequently, twos-complement code is by far the most popular code for representing signed binary numbers in computers.

Exceptional conditions. If the result of an arithmetic operation involving n-bit numbers is too large (small) to be represented by n bits, *overflow (underflow)* is said to occur. It is generally necessary to detect overflow and underflow, since they may indicate bad data or a programming error. Consider, for example, the addition operation

$$z_{n-1}z_{n-2}\ldots z_0 := x_{n-1}x_{n-2}\ldots x_0 + y_{n-1}y_{n-2}\ldots y_0$$

using n-bit twos-complement operands. Assume that bitwise addition is performed with a carry bit c_i generated by the addition of x_i, y_i, and c_{i-1}. The output bits z_i and c_i can be computed according to the full-adder logic equations

$$z_i = x_i \oplus y_i \oplus c_{i-1}$$

$$c_i = x_i y_i + x_i c_{i-1} + y_i c_{i-1}$$

Let v be a binary variable indicating overflow when $v = 1$. Figure 3.22 shows how the sign bit z_{n-1} and v are determined as functions of the sign bits x_{n-1}, y_{n-1} and the carry bit c_{n-2}. The overflow indicator v is therefore defined by the logic equation

$$v = \bar{x}_{n-1}\bar{y}_{n-1}c_{n-2} + x_{n-1}y_{n-1}\bar{c}_{n-2}$$

If the combinations $(x_{n-1},y_{n-1},c_{n-2}) = (0,0,1)$ and $(1,1,0)$, which make $v = 1$, are removed from the truth table of Figure 3.22, then z_{n-1} is defined correctly for all the remaining combinations by the equation

$$z_{n-1} = x_{n-1} \oplus y_{n-1} \oplus c_{n-2}$$

Consequently, during twos-complement addition the sign bits of the operands can be treated in the same way as the remaining (magnitude) bits.

A related issue in computer arithmetic is *round-off error,* which results from the fact that every number must be represented by a limited number of bits. An

Inputs			Outputs	
x_{n-1}	y_{n-1}	c_{n-2}	z_{n-1}	v
0	0	0	0	0
0	0	1	0	1
0	1	0	1	0
0	1	1	0	0
1	0	0	1	0
1	0	1	0	0
1	1	0	1	1
1	1	1	1	0

Figure 3.22
Computation of the sign bit z_{n-1} and the overflow indicator v in twos-complement addition.

operation involving n-bit numbers frequently produces a result of more than n bits. For example, the product of two n-bit numbers contains up to $2n$ bits, all but n of which must normally be discarded. Retaining the n most significant bits of the result without modification is called *truncation*. Clearly the resulting number is in error by the amount of the discarded digits. This error can be reduced by a process called *rounding*. One way of rounding is to add $r^j/2$ to the number before truncation, where r^j is the weight of the least significant retained digit. For instance, to round 0.346712 to three decimal places, add 0.0005 to obtain 0.347212 and then take the three most significant digits 0.347. Simple truncation yields the less accurate value 0.346. Successive computations can cause round-off errors to build up unless countermeasures are taken. The number formats provided in a computer should have sufficient precision that round-off errors are of no consequence to most users. It is also desirable to provide facilities for performing arithmetic to a higher degree of precision if required. Such high precision is usually achieved by using several words to represent a single number and writing special subroutines to perform multiword, or *multiple-precision*, arithmetic.

Decimal numbers. Since humans use decimal arithmetic, numbers being entered into a computer must first be converted from decimal to some binary representation. Similarly, binary-to-decimal conversion is a normal part of the computer's output processes. In certain applications the number of decimal-binary conversions forms a large fraction of the total number of elementary operations performed by the computer. In such cases, number conversion should be carried out rapidly. The various binary number codes discussed above do not lend themselves to rapid conversion. For example, converting an unsigned binary number $x_{n-1}x_{n-2}...x_0$ to decimal requires a polynomial of the form

$$\sum_{i=0}^{n-1} x_i 2^{k+i}$$

to be evaluated.

Several number codes exist that facilitate rapid binary-decimal conversion by encoding each decimal digit separately by a sequence of bits. Codes of this kind are called *decimal codes*. The most widely used decimal code is the BCD (*binary-coded decimal*) code. In BCD format each digit d_i of a decimal number is denoted by its 4-bit equivalent $b_{i,3}b_{i,2}b_{i,1}b_{i,0}$ in standard binary form, as in (3.7). Thus the BCD number representing 971 is 100101110001. BCD is a weighted (positional) number code, since $b_{i,j}$ has the weight $10^i 2^j$. Signed BCD numbers employ decimal versions of the sign-magnitude or complement formats. The 8-bit ASCII code represents the 10 decimal digits by a 4-bit BCD field; the remaining 4 bits of the ASCII code word have no numerical significance.

Two other decimal codes of moderate importance are shown in Figure 3.23. The *excess-three* code can be formed by adding 0011_2 to the corresponding BCD number—hence its name. The advantage of the excess-three code is that it may be processed using the same logic used for binary codes. If two excess-three numbers are added like binary numbers, the required decimal carry is automatically generated from the high-order bits. The sum must be corrected by adding +3. For

Decimal digit	Decimal code			
	BCD	ASCII	Excess-three	Two-out-of-five
0	0000	0011 0000	0011	11000
1	0001	0011 0001	0100	00011
2	0010	0011 0010	0101	00101
3	0011	0011 0011	0110	00110
4	0100	0011 0100	0111	01001
5	0101	0011 0101	1000	01010
6	0110	0011 0110	1001	01100
7	0111	0011 0111	1010	10001
8	1000	0011 1000	1011	10010
9	1001	0011 1001	1100	10100

Figure 3.23
Some important decimal number codes.

example, consider the addition $5 + 9 = 14$ using excess-three code.

$$
\begin{array}{rll}
& 1000 = 5 & \\
+ & 1100 = 9 & \\
\text{Carry } 1 \leftarrow & 0100 & \text{Binary sum} \\
+ & 0011 & \text{Correction} \\
\hline
& 0111 = 4 & \text{Excess-three sum}
\end{array}
$$

Binary addition of the BCD representations of 5 and 9 results in 1110 and no carry generation. (The binary sum of two BCD numbers can also be corrected to give the proper BCD sum as described later.) Some arithmetic operations are difficult to implement using excess-three code, mainly because it is a *nonweighted* code; that is, each bit position in an excess-three number does not have a fixed weight.

The final decimal code illustrated by Figure 3.23 is the *two-out-of-five* code. Each decimal digit is represented by a 5-bit sequence containing two 1s and three 0s; there are exactly 10 distinct sequences of this type. The particular merit of the two-out-of-five code is that it is single-error detecting, since changing any one bit results in a sequence that does not correspond to a valid code word. Its drawbacks are that it is a nonweighted code and uses 5 rather than 4 bits per decimal digit.

The main advantage of the decimal codes is ease of conversion between the internal computer representation that allows only the symbols 0, 1 and external representations using the 10 decimal symbols 0, 1, 2,..., 9. Decimal codes have two disadvantages.

1. They use more bits to represent a number than the binary codes. Decimal codes therefore require more memory space. An n-bit word can represent 2^n numbers using binary codes; approximately $10^{n/4} = 2^{0.830n}$ numbers can be represented if a 4-bit decimal code such as BCD or excess-three is used.
2. The circuitry required to perform arithmetic using decimal operands is more complex than that needed for binary arithmetic. For example, in adding BCD

numbers bit by bit, a uniform method of propagating carries between adjacent positions is not possible, since the weights of adjacent bits do not differ by a constant factor.

Hexadecimal numbers. One or two other numerical codes are encountered in the design or use of computers. Of particular importance is *hexadecimal* (hex) code, which is characterized by a base $r = 16$ and the use of 16 digits, consisting of the decimal digits $0,1,\ldots,9$ augmented by the six digits A,B,C,D,E, and F, which have the numerical values 10, 11, 12, 13, 14, and 15, respectively. The unsigned hexadecimal integer 2FA0C has the interpretation

$$2 \times 16^4 + F \times 16^3 + A \times 16^2 + 0 \times 16^1 + C \times 16^0$$
$$= 2 \times 65,536 + 15 \times 4,096 + 10 \times 256 + 0 \times 16 + 12 \times 1$$
$$= 195,084$$

Hence $2FA0C_{16} = 195,084_{10}$.

Hexadecimal code is useful for representing long binary numbers, a consequence of the fact that the base 16 is a power of two. A hexadecimal number is converted to binary simply by replacing each hex digit by the equivalent 4-bit binary form. For example, we can convert $2FA0C_{16}$ to binary by replacing the first digit 2 by 0010, the second digit F by 1111, the third digit A by 1010, and so on, yielding

$$2FA0C_{16} = 00101111101000001100_2$$

Conversely, we can convert a binary number to hex form by replacing each four-digit group by the corresponding hex digit. Clearly hexadecimal-binary number conversion is very similar to BCD-binary conversion. By treating any binary word as an unsigned integer, we can easily convert the word to hex form as indicated above. Hex code provides a very convenient shorthand for binary information.

3.2.3 Floating-Point Numbers

The range of numbers that can be represented by a fixed-point number code is insufficient for many applications, particularly scientific computations where very large and very small numbers are encountered. Scientific notation permits us to represent such numbers using relatively few digits. For example, it is easier to write a quintillion as

$$1.0 \times 10^{18} \tag{3.15}$$

than as the 19-bit, fixed-point integer 1 000 000 000 000 000 000. The floating-point codes used in computers are binary (or binary-coded) versions of (3.15).

Basic formats. Three numbers are associated with a floating-point number: a mantissa M, an *exponent E*, and a *base B*. The mantissa M is also referred to as the *significand* or *fraction* in the literature. These three components together represent the real number $M \times B^E$. For example, in (3.15) 1.0 is the mantissa, 18 is the exponent, and 10 is the base. For machine implementation the mantissa and exponent are encoded as fixed-point numbers with a base r that is usually 2 or 10. The base B

is also r, or some power of r, for reasons that will become obvious. Since B is a constant, it need not be included in the number code; it is simply built into the circuits that process the numbers. A floating-point number is therefore stored as a word (M,E) consisting of a pair of signed fixed-point numbers: a mantissa M, which is usually a fraction or an integer, and an exponent E, which is an integer. The number of digits in M determines the precision of (M,E); B and E determine its range. With a word size of n bits, 2^n is the most real numbers that (M,E) can represent. Increasing B increases the range of the representable real numbers but results in a sparser distribution of numbers over that range.

As a small example, suppose that M and E are both 3-bit, sign-magnitude integers and $B = 2$. Then M and E can each assume the values ± 0, ± 1, ± 2, and ± 3. All binary words of the form $(M,E) = (x00, xxx)$ represent zero, where x denotes either 0 or 1. The smallest nonzero positive number is $(001,111)$, denoting $1 \times 2^{-3} = 0.125$; $(101,111)$ denotes -0.125. The largest representable positive number is $(011,011)$, which denotes $3 \times 2^3 = 24$, while $(111,011)$ denotes the largest negative number -24. Observe that the left-most bit, which is the sign of the mantissa, is also the sign of the floating-point number. Figure 3.24 illustrates the real numbers representable by this 6-bit, floating-point format. As the figure shows, they are sparsely and nonuniformly distributed over the range ± 24.

The floating-point representation of most real numbers is only approximate. For instance, the 6-bit format of Figure 3.24 cannot represent the number 1.25; it is approximated by $(011,101)$, representing 1.5, or by either $(001,000)$ or $(001,100)$, representing 1.0. Moreover, the results of most calculations with floating-point arithmetic only approximate the correct result. For example, in the system of Figure 3.24, the exact result (18) of the addition $(011,001) + (011,010)$, which implements $6 + 12$, is not representable. The closest representable number, that is, the best approximation to 18, is $(010,011) = 16$. Overflow occurs in this small system when a result's magnitude exceeds 24, and underflow occurs when a nonzero result has a magnitude less than 0.125. In practice, floating-point numbers must have long mantissas (at least 20 bits), and the results of floating-point operations must be carefully rounded off to minimize the errors inherent in floating-point representation. It is common practice for floating-point processing circuits to include a few extra mantissa digits termed *guard digits* to reduce approximation errors; the guard digits are removed automatically from the final results.

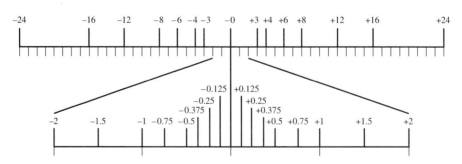

Figure 3.24
The real numbers representable by a hypothetical 6-bit, floating-point format.

Normalization and biasing. Floating-point representation is redundant in the sense that the same number can be represented in more than one way. For example, 1.0×10^{18}, 0.1×10^{19}, 1000000×10^{12}, and 0.000001×10^{24} are possible representations of a quintillion. It is generally desirable to have a unique or *normal* form for each representable number in a floating-point system. Consider the common case where the mantissa is a sign-magnitude fraction and a base of r is used. The mantissa is said to be *normalized* if the digit to the right of the radix point is not zero, that is, no leading zeros appear in the magnitude part of the number. Thus, for example, 0.1×10^{19} is the unique normal form of a quintillion using base 10, a decimal mantissa, and a decimal exponent. A binary fraction in twos-complement code is normalized when the sign bit differs from the bit to its right. This implies that no leading 1s appear in the magnitude part of negative numbers. Normalization restricts the magnitude $|M|$ of a fractional binary mantissa to the range

$$1/2 \le |M| < 1$$

Normal forms can be defined similarly for other floating-point codes. An unnormalized number is normalized by shifting the mantissa to the right or left and appropriately incrementing or decrementing the exponent to compensate for the mantissa shift.

The representation of zero poses some special problems. The mantissa must, of course, be zero, but the exponent can have any value, since $0 \times B^E = 0$ for all values of E. Often in attempting to compute zero, round-off errors result in a mantissa that is nearly, but not exactly, zero. For the entire floating-point number to be close to zero, its exponent must be a very large negative number $-K$. This requirement suggests that the exponent used for representing zero should be the negative number with the largest magnitude that can be contained in the exponent field of the number format. If k bits are allowed for the exponent including its sign, then 2^k exponent bit patterns are available to represent signed integers, which can range either from -2^{k-1} to $2^{k-1} - 1$ or from $-2^{k-1} + 1$ to 2^{k-1}, so that K is 2^{k-1} or $2^{k-1} - 1$.

A second complication arises from the desirability of representing zero by a sequence of 0-bits only. This convention gives zero the same representation in both fixed- and floating-point formats, which facilitates the implementation of instructions that test for zero. These considerations suggest that floating-point exponents should be encoded in excess-K code similar to the excess-three code of Figure 3.23, where the exponent field E contains an integer that is the desired exponent value plus K. The quantity K is called the *bias,* and an exponent encoded in this way is called a *biased exponent* or *characteristic.* Figure 3.25 shows the possible values of an 8-bit exponent with bias 127 and 128.

Standards. Until the 1980s floating-point number formats varied from one computer family to the next, making it difficult to transport programs between different computers without encountering small but significant differences in such areas as round-off errors. To deal with this problem, the Institute of Electrical and Electronics Engineers (IEEE) sponsored a standard format for 32-bit and larger floating-point numbers, known as the IEEE 754 standard [IEEE 1985], which has been widely adopted by computer manufacturers. Besides specifying the permissible formats for M, E, and B, the IEEE standard prescribes methods for handling round-off errors, overflow, underflow, and other exceptional conditions.

Exponent bit pattern E	Unsigned value	Number represented	
		Bias = 127	Bias = 128
111 ... 11	255	+128	+127
111 ... 10	254	+127	+126
. . .	. . .	. . .	
100 ... 01	129	+2	+1
100 ... 00	128	+1	0
011 ... 11	127	0	−1
011 ... 10	126	−1	−2
. . .	. . .	. . .	
000 ... 01	1	−126	−127
000 ... 00	0	−127	−128

Figure 3.25
Eight-bit biased exponents with bias = 127 (excess-127 code) and bias = 128 (excess-128 code).

EXAMPLE 3.4 THE IEEE 754 FLOATING-POINT NUMBER FORMAT [IEEE 1985; GOLDBERG 1991]. This standard format for 32-bit numbers is illustrated in Figure 3.26. It comprises a 23-bit mantissa field M, an 8-bit exponent field E, and a sign bit S. The base B is two. As in all signed binary number formats, both fixed-point and floating-point, S occupies the left-most bit position. M is a fraction that with S forms a sign-magnitude binary number. For the reasons discussed earlier, floating-point numbers are usually normalized, meaning that the magnitude field should contain no insignificant leading bits. Hence the magnitude part of a normalized sign-magnitude number always has 1 as its most significant digit. There is no need to actually store this leading 1 in floating-point numbers, since it can always be inserted by the arithmetic circuits that process the numbers. Consequently, in the IEEE 754 format the complete mantissa (called the *significand* in the standard) is actually 1.M, where the 1 to the left of the binary point is an implicit or *hidden* leading bit that is not stored with the number. Use of the hidden 1 means that the precision of a normalized number is effectively increased by 1 bit. The exponent representation is the 8-bit excess-127 code of Figure 3.25; hence the actual exponent value is computed as $E - 127$. The base B of the floating-point number is 2, so that a 1-bit left (right) shift of M corresponds to incrementing (decrementing) E by one.

Consequently, a 32-bit floating-point number conforming to the IEEE 754 standard represents the real number N given by the formula

$$N = (-1)^S 2^{E-127}(1.M) \tag{3.16}$$

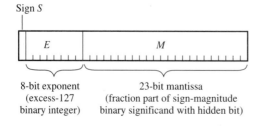

Sign S

E M

8-bit exponent
(excess-127
binary integer)

23-bit mantissa
(fraction part of sign-magnitude
binary significand with hidden bit)

Figure 3.26
IEEE 754 standard 32-bit floating-point number format.

provided $0 < E < 255$. For example, the number $N = -1.5$ is represented by

$$1 \quad 01111111 \quad 10000000000000000000000$$

where $S = 1$, $E = 127$, and $M = 0.5$, since from (3.16) we have $N = (-1)^1 2^{127-127}(1.5) = -1.5$. Nonzero floating-point numbers in this format have magnitudes ranging from $2^{-126}(1.0)$ to $2^{+127}(2 - 2^{-23})$, that is, from 1.18×10^{-38} to 3.40×10^{38} approximately. In contrast, 32-bit, fixed-point binary formats for integers can only represent nonzero numbers with magnitudes from 1 to $2^{31} - 1$ (approximately 2.15×10^9). The 64-bit version of the IEEE 754 standard is a straightforward extension of the 32-bit case. It employs an 11-bit exponent E and a 52-bit mantissa M and defines the number

$$N = (-1)^S 2^{E-1023}(1.M) \tag{3.17}$$

where $0 < E < 2047$.

The IEEE floating-point standard addresses a number of subtle problems encountered in floating-point arithmetic. Well-defined formats are specified for the results of overflow, underflow, and other exceptional conditions, which often yield unpredictable and unusable numbers in computers employing other floating-point formats. The IEEE standard's exception formats are intended to set flags in the host processor, which subsequent instructions can use for error control, in many cases with little or no loss of accuracy. If the result of a floating-point operation is not a valid floating-point number, then a special code referred to as *not a number* (NaN) is used. Examples of operations that result in NaNs are dividing zero by zero and taking the square root of a negative number. NaN formats are identified in the standard by $M \neq 0$, and $E = 255$ (32-bit format) or $E = 2047$ (64-bit format).

When overflow occurs, meaning that a number has been produced whose magnitude is too big to represent by the usual format, the result is referred to as *infinity,* or ∞, and is identified by $M = 0$, and $E = 255$ (32-bit format) or $E = 2047$ (64-bit format). The 754 standard stipulates that operations using the floating-point infinities $\pm\infty$ should follow certain properties of infinity in real-number theory, such as $-\infty + N = \infty$ and $-\infty < N < +\infty$ for any finite N. If underflow occurs, implying that a result is nonzero, but too small to represent as a normalized number, it is encoded in a *denormalized*[3] form characterized by $E = 0$ and a significand $0.M$ having a leading 0 instead of the usual leading 1. Denormalization reduces the effect of underflow to a systematic loss of precision equivalent to a small round-off error. Finally, floating-point zero is identified by an all-0 exponent and significand, but the sign S may be 0 or 1. Note that as the tiny denormalized numbers are diminished, they eventually reach zero.

In summary, the number N represented by a 32-bit IEEE-standard, floating-point number has the following set of interpretations.

If $E = 255$ and $M \neq 0$, then $N = \text{NaN}$.

If $E = 255$ and $M = 0$, then $N = (-1)^S \infty$.

If $0 < E < 255$, then $N = (-1)^S 2^{E-127}(1.M)$.

If $E = 0$ and $M \neq 0$, then $N = (-1)^S 2^{E-126}(0.M)$.

If $E = 0$ and $M = 0$, then $N = (-1)^S 0$.

The interpretation of 64-bit and larger floating-point numbers is similar.

---

[3]The term *unnormalized* applies to numbers with any value of E and a leading 0 instead of a leading 1 associated with their mantissas. Such numbers are encountered only as intermediate results during floating-point computations and are not relevant to the standard.

Typical of other floating-point number formats still in use is that of the IBM System/360-370. It consists of a sign bit S, a 7-bit exponent field E, and a mantissa field M containing 24, 56, or 112 bits. M is treated as a fraction, which with S forms a sign-magnitude number; there is no hidden leading 1. E is an integer in excess-64 code, corresponding to an exponent bias of 64. Unlike the IEEE 754 format where the base B of the representation is two, the System/360-370 has $B = 16$. Consequently, M is interpreted as a hexadecimal (base 16) number with every hexadecimal digit corresponding to 4 bits, and the exponent is treated as a power of 16. The value of a floating-point number in the normalized System/360-370 format is therefore given by

$$N = (-1)^S 16^{E-64}(0.M)$$

where M is a 6-, 14-, or 28-digit hexadecimal number. For example, the number 0.125×16^5 is encoded as

$$0 \quad 1000101 \quad 00100000\ldots0000$$

Note that the left-most four bits 0010 of the mantissa represent the nonzero hexadecimal digit 2; hence the above number is normalized. The number zero is always represented by the all-0 word, making the floating-point representation of zero identical to the System/360-370 fixed-point (twos-complement) representation. There are no equivalents of the IEEE 754 standard's NaN, infinity, and denormalized formats. While most floating-point instructions are performed with automatic normalization of the results, a few may be specified without normalization, thus providing some of the advantages of denormalization. Due to the larger value of B being used, the System/360-370 32-bit format can represent numbers with magnitudes ranging from 5.40×10^{-79} to 7.24×10^{75} approximately.

3.3
INSTRUCTION SETS

Next we turn to the representation, selection, and application of instruction sets. This topic embraces opcode and operand formats, the design of the instruction types to include in a processor's instruction set, and the use of instructions in executable programs.

3.3.1 Instruction Formats

The purpose of an instruction is to specify both an operation to be carried out by a CPU or other processor and the set of operands or data to be used in the operation. The operands include the input data or arguments of the operation and the results that are produced.

Introduction. Most instructions specify a register-transfer operation of the form

$$X_1 := op(X_1, X_2, \ldots, X_n)$$

which applies the operation op to n operands $X_1, X_2, \ldots, X_n$, where n ranges from zero to four or so. We can write the same instruction in the assembly-language notation

$$op \quad X_1, X_2, \ldots, X_n \qquad\qquad (3.18)$$

which defines the operation and its operands by specific "fields" within the instruction word (3.18). The operation *op* is specified by a field called the *opcode* (*op*eration *code*). The n $X_1, X_2, \ldots, X_n$ fields are referred to as *addresses*. An address X_i typically names a register or a memory location that stores an operand value. In some instances X_i itself *is* the desired value, in which case it is called an *immediate* address.

To reduce instruction size and thereby reduce program storage space, it is common to specify only $m < n$ operands explicitly in the instruction; the remaining operands are implicit. The explicit address fields refer to general-purpose CPU registers or memory locations, while the implicit ones refer to special-purpose registers. If m is the normal maximum number of explicit main-memory addresses allowed in any processor instruction, the processor is called an *m-address machine*. Implicit input operands must be placed in known locations before the instruction that refers to them is executed.

Inside the computer, instructions are stored as binary words. There can be several different sizes and formats, depending on the instruction type. RISCs tend to have few instruction formats, while CISCs tend to have many to accommodate more opcode types and operand addressing methods. The Motorola 680X0 (Example 3.3) is a CISC microprocessor series with many different instruction formats and sizes, a sampling of which appear in Figure 3.27 [Motorola 1989]. Instruction length in the 680X0 varies from 2 to 10 bytes. The 2-byte opcode field of the 680X0 is often used to hold one or two 3-bit register addresses, blurring the distinction between opcode and operand.

In the 680X0 family, simple instructions are assigned short formats. For example, the add-register instruction

$$\text{ADD.L} \quad \text{D1,D2} \qquad\qquad (3.19)$$

denotes register-to-register addition of 32-bit (long word) operands, that is,

$$\text{D2} := \text{D2} + \text{D1}$$

where D1 and D2 are two of the 680X0's data registers (Figure 3.11). This instruction fits in the third 2-byte format F3 of Figure 3.27, which accommodates two register-address fields. A variant of the same two-address instruction can also refer to an operand in memory:

$$\text{ADD.L} \quad \text{ADR1, D2} \qquad\qquad (3.20)$$

This instruction specifies the memory-to-register addition operation

$$\text{D2} := \text{D2} + \text{M(ADR1)}$$

and so combines the load and add operations. It uses the 6-byte format F6 to contain the 4-byte immediate address field ADR1. It also requires a memory access to obtain one of its input operands, the 4-byte long word with start address ADR1. Note that the binary (machine language) opcodes corresponding to (3.19) and (3.20) have to be different to distinguish their operand types.

The longest (10 byte) format F8 of the 680X0 is employed by such memory-to-memory move instructions as

$$\text{MOVE.B} \quad \text{ADR1,ADR2}$$

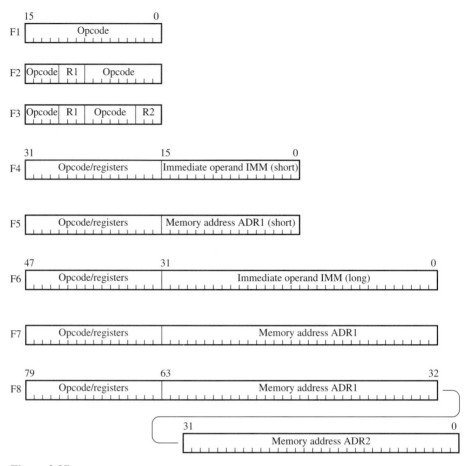

Figure 3.27
A selection of instruction formats of the Motorola 680X0.

which copies (via the CPU) the byte stored in memory location ADR1 to memory location ADR2, that is,

$$M(ADR2) := M(ADR1)$$

RISC formats. The instruction formats of the 680X0 accommodate a wide variety of operations and addressing modes. They also try to reduce object-program size by encoding the more common instructions in short formats and the less frequent and more complex instructions in longer formats. Since such instructions are often primitives in high-level programming languages, they serve to reduce both program length and what has been called the *semantic gap* between the user and the computer languages.

Complex instructions lead to several difficulties, which RISCs with their smaller and streamlined instruction sets attempt to minimize.

- The many instruction types and formats of a CISC complicate the program-control unit that decodes instruction opcodes and issues the control signals that govern their execution. The 68020 employs a large, two-level micropro-grammed PCU (Figure 3.11), whereas the ARM6 has a smaller hardwired circuit as its PCU.

- Fast, single-cycle instruction execution is harder to achieve with a complex instruction set, and it is more difficult for a compiler to optimize object-code performance.

A typical RISC employs instructions of fixed length. Memory addressing is restricted to load and store instructions, so the operands of most instructions are register addresses, which are short and easy to accommodate in a one-word format. Figure 3.28 shows the single 32-bit format used by instructions in the RISC 1 computer, a prototype RISC machine designed by David A. Patterson and his colleagues at the University of California, Berkeley, around 1980 [Patterson and Séquin 1982]. Most of the 31 instruction types defined for the RISC 1 perform register-to-register operations of the form

$$Rd := F(Rs,S2) \tag{3.21}$$

where Rd is the destination register, Rs is the first source register, and the right-most 5 bits of S2 define a second-source register. If bit 13 of the instruction is set to one, then S2 is interpreted as an immediate address, that is, as a 13-bit constant. The instructions of the ARM6 microprocessor (Example 3.2), like those of the RISC 1, are all 32 bits long, but they come in a large and CISC-like number of formats [Furber 1989].

Operand extension. A CPU is designed primarily to process data words and addresses of one specific length—a 32-bit word in the case of the ARM6 and RISC 1—although some instructions handle longer or shorter operands. Numerical operands can be unsigned binary number words, such as memory addresses, or signed data words that employ twos-complement code. (Recall from section 3.2.1 that the same arithmetic circuits can be used with unsigned and twos-complement numbers.) Instructions often contain operand fields that are shorter than the standard word size, for example, the 13-bit immediate address field S2 in the RISC 1 format of Figure 3.28. This problem is unavoidable in RISC instruction sets where the instruction length and the standard word size are the same. Consequently, a systematic method is needed to extend short operand values to full-size, signed or unsigned numbers.

When a short m-bit, twos-complement number is used in an n-bit arithmetic operation where $n > m$, a technique called *sign extension* is employed. This techniques replicates the left-most bit s of the short operand N, which corresponds to its sign bit, $n - m$ times and attaches $s^{n-m} = ss...s$ to the left side of N. Sign extension

Figure 3.28
Instruction format of the Berkeley RISC 1.

changes a 13-bit operand

$$N = 10101 \ 01010101 \tag{3.22}$$

in the S2 field of Figure 3.28 to the 32-bit word

$$N_{\text{sign-extended}} = 11111111 \ 11111111 \ 11110101 \ 01010101 \tag{3.23}$$

In this case $s = 1$ and $n - m = 19$. If s were 0, then sign extension would precede N by 19 leading 0s. The point of sign extension is that it does not change the numerical value of a twos-complement number. For instance, both (3.22) and (3.23) represent the *same* negative integer, namely, $-2,646_{10}$, in twos-complement code, as can readily be verified. Sign extension maintains a number's correct sign and magnitude because it introduces only numerically insignificant leading 0s (positive numbers) or insignificant leading 1s (negative numbers). If N is to be treated as an unsigned binary number, then it is always extended by leading 0s, independent of the value of s. This technique has been called *zero extension*. Applying zero extension to (3.22) yields

$$N_{\text{zero-extended}} = 00000000 \ 00000000 \ 00010101 \ 01010101$$

Next we ask: How is an n-bit memory address, which is a long (typically 32-bit) unsigned integer, constructed from a short m-bit address field, when $n > m$? Zero extension alone is sometimes used for this purpose, but it does not allow the m-bit address to refer to all 2^n possible addresses. The usual solution found in CISCs as well as in RISCs is to treat a short memory address as a modifier, or *offset*, which is added (in zero-extended form) to a full-length memory address stored in a designated CPU register, called a *base register*. The RISC 1 uses its Rs register for this purpose, with S2 serving as the offset. The following store-byte instruction

$$\text{STB} \quad \text{Rs,Rd(S2)} \tag{3.24}$$

is designed to copy the byte from the right end of register Rs to the memory location whose address is Rd $+\text{S2}_{\text{zero-extended}}$. In practice, sign extension is often implicit and Rd $+\text{S2}_{\text{zero-extended}}$ is written simply as Rd $+$ S2. Hence (3.24) is equivalent to

$$\text{M(Rd + S2)} := \text{Rs[24:31]}$$

The final memory address Rd + S2 is an example of an *effective address*. As we will see shortly in our discussion of addressing modes, many other techniques are employed for constructing effective addresses.

EXAMPLE 3.5 INSTRUCTION FORMATS OF THE MIPS RX000 SERIES [KANE AND HEINRICH 1992]. MIPS Computer Systems (now a division of Silicon Graphics) introduced the MIPS RX000 series of microprocessors in 1986. The first members of the series, the MIPS R2000 and R3000, are 32-bit machines that have most of the classic RISC features: a streamlined instruction set, a load/store architecture, and an instruction pipeline to support a performance target of one instruction completed every clock cycle. Later RX000 machines, such as the R10000 announced in 1994, add various extensions to the "MIPS I" architecture implemented in the R2000 and R3000; we will confine our discussion to the MIPS I case.

The RX000 is noteworthy for its simple and regular instruction formats, which we now examine in detail. As seen from Figure 3.29, all the RX000 instructions are one word (32 bits) in length and contain a 6-bit opcode in a fixed position. The remaining

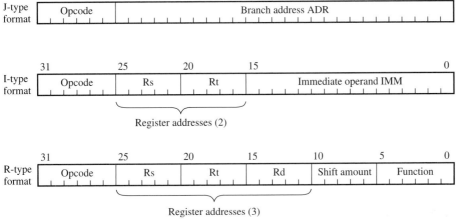

Figure 3.29
Instruction formats of the MIPS RX000.

26 bits are used in various ways, depending on the instruction type. Any operands included in the instruction must be less than a full word in length, so some way is needed to extend them to a full-size memory address or a twos-complement number.

In the case of a J-type (jump or branch) instruction, the 26 operand bits form a memory address ADR, which is the target or branch address. For example, a simple unconditional branch instruction has the J-type format

$$\text{J} \quad \text{ADR} \tag{3.25}$$

meaning **go to** ADR. Since RX000 memory addresses are 32 bits long, the PCU must extend the 26-bit address field ADR in (3.25) to 32 bits. This is done automatically by the following two-step process:

$$\text{Temp} := \text{PC[31:28].ADR.00;}$$
$$\text{PC} := \text{Temp;}$$

First the four high-order bits from the program counter PC are placed in front of ADR and 00 is appended to it. Then the resulting 32-bit word is made the new contents of PC.

The above address-extension method confines the possible branch addresses to a 2^{26}-word region of memory space near the location of the current branch instruction. However, this is not as restrictive as it might appear. First of all, recall that a 32-bit memory address refers to just one byte. Only 2^{30} instructions can be placed in a 2^{32}-byte memory, so only 30 bits are really needed to locate an instruction. The RX000 and similar machines always assign instructions to memory word locations with addresses that end in 00; that is, all instructions are aligned with the natural word boundaries in M. Moreover, while the 26-bit address field ADR is still 4 bits short of 30, the size of the accessible region for branching ($2^{26} \approx 6.71 \times 10^7$ different addresses) is more than adequate for most programming purposes—and can be increased by software means, if necessary.

The other two formats shown in Figure 3.29 specify register addresses using either two or three 5-bit fields. The RX000 has $2^5 = 32$ general-purpose registers in its register file, so register addresses can be fully specified with no difficulty. The second

(I type) format is used by ALU-immediate instructions such as

$$\text{ADDI} \quad \text{Rs,Rt,IMM}$$

which adds the contents of the instruction's immediate address field, that is, bits 15:0 of the instruction, to the contents of register Rs and places the result in register Rt. To convert the immediate operand IMM from 16 to 32 bits, it is sign-extended to 32 bits by duplicating its left-most bit to obtain bits 31:16.

The third (R type) format of the RX000 is used by data-processing instructions that have a natural three-address format to define operations of the form $X_1 := op(X_2, X_3)$. For instance, the add-register instruction

$$\text{ADD} \quad \text{Rd,Rs,Rt}$$

performs the 32-bit addition

$$\text{Rd} := \text{Rs} + \text{Rt}$$

using the contents of the named registers. Since the register addresses occupy only 15 bits of the instruction format, the remaining 11 bits are used in various ways to increase (and complicate) the range of operations that can be performed. In effect, they serve as extensions to the opcode. For example, there are six shift-register instructions, all of which use instruction bits 10:6 to specify the amount by which the target register's contents are to be shifted. The shift-left logical instruction

$$\text{SLL} \quad \text{Rd,Rt,Shamt}$$

shifts the contents of register Rt left by Shamt (shift amount) bits; it inserts 0s in the vacated positions on the right and places the result in Rd. In other words,

$$\text{Rt} := \text{Rd}[31-\text{Shamt}:0].0^{\text{Shamt}}$$

where 0^k denotes a string of k 0s.

For load and store instructions, the RX000 uses the typical RISC technique of providing a short address in the instruction, which serves as an offset to a full-length address stored in a CPU register. The I-type format of Figure 3.29 is used for load and store instructions. In this case Rs serves as the base register, and Rt serves as the data source (for store) or destination (for load). The instruction that loads a word into the CPU has the assembly-language format

$$\text{LW} \quad \text{Rt, IMM(Rs)}$$

which causes the 16-bit immediate address IMM, that is, the offset, to be sign-extended to 32 bits and added to the contents of Rs to form the effective address. This address is then used to read a word of data from M into register Rt. In HDL terms

$$\text{Rt} := \text{M(Rs + IMM)}$$

Addressing modes. The purpose of an address field is to point to the current value $V(X)$ of some operand X used by an instruction. This value can be specified in various ways, which are termed *addressing modes*. The addressing mode of X affects the following issues:

- The speed with which $V(X)$ can be accessed by the CPU.
- The ease with which $V(X)$ can be specified and altered.

Access speed is influenced by the physical location of $V(X)$—normally the CPU or the external memory M. Operand values located in CPU registers, such as the general-register file and the program counter PC, can be accessed faster than operands in M. It is therefore usual to favor instructions that address CPU registers, both in the design of instruction sets and in their use in computer programs. An operand's accessibility is also affected by the directness of its addressing mode: The address field X itself can be $V(X)$, it can specify directly the location of $V(X)$, or it can identify a location that specifies directly the location of $V(X)$. We can thus distinguish the number of *levels of indirection* associated with an address. The advantage of indirection, as we will see, is increased programming flexibility. We can achieve further flexibility by providing addresses that are automatically altered or *indexed*, for example, to step through an array of consecutive addresses.

If the value $V(X)$ of the target operand is contained in the address field itself, then X is called an *immediate operand* and the corresponding addressing mode is *immediate addressing*. By implication X is a constant, since it is very undesirable to modify instruction fields during execution.[4] More often than not, X is a variable in the usual mathematical sense, and the corresponding address field identifies the storage location that contains the required value $V(X)$. Thus X corresponds to a variable, and its value $V(X)$ can be varied without modifying the instruction address field. Operand specification of this type is called *direct addressing*.

The addressing modes of the operands appearing in a machine-language instruction, which can vary from operand to operand, are defined in the instruction's opcode. Some assembly languages allow addressing modes to be similarly defined by distinct opcodes. For example, the assembly language of the Intel 8085 series has the opcode MOV (move) to specify data transfers involving direct addressing only. Therefore, the register-to-register transfer $A := B$, for instance, is specified by

$$\text{MOV} \quad \text{A,B} \tag{3.26}$$

The A and B operands of (3.26) are considered to be directly addressed, since the contents of the named registers are the desired operand values. In contrast, to specify the operation A := 99, where 99 is an immediate operand, the 8085 instruction

$$\text{MVI} \quad \text{A,99} \tag{3.27}$$

with the opcode MVI (*move immediate*) must be used. Note that (3.27) uses both the direct and immediate addressing modes.

Most assembly languages take a different approach by specifying the addressing modes in the operand fields. For example, the Motorola 680X0 equivalents of (3.26) and (3.27), with D1 = A and D2 = B are

$$\text{MOVE} \quad \text{D2,D1}$$

and
$$\text{MOVE} \quad \text{\#99,D1} \tag{3.28}$$

respectively. (Note that the Motorola operand order is reversed with respect to the Intel convention.) In (3.28) the prefix # indicates that the immediate addressing mode is to be used for the operand in question. Deleting the # from (3.28) causes

---

[4]Self-modifying programs like the IAS code shown in Figure 1.15 (section 1.2.2) reflect the inadequacy of the addressing modes available in the earliest computers.

the first operand to refer to the data in memory location 99, that is, M(99), which would be an instance of direct memory addressing.

It is sometimes useful to change the location (as opposed to the value) of X without changing the address fields of any instructions that refer to X. This may be accomplished by *indirect addressing*, whereby the instruction contains the address W of a storage location, which in turn contains the address X of the desired operand value $V(X)$. By changing the contents of W, the address of the operand value required by the instruction is effectively changed. While direct addressing requires only one fetch operation to obtain an operand value, indirect addressing requires two. Figure 3.30 illustrates these different ways of specifying operands in the case of three load instructions that transfer the number 999 to the CPU register AC.

The ability to use all addressing modes in a uniform and consistent way with all opcodes of an instruction set or assembly language is a desirable feature termed *orthogonality*. Orthogonal instruction sets simplify programming both by reducing the number of distinct opcodes needed and by simplifying the rules for operand address specification. Many CISC computers like the 680X0 have little orthogonality, since processor costs can be reduced (at the expense of programming costs) by restricting instructions to a few frequently used addressing modes that vary from instruction to instruction.

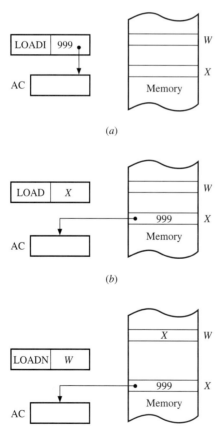

Figure 3.30
Three basic addressing modes: (*a*) immediate; (*b*) direct; (*c*) indirect.

Relative addressing. *Absolute addressing*, conceptually the simplest mode of direct address formation, requires the complete operand address to appear in the instruction operand field. This address is used without modification (except, perhaps, zero or sign extension in the case of a short address field) to access the desired data item. Frequently, only partial addressing information is included in the instruction, so the CPU must construct the complete (absolute) address. One of the commonest address construction techniques is *relative addressing,* in which the operand field contains a relative address, also called an *offset* or *displacement D.* The instruction also implicitly or explicitly identifies other storage locations R_1, $R_2,...,R_k$ (usually CPU registers) containing additional addressing information. The *effective address A* of an operand is then some function $f(D,R_1,R_2,...,R_k)$. In most cases of interest, each operand is associated with a single address register R from a set of general-purpose address registers, and A is computed by adding D to the contents of R, that is,

$$A := R + D$$

R may also be a special-purpose address register such as the program counter PC.
There are several reasons for using relative addressing.

1. Since all the address information need not be included in the instructions, instruction length is reduced.
2. By changing the contents of R, the processor can change the absolute addresses referred to by a block of instructions B. This address modification permits the processor to move (relocate) the entire block B from one region of main memory to another without invalidating the addresses in B. When used in this way, R may be referred to as a *base register* and its contents as a *base address.*
3. R can be used for storing indexes to facilitate the processing of indexed data. In this role R is called an *index register.* The indexed items $X(0)$, $X(1),...,X(k)$ are stored in consecutive addresses in memory. The instruction-address field D contains the address of the first item $X(0)$, while the index register R contains the index i. The address of item $X(i)$ is $D + R$. By changing the contents of the index register, a single instruction can be made to refer to any item $X(i)$ in the given data list.

The main drawbacks of relative addressing are the extra logic circuits and processing time needed to compute addresses.
So far we have assumed that each operand is a single memory word and can therefore be specified by a single address. If an instruction must process variable-length data consisting of many words, each operand specification is divided into two parts: an address field that points to the location of the first word of the operand and a length field L that indicates the number of words in the operand. The CPU automatically increments the instruction address field as successive words of the operand are accessed. The access is complete when L words have been accessed.
Indexed items are frequently accessed sequentially so that a reference to $X(k)$ stored in memory location A is immediately followed by a reference to $X(k + 1)$ or $X(k-1)$ stored in location $A + 1$ or $A -1$, respectively. To facilitate stepping through a sequence of items in this manner, addressing modes that automatically increment or decrement an address can be defined; the resulting address-modification process

is called *autoindexing*. In the case of the Motorola 680X0 series [Motorola 1989], the address field –(A3) appearing in an assembly-language instruction indicates that the contents of the designated address register A3 should be decremented automatically before the instruction is executed; this process is called *predecrementing*. Similarly, (A3)+ specifies that A3 should be incremented automatically after the current instruction has been executed (*postincrementing*). In each case the amount of the address increment or decrement is the length in bytes of the indexed operands.

Most processors have only a few, simple addressing modes for CPU registers, principally direct and immediate addressing. Immediate addresses represent data values that come with the instruction fetch and are placed in the instruction register IR. In *register direct addressing,* the address (name) R of the register containing the desired value $V(R)$ appears in the instruction. The Motorola 680X0 instruction

$$\text{MOVE} \quad \#99, \text{D1}$$

which means "move the constant 99 to data register D1," uses immediate addressing for 99 and register direct (or simply direct) addressing for D1.

The term *register indirect addressing* refers to indirect addressing with a register R name in the address field. It is often used to access memory, in which case R becomes a memory address register. For example,

$$\text{MOVE.B} \quad (\text{A0}), \text{D1}$$

uses parentheses to indicate that (A0) is an indirect address involving the 680X0's A0 addresss register. This move-byte instruction—the opcodes's .B suffix specifies a 1-byte operand—corresponds to

$$\text{D1}[7:0] := \text{M(A0)}$$

and copies the byte addressed by A0 into the low-order byte position of data register D1. (The other three bytes of D1 are unchanged.) An extension of this addressing mode is *register indirect with offset,* which can also be viewed as a type of base or indexed addressing. This mode is the only memory addressing mode employed by the MIPS RX000 series (Example 3.5). The RX000's store-word instruction, for example, is written as

$$\text{SW} \quad \text{Rt, OFFSET(Rs)} \tag{3.29}$$

where Rs is the base register and OFFSET is a number acting as an (immediate) offset operand. Instruction (3.29) is equivalent to the HDL statement

$$\text{M(Rs + OFFSET)} := \text{Rt}$$

where the offset is sign-extended before adding it to Rs to obtain the effective address Rs + OFFSET. The PowerPC has two addressing modes: register indirect with offset as described above (but called *register indirect with immediate index*) and a second mode (called *register indirect with index*) in which the effective address is Rs + Ri, where Ri is a register name.

The Motorola 680X0, like other CISC-style architectures, has many addressing modes, including the following: immediate, register direct, register indirect, register indirect with postincrement, register indirect with predecrement, register indirect with offset, register indirect with index, absolute short, absolute long, PC with offset, and PC with index. Its autoindexing features are illustrated in the following example.

EXAMPLE 3.6 STACK CONTROL IN THE MOTOROLA 680X0 [GILL, CORWIN AND LOGAR 1987; MOTOROLA 1989]. A *stack* is a sequence of storage locations that are accessible from only one end referred to as the *top of the stack*. A write operation addressed to a stack, termed a *push* operation, stores a new item at the top of the stack, while a read operation, termed a *pop* operation, removes the item stored at the top of the stack. Push or pop changes the position of the stack top by an amount that depends on the length of the operand pushed or popped. A stack is controlled by an address register called the *stack pointer* SP. This register stores the address of the last operand placed in the stack; that address is automatically adjusted after a push or pop operation so that SP contains the address of the new stack top.

Some computers—the Intel 80X86, for example—have special instructions and hardware for handling stacks that are intended as communication areas for program-control instructions like call and return. A few early computers such as the Burroughs B6500/7500 even employed stacks in place of general-register files; see Example 1.5 (section 1.2.3). The Motorola 680X0 has no explicit hardware for stack support, but, as we now show, its various addressing modes make it easy to treat any contiguous region of its external memory M as a stack.

Suppose that the programmer designates the address register A2 of the 680X0 to be a stack pointer and that the stack grows toward the low addresses of M. To push the contents of a data register, say, D6, into the stack requires the single instruction

$$\text{MOVE.L} \quad \text{D6}, -(\text{A2}) \tag{3.30}$$

The input operand is the 4-byte contents of D6, which is directly addressed in (3.30), while the output operand, which is the new contents of the top of the stack, is designated by –(A2), which denotes indirect addressing with predecrementing using address register A2. This push instruction is equivalent to the following HDL operations:

$$\text{A2} := \text{A2} - 4; \quad \text{M(A2)} := \text{D6};$$

Figure 3.31 shows the state of the affected parts of the CPU and M immediately before (Figure 3.31*a*) and immediately after (Figure 3.31*b*) execution of instruction (3.30). Observe how the data bytes are stored in M according to the big-endian convention.

It is easily seen that the pop instruction corresponding to (3.30) is

$$\text{MOVE.L} \quad \text{(A2)}+, \text{D6} \tag{3.31}$$

which is equivalent to

$$\text{D6} := \text{M(A2)}; \quad \text{A2} := \text{A2} + 4;$$

In this case the operand (A2)+ employs the register indirect with postincrement addressing mode.

Number of addresses. Some computers, notably CISCs like the 680X0, have instructions of several different lengths containing various numbers of addresses. A source of controversy in the early days was the question of how many explicit operand addresses to include in instructions. Clearly the fewer the addresses, the shorter the instruction format needed. However, limiting the number of addresses also limits the range of operations that an instruction can perform. Roughly speaking, fewer addresses mean more primitive instructions and therefore longer

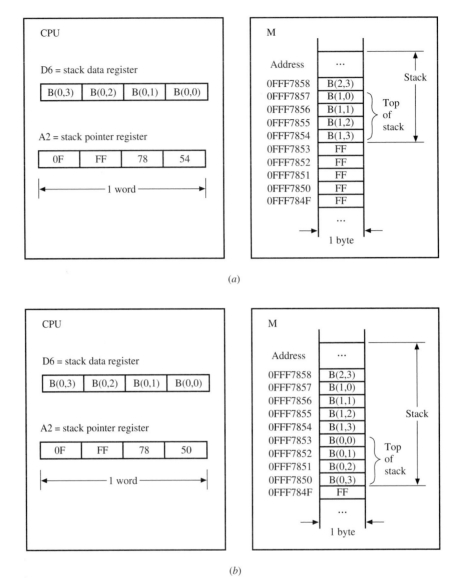

Figure 3.31
State of the Motorola 680X0 (*a*) immediately before and (*b*) immediately after
execution of the push instruction MOVE.L D6,–(A2).

programs to perform a given task. While the storage requirements of shorter
instructions and longer programs tend to balance, larger programs require longer
execution times. On the other hand, long instructions with multiple addresses
require more complex decoding and processing circuits. RISC instructions, with
the exception of load and store, contain short register addresses only, so two or
three addresses can be accommodated within a short and fixed-length instruction
word.

Most instructions require no more than three distinct operands. For example, the fundamental arithmetic operations—addition, subtraction, multiplication, and division—require three operands: two input operands and one output operand. A three-address instruction can therefore specify all needed operands. For example, the three-address add instruction

$$ADD \quad Z, X, Y$$

means add the contents of memory locations X and Y and place the result in location Z; that is, $Z := X + Y$. A one-address add instruction has the format

$$ADD \quad X$$

The unspecified operands are assumed to be stored in fixed locations such as the accumulator AC, in which case the instruction specifies the operation $AC := AC + X$. In the case of a two-address instruction, the accumulator is used to store the result (the sum) only.

$$ADD \quad X, Y$$

has the typical interpretation $AC := X + Y$. Another possibility is to use one address, say, X, to store both the addend X and the sum as follows: $X := X + Y$. In the latter case the addition operation destroys the X operand. Figures 3.32a, b, and c show how processors that employ one-address, two-address, and three-address instructions, respectively, might implement the operation

$$X := A \times B + C \times C \tag{3.32}$$

where the four operands A, B, C, and X are assumed to be stored in external memory.

A few computers have been designed so that most instructions contain no explicit addresses; they can be called *zero-address* machines; see also Example 1.5. Addresses are eliminated by storing operands in a push-down stack. All operands used by a zero-address instruction are required to be in the top locations in the stack. For example, the addition $X + Y$ is invoked by an instruction such as

$$ADD$$

that causes the top two operands, which should be X and Y, to be removed from the stack and added. The resulting sum $X + Y$ is then placed at the top of the stack. A stack pointer automatically keeps track of the stack top. Push and pop instructions are needed to transfer data to and from the stack. PUSH X causes the contents of X to be placed at the top of the stack. POP X causes the top word in the stack to be transferred to location X. Note that PUSH and POP are not themselves zero-address instructions; as implemented by (3.30) and (3.31), for instance, they are two-address instructions. Figure 3.33 shows how a program for (3.32) might be constructed for a zero-address, stack machine.

3.3.2 Instruction Types

We now turn to the question: What types of instructions should be included in a general-purpose processor's instruction set? We are concerned with the instructions

Instruction	Comments
LOAD A	Transfer A to accumulator AC.
MULTIPLY B	AC := AC × B
STORE T	Transfer AC to memory location T.
LOAD C	Transfer C to accumulator AC.
MULTIPLY C	AC := AC × C
ADD T	AC := AC + T
STORE X	Transfer result to memory location X.

(a) One-address machine

Instruction	Comments
MOVE T,A	T := A
MULTIPLY T,B	T := T × B
MOVE X,C	X := C
MULTIPLY X,C	X := X × C
ADD X,T	X := X + T

(b) Two-address machine

Instruction	Comments
MULTIPLY T,A,B	T := A × B
MULTIPLY X,C,C	X := C × C
ADD X,X,T	X := X + T

(c) Three-address machine

Figure 3.32
Programs to execute the operation $X := A \times B + C \times C$ in one-address, two-address, and three-address processors.

that are in the processor's machine language. All processors have a well-defined machine language, and some implement a lower-level "micromachine" language specified by microinstructions. A typical machine instruction defines one or two register transfer (micro) operations, and a sequence of such instructions is needed to implement a statement in a high-level programming language such as C. Because of the complexity of the operations, data types, and syntax of high-level languages, few attempts have been made to construct computers whose machine language directly corresponds to a high-level language. As noted earlier, there is a semantic gap between problem-specification languages and the machine instruction set that implements them, a gap that language-translation programs such as compilers and assemblers must bridge.

The requirements to be satisfied by an instruction set can be stated in the following general, but rather imprecise, terms:

Instruction	Comments
PUSH A	Transfer A to top of stack.
PUSH B	Transfer B to top of stack.
MULTIPLY	Remove A,B from stack and replace by $A \times B$.
PUSH C	Transfer C to top of stack.
PUSH C	Transfer second copy of C to top of stack.
MULTIPLY	Remove C,C from stack and replace by $C \times C$.
ADD	Remove $C \times C$, $A \times B$ from stack and replace by their sum.
POP X	Transfer result from top of stack to X.

Figure 3.33
Program to execute $X := A \times B + C \times C$ in a zero-address, stack processor.

- It should be *complete* in the sense that we should be able to construct a machine-language program to evaluate any function that is computable using a reasonable amount of memory space.
- It should be *efficient* in that frequently required functions can be performed rapidly using relatively few instructions.
- It should be *regular* in that the instruction set should contain expected opcodes and addressing modes; for example, if there is a left shift, there should be a right shift.
- To reduce both hardware and software design costs, the instructions may be required to be *compatible* with those of existing machines—previous members of the same computer family, for instance.

Because of the wide variation in CPU architectures between different computer families, standard machine or assembly languages do not exist. There are, nevertheless, broad similarities between all instruction sets, which go back to the IAS computer and other early machines.

Completeness. A function $f(x)$ is said to be *computable* if it can be evaluated in a finite number of steps by a Turing machine (see section 1.1.1). While real computers differ from Turing machines in having only a finite amount of memory, they can, in practice, evaluate any computable function to a reasonable degree of approximation. When viewed as instruction-set processors, Turing machines have a very simple instruction set. In our discussion of Turing machines, we defined four instruction types: write, move tape one square to the left, move tape one square to the right, and halt, all of which are conditional on the control processor's state. It follows that complete instruction sets can be constructed for finite-state machines using equally simple instruction types. In fact, computers have been proposed that employ only a single type of instruction; see problem 3.44. While very small instruction sets require simple, and therefore inexpensive, logic circuits to implement them, they lead to excessively complex programs. There is therefore a fundamental trade-off between processor simplicity and programming complexity.

Instructions are conveniently divided into the following five types:

1. *Data-transfer* instructions, which copy information from one location to another either in the processor's internal register set or in the external main memory.
2. *Arithmetic* instructions, which perform operations on numerical data.
3. *Logical* instructions, which include Boolean and other nonnumerical operations.
4. *Program-control* instructions, such as branch instructions, which change the sequence in which programs are executed.
5. *Input-output* (IO) instructions, which cause information to be transferred between the processor or its main memory and external IO devices.

These types are not mutually exclusive. For example, the arithmetic instruction $A := B + C$ implements the data transfer $A := B$ when C is set to zero.

Figure 3.34 lists representative instructions from the five types defined above, which have been culled from the instruction sets of various computers. The data-transfer instructions, particularly load and store, are the most frequently used instructions in computer programs, despite the fact that they involve no explicit computation. The arithmetic instructions cover a wide range of operations and are sometimes used as a rough measure of the complexity of an instruction set. The logical instructions include the word-based Boolean operations, as well as operations that have no obvious numerical interpretation. The major branch instructions are jump (un)conditionally and the call and return instructions used for subroutine linkage. The simplest IO instructions are data-transfer instructions addressed to IO ports, which transfer one or more words between an IO port and either the CPU or M. If the CPU delegates control of IO operations to an IO processor (IOP), the CPU needs instructions that enable it to supervise the execution of IO programs by the IOP. Instructions that are specific to particular IO devices, such as REWIND TAPE, PRINT LINE, and SCAN KEYBOARD, are treated as data by the CPU and IOP and are interpreted as instructions only by the IO devices to which they are transferred.

The completeness of an instruction set can be demonstrated informally by showing that it can program certain key operations in each of the five instruction groups. It must be possible to transfer a word between the processor and any memory location. It must be possible to add two numbers, so an add instruction is included in most instruction sets. Other arithmetic operations can readily be programmed using addition. As noted in section 3.2.2, subtraction of twos-complement numbers requires addition and logical complementation (NOT) only. More complex arithmetic operations such as multiplication, division, and exponentiation can be programmed using addition, subtraction, and shifting, as in Example 2.7. If a logically complete set of Boolean operations such as {AND,NOT} is in the instruction set, then any other Boolean operation can be programmed. Branching requires at least one conditional branch instruction that tests some stored quantity and alters the instruction execution sequence based on the test outcome. An unconditional branch can easily be realized by a conditional branch instruction.

RISC versus CISC. While an instruction set that is limited to two or three instructions is impractical, there is no agreement about the appropriate size or membership of a general-purpose instruction set. Early computers like the IAS had a small and simple instruction set forced by the need to minimize the amount of

Type	Operation name(s)	Description
Data transfer	MOVE	Copy word or block from source to destination.
	LOAD	Copy word from memory to processor register.
	STORE	Copy word from processor register to memory.
	SWAP (EXCHANGE)	Swap contents of source and destination.
	CLEAR	Transfer word of 0s to destination.
	SET	Transfer word of 1s to destination.
	PUSH	Transfer word from source to top of stack.
	POP	Transfer word from top of stack to destination.
Arithmetic	ADD	Compute sum of two operands.
	ADD WITH CARRY	Compute sum of two operands and a carry bit.
	SUBTRACT	Compute difference of two operands.
	MULTIPLY	Compute product of two operands.
	DIVIDE	Compute quotient (and remainder) of two operands.
	MULITPLY AND ADD	Compute product of two operands; add it to a third operand.
	ABSOLUTE	Replace operand by its absolute value.
	NEGATE	Change sign of operand.
	INCREMENT	Add 1 to operand.
	DECREMENT	Subtract 1 from operand.
	ARITHMETIC SHIFT	Shift operand left (right) with sign extension.
Logical	AND	
	OR	Perform the specified logical operation bitwise.
	NOT	
	EXCLUSIVE-OR	
	LOGICAL SHIFT	Shift operand left (right) introducing 0s at end.
	ROTATE	Left- (right-) shift operand around closed path.
	CONVERT (EDIT)	Change data format, for example, from binary to decimal.
Program control	JUMP (BRANCH)	Unconditional transfer; load PC with specified address.
	JUMP CONDITIONAL	Test specified conditions; if true, load PC with specified address.
	JUMP TO SUBROUTINE (BRANCH-AND-LINK)	Place current program control information including PC in known location, for example, top of stack; jump to specified address.
	RETURN	Restore current program control information including PC from known location, for example, from top of stack.
	EXECUTE	Fetch operand from specified location and execute as instruction; note that PC is not modified.
	SKIP CONDITIONAL	Test specified condition; if true, increment PC to skip next instruction.
	TRAP (SOFTWARE INTERRUPT)	Enter supervisor mode.
	TEST	Test specified condition; set flag(s) based on outcome.
	COMPARE	Make logical or arithmetic comparison of two or more operands; set flag(s) based on outcome.

Figure 3.34
List of common instruction types.

Type	Operation name(s)	Description
Program control	SET CONTROL VARIABLES	Large class of instructions to set controls for protection purposes, interrupt handling, timer control, and so forth (often privileged).
	WAIT (HOLD)	Stop program execution; test a specified condition continuously; when the condition is satisfied, resume instruction execution.
	NO OPERATION	No operation is performed, but program execution continues.
Input-output	INPUT (READ)	Copy data from specified IO port to destination, for example, output contents of a memory location or processor register.
	OUTPUT (WRITE)	Copy data from specified source to IO port.
	START IO	Transfer instuctions to IOP to initiate an IO operation.
	TEST IO	Transfer status information from IO system to specified destination.
	HALT IO	Transfer instructions to IOP to terminate an IO operation.

Figure 3.34
(continued).

CPU hardware. These instruction sets included only the most frequently used operations such as load a register from memory, store a result in memory, and add two fixed-point numbers. As hardware became cheaper, instructions tended to increase both in number and complexity so that by 1980 a typical computer had dozens of instruction types, with versions to handle several data types and addressing modes. These large instruction sets contain infrequently used but hard-to-program operations like floating-point divide. Since such operations are primitives in programming languages, they serve to reduce the semantic gap between the user's language and the computer's. However, complex instructions lead to a number of complications in both hardware and software design, which we now consider.

Suppose that a particular operation F can be implemented either by a single complex instruction I_F or by a multiinstruction routine P_F composed of simple instructions. Execution of P_F will generally be slower than execution of I_F because the processor must spend more time fetching the instructions of P_F and, depending on the nature of F, handling the intermediate data that links the instructions. A further drawback of P_F is that it occupies more memory space than I_F occupies. An obvious disadvantage of I_F is that it adds to the complexity of a processor's control unit, thereby increasing both the size of the processor and the time required to design it.

Clearly a program involving F is simplified by using I_F in place of P_F. When the program is written in a high-level language, however, as most programs are, the execution speedup that justifies a complex instruction like I_F may not be fully realizable. A compiler will typically translate F into the corresponding machine instruction I_F, if available, which uses fixed CPU registers and has a fixed execution time. On the other hand, if I_F is not available, an efficient or *optimizing* compiler may be able to generate object code Q_F corresponding to P_F that exploits information known at compilation time to reduce F's execution time. Suppose, for instance, that F is fixed-point multiplication and is implemented by both I_F and Q_F via a shift-and-add algorithm of the kind described in Example 2.7. If one of F's operands is a small constant or zero, then the compiler can easily generate a shorter form of P_F that is faster than the generic n-step multiply instruction I_F. The speed gap between I_F and P_F can also be narrowed by designing the small instruction set required for P_F to reduce the instruction fetch and execute cycle times as far as possible, preferably to one CPU clock cycle each. Another speed advantage of P_F over I_F is that P_F can be interrupted in midoperation at an appropriate instruction boundary, whereas I_F must proceed to termination before the CPU can respond to an interrupt.

Motivated by considerations of the foregoing sort, a number of computer designers advocated machines with relatively small and simple instruction sets, which have been dubbed *RISCs* for reduced instruction-set computers. *RISC* architecture is contrasted with the *complex instruction-set computer* (*CISC*) architecture found in most pre-1980 designs such as the IBM System/360-370 and the Motorola 680X0. The major attributes of RISCs have been defined as follows [Colwell et al. 1985]:

- Relatively few instruction types and addressing modes.
- Fixed and easily decoded instruction formats.
- Fast, single-cycle instruction execution.
- Hardwired rather than microprogrammed control.
- Memory access limited mainly to load and store instructions.
- Use of compilers to optimize object-code performance.

Several of these RISC attributes are closely related. For example, the small size and regularity of the instruction set simplifies the design of a hardwired program control unit, which in turn facilitates the achievement of fast single-cycle execution. The stress placed on efficient compilation requires the machine architects and compiler writers to cooperate closely in the design process.

RISC architectures restrict the instructions that access memory to load and store. Consequently, most RISC instructions involve only register-to-register operations that are internal to the CPU. To support them, a larger-than-usual number of registers may be placed in the CPU. This design facilitates single-cycle execution and minimizes the CPU cycle time. Pipelining the instruction execution process also supports single-cycle execution. Since complex instructions are not in the instruction set, they must be implemented by multiinstruction routines, which prompts the attention to efficient compilation. Machine code compiled for a RISC computer is likely to have more instructions than the corresponding CISC code but can execute more efficiently, especially if only fixed-point (integer) instructions are involved. However, if the frequency of complex operations is high, then the performance of the CISC machine may be better than that of the RISC machine.

EXAMPLE 3.7 INSTRUCTION SET OF THE MIPS RX000 [KANE AND HEINRICH 1992]. The RX000 microprocessor series and its instruction formats were introduced in Example 3.5 (section 3.3.1). A microprocessor in this family is implemented by a single IC and has the major components indicated in Figure 3.35. These include a file of 32 general-purpose 32-bit registers and the processing logic to perform the basic fixed-point ALU functions: add, subtract, multiply, divide and logical operations using 32-bit operands. Numerical operands are treated as unsigned or signed integers in twos-complement code. One register R0 in the register file permanently stores the constant zero. Some special-purpose arithmetic circuits perform address computation. The

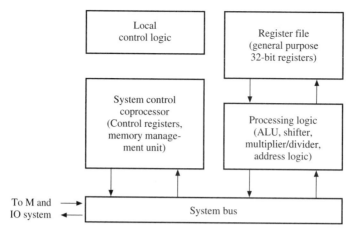

Figure 3.35
Overall organization of the MIPS RX000.

overall organization of the RX000 E-unit is similar to that of the ARM6 (Figure 3.9). As in the ARM6 case, the E-unit of the RX000 is pipelined to support the goal of executing instructions at a peak rate of one instruction per clock cycle. Floating-point operations meeting the requirements of the IEEE 754 standard are supported by an on-chip or off-chip floating-point unit (FPU).

In addition to the control logic needed for instruction execution, the RX000 contains a unit referred to as the *system control coprocessor* whose functions include communication with external memory (caches and main memory) and the automatic address translation logic needed to support a virtual memory system. The virtual memory feature uncouples the address space seen by the programmer from the computer's physical address space, making it possible, for example, to run a large program in a small amount of physical memory. The system control coprocessor is essentially invisible to the applications programmer. The RX000 can have several additional coprocessors implemented on additional ICs.

We now consider in detail the RX000's basic (MIPS I) instruction set, which is summarized in Figure 3.36. There are 74 types, divided almost equally between data-transfer, data-processing, and program-control instructions. All are 32 bits long and use one of the I, J, and R formats illustrated in Figure 3.29. The smallest addressable item in external memory M is, as usual, an 8-bit byte, which requires a 32-bit address to specify its location. Smaller address fields such as the 26-bit branch address field of J-type instructions are automatically extended to 32 bits before loading into the program counter PC. Note that to increment PC to point to the next sequential instruction of a program requires the step PC := PC + 4. The 16-bit (half-word) IMM field of I-type instructions serves either as an immediate data operand or else as an address offset. In either case it is also extended to 32 bits either by zero extension or by sign extension. During initialization, the microprocessor can be reset to store data according to either the big-endian or the little-endian convention.

Following the basic RISC philosophy, communication between the CPU and external memory M is via load and store instructions only, using the I-type format (Figure 3.29). The RX000 has instructions to load and store data in bytes and half-words (2 bytes), as well as full, 4-byte words. If a byte or half-word is to be loaded into a CPU register, then the loaded item is expanded to a full word by sign extension, unless the "unsigned" version of the load instruction is specified, in which case zero extension is

Type	Instruction	Assembly-language format	Narrative format (comment)
Data transfer	Load byte	LB Rt,Source	Load register Rt with sign-extended memory byte.
	Load byte unsigned	LBU Rt,Source	Load register Rt with zero-extended memory half-word.
	Load half-word	LH Rt,Source	Load register Rt with sign-extended memory half-word.
	Load half-word unsigned	LHU Rt,Source	Load register Rt with zero-extended memory half-word.
	Load word	LW Rt,Source	Load register Rt with memory word.
	Load word left	LWL Rt,Source	Load left side of register Rt with 1 to 3 memory bytes.
	Load word right	LWR Rt,Source	Load right side of register Rt with 1 to 3 memory bytes.
	Store byte	SB Rt,Dest	Store least significant byte of register Rt in memory.
	Store half-word	SH Rt,Dest	Store least significant half-word of register Rt in memory.
	Store word	SW Rt,Dest	Store register Rt in memory.
	Store word left	SWL Rt,Dest	Store left 1 to 3 bytes of register Rt in memory.
	Store word right	SWR Rt,Dest	Store right 1 to 3 bytes of register Rt in memory.
	Load upper immediate	LUI Rt,IMM	Move immediate operand IMM.0^{16} into register Rt.

(Four special register-move instructions for use with multiplication and division)

(Eight special data-transfer instructions for use with coprocessors, including the system control coprocessor)

Type	Instruction	Assembly-language format	Narrative format (comment)
Data processing	Add	ADD Rd,Rs,Rt	Add Rs to Rt; put result in Rd (trap on overflow).
	Add unsigned	ADDU Rd,Rs,Rt	Add Rs to Rt; put result in Rd.
	Add immediate	ADDI Rt,Rs,IMM	Add sign-extended IMM to Rs; put result in Rt (trap on overflow).
	Add immediate unsigned	ADDIU Rt,Rs,IMM	Add sign-extended IMM to Rs; put result in Rt.
	Subtract	SUB Rd,Rs,Rt	Subtract Rt from Rs; put result in Rd (trap on overflow).
	Subtract unsigned	SUBU Rd,Rs,Rt	Subtract Rt from Rs; put result in Rd.
	AND	AND Rd,Rs,Rt	Bitwise AND Rt and Rs; put result in Rd.
	AND immediate	ANDI Rt,Rs,IMM	Bitwise AND zero-extended IMM and Rs; put results in Rt.
	NOR	NOR Rd,Rs,Rt	Bitwise NOR Rt and Rs; put result in Rd.
	OR	OR Rd,Rs,Rt	Bitwise OR Rt and Rs; put result in Rd.
	OR immediate	ORI Rt,Rs,IMM	Bitwise OR zero-extended IMM and Rs; put result in Rt.
	XOR	XOR Rd,Rs,Rt	Bitwise XOR Rt and Rs; put result in Rd.

Figure 3.36
Instruction set of the MIPS RX000.

Type	Instruction	Assembly-language format	Narrative format (comment)
	XOR immediate	XORI Rt,Rs,IMM	Bitwise XOR zero-extended IMM and Rs; put result in Rt.
	Set on less than	SLT Rd,Rs,Rt	Compare Rt with Rs as signed integers; if Rs < Rt, then Rd := 1, else Rd := 0.
	Set on less than unsigned	SLTU Rd,Rs,Rt	Compare Rt with Rs as unsigned integers; if Rs < Rt, then Rd := 1, else Rd := 0.
	Set on less than immediate	SLTI Rt,Rs,IMM	Compare sign-extended IMM with Rs as signed integers; if IMM < Rs, then Rt := 1, else Rt := 0.
	Set on less than immediate unsigned	SLTIU Rt,Rs,IMM	Compare sign-extended IMM with Rs as unsigned integers; if IMM < Rs, then Rt := 1, else Rt := 0.
	(Two multiply and two divide instructions)		
	(Six logical and arithmetic shift instructions)		
Program control	Jump	J ADR	Jump unconditionally to address ADR.
	Jump and link	JAL ADR	Place PC + 8 in R31 and jump unconditionally to address ADR.
	Jump and link register	JALR Rd,Rs	Place PC + 8 in Rd and jump unconditionally to address in Rs.
	Branch on equal	BEQ Rs,Rt,IMM	If Rs = Rt, then jump to PC + 8 + IMM.
	Branch on not equal	BNE Rs,Rt,IMM	If Rs ≠ Rt, then jump to PC + 8 + IMM.
	Branch on less than 0	BLTZ Rs,IMM	If Rs < 0, then jump to PC + 8 + IMM.
	Branch on greater than 0	BGTZ Rs,IMM	If RS > 0, then jump to PC + 8 + IMM.
	Branch on less than or equal to 0	BLEZ Rs,IMM	If Rs ≤ 0, then jump to PC + 8 + IMM.
	Branch on greater than or equal to 0	BGEZ Rs,IMM	If Rs ≥ 0, then jump to PC + 8 + IMM.
	Branch on less than 0 and link	BLTZAL Rs,IMM	Place PC + 8 in R31; if Rs < 0, then jump to PC + 8 + IMM.
	Branch on greater than or equal to 0 and link	BGEZAL Rs,IMM	Place PC + 8 in R31; if Rs ≥ 0, then jump to PC + 8 + IMM.
	System call	SYSCALL	Jump unconditionally to the exception handler.
	Break	BREAK	Jump unconditionally to the exception handler.
	(10 miscellaneous coprocessor instructions)		

Figure 3.36
(continued)

used. For example, if M(Source) = 10101111, then the load byte instruction LB Rt,Source transfers

$$11111111\ 11111111\ 11111111\ 10101111$$

to the destination register Rt, whereas LBU Rt,Source transfers

$$00000000\ 00000000\ 00000000\ 10101111$$

to Rt. While most load and store instructions assume that full words are aligned on memory word boundaries, that is, their addresses terminate with 00, the RX000 provides four special instructions LWL, LWR, SWL, and SWR to load and store mis-aligned words.

The RX000's data-processing instructions include a typical set of arithmetic and logical operations. They employ two instruction types implying two different addressing modes: I type, in which case the instruction contains a 16-bit immediate operand in its IMM field, and R type, in which case all operands are stored in registers. For example, the logical OR instruction

OR Rd,Rs,Rt

implements the word-OR operation Rd := Rs *or* Rt, whereas the corresponding OR immediate instruction

ORI Rt,Rs,IMM

implements Rt := Rs *or* IMM, with IMM zero-extended to 32 bits.

The RX000 does not employ the usual set of status flags (zero, carry, overflow, and so on) to indicate special properties of results. The only exceptional condition that is automatically detected is twos-complement overflow in the case of ADD, ADDI, and SUB. When that happens, an automatic trap occurs, accompanied by a switch from user to supervisor state. To avoid such traps, "unsigned" versions of the preceding instructions are provided. ADDU, for example, is identical to ADD except that no overflow trap occurs under any circumstances.

Four compare or "set" instructions test register values and place the binary test outcome in a register Rd, effectively using Rd as a flag. For example, if Rt contains zero, then the "set on less than" instruction

SLT Rd,Rs,Rt

determines whether Rs contains a negative number. If Rs is less than Rt, then SLT sets Rd to 1; otherwise, it resets Rd to 0. While it seems a waste of hardware to use an entire 32-bit register to store a binary flag, such exception-indicating registers are more easily accessed by exception-handling software than individual flag bits. However, certain other common operations are complicated; see problem 3.41.

For simplicity, we will not discuss the RX000's shift instruction, which has no unusual features. We will also not discuss the multiply and divide instructions, which are unusual in that they require many cycles to execute and are handled by a special arithmetic unit within the CPU. Once execution of a multiply or divide instruction begins, other instructions may execute in parallel in the RX000's main arithmetic-logic circuitry.

In the program-control category, the RX000 has unconditional "jump" instructions, which employ absolute addressing with the J-type format, and conditional "branch" instructions, which employ PC-relative addressing and have the R format. The conditions tested by branch instructions are all determined by examining the contents of registers, which as noted above, serve as flags in this architecture. Consider, for example, the branch on less than or equal to zero instruction

BLEZ Rs,IMM

It is executed in two clock cycles t and $t+1$. In the first cycle t, a target address TARGET is determined as follows. The address offset IMM has 2 bits appended to its right end and the sign s of IMM (bit 15 of the instruction BLEZ) is extended by 14 bits to form a full 32-bit address. In other words, the branch address is given by

$$\text{TARGET} := s^{14}.\text{IMM}.00$$

In the second clock cycle $t + 1$, the CPU checks for the branch condition by examining the contents of the specified general register Rs. If Rs contains zero or if its sign bit is 1, indicating a negative number, then the operation PC := PC + TARGET is performed. Since PC is automatically incremented by four at the start of each clock cycle, we have effectively added TARGET plus eight to the contents of PC present at the start of cycle t; for brevity, this is indicated by PC + 8 + IMM in Figure 3.36.

The various branch instructions have "link" versions that unconditionally save the PC contents in a designated register. These are useful for implementing procedure calls and interrupts.

The design and control of instruction-processing logic are examined in Chapters 4 and 5.

3.3.3 Programming Considerations

To design programs using the instruction sets discussed in the preceding sections, a symbolic format called assembly language can be used. This section discusses the basic features of assembly language and their relationship both to the computer organization and to the machine-language programs that are actually executed by the host processor. Most computer programming is now done using higher-level languages such as C, which, like assembly language, must be translated (compiled) into machine language prior to execution.

Assembly language. Machine-language programs (object programs) are lists of instructions, each of which has the general form

opcode operand,operand,...,operand

For example, the machine-language version of the instruction for the Motorola 680X0 microprocessor series "Load the (immediate) decimal operand 2001 into address register A0," which is used in the program of Figure 3.13, has the 32-bit binary format

$$00100000\ 01111000\ 00000111\ 11010001 \qquad (3.33)$$

It may also be written more compactly in hexadecimal code thus:

$$2078\ 07D1 \qquad (3.34)$$

Here 2078 is the opcode word indicating "move long (32-bit) operand to register A0," while the operand field 07D1 is the hexadecimal equivalent of the decimal number 2001. Assembly-language versions of this instruction are

$$\text{MOVE.L \#2001,A0} \qquad (3.35)$$

and $$\text{MOVE.L \#\$07D1,A0} \qquad (3.36)$$

where the opcode and the operand A0 are represented in symbolic form. The prefix # denotes an immediate operand in the Motorola convention, while $ indicates that base 16 rather than base 10 is being used. Before they can be executed, assembly-language instructions like (3.35) and (3.36) must be translated into the equivalent machine-language form represented by (3.33) and (3.34). The translation or *assembly* process is carried out by a system program known as an *assembler,* which is analogous to a compiler that translates a high-level language program into machine code.

In addition to using symbolic names for opcodes and registers, assembly languages allow symbolic names to be assigned to user-defined constants and variables, such as the immediate operand appearing in (3.35) and (3.36). For example, many assembly languages use the statement

$$\text{A} \quad \text{EQU} \quad 2001 \tag{3.37}$$

to indicate that the symbol A is to be equivalent (EQU) to the decimal number 2001. If statement (3.37) is present in a program for the 680X0 microprocessor, then (3.35) and (3.36) can be replaced by

$$\text{MOVE.L} \quad \text{A,A0}$$

which is assembled into exactly the same machine code as before. This instruction also corresponds to the register-transfer operation denoted symbolically by A0 := A. Statement (3.37) is considered an assembly-language instruction but, unlike the MOVE instructions, does not translate into an executable instruction in machine language. Rather it is an instruction that tells the assembler how to treat the symbol A during the program-translation process. This type of nonexecutable assembly-language instruction is called a *directive* or *pseudoinstruction.*

The memory location to be assigned to an instruction can be indicated symbolically by means of a label at the beginning of an assembly-language statement. For example, the label L1 in

$$\text{L1} \quad \text{MOVE.L} \quad \text{A,A0} \quad \text{; Load initial value into A0} \tag{3.38}$$

is assigned to a physical memory address by the assembler, normally to the one immediately following the address assigned to the preceding instruction. Labels are generally used in an assembly-language instruction only when another instruction needs to refer to the first one. For example, the 680X0 instruction

$$\text{JMP L1} \quad \text{; Branch unconditionally to instruction labeled L1} \tag{3.39}$$

causes a branch to instruction (3.38), which has the label L1; JMP L1 is the assembly-language equivalent of the high-level language statement **go to** L1. All assembly languages allow the programmer to introduce comments, which have no effect on the assembly process but are useful for documenting a program to improve its readability. As illustrated by (3.38) and (3.39), 680X0 assembly language uses a semicolon as a prefix to mark comments.

Assemblers also allow the programmer to assign a symbolic name to a sequence of instructions, permitting those instructions to be treated as a single instructionlike entity termed a *macroinstruction,* or simply a *macro.* Assembly languages often have built-in macros that appear to the programmer to augment the machine's instruction set. For example, the MIPS RX000 machine language lacks the logical NOT instruction found in other computers. However, a NOT instruction of the form

$$\text{NOT} \quad \text{Rd, Rs} \quad \text{; Form bitwise logical complement } \overline{\text{Rs}} \text{ of Rs and place in Rd}$$

is easily synthesized from the RX000's NOR instruction, as follows:

NOR Rd, Rs, 0   ; Compute the NOR function $\overline{Rs + 0} = \overline{Rs}$ and place in Rd

Thus we conclude that assembly-language instructions have the following general format:

label   opcode   operand,operand,…,operand   comments

where the opcode can be an executable command corresponding to a machine-language opcode, a directive, or a macro. Like machine languages, assembly languages vary from computer to computer and are usually defined (not always consistently) by a computer's primary manufacturer.

Assembly process. The input to the assembler program is a source program written in assembly language. The output is an object program in machine language and an optional *assembly listing* that shows both the assembly-language and machine-language versions of the program and the correspondence between them. The object code can be combined with other machine-language programs to produce a final composite executable program. A system program called a *linker* performs the task of combining different programs in this fashion. The use of symbolic names for shared data and labels plays an important role in allowing the linker to merge different assembly-language programs, or perhaps to merge the work of different programmers.

Nonexecutable assembly-language instructions such as the EQU statement (3.37) are known as *directives*. They are used to define the values of program parameters, to assign programs and data to specific physical or symbolic memory locations, and to control the output of the assembly process. In the case of macro-assemblers, directives are also used to define macros. Figure 3.37 lists a representative set of the directives found in most assembly languages. The EQU directive tells the assembler to equate two different names for the same thing. In (3.37) EQU

Type	Opcode	Description
Symbol definition	EQU	Equate symbolic name (in label position) to operand value.
Memory assigment	ORG	Origin: use operand value as starting address for subsequent instructions.
	DS	Define storage: reserve the specified number of consecutive locations (bytes) in memory.
	DC	Define constant: store the operand values as constants.
Macro definition	MACRO	Start of macro definition.
	ENDM	End of macro definition.
Miscellaneous	END	End of program(s) to be assembled.
	TITLE	Use operand as title on each page of assembly listing.
	IF	Start of conditional block of instructions to be assembled only if a specified condition is met.
	ENDIF	End of conditional block.

Figure 3.37
List of representative assembly-language directives.

assigns a symbolic name to a constant; it can also be used to equate two symbolic names for variables, as in

ALPHA   EQU   BETA

which defines a new variable ALPHA that must always have the same value as a previously defined parameter BETA. The ORG (origin) directive tells the assembler which memory address to assign for storing the subsequent executable code or data. For example, in

ORG   100
L1   MOVE.L   A, A0

the ORG directive states that the MOVE instruction is to be assigned to memory location 100, which equates the symbolic address or label L1 to the physical address 100. The assembler needs this address value to translate into machine code the address fields of any instructions that refer to L1. Once the start address of a block of code has been established, the assembler automatically keeps track of the memory locations to be assigned to all items in the block.

Sometimes it is useful to reserve a block of memory for future use, for example, as a buffer storage area for IO data, without specifying its contents. The DS (define storage) instruction is provided for this purpose. Thus the directive

L2   DS   500

states that a block of 500 memory bytes should be reserved, beginning at the current location L2. If it is desired to actually define data to be placed in a program, the DC (define constant) directive is used. DS and DC typically exist in several versions depending on the word size to be used. For example, the 680X0 directive

L3   DC.B   1,2,3,4,5,6,7

causes the seven specified operand values to be placed (in binary form) in seven consecutive 1-byte memory locations starting with L3. If the same data is to be stored in the ASCII character code, then the format

L3   DC.B   '1234567'

is used. We now turn to an example that illustrates the directives discussed so far.

EXAMPLE 3.8 ASSEMBLY OF VECTOR ADDITION PROGRAM FOR THE MOTOROLA 680X0 . This particular programming task, which was considered earlier for the IAS computer (Example 1.4), the PowerPC (Example 1.7), as well as the 680X0 (Example 3.3), is to add two 1000-element vectors A and B creating a sum vector C. We assume again that the vectors are 1000-byte decimal (BCD) numbers. The 680X0 series has a 1-byte add instruction ABCD (add BCD), which is placed in a program loop and executed 1000 times to accomplish the desired vector addition. The program can be described abstractly in the following high-level language format:

$$\text{for } I = 1 \text{ to } 1000 \text{ do}$$
$$C[i] := A[i] + B[i] + \text{carry}; \tag{3.40}$$

We assume that A, B, and C are stored in three consecutive 1000-byte blocks of memory as depicted in Figure 3.38.

Hexadecimal
address

Decimal
address

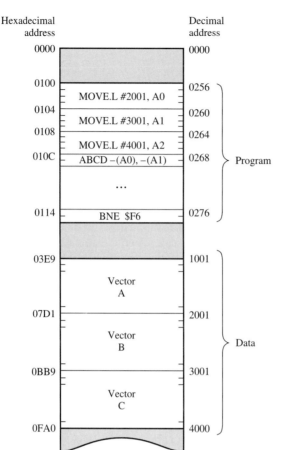

Figure 3.38
Memory allocation for
the 680X0 vector addition
program.

To determine how best to implement (3.40) in assembly language, the available instruction types and addressing modes must be examined carefully. The ABCD instruction, besides being limited to byte operands, allows only two operand addressing modes: direct register addressing and indirect register addressing with predecrementing. As explained earlier, the latter mode causes the contents of the designated address register to be automatically decremented just before the add operation is carried out. This approach is convenient for stepping through lists, in this case the elements of a vector, and hence it is selected here. Two of the address registers A0 and A1 are chosen to address or point to the current elements of A and B, respectively. Thus the basic addition step is implemented by the instruction

$$\text{ABCD} \quad -(\text{A0}),-(\text{A1}) \tag{3.41}$$

which is equivalent to

$$\text{A0} := \text{A0} -1, \text{A1} := \text{A1} - 1;$$
$$\text{M(A1)} := \text{M(A0)} + \text{M(A1)} + \text{carry};$$

A third address register A2 is used to point to vector C, and the result computed by (3.41) is stored in the C region by the 1-byte data transfer instruction

$$\text{MOVE.B} \quad (\text{A1}),-(\text{A2}) \tag{3.42}$$

Because addresses are predecremented, A0, A1, and A2 must be initialized to values that are one greater than the highest addresses assigned to A, B, and C, respectively. The foregoing instructions (3.41) and (3.42) are executed 1000 times, that is, until the lowest address (1001 in the case of vector A) is reached. This point can be detected by the CMPA (compare address) instruction

$$\text{CMPA} \quad \#1001, \text{A0}$$

which sets the zero-status flag Z to 1 if A0 = 1001 and to 0 otherwise. When Z ≠ 1, a branch is made back to (3.41) using the BNE (branch if not equal to 1) instruction. The resulting code, which also appears with comments in Figure 3.13, is as follows:

```
                MOVE.L      #2001, A0
                MOVE.L      #3001,A1
                MOVE.L      #4001,A2
      START     ABCD        –(A0),–(A1)
                MOVE.B      (A1),–(A2)
                CMPA        #1001,A0
      BNE       START
```

Figure 3.39 shows an assembly listing of the foregoing code with various directives added for both illustrative purposes and to complete the program. The assembly-language source code appears on the right side of Figure 3.39, while the assembled object program appears on the left in hexadecimal code. The left-most column contains the memory addresses assigned by the assembler to the machine-language instructions and data, which are then listed to the right of these memory addresses. The first ORG directive causes the assembler to fix the start of the program at the hexadecimal address 0100. The symbolic names A, B, and C are assigned by EQU directives to the addresses of the first elements of the three corresponding vectors. The subsequent MOVE.L (move long) instructions contain arithmetic expressions that are evaluated during assembly and replaced by the corresponding numerical value. For example, the expression A + 1000 appearing in the first MOVE.L instruction is replaced by 1001 + 1000 = 2001. In general, assembly languages allow arithmetic-logic expressions to be used as operands, provided the assembler can translate them to the form needed for the object program. The statement MOVE.L #2001, A0 is thus the first executable statement of the program, and its machine-language equivalent 2078 07D1 is loaded into memory locations 0100:0103 (hex), as indicated in Figures 3.38 and 3.39. The remainder of the short program is translated to machine code and allocated to memory in similar fashion.

Many 680X0 branch instructions use relative addressing, which means that the branch address is computed relative to the current address stored in the program counter PC. Consider, for instance, the conditional branch instruction BNE START, the last executable instruction in the vector-addition program. As shown by Figure 3.39, the corresponding machine-language instruction is 66F6 in which 66 is the opcode BNE and F6 is an 8-bit relative address derived from the operand START. Now $F6_{16} = 11110110_2$, which when interpreted as a twos-complement number is -10_{10} or $-0A_{16}$. After BNE START has been fetched from memory locations 0114_{16} and 0115_{16}, PC is automatically incremented to point to the next consecutive memory location 0116_{16}. Hence at this point $PC = 00000116_{16}$. Now when the CPU executes the branch instruction BNE, it computes the branch address as $PC + (-0A) = 0000010C_{16}$, which, as required, is the physical address of the instruction (ABCD) with the symbolic address START.

The remainder of the vector-addition program illustrates the assembly-language directives that define data regions. ORG is used again to establish a start address for the data region; in this case the start address is $1001_{10} = 03E9_{16}$. The DS.B (define storage

Machine language			Assembly language			
Location	Code/Data		; 68000/68020 program for vector addition			
			;			
			; The vectors are composed of a thousand 1-byte (two digit) decimal numbers. The starting (decimal) addresses of A, B, and C are 1001, 2001, and 3001, respectively.			
			;			
			; Define origin of program at hex address 100			
0100			ORG	$100		
			; Define symbolic vector start addresses			
03E9			A	EQU	1001	
07D1			B	EQU	2001	
0BB9			C	EQU	3001	
			; Begin executable code			
0100	2078	07D1		MOVE.L	A+1000,A0	; Set pointer beyond end of A
0104	2278	0BB9		MOVE.L	B+1000,A1	; Set pointer beyond end of B
0108	2478	0FA1		MOVE.L	C+1000,A2	; Set pointer beyond end of C
010C	C308		START	ABCD	–(A0), –(A1)	; Decrement pointers & add
010E	1511			MOVE.B	(A1), –(A2)	; Store result in C
0110	B0F8	03E9		CMPA	A,A0	; Test for termination
0114	66 F6			BNE	START	; Branch to START if Z ≠ 1
			; End executable code			
			;			
			; Begin data definition			
		03E9		ORG	A	; Define start of vector A
03E9				DS.B	1000	; Reserve 1000 bytes for A
07D1	01 01 01			DC.B	1,1,1	; Initialize elements 1:3 of B
07D4	16 16 16			DC.B	22,22,22	; Initialize elements 4:6 of B
				END		; End program

Figure 3.39
Assembly listing of the 680X0 program for vector addition.

in bytes) directive reserves a region of 1000 bytes. This directive merely causes the assembler's memory location counter, which it uses to keep track of memory addresses, to be incremented by the specified number of bytes. As indicated by Figure 3.38, this action makes the location counter point to the start of the region storing vector B. The two DC. B (define constant in bytes) commands initialize six elements of B to the specified constant values. Finally the END directive indicates the end of the assembly-language program.

Macros and subroutines. Two useful tools for simplifying program design by allowing groups of instructions to be treated as single entities are macros and subroutines. A macro is defined by placing a portion of assembly-language code between appropriate directives as follows:

name   MACRO operand,..., operand

$\left.\begin{array}{c} ... \end{array}\right\}$ Body of macro

ENDM

The macro is subsequently invoked by treating the user-defined macro name, which appears in the label field of the MACRO directive, as the opcode of a new (macro) instruction. Each time the macro opcode appears in a program, the assembler replaces it by a copy of the corresponding macro body. If the macro has operands, then the assembler modifies each copy of the macro body that it generates by inserting the operands included in the current macro instruction. Macros thus allow an assembly language to be augmented by new opcodes for all types of operations; they can also indirectly introduce new data types and addressing modes. A macro is typically used to replace a short sequence of instructions that occur frequently in a program. Note that although macros shorten the source code, they do not shorten the object code assembled from it.

Suppose, for example, that the following two-instruction sequence occurs in a program for the Intel 8085 [Intel 1979]:

```
LDHL   ADR     ;Load M(ADR) into address register HL
MOV    A,M     ;Load M(HL) into accumulator register A
```

This code implements the operation A := M(M(ADR)), which loads register A treating ADR as an indirect memory address. We can define it as a macro named LDAI (load accumulator indirect) as follows:

```
LDAI   MACRO  ADR
       LDHL   ADR  ;Load M(ADR) into address register HL
       MOV    A,M  ;Load M(HL) into register A
       ENDM
```

With this macro definition present in an 8085 program, LDAI becomes a new assembly-language instruction for the programmer to use. The subsequent occurrence of a statement such as

$$\text{LDAI} \quad \text{1000H} \tag{3.43}$$

in the same program causes the assembler to replace it by the macro body

```
LDHL   1000H
MOV    A,M
```

with the immediate address 1000_{16} from (3.43) replacing the macro's dummy input parameter ADR. Note that the macro definition itself is not part of the object program.

A subroutine or procedure is also a sequence of instructions that can be invoked by name, much like a single (macro) instruction. Unlike a macro, however, a subroutine definition is assembled into object code. It is subsequently used, not by replicating the body of the subroutine during assembly, but rather during program execution by establishing dynamic links between the subroutine object code and the points in the program where the subroutine is needed. The necessary links are established by means of two executable instructions named CALL or JUMP TO SUBROUTINE, and RETURN. Consider, for example, the following code segment:

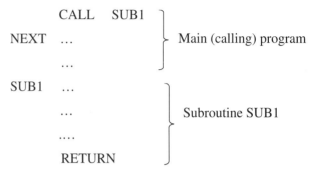

After CALL SUB1 has been fetched, the program counter PC contains the address NEXT of the instruction immediately following CALL; this *return address* must be saved to allow control to be returned later to the main program. Thus a call instruction first saves the contents of PC in a designated save area. It then transfers the address that forms the operand of the call statement, SUB1 in this case, into PC. SUB1 is the address of the first executable instruction in the subroutine and also serves as the subroutine's name. The processor then begins execution of the subroutine. Control is returned to the original program from the subroutine by executing RETURN, which simply retrieves the previously saved return address and restores it to PC.

CALL and RETURN may use specific CPU registers or main-memory locations to store return addresses. The RX000, for instance, uses a CPU register from its register file to save a return address on executing any of its jump/branch-and-link-register instructions, which serve as call instructions; see Figure 3.36. Many computers use a memory stack for this purpose. CALL then pushes the return address into the stack, from which it is subsequently retrieved by RETURN. The stack pointer SP automatically keeps track of the top of the stack, where the last return address was pushed by CALL and from which it will be popped by RETURN.

Figure 3.40 illustrates the actions taken by the CALL instruction in a stack realization. For simplicity, we assume that opcodes and the addresses are all one memory word long. The instruction CALL SUB1 is stored in memory locations 1000 and 1001, and we assume that the assembler has replaced SUB1 with the physical address 2000. Immediately before the CALL instruction cycle begins, the program counter PC contains the address 1000, as shown in Figure 3.40a. The CALL opcode is fetched and decoded, and PC is incremented to 1001. On identifying the instruction as a subroutine call, the CPU fetches the address part 2000 of the instruction and stores it in the (buffer) address register AR; again PC is incremented to 1002. At this point the system state is as shown in Figure 3.40b, and PC contains the return address to the main program. Next the contents of PC are pushed into the stack. Then the contents of AR are transferred to PC, and the stack

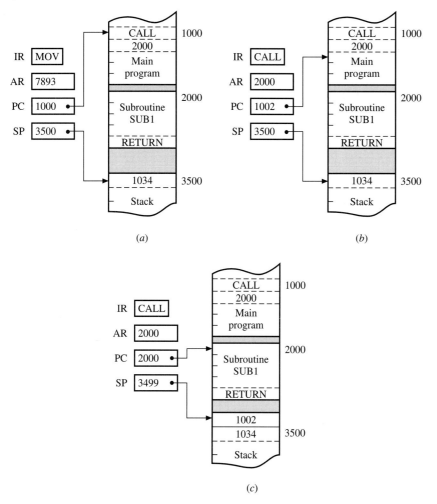

Figure 3.40
Processor and memory state during execution of a CALL instruction: (*a*) initial state,
(*b*) state immediately after fetching the instruction, and (*c*) final state.

pointer SP is decremented by one. The resulting state of the system is depicted in
Figure 3.40*c*.

3.4
SUMMARY

The main task of a CPU is to fetch instructions from an external memory M and
execute them. This task requires a program counter PC to keep track of the active
instruction, and registers to store the instructions and data as they are processed.
The simplest CPUs employ a central data register called an accumulator, along
with an ALU capable of addition, subtraction, and word-oriented logic operations.
In most CPUs a register file containing 32 or more general-purpose registers

replaces the accumulator. RISC processors such as the ARM and the MIPS RX000 allow only load and store instructions to access M, and use small instruction sets and techniques such as pipelining to improve performance. CISC processors such as the Motorola 680X0 have larger instruction sets and some more powerful instructions that improve performance in some applications but reduce it in others. The arithmetic capabilities of simpler processors are limited to the fixed-point (integer) instructions unless auxiliary coprocessors are used. More powerful CPUs have built-in hardware to execute floating-point instructions.

Computers store and process information in various formats. The basic unit of storage (the smallest addressable unit) is the 8-bit byte. The CPU is designed to handle data in a few fixed-word sizes, 32-bit words being typical. The two major formats for numerical data are fixed-point and floating-point. Fixed-point numbers can be binary (base 2) or, less frequently, decimal, meaning a binary code such as BCD that preserves the decimal weights found in ordinary (base 10) decimal numbers. The most common binary number codes are sign magnitude and twos complement. Each code simplifies the implementation of some arithmetic operations; twos complement, for example, simplifies the implementation of addition and subtraction and so is generally preferred. A floating-point number comprises a pair of fixed-point numbers, a mantissa M, and an exponent E and represents numbers of the form $M \times B^E$ where B is an implicit base. Floating-point numbers greatly increase the numerical range obtainable using a given word size but require much more complex arithmetic circuits than fixed-point numbers require. The IEEE 754 standard for floating-point numbers is widely used.

The functions performed by a CPU are defined by its instruction set. An instruction consists of an opcode and a set of operand or address fields. Various techniques called addressing modes are used to specify operands. An instruction's operands can be in the instruction itself (immediate addressing), in CPU registers, or in external memory M. Operands in registers can be accessed more rapidly than those in M. An instruction set should be complete, efficient, and easy to use in some broad sense. Instructions can be grouped into several major types: data transfer (load, store, move register, and input-output instructions), data processing (arithmetic and logical instructions), and program control (conditional and unconditional branches). All practical computers contain at least a few instructions of each type, although in theory one or two instruction types suffice to perform all computations. RISCs are characterized by streamlined instruction sets that are supported by fast hardware implementations and efficient software compilers. While CISCs have larger and more complex instruction sets, they simplify the programming of complex functions such as division. The use of subroutines (procedures) and macroinstructions can simplify assembly-language programming in all types of processors.

3.5
PROBLEMS

3.1. Show how to use the 10-member instruction set of Figure 3.4 to implement the following operations that correspond to single instructions in many computers; use as few instructions as you can. (*a*) Copy the contents of memory location X to memory location Y. (*b*) Increment the accumulator AC. (*c*) Branch to a specified address *adr* if AC $\neq 0$.

3.2. Use the instruction set of Figure 3.4 to implement the following two operations assuming that sign-magnitude code is used. (a) AC := –M(X). (b) Test the right-most bit b of the word stored in a designated memory location X. If b = 1, clear AC; otherwise, leave AC unchanged. [*Hint*: Use an AND instruction to mask out certain bits of a word.]

3.3. Consider the possibility of overlapping instruction fetch and execute operations when executing the multiplication program of Figure 3.5. (a) Assuming only one word can be transferred over the system bus at a time, determine which instructions can be overlapped with neighboring instructions. (b) Suppose that the CPU-memory interface is redesigned to allow one instruction fetch and one data load or store to occur during the same clock cycle. Now determine which instructions, if any, in the multiplication *cannot* be overlapped with neighboring instructions.

3.4. Write a brief note discussing one advantage and one disadvantage of each of the following two unusual features of the ARM6: (a) the inclusion of the program counter PC in the general register file; (b) the fact that execution of every instruction is conditional.

3.5. Use HDL notation and ordinary English to describe the actions performed by each of the following ARM6 instructions: (a) MOV R6,#0; (b) MVN R6,#0; (c) ADD R6,R6,R6; (d) EOR R6,R6,R6.

3.6. Suppose the ARM6 has the following initial register contents (all given in hex code):

R1 = 11110000; R2 = 0000FFFF; R3 = 12345678; NZCV = 0000

Identify the new contents of every register or flag that is changed by execution of the following instructions. Assume each is executed separately with the foregoing initial state. (a) MOV R1,R2; (b) MOVCS R1,R2; (c) MVNCS R2,R1; (d) MOV R3,#0; (e) MOV R3,R4, LSL#4.

3.7. Suppose the ARM6 has the following initial register and memory contents (all given in hex code):

R1 = 00000000; R2 = 87654321; R3 = A05B77F9; NZCV = 0000

Identify the new contents of every register or flag that is changed by execution of the following instructions. Assume each is executed separately with the foregoing initial state. (a) ADD R1,R2,R3; (b) ADDS R1,R3,R3; (c) SUBS R2,R1,#1; (d) ANDS R3,R2,R1; (e) EORCSS R1,R2,R3.

3.8. Use the instruction set for the ARM6 given in Figure 3.10 to write short code segments to perform the tasks given below. Note that an opcode can be followed by two optional suffixes, a two-character condition code to determine branching and S to activate the status flags. Figure 3.41 lists all possible condition fields. The required tasks are: (a) Replace the contents of register R1 by its absolute value. (b) Perform the 64-bit subtraction R5.R4 := R1.R0 – R3.R2, where the even-numbered registers contain the right (less significant) half of each operand.

3.9. Write the shortest ARM6 program that you can to implement the following conditional statement:

while $(x \neq y)$ **do** $x := y - 1$;

Assume that x and y are stored in CPU registers R1 and R2, respectively.

Code	Mnemonic	Flag test	Usual interpretation
0000	EQ	Z = 1	Result equal to zero.
0001	NE	Z = 0	Result not equal to zero.
0010	CS or HS	C = 1	Unsigned overflow: result higher or same.
0011	CC or LO	C = 0	No unsigned overflow: result lower.
0100	MI	N = 1	Result negative.
0101	PL	N = 0	Result positive or zero.
0110	VS	V = 1	Signed overflow.
0111	VC	V = 0	No signed overflow.
1000	HI	C = 1 and Z = 0	Unsigned result higher.
1001	LS	C = 0 or Z = 1	Unsigned result lower or same.
1010	GE	N = V	Signed result greater or equal.
1011	LT	$\bar{N} = V$	Signed result less than.
1100	GT	Z = 0 and N = V	Signed result greater than.
1101	LE	Z = 1 or $\bar{N} = V$	Signed result less than or equal.
1110	AL	None	Always (unconditional branch).
1111	NV	None	Never (no branching)

Figure 3.41
Condition codes of the ARM6 and their interpretation.

3.10. Identify five major differences between the instruction sets of the ARM6 and the 680X0 and comment on their impact on the CPU cost and performance.

3.11. Use HDL notation and ordinary English to write the actions performed by each of the following 680X0 instructions: (*a*) MOVE (A5)+,D5; (*b*) ADD.B $2A10,D0; (*c*) SUBI #10,(A0); (*d*) AND.L #$FF,D0.

3.12. The 680X0 has two types of unconditional branch instructions BRA (branch always) and JMP (jump). Therefore, branch to statement L can be implemented either by BRA L or JMP L. What is the difference between these two instructions? Under what circumstances is each type of branch instruction preferred?

3.13. Write a program for the 680X0 that replaces the word DATA stored in memory location ADR by its bitwise logical complement $\overline{\text{DATA}}$ if and only if DATA ≠ 0.

3.14. Modify the vector addition program of Figure 3.13 (Example 3.3) to compute the sum C := A + B for 100 instead of 1000 one-byte decimal numbers. Assume that the locations of the A and B operands are unchanged, but the result C is now required to replace (overwrite) B.

3.15. Suppose that the hex contents of two CPU registers in a 32-bit processor are as follows:

$$R0 = 01237654; \quad R1 = 7654EDCB$$

The following store-word instructions are executed to transfer the contents of these registers to main memory M.

STORE   R0,ADR

STORE   R1,ADR+4

215

CHAPTER 3
Processor
Basics

Assuming that M is byte-addressable, give the contents of all memory locations affected by the above code (*a*) if the computer is big-endian and (*b*) if the computer is little-endian.

3.16. Suppose that a 680X0-based computer C_1, which is big-endian, is communicating with another computer C_2, which is similar to C_1 except that it is little-endian. C_2 stores 4-byte (long) words from its register file into a common memory M, which C_1 subsequently loads into its data registers. Outline an efficient way to program C_1's load operations so that data words always appear in the correct form in its register file.

3.17. The usual objection to tagged architecture is that the presence of tags in stored data increases memory size and cost. It has been argued, however, that tags can actually reduce storage requirements by decreasing program size. Analyze the validity of this argument.

3.18. Figure 3.42 lists all the 16 code words of a code known as a Hamming code [Hamming 1986], which is designed to check 4-bit words using three check bits. Prove that all single-bit errors can be corrected and all double-bit errors can be detected by this code.

3.19. Consider the small Hamming code defined in Figure 3.42. Show that each check bit c_i can be expressed in the form $c_i = a_1d_1 \oplus a_2d_2 \oplus a_3d_3 \oplus a_4d_4$, where $a_j = 0$ or 1 and d_j is an information (data) bit. Hence the check bits for this (and other) Hamming codes can be generated by a set of EXCLUSIVE-OR (parity) circuits.

Information bits $d_1d_2d_3d_4$	Check bits $c_1c_2c_3$
0 0 0 0	0 0 0
0 0 0 1	1 1 1
0 0 1 0	1 1 0
0 0 1 1	0 0 1
0 1 0 0	1 0 1
0 1 0 1	0 1 0
0 1 1 0	0 1 1
0 1 1 1	1 0 0
1 0 0 0	0 1 1
1 0 0 1	1 0 0
1 0 1 0	1 0 1
1 0 1 1	0 1 0
1 1 0 0	1 1 0
1 1 0 1	0 0 1
1 1 1 0	0 0 0
1 1 1 1	1 1 1

Figure 3.42
Hamming SECDED code for 4-bit words.

3.20. Convert the following three 2^i-bit words to standard decimal form assuming they represent (*a*) sign-magnitude and (*b*) twos-complement integers: $FFFF_{16}$; $FEDCBA98_{16}$; $7EDCBA9_{16}$.

3.21. The following binary word $W = 10001011101001$ is stored in a 14-bit register. What is the decimal number represented by W if it is interpreted as an integer in each of the following codes: (*a*) unsigned binary; (*b*) sign-magnitude; (*c*) twos-complement?

3.22. Using 32-bit integer formats, give the sign-magnitude, twos-complement, and BCD representation of each of the following decimal numbers: +999, −999, +1000, −1000, zero. State your assumptions concerning sign representation.

3.23. (*a*) What are the decimal equivalents of the largest fixed-point binary numbers that can be represented in 32-, 64-, and 128-bit words? (*b*) Convert the following sign-magnitude words to decimal: 10111011, 01010101, 1011101010111010. (*c*) Repeat part (*b*) assuming this time that the numbers are in twos-complement code.

3.24. Figure 3.43 shows the single-precision number format used in the B6500/7500 and other early Burroughs computers. This format is used for both fixed- and floating-point numbers—an unusual feature. The total length of a number is 47 bits, including the exponent, mantissa, and two sign bits. The implicit number base $B = 8$. Fixed-point numbers are treated as a special case of floating point where the exponent E is always zero (encoded as 000000_2). The exponent and mantissa are treated as sign-magnitude integers and biasing is not used. Write a note listing the advantages and disadvantages of combining fixed- and floating-point representation in this way.

3.25. Consider again the B6500/7500 single-precision number format described in the preceding problem. (*a*) Give in decimal form the largest and the smallest nonzero numbers that can be represented, when no normalization is used. (*b*) Again calculate the largest and the smallest nonzero numbers, this time assuming that the numbers are normalized according to the following definition: a B6500/7500 number is normal if there are no leading-zero digits in the mantissa.

3.26. A floating-point processor is being designed with a number format that must meet the following requirements:

- Numbers in the range $\pm 1.0 \times 10^{\pm 64}$ must be represented.
- The precision required is eight decimal digits; that is, the eight most significant digits of the decimal equivalent of every number in the required range must be representable.

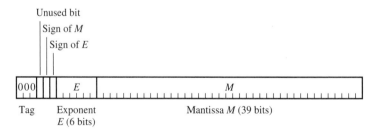

Figure 3.43
The B6500/7500 format for single-precision numbers.

- The representation of each number should be unique, with zero represented by a sequence of 0s.
- Binary arithmetic is to be used throughout with $B = 2$, where B is the floating-point number base.

Design a number format that satisfies these requirements and uses as few bits as possible. Indicate clearly the number codes used and why they were chosen.

3.27. Suppose that in the 6-bit floating-point format illustrated by Figure 3.24, $B = 2$, E is a 3-bit sign-magnitude integer as before, but M is now a 3-bit sign-magnitude fraction. (*a*) What are the decimal values of the largest and smallest nonzero real numbers that can be represented by this format? (*b*) How many different real numbers can be represented?

3.28. Consider the 6-bit floating-point format defined in Figure 3.24. Suppose that E and B are unchanged, but M is a 3-bit sign-magnitude fraction and that all floating-point numbers are normalized with an excess-K biased exponent. (*a*) What is a suitable value for this bias K and why? (*b*) How many different real numbers can be represented in this normalized format?

3.29. Obtain the (approximate) decimal values that conform to the IEEE 754 floating-point format of the following two numbers:

$$A = 1 \quad 00101111 \quad 10000000000000000000000$$

$$B = 0 \quad 10001110 \quad 00000000000000000000001$$

3.30. Derive the correct floating-point representation for the decimal numbers +3.25 and −3.25 using the 32-bit IEEE 754 floating-point standard.

3.31. Consider the 64-bit IEEE floating-point number format defined in section 3.2.3. Determine the largest positive number, the smallest nonzero positive number, and the negative number with the largest magnitude that can be represented in this format. Assume that the three numbers are to be normalized and give your answers in the form of 16-digit hexadecimal strings.

3.32. The floating-point number format used by the IBM System/360-370 series is defined in section 3.2.3. Determine the total number of different normalized numbers that the 32-bit version of this format can represent.

3.33. Consider a 32-bit RISC-style processor P whose only addressing modes for register-to-register instructions are immediate and direct and whose only addressing mode for load/store instructions is register indirect with offset. Assume also that the CPU has 64 general-purpose registers R0:R63 that can serve either as data or address registers. A single 32-bit instruction format contains four fields: an opcode, two register fields, and a 16-bit immediate address field. (*a*) What is the maximum number of opcode types? (*b*) Using an ad hoc but typical assembly-language notation with clear comments, describe how a single instruction of P might perform each of the following three operations: load a word from M; store a byte in M; double the number word stored in a register (there is no multiply opcode).

3.34. Consider the 32-bit RISC-style processor P sketched in the preceding problem. Describe how one or more instructions of P might perform each of the following three operations, assuming that P has no explicit clear, swap, or push opcodes: clear a register; swap the contents of two registers; push a word into a stack. Again use an ad hoc but typical assembly-language notation with clear explanatory comments. Use as few instructions as you can.

3.35. Suppose the memory data register DR in a CPU like that of Figure 3.3 transfers 32-bit words to M in a single clock cycle. The data item D to be stored may be 16 or 32 bits long. If a 16-bit data item D is placed in DR, it is automatically extended to 32 bits as it is transmitted from DR to M. The size of D is given by a flag S, whose 0 and 1 values denote 16 and 32 bits, respectively. The extension method is given by a second flag E, whose 0 and 1 values denote zero extension and sign extension, respectively. Design a register-level logic circuit to perform the needed extension, making it as simple and as fast as possible.

3.36. A memory data register DR can transfer 32-bit words to M in a single clock cycle. The data items to be stored can be 4, 8, 16, or 32 bits long, and short items are always sign-extended to 32 bits for transmission to M. A 2-bit flag S in the CPU is set to 00, 01, 10, or 11 to indicate a data size of 4, 8, 16, or 32 bits, respectively. Design an efficient logic circuit at the register level to implement the sign extension.

3.37. Consider the instruction formats of the MIPS RX000 defined in Example 3.5. Suppose that the currently executing instruction I in an RX000 CPU is stored at (hexadecimal) memory address $FFFFFF00_{16}$. (*a*) If I is not a branch instruction, what is the (hexadecimal) memory address of the instruction that will be executed immediately after I? (*b*) Suppose that I is an unconditional jump instruction that contains the 26-bit branch address field $ADR = 2A9FFFF_{16}$. Again what is the (hexadecimal) memory address of the instruction that will be executed immediately after I?

3.38. Use a figure similar to Figure 3.31 to show the state of the CPU and M in the Motorola 680X0 immediately before and after execution of the stack-pop instruction MOVE.L (A2)+,D6.

3.39. The stack shown in Figure 3.31 for a 680X0-based computer grows toward the low-address end of M. Suppose that the stack is required to grow in the opposite direction, that is, toward the high-address end of M. Construct the push and pop instructions needed for this case.

3.40. The 680X0 instruction JSR SUB pushes the contents of the program counter PC onto a stack using stack pointer register SP and then causes a jump to the instruction at memory location SUB. Its operation may be described as follows:

$$(-SP) := PC; \quad PC := SUB$$

(*a*) Show how to use the 680X0 MOVE instructions to simulate JSR, assuming that JSR can have SP and PC as operands. (*b*) The last instruction executed by a subroutine should be return from subroutine (RTS) which restores to PC the address saved earlier by JSR; this instruction should also update SP. Again use the 680X0 MOVE instructions to simulate RTS, again assuming that SP and PC can be operands of MOVE.

3.41. The MIPS RX000 has no status flag C to indicate whether an arithmetic instruction applied to an unsigned number generates a carry, that is, overflows a 32-bit register. In fact, the RX000 add unsigned instruction that computes Rd := Rs + Rt

$$ADDU \quad Rd,Rs,Rt$$

sets no status flags under *any* circumstances. Using standard instructions (but no flags), devise a short program that will determine whether the foregoing instruction causes overflow. A useful RX000 instruction for this purpose is the compare instruction

$$\text{SLTU} \quad \text{Rd,Rs,Rt}$$

which compares the contents of Rs and Rt, treating both as 32-bit unsigned numbers. If Rs < Rt, then Rd := $1 = 0^{31}1$; otherwise, Rd := $0 = 0^{32}$. The RX000 also has a typical set of conditional branch instructions that test the contents of a register for zero.

3.42. An *arithmetic* right shift (ARS) instruction—arithmetic left shifts are uncommon—shifts an operand D k bits to the right and fills the vacated positions by sign extension. The bits shifted out from the right end of D are discarded. It is often stated that a k-bit ARS implements division by 2^k when applied to a twos-complement integer D; that is, the shifted result SD is the integer quotient Q on dividing D by 2^k. The discarded bits represent the integer remainder R. (*a*) Show that this division-by-2^k interpretation is valid when D is positive. (*b*) Show that the division-by-2^k interpretation of ARS is invalid for negative D by considering operands of length 4 bits and finding a specific counterexample.

3.43. As noted in the preceding problem, ARS instructions cannot be used directly to implement division of twos-complement integers by 2^k. Some computers provide a special instruction—let us call it SI—such that if we apply SI to the result SD produced by a k-bit ARS, we obtain the correct integer quotient for division by 2^k. For this two-instruction combination to work, ARS is designed to set a special flag F when its input operand D is negative and the bits shifted out and discarded by ARS include at least one 1 bit. What is the function performed by SI? Explain informally how it works with ARS to implement division by 2^k.

3.44. *Single-instruction computers* (SICs) have attracted interest for many years. They are extreme cases of RISCs in which the instruction set has been reduced to the absolute minimum. One type of SIC is based on a conditional move (CMOVE) instruction. This instruction has the two-address format

$$\text{CMOVE} \quad \text{dest,source}$$

corresponding to **if** *cond* **then** dest := source, where *cond* is a condition code and all movable items are w-bit words stored in a common n-bit address space shared by M, IO devices, and CPU registers (which can be placed in M). CMOVE combines conditional load and store instructions of the type found in the ARM—it is a pure load/store architecture. The CPU contains the logic needed to fetch instructions (a PC and address-generation logic), but it does not contain the usual ALU logic. Instead, special "IO processors" execute all arithmetic and logical operations. For example, $A \times B$ is implemented by moving A, B, and any necessary control words to the input ports of an external multiplier *MULT* and subsequently moving the result from *MULT*'s output port. The tested conditions *cond* can include a flag C that is set by the sign bit of the last word moved. It is also desirable to have an always-true condition to implement an unconditional move. Most proposed CMOVE architectures support a few addressing modes, including indexing. Write a note analyzing the advantages and disadvantages of this type of SIC architecture.

3.45. Consider a set of four processors P_0, P_1, P_2, and P_3, where P_i is an i-address machine. P_0 is a zero-address stack machine, while P_1, P_2, and P_3 are conventional computers each with 16 general-purpose registers R0:R15 for data and address storage. All four processors have instructions with the (assembly language) opcodes ADD, SUB, MUL,

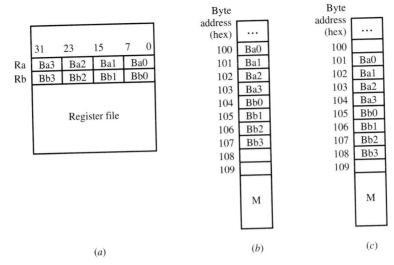

Figure 3.44
Snapshot of RX000 state.

and DIV to implement the operations +, –, ×, and /, respectively. (*a*) Using as few in-structions as you can, write a program for each of the four machines to evaluate the following arithmetic expression:

$$X := (A/B + C \times D)/(D \times E - F + C/A) + G \qquad (3.44)$$

Use standard names for any additional instructions that you need, for example, LOAD or PUSH. (*b*) Calculate the total object-program size in bits for each of your four programs assuming the following data on machine-language instruction formats: opcodes (which contain no addressing information) are 8 bits long; memory-address length is 16 bits; and register-address length is 4 bits. (For example, the two-address instruction LOAD R7,B for P_2, which denotes R7 := M(B), occupies 8 + 4 + 16 = 28 bits.)

3.46. Figure 3.44*a* shows the byte-by-byte contents of two registers in the RX000 general register file. (*a*) Construct a short program that transfers the data in question from the register file to memory M exactly as indicated in Figure 3.44*b*. (*b*) Suppose that the same two words must be stored as shown in Figure 3.44*c*, where they are not aligned with memory word boundaries. Suggest *two* methods for performing the two-word storage operation in this case.

3.47. Show how each of the following macroinstructions can be implemented by a single machine instruction from the RX000 instruction set.

(*a*) LI   Rdest,IMM   ; Load immediate: load IMM (sign-extended) into register Rdest

(*b*) MOVE Rdest,Rsource   ; Move contents of register Rsource to register Rdest

(*c*) NOP   ; No operation: execute an instruction cycle that does not change the
          ; CPU's state

3.48. A new microprocessor is being designed with a conventional architecture employing single-address instructions and 8-bit words. Due to physical size constraints, only eight distinct 3-bit opcodes are allowed. The use of modifiers or the address field to extend the opcodes is forbidden. (*a*) Which eight instructions would you implement? Specify the operations performed by each instruction as well as the location of its operands. (*b*) Demonstrate that your instruction set is functionally complete in some reasonable sense; or if it is not, describe an operation that cannot be programmed using your instruction set.

3.49. Write a short code segment for the RX000 to implement the following common macro, which computes the absolute value of the contents of register Rsource and puts the result in register Rdest.

ABS Rdest,Rsource

3.50. There are few well-defined general principles concerning hardware-software trade-offs in processor design. Two principles of this type are given below. Write a brief note on each, illustrating it with examples. (*a*) "Whenever there is a system function that is expensive and slow in all its generality, but where software can recognize a frequently occurring degenerate case (or can move the entire function from run time to compile time) that function [should be] moved from hardware to software, resulting in lower cost and improved performance." (George Radin, 1983) (*b*) "Simple, frequent, and highly-skew conditional branches [e.g., tests for arithmetic overflow] should be implemented in hardware [rather than software]." (Brian Randell, 1985)

3.51. (*a*) Explain how directives differ from other assembly-language instructions. (*b*) List the criteria for using macros instead of subroutines to structure assembly-language programs.

3.52. A program called a *disassembler* is sometimes useful for debugging programs. It is designed to convert object code to assembly-language format, thus reversing the work of an assembler. However, a disassembler cannot recover all the structure of the original assembly-language code. Explain in detail why this is so.

3.53. Consider the processor and memory state depicted in Figure 3.40 and suppose that execution of the subroutine continues to completion. Let the subroutine's RETURN instruction be stored in memory location 2500 (decimal). Draw a diagram similar to Figure 3.40 that shows the system state at the same three points during the execution of RETURN.

3.6
REFERENCES

1. Circello, J. et al. "The Superscalar Architecture of the MC68060." *IEEE Micro,* vol. 15 (April 1995) pp. 10–21.
2. Cohen, D. "On Holy Wars and a Plea for Peace." *IEEE Computer,* vol. 14 (October 1981) pp. 48–54.
3. Colwell, R. P. et al. "Computers, Complexity, and Controversy." *IEEE Computer,* vol. 18 (September 1985) pp. 8–19.
4. Feustel, E. A. "On the Advantages of Tagged Architecture." *IEEE Transactions on Computers,* vol. C-12 (July 1973) pp. 644–56.
5. Furber, S. B. *VLSI RISC Architecture and Organization.* New York: Marcel Dekker, 1989.

6. Gill, A., E. Corwin, and A. Logar. *Assembly Language Programming for the 68000*. Englewood Cliffs, NJ: Prentice-Hall, 1987.

7. Goldberg, D. "What Every Computer Scientist Should Know about Floating-Point Arithmetic." *ACM Computing Surveys,* vol. 23 (March 1991) pp. 5–48.

8. Hamming, R. W. *Coding and Information Theory*. 2nd ed. Englewood Cliffs, NJ: Prentice-Hall, 1986.

9. IEEE Inc. *IEEE Standard for Binary Floating-Point Arithmetic* (ANSI/IEEE Std 754-1985), New York, August 1985.

10. Intel Corp. *MCS-80/85 Family User's Manual*. Santa Clara, CA, 1979.

11. Kane, G. and J. Heinrich. *MIPS RISC Architecture*. Englewood Cliffs, NJ: Prentice-Hall, 1992.

12. Motorola Inc. *M68000 Family Programmer's Reference Manual*. Phoenix, AZ, 1989.

13. Myers, G. J. *Advances in Computer Architecture*. 2nd ed. New York: Wiley-Interscience, 1982.

14. Patterson, D. A. and C.H. Séquin. "A VLSI RISC." *IEEE Computer,* vol. 15 (September 1982) pp. 8–21.

15. Siewiorek, D. P. and R. S. Swarz. *Reliable Computer Systems*. 2nd ed. Burlington, MA: Digital Press, 1992.

16. van Someren A. and C. Atack. *The ARM RISC Chip.* Wokingham, England: Addison-Wesley, 1994.

CHAPTER 4

Datapath Design

An instruction-set processor consists of datapath (data processing) and control units. This chapter addresses the register-level design of the datapath unit, while Chapter 5 covers the control unit. The focus is on the arithmetic algorithms and circuits needed to process numerical data. These circuits are examined first for fixed-point numbers (integers) and then for floating-point numbers. The use of pipelining to speed up data processing is also discussed.

4.1
FIXED-POINT ARITHMETIC

The design of circuits to implement the four basic arithmetic instructions for fixed-point numbers—addition, subtraction, multiplication, and division—is the main topic of this section. It also discusses the implementation of logic instructions and ALU design.

4.1.1 Addition and Subtraction

Add and subtract instructions for fixed-point binary numbers are found in the instruction set of every computer. In smaller machines such as microcontrollers they are the only available arithmetic instructions. As we have seen in earlier chapters, addition and subtraction hardware (Example 2.7) or software (Example 3.1) can be used to implement multiplication and, in fact, any arithmetic operation. Beginning with Charles Babbage, computer designers have devoted considerable effort to the design of high-speed adders and subtracters. As we will see, these basic circuits can be designed in many different ways that involve various trade-offs between operating speed and hardware cost.

Basic adders. First consider the design of a circuit to add two n-bit unsigned binary numbers, a topic discussed in section 2.1.3. The fastest such adder is, in principle, a two-level combinational circuit in which each of the n sum bits is expressed as a (logical) sum of products or product of sums of the n input variables. In practice, such a circuit is feasible for very small values of n only, as it requires $c(n)$ gates with fan-in $f(n)$, where both $c(n)$ and $f(n)$ grow exponentially with n. Practical adders take the form of multilevel combinational or, occasionally, sequential circuits. They sacrifice operating speed for a reduction in circuit complexity as measured by the number and size of the components used. In general, the addition of two n-bit numbers X and Y is performed by subdividing the numbers into stages X_i and Y_i of length n_i, where $n > n_i > 1$. X_i and Y_i are added separately, and the resulting partial sums are combined to form the overall sum. The formation of this sum involves assimilation of carry bits generated by the partial additions.

The sum z_i, c_i of two 1-bit numbers x_i and y_i can be expressed by the *half-adder* logic equations

$$z_i = x_i \oplus y_i$$

$$c_i = x_i y_i$$

where z_i is the sum bit, c_i is the carry-out bit, $\oplus$ denotes EXCLUSIVE-OR, and juxtaposition denotes AND. If we introduce a third input bit c_{i-1} denoting a carry-in signal, we obtain the following *full-adder* equations:

$$z_i = x_i \oplus y_i \oplus c_{i-1}$$

$$c_i = x_i y_i + x_i c_{i-1} + y_i c_{i-1} \qquad (4.1)$$

(Note that + denotes logical OR—not plus—here.) A full adder, also called a *1-bit adder,* can be directly implemented from these equations in various ways, as demonstrated by Figure 2.9 (section 2.1.1). Figure 4.1 shows a fast AND-OR realization of a 1-bit adder, along with an appropriate circuit symbol for use in register-level designs.

The least expensive circuit in terms of hardware cost for adding two n-bit binary numbers is a serial adder, the design of which was covered in Example 2.2. A serial adder adds the numbers bit by bit and so requires n clock cycles to compute the complete sum of two n-bit numbers. As Figure 4.2 indicates, a serial adder consists of a full adder realizing Equations (4.1) and a flip-flop to store c_i. One sum bit is generated in each clock cycle; a carry is also computed and stored for use during the next clock cycle. Figure 4.2 presents a high-level view of a serial adder that has a D flip-flop as the carry store. Although this adder is slow, its circuit size is very small and is independent of n.

Circuits that, in one clock cycle, add all bits of two n-bit numbers, as well as an external carry-in signal c_{in}, are called n-bit *parallel* adders or simply n-bit adders. The simplest such adder is formed by connecting n full adders as in Figure 4.3. Each 1-bit adder stage supplies a carry bit to the stage on its left. A 1 appearing on the carry-in line of a 1-bit adder can cause it to generate a 1 on its carry-out line. Hence carry signals propagate through the adder from right to left, giving rise to the name *ripple-carry adder.* In the worst case a carry signal can ripple through all n stages of the adder. The input carry signal c_{in} is normally set to 0 for addition. The maximum signal propagation delay of an n-bit ripple-carry adder, which in synchronous circuit design determines the operating speed, is nd,

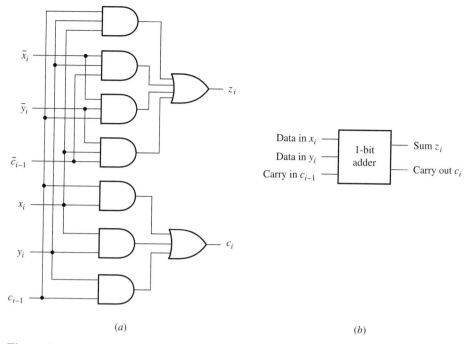

(a)

(b)

Figure 4.1
A 1-bit (full) adder: (a) two-level AND-OR logic circuit and (b) symbol.

where d is the delay of a full-adder stage. Unlike a serial adder, the amount of hardware in a ripple-carry adder increases linearly with n, the word size of the numbers being added.

Subtracters. Adders like those of Figures 4.2 and 4.3 operate correctly on both unsigned and positive numbers because the 0 sign bit of a positive number has the same effect as a leading zero in an unsigned number. The best way to add

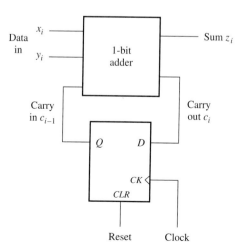

Figure 4.2
A serial binary adder.

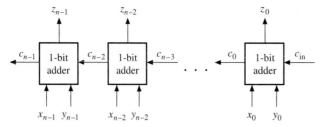

Figure 4.3
An n-bit ripple-carry adder composed of n 1-bit (full) adders.

negative numbers—these have 1 as the sign bit—depends on the number code in use. Adding $-X$ to Y is equivalent to subtracting X from Y, so the ability to add negative numbers implies the ability to do subtraction.

Subtraction is relatively simple with twos-complement code because negation (changing X to $-X$) is very easy to implement. As discussed in section 3.2.2, if $X = x_{n-1}x_{n-2}...x_0$ is a twos-complement integer, then negation is realized by

$$-X = \bar{x}_{n-1}\bar{x}_{n-2}...\bar{x}_0 + 1 \tag{4.2}$$

where + denotes addition modulo 2^n. An efficient way to obtain the ones-complement portion $\bar{X} = \bar{x}_{n-1}\bar{x}_{n-2}...\bar{x}_0$ of $-X$ in (4.2) uses the word-based EXCLUSIVE-OR function $X \oplus s$ with a control variable s. When $s = 0$, $X \oplus s = X$, but when $s = 1$, $X \oplus s = \bar{X}$. Suppose that Y and $X \oplus s$ are now applied to the inputs of an n-bit adder. The addition of 1 required by (4.2) to change $\bar{X}$ to $-X$ can be realized by applying s to the carry input line of the adder. In the resulting circuit shown in Figure 4.4, the control line s selects the addition operation $Y + X$ when $s = 0$ and the subtraction operation $Y - X = Y + \bar{X} + 1$ when $s = 1$. Thus extending a parallel adder to perform twos-complement subtraction as well as addition merely requires connecting n two-input EXCLUSIVE-OR gates to the adder's inputs; these gates are represented by a single n-bit word gate in Figure 4.4.

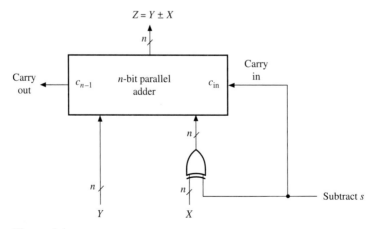

Figure 4.4
An n-bit twos-complement adder-subtracter.

As an example, let $X = 11101011$ and $Y = 00101000$, denoting -21_{10} and 40_{10}, respectively, in twos-complement code. Bit-by-bit addition produces

$$Z = X + Y = 11101011 + 00101000 = 00010011 \qquad (4.3)$$

which corresponds to $-21_{10} + 40_{10} = +19_{10}$. (Observe that the output carry $c_{n-1} = 1$ in (4.3) is ignored.) To subtract X from Y, we first compute

$$-X = \bar{1}\,\bar{1}\,\bar{1}\,\bar{0}\,\bar{1}\,\bar{0}\,\bar{1}\,\bar{1} + 1 = 00010101$$

and then the sum

$$Z = (-X) + Y = 00010101 + 00101000 = 00111101$$

which corresponds to $21_{10} + 40_{10} = +61_{10}$.

Subtraction is not so readily implemented in the case of unsigned or sign-magnitude numbers. It is sometimes useful to construct a subtracter for such numbers based on the *full (1-bit) subtracter* function $z_i = y_i - x_i - b_{i-1}$. This operation is defined by the logic equations:

$$z_i = x_i \oplus y_i \oplus b_{i-1}$$

$$b_i = x_i \bar{y}_i + x_i b_{i-1} + \bar{y}_i b_{i-1}$$

Here z_i is the difference bit, while b_{i-1} and b_i are the borrow-in and borrow-out bits, respectively. n-bit serial or parallel binary subtracters are constructed in essentially the same way as the corresponding adders with carry signals replaced by borrows. Subtracters are of minor interest compared with adders, because, as we have just seen, an adder suffices for both addition and subtraction when twos-complement number code is used.

Overflow. When the result of an arithmetic operation exceeds the standard word size n, overflow occurs. With n-bit *un*signed numbers, overflow is indicated by an output carry bit $c_{n-1} = 1$. For example, adding the unsigned numbers $X = 11101011 = 235_{10}$ and $Y = 00101010 = 42_{10}$ using an adder like that of Figure 4.3 yields

$$Z = X + Y = 11101011 + 00101010 = 00010101 \qquad (4.4)$$

with $c_{n-1} = c_7 = 1$. Now Z corresponds to 21_{10}, which is $235_{10} + 42_{10}$ (modulo 256) and is the result of addition that "wraps around" when the largest number $2^n - 1$, in this case $11111111 = 255_{10}$, is exceeded. On appending c_7 to Z, we get $c_7 Z = 100010101 = 277_{10} = 256_{10} + 21_{10}$, which is the sum in ordinary (modulo infinity) arithmetic. Unsigned arithmetic operations are often viewed as modulo-2^n operations only, and overflow is not explicitly detected. This is the case when computing memory addresses in a computer, for instance, where addresses simply wrap around to zero after the highest address is reached.

Overflow is indicated by a flag bit v in operations involving signed numbers; this flag is found in CPU status (condition code) registers. If we reinterpret the numbers in the preceding example as twos-complement rather than as unsigned, then $X = 11101011$ denotes -21_{10}, while $Y = 00101010$ denotes $+42_{10}$. The result Z computed in (4.4) now denotes $+21_{10}$, and the fact that $c_{n-1} = 1$ does not indicate overflow. In fact, we can never have overflow on adding a positive to a negative number. Overflow in modulo-2^n twos-complement addition can only result from adding two positive numbers or two negative numbers. In the first case overflow is indicated by a carry bit *into* the sign position, that is, by $c_{n-2} = 1$, since this indicates that the magnitude of the sum exceeds the $n - 1$ bits allocated to it. A little thought shows that overflow from adding two negative numbers is indicated by $c_{n-2} = 0$. We can thus conclude (as we did earlier in section 3.2.2) that the overflow condition is specified by the logic expression

$$v = \bar{x}_{n-1}\bar{y}_{n-1}c_{n-2} + x_{n-1}y_{n-1}\bar{c}_{n-2} \tag{4.5}$$

Now c_{n-1}, the carry output signal from the sign position, is defined by $x_{n-1}y_{n-1} + x_{n-1}c_{n-2} + y_{n-1}c_{n-2}$, from which it follows that

$$v = c_{n-1} \oplus c_{n-2} \tag{4.6}$$

Either (4.5) or (4.6) can be used to design overflow detection logic for twos-complement addition or subtraction. Overflow detection in the case of sign-magnitude numbers is similar and is left as an exercise (problem 4.6).

High-speed adders. The general strategy for designing fast adders is to reduce the time required to form carry signals. One approach is to compute the input carry needed by stage i directly from carrylike signals obtained from all the preceding stages $i - 1, i - 2, \ldots, 0$, rather than waiting for normal carries to ripple slowly from stage to stage. Adders that use this principle are called *carry-lookahead adders*. An n-bit carry-lookahead adder is formed from n stages, each of which is basically a full adder modified by replacing its carry output line c_i by two auxiliary signals called g_i and p_i, or *generate* and *propagate*, respectively, which are defined by the following logic equations:

$$g_i = x_i y_i \qquad p_i = x_i + y_i \tag{4.7}$$

The name *generate* comes from the fact that stage i generates a carry of 1 ($c_i = 1$) independent of the value of c_{i-1} if both x_i and y_i are 1; that is, if $x_i y_i = 1$. Stage i propagates c_{i-1}; that is, it makes $c_i = 1$ in response to $c_{i-1} = 1$ if x_i or y_i is 1—in other words, if $x_i + y_i = 1$.

Now the usual equation $c_i = x_i y_i + x_i c_{i-1} + y_i c_{i-1}$, denoting the carry signal c_i to be sent to stage $i + 1$, can be rewritten in terms of g_i and p_i.

$$c_i = g_i + p_i c_{i-1} \tag{4.8}$$

Similarly, c_{i-1} can be expressed in terms of g_{i-1}, p_{i-1}, and c_{i-2}.

$$c_{i-1} = g_{i-1} + p_{i-1}c_{i-2} \tag{4.9}$$

On substituting (4.9) into (4.8) we obtain

$$c_i = g_i + p_i g_{i-1} + p_i p_{i-1} c_{i-2}$$

Continuing in this way, c_i can be expressed as a sum-of-products function of the p and g outputs of all the preceding stages. For example, the carries in a four-stage carry-lookahead adder are defined as follows:

$$
\begin{aligned}
c_0 &= g_0 + p_0 c_{in} \\[4pt]
c_1 &= g_1 + p_1 g_0 + p_1 p_0 c_{in} \\[4pt]
c_2 &= g_2 + p_2 g_1 + p_2 p_1 g_0 + p_2 p_1 p_0 c_{in} \\[4pt]
c_3 &= g_3 + p_3 g_2 + p_3 p_2 g_1 + p_3 p_2 p_1 g_0 + p_3 p_2 p_1 p_0 c_{in}
\end{aligned}
\tag{4.10}
$$

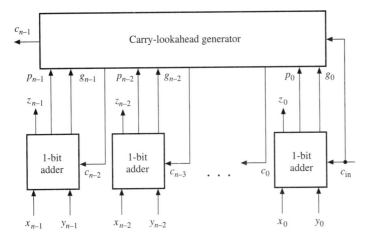

Figure 4.5
Overall structure of carry-lookahead adder.

Figure 4.5 shows the general form of a carry-lookahead adder circuit designed in this way.

We can further simplify the design by noting that the sum equation for stage i

$$z_i = x_i \oplus y_i \oplus c_{i-1}$$

is equivalent to

$$z_i = p_i \oplus g_i \oplus c_{i-1} \qquad (4.11)$$

Combining the pg equations (4.7), the carry-lookahead equations (4.10), and the modified sum equations (4.11) for $0 \le i \le 3$, we obtain the 4-bit carry-lookahead adder depicted in Figure 4.6. This design is found in practical adders such as the 74283 IC [Texas Instruments 1988]. It has four levels of logic gates, so the adder's maximum delay is $4d$, where d is the (average) gate delay. This delay is independent of the number of inputs n as long as carry generation is defined by two-level logic as in (4.10). However, the number of gates grows in proportion to n^2 as n increases. In contrast, the number of gates in a two-level adder of the sum-of-products type grows exponentially with n, while the number of gates in a ripple-carry adder grows linearly with n. The complexity of the carry-generation logic in the carry-lookahead adder, including its gate count, its maximum fan-in, and its maximum fan-out, increases steadily with n. Such practical cost considerations limit n in a single carry-lookahead adder module to four or so.

Adder expansion. The methods of handling carry signals in the two main combinational adder designs considered so far, namely, ripple-carry propagation (Figure 4.3) and carry-lookahead (Figure 4.5), can be extended to larger adders of the kind needed to execute add instructions in, say, a 64-bit computer. If we replace the n 1-bit (full) adder stages in the n-bit ripple-carry design of Figure 4.3 with n k-bit adders, we obtain an nk-bit adder. Four 4-bit adders such as the 4-bit carry-lookahead circuit of Figure 4.6 can be connected in this way to form the 16-bit adder appearing in Figure 4.7. This design represents a compromise between a 16-stage ripple-carry adder, which is cheap but slow, and a single-stage 16-bit

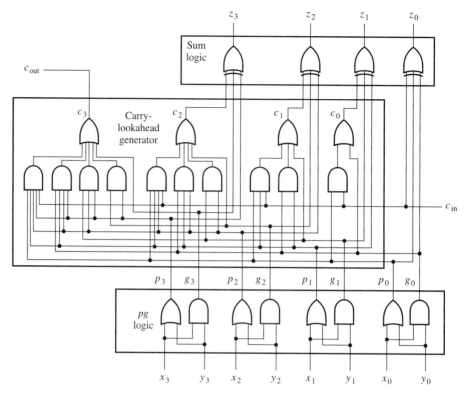

Figure 4.6
A 4-bit carry-lookahead adder.

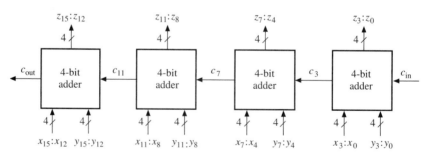

Figure 4.7
A 16-bit adder composed of 4-bit adders linked by ripple-carry propagation.

carry-lookahead adder, which is fast, expensive, and impractical because of the complexity of its carry-generation logic. The circuit of Figure 4.7 effectively combines sets of four $x_i y_i$ inputs into groups that are added via carry lookahead; the results computed by the various groups are then linked via ripple carries.

Comparing Figures 4.3 and 4.7, we see that we have effectively replaced components designed for 1-bit addition with similar but larger components intended for 4-bit addition. If we apply the same principle to the carry-lookahead circuit of Figure 4.5, we get the expanded design of Figure 4.8. Again we are replacing 1-bit

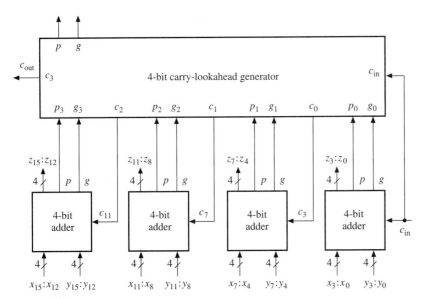

Figure 4.8
A 16-bit adder composed of 4-bit adders linked by carry lookahead.

adders with 4-bit adders, but now each adder stage produces a propagate-generate signal pair pg instead of c_{out}, and a carry-lookahead generator converts the four sets of pg signals to the carry inputs required by the four stages. The "group" g and p signals produced by each 4-bit stage are defined by

$$g = x_i y_i + x_{i-1} y_{i-1}(x_i + y_i) + x_{i-2} y_{i-2}(x_i + y_i)(x_{i-1} + y_{i-1})$$

$$+ x_{i-3} y_{i-3}(x_i + y_i)(x_{i-1} + y_{i-1})(x_{i-2} + y_{i-2}) \qquad (4.12)$$

$$p = (x_i + y_i)(x_{i-1} + y_{i-1})(x_{i-2} + y_{i-2})(x_{i-3} + y_{i-3})$$

which directly extend (4.7). It is not hard to show that the logic to generate the group carry signals c_{out}, c_{11}, c_7, and c_3 in Figure 4.8 is exactly the same as that of the carry-lookahead generator of Figure 4.6 and is therefore defined by Equations (4.10).

EXAMPLE 4.1 DESIGN OF A COMPLETE TWOS-COMPLEMENT ADDER-SUBTRACTER. To illustrate the preceding concepts, we will design a twos-complement adder-subtracter that computes the three quantities $X + Y$, $X - Y$, and $Y - X$, as well as overflow and zero flags. The design goal is to minimize the number of gates used; operating speed is not of concern. The circuit is required in several versions that handle different data word sizes, including 4, 8, and 16 bits. We will assume that we have standard gate-level and 4-bit register-level components available as building blocks.

The lowest cost adders employ ripple-carry propagation and can easily provide access to the internal signals needed by the flags. Recall that overflow detection uses c_{n-2}, the input carry to the sign position. Zero detection requires access to all the sum outputs and poses no special problems. Figure 4.9a shows the logic diagram of an appropriate 4-bit ripple-carry adder. The overflow flag is defined by Equation (4.6) as $v = c_3 \oplus c_2$ and is realized here by an XOR gate. The zero flag is defined by $z =$

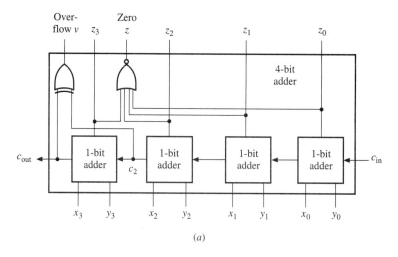

(a)

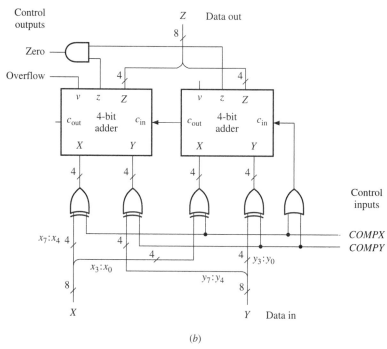

(b)

Figure 4.9
Low-cost addition and subtraction of twos-complement numbers: (a) 4-bit adder module
and (b) 8-bit adder-subtracter.

$\overline{z_3 + z_2 + z_1 + z_0}$ and implemented by a NOR gate. We can use k copies of this adder to
produce a $4k$-bit ripple-carry adder in the usual way. The overflow flag for the entire
circuit is taken from the v output of the left-most (most significant) stage, while the z
outputs of all the stages are ANDed to produce the zero flag.

To extend the adder to an adder-subtracter, the design of Figure 4.4 is a good starting point. It uses an XOR word gate to complement the X input, thereby enabling the
circuit to compute $X + Y$ and $Y - X$. To implement the third operation $X - Y$, we could

insert a two-way 4-bit multiplexer into each of the data-in buses so that both X and Y can be applied to each of the adder-subtracter's data inputs. A cheaper solution is to insert a second XOR word gate into the Y bus, enabling Y to be complemented independently. We can then compute $X - Y$ in the form $X + \bar{Y} + 1$.

The complete design of an 8-bit adder-subtracter along the foregoing lines is depicted in Figure 4.9b. It contains two 4-bit adders of the type in Figure 4.9a linked by their carry lines. Two lines *COMPX* and *COMPY* control the XOR gates that change X and Y to $\bar{X}$ and $\bar{Y}$, respectively. The OR gate sets the adder's carry-in line to 1 during subtraction. A two-input AND gate combines the two z outputs to produce the zero flag, which is 1 if and only if the entire 8-bit result $Z = 0$.

Three of the four signal combinations on *COMPX* and *COMPY* control lines implement the desired three arithmetic functions. The fourth combination 11 implements the sum $\bar{X} + \bar{Y} + 1$, which is an arithmetic function implemented by our design that has no obvious uses.[1] Such superfluous functions are common in the design of data processing circuits.

4.1.2 Multiplication

Fixed-point multiplication requires substantially more hardware than fixed-point addition and, as a result, is not included in the instruction sets of some smaller processors. Multiplication is usually implemented by some form of repeated addition. A simple but slow method to compute $X \times Y$ is to add the multiplicand Y to itself X times, where X is the multiplier. (A version of this technique using counters is discussed in problem 2.4.) Often multiplication is implemented by multiplying Y by X k bits at a time and adding the resulting terms. Figure 4.10 shows this process for unsigned binary numbers in pencil-and-paper calculations with $k = 1$. The main operations involved are shifting and addition. The algorithm of Figure 4.10 is inefficient in that the 1-bit products $x_j 2^i Y$ must be stored until the final addition step is completed. In machine implementations it is desirable to add each $x_j 2^i Y$ term as it is generated to the sum of the preceding terms to form a number P_{i+1} called a *partial product*. Figure 4.11 shows the calculation in Figure 4.10 implemented in this way. The computation involved in processing one multiplier bit x_j can be described by a register-transfer statement of the form

$$P_{i+1} := P_i + x_j 2^i Y \tag{4.13}$$

1010	Multiplicand Y
1101	Multiplier $X = x_3 x_2 x_1 x_0$
1010	$x_0 Y$
0000	$x_1 2Y$
1010	$x_2 2^2 Y$
1010	$x_3 2^3 Y$
10000010	Product $P = \displaystyle\sum_{j=0}^{3} x_j 2 Y^j$

Figure 4.10
Typical pencil-and-paper method for multiplication of unsigned binary numbers.

[1] On the other hand, it has been observed, that "there is no feature of a machine, however pathological, which cannot be exploited by a programmer." [Kampe 1960].

1010	Multiplicand Y
1101	Multiplier $X = x_3x_2x_1x_0$
00000000	$P_0 = 0$
1010	x_0Y
00001010	$P_1 = P_0 + x_0Y$
0000	x_12Y
00001010	$P_2 = P_1 + x_12Y$
1010	$x_22^2Y^j$
00110010	$P_3 = P_2 + x_22^2Y$
1010	x_32^3Y
10000010	$P_4 = P_3 + x_32^3Y = P$

Figure 4.11

The multiplication of Figure 4.10 modified for machine implementation.

where 2^iY is equivalent to Y shifted i positions to the left. In the version of this multiplication algorithm presented in Example 2.7 (section 2.2.3), P_i is shifted right with respect to a fixed multiplicand Y so that (4.13) is replaced by the equivalent two operations

$$P_i := P_i + x_jY; \quad P_{i+1} := 2^{-j}P_i; \tag{4.14}$$

The multiplication of sign-magnitude numbers requires a straightforward extension of the unsigned case discussed above. The magnitude part of the product $P = X \times Y$ is computed by the unsigned shift-and-add multiplication algorithm, and the sign p_s of P is computed separately from the signs of X and Y as follows: $p_s := x_s \oplus y_s$. The implementation of sign-magnitude multiplication using this sequential method is covered in Example 2.7.

Twos-complement multipliers. The multiplication of twos-complement numbers presents some difficulties in the case of negative operands. For example, when a negative P_i is right-shifted as in (4.14), leading 1s rather than leading 0s must be introduced at the left end of the number. More seriously, the multiplication process must treat positive and negative operands differently.

A conceptually simple approach to twos-complement multiplication is to negate all negative operands at the beginning, perform unsigned multiplication on the resulting (positive) numbers, and then negate the result if necessary. Twos-complement negation for an integer $X = x_{n-1}x_{n-2}x_{n-3}\ldots x_1x_0$ is specified by

$$-X = \bar{x}_{n-1}\bar{x}_{n-2}\bar{x}_{n-3}\ldots \bar{x}_1\bar{x}_0 + 000\ldots01 \quad (\text{modulo } 2^n) \tag{4.15}$$

and can easily be implemented by an adder and an EXCLUSIVE-OR word gate, as shown in Figure 4.4. However, up to four extra clock cycles are needed to negate X and Y and the double-length product P. Several faster schemes have been proposed to handle negative operands. Since these hinge on certain properties of the twos-complement representation, we consider the latter first.

Clearly $\bar{x}_i = 1 - x_i$ (modulo 2), so we can rewrite (4.15) as follows:

$$-X = 111\ldots11 - x_{n-1}x_{n-2}x_{n-3}\ldots x_1x_0 + 000\ldots01 \quad (\text{modulo } 2^n) \tag{4.16}$$

Since $2^n = 111\ldots11 + 000\ldots01$, this equation is equivalent to $-X = 2^n - X$, which, incidentally, indicates the origin of the term twos-complement. Now if X is positive

$(x_{n-1} = 0)$, we can express its value as

$$X = \sum_{i=0}^{n-2} 2^i x_i \tag{4.17}$$

If X is negative $(x_{n-1} = 1)$, then (4.17) does not hold. However, we can rewrite (4.16) as

$$-X = 111\ldots11 - (0x_{n-2}x_{n-3}\ldots x_1 x_0 + 100\ldots00) + 000\ldots01$$

$$= 2^{n-1} - x_{n-2}x_{n-3}\ldots x_1 x_0 \tag{4.18}$$

because $2^{n-1} = 111\ldots11 - 100\ldots00 + 000\ldots0$. Hence for negative X,

$$X = -2^{n-1} + x_{n-2}x_{n-3}\ldots x_1 x_0$$

$$= -2^{n-1} + \sum_{i=0}^{n-2} 2^i x_i \tag{4.19}$$

Finally, we combine (4.17) and (4.19) into a single formula

$$X = -2^{n-1}x_{n-1} + \sum_{i=0}^{n-2} 2^i x_i \tag{4.20}$$

which is valid for both positive and negative n-bit integers. For example, suppose that $n = 6$ and $X = 101101$. Evaluating X according to (4.20) yields

$$X = -2^5 \times 1 + 2^4 \times 0 + 2^3 \times 1 + 2^2 \times 1 + 2^1 \times 0 + 2^0 \times 1$$

$$= -32 + 8 + 4 + 1 = -19$$

Equation (4.20) implies that we can treat bits $x_{n-2}x_{n-3}\ldots x_1 x_0$ of a negative twos-complement integer in the same way as the corresponding (magnitude) bits of a positive number; each bit x_i has the positive weight 2^i. Weight $+2^{n-1}$ is assigned to the sign bit x_{n-1} of a positive number; however, since $x_{n-1} = 0$, its contribution to the number is zero. In the negative case, the sign x_{n-1} is assigned weight -2^{n-1}; this adds -2^{n-1} to the number, ensuring that it is negative.

If $X = x_{n-1}x_{n-2}\ldots x_1 x_0$ is a twos-complement fraction instead of an integer, then the negation formula (4.15) remains valid, but because bit i now has weight 2^{i-n+1} instead of 2^i, Equation (4.20) is replaced by

$$X = -2^0 x_{n-1} + \sum_{i=0}^{n-2} 2^{i-n+1} x_i \tag{4.21}$$

In effect we have multiplied (4.20) by the scaling factor $2^{-(n-1)}$. For example, let $n = 4$ and $X = 1011$, which represents the fraction -0.625_{10}. Application of (4.21) yields

$$X = -2^0 \times 1 + 2^{-1} \times 0 + 2^{-2} \times 1 + 2^{-3} \times 1$$

$$= -1.000 + 0.250 + 0.125 = -0.625$$

Suppose that X is the multiplier operand in a shift-and-add multiplication algorithm to compute $P = X \times Y$ for twos-complement numbers. Equations (4.20) and

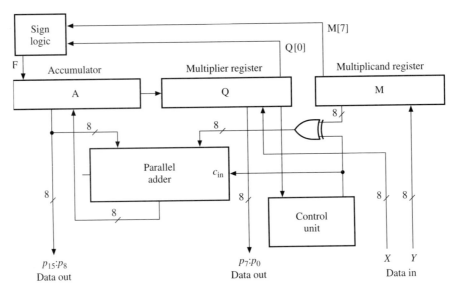

Figure 4.12
The datapath of the twos-complement multiplier.

(4.21) suggest that we can use an unsigned multiplication technique like those illustrated in Figures 4.12 and 4.13 with one change: When multiplying by the sign bit, perform subtraction rather than addition in the final step if a minus sign $x_{n-1} = 1$ is encountered. This observation is the basis of a twos-complement multiplication algorithm developed by James E. Robertson, which has been widely used in computer design [Robertson 1955; Cavanagh 1984]. We now show one way to adapt the circuit developed in Example 2.7 for sign-magnitude multiplication to deal with the twos-complement case.

2Cmultiplier	**(in:** INBUS; **out:** OUTBUS);
	register A[7:0], M[7:0], Q[7:0], COUNT[2:0], F;
	bus INBUS[7:0], OUTBUS[7:0];
BEGIN:	A := 0, COUNT := 0, F := 0,
INPUT:	M := INBUS;
	Q := INBUS;
ADD:	A[7:0] := A[7:0] + M[7:0] × Q[0],
	F := (M[7] **and** Q[0]) **or** F;
RSHIFT:	A[7] := F, A[6:0].Q := A.Q[7:1], COUNT := COUNT + 1;
TEST:	*if* COUNT ≠ 7 **then go to** ADD;
SUBTRACT:	A[7:0] := A[7:0] − M[7:0] × Q[0], Q[0] := 0;
OUTPUT:	OUTBUS := Q;
	OUTBUS := A;
	end *2Cmultiplier*;

Figure 4.13
HDL description of the multiplier for 8-bit twos-complement fractions.

EXAMPLE 4.2 DESIGN OF A MULTIPLIER FOR TWOS-COMPLEMENT FRACTIONS. Consider again the task of multiplying two 8-bit binary fractions $X = x_7 x_6 x_5 x_4 x_3 x_2 x_1 x_0$ and $Y = y_7 y_6 y_5 y_4 y_3 y_2 y_1 y_0$ to form the product $P = Y \times X$, this time using twos-complement code. (Example 2.7 analyzed this problem for the sign-magnitude case.) Assume that the multiplier will have a register-level structure similar to that in Figure 2.41, with registers A, M, and Q storing the various operands and A.Q forming a right-shift register. Since sign bits will be included in additions and subtractions, we need an 8-bit adder-subtracter, rather than the 7-bit magnitude-only adder used in the earlier design. Figure 4.12 shows the datapath of the proposed design at the register level.

To develop the required twos-complement multiplication algorithm for this machine, we consider the four possible cases determined by the signs of X and Y.

1. $x_7 = y_7 = 0$; that is, both X and Y are positive. The computation in this case is effectively unsigned multiplication with the product P computed in a series of add-and-shift steps of the form

$$P_i := P_i + x_i Y; \quad P_{i+1} := 2^{-1} P_i;$$

All partial products P_i are nonnegative, so leading 0s are introduced into A during the right-shift operation indicated by the factor 2^{-1}.

2. $x_7 = 0$, $y_7 = 1$; that is, X is positive and Y is negative. The partial product P_i will be zero, and leading 0s should be shifted into A as before, until the first 1 in X is encountered. Multiplication of Y by this 1 and addition of the result to A causes P_i to become negative, from which point on leading 1s rather than 0s must be shifted into A. These rules ensure that a right shift corresponds to division by 2 in twos-complement code.

3. $x_7 = 1$, $y_7 = 0$; that is, X is negative and Y is positive. This follows case 1 for the first seven add-and-shift steps yielding the partial product

$$P_7 = \sum_{i=0}^{6} 2^{i-7} x_i Y$$

For the final step, often referred to as a correction step, the subtraction $P := P_7 - Y$ is performed. The result P is then given by

$$P = -Y + \sum_{i=0}^{6} 2^{i-7} x_i Y = \left(-x_7 + \sum_{i=0}^{6} 2^{i-7} x_i \right) Y$$

which is $X \times Y$ by (4.21).

4. $x_7 = y_7 = 1$; that is, both X and Y are negative. The procedure used here follows case 2, with leading 0s (1s) being introduced into the accumulator whenever its contents are zero (negative). The correction (subtraction) step of case 3 is also performed, which ensures that the final product in A.Q is nonnegative.

Each addition/subtraction step can be performed in the usual twos-complement fashion by treating the sign bits like any other and ignoring overflow. Care is needed in the shift step to ensure that the correct new value is placed in the accumulator's sign position A[7]. This value must be a leading 0 if the current partial product in A.Q is positive or zero, and 1 if it is negative. We introduce a flip-flop F to control the values assigned to A[7]. F is initially set to 0, and is subsequently defined by

$$F := (y_7 \textbf{ \textit{and} } x_i) \textbf{ \textit{or} } F$$

Step	Action	F	Accumulator A	Register Q
0	Initialize registers	0	00000000	10110011 = multiplier X
1			11010101	= multiplicand Y = M
	Add M to A	1	11010101	10110011
	Right-shift F.A.Q	1	11101010	11011001
2			11010101	
	Add M to A	1	10111111	11011001
	Right-shift F.A.Q	1	11011111	11101100
3			00000000	
	Add zero to A	1	11011111	11101100
	Right-shift F.A.Q	1	11101111	11110110
4			00000000	
	Add zero to A	1	11101111	11110110
	Right-shift F.A.Q	1	11110111	11111011
5			11010101	
	Add M to A	1	11001100	11111011
	Right-shift F.A.Q	1	11100110	01111101
6			11010101	
	Add M to A	1	10111011	01111101
	Right-shift F.A.Q	1	11011101	10111110
7			00000000	
	Add zero to A	1	11011101	10111110
	Right-shift F.A.Q	1	11101110	11011111
8			11010101	
	Subtract M from A	1	00011001	11011111
	Set Q[0] to 0		00011001	11011110 = product P

Figure 4.14
Illustration of the Robertson multiplication algorithm for twos-complement fractions.

Here y_7 is the sign of the multiplicand stored in M[7], and x_i is the current multiplier bit being tested in Q[0]. Thus F is set to 1 if Y is negative and at least one nonzero x_i is encountered. Once set to 1, it remains at that value. A negative Y and a positive or negative X therefore produce a series of negative partial products. This situation is to be expected, since bits $x_6{:}x_0$ of the multiplier X are always treated as if they were positive. A positive Y, or $X = 0$, causes F to remain permanently at 0. Note that the sign p_{15} of the product P requires no separate computational step. As in Example 2.7, the least significant bit p_0 of P is set to 0 to make the result exactly 16 bits long.

Figure 4.13 presents an HDL description of the twos-complement multiplication algorithm, which summarizes the foregoing analysis; compare the corresponding sign-magnitude algorithm in Figure 2.39. An application of the present algorithm to the case $X = 10110011$ and $Y = 11010101$ appears in Figure 4.14. The sign bit x_7 of the multiplier X is underlined to show its passage through Q. Observe how F becomes 1 in step 1, when the negative multiplicand is first added to the accumulator. F continues to supply leading 1s to the A register until step 8. Then because Q[7] = x_7 = 1, a subtraction is performed that produces the proper sign $p_{15} = 0$ in A(0). Setting Q[0] = p_0 to 0 completes the multiplication process.

Booth's algorithm. Another interesting and widely used scheme for twos-complement multiplication was proposed by Andrew D. Booth in the 1950s

[Booth 1951]. Like Robertson's method in Example 4.2, Booth's algorithm employs both addition and subtraction, but it treats positive and negative operands uniformly—no special actions are required for negative numbers. Booth's algorithm can also be readily extended in various ways to speed up the multiplication process; see problems 4.16 and 4.17. A version of this algorithm implements the ARM6's multiply instruction.

The multiplication algorithms we have considered so far involve scanning the multiplier X from right to left and using the value of the current multiplier bit x_i to determine which of the following operations to perform: add the multiplicand Y, subtract Y, or add zero, that is, no operation. In Booth's approach two adjacent bits $x_i x_{i-1}$ are examined in each step. If $x_i x_{i-1} = 01$, then Y is added to the current partial product P_i, while if $x_i x_{i-1} = 10$, Y is subtracted from P_i. If $x_i x_{i-1} = 00$ or 11, then neither addition or subtraction is performed; only the subsequent right shift of P_i takes place. Thus Booth's algorithm effectively skips over runs of 1s and runs of 0s that it encounters in X. This skipping reduces the average number of add-subtract steps and allows faster multipliers to be designed, although at the expense of more complex timing and control circuitry.

The validity of Booth's method can be seen as follows. Suppose that X is a positive integer and contains a subsequence X^* consisting of a run of k 1s flanked by two 0s.

$$X^* = x_i x_{i-1} x_{i-2} \cdots x_{i-k+1} x_{i-k} x_{i-k-1}$$

$$= 0\,1\,1\,\ldots\,1\,1\,0$$

In a direct add-and-shift multiplication algorithm such as Robertson's, Y is multiplied by each bit of X^* in sequence and the results are summed so that X^*'s contribution to the product $P = X \times Y$ is

$$\sum_{j=i-k}^{i-1} 2^j Y \tag{4.22}$$

Now when Booth's algorithm is applied to X^*, it performs an addition when it encounters $x_i x_{i-1} = 01$, which contributes $2^i Y$ to P. It performs a subtraction at $x_{i-k} x_{i-k-1} = 10$, which contributes $-2^{i-k} Y$ to P. Thus the net contribution of X^* to the product P in this case is

$$2^i Y - 2^{i-k} Y = 2^{i-k} Y (2^k - 1) Y$$

$$= 2^{i-k} \sum_{m=0}^{k-1} 2^m Y$$

$$= \sum_{m=0}^{k-1} 2^{m+i-k} Y \tag{4.23}$$

Suppose the index m is replaced by $j = m + i - k$. Then the upper and lower limits of the summation in (4.23) change from $k-1$ and 0 to $i-1$ and $i-k$, respectively, implying that (4.22) and (4.23) are, in fact, the same. It follows that Booth's algorithm correctly computes the contribution of X^*, and hence of the entire multiplier X, to the product P. Equation (4.20) implies that the contribution of a negative X^*

BoothMult	(**in:** INBUS; **out:** OUTBUS);
	register A[7:0], M[7:0], Q[7:–1], COUNT[2:0],
	bus INBUS[7:0], OUTBUS[7:0];
BEGIN:	A := 0, COUNT := 0,
INPUT:	M := INBUS;
	Q[7:0] := INBUS, Q[–1] := 0;
SCAN:	**if** Q[1] Q[0] = 01 **then** A[7:0] := A[7:0] + M[7:0], **go to** TEST;
	else if Q[1] Q[0] = 10 **then** A[7:0] := A[7:0] – M[7:0];
TEST:	**if** COUNT = 7 **then go to** OUTPUT,
RSHIFT:	A[7] := A[7], A[6:0].Q = A.Q[7:0],
INCREMENT:	COUNT := COUNT + 1, **go to** SCAN;
OUTPUT:	OUTBUS := A, Q[0] := 0;
	OUTBUS := Q[7:0];
end *BoothMult;*	

Figure 4.15

HDL description of an 8-bit multiplier implementing the basic Booth algorithm.

to P can also be expressed in the formats of (4.20) and (4.23); a similar argument demonstrates the correctness of the algorithm for negative multipliers. The argument for fractions is essentially the same as that for integers.

The twos-complement multiplication circuit of Figure 4.12 can easily be modified to implement Booth's algorithm. Figure 4.15 describes a straightforward implementation of the Booth algorithm using the above approach with $n = 8$ and a circuit based on Figure 4.12. An extra flip-flop Q[–1] is appended to the right end of the multiplier register Q, and the sign logic for A is reduced to the simple sign extension A[7] := A[7]. In each step the two adjacent bits Q[0]Q[–1] of Q are examined, instead of Q[0] alone as in Robertson's algorithm, to decide the operation (add Y, subtract Y, or no operation) to be performed in that step. For comparison with Robertson's method in Figure 4.13, the operands are assumed to be fractions. The application of this algorithm to the example solved by Robertson's method in Figure 4.14 appears in Figure 4.16, where the bits stored in Q[0]Q[–1] in each step are underlined.

Combinational array multipliers. Advances in VLSI technology have made it possible to build combinational circuits that perform $n \times n$-bit multiplication for fairly large values of n. An example is the Integrated Device Technology IDT721CL multiplier chip, which can multiply two 16-bit numbers in 16 ns [Integrated Device Technology 1995]. These multipliers resemble the n-step sequential multipliers discussed above but have roughly n times more logic to allow the product to be computed in one step instead of in n steps. They are composed of arrays of simple combinational elements, each of which implements an add/subtract-and-shift operation for small slices of the multiplication operands.

Suppose that two binary numbers $X = x_{n-1}x_{n-2}...x_1x_0$ and $Y = y_{n-1}y_{n-2}...y_1y_0$ are to be multiplied. For simplicity, assume that X and Y are unsigned integers. The product $P = X \times Y$ can therefore be expressed as

Step	Action	Accumulator	Register Q
0	Initialize registers	00000000	10110011 = multiplier X
	Set Q[–1] to 0	00000000	101100110
1		11010101	= mulitplicand Y = M
	Subtract M from A	00101011	10110010
	Right-shift A.Q	00010101	110110011
2	Skip add/subtract	00010101	11011001
	Right-shift A.Q	00001010	111011001
3		11010101	
	Add M to A	11011111	11101100
	Right-shift A.Q	11101111	111101100
4	Skip add/subtract	11101111	11110100
	Right-shift A.Q	11110111	111110110
5		11010101	
	Subtract M from A	00100010	11111010
	Right-shift A.Q	00010001	011111011
6	Skip add/subtract	00010001	01111011
	Right-shift A.Q	00001000	101111101
7		11010101	
	Add M to A	11011101	10111101
	Right-shift A.Q	11101110	110111110
8		11010101	
	Subtract M from A	00011001	11011110
	Set Q[0] to 0	00011001	110111100 = product P

Figure 4.16

Illustration of the Booth multiplication algorithm.

$$P = \sum_{i=0}^{n-1} 2^i x_i Y \qquad (4.24)$$

corresponding to the bit-by-bit multiplication style of Figure 4.10. Now (4.24) can be rewritten as

$$P = \sum_{i=0}^{n-1} 2^i \left(\sum_{j=0}^{n-1} x_i y_j 2^j \right) \qquad (4.25)$$

Each of the n^2 1-bit product terms $x_i y_j$ appearing in (4.25) can be computed by a two-input AND gate—observe that the arithmetic and logical products coincide in the 1-bit case. Hence an $n \times n$ array of two-input ANDs of the type shown in Figure 4.17 can compute all the $x_i y_j$ terms simultaneously. The terms are summed according to (4.25) by an array of $n(n-1)$ 1-bit full adders as shown in Figure 4.18; this circuit is a kind of two-dimensional ripple-carry adder. The shifts implied by the 2^i and 2^j factors in (4.25) are implemented by the spatial displacement of the adders along the x and y dimensions. Note the similarities between the circuit of Figure 4.17 and the multiplication examples of Figures 4.10 and 4.11.

The AND and add functions of the array multiplier can be combined into a single component (cell) as illustrated in Figure 4.19. This cell realizes the arithmetic expression

$$c_{out}s = a\ \textbf{plus}\ b\ \textbf{plus}\ xy \tag{4.26}$$

An $n \times n$-bit multiplier can be built using n^2 copies of this cell as the sole component, although, as in Figure 4.18, some cells on the periphery of the array have inputs set to 0 or 1, effectively reducing their operation from (4.26) $a\ \textbf{plus}\ b\ \textbf{plus}\ xy$ to $a\ \textbf{plus}\ b$ (a half adder). The multiplication time for this multiplier is determined by the worst-case carry propagation and, ignoring the differences between the internal and peripheral cells, is $(2n-1)D$, where D is the delay of the basic cell.

Multiplication algorithms for twos-complement numbers, such as Robertson's and Booth's, can also be realized by arrays of combinational cells as the next example shows.

**EXAMPLE 4.3 ARRAY IMPLEMENTATION OF THE BOOTH MULTIPLICA-
TION ALGORITHM** [KOREN 1993]. Implementing the Booth method by a combinational array requires a multifunction cell capable of addition, subtraction, and no operation (skip). Such a cell B is shown in Figure 4.20a. Its various functions are selected by a pair of control lines H and D as indicated. It is easily seen that the required functions of B are defined by the following logic equations.

$$z = a \oplus bH \oplus cH$$

$$c_{out} = (a \oplus D)(b + c) + bc$$

When $HD = 10$, these equations reduce to the usual full-adder equations (4.1); when $HD = 11$, they reduce to the corresponding full-subtracter equations

$$z = a \oplus b \oplus c$$

$$c_{out} = \bar{a}b + \bar{a}c + bc$$

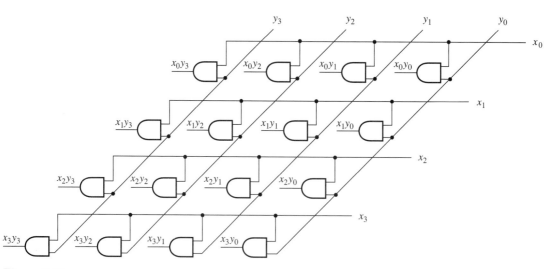

Figure 4.17
AND array for 4×4-bit unsigned multiplication.

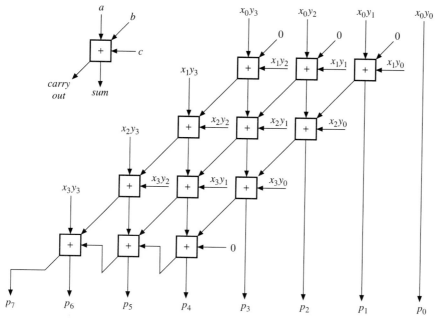

Figure 4.18
Full-adder array for 4×4-bit unsigned multiplication.

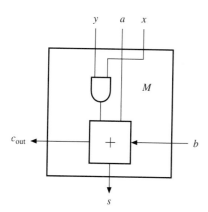

Figure 4.19
Cell M for an unsigned array multiplier.

in which c and c_{out} assume the roles of borrow-in and borrow-out, respectively. When $H = 0$, z becomes a, and the carry lines play no role in the final result.

An n-bit multiplier is constructed from $n^2 + n(n - 1)/2$ copies of the B cell connected as shown in Figure 4.20b. The extra cells at the top left change the array's shape from the parallelogram of Figure 4.18 to a trapezium and are employed to sign-extend the multiplicand Y for addition and subtraction. Note how the diagonal lines marked b deliver the sign-extended Y directly to every row of B cells. When Y is positive, it is sign-extended by leading 0s; this is implicit in the array of Figure 4.18. In the present case, when Y is negative, it must be explicitly sign-extended by leading 1s.

The operation to be performed by each row i of B cells is decided by bits $x_i x_{i-1}$ of the operand X. To allow each possible $x_i x_{i-1}$ pair to control row operations, we

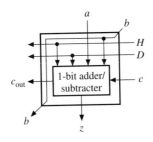

H	D	Function
0	X	$z = a$ (no operation)
1	0	$c_{out}z = a$ **plus** b **plus** c (add)
1	1	$c_{out}z = a - b - c$ (subtract)

(a)

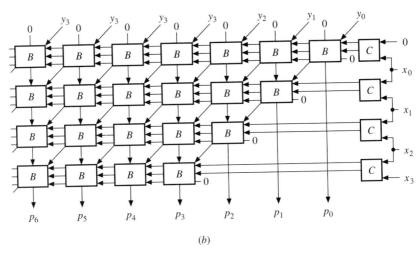

(b)

Figure 4.20
Combinational array implementing Booth's algorithm: (a) main cell B and
(b) array multiplier for 4×4-bit numbers.

introduce a second cell type denoted C in Figure 4.20b to generate the control input
signal H and D required by the B cells. Cell C compares x_i with x_{i-1} and generates
the values of HD required by Figure 4.20a; these values are as follows:

$$H = \overline{x_i \oplus x_{i-1}}$$
$$D = \overline{x_i}x_{i-1}$$

4.1.3 Division

In fixed-point division two numbers, a divisor V and a dividend D, are given. The
object is to compute a third number Q, the quotient, such that $Q \times V$ equals or is
very close to D. For example, if unsigned integer formats are being used, Q is computed so that

$$D = Q \times V + R$$

where R, the remainder, is required to be less than V, that is, $0 \le R < V$. We can then write

$$D/V = Q + R/V \qquad (4.27)$$

Here R/V is a small quantity representing the error in using Q alone to represent D/V; this error is zero if $R = 0$.

Preliminaries. The relationship $D \approx Q \times V$ suggests that a close correspondence exists between division and multiplication, specifically the dividend, quotient, and divisor correspond to the product, multiplicand, and multiplier, respectively. This correspondence means that similar algorithms and circuits can be used for multiplication and division. In multiplication the shifted multiplier is added to the multiplicand to form the product. In division the shifted divisor is subtracted from the dividend to form the quotient. Just as multiplication ends with a double-length product, division often begins with a double-length dividend. Despite these similarities, division is a more difficult operation than multiplication because to determine a particular quotient bit q_i, we have to answer the question: How many multiples is the divisor V of the current partial dividend D_i? This question is typically answered by trial and error: Multiply V by a trial value for q_i, subtract the result from D_i, and check the value of the remainder. Note too that the next quotient bit q_{i+1} cannot be determined until q_i is known. Thus division has an element of uncertainty not found in multiplication.

One of the simpler binary division methods is a sequential digit-by-digit algorithm similar to that used in pencil-and-paper methods with decimal numbers. Figure 4.21 illustrates this approach for a 3-bit divisor $V = 101$ and a 6-bit dividend $D = 100110$. The dividend is scanned from left to right, and the quotient is computed bit by bit. In each step divisor V is compared to the current partial dividend D_i, referred to here as the partial remainder R_i.[2] The current quotient bit q_i is either 0 or 1, and is determined by comparing V with R_i; this comparison is the hard part of division. Note that decimal division is harder than binary in this

	0111	Quotient $Q = q_3 q_2 q_1 q_0$
Divisor $V = 101$	100110	Dividend $D = R_0$
	000	$q_3 V$
	100110	R_1
	101	$q_2 2^{-1} V$
	10010	R_2
	101	$q_1 2^{-2} V$
	1000	R_3
	101	$q_0 2^{-3} V$
	011	$R_4 = $ remainder R

Figure 4.21
Typical pencil-and-paper method for division of unsigned numbers.

---

[2]We use the terms *partial dividend* and *partial remainder* interchangeably because the remainder from step i is used as the dividend in step $i + 1$.

regard because q_i must be selected from 10 possible digit values instead of from two. If the numbers appearing in the division calculation of Figure 4.21 are unsigned binary integers of length six, then (4.27) becomes

$$100110. / 000101. = 000111. + 000011./ 000101.$$

corresponding to the decimal division $38/5 = 7 + 3/5$. If the numbers are unsigned 6-bit fractions, then Figure 4.21 is interpreted as

$$.100110/.101000 = .111000 + .000011/.101000$$

corresponding to $.59375/.625 = .875 + .046875/.625$.

In integer arithmetic Q and R are always integers of the standard word size. If fraction formats are used, however, the number of bits of Q is not necessarily bounded. For example, $.2000/.3000 = .66666...$, a repeating fraction. It is necessary, therefore, to limit the number of quotient bits generated by the division process. Division of $.2000$ by $.3000$ might be required to yield a four-digit quotient Q with truncation or rounding determining the final digit of Q. Several other difficulties occur in division. If D is too large relative to V, then Q will not fit in the standard word size, resulting in *quotient overflow*. For instance, the four-digit fraction division $.2000/.0100$ produces a nonfraction six-digit result 20.0000. When $V = 0$, the quotient Q is treated as undefined or infinity and a *divide-by-zero error* is said to occur. Special circuits are employed to check for, and flag, quotient overflow and zero divisors before division begins.

Basic algorithms. Suppose that the divisor V and dividend D are unsigned integers and the quotient $Q = q_{n-1}q_{n-2}q_{n-3}...$ is to be computed one bit at a time. At each step i, $2^{-i}V$, which represents the divisor shifted i bits to the right, is compared with the current partial remainder R_i. The quotient bit q_i is set to 1 (0) if $2^{-i}V$ is less (greater) than R_i, and a new partial remainder R_{i+1} is computed according to the relation

$$R_{i+1} := R_i - q_i 2^{-i}V \qquad (4.28)$$

In machine implementations it is more convenient to shift the partial remainder to the left relative to a fixed divisor, in which case (4.28) is replaced by

$$R_{i+1} := 2R_i - q_i V$$

Figure 4.22 shows the calculation of Figure 4.21 modified in this way. The final partial remainder R_4 is now the overall remainder R shifted three bits to the left, so that $R = 2^{-3}R_4$.

As observed above, the central problem in division is finding the quotient digit q_i. If radix-r numbers are being represented, then q_i must be chosen from among r possible values. When $r = 2$, q_i can be generated by comparing V and $2R_i$ in the ith step, as is done implicitly in Figure 4.22. If $V > 2R_i$, then $q_i = 0$; otherwise, $q_i = 1$. If V is long, a combinational magnitude comparator circuit may be impractical, in which case q_i is usually determined by subtracting V from $2R_i$ and examining the sign of $2R_i - V$. If $2R_i - V$ is negative, $q_i = 0$; otherwise, $q_i = 1$.

The circuit used for multiplication in Example 4.2 (Figure 4.12) is easily modified to perform division, as shown in Figure 4.23. The $2n$-bit shift register A.Q stores the partial remainders. Initially the dividend (which can contain up to $2n$

Divisor V			Quotient Q
101	100110	Dividend $D = 2R_0$	
	000	$q_3 V$	0
	100110	R_1	
	1001100	$2R_1$	
	101	$q_2 V$	01
	100100	R_2	
	1001000	$2R_2$	
	101	$q_1 V$	011
	100000	R_3	
	1000000	$2R_3$	
	101	$q_0 V$	0111
	011000	$R_4 = 2^3 R$	

Figure 4.22
The division of Figure 4.21 modified for machine implementation.

bits) is placed in A.Q. The divisor V is placed in the M register where it remains throughout the division process. In each step A.Q is shifted to the left. The positions vacated at the right-most end of the Q register can be used to store the quotient bits as they are generated. When the division process terminates, Q contains the quotient, while A contains the (shifted) remainder.

As noted already, the quotient bit q_i can be determined by a trial subtraction of the form $2R_i - V$. This subtraction also yields the new partial remainder R_{i+1} when $2R_i - V$ is positive; that is, when $q_i = 1$. Clearly, the process of determining q_i and R_{i+1} can be integrated. Two major division algorithms are distinguished by the way they combine the computation of q_i and R_{i+1}. If $q_i = 0$, then the result of the trial

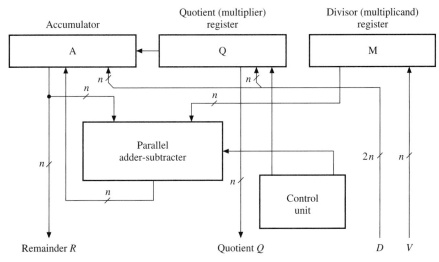

Figure 4.23
The datapath of a sequential n-bit binary divider.

subtraction is $2R_i - V$; however, the required new partial remainder R_{i+1} is $2R_i$. The partial remainder R_{i+1} can be obtained by adding V back to the result of the trial subtraction. This straightforward technique is called *restoring division*. In every step the operation

$$R_{i+1} := 2R_i - V \qquad (4.29)$$

is performed. When the result of the subtraction is negative, a restoring addition is performed as follows:

$$R_{i+1} := R_{i+1} + V$$

If the probability of $q_i = 1$ is 1/2, then this algorithm requires n subtractions and an average of $n/2$ additions.

The restoration step of the preceding algorithm is eliminated in a slightly different technique called *nonrestoring division*. This method is based on the observation that a restoration of the form

$$R_i := R_i + V \qquad (4.30)$$

is followed in the next step by the subtraction (4.29). Operations (4.29) and (4.30) can be merged into the single operation

$$R_{i+1} := 2R_i + V \qquad (4.31)$$

Thus when $q_i = 1$, which is indicated by a positive value of R_i, R_{i+1} is computed using (4.29). When $q_i = 0$, R_{i+1} is computed using (4.31). The calculation of each quotient bit involves either an addition or a subtraction, but not both. Nonrestoring division therefore requires n additions or subtractions, whereas restoring division requires an average of $3n/2$ additions and subtractions.

Figure 4.24 presents a nonrestoring division algorithm designed for the circuit of Figure 4.23 with unsigned integers. The divisor V and quotient Q are n bits long (with leading 0s if necessary), while the dividend D is up to $2n - 1$ bits long, which is the maximum length of the product of two n-bit integers. The flip-flop S is appended to the accumulator A to record the sign of the result of an addition or subtraction and to determine the quotient bit. Each new quotient bit is placed in $Q[0]$, and the final values of the quotient Q and the remainder R are in the Q and A registers, respectively. An application of this algorithm when $n = 4$ appears in Figure 4.25 with $D = 1100001_2 = 97_{10}$ and $V = 1010_2 = 10_{10}$.

The restoring and nonrestoring division techniques can be extended to signed numbers in much the same way as multiplication. Sign-magnitude numbers present few difficulties; the magnitudes of the quotient and remainder can be computed as in the unsigned number case, while their signs are determined separately. As remarked in [Cavanagh 1984], there are no simple division algorithms for handling negative numbers directly in twos-complement code because of the difficulty of selecting the quotient bits so that the quotient has the correct positive or negative representation. The most direct approach to signed division is to negate any negative operands, perform division on the resulting positive numbers, and then negate the results, as needed. A fast division algorithm for twos-complement numbers based on the nonrestoring approach was devised independently in 1958 by Dura W. Sweeney, James E. Robertson, and Keith D. Tocher and is called the SRT method in their honor; see [Cavanagh 1984; Koren 1993] for details.

NRdivider	(**in:** INBUS; **out:** OUTBUS);			

register S, A[$n-1$:0], M[$n-1$:0], Q[$n-1$:0], COUNT[$\lceil \log_2 n \rceil$:0];

bus INBUS[$n-1$:0], OUTBUS[$n-1$:0];

BEGIN: COUNT := 0, S := 0,

INPUT: A := INBUS; {Input the left half of the dividend D}

                   Q := INBUS; {Input the right half of the dividend D}

                   M := INBUS; {Input the divisor V}

SUBTRACT: S.A := S.A – M; {S is the sign of the result}

TEST: **if** S = 0 **then**

          begin Q[0] := 1;

          if COUNT = $n - 1$ **then go to** CORRECTION; **else**

             begin COUNT := COUNT + 1, S.A.Q[$n-1$:1] := A.Q; **end**

          S.A := S.A – M, **go to** TEST; **end**

       else {**if** S = 1}

          begin Q[0] := 0;

          if COUNT = $n - 1$ **then go to** CORRECTION; **else**

             begin COUNT := COUNT + 1, S.A.Q[$n-1$:1] := A.Q; **end**

          S.A := S.A + M, **go to** TEST; **end**

CORRECTION: **if** S = 1 **then** S.A := S.A + M;

OUTPUT: OUTBUS := Q; {Output the quotient Q}

                 OUTBUS := A; {Output the remainder R}

end *NRdivider;*

Figure 4.24
Nonrestoring division algorithm for unsigned integers.

Step	Action	S	A	Q
0	Initialize registers	0	1100	0010 = dividend D
1			1010	= divisor V = M
	Subtract M from A	0	0010	0010
	Reset Q[0]	0	0010	0011
	Left shift S.A.Q	0	0100	0110
2			1010	
	Subtract M from A	1	1010	0110
	Set Q[0]	1	1010	0110
	Left shift S.A.Q	1	0100	1100
3			1010	
	Add M to A	1	1110	1100
	Set Q[0]	1	1110	1100
	Left shift S.A.Q	1	1101	1000
4			1010	
	Add M to A	0	0111	1000
	Reset Q[3]	0	0111	1001
				1001 = quotient Q
			0111	= remainder R

Figure 4.25
Illustration of the nonrestoring division algorithm for unsigned integers.

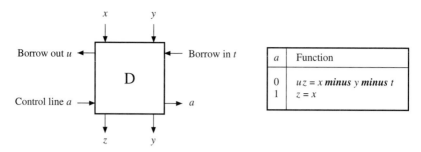

Figure 4.26
A cell D for array implementation of restoring division.

Combinational array dividers. Combinational array circuits can be used for division as well as for multiplication. Figure 4.26 shows a cell D suitable for implementing a version of the restoring division algorithm. This cell is basically a full subtracter with t and u being the borrow-in and borrow-out bits, respectively. The main output z is controlled by input a. When $a = 1$, z is the difference bit defined by the arithmetic equation

$$z = x \ \textbf{\textit{minus}} \ y \ \textbf{\textit{minus}} \ t$$

When $a = 0$, $z = x$. Thus the behavior of the cell D is given by the logic equations

$$z = x \oplus \bar{a}\,(y \oplus t)$$

$$u = \bar{x}y + \bar{x}t + yt$$

Figure 4.27 shows an array of D cells to divide 3-bit unsigned integers and generate a 4-bit quotient. Each row of the array subtracts the divisor V from the shifted partial remainder $2R_i$ generated by the row above. The sign of the result, and therefore of the quotient bit, is indicated by the borrow-out signal from the left-most cell in the row. This signal u_i is connected to the control inputs a of all cells in the same row. If $u_i = 0$, then the output from the row is $2R_i - V$ and $q_i = \bar{u}_i = 1$. If $u_i = 1$, then the output from the row is restored to $2R_i$, and again $q_i = \bar{u}_i = 0$. Thus the output of each row is initially $2R_i - V$, but it is restored to $2R_i$ when required. Restoration is achieved by overriding the subtraction performed by the row rather than by explicitly adding back the divisor.

Let d and d' be the carry (borrow) propagation and restore times of a cell, respectively. Let the divisor and dividend be n bits long. Each row of the divider array functions as an n-bit ripple-borrow subtracter, so the maximum time required to compute one quotient bit is $nd + d'$. The time required to compute an m-bit quotient and the corresponding remainder is therefore $m(nd + d')$, and the number of cells needed is $m(n + 1) - 1$.

Division by repeated multiplication. In systems containing a high-speed multiplier, division can be performed efficiently and at low cost using repeated multiplication. In each iteration a factor F_i is generated and used to multiply both the divisor V and the dividend D. Therefore

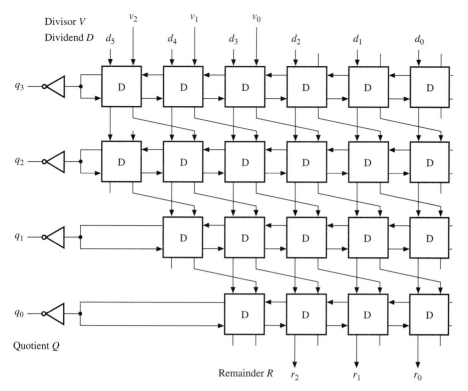

Figure 4.27
A divider array for 3-bit unsigned numbers using the cell D of Figure 4.26.

$$Q = \frac{D \times F_0 \times F_1 \times F_2 \times \ldots}{V \times F_0 \times F_1 \times F_2 \times \ldots}$$

F_i is chosen so that the sequence $V \times F_0 \times F_1 \times F_2 \ldots$ converges rapidly toward one. Hence $D \times F_0 \times F_1 \times F_2 \ldots$ must converge toward the desired quotient.

The convergence of the method depends on the selection of the F_i's. For simplicity, assume that D and V are positive normalized fractions so that $V = 1 - x$, where $x < 1$. Set $F_0 = 1 + x$. We can now write

$$V \times F_0 = (1 - x)(1 + x) = 1 - x^2$$

Clearly $V \times F_0$ is closer to one than to V. Next set $F_1 = 1 + x^2$. Hence

$$V \times F_0 \times F_1 = (1 - x^2)(1 + x^2) = 1 - x^4$$

and so on. Let V_i denote $V \times F_0 \times F_1 \times \ldots \times F_i$. The multiplication factor at each stage is computed as $F_i = 2 - V_{i-1}$, which is simply the twos-complement of V_{i-1}. Hence

$$F_i = 1 + x^{2^i} \text{ and } V_i = 1 - x^{2^{i+1}}$$

As i increases, V_i converges quickly toward one. The process terminates when $V_i = 0.11\ldots11$, the number closest to one for the given word size.

4.2
ARITHMETIC-LOGIC UNITS

The various circuits used to execute data-processing instructions are usually combined in a single circuit called an arithmetic-logic unit or ALU. The complexity of an ALU is determined by the way in which its arithmetic instructions are realized. Simple ALUs that perform fixed-point addition and subtraction, as well as word-based logical operations, can be realized by combinational circuits. ALUs that also perform multiplication and division can be constructed around the circuits developed for these operations in the preceding section. Much more extensive data-processing and control logic is necessary to implement floating-point arithmetic in hardware, as we will see later. Some processors having fixed-point ALUs employ special-purpose auxiliary units called arithmetic (co)processors to perform floating-point and other complex numerical functions.

4.2.1 Combinational ALUs

The simplest ALUs combine the functions of a twos-complement adder-subtracter with those of a circuit that generates word-based logic functions of the form $f(X,Y)$, for example, AND, XOR, and NOT. They can thus implement most of a CPU's fixed-point data-processing instructions. Figure 4.28 outlines an ALU that has separate subunits for logical and arithmetic operations. The particular class of operation (logical and arithmetic) to be performed is determined by a "mode" control line M attached to a two-way multiplexer that channels the required result to the

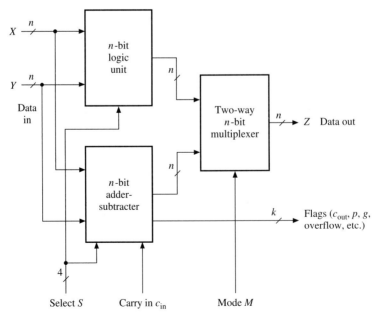

Figure 4.28
A basic n-bit arithmetic-logic unit (ALU).

output bus Z. The specific operation performed by the desired subunit is determined by a "select" control line S as shown. The ALU's logical operations are performed bitwise; that is, the same operation f is applied to every pair of data lines $x_i y_i$. The maximum number of distinct logical operations of the form $f(x_i, y_i)$ is 16, which is the number of distinct truth tables of two Boolean variables. Hence the select bus S needs to be of size 4 at most, as in Figure 4.28. S can also be used to select up to 16 different arithmetic operations such as $X + Y$, $X - Y$, $Y - X$, $X + 1$ (increment), $X - 1$ (decrement), and so on, as needed.

The logical operations in Figure 4.28 can be obtained by generating all four minterms of $f(x_i, y_i)$, namely,

$$m_3 = x_i y_i \quad m_2 = x_i \overline{y_i} \quad m_1 = \overline{x_i} y_i \quad m_0 = \overline{y_i}\, \overline{y_i}$$

for every pair $x_i y_i$ of data bits and by using the control lines $S = S_3 S_2 S_1 S_0$ to select desired subsets of the minterms to be ORed together. In particular, if we construct the sum-of-products expression

$$f(x_i, y_i) = m_3 S_3 + m_2 S_2 + m_1 S_1 + m_0 S_0$$

$$= x_i y_i S_3 + x_i \overline{y_i} S_2 + \overline{x_i} y_i S_1 + \overline{x_i}\, \overline{y_i} S_0 \qquad (4.32)$$

then we see that every combination of $S_3 S_2 S_1 S_0$ produces a different function. For example, $S = 0110$ makes $f(x_i, y_i) = x_i \overline{y_i} + \overline{x_i} y_i$, which is EXCLUSIVE-OR. Because of the bitwise nature of the logic operations, we can replace x_i and y_i in (4.32) with the n-bit words X and Y.

$$f(X,Y) = XYS_3 + X\overline{Y}S_2 + \overline{X}YS_1 + \overline{X}\,\overline{Y}S_0 \qquad (4.33)$$

We can now implement the logic unit directly from Equation (4.33), using several n-bit word gates as in Figure 4.29. The adder-subtracter can be designed by any of the techniques presented earlier, with appropriate additional connections to X, Y, and S.

Despite its conceptual simplicity, the ALU of Figure 4.28 is more expensive and slower than necessary. For $n = 4$, the logic subunit employs about 25 gates and inverters. If the arithmetic subunit is designed with carry lookahead in the style of Figure 4.6, around 60 gates are needed, depending on the variants of add and subtract that are implemented. The multiplexer in Figure 4.28 also requires additional

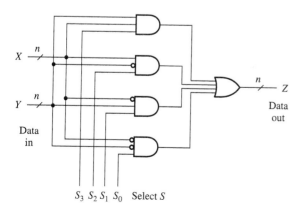

Figure 4.29
An n-bit logic unit that realizes
all 16 two-variable functions.

gates. The complete 4-bit ALU can therefore be expected to contain more than 100 gates of various kinds and have depth 9 or so. By judicious sharing of functions between the two main subunits, both of these figures can be reduced by a third, as the next example shows.

EXAMPLE 4.4 DESIGN OF A COMBINATIONAL ARITHMETIC-LOGIC UNIT [HANSEN AND HAYES 1995]. We now examine the structure of a well-known combinational ALU design that is found in many commercial products including the 74181, an IC referred to as a 4-bit ALU/function generator [Texas Instruments 1988]. Like the circuit of Figure 4.29, this design implements all 16 two-variable logic functions, as well as 16 arithmetic functions (some of which, like $X \bar{Y}$ *plus A,* are of questionable value). Its standard realization has about 60 gates and depth 6; see problem 4.21. We will describe its structure at the register level, following the model developed in [Hansen and Hayes 1995].

The main internal features of the 74181 appear in Figure 4.30. The key arithmetic operation of twos-complement addition is implemented by the carry-lookahead method. As in the design of Figure 4.6, the adder consists of propagate-generate logic feeding a lookahead circuit that computes carries, and a set of XOR gates that compute the final sum. The 74181's carry-lookahead generator is the same as that given earlier with the addition of propagate and generate outputs (denoted p and g) for extension purposes. However, the pg and sum circuits are also designed to be shared with the logic unit in an efficient, but nonobvious fashion. The modules labeled M_1 and M_2 generate a pair of 4-bit signals IP and IG that serve as internal propagate and generate, respectively, in the arithmetic mode and as minterm sources in the logic mode. From Figure 4.30 we see that each data output function F_i is defined by

$$F_i = IP_i \oplus IG_i \oplus (IC_{i-1} + M) \qquad (4.34)$$

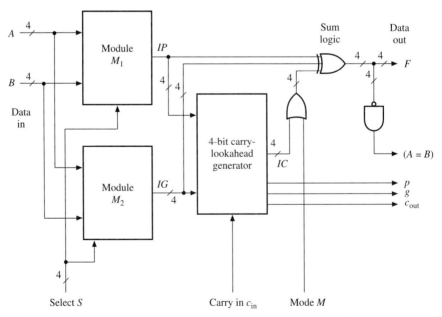

Figure 4.30
A register-level view of the 74181 4-bit ALU.

for $3 \geq i \geq 0$, where IC denotes the set of four internal carries produced by the carry-lookahead generator. The IP and IG functions are defined by

$$IP_i = A_i + B_i S_0 + \bar{B}_i S_1 \qquad (4.35)$$

$$IG_i = A_i \bar{B}_i S_2 + A_i B_i S_3 \qquad (4.36)$$

(See Figure 4.64 in this chapter's problem set for the gate-level implementation of these functions.)

In the logic mode of operation, $M = 1$, so (4.34) becomes

$$F_i = IP_i \oplus \overline{IG}_i \qquad (4.37)$$

On substituting (4.35) and (4.36) into (4.37) and simplifying, we obtain

$$F_i = \bar{A}_i B_i \bar{S}_0 + \bar{A}_i \bar{B}_i \bar{S}_1 + A_i \bar{B} S_2 + A_i B_i S_3 \qquad (4.38)$$

This expresses $F_i(A_i, B_i)$ in sum-of-minterms form, with a distinct (possibly complemented) select variable controlling each minterm. It therefore produces a different logic function for each of the 16 possible combinations of the S variables, and so is essentially the same as (4.33). Hence with $M = 1$, the 74181 acts as a universal function generator capable of producing any two-variable Boolean function $F(A,B)$.

In the arithmetic mode $M = 0$, and (4.34) changes to

$$F_i = IP_i \oplus IG_i \oplus IC_{i-1}$$

This has the general form of a sum (or difference) output—compare Equation (4.11). We can interpret the entire output function $F = F_3 F_2 F_1 F_0$ more easily using the arithmetic expression

$$F = \overline{IP} \text{ **plus** } \overline{IG} \text{ **plus** } c_{\text{in}} \qquad (4.39)$$

which is implied by (4.35) to (4.37) when $M = 1$. Here **plus** denotes twos-complement addition to distinguish it from + denoting logical OR. When $S = 1001$, Equations (4.35) and (4.36) imply that IP_i and IG_i become the usual propagate and generate functions, $IP_i = A_i + B_i$ and $IG_i = A_i B_i$, respectively. Hence the control settings $M = 1$ and $S = 1001$ make the 74181 behave like a carry-lookahead adder that computes

$$F = A \text{ **plus** } B \text{ **plus** } c_{\text{in}}$$

Changing S to 0110 produces the twos-complement subtraction

$$F = A \text{ **minus** } B \text{ **minus** } c_{\text{in}}$$

and effectively reconfigures the ALU as shown in Figure 4.4.

The various combinations of S produce a total of 16 different functions in the arithmetic mode, only a few of which are useful. For example, with $S = 0100$, Equation (4.39) becomes

$$F = 1111 \text{ **plus** } 0000 \text{ **plus** } c_{\text{in}}$$

which is 1111 when $c_{\text{in}} = 0$, that is, the constant minus-one in twos-complement code. When $c_{\text{in}} = 1$, F changes to 0000, since we are adding plus-one to minus-one. The ability to generate constants like ±1 and 0 in this way is useful for implementing some types of instructions.

The 74181's p, g, and c_{out} outputs are intended to allow k copies of the 74181 to be combined either using ripple-carry propagation or carry-lookahead to form a $4k$-bit ALU. Figure 4.31 shows a 16-bit ALU composed of four 74181 stages, with ripple-carry propagation between stages; compare Figure 4.3. Note how the S and M control lines are shared, while the data lines are separate. Note too that no interstage connections are needed for the logic operations because of their bitwise, word-oriented nature. Another interesting feature of the 74181 is its ability to act as a magnitude comparator in conjunction with the carry output c_{out}; see problem 4.23. The electronic circuits driving the 74181's $(A = B)$ output are designed so that when several $(A = B)$ lines are wired together as in Figure 4.31, the wired connection outputs the AND function of all its input signals. In other words, the overall $(A = B)$ output signal is 1 if and only if each 74181 slice produces $(A = B) = 1$. This type of technology-specific connection is called a *wired AND*. No extra gates or other "glue" logic are needed for ripple-carry expansion of the 74181.

4.2.2 Sequential ALUs

Although, as we have seen, both multiplication and division can be implemented by combinational logic, it is generally impractical to merge these operations with addition and subtraction into a single, combinational ALU. The reason is twofold. Combinational multipliers and dividers are costly in terms of hardware. They are also much slower than addition and subtraction circuits, a consequence of their many logic levels. An n-bit combinational multiplier or divider is typically composed of n or more levels of add-subtract logic, making multiplication and division at least n times slower than addition or subtraction. The number of gates in the multiply-divide logic is also greater by a factor of about n. Hence except when n is very small, complete ALUs are usually constructed from low-cost sequential circuits where add and subtract each take one clock cycle, while multiplication and division are multicycle operations.

Basic design. Figure 4.32 shows a widely used sequential ALU design that aims at minimizing hardware costs. This ALU organization is found in the IAS computer (Figure 1.11) and in many computers built after IAS. It is intended to

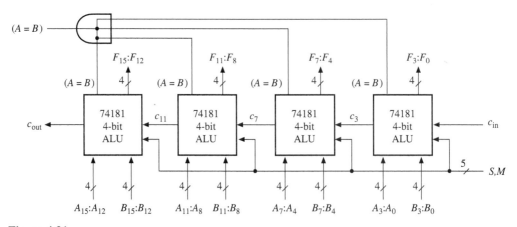

Figure 4.31
A 16-bit combinational ALU composed of four 74181s linked by ripple-carry propagation.

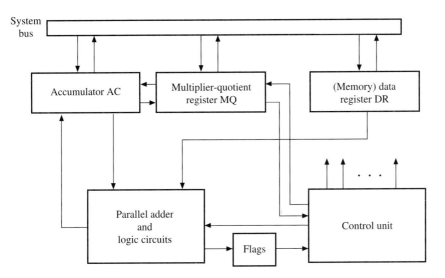

Figure 4.32
Structure of a basic sequential ALU.

implement multiplication and division using one of the sequential digit-by-digit shift-and-add/subtract algorithms discussed earlier. Three one-word registers are used for operand storage: the accumulator AC, the multiplier-quotient register MQ, and the data register DR. AC and MQ are organized as a single register AC.MQ capable of left- and right-shifting. Additional data processing is provided by a combinational ALU capable of addition, subtraction, and logical operations; we will refer to this unit as the add-subtract unit. This unit derives its inputs from AC and DR and places its results in AC. The MQ register is so-called because it stores the multiplier during multiplication and the quotient during division. DR stores the multiplicand or divisor, while the result (product or quotient and remainder) is stored in the register-pair AC.MQ. The role of these registers is defined concisely as follows:

Addition	$AC := AC + DR$
Subtraction	$AC := AC - DR$
Multiplication	$AC.MQ := DR \times MQ$
Division	$AC.MQ := MQ/DR$
AND	$AC := AC$ *and* DR
OR	$AC := AC$ *or* DR
EXCLUSIVE-OR	$AC := AC$ *xor* DR
NOT	$AC := \textbf{\textit{not}}(AC)$

DR can serve as a memory data register to store data addressed by an instruction address field ADR. Then DR can be replaced by M(ADR) in the above list of ALU operations, resulting in a one-address memory-referencing format.

Register files. Modern CPUs retain special registers like the multiplier-quotient register MQ for multiplication and division, but the accumulator AC and the data register DR are usually replaced by a set of general-purpose registers $R_0:R_{m-1}$

known as a register file RF. Each register R_i in RF is individually addressable—its address is the subscript i—so that arithmetic-logic instructions can take the generic two- and three-address forms

$$R_2 := f(R_1, R_2) \qquad (4.40)$$

$$R_3 := f(R_1, R_2) \qquad (4.41)$$

respectively. Hence the processor can retain intermediate results in fast, easily accessed registers, rather than having to pack them off to external memory M. Clearly RF functions as a small random-access memory (RAM) and, in fact, is often implemented using a fast RAM technology. RF differs from M in one important respect: RF requires two or three operands to be accessible simultaneously. For example, to implement (4.40) as a single-cycle instruction, we must be able to read R_1 and R_2, and write to R_2 in the same clock cycle. RF then needs several access ports for simultaneously reading from or writing to several different registers. Hence a register file is often realized as a *multiport RAM*. A standard RAM has just one access port with an associated address bus *ADR* and data bus *D*. This port can be used to read or write the data word in the single word location we denote by M(*ADR*).

To build a multiport register file requires a set of registers of the appropriate size and several multiplexers and demultiplexers that allow data words to be steered from any desired registers to the various output ports (read operations) or from the various input ports to registers (write operations). Of course, we don't want several devices writing to the same register R_i simultaneously, although they may read from several R_i's simultaneously. Figure 4.33 shows a three-port register file that supports simultaneous reads from two ports *A* and *B*, while writing can take place via a third port *C*. This file contains four 16-bit registers and meets the data access requirements of (4.40) and (4.41). In the two-address case (4.40), the address of R_1 is applied to port *A*, while that of R_2 is applied to ports *B* and *C*.

Figure 4.34 shows a representative datapath unit for implementing logical and fixed-point operations; it is often referred to as an *integer* or *fixed-point unit*. It contains a register file RF and a (combinational) ALU capable at least of addition and subtraction. Often specialized circuitry is added for multiplication and division because the longer delay of these operations and their use of double-length operands make it difficult to include their registers in RF. Also shown are links that connect the datapath unit to the external memory M (a cache or main memory) and the IO system. These links can also connect to other functional units such as a floating-point unit.

ALU expansion. It is quite feasible to manufacture an entire sequential ALU for fixed-point m-bit numbers on a single IC chip. Moreover, the ALU can easily be designed for expansion to handle operands of size $n = km$, or indeed any word size $n > m$, in two ways:

1. *Spatial expansion*: Connect k copies of the m-bit ALU in the manner of a ripple-carry adder to form a single ALU capable of processing km-bit words directly. The resulting array-like circuit is said to be *bit sliced* because each component ALU concurrently processes a separate "slice" of m bits from each km-bit operand.

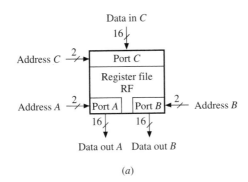

(a)

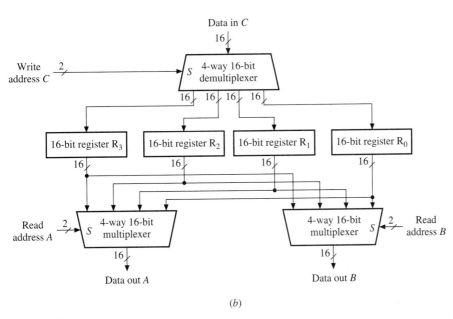

(b)

Figure 4.33
A register file with three access ports: (a) symbol and (b) logic diagram.

2. *Temporal expansion*: Use one copy of the *m*-bit ALU chip in the manner of a serial adder to perform an operation on *km*-bit words in *k* consecutive steps (clock cycles). In each step the ALU processes a separate *m*-bit slice of each operand. This processing is called *multicycle* or *multiple-precision* processing.

The 16-bit ALU in Figure 4.31 composed of four copies of the 4-bit 74181 IC is an example of a bit-sliced combinational ALU. The hardware cost of a bit-sliced ALU such as this increases directly with *k*, the number of slices, but the ALU's performance measured, say, in cycles per instruction (CPI), remains essentially constant. The cycle period does increase slowly with *k*, however. In a multicycle ALU, on the other hand, the performance decreases directly with *k*, but the amount of hardware remains constant. A multicycle ALU must be controlled by a (micro) program that repeatedly applies the same basic instruction to all slices of the operands, which must be supplied serially (slice by slice) to the ALU.

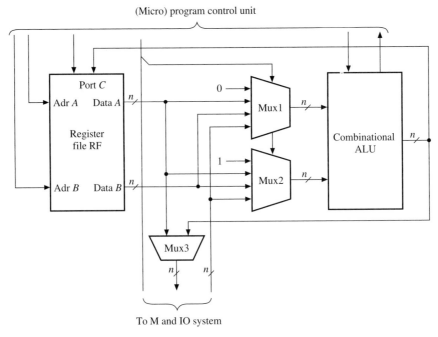

Figure 4.34
A generic datapath unit with an ALU and a register file.

Figure 4.35 shows how a 16-bit ALU can be constructed from four 4-bit sequential ALU slices. The data buses and register files of the individual slices are effectively juxtaposed to increase their size from 4 to 16 bits. The control lines that select and sequence the operations to be performed are connected to every slice so that all slices execute the same actions in lockstep with one another. Each slice thus performs the same operation on a different 4-bit part (slice) of the input operands and produces only the corresponding part of the results. The required control signals are derived from an external control unit, which can be hardwired or microprogrammed. Certain operations require information to be exchanged between slices. For example, to implement a shift operation, each slice must be able to send a bit to, and receive a bit from, its left or right neighbors. Similarly, when performing addition or subtraction, carry bits must be transmitted between neighboring slices. For this purpose horizontal connections are provided between the slices as shown in Figure 4.35.

A multicycle implementation of the 16-bit ALU of Figure 4.35 would require the basic 4-bit ALU to store internally all the information that needs to be exchanged between slices. Add and shift operations require only modest changes like extra flip-flops to store the output carry and shift signals, as well as (micro) instructions of the add-with-carry type that make use of these stored signals. Multiplication and division require more significant changes.

EXAMPLE 4.5 THE ADVANCED MICRO DEVICES 2901 BIT-SLICED ALU
[MICK AND BRICK 1980]. AMD introduced the 2900 series of ICs for bit-sliced processor design in the mid-1970s. Its elegant design has been widely imitated, and its

principal members are included in recent VLSI cell libraries [AT&T Microelectronics 1994]. The 2901 IC is the simplest of several 4-bit ALU slices in the 2900 family. It has the internal organization depicted in Figure 4.36 and executes a small set of operations usually specified by microinstructions. A combinational arithmetic-logic circuit C performs three arithmetic operations (twos-complement addition and subtraction) and five logical operations on 4-bit operands. The particular operation to be carried out by C is defined by a 9-bit (micro) instruction bus I intended to be driven by an external control unit. A pair of combinational shifters allow results generated by C to be left- or right-shifted to facilitate the implementation of multiplication, division, and so on via shift-and-add/subtract algorithms. The 2901 has a general-register organization with sixteen 4-bit registers organized as a 16×4-bit register file R[0:15], referred to as "the RAM." An additional register designated Q is designed to act as the multiplier-quotient register when implementing multiplication or division. C obtains its inputs either from the RAM, Q, or an external input data bus D; all-0 constant input operands may also be

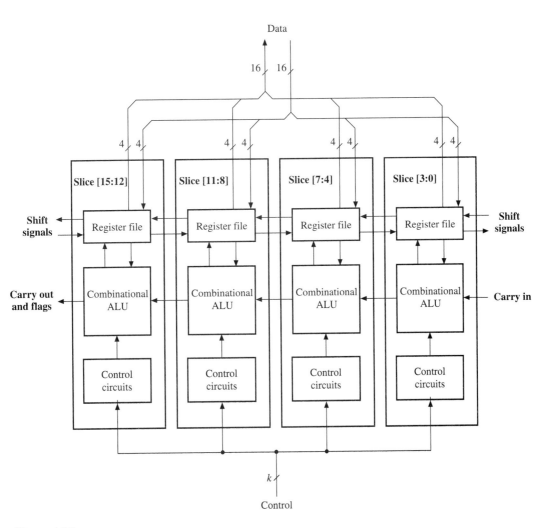

Figure 4.35
Sixteen-bit ALU composed of four 4-bit slices.

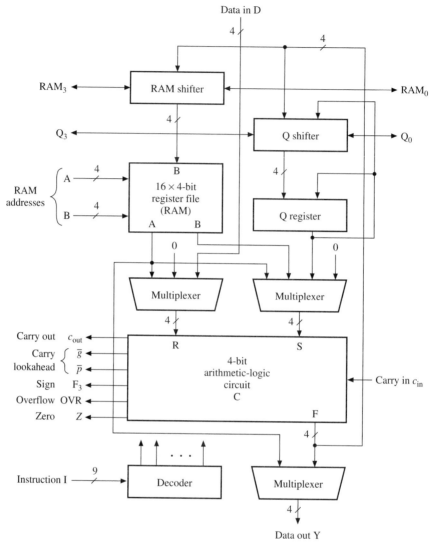

Figure 4.36
Organization of the 2901 4-bit ALU slice.

specified. The RAM registers to be used as operand sources or destinations are specified by the 4-bit A and B address buses, which are also derived from an external micro-instruction. The results generated by C can be stored internally in the 2901 and/or placed on the external output data bus Y.

A set of k 2901s can be interconnected according to the one-dimensional array structure of Figure 4.35 to form a processor with essentially the same properties as the 2901 but handling $4k$-bit instead of 4-bit data. The instruction bus I and the RAM address buses A and B are the main control lines that are connected in common to all slices. Direct connections between the shifters on adjacent slices permit shifting to be extended across the entire processor array. Each slice produces a carry-out signal c_{out}

that can be connected to the carry-in line c_{in} of the slice on its left, allowing arithmetic operations to be extended across the array via the bit-sliced scheme of Figure 4.7.

Ripple-carry connections between slices have the drawback that carry-propagation time increases rapidly with the number of slices. Consequently, the 2901 and other bit-sliced ALUs also support the implementation of carry lookahead in the style of Figure 4.5. To this end, the 2901 produces (in complemented form) the g and p signals required for carry lookahead, and an external carry-lookahead circuit generates the c_{in} signals for the slices (except the right-most one) from the g's and p's of all preceding slices. The 2900 series has an IC for this purpose, namely, the 2902 4-bit carry-lookahead generator, which is a fast, two-level logic circuit that implements Equations (4.10). The 2901 also produces three flag signals providing status information on the current result F from the arithmetic-logic circuit C. The zero flag Z indicates whether the all-0 result F = 0000 occurred; the overflow flag OVR indicates whether overflow occurred during arithmetic operations; and the sign flag F_3 is the value of the left-most bit of F. A 16-bit ALU composed of four copies of the 2901 appears in Figure 4.37. This circuit employs carry lookahead, and also shows how the flag signals for the array are produced (compare Figure 4.31).

The 2901's 9-bit control bus I contains three 3-bit fields—I_S, I_F, and I_D—which specify the operand sources, the ALU function, and the result destinations, respectively; see Figure 4.38. I_D is also used to control shifting of the result; this is indicated by multiplication by 2 (left shift) or division by 2 (right shift) in the figure. The various possible combinations of the three I fields define the 2901's microinstruction set and enable a large number of distinct register-transfer operations to be specified. For example, the subtraction

$$R[6] := R[7] - R[6]$$

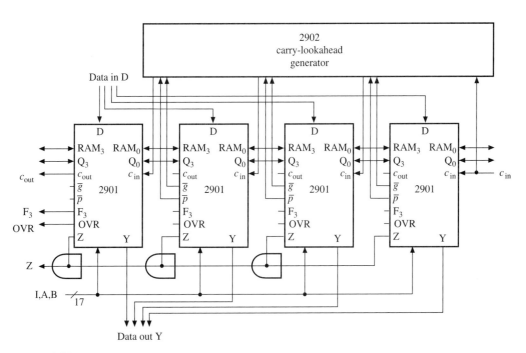

Figure 4.37
A 16-bit 4-slice array of 2901s employing carry lookahead.

Inputs						Outputs		
I_S	R	S	I_F	Function	I_D	Y	R(B)	Q
000	R(A)	Q	000	$R + S + C_{in}$	000	F	–	F
001	R(A)	R(B)	001	$S - R - \bar{C}_{in}$	001	F	–	–
010	0	Q	010	$R - S - \bar{C}_{in}$	010	R(A)	F	–
011	0	R(B)	011	R or S	011	F	F	–
100	0	R(A)	100	R and S	100	F	$2^{-1}F$	$2^{-1}Q$
101	D	R(A)	101	$\bar{R}$ and S	101	F	$2^{-1}F$	–
110	D	Q	110	R xor S	110	F	2F	2Q
111	D	0	111	R xnor S	111	F	2F	–

Figure 4.38
Microoperations performed by the 2901.

is specified by the (partial) microinstruction

$$A,B,I_S,I_F,I_D,C_{in} = 0111,0110,001,010,011,0$$

This microinstruction applies the contents of registers R[7] and R[6] to the R and S inputs, respectively, of C and selects the ALU function $R - S - \bar{C}_{in}$ (subtract with borrow); it also causes the result that appears on F to be stored back into R[6]. Although no data-transfer operations are explicitly specified in Figure 4.38, they are easily obtained from the specified functions. For instance, the operation

$$Q := D$$

loads register Q from an external data source; it can be realized via the logical OR operation Q := D or 0 as follows:

$$A,B,I_S,I_F,I_D,C_{in} = = dddd,dddd,111,011,000,d \tag{4.42}$$

where d denotes a don't-care value.

Multiplication and division cannot be bit sliced in the same way as addition, subtraction, or shifting. However, these operations can be performed by a bit-sliced ALU under the control of a microprogram that implements one of the shift-and-add/subtract algorithms described earlier. This topic is discussed further in Chapter 5.

Figure 4.39 gives an example of a more recent ALU chip, the GEC Plessey PDSP1601, which, for brevity, we call the 1601 [GEC Plessey Semiconductors 1990]. This single IC is housed in an 84-pin PGA package and is designed to process 16-bit words directly, and bigger words indirectly via either bit slicing or via multicycle expansion. The 1601 supports 32 arithmetic and logical operations that are broadly similar to those of the 2901 (Figure 4.38). The arithmetic instructions include various types of add, subtract, and shift applied to 16-bit twos-complement operands. The 1601 contains a 16-bit combinational ALU and two small register files. It also has a combinational "barrel" shifter that can shift a 16-bit operand from 1 to 16 places to the left or right. The barrel shifter roughly corresponds to the 2901's Q shifter but is much more powerful. Shifters of this sort are useful when implementing the shifts associated with multiplication, division, and floating-point operations. For extension via bit slicing, the 1601 provides carry and shift IO lines

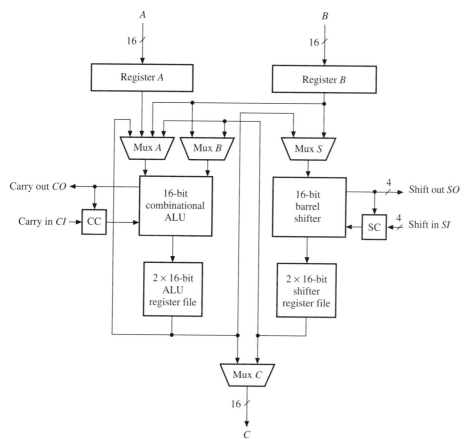

Figure 4.39
Organization of GEC Plessey 1601 ALU and barrel shifter.

that allow k copies of the 1601 to be chained to form a $16k$-bit bit-sliced ALU that can operate at the same speed as a single 1601 slice. For multicycling, the output carry and shift bits are stored internally in the circuits denoted CC and SC in Figure 4.39.

To perform, say, a 64-bit addition in bit-slice mode (referred to as *cascade* mode in the 1601 manufacturer's literature), a microinstruction APBCI, denoting *A plus B plus CI,* is executed simultaneously by each of four cascaded 1601 slices. The carry-in line *CI* is set to 0 in the least significant slice; each of the other slices has its *CI* line connected to its right neighbor's carry-out line *CO*. To perform the same 64-bit addition in multicycle mode, a single copy of the 1601 is used. It is supplied with four 16-bit slices of the input operands at its *A* and *B* ports in four successive clock cycles. In the first cycle the microinstruction APBCI is applied with *CI* = 0. In the remaining three cycles the microinstruction APBCO, denoting *A plus B plus CO,* is executed, which includes in the sum the output carry bit generated in the preceding clock cycle and stored in CC.

4.3
ADVANCED TOPICS

This section studies several additional aspects of datapath design. First we discuss the implementation of floating-point operations. Then we examine the use of pipelining to increase the throughput of a datapath unit.

4.3.1 Floating-Point Arithmetic

Let (X_M, X_E) be the floating-point representation of a number X, which therefore has the numerical value $X_M \times B^{X_E}$. Recall from section 3.2.3 that the mantissa (significand) X_M and the exponent X_E are fixed-point numbers and that the base B is the same as the base (radix) of X_M. To simplify the discussion, we make the following realistic assumptions:

1. X_M is an n_M-bit binary (twos-complement or sign-magnitude) fraction.
2. X_E is an n_E-bit integer in excess-$2^{n_E - 1}$ code, implying an exponent bias of $2^{n_E - 1}$.
3. $B = 2$.

We also assume that the floating-point numbers are stored in normal form only; hence the final result of each floating-point arithmetic operation should be normalized.

Basic operations. General formulas for floating-point addition, subtraction, multiplication, and division are given in Figure 4.40. Multiplication and division are relatively simple because the mantissas and exponents can be processed independently. Floating-point multiplication requires a fixed-point multiplication of the mantissas and a fixed-point addition of the exponents. For example, if $X = 1.32400111 \times 10^{17}$ and $Y = 1.04799245 \times 10^{21}$, the product $X \times Y$ is given by $(1.32400111 \times 1.04799245) \times 10^{(17 + 21)} = 1.38758607 \times 10^{38}$. Floating-point division requires a fixed-point division involving the mantissas and a fixed-point subtraction involving the exponents. Thus multiplication and division are not much harder to implement than the corresponding fixed-point operations.

Floating-point addition and subtraction are complicated by the fact that the exponents of the two input operands must be made equal before the corresponding mantissas can be added or subtracted. As suggested by Figure 4.40, this exponent equalization can be done by right-shifting the mantissa X_M associated with the smaller exponent X_E a total of $Y_E - X_E$ digit positions to form a new mantissa

Addition	$X + Y = (X_M 2^{X_E - Y_E} + Y_M) \times 2^{Y_E}$	where $X_E \leq Y_E$
Subtraction	$X - Y = (X_M 2^{X_E - Y_E} - Y_M) \times 2^{Y_E}$	
Multiplication	$X \times Y = (X_M \times Y_M) \times 2^{X_E + Y_E}$	
Division	$X/Y = (X_M / Y_M) \times 2^{X_E - Y_E}$	

Figure 4.40
The four basic arithmetic operations for floating-point numbers.

$X_M 2^{X_E - Y_E}$, which can then be combined directly with Y_M. Thus floating-point addition and subtraction have three main steps:

1. Compute $Y_E - X_E$, a fixed-point subtraction.
2. Shift X_M by $Y_E - X_E$ places to the right to form $X_M 2^{X_E - Y_E}$.
3. Compute $X_M 2^{X_E - Y_E} \pm Y_M$, a fixed-point addition or subtraction.

For example, to add the decimal floating-point numbers $X = 1.32400111 \times 10^{17}$ and $Y = 1.04799245 \times 10^{21}$, we first compute $Y_E - X_E = 21 - 17 = 4$, identifying X_E as the smaller exponent. We then right-shift X_M by four places to obtain $X_M 2^{-4} = 0.00013240$. Finally, we perform the mantissa addition $X_M 2^{-4} + Y_M = 0.00013240 + 1.04799245 = 1.04812485$, so the final result has mantissa 1.04812485 and exponent 21.

Each floating-point arithmetic operation needs an extra step in order to normalize the result. A number $X = (X_M, X_E)$ is normalized by left-shifting (right-shifting) X_M and decrementing (incrementing) X_E by 1 to compensate for each one-digit shift of X_M. As noted earlier, a twos-complement fraction is normalized when the sign bit x_{n-1} differs from the bit x_{n-2} on its right, a fact used to terminate the normalization process. A sign-magnitude fraction is normalized by left-shifting the magnitude part until there are no leading 0s, that is, until $x_{n-2} = 1$. (The normalization rules are different if the base B is not two.) The left-most bit of the mantissa may be hidden, since normalization fixes its value; see the discussion of the IEEE 754 floating-point standard in Example 3.4.

Difficulties. Several minor problems are associated with exponent biasing. If biased exponents are added or subtracted using fixed-point arithmetic in the course of a floating-point calculation, the resulting exponent is doubly biased and must be corrected by subtracting the bias. For example, let the exponent length be 4, and let the bias be $2^{4-1} = 8$. Suppose that exponents $X_E = 1111$ and $Y_E = 0101$ denoting $+7$ and -3, respectively, are to be added. If ordinary binary addition is used, we obtain the sum $X_E + Y_E = 10100$, which denotes $12 = 4 + 8$ in excess-8 code. The sum 10100 is now corrected by subtracting the bias 1000 to produce 1100, which is the correct biased representation of $X_E + Y_E = 4$.

Another problem arises from the all-0 representation usually required of zero. If $X \times Y$ is computed as $(X_M \times Y_M) \times 2^{X_E + Y_E}$ and either X_M or Y_M is zero, the resulting product has an all-0 mantissa but may not have an all-0 exponent. A special step is then needed to make the exponent bits 0.

A floating-point operation causes overflow or underflow if the result is too large or too small to be represented. Overflow or underflow resulting from mantissa operations can usually be corrected by shifting the mantissa of the result and modifying its exponent; this is done automatically during floating-point processing. For instance, adding the normalized decimal numbers $X = 5.1049 \times 10^7$ and $Y = 7.9379 \times 10^7$ produces the sum 13.0428×10^7, which is normalized to 1.3043×10^8 by shifting X_M one digit to the right (and rounding off the result) and incrementing the exponent by one. If, however, the exponent overflows or underflows, an error signal indicating floating-point overflow or underflow is generated. A floating-point result that has overflowed may sometimes be retained in "denormalized" form, as discussed in Example 3.4.

To preserve accuracy during floating-point calculations, one or more extra bits called *guard bits* are temporarily attached to the right end of the mantissa

$x_{n-1}x_{n-2}...x_1x_0$. For example, a guard bit x_{-1} is needed when results are to be rounded rather than truncated to n bits. Rounding is accomplished by adding 1 to x_0 and truncating the result to n bits. When a mantissa is right-shifted during the alignment step of addition or subtraction, the bits shifted from the right end can be retained as guard bits. In the case of floating-point multiplication, bits from the right half of the $2n$-bit result of multiplying two n-bit (unsigned) mantissas serve as guard bits. Suppose, for instance, that $X_M = 0.1...$ and $Y_M = 0.1...$ are normalized positive mantissas (fractions). Multiplying them by a standard fixed-point multiplication algorithm yields an unnormalized double-length result of the form

$$P_M = X_M \times Y_M = 0.01... \qquad (4.43)$$

which contains a leading 0. If P_M is now truncated or rounded to n bits, then the precision of the result is only $n-1$ bits. It is clearly desirable to retain an additional bit from the double-length product so that when (4.43) is normalized by a left shift, the result contains n significant bits. We therefore employ two guard bits in this case, one to maintain precision during normalization and one for rounding purposes.

Floating-point units. Floating-point arithmetic can be implemented by two loosely connected fixed-point datapath circuits, an exponent unit and a mantissa unit. The mantissa unit performs all four basic operations on the mantissas; hence a generic fixed-point arithmetic circuit such as that of Figure 4.32 can be used. A simpler circuit capable of only adding, subtracting, and comparing exponents suffices for the exponent unit. Exponent comparison can be done by a comparator or by subtracting the exponents. Figure 4.41 outlines the structure of a floating-point unit employing the foregoing approach. The exponents of the input operands are put in registers E1 and E2, which are connected to an adder that computes E1 + E2. The exponent comparison required for addition and subtraction is made by computing E1 − E2 and placing it in a counter register E. The larger exponent is then determined from the sign of E. The shifting of one mantissa required before the

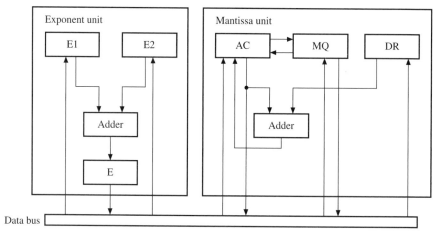

Figure 4.41
Datapath of a floating-point arithmetic unit.

mantissa addition or subtraction can occur is controlled by E. The magnitude of E is sequentially decremented to zero. After each decrement, the appropriate mantissa (whose location in the mantissa unit varies with the operation being performed) is shifted one digit position. Once the mantissas have been aligned, they are processed in the usual manner. The exponent of the result is also computed and placed in E.

All computers with floating-point instructions also have fixed-point instructions, so it is sometimes desirable to design a single ALU to execute both fixed-point and floating-point instructions. This design takes the form of a fixed-point arithmetic unit in which the registers and the adder can be partitioned into exponent and mantissa parts as in Figure 4.41 when floating-point operations are being performed. In recent years it has become more common to implement fixed-point and floating-point instruction in separate units, a fixed-point or integer unit FXU and a floating-point unit FPU. This separation makes it possible for fixed-point and floating-point instructions to be executed in parallel.

Addition. We now consider the implementation of floating-point addition in more detail. Figure 4.42 presents an addition algorithm intended for use with the floating-point unit of Figure 4.41; with minor modifications it can also be used for floating-point subtraction. The mantissa is assumed to be a binary fraction, and the exponent a biased integer; the base B is 2. The first step of the algorithm is equalization of the exponents, which is done by subtracting them and aligning the mantissas by shifting one of them until the difference between the exponents has been reduced to zero. Next the aligned mantissas are added. Finally the result is normalized, if necessary, by again shifting the mantissa and making a compensating change in the exponent. The mantissa and exponent of the final result are placed in the AC and E registers, respectively. Tests are also performed for floating-point overflow and underflow; if either occurs, a flag ERROR is set to 1. A separate test is made for a zero result which, if indicated by AC = 0, causes E to be set to 0 also.

Several improvements can be made to this algorithm; these are left as an exercise (problem 4.29). We can save time by checking to see whether one of the input operands X or Y is zero at the start and simply making the nonzero operand the result. If both X and Y are zero, either operand may be used as the result. If the difference between exponents is very large ($|E| > n_M$), then the shifting process to align one of the mantissas, say, X_M in AC, will result in AC = 0 after n_M steps. Continued shifting to make E = 0 will not affect the result, which in this case will be Y_M. Note also that it is more efficient to terminate the shifting after n_M steps instead of $|E|$ steps, as is done in Figure 4.42.

Figure 4.43 shows the step-by-step application of the addition algorithm of Figure 4.42 to two 32-bit floating-point numbers. The numbers have the 32-bit format of the IEEE Standard 754 described in Example 3.4. In this format each number N has a 23-bit fractional mantissa M with a hidden bit, an 8-bit exponent E in excess-127 code, and a base $B = 2$. The value of N is therefore given by the formula

$$N = (-1)^S 2^{E-127}(1.M)$$

The numbers to be added in this instance are

$$X = 0 \ 01111111 \ 10000000000000000000000$$
$$Y = 0 \ 10000111 \ 00101011010000000000000$$

register AC $[n_M-1:0]$, DR$[n_M-1:0]$, E$[n_E-1:0]$, E1$[n_E-1:0]$, E2$[n_E-1:0]$,

AC_OVERFLOW, ERROR;

BEGIN: AC_OVERFLOW := 0, ERROR := 0,

LOAD: E1 := X_E, AC := X_M;

E2 := Y_E, DR := Y_M;

{Compare and equalize exponents}

COMPARE: E := E1 – E2;

EQUALIZE: **if** E < 0 **then** AC := **right-shift**(AC), E := E + 1,
go to EQUALIZE; **else**
if E > 0 **then** DR := **right-shift**(DR), E := E – 1,
go to EQUALIZE;

{Add mantissas}

ADD: AC := AC + DR, E := **max**(E1,E2);

{Adjust for mantissa overflow and check for exponent overflow}

OVERFLOW: **if** AC_OVERFLOW = 1 **then begin**
if E = E_{MAX} **then go to** ERROR;
AC := **right-shift**(AC), E := E + 1, **go to** END; **end**

{Adjust for zero result}

ZERO: **if** AC = 0 **then** E := 0, **go to** END;

{Normalize result}

NORMALIZE: **if** AC is normalized **then go to** END;

UNDERFLOW: **if** E > EMIN **then**
AC := **left-shift**(AC), E := E – 1, **go to** NORMALIZE;

{Set error flag indicating overflow or underflow}

ERROR: ERROR := 1;

END: . . .

Figure 4.42
Algorithm for floating-point addition.

which denote $+1.5_{10}$ and $+299.25_{10}$, respectively. The exponent subtraction $X_E - Y_E$ in the COMPARE step is done using excess-127 code and produces $11110111 = -8_{10}$. Note that a 0 in the left-most bit position of E always indicates a negative number in this code (see Figure 3.25). Now the EQUALIZE step is executed, causing E to be incremented and AC, which contains the mantissa of X (including its hidden bit), to be right-shifted. After eight shifts, E reaches zero, indicated by its left-most bit changing from 0 to 1. Then the mantissa addition takes place, and the larger exponent is transferred from E1 to E. The sum appearing in AC is normalized, so the final result $X + Y = 300.75_{10}$ has its exponent in E and its mantissa in AC. The sum is eventually stored in the following standard format.

$$X + Y = 0 \quad 10000111 \quad 00101100110000000000000$$

EXAMPLE 4.6 FLOATING-POINT ADD UNIT OF THE IBM SYSTEM/360 MODEL 91 [ANDERSON ET AL. 1967]. We now briefly describe the floating-point

| Step | Exponent registers | | | Mantissa registers | |
	E1	E2	E	AC	DR
LOAD	01111111	10000111	00000000	11000000000000 . . . 00	10010101101000 . . . 00
	$= X_E$	$= Y_E$		$= 1.X_M$	$= 1.\ Y_M$
COMPARE			01110111		
			$= X_E - Y_E$		
EQUALIZE			01111000	01100000000000 . . . 00	
			01111001	00110000000000 . . . 00	
			01111010	00011000000000 . . . 00	
			01111011	00001100000000 . . . 00	
			01111100	00000110000000 . . . 00	
			01111101	00000011000000 . . . 00	
			01111110	00000001100000 . . . 00	
			01111111	00000000110000 . . . 00	
			10000000		
ADD			10000111	10010110011000 . . . 00	
			$= Y_E$	$= AC + DR$	
Result			10000111	10010110011000 . . . 00	
			$= (X + Y)_E$	$= 1.\ (X + Y)_M$	

Figure 4.43
Illustration of the floating-point addition algorithm of Figure 4.42.

adder of the IBM System/360 Model 91, a mainframe computer of the mid-1960s whose advanced design features, including caches and several types of instruction-level parallelism, were very influential. Figure 4.44 shows the datapath of the Model 91's add unit. It adds or subtracts 32-bit and 64-bit numbers having the floating-point format specific to the System/360 family and its successors (see section 3.2.3). The general algorithm of Figure 4.42 is used with some changes to increase speed. In particular, the shifting needed to align the mantissas and subsequently to normalize their sum is carried out by combinational logic (barrel shifters) rather than by shift registers. These shifters allow k hexadecimal digits (recall that the base B is 16) to be shifted simultaneously. The corresponding subtraction of k from the exponent required for normalization is also done in one clock cycle by using an extra adder (adder 3).

The operation of this floating-point adder unit is as follows. The exponents of the input operands are placed in registers E1 and E2, and the corresponding mantissas are placed in M1 and M2. Next E2 is subtracted from E1 using adder 1; the result is used to select the mantissa to be right-shifted by shifter 1 and also to determine the length of the shift. For example, if E1 > E2 and E1 − E2 = k, M2 is right-shifted by k digit positions, that is, $4k$ bit positions. The shifted mantissa is then added to or subtracted from the other mantissa via adder 2, a 56-bit parallel adder with several levels of carry look-ahead. The resulting sum or difference is placed in a temporary register R where it is examined by a special combinational circuit, the zero-digit checker. The output z of this circuit indicates the number of leading 0 digits (or leading Fs in the case of negative numbers) of the number in R. The number z is then used to control the final normalization step. The contents of R are left-shifted z digits by shifter 2, and the result is placed in register M3. The corresponding adjustment is made to the exponent by subtracting z using adder 3. In the event that R = 0, adder 3 can be used to set all bits of E3 to 0, which denotes an exponent of −64.

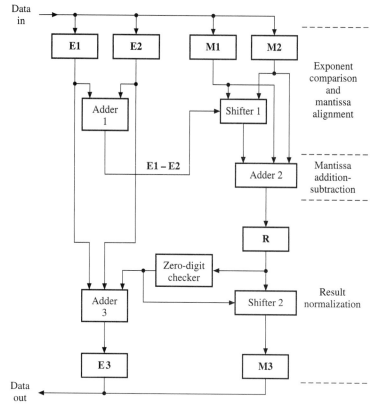

Figure 4.44
Floating-point add unit of the IBM System/360 Model 91.

Coprocessors. Complicated arithmetic operations like exponentiation and trigonometric functions are costly to implement in CPU hardware, while software implementations of these operations are slow. A design alternative is to use auxiliary processors called arithmetic coprocessors to provide fast, low-cost hardware implementations of these special functions. In general, a *coprocessor* is a separate instruction-set processor that is closely coupled to the CPU and whose instructions and registers are direct extensions of the CPU's. Instructions intended for the coprocessor are fetched by the CPU, jointly decoded by the CPU and the coprocessor, and executed by the coprocessor in a manner that is transparent to the programmer. Specialized coprocessors like this are used for tasks such as managing the memory system or controlling graphics devices. The MIPS RX000 series, for example, was designed to allow the CPU to operate with up to four coprocessors [Kane and Heinrich 1992]. One of these is a conventional floating-point processor, which is implemented on the main CPU chip in later members of the series.

Coprocessor instructions can be included in assembly or machine code just like any other CPU instructions. A coprocessor requires specialized control logic to link the CPU with the coprocessor and to handle the instructions that are executed by the coprocessor. A typical CPU-coprocessor interface is depicted in Figure 4.45. The coprocessor is attached to the CPU by several control lines that allow the

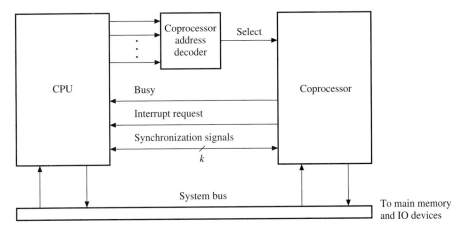

Figure 4.45
Connections between a CPU and a coprocessor.

activities of the two processors to be coordinated. To the CPU, the coprocessor is a passive or slave device whose registers can be read and written into in much the same manner as external memory. Communication between the CPU and coprocessor to initiate and terminate execution of coprocessor instructions occurs automatically as coprocessor instructions are encountered. Even if no coprocessor is actually present, coprocessor instructions can be included in CPU programs, because if the CPU knows that no coprocessor is present, it can transfer program control to a predetermined memory location where a software routine implementing the desired coprocessor instruction is stored. This type of CPU-generated interruption of normal program flow is termed a *coprocessor trap*. Thus the coprocessor approach makes it possible to provide either hardware or software support for certain instructions without altering the source or object code of the program being executed.

A coprocessor instruction typically contains the following three fields: an opcode F_0 that distinguishes coprocessor instructions from other CPU instructions, the address F_1 of the particular coprocessor to be used if several coprocessors are allowed, and finally the type F_2 of the particular operation to be executed by the coprocessor. The F_2 field can include operand addressing information. By having the coprocessor monitor the system bus, it can decode and identify a coprocessor instruction at the same time as the CPU; the coprocessor can then proceed to execute the coprocessor instruction directly. This approach is found in some early coprocessors but has the major drawback that the coprocessor, unlike the CPU, does not know the contents of the registers defining the current memory addressing modes. Consequently, it is common to have the CPU partially decode every coprocessor instruction, fetch all required operands, and transfer the opcode and operands directly to the coprocessor for execution. This is the protocol followed in 680X0-based systems employing the 68882 floating-point coprocessor, which is the topic of the next example.

EXAMPLE 4.7 THE MOTOROLA 68882 FLOATING-POINT COPROCESSOR [MOTOROLA 1989]. The Motorola 68882 coprocessor extends 680X0-series CPUs

Type	Opcode	Operation specified
Data transfer	FMOVE	Move word to/from coprocessor data or control register
	FMOVECR	Move word to/from ROM storing constants (0.0, π, e, etc.)
	FMOVEM	Move multiple words to/from coprocessor
Data processing	FADD	Add
	FCMP	Compare
	FDIV	Divide
	FMOD	Modulo remainder
	FMUL	Multiply
	FREM	Remainder (IEEE format)
	FSCALE	Scale exponent
	FSGLMUL	Single-precision multiply
	FSGLDIV	Single-precision divide
	FSUB	Subtract
	FABS	Absolute value
	FACOS	Arc cosine
	FASIN	Arc sine
	FATAN	Arc tangent
	FATANH	Hyperbolic arc tangent
	FCOS	Cosine
	FCOSH	Hyperbolic cosine
	FETOX	e to the power of x
	FETOXMI	(e to the power of x) minus 1
	FGETEXP	Extract exponent
	FGETMAN	Extract mantissa
	FINT	Extract integer part
	FINTRZ	Extract integer part rounded to zero
	FLOGN	Logarithm of x to the base e
	FLOGNP1	Logarithm of $x + 1$ to the base e
	FLOG10	Logarithm to the base 10
	FLOG2	Logarithm to the base 2
	FNEG	Negate
	FSIN	Sine
	FSINCOS	Simultaneous sine and cosine
	FSINH	Hyperbolic sine
	FSQRT	Square root
	FTAN	Tangent
	FTANH	Hyperbolic tangent
	FTENTOX	10 to the power of x
	FTWOTOX	2 to the power of x
	FLOGN	Logarithm of x to the base e
Program control	FBcc	Branch if condition code (status) cc is 1
	FDBcc	Test, decrement count, and branch on cc
	FNOP	No operation
	FRESTORE	Restore coprocessor state
	FSAVE	Save coprocessor state
	FScc	Set ($cc = 1$) or reset ($cc = 0$) a specified byte
	FTST	Set coprocessor condition codes to specified values
	FTRAPcc	Conditional trap

Figure 4.46
Instruction set of the Motorola 68882 floating-point coprocessor.

like the 68020 (section 3.1.2) with a large set of floating-point instructions. The 68882 and the 68020 are physically coupled along the lines indicated by Figure 4.45. While decoding the instructions it fetches during program execution, the 68020 identifies coprocessor instructions by their distinctive opcodes. After identifying a coprocessor instruction, the 68020 CPU "wakes up" the 68882 by sending it certain control signals. The 68020 then transmits the opcode to a predefined location in the 68882 that serves as an instruction register. The 68882 decodes the instruction and begins its execution, which can proceed in parallel with other instructions executed within the CPU proper. When the coprocessor needs to load or store operands, it asks the CPU to carry out the necessary address calculations and data transfers.

The 68882 employs the IEEE 754 floating-point number formats described in Example 3.4 with certain multiple-precision extensions; it also supports a decimal floating-point format. From the programmer's perspective, the 68882 adds to the CPU a set of eight 80-bit floating-point data registers FP0:FP7 and several 32-bit control registers, including instruction (opcode) and status registers. Besides implementing a wide range of arithmetic operations for floating-point numbers, the 68882 has instructions for transferring data to and from its registers, and for branching on conditions it encounters during instruction execution. Figure 4.46 summarizes the 68882's instruction set. These coprocessor instructions are distinguished by the prefix F (floating-point) in their mnemonic opcodes and are used in assembly-language programs just like regular 680X0-series instructions; see Fig. 3.12. The status or condition codes cc generated by the 68882 when executing floating-point instructions include invalid operation, overflow, underflow, division by zero, and inexact result. Coprocessor status is recorded in a control register, which can be read by the host CPU at the end of a set of calculations, enabling the CPU to initiate the appropriate exception-processing response. As some coprocessor instructions have fairly long (multicyle) execution times, the 68882 can be interrupted in the middle of instruction execution. Its state must then be saved and subsequently restored to complete execution of the interrupted instruction.

The appearance of coprocessors stems in part from the fact that until the 1980s IC technology could not provide microprocessors of sufficient complexity to include on-chip floating-point units. Once such microprocessors became possible, arithmetic coprocessors began to migrate onto CPU chips, losing some of their separate identity in the process —especially in the case of CISC processors. For example, the 1990-vintage Motorola 68040 microprocessor integrates a 68882-style floating-point coprocessor with a 68020-style CPU in a single microprocessor chip [Edenfield et al. 1990]. Arithmetic coprocessors provide an attractive way of augmenting the performance of a RISC CPU without affecting the simplicity and efficiency of the CPU itself. The multiple function (execution) units in superscalar microprocessors like the Pentium resemble coprocessors in that each unit has an instruction set that it can execute independently of the program control unit and the other execution units.

4.3.2 Pipeline Processing

Pipelining is a general technique for increasing processor throughput without requiring large amounts of extra hardware [Kogge 1981; Stone 1993]. It is applied to the design of the complex datapath units such as multipliers and floating-point adders. It is also used to improve the overall throughput of an instruction set processor, a topic to which we return in Chapter 5.

Introduction. A pipeline processor consists of a sequence of m data-processing circuits, called *stages* or *segments*, which collectively perform a single operation on a stream of data operands passing through them. Some processing takes place in each stage, but a final result is obtained only after an operand set has passed through the entire pipeline. As illustrated in Figure 4.47, a stage S_i contains a multiword input register or latch R_i, and a datapath circuit C_i that is usually combinational. The R_i's hold partially processed results as they move through the pipeline; they also serve as buffers that prevent neighboring stages from interfering with one another. A common clock signal causes the R_i's to change state synchronously. Each R_i receives a new set of input data D_{i-1} from the preceding stage S_{i-1} except for R_1 whose data is supplied from an external source. D_{i-1} represents the results computed by C_{i-1} during the preceding clock period. Once D_{i-1} has been loaded into R_i, C_i proceeds to use D_{i-1} to compute a new data set D_i. Thus in each clock period, every stage transfers its previous results to the next stage and computes a new set of results.

At first sight a pipeline seems a costly and slow way to implement the target operation. Its advantage is that an m-stage pipeline can simultaneously process up to m independent sets of data operands. These data sets move through the pipeline stage by stage so that when the pipeline is full, m separate operations are being executed concurrently, each in a different stage. Furthermore, a new, final result emerges from the pipeline every clock cycle. Suppose that each stage of the m-stage pipeline takes T seconds to perform its local suboperation and store its results. Then T is the pipeline's clock period. The *delay* or *latency* of the pipeline, that is, the time to complete a single operation, is therefore mT. However, the *throughput* of the pipeline, that is, the maximum number of operations completed per second is $1/T$. Equivalently, the number of clock cycles per instruction or *CPI* is one. When performing a long sequence of operations in the pipeline, its performance is determined by the delay (latency) T of a single stage, rather than by the delay mT of the entire pipeline. Hence an m-stage pipeline provides a speedup factor of m compared to a nonpipelined implementation of the same target operation.

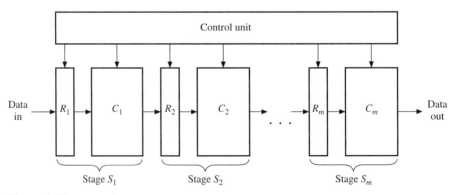

Figure 4.47
Structure of a pipeline processor.

Any operation that can be decomposed into a sequence of suboperations of about the same complexity can be realized by a pipeline processor. Consider, for example, the addition of two normalized floating-point numbers x and y, a topic discussed in section 4.3.1. This operation can be implemented by the following four-step sequence: compare the exponents, align the mantissas (equalize the exponents), add the mantissas, and normalize the result. These operations require the four-stage pipeline processor shown in Figure 4.48. Suppose that x has the normalized floating-point representation (x_M, x_E), where x_M is the mantissa and x_E is the exponent with respect to some base $B = 2^k$. In the first step of adding $x = (x_M, x_E)$ to $y = (y_M, y_E)$, which is executed by stage S_1 of the pipeline, x_E and y_E are compared, an operation performed by subtracting the exponents, which requires a fixed-point adder (see Example 4.6). S_1 identifies the smaller of the exponents, say, x_E, whose mantissa x_M can then be modified by shifting in the second stage S_2 of the pipeline to form a new mantissa x'_M that makes $(x'_M, y_E) = (x_M, x_E)$. In the third stage the mantissas x'_M and y_M, which are now properly aligned, are added. This fixed-point addition can produce an unnormalized result; hence a fourth and final step is needed to normalize the result. Normalization is done by counting the number k of leading zero digits of the mantissa (or leading ones in the negative case), shifting the mantissa k digit positions to normalize it, and making a corresponding adjustment in the exponent.

Figure 4.49 illustrates the behavior of the adder pipeline when performing a sequence of N floating-point additions of the form $x_i + y_i$ for the case $N = 6$. Add sequences of this type arise when adding two N-component real (floating-point) vectors. At any time, any of the four stages can contain a pair of partially processed scalar operands denoted (x_i, y_i) in the figure. The buffering of the stages ensures that S_i receives as inputs the results computed by stage S_{i-1} during the preceding clock period only. If T is the pipeline's clock period, then it takes time $4T$ to compute the single sum $x_i + y_i$; in other words, the pipeline's delay is $4T$. This value is approximately the time required to do one floating-point addition using a nonpipelined processor plus the delay due to the buffer registers. Once all four stages of the pipeline have been filled with data, a new sum emerges from the last stage S_4 every T seconds. Consequently, N consecutive additions can be done in time $(N + 3)T$, implying that the four-stage pipeline's speedup is

$$S(4) = \frac{4N}{N + 3}$$

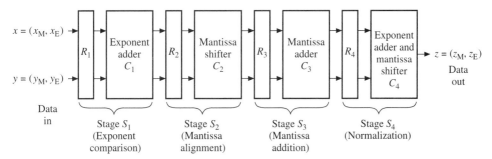

Figure 4.48
Four-stage floating-point adder pipeline.

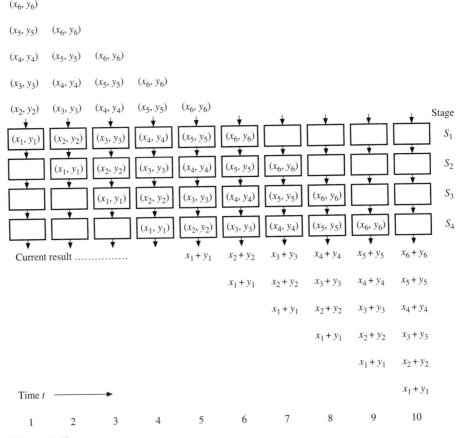

Figure 4.49
Operation of the four-stage floating-point adder pipeline.

For large N, $S(4) \approx 4$ so that results are generated at a rate about four times that of a comparable nonpipelined adder. If it is not possible to supply the pipeline with data at the maximum rate, then the performance can fall considerably, an issue to which we return in Chapter 5.

Pipeline design. Designing a pipelined circuit for a function involves first finding a suitable multistage sequential algorithm to compute the given function. This algorithm's steps, which are implemented by the pipeline's stages, should be balanced in the sense that they should all have roughly the same execution time. Fast buffer registers are placed between the stages to allow all necessary data items (partial or complete results) to be transferred from stage to stage without interfering with one another. The buffers are designed to be clocked at the maximum rate that allows data to be transferred reliably between stages.

Figure 4.50 shows the register-level design of a floating-point adder pipeline based on the nonpipelined design of Figure 4.44 and employing the four-stage organization of Figure 4.48. The main change from the nonpipelined case is the inclusion of buffer registers to define and isolate the four stages. A further modification has been made to implement fixed-point as well as floating-point addition.

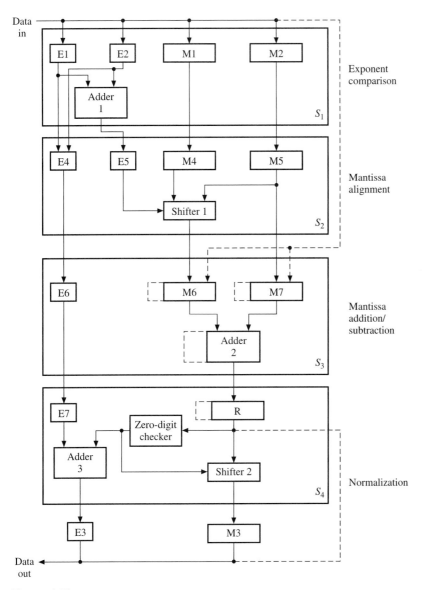

Figure 4.50
Pipelined version of the floating-point adder of Figure 4.44.

The circuits that perform the mantissa addition in stage S_3 and the corresponding buffers are enlarged, as shown by broken lines in Figure 4.50, to accommodate full-size fixed-point operands. To perform a fixed-point addition, the input operands are routed through S_3 only, bypassing the other three stages. Thus the circuit of Figure 4.50 is an example of a *multifunction pipeline* that can be configured either as a four-stage floating-point adder or as a one-stage fixed-point adder. Of course, fixed-point and floating-point subtraction can also be performed by this circuit; subtraction and addition are not usually regarded as distinct functions in this context, however.

The same function can sometimes be partitioned into suboperations in several different ways, depending on such factors as the data representation, the style of the logic design, and the need to share stages with other functions in a multifunction pipeline. A floating-point adder can have as few as two stages and as many as six. For example, five-stage adders have been built in which the normalization stage (S_4 in Figure 4.50) is split into two stages: one to count the number k of leading zeros (or ones) in an unnormalized mantissa and a second stage to perform the k shifts that normalize the mantissa.

Whether or not a particular function or set of functions F should be implemented by a pipelined or nonpipelined processor can be analyzed as follows. Suppose that F can be broken down into m independent sequential steps $F_1, F_2, \ldots, F_m$ so that it has an m-stage pipelined implementation P_m. Let F_i be realizable by a logic circuit C_i with propagation delay (execution time) T_i. Let T_R be the delay of each stage S_i due to its buffer register R_i and associated control logic. The longest T_i times create bottlenecks in the pipeline and force the faster stages to wait, doing no useful computation, until the slower stages become available. Hence the delay between the emergence of two results from P_m is the maximum value of T_i. The minimum clock period (the *pipeline period*) T_C is defined by the equation

$$T_C = \max\{T_i\} + T_R \quad \text{for } i = 1, 2, \ldots, m \tag{4.44}$$

The throughput of P_m is $1/T_C = 1/(\max\{T_i\} + T_R)$. A nonpipelined implementation P_1 of F has a delay of $\Sigma_{i=1}^{m} T_i$ or, equivalently, a throughput of $1/(\Sigma_{i=1}^{m} T_i)$. We conclude the m-stage pipeline P_m has greater throughput than P_1; that is, pipelining increases performance if

$$T_C < \Sigma_{i=1}^{m} T_i$$

Equation (4.44) also implies that it is desirable for all T_i times to be approximately the same; that is, the pipeline stages should be balanced.

Feedback. The usefulness of a pipeline processor can sometimes be enhanced by including feedback paths from the stage outputs to the primary inputs of the pipeline. Feedback enables the results computed by certain stages to be used in subsequent calculations by the pipeline. We next illustrate this important concept by adding feedback to a four-stage floating-point adder pipeline like that of Figure 4.50.

EXAMPLE 4.8 SUMMATION BY A PIPELINE PROCESSOR . Consider the problem of computing the sum of N floating-point numbers $b_1, b_2, \ldots, b_N$. It can be solved by adding consecutive pairs of numbers using an adder pipeline and storing the partial sums temporarily in external registers. The summation can be done much more efficiently by modifying the adder as shown in Figure 4.51. Here a feedback path has been added to the output of the final stage S_4, allowing its results to be fed back to the first stage S_1. A register R has also been connected to the output of S_4, so that stage's results can be stored indefinitely before being fed back to S_1. The input operands of the modified pipeline are derived from four separate sources: a variable X that is typically obtained from a CPU register or a memory location; a constant source K that can apply such operands as the all-0 and all-1 words; the output of stage S_4, representing the result computed by S_4 in the preceding clock period; and, finally, an earlier result computed by the pipeline and stored in the output register R.

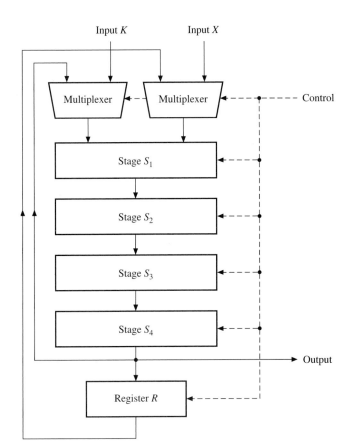

Input K Input X

Multiplexer   Multiplexer   - - - - - Control

Stage S_1

Stage S_2

Stage S_3

Stage S_4

Output

Register R

Figure 4.51
Pipelined adder with feedback paths.

The N-number summation problem is solved by the pipeline of Figure 4.51 in the following way. The external operands $b_1, b_2, \ldots, b_N$ are entered into the pipeline in a continuous stream via input X. This process requires a sequence of register or memory fetch operations, which are easily implemented if the operands are stored in contiguous register/memory locations. While the first four numbers b_1, b_2, b_3, b_4 are being entered, the all-0 word denoting the floating-point number zero is applied to the pipeline input K, as illustrated in Figure 4.52 for times $t = 1{:}4$. After four clock periods, that is, at time $t = 5$, the first sum $0 + b_1 = b_1$ emerges from S_4 and is fed back to the primary inputs of the pipeline. At this point the constant input $K = 0$ is replaced by the current result $S_4 = b_1$. The pipeline now begins to compute $b_1 + b_5$. At $t = 6$, it begins to compute $b_2 + b_6$; at $t = 7$, computation of $b_3 + b_7$ begins, and so on. When $b_1 + b_5$ emerges from the pipeline at $t = 8$, it is fed back to S_1 to be added to the latest incoming number b_9 to initiate computation of $b_1 + b_5 + b_9$. (This case does not apply to Figure 4.52, where $b_8 = b_N$ is the last item to be summed.) In the next time period, the sum $b_2 + b_6$ emerges from the pipeline and is fed back to be added to the incoming number b_{10}. Thus at any time, the pipeline is engaged in computing in its four stages four partial sums of the form

$$
\begin{aligned}
&b_1 + b_5 + b_9 + b_{13} + \ldots \\
&b_2 + b_6 + b_{10} + b_{14} + \ldots \\
&b_3 + b_7 + b_{11} + b_{15} + \ldots \\
&b_4 + b_8 + b_{12} + b_{16} + \ldots
\end{aligned}
\qquad (4.45)
$$

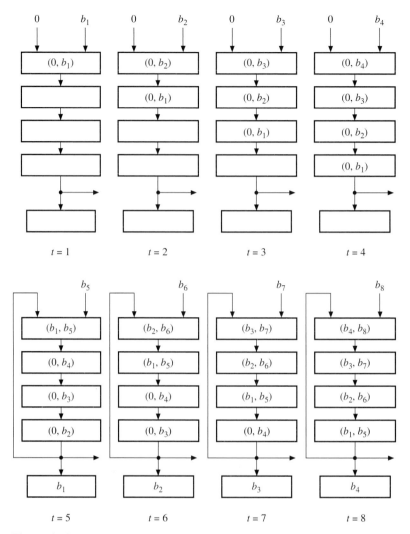

Figure 4.52
Summation of an eight-element vector.

When the last input operand b_N has entered the pipeline, the feedback structure is again altered to allow the four partial sums in (4.45) to be added together to produce the desired result $b_1 + b_2 + \ldots + b_N$. The necessary modification to the feedback structure is shown in Figure 4.52 for the case $N = 8$. At $t = 9$, the external inputs to the pipeline are disabled by setting them to zero, and the first of the four partial sums $b_1 + b_5$ at the output of stage S_4 is stored in register R. Then at $t = 10$, the new result $b_2 + b_6$ from S_4 is fed back to the pipeline inputs, along with the previous result $b_1 + b_5$ obtained from R. Thus computation of $b_1 + b_5 + b_2 + b_6$, which is the sum of half of the input operands, begins at this point. After a further delay of one time period, computation of the other half-sum $b_3 + b_7 + b_4 + b_8$ begins. When $b_1 + b_5 + b_2 + b_6$ emerges from S_4 at $t = 14$, it is stored in R until $b_4 + b_8 + b_3 + b_7$ emerges from S_4 at $t = 16$. At this point the outputs of S_4 and R are fed back to S_1. The final result is produced four time periods later—at $t = 20$ in the case of $N = 8$.

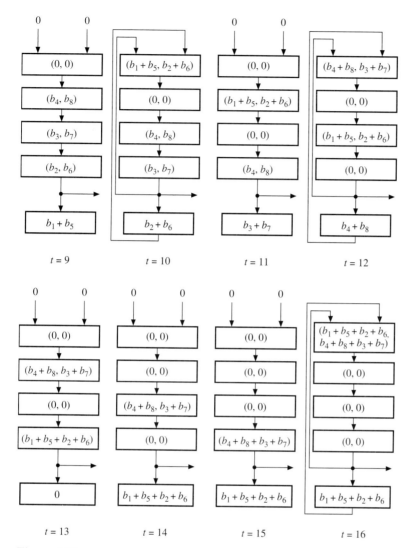

$t = 9$ $t = 10$ $t = 11$ $t = 12$

$t = 13$ $t = 14$ $t = 15$ $t = 16$

Figure 4.52
(continued)

It is easily seen that for the general case of N operands, the scheme of Figure 4.52 can compute the sum of $N > 4$ floating-point numbers in time $(N + 11)T$, where T is the pipeline's clock period, that is, the delay per stage. Since a comparable nonpipelined adder requires time $4NT$ to compute SUM, we obtain a speedup here of about $4N/(N + 11)$, which approaches 4 as N increases.

The foregoing summation operation can be invoked by a single *vector instruction* of a type that characterized the vector-processing, pipeline-based "supercomputers" of the 1970s and 1980s [Stone 1993]. For instance, Control Data Corp.'s STAR-100 computer [Hintz and Tate 1972] has an instruction SUM that computes the sum of the elements of a specified floating-point vector $B = (b_1, b_2,...,b_N)$ of arbitrary length N and places the result in a CPU register. The starting (base) address of B, which corresponds to a block of main memory, the name C of the result register, and the vector length N are all specified by operand fields of SUM. We can see from Figure 4.52 that a relatively complex pipeline control sequence is needed to implement a vector instruction of this sort. This complexity contributes significantly to both the size and cost of vector-oriented computers. Moreover, to achieve maximum speedup, the input data must be stored in a way that allows the vector elements to enter the pipeline at the maximum possible rate—generally one number-pair per clock cycle.

The more complex arithmetic operations in CPU instruction sets, including most floating-point operations, can be implemented efficiently in pipelines. Fixed-point addition and subtraction are too simple to be partitioned into suboperations suitable for pipelining. As we see next, fixed-point multiplication is well suited to pipelined design.

Pipelined multipliers. Consider the task of multiplying two n-bit fixed-point binary numbers $X = x_{n-1}x_{n-2}...x_0$ and $Y = y_{n-1}y_{n-2}...y_0$. Combinational array multipliers of the kind described in section 4.1.2 are easily converted to pipelines by the addition of buffer registers. Figure 4.53 shows a pipelined array multiplier that employs the 1-bit multiply-and-add cell M of Figure 4.19 and has $n = 3$. Each cell M computes a 1-bit product x_iy_j and adds it to both a product bit from the preceding stage and a carry bit generated by the cell on its right. Thus the n cells in each stage S_i, $0 \le i \le n - 1$, compute a partial product of the form

$$P_i = P_{i-1} + x_i2^iY \tag{4.46}$$

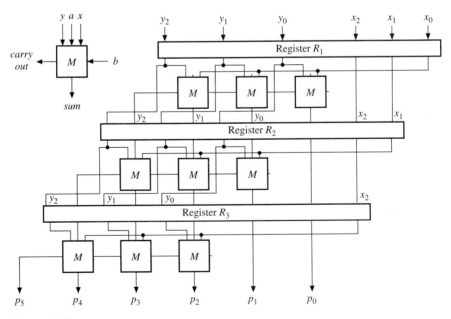

Figure 4.53
Multiplier pipeline using ripple-carry propagation.

with the final product $P_{n-1} = XY$ being computed by the last stage. In addition to storing the partial products in the buffer registers denoted R_i, the multiplicand Y and all hitherto unused multiplier bits must also be stored in R_i.

An n-stage multiplier pipeline of this type can overlap the computation of n separate products, as required, for example, when multiplying fixed-point vectors, and can generate a new result every clock cycle. Its main disadvantage is the relatively slow speed of the carry-propagation logic in each stage. The number of M cells needed is n^2, and the capacity of all the buffer registers is approximately $3n^2$ (see problem 4.31); hence this type of multiplier is also fairly costly in hardware. For these reasons, it is rarely used.

Multipliers often employ a technique called *carry-save addition,* which is particularly well suited to pipelining. An n-bit carry-save adder consists of n disjoint full adders. Its input is three n-bit numbers to be added, while the output consists of the n sum bits forming a word S and the n carry bits forming a word C. Unlike the adders discussed so far, there is no carry propagation within the individual adders. The outputs S and C can be fed into another n-bit carry-save adder where, as shown in Figure 4.54, they can be added to a third n-bit number W. Observe that the carry connections are shifted to the left to correspond to normal carry propagation. In general, m numbers can be added by a treelike network of carry-save adders to produce a result in the form (S,C). To obtain the final sum, S and C must be added by a conventional adder with carry propagation.

Multiplication can be performed using a multistage carry-save adder circuit of the type shown in Figure 4.55; this circuit is called a *Wallace tree* after its inventor [Wallace 1964]. The inputs to the adder tree are n terms of the form $M_i = x_i Y 2^k$. Here M_i represents the multiplicand Y multiplied by the ith multiplier bit weighted by the appropriate power of 2. Suppose that M_i is $2n$ bits long and that a full double-length product is required. The desired product P is $\sum_{i=0}^{n-1} M_i$. This sum is computed by the carry-save adder tree, which produces a $2n$-bit sum and a

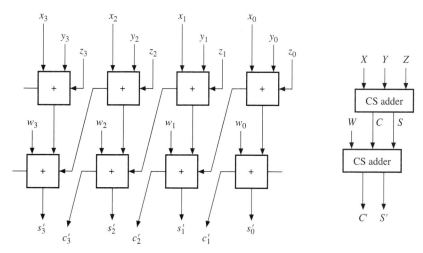

Figure 4.54
A two-stage carry-save adder.

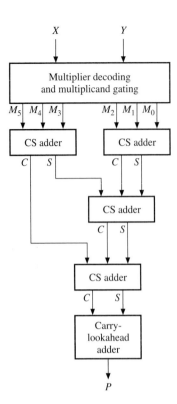

Figure 4.55
A carry-save (Wallace tree) multiplier.

$2n$-bit carry word. The final carry assimilation is performed by a fast adder—a carry-lookahead adder, for instance—with normal internal carry propagation.

The strictly combinational multiplier of Figure 4.55 is practical for moderate values of n, depending on the level of circuit integration used. For large n, the number of carry-save adders required can be excessive. Carry-save techniques can still be used, however, if the multiplier is partitioned into k m-bit segments. Only m terms M_i are generated and added via the carry-save adder circuits. The process is repeated k times, and the resulting sums are accumulated. The product is therefore obtained after k iterations.

Carry-save multiplication is well suited to pipelined implementation. Figure 4.56 shows a four-stage pipelined version of the carry-save multiplier of Figure 4.55. The first stage decodes the multiplier and transfers appropriately shifted copies of the multiplicand into the carry-save adders. The output of the first stage is a set of numbers (partial products) that are then summed by the carry-save adder tree. The carry-save logic has been subdivided into two stages by the insertion of buffer registers (denoted R in the figure). The fourth and final stage contains a carry-lookahead adder to assimilate the carries. This type of multiplier is easily modified to handle floating-point numbers. The input mantissas are processed in a fixed-point multiplier pipeline. The exponents are combined by a separate fixed-point adder, and a normalization circuit is also introduced.

The next example describes the pipelined floating-point unit of the Motorola 68040 microprocessor, which integrates the functions of the 68020 microprocessor (section 3.1.2 and Examples 3.3, 3.6, and 3.8) and its 68882 floating-point coprocessor (Example 4.7) in a single IC containing more than 1.2 million transistors.

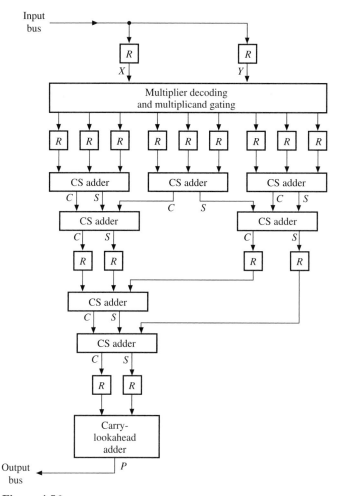

Figure 4.56
A pipelined carry-save multiplier.

This floating-point unit also implements many of the design techniques covered in this section.

EXAMPLE 4.9 THE PIPELINED FLOATING-POINT UNIT OF THE MOTOR-OLA 68040 [EDENFIELD ET AL. 1990]. This member of the 680X0 series of one-chip 32-bit microprocessors was introduced in 1990. It executes the combined instruction sets of the 68020 CPU and the 68882, which are listed in Figures 3.12 and 4.46, respectively, and is about four times as fast as the 68020 for a fixed clock rate. The 68040 contains two pipelined arithmetic processors: an integer unit (IU), which handles integer instructions, logical instructions, and address calculations, and a floating-point unit (FPU), which we now examine. A key design goal of the FPU is compatibility with object code written for the 68020 and 68882, as well as compatibility with the IEEE 754 floating-point standard. Only the subset of the 68882's instructions listed in Figure 4.57, including the four basic arithmetic operations and square root, are actually realized in hardware. Also included is a small set of data-transfer and program-control

Type	Opcode	Operation specified
Data transfer	FMOVE	Move word to/from coprocessor data or control register
	FMOVEM	Move multiple words to/from coprocessor
Data processing	FADD	Add
	FCMP	Compare
	FDIV	Divide
	FMUL	Multiply
	FSUB	Subtract
	FABS	Absolute value
	FNEG	Negate
	FSQRT	Square root
Program control	FB*cc*	Branch if condition code (status) *cc* is 1
	FDB*cc*	Test, decrement count, and branch on *cc*
	FRESTORE	Restore coprocessor state
	FSAVE	Save coprocessor state
	FS*cc*	Set (*cc* = 1) or reset (*cc* = 0) a specified byte
	FTST	Set coprocessor condition codes to specified values
	FTRAP*cc*	Conditional trap

Figure 4.57
Subset of the 68882 floating-point instruction set implemented by the 68040.

instructions to support floating-point operations. The remaining 68882 instructions must be simulated by software, for which the 68040 provides some hardware support.

The 68040's FPU has the three-stage pipeline organization shown in Figure 4.58. It is designed to handle floating-point number sizes of 32, 64, and 80 bits. The FPU is divided into two largely independent subunits: one for 64-bit mantissas (which expand to 67 bits when guard digits are included) and the other for 16-bit exponents. The FPU obtains its operands from and sends its results to the IU in a way that mimics the 68882's communication with its host CPU. The pipeline's first stage S_1 (referred to as the floating-point conversion unit) reformats input and output operands to meet IEEE 754 requirements, and is the only stage that communicates with the IU. Stage S_1 also has an ALU for comparing input exponents, as required in floating-point addition or subtraction. The second stage S_2 (the floating-point execution unit) contains a large (67 bit) ALU, a fast barrel shifter, and an array multiplier; this stage is responsible for executing all major operations on mantissas. The final stage S_3 (the floating-point normalization unit) rounds off and normalizes results; it also deals with exceptional cases. Various buses shown in simplified form in Figure 4.58 provide bypass and feedback paths through the pipeline. The clocking of the pipeline is complicated by the need to use several cycles to transfer long operands so that the minimum delay of each stage is two cycles. The delay of a floating-point operation can vary from 2 clock cycles to more than 100 in the case of the FSQRT instruction.

Certain instructions such as FABS, FMOVE, and FNEG are executed entirely within stage S_1 and thus have a delay of two clock cycles. The add and subtract instructions FADD and FSUB use all three stages of the FPU and have a delay of three. These instructions see a pipeline whose organization resembles that of Figure 4.50, with the latter's middle stages S_2 and S_3 merged into the 68040's second (execution) stage S_2. FMUL is executed primarily by the 64 × 8-bit, fixed-point multiplier in S_2. The multiplication of two mantissas requires several passes through the multiplier circuit, which implements the carry-save multiplication method discussed earlier. Two passes can be made per clock cycle of the pipeline, so that the final set of sum-carry pairs is generated in four clock cycles. An additional cycle through S_2's ALU assimilates the carries and yields the final product. The floating-point division instruction FDIV is implemented by a shift-and-subtract algorithm of the non-restoring type, which requires no special division hardware but takes up to 38 clock cycles.

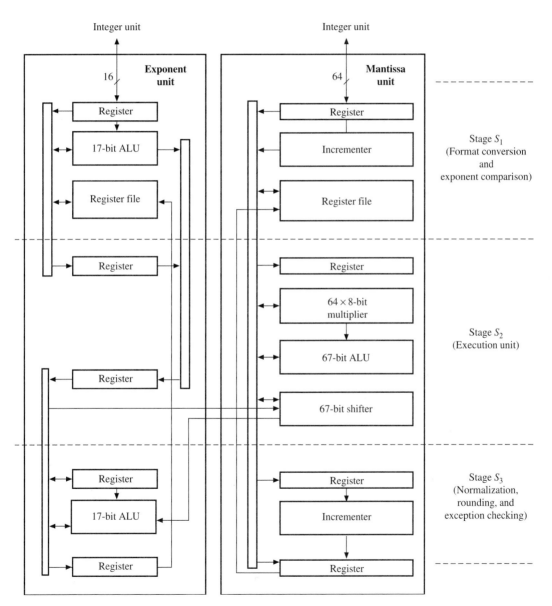

Figure 4.58
Pipelined floating-point unit of the Motorola 68040.

Systolic arrays. Closely related conceptually to arithmetic pipelines are the data-processing circuits called *systolic arrays* [Johnson, Hurson, and Shirazi 1993] formed by interconnecting a set of identical data-processing cells in a uniform manner. Data words flow synchronously from cell to cell, with each cell performing a small step in the overall operation of the array. The data are not fully processed until the end results emerge from the array's boundary cells. A one-dimensional systolic array is therefore a kind of pipeline with identical stages. A two-dimensional systolic array has a structure not unlike the divider array in Figure 4.27, but its cells are sequential rather than combinational. In general, a systolic array permits data to flow through the cells in several directions at once. As in pipelines, buffering must be included within the cells to isolate different sets of operands from one another. The name *systolic* derives from the rhythmic nature of the data flow, which can be compared with the rhythmic contraction of the heart (the systole) in pumping blood through the body. Systolic processors have been designed to implement various complex arithmetic operations such as convolution (problem 4.34), matrix multiplication, and solution techniques for linear equations. We illustrate the concepts involved by a two-dimensional systolic array that performs matrix multiplication.

Let X be an $n \times n$ matrix of fixed-point or floating-point numbers defined by

$$X = \begin{bmatrix} x_{1,1} & x_{1,2} & \dots x_{1,n} \\ x_{2,1} & x_{2,2} & \dots x_{2,n} \\ & \dots & \\ x_{n,1} & x_{n,2} & \dots x_{n,n} \end{bmatrix}$$

For brevity we write $X = [x_{i,j}]$, where $x_{i,j}$ is the element in the ith row and jth column of X. The product of X and another $n \times n$ matrix $Y = [y_{i,j}]$ is the $n \times n$ matrix $Z = [z_{i,j}]$ given by

$$z_{i,j} = \sum_{k=1}^{n} x_{i,k} \times y_{k,j} \tag{4.47}$$

A systolic array for matrix multiplication may be constructed from a cell (Figure 4.59*a*) that executes the following multiply-and-add operation on individual numbers (scalars):

$$z := z' + x \times y \tag{4.48}$$

Note that the same type of operation appears in the cell M of the fixed-point array multiplier in Figure 4.53, with 1-bit operands replacing the n-bit numbers used here. Multiply-and-add is also a basic instruction type in recent CPUs such as the PowerPC.

Each cell $C_{i,j}$ of the matrix multiplier receives its x and y operands from the left and top, respectively. In addition to computing z, $C_{i,j}$ propagates its x and y input operands rightward and downward, respectively. The systolic matrix multiplier is constructed from $n(2n - 1)$ copies of $C_{i,j}$, which are connected in the two-dimensional mesh configuration depicted in Figure 4.59*b*. The n operands forming the ith row of X flow horizontally from left to right through the ith row of cells as they might through a one-dimensional pipeline. The n operands forming the jth column of **Y** flow vertically through the *j*th column of cells in a similar manner. The *x* and *y* operands are carefully ordered and separated by zeros as shown in the figure so that the specific operand pairs $x_{i,k}, y_{k,j}$ appearing in (4.47) meet at an appropriate cell of the array, where they are multiplied according to (4.48) and added to a running sum z'. The z's emerge from the left side of $C_{i,j}$, so that there is a flow of partial results from right to left through the cell array. Each row of cells eventually issues the corresponding row of the matrix product **Z** from its left side.

To illustrate the operation of the matrix multiplier, consider the computation of $z_{1,1}$ in Figure 4.59*b*. Specializing Equation (4.47) for the case where $n = 3$, we get

$$z_{1,1} = x_{1,1}y_{1,1} + x_{1,2}y_{2,1} + x_{1,3}y_{3,1}$$

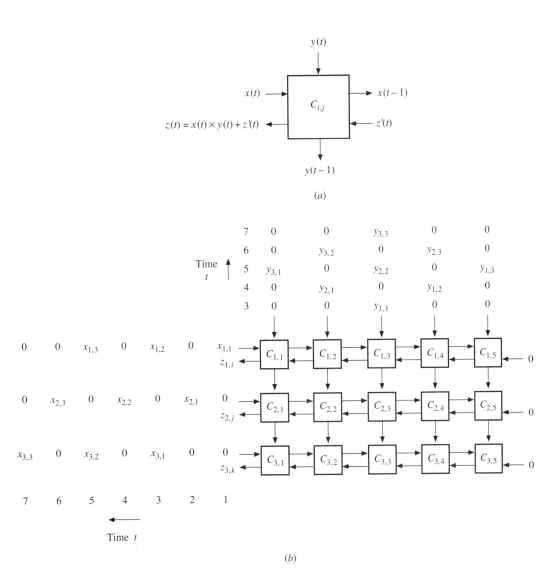

Figure 4.59
Systolic array for matrix multiplication: (*a*) basic cell and (*b*) 3 × 5 array.

The operand $x_{1,1}$ flows rightward through the top row of cells meeting only zero values of y and z until it encounters $y_{1,1}$ at cell $C_{1,3}$ at time $t = 3$. This cell then computes $z = x_{1,1}y_{1,1} + 0$, which it sends to the cell $C_{1,2}$ on its left. At the same time $C_{1,3}$ forwards $y_{1,1}$ to the second row of cells for use in computing the second row of the result matrix $\mathbf{Z}$; it also forwards $x_{1,1}$ to its right neighbor $C_{1,4}$. In the next clock cycle ($t = 4$), $x_{1,2}$ and $y_{2,1}$ are applied to $C_{1,2}$. This cell therefore computes $z = x_{1,2}y_{2,1} + z'$, where $z' = x_{1,1}y_{1,1}$. Finally at $t = 5$, the last pair of operands $x_{1,3}$ and $y_{3,1}$ converge at the boundary cell $C_{1,1}$, which computes $z = x_{1,3}y_{3,1} + z'$, using the value $z' = x_{1,1}y_{1,1} + x_{1,2}y_{2,1}$ supplied by $C_{1,2}$; z is the desired result $z_{1,1}$. At time $t = 6$, $C_{1,1}$ emits a zero, and at $t = 7$, it emits the next element $z_{1,2}$ of $\mathbf{Z}$. This process continues until all the elements of the first row of $\mathbf{Z}$ have been generated. Concurrently and in a similar way, the remaining rows of cells compute the other rows of $\mathbf{Z}$. Note, however, that $x_{i+1,j}$ is produced two cycles later than $x_{i,j}$. The last result $z_{n,n}$ emerges from the array at $t = 4n - 3$. Thus using $O(n^2)$ cells, this systolic array performs matrix multiplication in $O(n)$ time, that is, linear time. Roughly speaking, the array generates n elements of the product matrix $\mathbf{Z}$ in one step (two clock cycles in the present example).

The major characteristics of a systolic array can be deduced from the preceding example.

1. It provides a high degree of parallelism by processing many sets of operands concurrently.
2. Partially processed data sets flow synchronously through the array in pipeline fashion, but possibly in several directions at once, with complete results eventually appearing at the array boundary.
3. The use of uniform cells and interconnection simplifies implementation, for example, when using single-chip VLSI technology.
4. The control of the array is simple, since all cells perform the same operations; however, care must be taken to supply the data in the correct sequence for the operation being implemented.
5. If the X and Y matrices are generated in real time, it is unnecessary to store them before computing $X \times Y$, as with most sequential or parallel processing techniques. Thus the use of systolic arrays reduces overall memory requirements.
6. The amount of hardware needed to implement a systolic array like that of Figure 4.59 is relatively large, even taking maximum advantage of VLSI.

Systolic arrays have found successful application in the design of special-purpose arithmetic circuits for digital signal processing, where data must be processed in real time at very high speeds using operations like matrix multiplication.

4.4
SUMMARY

The datapath or data-processing part of a CPU is responsible for executing arithmetic and logical (nonnumerical) instructions on various operand types, including fixed-point and floating-point numbers. The power of an instruction set is often measured by the arithmetic instructions it contains. The arithmetic functions of simpler machines such as RISC processors may be limited to the addition and subtraction of fixed-point numbers. More powerful processors incorporate multiply and divide instructions and in many cases have the hardware needed to process floating-point instructions as well.

Arithmetic circuit design is a well-developed field. Fixed-point adders and subtracters are easily constructed from combinational logic. The simplest but slowest adder circuits employ ripple-carry propagation. High-speed adders reduce carry-propagation delays by techniques such as carry lookahead. Fixed-point multiplication and division can be implemented by shift-and-add/subtract algorithms that resemble manual methods. The product or quotient of two km-bit numbers is formed in k sequential steps, where each step involves an m-bit shift and, possibly, a km-bit addition or subtraction. Division is inherently more difficult than multiplication due to the problem of determining quotient digits. Both multipliers and dividers can be implemented by combinational logic array circuits but at a substantial increase in the amount of hardware required.

The simplest ALU is a combinational circuit that implements fixed-point addition and subtraction, typically using the carry-lookahead method; it also implements a set of bitwise (word) logical operations. Multiplication and division algorithms of the shift-and-add/subtract type can be realized by adding a few operand registers—an accumulator AC, a multiplier-quotient register MQ, and a multiplicand-dividend register MD—as well as a small control unit. Datapath units usually contain an addressable register file—in effect, a small, high-speed RAM—to store ALU operands. The register file has several IO ports to allow operands in several different registers to be accessed simultaneously. Bit slicing is a useful technique for constructing a large ALU from multiple copies of a small ALU slice. Multicycling allows a small ALU to process large operands at lower hardware cost but more slowly than bit slicing.

Floating-point and other complex operations can be implemented by an autonomous execution unit within the CPU or by a program-transparent extension to the CPU called a coprocessor. A floating-point processor is typically composed of a pair of fixed-point ALUs—one to process exponents and the other to process mantissas. Special circuits are needed for normalization and, in the case of floating-point addition and subtraction, exponent comparison and mantissa alignment.

Finally, the throughput of a complex datapath circuit such as a floating-point processor can be substantially increased with low hardware overhead by a technique called pipelining. The operations of interest are broken into a sequence of steps, each of which is implemented by a pipeline stage. Buffering between the stages allows an n-stage pipeline to execute up to n separate instructions concurrently. Hence the pipeline's throughput when executing a long sequence of instructions exceeds by a factor of up to n that of a similar but nonpipelined processor. Systolic arrays extend the pipeline concept from one to two or more data-processing dimensions.

4.5
PROBLEMS

4.1. Figure 4.60 gives the logic diagram of a small arithmetic circuit found in a commercial IC with the IO signals renamed to conceal their identities. (*a*) What is the overall function of this circuit? (*b*) Identify the purpose of every IO signal. (*c*) Why do all input

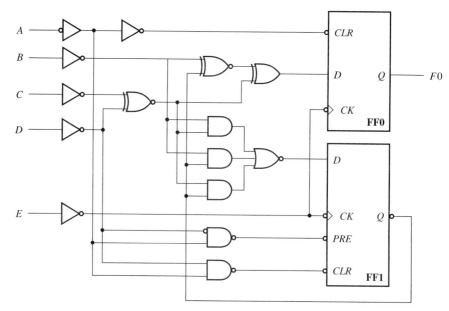

Figure 4.60
Small arithmetic circuit from a commercial IC.

lines contain inverters, which apparently increase the circuit's gate count without contributing to its functionality?

4.2. A 1-bit or *full subtracter* implements the arithmetic equation

$$b_i z_i = x_i - y_i - b_{i-1}$$

where z_i and b_i denote the difference and borrow functions, respectively. (*a*) Derive a pair of logic equations defining z_i and b_i. (*b*) Design an *n*-bit subtracter whose operation is analogous to that of a ripple-carry adder.

4.3. Redesign the *n*-bit twos-complement adder-subtracter of Figure 4.4 so that it can compute any of the three operations $X + Y$, $X - Y$, or $Y - X$, as specified by a 2-bit *MODE* control input.

4.4. Addition and subtraction of sign-magnitude numbers is complicated by the fact that to compute $X + Y$, the magnitudes $|X|$ and $|Y|$ must be compared to determine the operation to perform and the order of the operands. This can be seen from Figure 4.61 which gives a complete procedure for addition of *n*-bit, sign-magnitude numbers. Design a register-level circuit to compute the three functions $X + Y$, $X - Y$, and $Y - X$. Assume that the word size *n* is 16 bits and that the standard design components are available, including a 16-bit (unsigned) adder, a 16-bit (unsigned) subtracter, and a 16-bit magnitude comparator.

4.5. Suppose that the adder-subtracter circuit of Figure 4.62 has been designed for twos-complement numbers. It computes the sum $Z = X + Y$ when control line $SUB = 0$ and the difference $Z = X - Y$ when $SUB = 1$. An overflow flag v is to be added to the circuit, but it is not possible to access internal lines. In other words, only those data and control

1. X and Y both positive: Add $X = x_{n-1}x_{n-2}...x_0$ and $Y = y_{n-1}y_{n-2}...y_0$ (modulo 2^n) to form the result $Z = z_{n-1}z_{n-2}...z_0$. (This is n-bit unsigned addition).
2. X positive; Y negative: Let $|X| = x_{n-2}x_{n-3}...x_0$ and $|Y| = y_{n-2}y_{n-3}...y_0$. If $|X| < |Y|$, subtract X from Y (modulo 2^n). If $|X| \geq |Y|$, then set y_{n-1} to 0 and subtract Y from X (modulo 2^n).
3. X negative; Y positive: If $|Y| < |X|$, subtract Y from X (modulo 2^n). If $|Y| \geq |X|$, set x_{n-1} to 0 and subtract X from Y (modulo 2^n).
4. X and Y both negative: Add X and Y (modulo 2^n) and set z_{n-1} to 1.

Figure 4.61
Algorithm for subtracting sign-magnitude numbers.

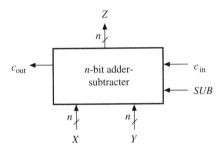

Figure 4.62
An n-bit adder-subtracter circuit.

lines appearing in the figure can be used to compute v. Construct a suitable logic circuit for v.

4.6. Consider again the adder-subtracter of Figure 4.62, assuming now that it has been designed for sign-magnitude numbers. It computes $Z = X + Y$ when $SUB = 0$ and $Z = X - Y$ when $SUB = 1$. Assume that the circuit contains an n-bit ripple-carry adder and a similar n-bit ripple-borrow subtracter and that you have access to all internal lines. Derive a logic equation that defines an overflow flag v for this circuit.

4.7. Give an informal interpretation and proof of correctness of the two expressions (4.12) for p and g that define the propagate and generate conditions, respectively, for a 4-bit carry-lookahead generator.

4.8. Show how to extend the 16-bit design of Figure 4.8 to a 64-bit adder using the same two component types: a 4-bit adder module and a 4-bit carry-lookahead generator.

4.9. Stating your assumptions and showing your calculations, obtain an good estimate for each of the following for both an n-bit carry-lookahead adder and an n-bit ripple-carry adder: (*a*) the total number of gates used; (*b*) the circuit depth (number of levels); and (*c*) the maximum gate fan-in.

4.10. Another useful technique for fast binary addition is the *conditional-sum* method. It and a closely related method called *carry-select* addition are based on the idea of simultaneously generating two versions of each sum bit s_i: a version s_i^1, which assumes that its input carry $c_{i-1} = 1$, and a second version s_i^0, which assumes that $c_{i-1} = 0$. A multiplexer controlled by c_{i-1} then selects either s_i^1 or s_i^0 to be s_i. The advantage of this method is that the sums (and carries) can be generated without waiting for their

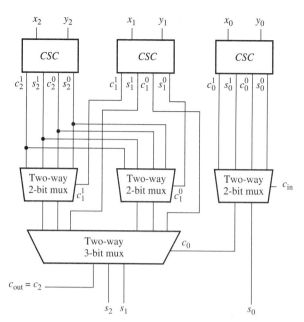

Figure 4.63
Three-bit conditional-sum adder.

incoming carries to arrive. Figure 4.63 shows a 3-bit conditional-sum adder from which its general structure and operation can readily be deduced. (*a*) Construct a gate-level logic circuit for the *CS* module. (*b*) Show how to extend the circuit of Figure 4.63 from 3 to 7 bits. (*c*) Briefly compare the conditional-sum and carry-lookahead techniques in terms of speed and hardware costs.

4.11. Suppose the combinational array multiplier of Figures 4.17 and 4.18 is given the unsigned integer operands $X = 1010$ and $Y = 1001$. Determine the output signals generated by every adder cell when the array computes $X \times Y$.

4.12. Use the multiplier cell of Figure 4.19 to construct a combinational array multiplier for 5-bit unsigned numbers. Draw a logic diagram for the multiplier and show all the signals (including constant signals) applied to every cell.

4.13. Suppose a multiplier MULT_{16} for 16-bit unsigned numbers is constructed from AND and adder arrays as illustrated by Figures 4.17 and 4.18, respectively. Let d denote the propagation delay of a single gate G and let $D = 4d$ be the delay of a full adder FA. (*a*) How many copies of FA are needed to build MULT_{16}? (*b*) What is the worst-case delay of MULT_{16}? (*c*) Observe that the bottom row of full adders in Figure 4.17 is a simple ripple-carry adder ADD. Stating all your assumptions, estimate the speedup in multiplication that results from replacing ADD in MULT_{16} by a carry-lookahead adder of standard design.

4.14. Suppose the Booth array multiplier of Figure 4.20 is given the signed integer operands $X = 1010$ and $Y = 1001$. Determine the output signals generated by every M cell when the array computes $X \times Y$.

4.15. In bit-by-bit multiplication of Y by X, bit $x_i = 1$ in position i of X causes an addition that contributes $2^i Y$ to the solution P. Clearly $x_i = 0$ contributes nothing to P. In the Booth algorithm $x_i = 1$ causes either addition or subtraction; in the latter case it contributes

$-2^i Y$ to the solution. Thus $X \times Y$ is computed in the form $(\pm 2^{i1} Y \pm 2^{i2} Y \pm \ldots \pm 2^{ik} Y) =$ $(\pm 2^{i1} \pm 2^{i2} \pm \ldots \pm 2^{ik}) \times Y$. Booth's algorithm effectively multiplies by a number X^* that has digits weighted by -2^i as well as the usual $+2^i$. We can make this weighting explicit by "recoding" X into X^* using the three digits $0, 1$, and $\bar{1}$, where $\bar{1}$ in position i denotes a weight of -2^i. For example, $X^* = 1\ \bar{1}00100\ \bar{1}0$ is evaluated as $+2^8 - 2^7 + 2^4 - 2^1 = 70_{10} = 01001110_2$. X^* is an instance of a *signed-digit number*, a useful concept in designing multipliers and dividers. Using the recoding rules implicit in Booth's algorithm, obtain signed-digit representations of the twos-complement integers $A = 011010001$ and $B = 101011110$.

4.16. Booth multiplication skips over runs of zeros and ones, which reduces the number of add and subtract steps needed to multiply two n-bit numbers from n to a variable number whose average value n_{ave} is less than n. Some designers argued that this fact can be exploited to reduce the average multiplication time from n to n_{ave} steps. (*a*) Show that $n_{ave} = n/2$. (*Hint*: Assume n_{ave} is known and use it to determine $[n + 1]_{ave}$). (*b*) Explain why practical multipliers are rarely designed to use this speedup technique. (See the following problem for a practical speedup technique for Booth multipliers.)

4.17. A faster version of Booth's multiplication algorithm for twos-complement numbers, known as the *modified Booth algorithm* (MBA), examines three adjacent bits $x_{i+1} x_i x_{i-1}$ of the multiplier X at a time, instead of two. Besides the three basic actions performed by the original Booth algorithm, which can be expressed as add 0, Y, or $-Y$ to A (the accumulated partial products), MBA performs two more actions: add $+2Y$ or $-2Y$ to A. These have the effect of increasing the radix from two to four and allow an n-bit multiplication to be done in $n/2$ clock cycles instead of n (at the usual cost of more hardware). Figure 4.64 shows a pencil-and-paper application of MBA to two 8-bit twos-complement integers X and Y. (*a*) Construct a truth table that defines the basic actions of MBA as a function of $x_{i+1} x_i x_{i-1}$. (*b*) Give an HDL description of MBA along the lines of Figure 4.15.

4.18. Division circuits usually include logic to detect a dividend-divisor combination that will cause the quotient to overflow. Suppose that a divider for n-bit unsigned integers has a double-word ($2n$-bit) dividend D and a single-word divisor V. (*a*) What general condition must be satisfied for quotient overflow to occur? (*b*) How would you modify

Operands	Values	i	$x_{i+1} x_i x_{i-1}$	Action
Multiplicand Y	10101010			
Multiplier X	11001110			
P_0	0000000010101100	0	100	Add $-2Y$ to A
P_2	00000000000000	2	111	Add 0 to A
P_4	111110101010	4	001	Add $+Y$ to A
P_6	0001010110	6	110	Add $-Y$ to A
P	0001000011001100 $= P_0 + P_2 + P_4 + P_6$			

Figure 4.64
Illustration of the modified (radix-4) Booth method of multiplication.

the sequential division circuit of Figure 4.23 to introduce an overflow detector using as little extra logic as possible?

4.19. Suppose the restoring array divider of Figure 4.27 has the integer operands $D = 100110$ and $V = 101$. Determine the results Q and R, as well as the vertical output signals generated by every D cell when the array computes D/V.

4.20. Consider the divider array of Figure 4.27 that is designed to handle a word size of $n = 3$ with a double-length (6 bit) dividend D. (*a*) Why are there four rows of D cells instead of three? (*b*) Suppose that dividends are restricted to 3 bits instead of 6. Which cells can then be deleted from the array?

4.21. Figure 4.65 shows a gate-level logic diagram for the 74181 ALU/function generator. The inputs have been assigned the names used in Figure 4.30, but the eight outputs are abstractly labeled $f_1{:}f_8$. Deduce (without using any outside sources) the correspondence between the output signal names in the two figures; that is, identify all the outputs in Figure 4.65 and explain your reasoning.

4.22. (*a*) What arithmetic and logic functions are computed by the 74181 ALU when $S = S_3S_2S_1S_0 = 1100$? (*b*) A useful logic operation of the 74181 is the EXCLUSIVE-OR function $A \oplus B$. What values should S, M, and c_{in} have in this case? Briefly explain your reasoning.

4.23. The 74181 ALU is designed for use as a 4-bit magnitude comparator. For this purpose it must be set to its arithmetic subtract mode ($M = 1$, $S = 0110$) with $c_{in} = 1$. The relations between the magnitudes of A and B can then be determined from the combined values of the two outputs ($A = B$) and c_{out}. Identify the specific output values that indicate each of the following: $A = B$, $A < B$, $A \le B$, $A > B$, and $A \ge B$.

4.24. Show how to connect four copies of the 74181 to form a 16-bit ALU with carry lookahead across all stages.

4.25. Design a register file in the style of Figure 4.33 that stores eight 32-bit numbers and has one read port A and one write port B.

4.26. Suppose the register file RF_{16} of Figure 4.33 is to be built out of four identical 4-bit slices denoted RF_4. (*a*) Give a register-level diagram showing the internal structure of RF_4. (*b*) Show how four copies of RF_4 are interconnected to form RF_{16}.

4.27. Design a 16-bit bit-sliced ALU using four copies of the AMD 2901 4-bit slice. Use carry lookahead and use NAND gates to design the necessary carry-generation logic. Give a block diagram of your design and give a set of Boolean equations that specify the carry-lookahead function.

4.28. Suppose the 1601 ALU of Figure 4.39 operating at a clock frequency of 20 MHz is used to build an ALU intended to execute a long sequence of 80-bit additions. What is the maximum throughput in operations per second if the 1601-based ALU is set up to perform 80-bit operations (*a*) in bit-sliced mode and (*b*) in multicycling mode.

4.29. Modify the algorithm for floating-point addition in Figure 4.42 to make the following improvements: (*a*) Perform either addition or subtraction as specified by an opcode in the instruction register IR. (*b*) Test for zero operands at the start and skip as much computation as possible when X and/or Y is zero. (*c*) Modify the mantissa assignment

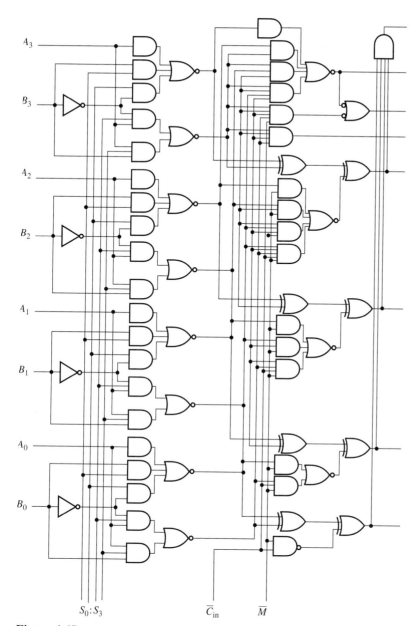

A_3

B_3

A_2

B_2

A_1

B_1

A_0

B_0

$S_0{:}S_3$ $\overline{C}_{\mathrm{in}}$ $\overline{M}$

Figure 4.65
Logic diagram for the 74181 ALU/function generator.

strategy to reduce the amount of shifting when $|E| > n_M$. (d) Introduce separate flags OVR_ERROR and UND_ERROR to indicate overflow and underflow, respectively; these flags replace ERROR.

4.30. (a) List the advantages and disadvantages of designing a floating-point processor in the form of a k-stage pipeline. (b) A floating-point pipeline has five stages S_1, S_2, S_3, S_4, and S_5 whose delays are 120, 90, 100, 85, and 110 ns, respectively. What is the pipeline's maximum throughput in millions of floating-point operations per second (MFLOPS)?

4.31. Consider the logic diagram for a pipelined 3×3-bit multiplier appearing in Figure 4.53. (a) The six unconnected line stubs attached to some of the M cells are redundant in that they always carry the logic value 0. Certain connected lines are also redundant in this sense and are included only to make the stages uniform. Identify all such redundant connections. (b) Consider a general $n \times n$ version of this multiplier pipeline. Assuming that the stages are identical and are labeled $S_0, S_1, \ldots, S_{n-1}$, show that the total number of 1-bit buffer registers of type R needed is $3n^2 - n$.

4.32. In digital signal processing it is sometimes necessary to multiply a high-speed stream of n-bit numbers $Y_1, Y_2, Y_3, \ldots$ by a single number X. The output should be a stream of n-bit results $Y_1X, Y_2X, Y_3X, \ldots$ moving at the same rate as the input stream. Assuming that X and Y_i are positive n-bit binary fractions, design a pipeline processor to carry out this type of multiplication efficiently. If the pipeline is constructed from gates of average delay d, estimate its throughput.

4.33. Outline how the Motorola 68040's FPU can be used to multiply two 32-bit mantissas to produce a 64-bit product, given that its mantissa multiplier is designed for 64×8-bit numbers.

4.34. Let $X = x_0, x_1, \ldots, x_{n-1}$ and $Y = y_0, y_1, \ldots, y_{n-1}$ be two fixed-point vectors of length n. The double-length vector $Z = z_0, z_1, \ldots, z_{2n-2}, z_{2n-1}$ defined by

$$z_i = \sum_{j=0}^{n-i} x_i \times y_{i-j}$$

where $x_j = y_j = 0$ if $j < 0$ is called the *convolution* of X and Y. This operation is useful in applications such as digital signal processing. Design a one-dimensional systolic array to implement convolution. The array should have the general structure of a pipeline with the X, Y, and Z vectors flowing horizontally. Describe the functions of the processing cell (stage) and draw a diagram illustrating the operation of the systolic array in the style of Figure 4.59.

4.35. The COordinate Rotation DIgital Computer (CORDIC) technique [Volder 1959] is a fast, low-cost way to compute trigonometric functions. It treats a number Z as a vector represented by Cartesian coordinates (X, Y), and operations analogous to vector rotation calculate the required functions of Z. Suppose that the vector Z is rotated through an angle θ. The result $Z' = (X', Y')$ is defined by the equations

$$X' = X \cos\theta \pm Y \sin\theta$$
$$Y' = Y \cos\theta \mp X \sin\theta \qquad (4.49)$$

where the upper and lower signs correspond to clockwise and counterclockwise rotation, respectively. These equations imply that

$$X'' = X'/\cos\theta = X \pm Y \tan\theta$$
$$Y'' = Y'/\cos\theta = Y \pm X \tan\theta \qquad (4.50)$$

$Z'' = (X'', Y'')$ can be interpreted as the original vector Z after rotation through an angle θ and a magnitude increase by the factor $K = 1/\cos\theta$. If $\tan\theta$ is a power of 2, then the multiplication by $\tan\theta$ in (4.50) can be realized by shifting. The essence of CORDIC is to implement the rotation described by (4.50) as a sequence of $n + 1$ rotations through angles α_i such that

$$\theta = \alpha_0 \pm \alpha_1 \pm \alpha_2 \pm \dots \pm \alpha_n \tag{4.51}$$

and $$\alpha_i = \tan^{-1}(2^{-i}) \tag{4.52}$$

Then if $Z = (X_0, Y_0)$, rotation through angle α_i is defined by (4.51) and (4.52) and has the form

$$X_{i+1} = X_i \pm Y_i 2^{-i}$$

$$Y_{i+1} = Y \mp X 2^{-i} \tag{4.53}$$

The resulting vector Z_n has magnitude $K_n|Z_0|$, where $K_n = \Pi_{i=0}^{n}(\cos\alpha_i)^{-1}$ is a constant depending on n, which converges toward 1.6468. Observe that the only operations in (4.53) are addition, subtraction, and shifting.

The signs appearing in (4.51) depend on θ and must be computed in order to determine the operations needed to evaluate (4.53). The sign computation is done by storing the constants $\{\alpha_i\}$ in a table. In each iteration it is determined which of $+\alpha_i$ and $-\alpha_i$ causes $|\theta + (\alpha_0 \pm \alpha_1 \pm \dots \pm \alpha_i)|$ to converge toward zero. If $+\alpha_i$ ($-\alpha_i$) is selected, then the upper (lower) signs in (4.51) are used, which correspond to a clockwise (counterclockwise) rotation through the angle α_i. Each iteration increases the accuracy of (X_i, Y_i) by about 1 bit.

CORDIC is used to calculate $\sin\theta$, $\cos\theta$, and $\tan\theta$ as follows: Let $X_0 = K_{n-1} \approx 0.6073$ and $Y_0 = 0.0$, where n has been chosen to achieve the desired accuracy. Compute (X_n, Y) according to (4.53). From (4.49) and (4.50) we see that $X_n = K_n X_0 \cos\theta$ and $Y_n = K_n X_0 \sin\theta$; hence X_n and Y_n are the required values of $\cos\theta$ and $\sin\theta$, respectively. $\tan\theta$ can now be computed by Y_n/X_n. (a) Give in tabular form all the calculations required by CORDIC to compute $\sin 33°$ to three decimal places. (b) Draw a register-level logic circuit for a simple CORDIC arithmetic unit that computes $\sin\theta$ and $\cos\theta$.

4.36. Describe how the CORDIC technique presented in the preceding problem can be adapted to compute the inverse trigonometric functions $\sin^{-1}x$, $\cos^{-1}x$, and $\tan^{-1}x$.

4.6
REFERENCES

1. Anderson, S. F. et al. "The IBM System/360 Model 91: Floating-Point Execution Unit." *IBM Journal of Research and Development,* vol.2 (January 1967) pp. 34–53.
2. AT&T Microelectronics. *HS600C and LP600C CMOS Standard Cell Libraries Data Book.* Allentown, PA, April 1994.
3. Booth, A. D. "A Signed Binary Multiplication Technique." *Quarterly Journal of Mechanics and Applied Mathematics.* vol. 4, pt. 2 (1951) pp. 236–40.
4. Cavanagh, J. J. F. *Digital Computer Arithmetic.* New York: McGraw-Hill, 1984.
5. Edenfield, R. W. et al. "The 68040 Processor: Part I, Design and Implementation." *IEEE Micro* vol. 10, (February 1990) pp. 66–78.
6. GEC Plessey Semiconductors. *Digital Signal Processing IC Handbook.* Swindon, UK, 1990.
7. Hansen, M. C. and J. P. Hayes. "High-Level Test Generation Using Physically-Induced Faults." *Proc. 13th VLSI Test Symp.* Princeton, NJ, 1995, pp. 20–28.
8. Hintz, R. G. and D. P. Tate. "Control Data STAR-100 Processor Design." *Proc. 6th IEEE Computer Soc. Conf.* (Compcon 72), San Francisco, CA, September 1972, pp. 1–4.

9. Integrated Device Technology Inc. "16 × 16 parallel CMOS multipliers IDT7216L/IDT7217L." data sheet, Santa Clara, CA, August 1995.

10. Johnson, K. T., A. R. Hurson, and B. Shirazi. "General Purpose Systolic Arrays." *IEEE Computer,* vol. 26 (November 1993) pp. 20–31.

11. Kampe, T. W. "The Design of a General-Purpose Microprogrammable Computer with Elementary Structure." *IEEE Transactions on Electronic Computers,* vol. EC-9 (June 1960), pp. 208–13.

12. Kane, G. and J. Heinrich. *MIPS RISC Architecture.* Englewood Cliffs, NJ: Prentice-Hall, 1992.

13. Kogge, P. M. *The Architecture of Pipelined Computers.* New York: McGraw-Hill, 1981.

14. Koren, I. *Computer Arithmetic Algorithms.* Englewood Cliffs, NJ: Prentice-Hall, 1993.

15. Mick, J. and J. Brick. *Bit-Slice Microprocessor Design.* New York: McGraw-Hill, 1980.

16. Motorola Inc. *MC68881/MC68882 Floating-Point Coprocessor User's Manual.* Englewood Cliffs, NJ: Prentice-Hall, 1989.

17. Robertson, J. E. "Twos Complement Multiplication in Binary Parallel Computers." *IRE Transactions on Electronic Computers,* vol. EC-4 (September 1955) pp. 118–19.

18. Stone, H. S. *High-Performance Computer Architecture.* 3rd ed. Reading, MA: Addison-Wesley, 1993.

19. Texas Instruments Inc. *The TTL Logic Data Book.* Dallas, TX, 1988.

20. Volder, J. E. "The CORDIC Trigonometric Computing Technique." *IRE Transactions on Electronic Computers,* vol. EC-8 (September 1959) pp. 330–34.

21. Wallace, C. S. "A Suggestion for a Fast Multiplier." *IEEE Transactions on Electronic Computers,* vol. EC-13 (February 1964) pp. 14–17.

CHAPTER 5

Control Design

In this chapter we study the register-level design of the control part of an instruction-set processor; the data-processing part was covered in Chapter 4. The two basic approaches to control-unit design—hardwired and microprogrammed—are discussed in detail. The complex task of controlling pipelined and superscalar processors is also examined.

5.1
BASIC CONCEPTS

First we discuss the general structure and behavior of control units. Then we examine the design of hardwired controllers, which are characterized by the use of fixed (nonprogrammable) logic circuits.

5.1.1 Introduction

We saw in section 2.1.1 that it is useful to separate a digital system into two parts: a datapath (data processing) unit and a control unit. The datapath is a network of functional and storage units capable of performing certain (micro) operations on data words. The purpose of the control unit is to issue control signals to the datapath. These control signals enter the datapath at "control points," where they select the functions to be performed at specific times and route the data through the appropriate parts of the datapath unit. In other words, the control unit logically reconfigures the datapath to implement some specified instruction or program.

A CPU's datapath contains circuits to perform arithmetic and logical operations on words such as fixed-point or floating-point numbers. The internal struc-

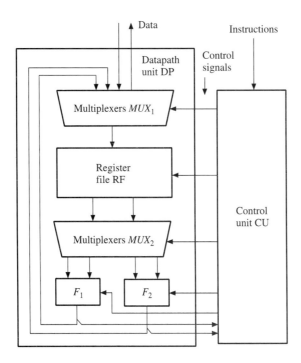

Figure 5.1
Processor composed of a datapath unit DP and a control unit CU.

ture of the datapath circuit DP of a small microprocessor is depicted in Figure 5.1. It contains a register file RF for temporary storage of operands, two functional units F_1 and F_2 responsible for data processing, and multiplexers to allow the data to be steered through DP. Typical functional units are an ALU performing addition, subtraction, and logical operations; a shifter; or a multiplier. The control unit CU receives external instructions or commands, which it converts into a sequence of control signals that the CU applies to DP to implement a sequence of register-transfer operations.

Figure 5.2 shows the control signals that implement an addition instruction of the form ADD A,B, which we write as

$$A := A + B; \tag{5.1}$$

in our HDL notation. Assume that this operation can be executed in a single clock cycle, whose timing details are not of concern at this level of abstraction. The input variables A and B are obtained from registers of the same name in RF, and the result is stored back into register A. Observe that the registers of RF permit their contents to be read from and written into in the same clock cycle, a basic property of the (edge-triggered) flip-flops from which such registers are constructed. RF is configured with one input and two output ports to support operations like (5.1) with two or three addresses. Besides selecting the data registers to be used, the control unit CU must also select the operation to be performed on the data, in this case, functional unit F_1's ADD operation. Finally the necessary logical connections for the data to flow through DP must be established by applying appropriate control signals to the multiplexers.

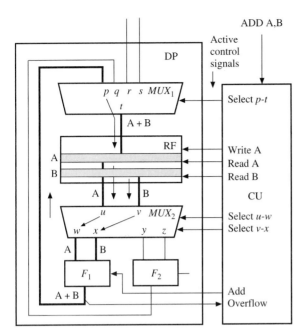

Figure 5.2
The processor of Figure 5.1 configured to implement the add operation A := A + B.

Thus we see that CU must activate the following three types of control signals during the clock cycle in which the ADD A,B instruction is executed.

- Function select: Add.
- Storage control: Read A, Read B, Write A.
- Data routing: Select p-t, Select u-w, Select v-x.

There is usually some feedback of control information from DP to CU to indicate exceptional conditions encountered during instruction execution. In the example of Figure 5.2, the functional unit F_1 performing the addition sends an overflow signal to CU whenever the sum A + B exceeds the normal word size.

Multicycle operations. Many types of instructions are executed in a single clock cycle—indeed, single-cycle execution is a central goal of RISC design. Some instructions require more than one clock cycle for their execution, however. For example, double-precision addition can be implemented by a two-instruction sequence (program) of the form

$$\begin{matrix} \text{ADD} & \text{AL, BL} \\ \text{ADDC} & \text{AH, BH} \end{matrix} \qquad (5.2)$$

which involves two double-word operands A and B. The first (ADD) instruction in (5.2) adds the low-order half (right word) of B to the low-order half of A, implicitly generating and storing a carry-out signal C. The second (ADDC) instruction adds the high-order half of B to the high-order half of A along with the carry C, thus ensuring that carries are propagated across the full double-length result. This short program is implemented in two consecutive clock cycles by activating the control signals listed below, not all of which appear in Figure 5.2.

Cycle	Function select	Storage control	Data routing
1	Add	Read AL, Read BL, Write AL	Select p-t, Select u-w, Select v-x
2	Add with carry	Read AH, Read BH, Write AH	Select p-t, Select u-w, Select v-x

(5.3)

This low-level description of the double-precision addition in terms of the control signals to be activated is an example of a *microprogram* and is contrasted with the higher-level *program* for the same operation appearing in (5.2). Each line of (5.3) is an example of a *microinstruction* specifying a set of low-level *microoperations*.

A further complication arises when the execution of a microoperation is conditional on the values of certain data or control signals. For example, the various sequential multiplication algorithms covered in the preceding chapters are specified by multistep algorithms that can be viewed as multicycle microprograms. The Booth multiplication algorithm (Figure 4.15), for instance, has statements of the following type:

> LOOP: **if** COND1 = **true then** ADD A,B
>   **else** SUB A,B;
>
>   **if** COND2 = **true then** **go to** OUTPUT
>   **else** LOOP;
>
> OUTPUT: . . .

We can expand the microinstruction format of (5.3) to accommodate conditional operations in the following straightforward (but inefficient) way:

Current address	Condition select C	Next address		Function select		Storage control	Data routing
		C = true	$C \neq$ true	C = true	$C \neq$ true		
ADR1	COND1	ADR2	ADR2	ADD	SUB	. . .	. . .
ADR2	COND2	ADR3	ADR1	. . .	. . .	. . .	. . .
ADR3	. . .	. . .	. . .	. . .	. . .	. . .	. . .

(5.4)

Here we are introducing some new fields to specify a condition C to be tested, as well as alternative control signals to be activated depending on the current value of C. Typically, C corresponds to a status control signal from DP, or to a special signal generated within CU, such as an end-of-loop condition. If, for instance, C = COND1 in the preceding example, then one of the two function-select signals, ADD or SUB, is activated. To vary the order in which the microinstructions are executed, a pair of next-address fields is also provided, one of which is selected by the current value of C. This technique requires attaching an address to every microinstruction, thus completing the analogy between microinstructions and higher-level (assembly language) formats.

Implementation methods. Historically, two general approaches to control unit design have evolved. One approach views the controller as a sequential logic circuit or finite-state machine that generates specific sequences of control signals in response to externally supplied instructions; see Figure 5.3a. It is designed with the usual goals of minimizing the number of components used and maximizing the speed of operation. Once the unit is constructed, the only way to implement changes in control-unit behavior is by redesigning the entire unit. Such a circuit is therefore said to be *hardwired*. The format of (5.4) is essentially similar to the state-table format for describing the behavior of a (hardwired) sequential circuit, as illustrated in (5.5).

Current state	Current input	Next state	Current outputs		
			Function	Storage	Routing
ADR1	COND1 = 1	ADR2	ADD	...	...
ADR1	COND1 = 0	ADR2	SUB	...	...
ADR2	COND2 = 1	ADR3	...	...	...
ADR2	COND2 = 0	ADR1	...	...	...
ADR3	...	...	...	...	...

(5.5)

Microprogramming provides an alternative method of designing program control units. A *microprogrammed control unit* has the structure shown in Figure 5.3b. It is built around a storage unit called a *control memory*, where all the control signals are stored in a programlike format resembling (5.4). The control memory stores a set of microprograms designed to implement or *emulate* the behavior of the given instruction set. Each instruction causes the corresponding microprogram to be fetched and its control information extracted in a manner that resembles the fetching and execution of a program from the computer's main memory.

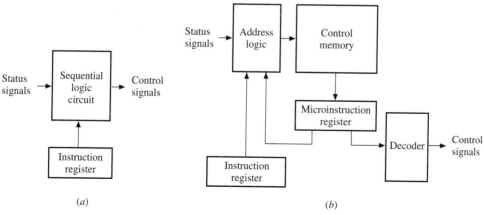

Figure 5.3
General structure of (*a*) a hardwired and (*b*) a microprogrammed control unit.

Microprogramming makes control unit design more systematic by organizing control signals into formatted words (microinstructions). Since the control signals are embedded in a kind of low-level software—this is referred to as *firmware*—design changes can be easily made just by altering the contents of the control memory. On the negative side, microprogrammed control units are more costly to manufacture than hardwired units due to the presence of the control memory and its access circuitry. Microprogrammed units also tend to be slower because of the extra time required to fetch microinstructions from the control memory. RISC processors, with their emphasis on small, fast instruction sets, favor the use of hardwired control units.

CPU control units, both hardwired and microprogrammed, are often organized as (*micro*) *instruction pipelines* in order to improve their performance. As we saw in section 4.3.2, pipelining is a relatively low-cost way of increasing a processor's throughput by decomposing its operation into a sequence of relatively independent steps. Program control naturally involves a sequence of steps (instruction fetching and decoding, input operand fetching, operation execution, and result storage) that can be carried out concurrently with different instructions. Modern CPUs make extensive use of pipelines to increase their effective instruction execution rate [Stone 1993].

5.1.2 Hardwired Control

Next we examine the design of control units that use fixed logic circuits to interpret instructions and generate control signals from them.

Design methods. Control-unit design involves various trade-offs between the amount of hardware used, the speed of operation, and the cost of the design process itself. To illustrate these issues, we consider two systematic approaches to the design of hardwired controllers [Hayes 1993; Baranov 1994]. These methods are representative of those used in practice, but by themselves are suitable only for small control units such as might be encountered in simple RISC processors or application-specific controllers.

- Method 1: The *classical method* of sequential circuit design, which was discussed briefly in section 2.1.3. It attempts to minimize the amount of hardware, in particular, by using only $\lceil \log_2 P \rceil$ flip-flops to realize a P-state circuit.
- Method 2: An approach that uses one flip-flop per state and is known as the *one-hot method*. While expensive in terms of flip-flops, this method simplifies CU design and debugging.

In practice, processor control units are often so complex that no one design method by itself can yield a satisfactory circuit at an acceptable cost. The most acceptable design may consist of several linked, but independently designed, sequential circuits.

State tables. The behavior required of a control unit, like that of any finite-state machine, can be represented by a state table of the general type shown in Figure 5.4a. The rows of the state table correspond to the set of internal states $\{S_i\}$. These states are determined by the information stored in the machine at discrete points of time (clock cycles). Let X and Z denote the input and output variables.

State	Inputs			
	I_1	I_2		I_m
S_1	$S_{1,1}, O_{1,1}$	$S_{1,2}, O_{1,2}$	$\ldots$	$S_{1,m}, O_{1,m}$
S_2	$S_{2,1}, O_{2,1}$	$S_{2,2}, O_{2,2}$	$\ldots$	$S_{2,m}, O_{2,m}$
		$\ldots$		
S_n	$S_{n,1}, O_{n,1}$	$S_{n,2}, O_{n,2}$	$\ldots$	$S_{n,m}, O_{n,m}$

(a)

State	Inputs				Outputs
	I_1	I_2		I_m	
S_1	$S_{1,1}$	$S_{1,2}$	$\ldots$	$S_{1,m}$	O_1
S_2	$S_{2,1}$	$S_{2,2}$	$\ldots$	$S_{2,m}$	O_2
		$\ldots$			
S_n	$S_{n,1}$	$S_{n,2}$	$\ldots$	$S_{n,m}$	O_n

(b)

Figure 5.4
State tables for a finite-state machine: (a) Mealy type and (b) Moore type.

The columns correspond to the combinations of the X signals that can be applied to the machine and are denoted here by $\{I_j\}$. The entry in row S_i and column I_j has the form $S_{i,j}, O_{i,j}$, where $S_{i,j}$ is the next state of the machine that results from the application of input combination I_j, and $O_{i,j}$ denotes the output signals that appear on Z whenever the machine is in state S_i with input I_j applied. In general, an entry in the state table defines a specific, one-cycle transition between two states.

Control units have a feature that favors a slightly different style of state table: Their output signal values often depend on the current state S_i only and so are independent of the input combination I_j. If all outputs are of this type, the circuit is called a *Moore machine*, in contrast with the more general *Mealy machine* of Figure 5.4a. (These names honor G. H. Mealy and E. F. Moore who were early researchers into finite-state machine theory [Mealy 1955; Moore 1956].) The state table of Figure 5.4a becomes a Moore machine if for every row i, we have $O_{i,j} = O_{i,k} = O_i$ for all j, $k = 1,2,\ldots,m$. In that case we can represent the machine's behavior in the more compact format of Figure 5.4b, where the output signals associated with each row are placed in a separate column.

GCD processor. To illustrate the classical and one-hot approaches to control-unit design, we will apply them to a special-purpose processor that computes the greatest common divisor $gcd(X,Y)$ of two positive integers X and Y; $gcd(X,Y)$ is defined as the largest integer that divides exactly into both X and Y. For example, $gcd(12,18) = 6$, and $gcd(12,17) = 1$. It is customary to assume that $gcd(0,0) = 0$.

We use a variant of Euclid's algorithm [Cormen, Leiserson, and Rivest 1990] to calculate $gcd(X,Y)$. Figure 5.5 gives an HDL description of this method.

```
gcd(in: X,Y; out: Z);
  register XR, YR, TEMPR;
  XR := X;                    {Input the data}
  YR := Y;
  while XR > 0 do begin
    if XR ≤ YR then begin     {Swap XR and YR}
      TEMPR := YR;
      YR := XR;
      XR := TEMPR; end
      XR := XR − YR;          {Subtract YR from XR}
  end
  Z := YR;                    {Output the result}
end gcd;
```

Figure 5.5

Procedure *gcd* to compute the greatest common divisor of two numbers.

The basic idea is to subtract the smaller of the two numbers from the other repeatedly—recall that division corresponds to repeated subtraction—until we obtain a number that divides the other. For example, with $X = 20$ and $Y = 12$, our *gcd* algorithm proceeds as follows:

Conditions		Actions		
		$XR := 20; YR := 12;$		
$XR > 0$:	$XR > YR$:	$XR := XR − YR = 8;$		
$XR > 0$:	$XR \leq YR$:	$YR := 8; XR := 12;$	$XR := XR − YR = 4;$	
$XR > 0$:	$XR \leq YR$:	$YR := 4; XR := 8;$	$XR := XR − YR = 4;$	
$XR > 0$	$XR \leq YR$:	$YR := 4; XR := 4;$	$XR := XR − YR = 0;$	
$XR \leq 0$:		$Z := 4;$		

Hence we conclude that $gcd(20,12) = 4$.

Analysis of the *gcd* procedure suggests that its datapath unit DP should contain a pair of registers XR and YR to store the corresponding variables, one or more functional units to perform subtraction and magnitude comparison, and multiplexers for data routing, as indicated in Figure 5.6. We do not need to include a register for the "temporary" variable *TEMPR,* as we would in a typical programmed implementation, because we can read from and write to a register in the same clock cycle. The swap operation can therefore be done without conflict in one cycle thus:

$$X := Y, \quad Y := X; \tag{5.6}$$

The control unit CU generates control signals *Load XR* and *Load YR* to load each register independently with the input data X and Y. A control signal *Select XY* routes X and Y to XR and YR, respectively. Another signal *Swap* controls the swap operation defined by (5.6), which requires routing the outputs of the XR and YR registers to each other's inputs. A final signal *Subtract* is assumed to control the subtraction $XR := XR − YR$ by routing the output of the subtracter to XR. The input signals to CU are an asynchronous *Reset* signal, two comparison signals $(XR \geq YR)$ and $(XR > 0)$ generated by DP, and the usual, implicit clock signal.

We can identify a set of states for CU by examining the behavior defined in the HDL specification (refer to Figure 5.5)—a simple process here, but one that is

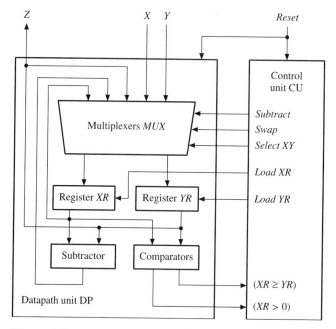

Figure 5.6
Hardware needed to implement the *gcd* procedure.

tedious and error-prone in the case of large control units. A start state S_0 is entered when *Reset* becomes 1; this state also loads X and Y into the DP registers. The subsequent actions of the *gcd* processor are either a swap or a subtraction, for which we define the states S_1 and S_2, respectively. A final state S_3 is entered when $gcd(X,Y)$ has been computed. Figure 5.7 gives a Moore-type state table defining the CU's behavior. Each state transition is deduced directly from the HDL description. If the input control signal $(XR > 0) = 0$, indicating that the **while** loop should be skipped, a transition is made from S_0 to S_3; this yields the first next-state entry in the top row of Figure 5.7. If, on the other hand, $(XR > 0) = 1$, the **while** loop is entered, and a transition is made to S_1 to perform a swap if $(XR \geq YR) = 0$; otherwise, the transition is to S_2 to perform a subtraction. The latter case defines to the third entry of the state table, whose input combination is $(XR > 0)(XR \geq YR) = 11$.

| State | Inputs $(XR > 0)$ $(XR \geq YR)$ | | | Outputs | | | | |
	0–	10	11	Subtract	Swap	Select XY	Load XR	Load YR
S_0 (Begin)	S_3	S_1	S_2	0	0	1	1	1
S_1 (Swap)	S_2	S_2	S_2	0	1	0	1	1
S_2 (Subtract)	S_3	S_1	S_2	1	0	0	1	0
S_3 (End)	S_3	S_3	S_3	0	0	0	0	0

Figure 5.7
State table defining the control unit of the *gcd* processor.

Since a subtraction always follows a swap, all next-state entries in the second row are S_2. The corresponding active outputs are the two register-load signals *Load XR* and *Load YR*, along with *Swap*, which route the outputs of *XR* and *YR* to *YR* and *XR*, respectively. The next states for state S_2 are the same as those for S_0; the active outputs are *Subtract*, which routes the output $XR - YR$ of the subtracter to *XR*, and *Load XR*. The final state S_3 is assumed to be a "dead" state that is unaffected by all inputs (except *Reset*) and produces no active outputs.

Classical method. The major steps of the classical design method are as follows:

1. Construct a *P*-row state table that defines the desired input-output behavior.
2. Select the minimum number p of D-type flip-flops and assign a p-bit binary code to each state.
3. Design a combinational circuit C that generates the primary output signals $\{z_i\}$ and the secondary outputs $\{D_i\}$ that must be applied to the flip-flops.

We now apply this method to the design of the control unit CU for the *gcd* processor. We have already constructed the necessary state table (Figure 5.7). Since there are four states, we require two flip-flops, whose outputs $D_1 D_0 = y_1 y_0$ define CU's internal states. We assign the binary patterns to the four states in the following obvious way:

$$S_0 = 0\ 0$$
$$S_1 = 0\ 1$$
$$S_2 = 1\ 0 \tag{5.7}$$
$$S_3 = 1\ 1$$

We note in passing that the state assignment pattern affects the complexity of the circuit in subtle ways.

At this point we can construct a binary version of the state table, the *excitation table,* as shown in Figure 5.8. The D flip-flop's characteristic equation $D_i^+(t + 1) = D_i(t)$ defines the inputs D_1^+ and D_0^+ to the flip-flops. CU's combinational logic C can now be derived from the excitation table using any available manual or automatic method. Suppose, for instance, that we use two-level sum-of-products (SOP) minimization. It is easily checked that C is defined by the following SOP equations, which lead directly to the design of Figure 5.9. Note that all gates in an AND-OR SOP circuit can be changed to NANDs to produce a NAND-NAND realization of the original function.

$$D_1^+ = (\overline{XR > 0}) + (XR \geq YR) + D_0$$
$$D_0^+ = D_1 \cdot D_0 + (\overline{XR \geq XR}) \cdot \overline{D}_0 + (\overline{XR > 0}) \cdot \overline{D}_0$$
$$Subtract = D_1 \cdot \overline{D}_0 \tag{5.8}$$
$$Swap = \overline{D}_1 \cdot D_0$$
$$Select\ XY = \overline{D}_1 \cdot \overline{D}_0$$
$$Load\ XR = \overline{D}_0 + \overline{D}_1$$
$$Load\ YR = \overline{D}_1$$

Inputs		Present state		Next state		Outputs				
$(XR > 0)$	$(XR \geq YR)$	D_1	D_0	D_1^+	D_0^+	Subtract	Swap	Select XY	Load XR	Load YR
0	d	0	0	1	1	0	0	1	1	1
0	d	0	1	1	0	0	1	0	1	1
0	d	1	0	1	1	1	0	0	1	0
0	d	1	1	1	1	0	0	0	0	0
1	0	0	0	0	1	0	0	1	1	1
1	0	0	1	1	0	0	1	0	1	1
1	0	1	0	0	1	1	0	0	1	0
1	0	1	1	1	1	0	0	0	0	0
1	1	0	0	1	0	0	0	1	1	1
1	1	0	1	1	0	0	1	0	1	1
1	1	1	0	1	0	1	0	0	1	0
1	1	1	1	1	1	0	0	0	0	0

Figure 5.8
Excitation table for the control unit of the *gcd* processor.

One-hot method. While the classical design method minimizes a control unit's memory elements, its effect on the amount of combinational logic C is less obvious. Furthermore, control units designed by this technique tend to have a complicated, "random" structure, which makes design debugging and subsequent maintenance of the circuit difficult. An alternative approach that simplifies the

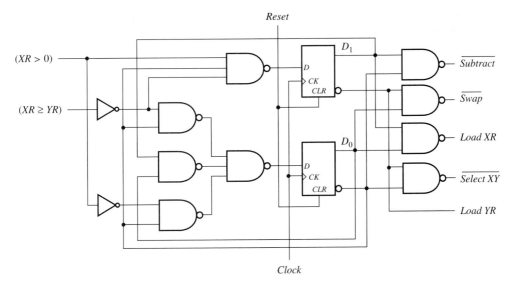

Figure 5.9
All-NAND classical design for the control unit of the *gcd* processor.

design process and gives C a regular and predictable structure, is the one-hot method, so called because its binary state assignment always contains a single 1—the "hot" bit—while all the remaining bits are 0. Thus the state assignment for a four-state machine like the *gcd* processor takes the following form:

$$S_0 = 0\,0\,0\,1$$
$$S_1 = 0\,0\,1\,0$$
$$S_2 = 0\,1\,0\,0 \qquad\qquad (5.9)$$
$$S_3 = 1\,0\,0\,0$$

In general, P flip-flops are needed to represent P states, so the one-hot method is restricted to fairly small values of P.

A key feature of this technique is that the next-state and output equations have a simple, systematic form and can be written down directly from the control unit's original symbolic state table. Because the binary pattern assigned to each state is, in effect, fully decoded, we can find out whether the machine is in state S_i merely by inspecting the corresponding hot state variable D_i. The classical method requires us to check all state variables to get this information.

Suppose that state S_i in a one-hot design has the hot variable D_i. Further, suppose that $I_{j,1}, I_{j,2}, \ldots, I_{j,n_j}$ denote all input combinations that cause a state transition from S_j to S_i. Then each AND combination of the form $D_j \cdot I_{j,k}$ must make $D_i = 1$. Hence, considering all such combinations that cause transitions to S_i, we can write

$$D_i^+ = D_1(I_{1,1} + I_{1,2} + \ldots + I_{1,n_1}) + D_2(I_{2,1} + I_{2,2} + \ldots + I_{2,n_2}) + \ldots \quad (5.10)$$

This immediately yields the SOP form

$$D_i^+ = D_1 I_{1,1} + D_1 I_{1,2} + \ldots + D_1 I_{1,n_1} + D_2 I_{2,1} + D_2 I_{2,2} + \ldots + D_2 I_{2,n_2} + \ldots$$

which is practical to implement by an AND-OR or NAND-NAND circuit, provided that each state transition is determined by relatively few states and input variables, as is common in control-unit behavior. Equation (5.10) can also lead directly to fairly simple factored forms. Consider the state table of Figure 5.7 for the *gcd* processor's CU. State S_1 appears as a next state only for S_0 and S_2, in each case with the input combination $(XR > 0) \cdot (\overline{XR \geq XR})$. Hence (5.10) becomes

$$D_1^+ = D_0 \cdot (XR > 0) \cdot (\overline{XR \geq XR}) + D_2 \cdot (XR > 0) \cdot (\overline{XR \geq XR})$$
$$= (D_0 + D_2) \cdot (XR > 0) \cdot (\overline{XR \geq XR})$$

The primary output equations are even easier to derive for one-hot designs. If output signal z_k is 1 (active) only in rows k,h for $h = 1,2,\ldots,m_k$, then we have

$$z_k = D_{k,1} + D_{k,2} + \ldots + D_{k,m_k} \qquad\qquad (5.11)$$

De Morgan's law of Boolean algebra allows us to rewrite this OR equation as

$$z_k = \overline{\overline{D}_{k,1} \overline{D}_{k,2} \ldots \overline{D}_{k,m_k}}$$

in which form it can be generated by a single NAND whose inputs are the complemented outputs of the flip-flops. In the *gcd* processor case, output *Load YR* = 1 in states S_0 and S_1 only; therefore

$$Load\ YR = D_0 + D_1 = \overline{\overline{D}_0 \overline{D}_1}$$

The entire set of next-state and output equations obtained by applying (5.10) and (5.11) to the *gcd* processor's CU follows.

$$D_0^+ = 0$$

$$D_1^+ = D_0 \cdot (XR > 0) \cdot (\overline{XR \geq XR}) + D_2 \cdot (XR > 0) \cdot (\overline{XR \geq XR})$$

$$D_2^+ = D_0 \cdot (XR > 0) \cdot (XR \geq XR) + D_1 + D_2 \cdot (XR > 0) \cdot (XR \geq XR)$$

$$D_3^+ = D_0 \cdot (\overline{XR > 0}) + D_2 \cdot (\overline{XR > 0}) + D_3$$

$$Subtract = D_2$$

$$Swap = D_1$$

$$Select\ XY = D_0$$

$$Load\ XR = D_0 + D_1 + D_2$$

$$Load\ YR = D_0 + D_1$$

A NAND implementation of these equations appears in Figure 5.10. Note that the asynchronous *Reset* line must set D_0 to 1 and all other state variables to 0.

The steps of the one-hot design method for a Moore machine can be summarized as follows:

1. Construct a *P*-row state table that defines the desired input-output behavior.
2. Associate a separate D-type flip-flop D_i with each state S_i, and assign the *P*-bit one-hot binary code $D_1, D_2, \ldots, D_{i-1}, D_i, D_{i+1}, \ldots, D_P = 0,0,\ldots,0,1,0,\ldots,0$ to S_i.
3. Design a combinational circuit C that generates the primary and secondary output signals $\{D_i\}$ and $\{z_k\}$, respectively. D_i^+ is defined by the logic equation

$$D_i^+ = \sum_{i=1}^{P} D_i (I_{j,1} + I_{j,2} + \ldots + I_{j,n_j})$$

where $I_{j,1}, I_{j,2}, \ldots, I_{j,n_j}$ denote all input combinations that cause a transition from S_j to S_i. If $z_k = 1$ (active) only in rows k,h for $h = 1,2,\ldots,m_k$, then z_k is defined by

$$z_k = D_{k,1} + D_{k,2} + \ldots + D_{k,m_k} = \overline{\overline{D}_{k,1} \overline{D}_{k,2} \ldots \overline{D}_{k,m_k}}$$

We next present an example that illustrates the application of the one-hot method to a computer's IO interface, specifically to a direct-memory access (DMA) controller, which handles data transfers between main memory and high-speed IO devices. (DMA communication is discussed in Chapter 7.)

EXAMPLE 5.1 DESIGN OF A DMA CONTROLLER. This problem, which is adapted from [Actel 1994], is representative of control units that link several interacting systems—in this case, main memory and a set of IO devices. The target machine is the control part of a four-channel DMA controller of the kind found in the IO subsystem of most computers. It is a six-state Moore-type machine with four input and five output signals, which are identified as follows:

Inputs: *IOREQ*   Any of four data-transfer request signals
           CONT   Continue (indicates pending, unprocessed requests)

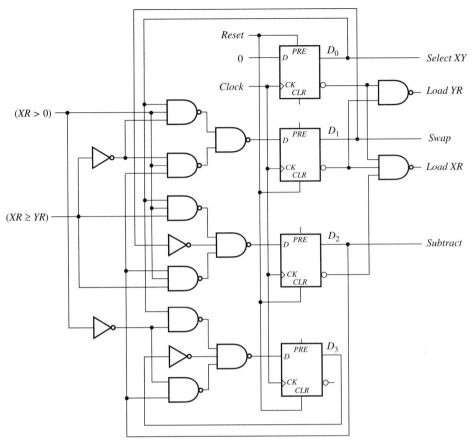

Figure 5.10
All-NAND one-hot design for the control unit of the *gcd* processor.

	MACK	Memory transfer acknowledgment
	PBGNT	Processor bus grant (indicates availability of data-transfer bus)
Outputs:	*CE*	Count enable (bookkeeping function)
	CMREQ	Channel memory request
	CNTLD	Counter load (bookkeeping function)
	RLD	Register load (bookkeeping function)
	PBREQ	Processor bus request for control of data-transfer bus

The behavior of the DMA controller is given by the state transition diagram of Figure 5.11*a*. Each transition is marked with the corresponding active input control signals. Since every transition is triggered by only one such signal, this notation is quite compact. Each state is marked with the (boxed) name of the output control signals that it activates—the number of such signals ranges from zero to two. A state table in the style of Figure 5.4 that is equivalent to Figure 5.11*a* is easy to construct, but it is large because of the many possible input combinations. Noting that most input signals do not affect a given state transition, and so are assigned the don't-care value *d*, we can condense the state table into the compact form of Figure 5.11*b*.

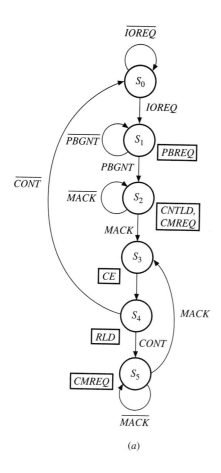

(a)

Inputs				Present state	Next state	Outputs				
IOREQ	CONT	MACK	PBGNT			PBREQ	CNTLD	CMREQ	RLD	CE
0	d	d	d	S_0	S_0	0	0	0	0	0
1	d	d	d	S_0	S_1	0	0	0	0	0
d	d	d	0	S_1	S_1	1	0	0	0	0
d	d	d	1	S_1	S_2	1	0	0	0	0
d	d	0	d	S_2	S_2	0	1	1	0	0
d	d	1	d	S_2	S_3	0	1	1	0	0
d	d	d	d	S_3	S_4	0	0	0	0	1
d	0	d	d	S_4	S_0	0	0	0	1	0
d	1	d	d	S_4	S_5	0	0	0	1	0
d	d	0	d	S_5	S_5	0	0	1	0	0
d	d	1	d	S_5	S_3	0	0	1	0	0

(b)

Figure 5.11
State behavior of the DMA controller: (a) state transition graph and (b) condensed
state table.

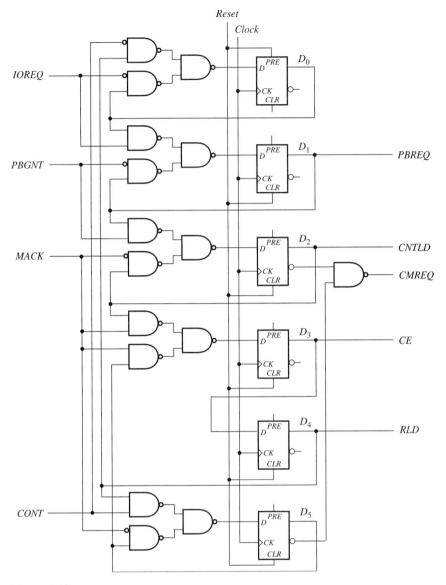

Figure 5.12
One-hot design for the DMA controller.

Now we assign a D flip-flop D_i to each state S_i and write down the six state-transition equations directly from Figure 5.11.

$$D_0{}^+ = D_0 \cdot \overline{IOREQ} + D_4 \cdot \overline{CONT}$$

$$D_1{}^+ = D_0 \cdot IOREQ + D_1 \cdot \overline{PBGNT}$$

$$D_2{}^+ = D_1 \cdot PBGNT + D_2 \cdot \overline{MACK}$$

$$D_3{}^+ = D_2 \cdot MACK + D_5 \cdot MACK$$

$$D_4^+ = D_3$$

$$D_5^+ = D_4 \cdot CONT + D_5 \cdot \overline{MACK}$$

The output equations are also immediately obtained from Figure 5.11.

$$CE = D_3$$

$$CMREQ = D_2 + D_5$$

$$CNTLD = D_2$$

$$RLD = D_4$$

$$PBREQ = D_1$$

Figure 5.12 shows an all-NAND circuit derived from these equations. Note the regular structure of the combinational logic, which is typical of one-hot designs. An equivalent classical design has three flip-flops but a much more irregular combinational part.

5.1.3 Design Examples

This section presents some examples to illustrate the foregoing methods for designing hardwired control units. We will use these examples again in our discussion of microprogrammed control.

Multiplier control. First consider the design of a control unit CU for the twos-complement (Robertson) multiplier introduced in Example 4.2 (section 4.1.2). The block diagram of the multiplier's datapath unit DP (Figure 4.12) is redrawn in expanded form in Figure 5.13 to show a set of control points, which represent abstractly the control signals and associated logic circuits needed to link CU and DP. These control signals are derived from the multiplication algorithm in Figure 4.13 and are listed in Figure 5.14. In general, a control point can be associated with each distinct action (register-transfer operation) op_i appearing in the algorithm being implemented. Its enabling control signal c_i is inserted into the component or interconnections associated with op_i. Operations that take place simultaneously may be able to share control signals. (Procedures to eliminate redundant control signals are considered later.) The statement labeled BEGIN in Figure 4.13, for instance, requires the registers A, COUNT, and F to be reset simultaneously to the all-zero state. A single control signal c_{10} is therefore provided for this purpose. It can be connected directly to the CLEAR inputs of the three registers in question, so no additional logic is needed to implement the c_{10} control point. Control signals c_8 and c_9 transfer a data word from the input bus INBUS to registers Q and M, respectively, and are shown in the corresponding data paths of Figure 5.13; these signals may be connected to the registers' (parallel) LOAD inputs. Control signal c_5 serves to change the function performed by the parallel adder from addition to subtraction for the correction step; it also resets Q[0] to 0. The remaining control signals of Figure 5.14 are defined similarly. Figure 5.13 introduces a control signal called COUNT7, which is set to 1 when COUNT = 111_2 and is set to 0 otherwise. COUNT7, the right-most bit Q[0] of the multiplier register Q and the external BEGIN signal serve as the primary inputs to CU.

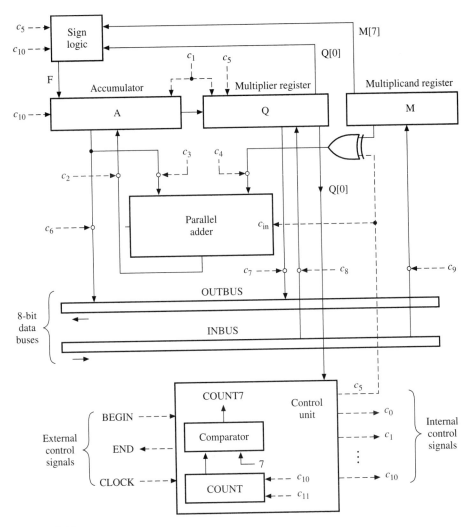

Figure 5.13
Twos-complement multiplier with a set of control points.

The multiplication algorithm is reformulated as a flowchart in Figure 5.15 to display the control signals from Figure 5.14 and indicate when each one is activated. The flowchart resembles a state transition graph that describes the behavior of both the control and datapath units. To obtain a state table for the control unit CU, we associate a state S_i with every operation block in Figure 5.15, leading to the seven states labeled S_1:S_7. An additional state S_0 represents the reset or waiting condition of the control unit. CU has three primary input signals—BEGIN, Q[0], and COUNT7; hence there are eight possible input combinations. Figure 5.16 shows an eight-state Moore-type state table in the style of Figure 5.7, which is derived directly from Figure 5.15. This state table is not necessarily the smallest such table defining the desired control function. In fact, the 13 output control signals c_0:c_{11}, END can be immediately reduced to 8 because several sets are equivalent in that they are always activated together, specifically $c_0 = c_1 = c_{11}$, $c_2 = c_3 = c_4$, and $c_9 =$

Control Signal	Operation controlled
c_0	Set sign bit of A to F.
c_1	Right-shift register-pair A.Q.
c_2	Transfer adder output to A.
c_3	Transfer A to left input of adder.
c_4	Transfer M to right input of adder.
c_5	Perform subtraction (correction). Clear Q[0].
c_6	Transfer A to output bus.
c_7	Transfer Q to output bus.
c_8	Transfer word on input bus to Q.
c_9	Transfer word on input bus to M.
c_{10}	Clear A, COUNT, and F registers.
c_{11}	Increment COUNT.
END	Completion signal (CU idle).

Figure 5.14

Control signals for the twos-complement multiplier.

c_{10}. Methods also exist that attempt to reduce the number of states by merging "compatible" states; see Problem 5.8. To eliminate a flip-flop in this case, we would need to reduce the number of states of CU from eight to four or fewer, which is not possible.

In the following example, we apply the two basic hardwired design techniques, classical and one hot, to the multiplier, taking Figures 5.15 and 5.16 as starting points.

EXAMPLE 5.2 IMPLEMENTING A MULTIPLIER CONTROL UNIT. The multiplier control unit CU is small enough that the classical design approach can be applied to it. This technique uses the minimum number of flip-flops, in this case three, whose outputs $D_2D_1D_0$ denote CU's internal state. We make the natural assignment of the bit-pattern $D_2D_1D_0 = i$ to state S_i, yielding $S_0 = 000$, $S_1 = 001$, $S_2 = 010$, and so on. The remaining problem is to design the combinational logic circuit portion C of CU, a straightforward but fairly tedious task, because C has six inputs BEGIN, Q[0], COUNT7,D_2,D_1,D_0 and 11 outputs: $D_2^+,D_1^+,D_0^+,c_0,c_2,c_5,c_6,c_7,c_8,c_{11}$,END.

The behavior of CU's combinational logic C is defined by an excitation table, which is obtained by replacing the symbolic states of Figure 5.16 with the corresponding 3-bit patterns. It remains to design C. Figure 5.17 shows the results of applying the two-level optimization program *espresso* to this problem. The *espresso* program implements an efficient algorithm that finds a minimum or near-minimum number of product terms (prime implicants), in this case only 13, needed to define C. The input description (Figure 5.17a) is a 64-row excitation table for C written in *espresso*'s PLA-style format. For example, the last row of Figure 5.17a

$$111111 \quad 00000001000$$

specifies the state transition from S_7 to S_0, with input combination BEGIN Q[0] COUNT7 = 111 and active output $c_7 = 1$. The last row of *espresso*'s solution (Figure 5.17b)

$$---110 \quad 11100010000$$

specifies the transition from S_6 to S_7, with input combination BEGIN Q[0] COUNT7 = --- denoting don't cares, and active output signal $c_6 = 1$. This captures the fact that S_6 is always followed by S_7, independent of CU's primary input signals. A NAND realization of the multiplier CU appears in Figure 5.18, which directly realizes the minimum SOP form obtained via *espresso*.

We can also implement CU directly from the state table of Figure 5.16, or, equally easily, from the flowchart of Figure 5.15 by the one-hot method. Eight flip-flops are needed to accommodate CU's eight states $S_0:S_7$. Equations (5.10) and (5.11) give the next-state and output equations. The next-state equations are

$$D_0^+ = D_0 \cdot \overline{BEGIN} + D_7$$

$$D_1^+ = D_0 \cdot BEGIN$$

$$D_2^+ = D_1$$

$$D_3^+ = D_2 \cdot Q[0] + D_4 \cdot Q[0] \cdot \overline{COUNT7}$$

$$D_4^+ = D_2 \overline{Q[0]} + D_3 + D_4 \cdot \overline{Q[0]} \cdot \overline{COUNT7}$$

$$D_5^+ = D_4 \cdot Q[0] \cdot COUNT7$$

$$D_6^+ = D_5 + D_4 \cdot \overline{Q[0]} \cdot \overline{COUNT7}$$

$$D_7^+ = D_6$$

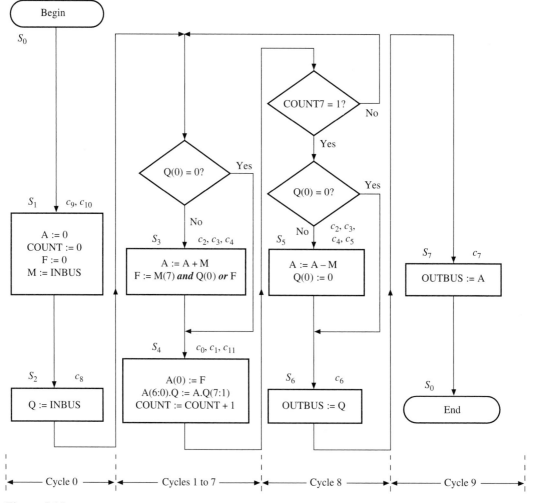

Figure 5.15
Flowchart for the twos-complement multiplier.

State	000	001	010	011	100	101	110	111	c_0	c_1	c_2	c_3	c_4	c_5	c_6	c_7	c_8	c_9	c_{10}	c_{11}	END
	Inputs: BEGIN Q[0] Count7								**Outputs**												
S_0	S_0	S_0	S_0	S_0	S_1	S_1	S_1	S_1	0	0	0	0	0	0	0	0	0	0	0	0	1
S_1	S_2	S_2	S_2	S_2	S_2	S_2	S_2	S_2	0	0	0	0	0	0	0	0	0	1	1	0	0
S_2	S_4	S_4	S_3	S_3	S_4	S_4	S_3	S_3	0	0	0	0	0	0	0	0	1	0	0	0	0
S_3	S_4	S_4	S_4	S_4	S_4	S_4	S_4	S_4	0	0	1	1	1	0	0	0	0	0	0	0	0
S_4	S_4	S_6	S_3	S_5	S_4	S_6	S_3	S_5	1	1	0	0	0	0	0	0	0	0	0	1	0
S_5	S_6	S_6	S_6	S_6	S_6	S_6	S_6	S_6	0	0	1	1	1	1	0	0	0	0	0	0	0
S_6	S_7	S_7	S_7	S_7	S_7	S_7	S_7	S_7	0	0	0	0	0	0	1	0	0	0	0	0	0
S_7	S_0	S_0	S_0	S_0	S_0	S_0	S_0	S_0	0	0	0	0	0	0	0	1	0	0	0	0	0

Figure 5.16
State table for the multiplier control unit.

```
.model  mult007.pla
.inputs  BGN Q0 CT7 D2 D1 D0
.outputs  D2+ D1+ D0+ c0 c2 c5 c6
          c7 c8 c9 END
.i 6
.o 11
.p 64
000000  00000000001
001000  00000000001
010000  00000000001
011000  00000000001
100000  00100000001
101000  00100000001
110000  00100000001
111000  00100000001
000001  01000000010
001001  01000000010
010001  01000000010
011001  01000000010
100001  01000000010
101001  01000000010
110001  01000000010
111001  01000000010
000010  10000000100
001010  10000000100
 .   .   .   .   .
101111  00000001000
110111  00000001000
111111  00000001000
.end
        (a)
```

```
model  mult005.pla
.inputs  BGN Q0 CT7 D2 D1 D0
.outputs  D2+ D1+ D0+ c0 c2 c5 c6
          c7 c8 c9 END
.i 6
.o 11
.p 13
-011-0  01000000000
1--000  00100000000
-10100  01110000000
-11100  10110000000
---111  00000001000
-0-010  10000000100
-0-100  10010000000
---011  10001000000
-1-010  01100000100
---000  00000000001
---001  01000000010
---101  11001100000
---110  11100010000
.e
        (b)
```

Figure 5.17
Design of combinational part of the multiplier control unit by *espresso*: (a) input data
(excitation table) and (b) output data (optimized SOP specification).

The output equations are

$$c_0 = c_1 = c_{11} = D_4$$

$$c_2 = c_3 = c_4 = D_3 + D_5$$

$$c_5 = D_5$$

$$c_6 = D_6$$

$$c_7 = D_7$$

$$c_8 = D_2$$

$$c_9 = c_{10} = D_1$$

$$END = D_0$$

The NAND circuit implied by these equations appears in Figure 5.19.

Despite having more flip-flops, the one-hot design is better in many ways than the classical design. The one-hot design has fewer and generally smaller gates in its combi-

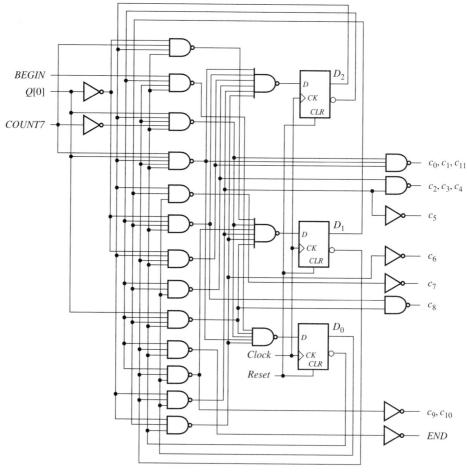

Figure 5.18
All-NAND classical design for the multiplier control unit.

national logic because entry to a particular state depends on a small number of primary and secondary (state) input variables—as few as one state variable in several cases. This dependence also holds for the output functions, since most of the primary output signals can be taken directly from the corresponding hot-state variable. Another point worth noting is that the one-hot CU's structure closely follows that of its state behavior, as exemplified by the flowchart specification (Figure 5.15). Consequently, the one-hot design is easier to understand and easier to modify (should that be necessary) than the classical design.

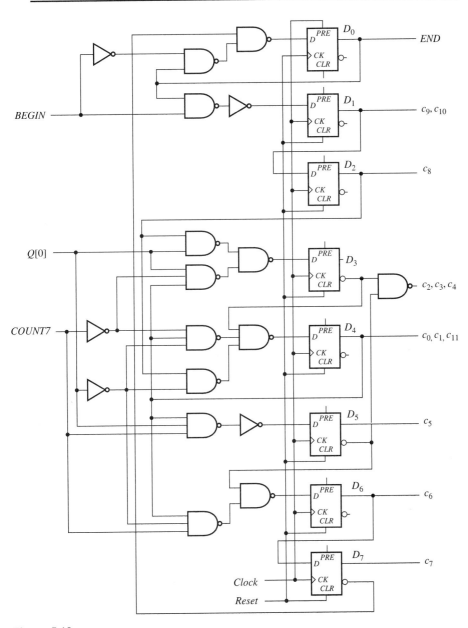

Figure 5.19
All-NAND one-hot design for the multiplier control unit.

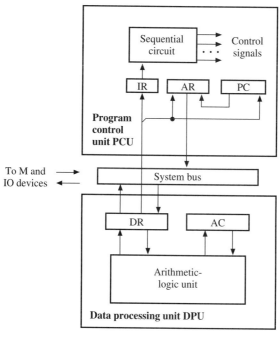

(a)

Type	HDL format	Assembly format	Comment
Data transfer	AC := M(X)	LD X	Load X from M into AC
	M(X) := AC	ST X	Store contents of AC in M as X
	DR := AC	MOV DR, AC	Copy contents of AC to DR
	AC := DR	MOV AC, DR	Copy contents of DR to AC
Data processing	AC := AC + DR	ADD	Add DR to AC
	AC := AC – DR	SUB	Subtract DR from AC
	AC := AC *and* DR	AND	And DR to AC
	AC := *not* AC	NOT	Complement contents of AC
Program control	PC := M(*adr*)	BRA adr	Jump to instruction with address *adr*
	if AC = 0 **then**	BZ adr	Jump to instruction *adr* if AC = 0
	PC := M(*adr*)		

(b)

Figure 5.20
An accumulator-based CPU: (*a*) organization and (*b*) instruction set.

CPU control unit. The design of the CU for a basic, nonpipelined CPU differs mainly in degree—the CPU is a multifunction unit that can contain hundreds of control lines—but not in kind from the multiplier control unit. Here we examine a few of the design issues involved, using an accumulator-based CPU as an example. In section 5.3.3 we will discuss the complex control problems associated with pipelined CPUs.

The accumulator-based CPU introduced in section 3.1.1 has the overall organization depicted in Figure 5.20a (which repeats Figure 3.3). This CPU consists of a datapath unit DPU designed to execute the set of 10 basic single-address instructions listed in Figure 5.20b. The instructions are assumed to be of fixed length and to act on data words of the same fixed length, say 32 bits. The program control unit PCU is responsible for managing the control signals linking the PCU to the DPU, as well as the control signals between the CPU and the external memory M.

To design the PCU, we must first identify the relevant control actions (microoperations) needed to process the given instruction set using the hardware from Figure 5.20a. A flowchart description of the behavior of the CPU appears in Figure 5.21, which is similar in form to the multiplier's flowchart (Figure 5.15). All instructions require a common instruction-fetch step, followed by an execution step that varies with each instruction type. The fetch step copies the contents of the program counter PC to the memory address register AR. A memory-read operation is then executed, which transfers the instruction word I to memory data register DR; this is expressed by DR := M(AR). I's opcode is transferred to the instruction register IR, where it is decoded; at the same time PC is incremented to point to the next consecutive instruction in M.

The subsequent operations depend on the opcode pattern. For example, the store instruction ST X is executed in three steps: the address field of ST X is transferred to AR, the contents of the accumulator AC are transferred to DR, and finally the memory write operation M(AR) := DR is performed. The branch-on-zero instruction BZ adr is executed by first testing AC. If AC $\neq$ 0, no action is taken; if AC = 0, the address field adr, which is in DR(ADR), is transferred to PC, thus effecting the branch operation. Figure 5.21 implies that instruction fetching takes three cycles, while instruction execution takes from one to three cycles. As we will see later, RISC processors are usually designed so that all instruction execution times are equalized to one CPU clock period T_C in length, making the cycles associated with the register-transfer operations in Figure 5.21 into subcycles of T_C.

The microoperations appearing in the flowchart implicitly determine the control signals and control points needed by the CPU. Figure 5.22b lists a suitable set of control signals for the CPU and their functions, while Figure 5.22a shows the approximate positions of the corresponding control points in both the PCU and DPU. These control lines can be placed in the three basic groups defined earlier.

- Function select: $c_2, c_9, c_{10}, c_{11}, c_{12}$.
- Storage control: c_1, c_8.
- Data routing: $c_0, c_3, c_4, c_5, c_6, c_7$.

Here *storage control* refers to the external memory M. Many of the control signals transfer information between the CPU's internal data and control registers.

Control unit design. The overall organization of a hardwired control unit that implements the flowchart of Figure 5.21 appears in Figure 5.23. It is assumed that the opcode stored in the instruction register IR is decoded into 10 signals, one per instruction type, which along with BEGIN and a status signal (AC = 0) form the inputs to the main sequential circuit FSM that generates the control signals $c_0:c_{12}$. Hence FSM has 12 primary inputs and 13 primary outputs. The number of internal states can be estimated from Figure 5.21. If each distinct action box is assigned to a different state,

AC = Accumulator
AR = Memory address register
DR = Memory data register
DR(OP) = Opcode field of DR
DR(ADR) = Address field of DR
IR = Instruction (opcode) register
M = Main memory
PC = Program counter

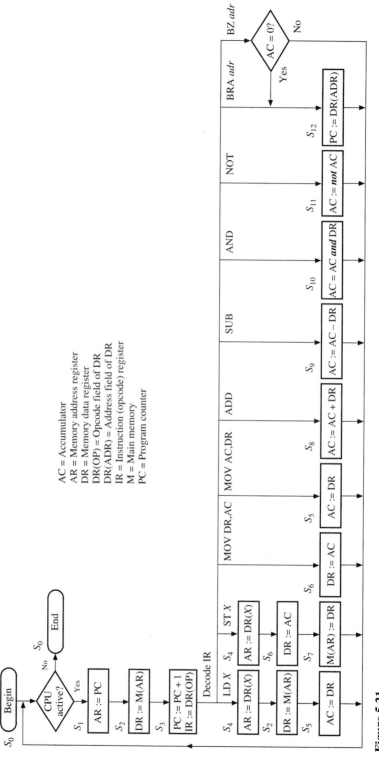

Figure 5.21
Flowchart of the accumulator-based CPU.

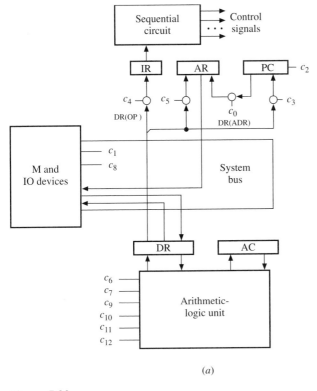

Control signal	Operation controlled
c_0	AR := PC
c_1	DR := M(AR)
c_2	PC := PC + 1
c_3	PC := DR(ADR)
c_4	IR := DR(OP)
c_5	AR := DR(ADR)
c_6	DR := AC
c_7	AC := DR
c_8	M(AR) := DR
c_9	AC := AC + DR
c_{10}	AC := AC − DR
c_{11}	AC := AC *and* DR
c_{12}	AC := *not* AC

(a)   (b)

Figure 5.22
(a) Control points and (b) control signal definitions for the accumulator-based CPU.

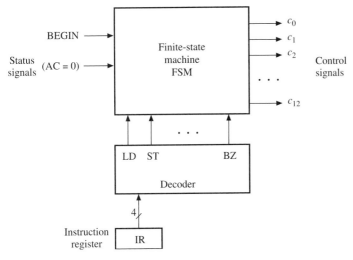

Figure 5.23
Organization of a hardwired control unit for the accumulator-based CPU.

then there are 13 states $S_0:S_{12}$, as indicated on the flowchart. Implementing the resulting 13-state machine via the classical or one-hot methods is straightforward.

EXAMPLE 5.3 IMPLEMENTING A PROGRAM CONTROL UNIT. The circuit FSM of Figure 5.23 issues the control signals governing instruction processing in the 10-instruction accumulator-based CPU. Its behavior is defined by the flowchart in Figure 5.21. We will implement FSM using a minor variant of our earlier one-hot method that reduces the number of flip-flops needed, while maintaining the simplicity of a one-hot design. Most of the states $S_4:S_{12}$ identified in Figure 5.21 for the execution phase of the instruction can be distinguished by the opcode-type signals LD, ST, and so on, which are primary inputs of FSM. If we do not require FSM to be a Moore machine, we can coalesce the states into a smaller set whose output actions (the control signals they activate) are determined by FSM's primary inputs as well as its states. Specifically, we can replace the states in the execution phase by just three states S_4^*, S_5^*, S_6^*, all of which are visited in sequence by the load and store instructions, but which reduce to a single state S_4^* for the remaining instructions. We can also reduce the instruction-fetch phase to a sequence of three states by merging S_0 and S_1 into one state S_1^* so that, whether active or inactive, FSM performs the operation AR := PC.

The resulting machine has the state behavior depicted by a Mealy-type state transition graph in Figure 5.24. This figure follows the condensed style of Figure 5.11 where only the signals that directly affect or are affected by each state are shown. For example, the state transition graph implies that when in state S_5^*, a transition is made to S_6^* with output $c_1 = 1$ (the only active output) if the current instruction is of type LD. This event is indicated by the label LD/c_1 on the S_5^*-to-S_6^* transition arrow. If the current instruction is ST, however, then only c_6 becomes 1, as indicated by the label ST/c_6. No other instruction types allow FSM to enter state S_5^*. When the transition from state S_i to S_j is automatic, that is, it is independent of the primary input signals, we used a label of the form $\emptyset/O_j$.

Let us implement FSM using six D flip-flops, with the output D_i of the ith flip-flop forming the hot variable for state S_i or S_i^*. We can now write down a set of logic equations directly from Figure 5.24 that define FSM.

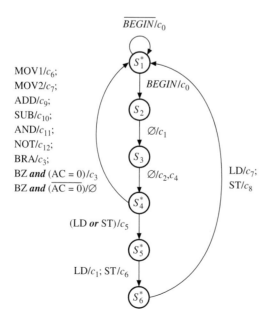

Figure 5.24
State transition graph for the accumulator-based CPU.

$$D_1^+ = D_1 \cdot \overline{BEGIN} + D_4 \cdot (MOV1 + MOV2 + ADD + SUB + AND$$
$$+ NOT + BRA + BZ) + D_6$$
$$D_2^+ = D_1 \cdot BEGIN$$
$$D_3^+ = D_2$$
$$D_4^+ = D_3$$
$$D_5^+ = D_4 \cdot (LD + ST)$$
$$D_6^+ = D_5$$

The output equations also follow immediately from Figure 5.24.

$$c_0 = D_1 \qquad\qquad c_1 = D_2 + D_5 \cdot LD$$
$$c_2 = c_4 = D_3 \qquad\qquad c_3 = D_4 \cdot (BRA + BZ \cdot (AC = 0))$$
$$c_5 = D_4 \cdot (LD + ST) \qquad\qquad c_6 = D_4 \cdot MOV1 + D_5 \cdot ST$$
$$c_7 = D_4 \cdot MOV2 + D_6 \cdot LD \qquad\qquad c_8 = D_6 \cdot ST$$
$$c_9 = D_4 \cdot ADD \qquad\qquad c_{10} = D_4 \cdot SUB$$
$$c_{11} = D_4 \cdot AND \qquad\qquad c_{12} = D_4 \cdot NOT$$

These equations lead to the logic circuit in Figure 5.25.

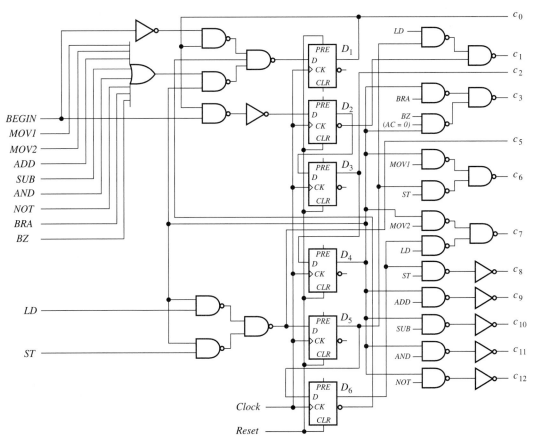

Figure 5.25
One-hot implementation of the CPU state transition graph of Figure 5.24.

5.2
MICROPROGRAMMED CONTROL

We turn next to the design of control units that use microprograms to select, interpret, and execute a processor's instruction set.

5.2.1 Basic Concepts

An instruction is implemented by a sequence of one or more sets of concurrent microoperations. Each microoperation is associated with a group of control lines that must be activated in a prescribed sequence to trigger the microoperations. As the number of instructions and control lines can be in the hundreds, a hardwired control unit is difficult to design and verify, even with good CAD tool support. Furthermore, such a control unit is inherently inflexible in the sense that changes, for example, to correct design errors or update the instruction set, require that the control unit be redesigned.

Microprogramming [Lynch 1993] is a method of control-unit design in which the control signal selection and sequencing information is stored in a ROM or RAM called a *control memory* CM. The control signals to be activated at any time are specified by a *microinstruction*, which is fetched from CM in much the same way an instruction is fetched from main memory. Each microinstruction also explicitly or implicitly specifies the next microinstruction to be used, thereby providing the necessary information for microoperation sequencing. A set of related microinstructions forms a *microprogram*. Microprograms can be changed relatively easily by changing the contents of CM; hence microprogramming yields control units that are more flexible than their hardwired counterparts. This flexibility is achieved at some extra hardware cost due to the control memory and its access circuitry. There is also a performance penalty due to the time required to access the microinstructions from CM. These disadvantages have discouraged the use of microprogramming in RISCs and other high-speed processors, where chip area and circuit delay must both be minimized. Microprogramming continues to be used in such CISCs as the Pentium and 680X0.

In a microprogrammed CPU, each machine instruction is executed by a microprogram which acts as a real-time interpreter for the instruction. The set of microprograms that interpret a particular instruction set or machine language L is called an *emulator* for L. A microprogrammed computer C_1 can be made to execute programs written in the machine language L_2 of another, very similar computer C_2 by placing an emulator for L_2 in the control memory of C_1. In that case C_1 is said to be able to *emulate* C_2.

As a design activity, microprogramming can be compared with assembly-language programming; however, the microprogrammer requires a more detailed knowledge of the processor hardware than the assembly-language programmer. Symbolic languages similar to assembly languages are used to write microprograms: these are called *microassembly languages*. A *microassembler* is necessary to translate microprograms into executable programs that can be stored in the control memory.

Control unit organization. In its simplest form a microinstruction has two parts: a set of *control fields* that specify the control signals to be activated and an

address field that contains the address in CM of the next microinstruction to be
executed. In the original scheme proposed by Maurice V. Wilkes, the inventor of
microprogramming, each bit k_i of a control field corresponds to a distinct control
line c_i [Wilkes 1951]. When $k_i = 1$ in the current microinstruction, c_i is activated;
otherwise c_i remains inactive. Figure 5.26 shows a microprogrammed control unit
designed in this style. The control memory CM is implemented by a ROM of the
type discussed in section 2.2.2. The left part (AND plane) of the ROM decodes an
address obtained from the *control memory address register* (CMAR). Each address
selects a particular row in the right part (OR plane) of the ROM that contains a
microinstruction composed (in this small example) of a 6-bit control field and a 3-
bit address field. When the top-most row in Figure 5.26, which represents the
microinstruction with address 000, is selected, the control signals c_0, c_2, and c_4 are
activated, as indicated by the ×s in the control field. At the same time, the contents
of the address field $a_2a_1a_0 = 001$ are sent to the CMAR, where they are stored and
used to address the next microinstruction to be executed.

As Figure 5.26 indicates, the CMAR can be loaded from an external source as
well as from the address field of a microinstruction. The external source typically
provides the starting address of a microprogram in the CM. A specific microprogram prestored in CM executes (interprets) each instruction of a microprogrammed

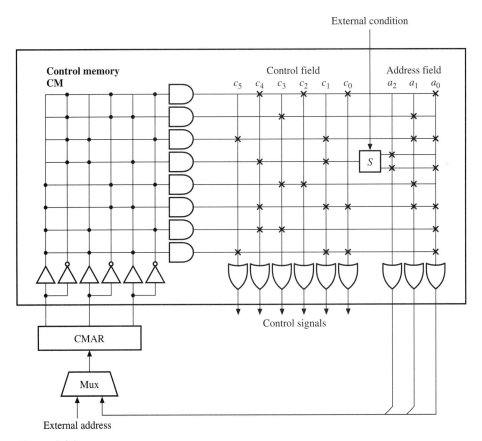

Figure 5.26
Basic structure of a microprogrammed control unit.

CPU. The instruction's opcode, after suitable encoding, provides the starting address for its microprogram.

Every program control unit should be able to respond to external signals or conditions. We can satisfy this requirement by introducing some form of switch S controlled by an external condition that allows the current microinstruction to select one of two possible address fields. Thus in Figure 5.26, the third microinstruction may be followed by the microinstruction with address 100 or 101, as determined by the external condition. This feature makes conditional branches within a microprogram possible.

Many modifications to the preceding design have been proposed over the years. A major area of concern is the microinstruction's word length, since it greatly influences the size and cost of the CM. Microinstruction length is determined by three factors:

- The maximum number of simultaneous microoperations that must be specified, that is, the degree of parallelism required at the microoperation level.
- The way in which the control information is represented or encoded.
- The way in which the next microinstruction address is specified.

Control memories are usually ROMs, so their contents cannot be altered online. Normally there is no need to change the CM except to correct design errors or to make minor enhancements to the system. It was recognized from the beginning, however, that the CM could be a read-write memory or RAM. Wilkes observed that such a device, called a *writable control memory* (WCM), would have a number of "fascinating possibilities," but doubted that its cost could be justified [Wilkes 1951]. Perhaps the most interesting feature of a WCM is that it allows us to change a processor's instruction set by changing the microprograms that interpret the instruction set. Thus we can, in principle, provide the same machine with several different instruction sets that can be tailored to specific applications. A processor with a WCM is said to be *dynamically microprogrammable* because the control memory contents can be altered under program control.

Parallelism in microinstructions. Microprogrammed processors are frequently characterized by the maximum number of microoperations that a single microinstruction can specify. This number ranges from one to several hundred.

Microinstructions that specify a single microoperation are similar to conventional machine instructions. They are relatively short, but due to their lack of parallelism, more microinstructions are needed to perform a given operation. The format of the IBM System/370 Model 145, which is shown in Figure 5.27, is representative of this type of microinstruction. It consists of 4 bytes (32 bits). The left-most byte (shaded) is an opcode that specifies the microoperation to be performed. The next 2 bytes specify operands, which, in most cases, are the addresses of CPU registers. The right-most byte contains information used to construct the address of the next microinstruction.

Microinstruction formats take advantage of the fact that, at the microprogramming level, many operations can be performed in parallel. If all useful combinations of parallel microoperations were specified by a single opcode, the number of opcodes would, in most cases, be enormous. Furthermore, an opcode decoder of considerable complexity would be needed. To avoid these difficulties, it is usual to

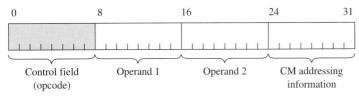

Control field (opcode)   Operand 1   Operand 2   CM addressing information

Figure 5.27
Microinstruction format of the IBM System/370 Model 145.

divide the microoperation specification part of a microinstruction into k disjoint control fields. Each control field handles a limited set of microoperations, any one of which can be performed simultaneously with the microoperations specified by the remaining control fields. A control field often specifies the control-line values for a single device such as an adder, a register, or a bus. In the extreme case represented by Figure 5.26, there is a 1-bit control field for every control line in the system.

Figure 5.28 shows another microinstruction style, that of the IBM System/360 Model 50. It encompasses 90 bits, which are partitioned into separate fields for various purposes. There are 21 fields, shown shaded in Figure 5.28, which constitute the control fields. The remaining fields are used to generate the next microinstruction address and to detect errors by means of parity bits. For example, the 3-bit control field consisting of bits 65:67 controls the right input to the main adder of the CPU in question. This field indicates which of several possible registers should be connected to the adder's right input. Bits 68:71 identify the function to be performed by the adder; the possibilities include binary addition and decimal addition with various ways of handling input and output carry bits.

The scheme of Figure 5.26 with a control field for every control signal is wasteful of control memory space because most of the possible combinations of control signals are never used. Consider, for instance, the register R of Figure 5.29,

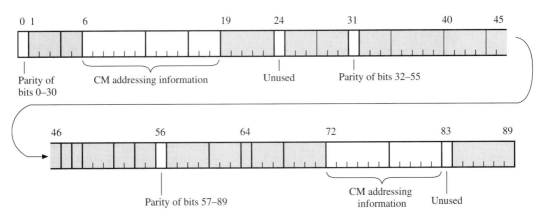

Figure 5.28
Ninety-bit microinstruction format of the IBM System/360 Model 50 (shaded areas are control fields).

which can be loaded from any of four independent sources under the control of the four separate signals c_0, c_1, c_2, c_3, as indicated abstractly in Figure 5.29a. A straightforward implementation of the associated control points using an encoder and a multiplexer appears in Figure 5.29b. Suppose that the c_i's are derived from a microinstruction control field in which there is 1 bit for each control signal. This results in the 4-bit control field shown in Figure 5.30a. Only the five control-field patterns shown in Figure 5.30a are valid, since any other pattern will create a conflict by attempting to load R from two or more independent sources simultaneously. These five patterns can be also encoded into a field $K = k_0 k_1 k_2$ of width $\lceil \log_2 5 \rceil = 3$ bits, as shown in Figure 5.30b, thus reducing the width of the control field from 4 to 3 bits. In general, any n independent control signals or microoperations can be encoded in a control field of $\lceil \log_2(n + 1) \rceil$ bits, assuming the need to specify a no-operation condition when no control signal is active.

The unencoded format of Figure 5.30a has the advantage that all the control signals are individually identified in, and can be obtained directly from, the microinstruction. The encoded control signals k_0, k_1, k_2 of Figure 5.30b must be passed through a decoder if we wish to extract the four original control signals c_0, c_1, c_2, c_3.

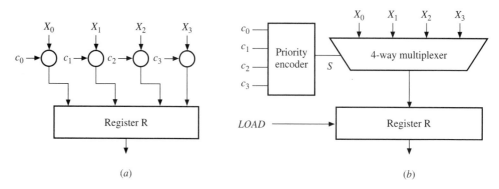

Figure 5.29
A register that can be loaded from four independent sources: (a) abstract representation and (b) possible implementation.

c_0	c_1	c_2	c_3	
1	0	0	0	$R := X_0$
0	1	0	0	$R := X_1$
0	0	1	0	$R := X_2$
0	0	0	1	$R := X_3$
0	0	0	0	No operation

(a)

k_0	k_1	k_2	
0	0	0	$R := X_0$
0	0	1	$R := X_1$
0	1	0	$R := X_2$
0	1	1	$R := X_3$
1	0	0	No operation

(b)

Figure 5.30
Control field for the circuit of Figure 5.29: (a) unencoded format and (b) encoded format.

Often we can use the encoded control signals directly so that no decoding is needed. For example, in the present example, we can connect the two signals $k_1 k_2$ of Figure 5.30b directly to the select inputs S of the multiplexer in Figure 5.29b, thereby eliminating the priority encoder. The complemented control signal $\bar{k}_0$ can then be connected directly to the *LOAD* input of the register R to complete the design.

Horizontal versus vertical. Microinstructions are commonly divided into two types. *Horizontal* microinstructions have the following general attributes:

- Long formats.
- Ability to express a high degree of parallelism.
- Little encoding of the control information.

Vertical microinstructions, on the other hand, are characterized by

- Short formats.
- Limited ability to express parallel microoperations.
- Considerable encoding of the control information.

The format of the IBM System/360 Model 50 shown in Figure 5.28 is representative of horizontal microinstructions, while that of the System/370 Model 145 shown in Figure 5.27 is representative of vertical microinstructions.

Other definitions of horizontal and vertical are found in the literature. One is based on the degree of encoding: a horizontal microinstruction format allows no encoding of control information, whereas a vertical format does. An alternative definition is based on the degree of parallelism. A vertical microinstruction can specify only one microoperation (no parallelism), while a horizontal microinstruction can specify many microoperations. These definitions are not independent, since a large amount of parallelism implies little encoding, and vice versa. For example, the format of Figure 5.31a is horizontal and that of Figure 5.31c is vertical under both of the preceding definitions.

Vertical microinstructions are broadly similar to RISC instructions, both in the small amount of parallelism they specify and in their single-cycle execution style. Computers have also been designed with long and highly parallel instruction formats that resemble horizontal microinstructions; see problem 5.36.

Microinstruction addressing. Each microinstruction in the basic design of Figure 5.26 contains within itself the address of the next microinstruction to be executed. In the case of branch microinstructions, two possible next addresses are included. This explicit address specification has the advantage that no time is lost in microinstruction address generation, but it is wasteful of control memory space. The address fields can be eliminated from all but branch instructions by using a *microprogram counter* μPC as the primary source of microinstruction addresses. Its role is analogous to that of the program counter PC at the instruction level. Since only instructions have to be fetched from the control memory, μPC is also used as the control memory address register CMAR.

Conditional branching is a desirable feature in microprograms just as it is in programs, and it can be implemented in various ways. The condition to be tested is often a status signal generated by the datapath being controlled. If several such

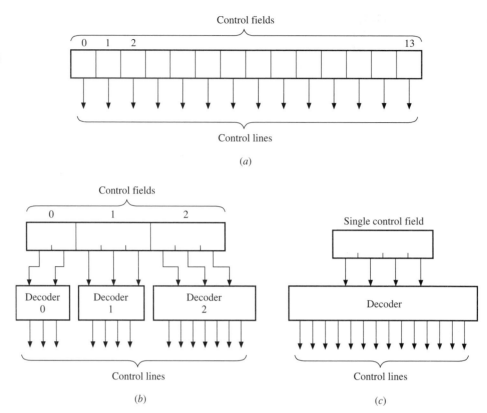

Figure 5.31
Control-field formats: (*a*) no encoding; (*b*) some encoding; (*c*) complete encoding.

conditions exist, a *condition-select* subfield is included in the microinstruction format to specify which of the possible conditions is to be tested. The branch address can be in the microinstruction itself, in which case it is loaded into CMAR when a branch condition is satisfied. Control memory space can be conserved by not storing a complete address field in the microinstruction, but by storing instead some low-order bits of the address. This technique restricts the range of branch instructions to a small region of the control memory.

An alternative approach to conditional branching is to allow the condition variables to modify the contents of CMAR directly, thus eliminating wholly or in part the need for branch addresses in microinstructions. For example, let the condition variable *OVF* indicate an overflow condition when $OVF = 1$, and the normal no-overflow condition when $OVF = 0$. Suppose we want to execute a SKIP ON OVERFLOW microinstruction. We can connect *OVF* to the count-enable input of µPC at an appropriate point in the microinstruction cycle, thereby allowing the overflow condition to increment µPC an extra time, thus performing the desired skip operation.

Microoperation timing. So far we have assumed that a microinstruction activates a set of control signals for an unspecified time during the microinstruction's execution cycle. A single clock signal synchronizes the control signals, and its period can be the same as the microinstruction cycle period. This mode of control has been termed *monophase*. The number of microinstructions to specify a particular operation can be reduced by dividing the microinstruction cycle into several sequential subperiods or (clock) *phases*. A control signal is typically active during only one of the phases. This *polyphase* mode of operation permits a single microinstruction to specify a short sequence of microoperations for some increase in the complexity of the microinstruction format.

Consider a microinstruction that controls the register-transfer operation

$$R := f(R_1, R_2)$$

where R can be R_1 or R_2. This operation can be performed in several phases; the following four-phase interpretation is representative.

- *Phase Φ_1*: Fetch the next microinstruction from the control memory CM.
- *Phase Φ_2*: Transfer the contents of registers R_1 and R_2 to the inputs of the f unit.
- *Phase Φ_3*: Store the result generated by the f unit in a temporary register or latch L.
- *Phase Φ_4*: Transfer the contents of L to the destination register R.

Figure 5.32 shows the timing signals associated with these four phases.

We have also assumed that the influence of a microinstruction control field is limited to the period during which the microinstruction is executed. We can lift this restriction by storing the control field in a register that continues to exercise control until a subsequent microinstruction modifies it. This technique is called *residual control* and is particularly useful when microinstructions are used to allocate the resources of a system. For example, a connection between two units can be established by a microinstruction and maintained for an arbitrarily long period of time via residual control.

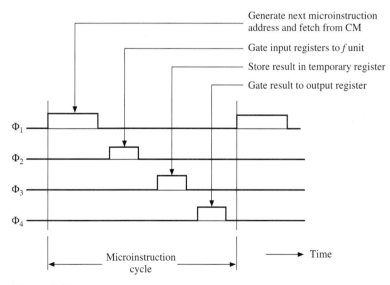

Figure 5.32
Timing diagram for a four-phase microinstruction.

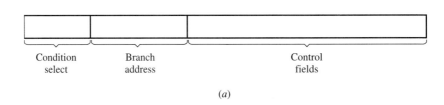

(a)

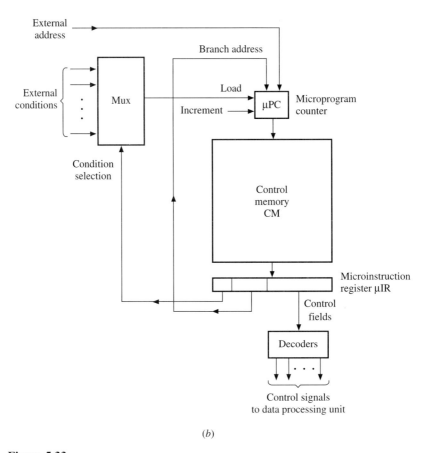

(b)

Figure 5.33
Typical microprogrammed controller: (a) microinstruction format and (b) control
unit organization.

    Control unit organization. We now describe the design of a typical micropro-
grammed control unit. We use the microinstruction format shown in Figure 5.33a,
which has three parts arranged as follows:

- A condition-select field specifies the external condition to be tested in the case of
  conditional branch microinstructions.
- An address field contains the next-address field to be used when a branch condition is satisfied. A microprogram counter μPC provides the next microinstruction address when no branching is needed.
- The rest of the microinstruction specifies in encoded or unencoded format the
  control signals that are activated to perform the desired microoperations.

Figure 5.33*b* depicts a control unit designed around this microinstruction format. The counter μPC is the address register for the control memory CM. The contents of the addressed word in CM are transferred to the microinstruction register μIR. The control fields are decoded if necessary and produce control signals for the data-processing unit; μPC is then incremented. If a branch is specified by the microinstruction in μIR, the contents of the microinstruction's address field are loaded into μPC.

In the scheme of Figure 5.33*a*, the condition-select field controls a multiplexer that activates the parallel-load control input of μPC based on the status of some external condition variables. Suppose that two condition variables v_1, v_2 must be tested. A condition-select field $s_0 s_1$ of 2 bits suffices, with the following interpretation:

s_0	s_1	Meaning
0	0	No branching
0	1	Branch if $v_1 = 1$
1	0	Branch if $v_2 = 1$
1	1	Unconditional branch

The multiplexer has four inputs x_0, x_1, x_2, x_3, where x_i is routed to the multiplexer's output when $s_0 s_1 = i$. Hence we require $x_0 = 0$, $x_1 = v_1$, $x_2 = v_2$, and $x_3 = 1$ to control the loading of microinstruction branch addresses into μPC in this case.

Finally, a provision is made for loading μPC with an address from an external source. This address is used to enter the starting address of the desired microprogram in cases where CM contains more than one microprogram.

EXAMPLE 5.4 THE AMD 2909 BIT-SLICED MICROPROGRAM SEQUENCER [MICK AND BRICK 1980; ADVANCED MICRO DEVICES 1985]. Like the 2901 4-bit ALU slice (Example 4.5), the 2909 microprogram sequencer is a member of the 2900 family of microprocessor components, now found mainly in VLSI cell libraries. It generates microinstruction addresses for a control memory CM and comprises a microprogram counter μPC and all the logic needed for next-address generation. Devices of this type are termed *microprogram sequencers*. The 2909 thus replaces μPC and the multiplexer appearing in Figure 5.33; it also adds a stack to implement subroutine calls at the microprogram level. Figure 5.34 shows the internal organization of the 2909. It handles addresses that are only 4 bits long, thus limiting a single copy of the 2909 to controlling a 16-word CM. However, the 2909 is bit sliced, so k copies of the 2909 can be cascaded to make a microprogram sequencer for $4k$-word addresses. Three copies of the 2909 connected as in Figure 5.35 can process 12-bit addresses and support a 4096-word control memory.

The function of a microprogram sequencer is to transfer an address from one of several internal and external address sources to an output bus—the 4-bit bus Y in the 2909 case—that is connected to the address bus of CM. The 2909 has four separate address sources: its microprogram counter μPC, an external bus D, a register R that is attached to a second external bus, and a four-word internal stack ST. μPC is actually implemented by a 4-bit register of the same name and by a separate incrementer, as shown in Figure 5.34. In every clock cycle this logic circuit performs the operation

$$c_{out} \cdot \mu PC := Y + c_{in} \tag{5.12}$$

where c_{in} and c_{out} are carry-in and carry-out signals, respectively. By connecting the c_{out} output line of each 2909 in an array of k 2909s to the c_{in} input of the 2909 to its left, the operation (5.12) can be extended to addresses of arbitrary length.

If a sequence of microinstructions without branches is being executed, then (5.12) alone suffices for microinstruction sequencing. Many microprograms, however, involve some branching to nonconsecutive addresses in CM. A branch address is made available as the address of the next microinstruction by connecting the appropriate address field of the current microinstruction in the external microinstruction register µIR to the 2909's D or R bus in the manner of Figure 5.33b. The stack ST serves as the

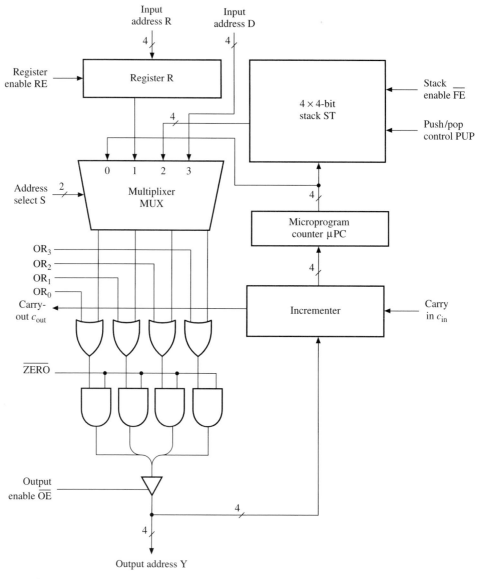

Figure 5.34
Structure of the 2909 microprogram sequencer.

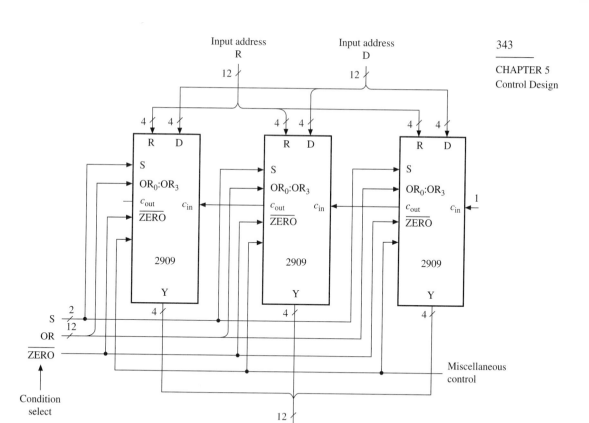

Figure 5.35
Bit-sliced microprogram sequencer for 12-bit addresses.

remaining address source. ST is intended to support subroutine (procedure) calls within microprograms. CALL X is implemented by pushing the contents of μPC into ST and taking the next address X from the D or R source. A subsequent return from the micro-subroutine requires popping ST into μPC. Four addresses can be stored in ST, which allows up to four procedure calls to be nested within a microprogram.

The four possible address sources—μPC, D, R, and ST—are connected to a multi-plexer MUX which, as shown in Figure 5.34, is controlled by the two external select lines S. These lines are typically driven from a 2-bit condition-select field in the current microinstruction; they can also connect to CPU status flags or interrupt request lines. The 2909 has five control lines, denoted $OR_0:OR_3$ and $\overline{ZERO}$, that permit external conditions to modify the address selected by MUX. For example, if $\overline{ZERO}$ is activated ($\overline{ZERO} = 0$), then Y becomes 0000. This line is typically connected to a reset signal, which forces the control unit to begin execution of a microprogram whose starting address is all 0s. The OR_i lines can force selected bits of Y to 1 to implement conditional branches relative to the current address, for instance, to skip the next microinstruction. The stack ST is enabled by the $\overline{FE}$ (file enable) line, while the push-pop select line PUP causes a push (pop) to be performed when PUP = 1 (0).

Thus microinstruction sequencing by the 2909 is controlled by signals derived from a combination of microinstruction control fields and external conditions. For example, suppose the address X is applied to the 2909's input bus D. The following microinstruction control fields

$$S,\overline{FE},PUP,OR,\overline{ZERO} = 11,1,d,0000,1 \tag{5.13}$$

implement the operation **go to** X. The effect of (5.13) is to disable ST and the OR-AND address-modification logic while routing the desired branch address X from D to Y. The microoperation CALL X, where X is stored in the R register, is specified by

$$S,\overline{FE},PUP,OR,\overline{ZERO} = 01,0,1,0000,1$$

while RETURN is implemented by

$$S,\overline{FE},PUP,OR,\overline{ZERO} = 10,0,0,0000,1$$

5.2.2 Multiplier Control Unit

Several hardwired control unit designs for a sequential twos-complement multiplication circuit were presented in Example 5.2. Now we examine the design of a microprogrammed control unit for the same multiplier. The design process can begin with either the flowchart of Figure 5.15 or the state table of Figure 5.16, both of which define the flow of control and identify the control signals to be activated. An HDL description like that of Figure 4.13 may be more appropriate, however, since it is essentially the required microprogram written in symbolic form. Figure 5.36a repeats this HDL description of the multiplier in a format in which every statement corresponds to a distinct microinstruction, implying that a microprogram of 10 microinstructions is sufficient.

Microprogram structure. As a first attack, we use the microinstruction format of Figure 5.33a, which has three parts: a condition-select field, a branch address, and a set of control fields. An address field of 4 bits can address up to 16 microinstructions. Initially, no encoding of control signals will be done, so that there are thirteen 1-bit control fields, one for each of the control lines $c_0,c_1,\ldots,c_{11}$,END. The control unit has the general organization of Figure 5.33b, which has a microprogram counter μPC as the control memory address register. During each microinstruction cycle, μPC is incremented to produce the address of the next microinstruction. In the case of a branch microinstruction, the address stored in the current microinstruction is the branch address. We eliminate the need for an external address input by storing the first microinstruction in address 0 of CM and simply resetting μPC to 0 at the start of multiplication.

Every microinstruction can specify a branch address and so can implement a conditional or unconditional branch. The condition-select field has to indicate one of four conditions:

- No branching
- Branch if Q[0] = 0
- Branch if COUNT7 = 0
- Unconditional branch

Hence a 2-bit condition-select field is needed. We conclude that a 19-bit microinstruction word is sufficient when a full horizontal version of the format in Figure 5.33a is used.

Address	Microoperations	Control signals activated
BEGIN:	A := 0, COUNT := 0, F := 0, M := INBUS;	c_9, c_{10}
INPUT:	Q := INBUS;	c_8
TEST1:	**if** Q[0] = 0 **then go to** RSHIFT:	
ADD:	A[7:0] := A[7:0] + M[7:0], F := (M[7] **and** Q[0]) **or** F;	c_2, c_3, c_4
RSHIFT:	A[7] := F, A[6:0].Q := A.Q[7:1], COUNT := COUNT + 1, **if** COUNT7 = 0 **then go to** TEST1;	c_0, c_1, c_{11}
TEST2:	**if** Q[0] = 0 **then go to** OUTPUT1;	
SUBTRACT:	A[7:0] := A[7:0] − M[7:0], Q[0] := 0;	c_2, c_3, c_4, c_5
OUTPUT1:	OUTBUS := A;	c_6
OUTPUT2:	OUTBUS := Q;	c_7
END:	Halt;	END

(a)

Address in CM	Condition select	Branch address	c_0	c_1	c_2	c_3	c_4	c_5	c_6	c_7	c_8	c_9	c_{10}	c_{11}	END
0000	00	0000	0	0	0	0	0	0	0	0	0	1	1	0	0
0001	00	0000	0	0	0	0	0	0	0	0	1	0	0	0	0
0010	01	0100	0	0	0	0	0	0	0	0	0	0	0	0	0
0011	00	0000	0	0	1	1	1	0	0	0	0	0	0	0	0
0100	10	0010	1	1	0	0	0	0	0	0	0	0	0	1	0
0101	01	0111	0	0	0	0	0	0	0	0	0	0	0	0	0
0110	00	0000	0	0	1	1	1	1	0	0	0	0	0	0	0
0111	00	0000	0	0	0	0	0	0	1	0	0	0	0	0	0
1000	00	0000	0	0	0	0	0	0	0	1	0	0	0	0	0
1001	11	1001	0	0	0	0	0	0	0	0	0	0	0	0	1

(b)

Figure 5.36
(a) Symbolic and (b) binary microprogram for twos-complement multiplication.

It is now easy to construct a binary microprogram that implements the multiplication algorithm. The symbolic microprogram of Figure 5.36a is converted line by line into the bit patterns shown in Figure 5.36b. Consecutive microinstructions are assigned to consecutive addresses, and the appropriate condition-select bits are inserted (00 denotes no branching; the remaining condition codes are easily deduced). When multiplication is completed, the microprogram enters a waiting (halt) state by repeatedly executing the no-operation microinstruction in CM location 1001. It remains in this state until μPC is reset by the arrival of an external BEGIN signal. The structure of the resulting control unit appears in Figure 5.37.

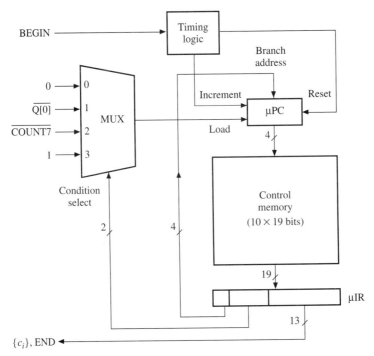

Figure 5.37
Microprogrammed control unit for the twos-complement multiplier.

Control-field encoding. Few of the 2^{13} possible control-field patterns allowed by the microinstruction format of Figure 5.37 are actually useful or needed. Figure 5.36 shows that several sets of control signals are always activated simultaneously; hence a single 1-bit control field suffices for each such set. The 8 bits reserved for the 3 sets $\{c_0, c_1, c_{11}\}$, $\{c_2, c_3, c_4\}$, and $\{c_9, c_{10}\}$ can be replaced by 3 bits, yielding the short, horizontal format given in Figure 5.38.

The number of control bits can be reduced further by encoding the control fields. Since there are only 10 distinct microinstructions in the multiplication microprogram (Figure 5.36), we can encode the control signals in a single 4-bit control field, yielding a purely vertical format. However, this design severely

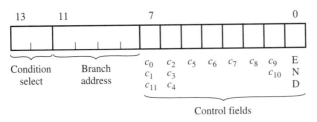

Figure 5.38
Horizontal microinstruction format after removing redundant control fields.

limits our ability to subsequently modify the microinstruction set. Suppose that the microinstruction format we are designing will be used for more applications than the control of multiplication—note that the multiplier has most of the components of a sequential ALU. It is therefore of interest to encode the microinstructions so that microinstructions as yet unspecified can easily be added later.

A systematic method of encoding is to divide the control signals into sets that are *compatible* in the sense that no two members of set, called a *compatibility class*, are ever active at the same time. The four control signals c_0, c_1, c_2, c_3 that load the same register R in Figure 5.33 are examples of a compatibility class. We can now state the following optimization problem, which aims to minimize the total size of the control fields needed to implement a particular set of microinstructions: Find a collection of compatibility classes $\{C_i\}$ of control signals such that

- Every control signal is contained in at least one $\{C_i\}$.
- The function $W = \sum_i \lceil \log_2(|C_i| + 1) \rceil$ is a minimum, where $|C_i|$ is the number of signals in $\{C_i\}$.

Here W represents the combined width of all the microinstruction's control fields. A solution to this problem minimizes the number of control bits while keeping the maximum degree of parallelism inherent in the original microinstruction set. Only the control fields are being minimized; the next-address and condition-select fields are unaffected.

Many general solutions, both exact and heuristic, to the foregoing problem are discussed in the literature on microprogramming [Lynch 1993]. The problem is easy to solve in the case of the twos-complement multiplier, where we have 10 microinstructions and, after eliminating redundant bits from the control field, eight control signals $\{c_0, c_2, c_5, c_6, c_7, c_8, c_9, \text{END}\}$; see Figure 5.38. There are only two incompatible microoperations, namely c_2 and c_5, which are activated together in the SUBTRACT microinstruction. Hence the two largest or *maximal compatibility classes* (MCCs) are $C_0 = \{c_0, c_2, c_6, c_7, c_8, c_9, \text{END}\}$ and $C_1 = \{c_0, c_5, c_6, c_7, c_8, c_9, \text{END}\}$, so a format containing two encoded control fields suffices. There are several ways to choose subsets of C_0 and C_1 that cover all control signals and yield a value of five for the cost function W. For example, we can set $C_0' = \{c_0, c_2, c_6\}$ and $C_1' = \{c_5, c_7, c_8, c_9, \text{END}\}$. The resulting microinstruction has the format shown in Figure 5.39 and requires a pair of decoders to extract the control signals. The fact that there are only two control fields indicates that little inherent parallelism exists in the multiplication algorithm.

Encoding by function. A drawback of the minimum-width control format of Figure 5.39 is that functionally unrelated control signals are combined in the same control field, while related signals are derived from different control fields. For example, both C_0' and C_1' control the transfer of information to OUTBUS. This lack of functional separation makes the writing of microprograms difficult, since the microprogrammer must associate several unrelated opcodes with each control field. An encoded format in which each control field specifies the control signals for one component or for a related set of operations is preferred, even though more control bits may be needed.

On examining the multiplier circuit, we see that there are five components to be controlled: the adder, the A.Q register-pair, the external iteration counter COUNT, and the two data buses INBUS and OUTBUS. Each component has its

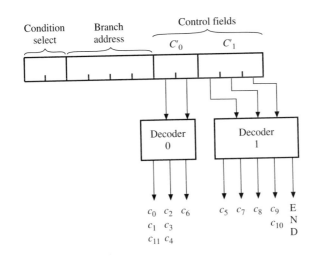

Condition
select

Branch
address

Control fields

C'_0 C'_1

Decoder
0

Decoder
1

c_0 c_2 c_6 c_5 c_7 c_8 c_9 E
c_1 c_3 c_{10} N
c_{11} c_4 D

Figure 5.39
Vertical microinstruction format
with maximum parallelism and
minimum control-field width.

own set of functions, suggesting the *encoding-by-function* format of Figure 5.40a.
Possible control-field assignments and their interpretation appear in Figure 5.40b.
Note that this ad hoc encoding has combined the "incompatible" control signals c_2
and c_5. This is unlikely to be of concern, however, if the microinstruction set is
later enlarged—there is no obvious functional advantage in keeping c_2 and c_5 in
separate fields. The assignment of a separate control field to INBUS is of questionable wisdom. It prevents INBUS from transferring data to two or more destinations, such as Q and M, simultaneously. Such a transfer could be useful, for
example, to clear both registers at once. It might be better to associate a control
field with each register that is a potential destination of INBUS rather than with
INBUS itself.

Multiple microinstruction formats. In the original multiplication microprogram, several microinstructions are used only for next-address generation and do
not activate any control lines. This suggests that we can reduce microinstruction
size by using a single field to contain either control information or address
information. We then obtain two distinct microinstruction types—branch microinstructions, which specify no control information, and action or *operate* microinstructions, which activate control lines but have no branching capability. Note
that this approach is almost always used at the instruction level. The division of
microinstructions into the branch and operate types is rather natural, since the
branch microinstructions control the internal operations of the control unit, while
the operate microinstructions control the external datapath.

Suppose that we want to use unencoded control fields for the twos-complement multiplier, which requires 8 control bits, as seen from Figure 5.38. Now we
define a microinstruction format having two parts, a 2-bit condition-select field
with the same meaning as before, and an 8-bit field that can contain either a branch
address or control information. The condition-select code 00, which denotes no
branching, serves to identify the operate microinstructions. The remaining three
select field codes identify conditional and unconditional branches. We thus obtain
the two 10-bit microinstruction formats of Figure 5.41a. Note that the additional
address bits enable us to write microprograms containing up to $2^8 = 256$ instruc-

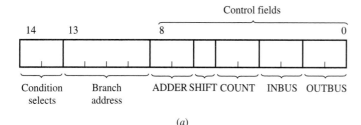

(a)

Control field	Bits used	Code	Microoperations specified	Control signals activated
ADDER	7,8	00	No operation	
		01	A := A + M, set F	c_2, c_3, c_4
		10	A := A − M, Q[0] := 0	c_2, c_3, c_4, c_5
		11	Unused	
SHIFT	6	0	No operation	
		1	Right-shift A.Q, set A[7]	c_0, c_1
COUNT	5,4	00	No operation	
		01	Clear COUNT, A, F	c_{10}
		10	COUNT := COUNT + 1	c_{11}
		11	Unused	
INBUS	3,2	00	No operation	
		01	Q := INBUS	c_8
		10	M := INBUS	c_9
		11	Unused	
OUTBUS	1,0	00	No operation	
		01	OUTBUS := A	c_6
		10	OUTBUS := Q	c_7
		11	Unused	

(b)

Figure 5.40
(a) Microinstruction format with control fields encoded by function and (b) their interpretation.

tions. Because we have destroyed the capability of every microinstruction to implement a two-way branch, some operations need more microinstructions.

Figure 5.41b shows a microprogram for twos-complement multiplication using the formats of Figure 5.41a. This microprogram is somewhat easier to derive from the flowchart (Figure 5.15) than was the earlier microprogram (Figure 5.36) because we can now transform decision blocks directly into branch microinstructions, while activity boxes are transformed into operate microinstructions. The control unit of Figure 5.37 is easily modified to handle these new microinstruction formats: The condition-select field is used to control a demultiplexer that routes bits 0:7 either to external control lines (operate microinstructions) or to the branch address logic (branch microinstructions).

Multiplication and division cannot be bit sliced in the same way as addition, subtraction, or shifting. However, these operations can be implemented in a bit-

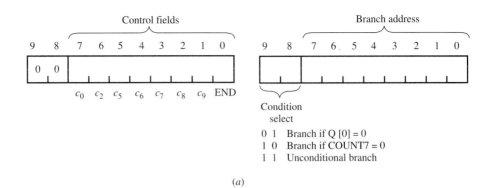

Condition
select

0 1   Branch if Q [0] = 0
1 0   Branch if COUNT7 = 0
1 1   Unconditional branch

(a)

Address	Condition select		Branch address or control bits								Comment
in CM	9	8	7	6	5	4	3	2	1	0	
0000	0	0	0	0	0	0	0	0	1	0	BEGIN
0001	0	0	0	0	0	0	0	1	0	0	INPUT
0010	0	1	0	0	0	0	0	1	0	0	TEST1
0011	0	0	0	1	0	0	0	0	0	0	ADD
0100	0	0	1	0	0	0	0	0	0	0	RSHIFT
0101	1	0	0	0	0	0	0	0	1	0	RSHIFT BRANCH
0110	0	1	0	0	0	0	1	0	0	0	TEST2
0111	0	0	0	1	1	0	0	0	0	0	SUBTRACT
1000	0	0	0	0	0	1	0	0	0	0	OUTPUT1
1001	0	0	0	0	0	0	1	0	0	0	OUTPUT2
1010	0	0	0	0	0	0	0	0	0	1	END
1011	1	1	0	0	0	0	1	0	1	1	HALT

(b)

Figure 5.41
(a) Multiple microinstruction formats and (b) multiplication microprogram that uses these
formats.

sliced ALU under the control of a microprogram that implements one of the shift-
and-add/subtract algorithms described in section 4.1, as the next example demonstrates.

EXAMPLE 5.5 TWOS-COMPLEMENT MULTIPLICATION IN A BIT-SLICED
ALU [MICK AND BRICK 1980]. The AMD 2901 is a 4-bit ALU slice, which is
described in Example 4.5. A set of k copies of the 2901 can easily be connected to perform the basic ALU operations (twos-complement addition and subtraction, as well as
the standard logical operations) on $4k$-bit data words. We now explain how such an
array can implement twos-complement multiplication under microprogram control.

   Figure 5.42 shows a four-slice 2901 circuit that is configured to multiply 16-bit
twos-complement numbers via the Robertson algorithm. The roles of the accumulator
A, the multiplicand register M, and the multiplier register Q are assigned to the 2901's
R(B), R(A), and Q registers, respectively. R(A) and R(B) are in the 2901's register file
(referred to as the RAM in 2900 literature), while Q is a "quotient" register intended to
support sequential multiplication and division algorithms. The register addresses A
and B are determined by external signals placed on the corresponding 4-bit RAM
address buses. The shift lines Q_0 and Q_3 serve to link the Q registers in the four 2901s

to form a 16-bit Q register that can be right shifted via the 2901's Q shifter (Figure 4.36). In the same fashion the RAM_0 and RAM_3 shift lines effectively link the slices of R(B), allowing it to serve as the 16-bit accumulator. A connection from RAM_0 on the right-most (least significant) slice to Q_3 on the left-most (most significant) slice links the 16-bit R(B) and Q registers to form the 32-bit shift register—A.Q in the original design—where the product will eventually be stored. Finally, as the contents of the A.Q register-pair are right shifted by the 2901's RAM shifter, the sign bit of the partial product should be entered into the most significant bit position of A.Q, that is, A[15].

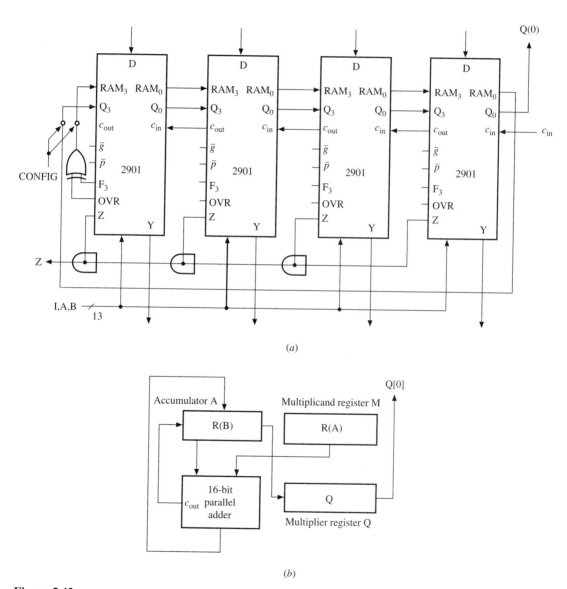

Figure 5.42

A four-slice 2901 array configured for 16-bit multiplication: (*a*) slice interconnections and (*b*) register assignments.

In our previous implementations of Robertson's algorithm, for example, in the microprograms of Figures 5.36 and 5.41, this bit was computed via the formula

$$F := (M[n-1] \textbf{ and } Q[0]) \textbf{ or } F \tag{5.14}$$

It can be shown that (5.14) is equivalent to

$$F := F[n-1] \textbf{ xor } OVF \tag{5.15}$$

where $F[n-1]$ is the sign bit F_3 of the result generated by the most significant 2901 slice and OVF is the overflow signal (based on twos-complement addition) produced by that same slice. Equation (5.15) is implemented by the XOR gate appearing in Figure 5.42a.

The microoperations performed by the 2901 are specified by the set of control signals $I = I_S, I_F, I_D$ listed in Figure 4.38; these are typically used as microinstruction control fields of the encoding-by-function type illustrated by Figure 5.40. The design of the 2901 control fields makes it possible to implement conditional microinstructions in clever ways. In particular, if the bits of the I_F function-select field are treated as condition variables, then the selected operation varies with the condition values. For instance, $I_F = 000$ specifies add with carry; if the middle bit of I_F is a condition variable and is changed to 1, we get $I_F = 010$, which specifies subtract with borrow.

The central operation in binary multiplication, which is a conditional add followed by a right shift, where the condition variable is the current multiplier bit x_i stored in $Q[0]$, can be implemented by a single, carefully constructed 2901 microinstruction. This operation is expressed as follows in HDL format:

$$\textbf{if } Q[0] = 1 \textbf{ then } R(B) := R(B) + R(A); \quad R(B).Q := R(B).Q/2; \tag{5.16}$$

Let $Q[0]$ be applied as a condition variable to the middle line of the 2901's input source control field I_S. Then (5.16) is realized by the following microinstruction:

$$I_S, I_F, I_D = 0 \ \overline{Q}[0]1,000,100 \tag{5.17}$$

$I_F = 000$ specifies the add-with-carry operation whose source and destination operands are determined by I_S and I_D, respectively. Changing I_S from 001 to 011 changes the operation defined by (5.17) from $Y := R(A) + R(B)$ to $Y := 0 + R(B)$, effectively skipping the add step. $I_D = 100$ causes the result F to be right shifted before loading into $R(B)$; it also right shifts Q as required by (5.16).

Since we also need to make I_S a constant at other times, we would implement (5.17) by connecting the middle bit of the I_S control field and $\overline{Q}[0]$ to the data inputs of a two-way 1-bit multiplexer MUXQ. The output of MUXQ would be the final control signal c. Another 1-bit control field CQ would be added to the microinstruction format to drive the select input of MUXQ and thus determine whether $c = \overline{Q}[0]$ or the current value in the I_S field.

Sixteen-bit multiplication requires (5.16) to be executed 15 times and be followed by a subtraction step that is again conditional on the value of $Q[0]$. A complete microprogram along these lines appears in Figure 5.43. It implements the same basic algorithm we have used earlier, with various modifications geared to the particular features of the 2900 series, and is designed to produce a very short multiplication microprogram. It must be possible to configure the 2901 ALU as in Figure 5.42 under control of a microprogram sequencer such as the AMD 2909 (Example 5.4) or 2910. The latter includes a counter that can be automatically decremented in every clock cycle and so can serve as the multiplier's iteration counter COUNT. On setting the 2910 to a special repeat mode, the microprogram sequencer will continue to output the address of the current microinstruction, and so repeatedly execute that microinstruction, until COUNT becomes zero.

Microoperations	Comment
Q := 0 *or* R(A)	Move multiplier *X* to Q from R(A)
R(B) := 0 *and* R(B)	Clear accumulator A = R(B)

COUNT := 15; **while** COUNT ≠ 0 **do**
    begin A := A × Q[0] + M; right-shift A.Q;
    COUNT := COUNT − 1 **end**
	Conditional add and shift repeated
	    15 times

A := A × Q[0] − M	Conditional subtract. Product = A.Q
R(B) := 0 *or* Q	Move low half-product from Q to R(B)

(*a*)

COUNT	A	B	I_S	I_F	I_D	c_{in}	CONFIG	REPEAT	Comment
...ddddd	0000	dddd	100	011	000	d	0	0	Move multiplier *X* to Q from R[0]
...ddddd	dddd	0011	011	100	011	d	0	0	Clear accumulator R[3]
...01111	0001	0011	0d0	000	100	0	1	1	Conditional add and shift repeated 15 times
...ddddd	0001	0011	0d0	001	100	1	1	0	Conditional subtract. Product = R[3].Q
...ddddd	dddd	0010	010	011	010	d	0	0	Move low half-product from Q to R[2]

(*b*)

Figure 5.43
(*a*) Symbolic and (*b*) binary microprogram for twos-complement
multiplication in the 2901-based processor.

Figure 5.43 gives in both symbolic (HDL) and binary form a multiplication micro-program containing only five microinstructions. The first two microinstructions initial-ize the multiplication, assuming that the multiplicand M is already stored in register R[1]. The third microinstruction implements (5.17) and is executed 15 times. The fourth microinstruction implements the conditional subtraction (correction step) needed to accommodate a negative *X*, while the last instruction transfers the contents of the Q register to the register file; at the end the data is stored as follows: R[0] = multi-plier, R[1] = multiplicand, and R[3].R[2] = product.

Most of the control fields appearing in Figure 5.43*b* specify control signals applied to the 2901 ALU. The CONFIG field is intended to produce the special multi-plication configuration of Figure 5.42, which requires various control points (not all shown) to establish links such as that from the output of the XOR gate to the RAM_3 input of the left-most slice, from $\overline{Q[0]}$ to the middle signal derived from I_S, and so on. An address field called REPEAT is also defined, with REPEAT = 0 meaning that the next microinstruction, whose address is generated by the microprogram counter μPC, immediately follows the current microinstruction. REPEAT = 1 means that the current microinstruction is to be repeated until the automatically decremented COUNT register reaches zero.

5.2.3 CPU Control Unit

This section considers the design of the microprogrammed control units and micro-programs for use in the CPU of nonpipelined, general-purpose computers.

Basic emulator. First we reexamine the accumulator-based CPU for which we developed a hardwired program control unit in section 5.1.3. The organization of this CPU and its 10-member instruction set appear in Figure 5.20. The 13 control signals listed in Figure 5.22 define the basic microoperations that are available to the microprogrammer. (We will later extend this to a more realistic set.) To simplify the presentation, we will give the microinstructions only in symbolic form using our HDL.

Suppose that you want to write an emulator for the target instruction set whose members, which are defined in Figures 5.20 and 5.21, are LD, ST, MOV1, MOV2, ADD, SUB, AND, NOT, BRA, and BZ. The microoperations that implement the various instructions appear in Figure 5.22, from which the required microprograms are easily deduced. The microprogram selected to emulate each instruction is identified by the instruction's opcode; hence the contents of the instruction register IR determine the microprogram's starting address. We will use the unmodified contents of IR as the microprogram address for the current instruction. We will further assume that each microinstruction can specify a branch condition, a branch address that is used only if the branch condition is satisfied, and a set of control fields defining the microoperations to be performed. These microinstruction fields can easily be adapted to a variety of formats (horizontal, vertical, encode-by-function, and so on) as discussed earlier.

Figure 5.44 lists a complete emulator for the given instruction set in symbolic form; the conversion of each microinstruction to binary code is straightforward.

FETCH:	AR := PC; DR := M(AR); PC := PC + 1, IR := DR(OP); **go to** IR;
LD:	AR := DR(ADR); DR := M(AR); AC := DR, **go to** FETCH;
ST:	AR := DR(ADR); DR := AC; M(AR) := DR, **go to** FETCH;
MOV1:	DR := AC, **go to** FETCH;
MOV2:	AC := DR, **go to** FETCH;
ADD:	AC := AC + DR, **go to** FETCH;
SUB:	AC := AC – DR, **go to** FETCH;
AND:	AC := AC *and* DR, **go to** FETCH;
NOT:	AC := *not* AC, **go to** FETCH;
BRA:	PC := DR(ADR), **go to** FETCH;
BZ:	**if** AC = 0 **then** PC := DR(ADR), **go to** FETCH;

Figure 5.44
A microprogrammed emulator for a small instruction set.

This emulator contains a distinct microprogram for each of the ten possible instruction execution cycles and another microprogram called FETCH—note how the name of the microprogram corresponds to its address in the emulator code—which controls the instruction fetch cycle. The **go to** IR microoperation is implemented by $\mu PC := IR$, which transfers control to the first microinstruction in the microprogram that interprets the current instruction. Depending on the microinstruction format chosen, either such branch operations can be included in a general operate-with-branching format or separate branch microinstructions can be defined. Figure 5.44 assumes that μPC is the default address source for microinstructions and is incremented automatically in every clock cycle.

Suppose that because of a design error, or because of a late modification to the specifications of the instruction set, we need to introduce a new instruction called CLEAR whose function is to reset all bits of the accumulator AC to 0. Although no control line to clear AC was included in the CPU, we can still write a microprogram to implement the CLEAR instruction using only the preexisting microoperations.

$$\text{CLEAR:} \quad DR := AC;$$

$$AC := \textit{not } AC;$$

$$AC := AC \textit{ and } DR, \textbf{ go to } \text{FETCH};$$

By storing this new microprogram in the control memory, CLEAR can be added to the instruction set with either no changes, or very minor ones, to the CPU hardware. Such flexibility is a key advantage of microprogramming over hardwired control.

Extensions. We will now add to the CPU structure of Figure 5.22 the circuits to implement fixed-point multiplication and division using sequential algorithms of the type discussed in Chapter 4. Two major new registers are required—a multiplier-quotient register MQ and a counter called COUNT, which counts the number of iterations (add/subtract and shift steps) used during multiplication or division. The memory data register DR will be assigned the role of multiplicand or divisor register MD when appropriate.

Figure 5.45a shows the modified CPU; the number of control signals has more than doubled to 29. These signals are denoted $c_0:c_{28}$ and defined in Figure 5.45b: $c_0:c_{12}$ correspond to the control signals of the original CPU in Figure 5.22. Several of the control signals listed in Figure 5.45b implicitly cause flag (status) bits to be set or reset. For example, if overflow occurs during addition or subtraction, which are controlled by c_9 and c_{10}, respectively, then OVR is set to 1; otherwise OVR is reset to 0. The three flag bits FLAGS, the least significant bit MQ[0] of the multiplier-quotient register, and the signal COUNT $= n - 1$ all serve as branch conditions that the microprogrammed control unit can test.

Figure 5.46 lists a symbolic microprogram for this CPU that implements the Robertson multiplication algorithm for twos-complement numbers first introduced in Example 4.2. A special-purpose microprogrammed controller for this type of multiplication was developed in section 5.2.2. The microprogram *2Cmult* given here is essentially the same as the one defined previously for the stand-alone multiplier (refer to Figure 5.42a). In this symbolic form, the microprogram is also similar to the original HDL description of the Robertson algorithm (Figure 4.13). We assume that before *2Cmult* is executed, the multiplier operand X is placed in MQ and the multiplicand Y is in DR. Each statement in Figure 5.46 represents a single microinstruction.

The general three-part microinstruction format comprising a condition-select field, a branch-address field, and a set of control fields will be used for *2Cmult*. Five conditions to be tested are identified in Figure 5.45a: AC = 0, AC < 0, MQ[0], COUNT = $n - 1$, and OVR, the overflow indicator. Adding the possibilities of an unconditional branch and no branching, we obtain seven branch-condition codes that can be represented by a 3-bit condition-select field.

Various control signals can be grouped together in common encoded fields to reduce the microinstruction size. We can identify many of these fields from the list of control signals without reference to the actual microinstructions that are to be implemented. For example, three control signals c_1, c_6, and c_{20} transfer data to DR. Since they are mutually exclusive (compatible), we can encode them in a

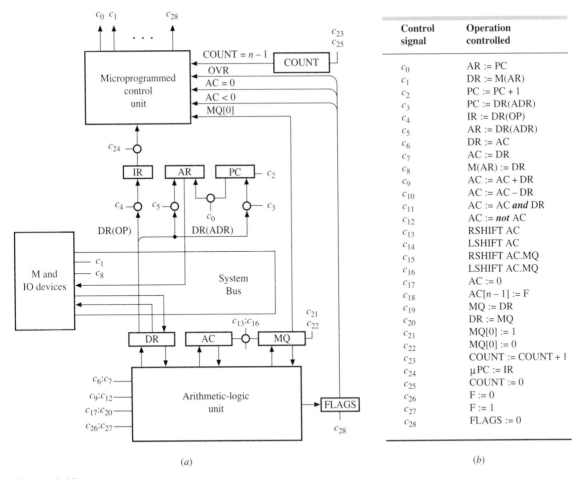

Control signal	Operation controlled
c_0	AR := PC
c_1	DR := M(AR)
c_2	PC := PC + 1
c_3	PC := DR(ADR)
c_4	IR := DR(OP)
c_5	AR := DR(ADR)
c_6	DR := AC
c_7	AC := DR
c_8	M(AR) := DR
c_9	AC := AC + DR
c_{10}	AC := AC − DR
c_{11}	AC := AC *and* DR
c_{12}	AC := *not* AC
c_{13}	RSHIFT AC
c_{14}	LSHIFT AC
c_{15}	RSHIFT AC.MQ
c_{16}	LSHIFT AC.MQ
c_{17}	AC := 0
c_{18}	AC[$n - 1$] := F
c_{19}	MQ := DR
c_{20}	DR := MQ
c_{21}	MQ[0] := 1
c_{22}	MQ[0] := 0
c_{23}	COUNT := COUNT + 1
c_{24}	µPC := IR
c_{25}	COUNT := 0
c_{26}	F := 0
c_{27}	F := 1
c_{28}	FLAGS := 0

(*a*)

(*b*)

Figure 5.45

(*a*) Control points and (*b*) control signal definitions for the extended CPU.

Address	Microinstruction
BEGIN:	A := 0, COUNT := 0, F := 0;
TEST1:	**if** MQ[0] = 0 **then go to** RSHIFT:
ADD:	AC := AC + DR, F := (DR[n–1] **and** MQ[0]) **or** F;
RSHIFT:	AC [n–1] := F, AC.MQ := RSHIFT(AC.MQ), COUNT := COUNT + 1, **if** COUNT ≠ n–1 **then go to** TEST1;
TEST2:	**if** MQ[0] = 0 **then go to** FETCH;
SUBTRACT:	AC := AC – DR, MQ[0] := 0, **go to** FETCH;

Figure 5.46
Twos-complement multiplication microprogram *2Cmult* for the extended CPU.

2-bit field. Note that one more bit pattern must be reserved for the no-operation case. Similarly, we can combine the many control signals that alter the contents of AC.

Suppose that we have decided not to encode the control signals. This decision implies that the condition-select and control fields occupy 32 bits of each microinstruction. Suppose further that an 8-bit branch address denoting a complete CM address is included in each microinstruction; a CM storing up to 256 forty-bit words is therefore supported. Figure 5.47 shows a possible organization for the CPU control unit with the foregoing design assumptions. As in our previous designs, external conditions control the loading of branch addresses into the μPC. In addition, the μPC can be loaded from the instruction register IR via a logic circuit K (typically a ROM or PLA), which maps instruction opcodes onto microinstruction addresses.

Microprogram sequencers. It is possible to place all the circuitry required to generate microinstruction addresses in a single IC or cell called a *microprogram sequencer*, a simple example of which, the AMD 2909, was discussed earlier (Example 5.4). A microprogram sequencer is a general-purpose building block for microprogrammed control units. It contains a microprogram counter μPC, as well as the logic needed for conditional branching and transferring control between microprograms. A control unit can be constructed from three components: a RAM or ROM used as the control memory, a microinstruction register, and a microprogram sequencer. Figure 5.48 shows a microprogrammed CU designed in this way. The microinstruction register can be implemented as a two-stage pipeline to allow microinstruction fetching and execution to be overlapped.

Microprogram sequencers are mainly found in standard-cell families like the 2900 series intended for the design of both general-purpose and application-specific processors. They are also used in CISC CPUs such as the Motorola 680X0. Because of IC component density and pin restrictions, early microprogram sequencers like the 2909 were relatively simple and had to be bit sliced to allow control units of practical size to be constructed from them. Subsequent advances in VLSI technology have enabled more powerful and self-contained control units of this kind to be built.

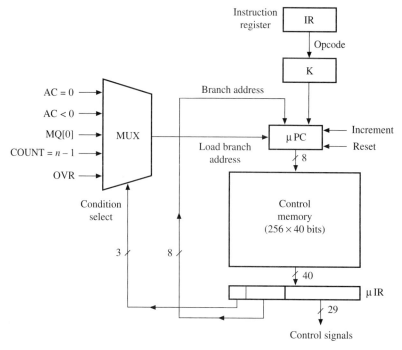

Figure 5.47
Microprogrammed control unit for the extended CPU.

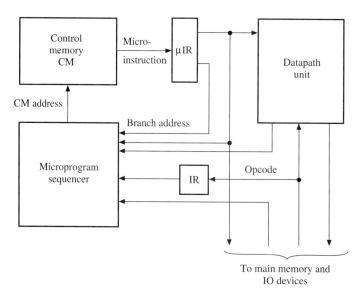

Figure 5.48
Microprogrammed CPU employing a microprogram sequencer.

EXAMPLE 5.6 THE TEXAS INSTRUMENTS 890 MICROPROGRAM SEQUENCER [TEXAS INSTRUMENTS 1985, LACKZO ET AL. 1986]. This circuit, whose full designation is the SN74AS890, is a member of the Texas Instruments 88X microprocessor component family, which was introduced in the mid-1980s aimed at the design of general-purpose CPUs. It can be considered a natural evolution of the 2909-class microprogram sequencers to accommodate larger address sizes (and hence larger control memories), more address sources, and more-flexible operating modes. Packaged in a single 70-pin IC, the 890 has a number of features intended to simplify the development of microprograms. The address size is 14 bits, enabling a single 890 to manage a control unit containing a 16K-word CM for the storage of microprograms; consequently, it is not bit sliced. The corresponding datapath member of the 88X series is the 888 (SN74AS888), an 8-bit ALU slice. The architecture of the 888 is almost identical to that of the 2901 4-bit ALU considered earlier (Examples 4.5 and 5.5) except for its larger word size.

Figure 5.49 depicts the internal organization of the 890. Like the 2909 (Figure 5.34), the CM address sources are a small set of external buses and internal registers, including a microprogram counter µPC and a LIFO stack. The µPC is implemented as

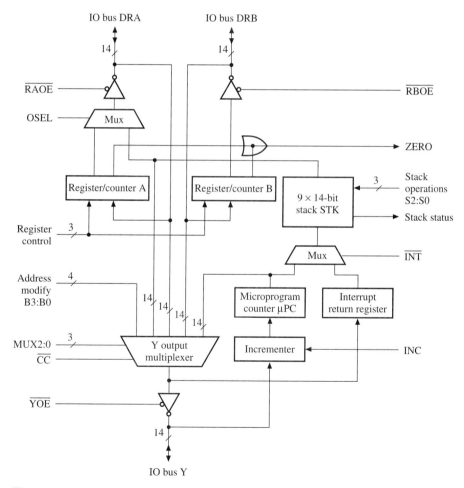

Figure 5.49
Structure of the Texas Instruments 890 microprogram sequencer.

a 14-bit register with a separate incrementer, as in the 2909, and is the usual source of microinstruction addresses. There are two main external sources of branch addresses, the buses DRA and DRB, while the Y bus serves as the main output address bus. All three buses are 14 bits wide and, for added flexibility, all are bidirectional. DRA, DRB, and Y may be compared with the 2909's D, R, and Y buses, respectively. The 4-bit B (branch) bus replaces the four least significant bits of addresses on the DRA and DRB buses to implement conditional 32-way branches; the B3:B0 lines therefore correspond roughly to the $OR_3:OR_0$ and $\overline{ZERO}$ lines used for address modification in the 2909. The DRA and DRB buses also have registers/counters A and B, respectively, associated with them. A and B can serve either as independent address sources or else as iteration counters when executing a loop in a microprogram.

The 890 has a nine-word stack STK to implement subroutine calls and interrupts. Three control lines S2:S0 allow various stack operations including push, pop, reset, and hold to be specified by microinstruction control fields. A push operation (with $\overline{INT}$ = 0) places the contents of μPC at the top of the stack; a pop operation transfers the address at the top of the stack to the Y bus via the Y multiplexer. In addition to the usual stack pointer SP for automatically tracking the top of the stack, a second pointer register, the read pointer RP, reads out the contents of the stack word by word to the 890's DRA port. This readout process, which does not alter the contents of the stack or SP, can be used to backtrack through a sequence of subroutine calls or interrupts to identify the cause (for instance, overflow) and the location in CM of a problem occurring during microprogram execution.

In summary, the 890 can output to the Y bus a 14-bit microinstruction address derived from four sources: the microprogram counter μPC, the stack STK, the DRA bus, or the DRB bus. The addresses on the DRA and DRB buses can be obtained either externally or from the 890's internal A and B registers. The DRA/DRB addresses can also be modified by the B3:B0 lines, which, in conjunction with the control inputs MUX2:MUX0 and $\overline{CC}$ of the Y multiplexer, support the implementation of many kinds of conditional and unconditional branching. The "condition code" bit $\overline{CC}$ is designed to add a simple two-way branch option to most microinstructions.

Consider the execution in cycle i of a microinstruction $I(ADR)$ stored at control memory address ADR. If no branching is specified, then during clock cycle i, μPC writes the address ADR to the Y bus; at the same time it reads in the next address ADR + 1 from the incrementer. In this way the 890 is ready to execute the instruction $I(ADR + 1)$ in cycle $i + 1$. Sometimes it is desirable to allow a status signal F from the datapath unit to control the operation of the incrementer so that under certain conditions (illustrated later) no incrementing occurs; in such a case the execution of $I(ADR)$ is repeated in cycle $i + 1$. The action (the execution of some microinstruction) that sets up the relevant value of F to block the increment in cycle i must therefore occur in cycle $i - 1$ or earlier.

Figure 5.50 presents a few examples of the huge number of possible branch microoperations that the 890 can implement (along with a full range of datapath operations that we do not consider here). We show only the principal control fields associated with program control in microinstructions. The first "continue" or "no operation" (NOP) microinstruction is intended merely to replace the current contents of μPC by $\mu PC + 1$; that is,

$$\mu I_1: \quad \mu PC := \mu PC + 1; \quad \{Continue\}$$

The condition code $\overline{CC}$ and increment bit INC must be set to 1 at least one cycle earlier. The control signal combination MUX2:MUX0,$\overline{CC}$ =1001 selects μPC as the data input of the Y multiplexer and applies it to the incrementer, which then outputs μPC + INC to μPC. The control field values S2:S0 = 111 and OSEL = 0 are needed to inactivate stack operations. The remaining control bits denoted by d are don't cares. The sec-

Instruction	CM address	MUX2: MUX0	S2:S0	R2:R0	OSEL	$\overline{CC}$	INC	DRA	DRB
(Setup)		ddd	ddd	ddd	d	1	1	...ddd	...ddd
Continue (NOP)	0001	100	111	ddd	0	d	d	...ddd	...ddd
(Setup)		ddd	ddd	ddd	d	1	d	...ddd	...ddd
Branch to 5	0001	000	111	ddd	0	d	d	...0101	...ddd
(Setup)		ddd	ddd	ddd	d	1	1	...ddd	...ddd
Branch to 5 if CC = 1	0001	110	111	000	0	d	d	...0101	...ddd
(Setup)		ddd	ddd	ddd	d	1	1	...ddd	...ddd
Loop until A = 0	0001	110	100	ddd	0	1	1	...ddd	...ddd
	0010	110	111	010	0	0	1	...ddd	...ddd
	0011	000	010	000	1	1	1	...ddd	...ddd
(Setup)		ddd	ddd	ddd	d	1	1	...ddd	...ddd
Call subroutine (at 5)	0001	000	110	ddd	d	d	d	...0101	...ddd
(Setup)		ddd	ddd	ddd	d	0	d	...ddd	...ddd
Return from subroutine	0001	010	011	000	d	0	d	...ddd	...ddd

Figure 5.50
Sample branch microinstructions for the 890 microprogram sequencer.

ond example in Figure 5.50 is a simple unconditional branch to the address on the DRA bus; the combination MUX2:MUX0,$\overline{CC}$ = 0000 makes Y = DRA. Changing MUX2:MUX0 to 110 as is done for the third microinstruction "branch to 5 if CC = 1," ensures that the branch occurs only if $\overline{CC}$ = 0; that is,

$$\mu I_3: \quad \textbf{if } \overline{CC} = 0 \textbf{ then } Y = DRA \textbf{ else } \mu PC := \mu PC + 1;$$

The fourth example employs a sequence (microprogram) of three microinstructions $\mu I_{4,1}:\mu I_{4,3}$ to implement "loop until A = 0" as follows:

$$\mu I_{4,1}: \quad \mu PC := \mu PC + 1, STK(SP) := \mu PC, SP := SP + 1; \quad \{\text{Continue, push } \mu PC\}$$

$$\mu I_{4,2}: \quad \mu PC := \mu PC + 1, A := DRA; \quad \{\text{Continue, load register A}\} \qquad (5.18)$$

$$\mu I_{4,3}: \quad A := A - 1, \textbf{if } A \neq 0 \textbf{ then } Y = STK(SP)$$
$$\textbf{else } \mu PC := \mu PC + 1, SP := SP - 1; \quad \{\text{Decrement A, branch to stack if } A = 0, \text{pop}\}$$

The call and return microinstructions have similar interpretations.

Normally μPC contains the address whose value is one plus the address ADR of the currently executing microinstruction. The interrupt return register IRR is designed to operate in parallel with μPC but contains the current address ADR rather than ADR + 1. This feature permits an interrupt to be implemented in the following way that has zero latency. The interrupting device disables the 890's Y bus by setting $\overline{YOE}$ to one. It then places a new address ADR1 (the interrupt vector) on Y, forcing a transfer to CM address ADR1, which is the start address of the interrupt-servicing routine P. The microinstruction at address ADR1 must be designed to push IRR into the stack (which requires $\overline{INT}$ = 1), thus saving the return address of the interrupted program.

Nanoprogramming. In most microprogrammed processors, an instruction fetched from memory is interpreted by a microprogram stored in a single control memory CM. In a few machines, however, the microinstructions do not directly issue the signals that control the hardware. Instead, they are used to access a *second* control memory called a *nanocontrol memory* nCM that directly controls the hardware. In such cases there are two levels of control memories, a higher-level one termed a *microcontrol memory* μCM whose contents are microinstructions and the lower-level nCM that stores *nanoinstructions*—see Figure 5.51. The nanoprogramming concept was first used in the QM-l computer designed around 1970 by Nanodata Corp. It is also employed in the Motorola 680X0 microprocessors series [Stritter and Tredennick 1978].

Consider a nanoprogrammed computer in which μCM and nCM have dimensions $H_m \times W_m$ and $H_n \times W_n$, respectively. The advantage of this two-level control design technique is that it can reduce the total size $S_2 = H_m \times W_m + H_n \times W_n$ of the control memories, which translates to smaller chip area in the case of a one-chip CPU like the 680X0. Typically, the microprograms are encoded in a narrow vertical format so that although H_m is large, W_m is small. Nanoinstructions, on the other hand, usually have a highly parallel horizontal format making W_n large. If one nanoprogram can interpret many microinstructions, then H_n can be kept relatively small so that $S_2 < S_1 = H_m \times W_n$, which is roughly the size of a comparable single-level control unit. The potential for reducing the total size of the control memories is the main reason for the use of nanoprogramming in the 680X0 series. Another advantage is the greater design flexibility that results from loosening the bonds between instructions and hardware with two intermediate levels of control rather than one. These advantages motivated the QM-1, which had the goal of efficiently emulating the instruction sets of a wide variety of different computers. The main disadvantages of the two-level approach are a loss of speed due to the extra memory access for nCM and a more complex control-unit organization.

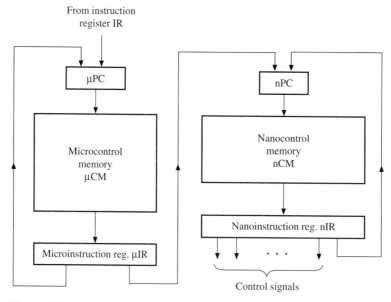

Figure 5.51
Two-level control store organization for nanoprogramming.

To see the savings in control-memory size that can result from the use of nano-programming, consider the analysis carried out by the designers of the 68000 microprocessor [Stritter and Tredennick 1978]. Suppose that one- and two-level control stores are characterized by the parameters shown in Figure 5.52. A one-level conventional CM is assumed to store H_m horizontal microinstructions each with a format consisting of N control bits and $\lceil \log_2 H_m \rceil$ next-address bits. The size of this memory is therefore

$$S_1 = H_m(N + \lceil \log_2 H_m \rceil) \tag{5.19}$$

In the two-level organization (Figure 5.52b), the microcontrol memory μCM again stores H_m microinstructions, but the N-bit control fields are transferred to nCM. In place of the latter, each microinstruction in μCM contains a $\lceil \log_2 H_n \rceil$-bit address to specify any nanoinstruction location in nCM. It is assumed that little or no branching takes place among nanoinstructions, so no explicit address bits are included in the model of nCM. Thus the size of the two-level control store is

$$S_2 = H_m(\lceil \log_2 H_m \rceil + \lceil \log_2 H_n \rceil) + NH_n \tag{5.20}$$

Suppose that all the control-bit patterns in nCM are different so that each represents a unique control state associated with the given instruction set. We can write $H_n = rH_m$, where r is the ratio of the number of unique control states to the total number H_n of control states needed to implement all instructions. Substituting into (5.20) yields

$$S_2 = H_m(\lceil \log_2 H_m \rceil + \lceil \log_2 rH_n \rceil + rN)$$

$$= H_m(2\lceil \log_2 H_m \rceil + \lceil \log_2 r \rceil + rN) \tag{5.21}$$

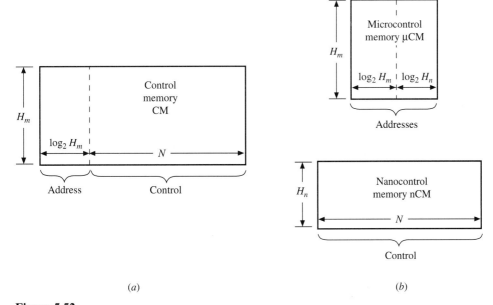

(a) (b)

Figure 5.52
Control memory models: (a) one level and (b) two level.

The following parameters are cited for the 68000 design: $N = 70$, $H_m = 650$, and $r = 0.4$ so that $H_n = 260$. Substituting into (5.20) and (5.21), we obtain $S_1 = 52,450$ and $S_2 = 30,550$. Consequently, the use of nanoprogramming saves a total of $52,450 - 30,550 = 21,850$ bits of control storage (42 percent of S_1). In general, two levels of control memory require less memory space if $S_2 < S_1$. Hence from (5.19) and (5.21), we conclude that the inequality

$$N \geq \lceil \log_2 H_m \rceil + \lceil \log_2 r \rceil + rN$$

must be satisfied.

5.3
PIPELINE CONTROL

Pipelining provides a basic way to speed up arithmetic operations, as we saw in Chapter 4. It is also used to implement the entire instruction-processing behavior of high-performance CPUs, a topic we examine in this section.

5.3.1 Instruction Pipelines

During program execution, instructions pass through a sequence of processing steps that lend themselves naturally to pipelining. Consequently, a CPU can be organized as one or more pipelines, whose various stages fetch opcodes and operands, execute instructions, and store results in local registers or external memory. In general, an *instruction pipeline* is a multifunction, reconfigurable pipeline designed to speed up a computer's performance by efficiently overlapping the processing of instructions. Such pipelines are contrasted with *arithmetic pipelines* of the type covered in section 4.3.2, which can, however, be built into instruction pipelines to implement the execution stages. An instruction pipeline is normally invisible to programmers and managed automatically by program compilers and by the CPU's internal program-control unit. Instruction pipelines were first used in the IBM 7030 (also known as Stretch) and a few other computers of the 1960s. They reemerged in the 1980s as key contributors to the high performance achieved by RISCs. Instruction pipelining has also been successfully incorporated into CISCs such as the 80X86/Pentium series, beginning with the 80486 microprocessor in 1989.

Pipeline structure. The general structure of a pipeline of m stages $S_1, S_2, \ldots, S_m$ appears in Figure 5.53 (which repeats Figure 4.47). When S_i has computed its results, it passes them, along with any unprocessed input operands, to S_{i+1} for further processing, and S_i receives a new set of operands from S_{i-1}. Thus the pipeline can contain up to m independent data sets, all in different stages of computation. Buffer registers and other synchronization logic are placed between stages so that the stages do not interfere with one another. The performance speedup of an instruction pipeline derives from the fact that up to m independent instructions can be in progress simultaneously in the m stages.

The simplest instruction pipeline breaks instruction processing into two parts: a fetch stage S_1 and an execute stage S_2. Thus a two-stage pipeline increases

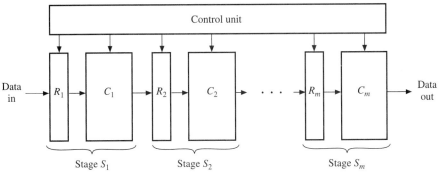

Figure 5.53
Structure of an *m*-stage pipeline.

throughput by overlapping instruction fetching and instruction execution. While instruction I_i with address A_i is being executed by stage S_2, the instruction I_{i+1} with the next consecutive address A_{i+1} is fetched from memory by stage S_1. If on executing I_i in S_2 it is determined that a branch must be made to a nonconsecutive address $A_j \neq A_{i+1}$, then the prefetched instruction I_{i+1} in S_1 has to be discarded. As we will see later, techniques exist to minimize the negative effect of branch instructions on pipeline performance.

Figure 5.54 shows an implementation of a two-stage instruction pipeline that is common in microprogrammed CPUs. It is the generic microprogrammed control unit of Figure 5.47 repackaged into two sequential stages. The fetch stage S_1 consists of the microprogram counter μPC, which is the source for microinstruction addresses, and the control memory CM, which stores the microinstructions. (CM is sometimes considered to lie outside the pipeline proper, with the task of feeding microinstructions "into" the pipeline.) Observe how μPC is appropriately positioned to be the buffer register for S_1. It is only necessary to increment μPC to obtain the next consecutive microinstruction address, which is then fetched while the current microinstruction is being executed in stage S_2. The execution stage S_2 contains the microinstruction register μIR, the decoders that extract control signals from the microinstructions in μIR, and the logic for choosing branch addresses. Another preexisting register, this time μIR, acts as the buffer register for stage S_2. Microinstruction execution is much simpler than the corresponding task at the instruction level. It involves decoding the control and condition-select fields of the current microinstruction μI stored in μIR, as well as distributing the resulting control signals. If μI specifies branching, the branch address is obtained directly from μI itself and fed back to S_1. There the branch address is loaded into μPC, replacing μPC's previous contents and causing any ongoing fetch operation in S_1 to be aborted.

Multistage pipelines. An *m*-stage instruction pipeline can overlap the processing of up to *m* instructions, so it is desirable to use more than two stages to maximize instruction throughput. The value of *m* depends on the maximum number of stages into which instruction processing can be efficiently broken. This number in turn depends on the complexity of the instruction set, the organization

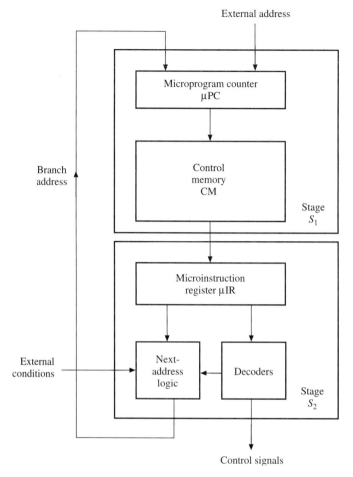

External address

Microprogram counter
μPC

Control
memory
CM

Branch
address

Stage
S_1

Microinstruction
register μIR

External
conditions

Next-
address
logic

Decoders

Stage
S_2

Control signals

Figure 5.54
Two-stage pipelined microprogram control unit.

of the external memory M, and the way in which the CPU's datapath is implemented. In practice, the number of pipeline stages ranges from three (in the case of the ARM6) to a dozen or more. Pipeline structure is complicated by the provision of alternative (parallel) stages, feedback paths, and feedforward (bypass) features.

Figure 5.55 shows a CPU organization that implements a four-stage instruction pipeline. We assume that the CPU is directly connected to a cache memory, which is split into instruction and data parts, called the I-cache and D-cache, respectively. This splitting of the cache permits both an instruction word and a memory data word to be accessed in the same clock cycle. Each stage makes use of certain common resources such as the cache and the register file RF, which can be regarded as external to the pipeline proper. The four stages $S_1:S_4$ of Figure 5.55 perform the following functions:

1. IF: instruction fetching and decoding using the I-cache.
2. OL: operand loading from the D-cache to RF.

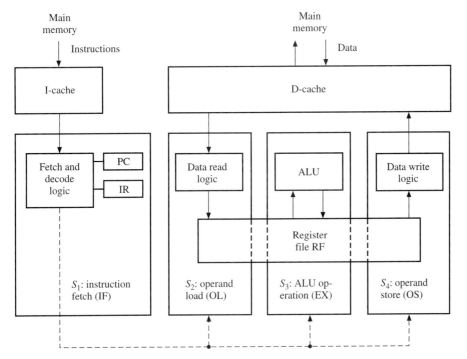

Figure 5.55
Organization of a CPU incorporating a four-stage instruction pipeline.

3. EX: data processing using the ALU and RF.
4. OS: operand storing to the D-cache from RF.

Stages S_2 and S_4 implement memory load and store operations, respectively, and are tailored to a load-store architecture. Stages S_2, S_3, and S_4 share the CPU's local registers in RF; these registers act as interstage buffer registers. The CPU's ALU is in stage S_3 and implements data-transfer and data-processing operations of the register-to-register type. If each stage completes its operation in a single CPU clock cycle of period T_C, the pipeline and the CPU as a whole can be clocked at a frequency of $f = 1/T_C$. At its maximum execution rate, which implies that no delays occur due to instruction branching, cache misses, or other causes, an ideal performance level of 1 clock cycle per instruction, or a *CPI* of 1, can be achieved.

We can vary the organization shown in Figure 5.55 in many ways to trade hardware cost for performance. For example, a less expensive D-cache cannot perform loads and stores simultaneously, in which case we can implement D-cache accesses in a single stage, thus merging S_2 and S_4 into a single load-store stage. Memory or register-file accesses are complicated by addressing modes such as indexing, which require an ALU to calculate a memory address before the access operation proper can be initiated. In such cases it may be desirable to add a stage, that is, a separate clock cycle, for operand address calculation. Instructions such as the more complicated arithmetic operations require multiple clock cycles for their execution; hence they require multiple cycles through the execution stage of a pipelined CPU. Such considerations, and the hardware/performance trade-offs they entail, give rise to the many different instruction pipeline organizations in contemporary computers.

EXAMPLE 5.7 PIPELINE ORGANIZATION OF THE MIPS R2/3000 [KANE AND HEINRICH 1992]. The R2000 and R3000 are early members of the MIPS RX000 series of RISC microprocessors, which we discussed in Examples 3.5 and 3.7. They implement the same MIPS-I instruction-set architecture and have nearly identical CPU organizations, so we will treat them as a single machine denoted by R2/3000. Later members of the same series have numerous architectural extensions and far more complex instruction pipelines.

The R2/3000 employs a five-stage instruction pipeline whose stages have the following functions designed to meet the goal of completing one instruction per clock cycle:

1. IF: instruction fetching using the I-cache.
2. RD: operand loading (reading) from the register file RF while decoding the fetched instruction.
3. EX: data processing using the ALU and RF as needed.
4. MA: operand accessing (load or store) using the D-cache.
5. WB: operand storing (writing back) to RF.

Comparing this pipeline organization with that of Figure 5.55, we see that the first and third stages are roughly the same. The R2/3000's instruction-fetch (IF) stage is complicated by the use of virtual memory, which requires that the (virtual) addresses appearing in the input instruction stream be translated on the fly into physical addresses corresponding to the available main memory. Consequently, instruction decoding is deferred to the second stage of the pipeline. This operand-read (RD) stage also transfers any needed input operands from the CPU's 32-word register file RF in preparation for execution in stage 3 (EX). All memory data accesses (D-cache loads and stores) use stage 4 (MA), which transfers a data word between the CPU and the D-cache. The fifth or "write back" (WB) stage is used by load instructions to write a word fetched from the data cache into RF. The result of an ALU operation is also stored in RF during the WB stage.

Like other RISCs, the R2/3000 aims at single-cycle execution of its instructions. Figure 5.56 shows the ideal situation when, after a start-up phase during which it fills up, the instruction pipeline is fully utilized and outputs a new result every clock cycle.

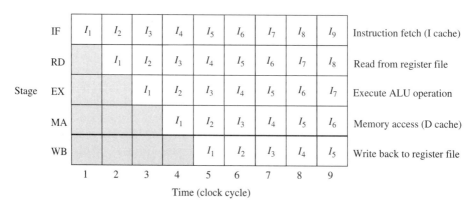

Figure 5.56

Maximum-rate instruction execution in the R2/3000 instruction pipeline.

If, in this "streaming" mode of operation, an instruction computes a new result in clock cycle i during the instruction's EX phase, that result can be used by another instruction in cycle $i + 1$. In some cases, notably load and branch instructions, this is not true, and delays occur due to the effects of an instruction on a subsequent one. For example, suppose that an instruction that loads a data word X into a register is immediately followed by an instruction that uses X in its EX stage. Then, as illustrated in Figure 5.57a, a one-cycle gap or *delay slot* occurs in the instruction stream because an LD (load) instruction's data is not available until after its MA cycle.

Several actions can be taken to deal with this situation:

- The pipeline can be temporarily halted or *stalled* whenever a load or branch instruction is executed. This action, however, complicates control of the pipeline and the synchronization of CPU operation and causes a loss in performance.
- A NOP (no operation) instruction can be inserted as shown in Figure 5.57b, which has the effect of synchronizing the issuing and execution of all instructions, none of which now needs to be delayed. This action does not improve the pipeline's performance, however.
- A nearby instruction that does not depend on X can be taken and repositioned in the instruction stream—which requires a smart compiler—immediately after the LD instruction. This approach is illustrated in Figure 5.57c, where the SUB instruction has been moved to fill LD's delay slot. Restructuring of this type is valid only if it does not alter the program's final results; for example, it requires that SUB not use the data fetched by LD as an input operand. The net effect is to make the pipeline operate at its maximum rate and to complete the four indicated instructions using one cycle fewer than before.

A similar delay problem arises in the case of branch instructions. The branch address computed by an R2/3000 branch instruction I does not become available for use until I's third (EX) stage, which creates a delay slot in I's second (RD) stage. Another instruction falling into this delay slot is executed, regardless of whether the branch is taken or not. Consequently, a compiler inserts a NOP into this slot unless, as in Figure 5.57c, the delay slot can be filled in some useful way that does not change the program's overall behavior.

Figure 5.58 summarizes the structure of another multistage instruction pipeline, that of the Amdahl 470V/7, a 1978-vintage machine designed to be compatible with the IBM System/370 series of mainframe computers [Amdahl 1978]. The 470V/7's memory system comprises a main memory and a single or *unified* cache (termed the high-speed buffer in Amdahl literature) intended for both instruction and data storage. The CPU is partitioned into a 12-stage pipeline, whose stages have the roles listed in Figure 5.58. These perform the same four functions as the generic pipeline of Figure 5.55, namely, instruction fetching and decoding (IF), operand loading (OL), instruction execution (EX), and, finally, operand storage (OS). Because of the many addressing modes and instruction types needed to support the 470V/7's CISC architecture, each of the preceding functions is subdivided into several pipeline stages. The first two stages S_1 and S_2 communicate with a memory control unit that is responsible for all accesses to main memory and the cache. These stages transfer instructions or data operands between the pipeline and the cache. All results are checked for errors in stage S_{11} using parity-check codes in most cases. If an error is detected, the instruction in question is automatically re-executed, an error-recovery technique called *instruction retry*.

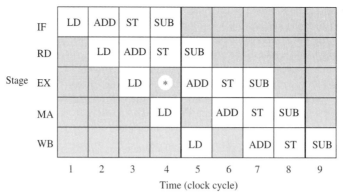

*Input operand of
ADD unavailable

(a)

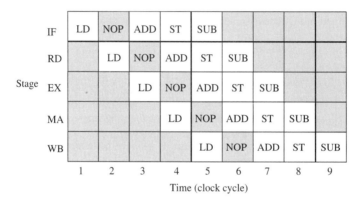

(b)

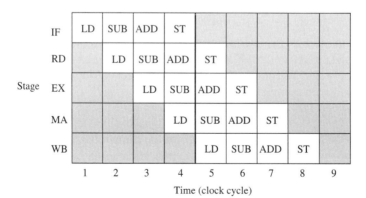

(c)

Figure 5.57
(a) R2/3000 pipeline delay slot caused by load instruction LD;
(b) use of NOP instruction to fill the delay slot; (c) use of SUB
instruction to eliminate the delay slot.

Function	Stage	Name	Action performed
Instruction fetch IF	S_1	Instruction address	Request next instruction from memory control unit
	S_2	Start buffer	Initiate cache to read instruction
	S_3	Read buffer	Read instruction from cache into I-unit
	S_4	Decode instruction	Decode opcode of instruction
Operand load OL	S_5	Read register	Read address (base and index) registers
	S_6	Compute address	Compute address of current memory operand
	S_7	Start buffer	Initiate cache to read memory operand
	S_8	Read buffer	Read operands from cache and register file
Execute instruction EX	S_9	Execute 1	Pass data to E-unit and begin instruction execution
	S_{10}	Execute 2	Complete instruction execution
Operand store OS	S_{11}	Check result	Perform code-based error check on result
	S_{12}	Write result	Store result

Figure 5.58
The stages of the Amdahl 470V/7 instruction pipeline.

In recent years the large number of pipeline stages illustrated by the 470V/7 have become common, because such fine-grained stages enable a pipeline to operate at higher clock frequencies. Multiple-instruction pipelines are also common, especially in *superscalar* processors, which can issue (dispatch) two or more instructions simultaneously. For example, each of the three functional units (E-units) of the PowerPC 601 microprocessor (Example 1.7) is implemented as a distinct pipeline; the structure and relationship of these pipelines are outlined in Figure 5.59 [Becker et al. 1993]. The 601 has an instruction buffer or queue that stores up to eight instructions which are prefetched from the single (unified) cache memory. In each clock cycle this buffer can send a separate instruction to each of the pipelined E-units. The two-stage branch-processing unit fetches and processes branch instructions. The five-stage fixed-point unit processes fixed-point ALU operations and also handles cache data accesses both for itself and for the floating-point unit. Some operations, such as multiply and divide, circulate repeatedly through the execute stage. The floating-point unit supports a full range of floating-point instructions, including a compound multiply-and-add instruction.

5.3.2 Pipeline Performance

The goal in controlling a pipelined CPU is to maximize its performance with respect to target workloads. After reviewing the performance measures applicable to instruction pipelines, we consider the factors that reduce performance and how they can be overcome.

Performance measures. A pipeline's performance can be measured by its *throughput* in terms of millions of instructions executed per second or *MIPS*. Another popular measure of performance is the number of clock cycles per instruction or *CPI*. These quantities are related by the equation

$$CPI = f/MIPS \qquad\qquad (5.22)$$

where f is the pipeline's clock frequency in MHz, and the values of *CPI* and *MIPS* are average figures that can be determined experimentally by processing suites of representative programs (benchmarks). The maximum value of *CPI* for a single pipeline is one, making the pipeline's maximum possible throughput equal to f. This throughput is attained only when the pipeline is supplied with a continuous stream of instructions that keep all its stages busy. Superscalar machines reduce *CPI* below one by executing several instruction streams simultaneously using multiple pipelines.

Figures 5.56 and 5.57 illustrate a useful way to visualize pipeline behavior called a *space-time diagram,* which shows the utilization of each pipeline stage as a function of time. In general, a space-time diagram for an *m*-stage pipeline has the form of an $m \times n$ grid, where n is the number of clock cycles to complete the processing of some sequence of N instructions of interest. Figure 5.60 shows a space-time diagram for the four-stage arithmetic pipeline of Example 4.8, which is executing a complex vector summation instruction denoted I. An unshaded box in these figures marks a busy stage S_i, and the box's entry denotes the particular instruction being processed by S_i. As the shading shows, some stages are not utilized at the beginning and end of the instruction sequence, when the pipeline must be filled and emptied (flushed), respectively. The stages are also underutilized if operands are not available when needed. The ratio of the unshaded (busy) area to

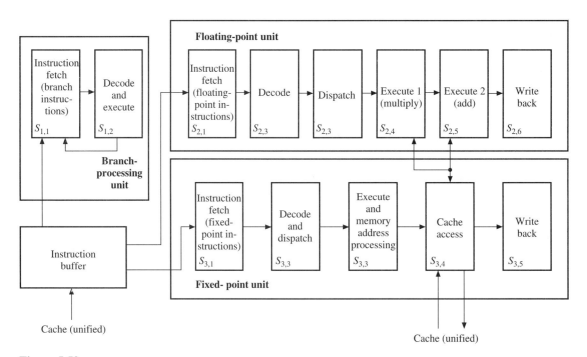

Figure 5.59
Instruction pipelining in the PowerPC 601.

the total (shaded and unshaded) area of a space-time diagram for an m-stage pipeline is defined as the *efficiency* or *utilization* $E(m)$ of the pipeline. In other words, $E(m)$ is the fraction of time the pipeline is busy. In the case of Figure 5.60, the efficiency is $E(4) = 44/76 = 0.58$. Note how the instruction reordering shown in Figure 5.57c improves the pipeline's efficiency by eliminating the delay slot.

Another general measure of pipeline performance is the *speedup S(m)* defined by

$$S(m) = \frac{T(1)}{T(m)} \qquad (5.23)$$

where $T(m)$ is the execution time for some target workload on an m-stage pipeline and $T(1)$ is the execution time for the same workload on a similar, nonpipelined processor. It is reasonable to assume that $T(1) \leq mT(m)$, in which case $S(m) \leq m$. A pipeline's efficiency and speedup are related as follows:

$$S(m) = m \times E(m) \qquad (5.24)$$

Hence for the example in Figure 5.60 where $m = 4$ and $E(4) = 0.58$, the speedup $S(4) = 4 \times 0.58 = 2.32$ and cannot exceed 4. In general, speedup and efficiency provide rough performance estimates which should be used with caution, since they depend on the programs being run. Their values can change drastically from program to program, or from one part of a program to another.

Optimizing m. Equation (5.24) suggests that an easy way to improve a pipeline's performance is to increase the number of stages m. This assumes that the pipeline's processing tasks can be subdivided in a useful way and that the cost of doing so is acceptable. Each new stage S_i introduces some new hardware cost and delay due to its buffer register R_i and associated control logic. We now analyze the trade-offs involved in doing this [Kogge 1981; Hwang 1993]. In particular, we will determine the pipeline's *performance/cost ratio PCR* defined as

$$PCR = \frac{f}{K} \qquad (5.25)$$

where f is the pipeline's clock frequency and K is its hardware cost.

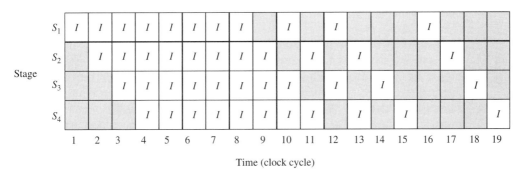

Figure 5.60
Space-time diagram for a four-stage pipeline.

Suppose the pipeline P has m stages and implements a particular set of operations (instructions) SI. Let a be the delay (latency) of an efficient, nonpipelined processor that also implements SI. It is reasonable to assume that each stage S_i of P has delay a/m—that is, m times less than the corresponding nonpipelined processor—plus some extra delay b due to S_i's buffer register R_i. Hence if $T_C = 1/f$ is P's clock period, we can write

$$T_C = a/m + b \qquad (5.26)$$

The pipeline's hardware cost can be estimated by

$$K = cm + d \qquad (5.27)$$

where c is the buffer-register cost per stage and d is the cost of the pipeline's (combinational) data-processing logic. Hence from (5.25), (5.26), and (5.27) we have $PCR^{-1} = T_C K = (a/m + b)(cm + d)$, so

$$PCR = m/[bcm^2 + (ac + bd)m + ad] \qquad (5.28)$$

To maximize PCR with respect to the number of stages m, we differentiate (5.28) with respect to m and equate the result to zero. Using the standard differentiation-by-parts formula

$$\frac{d}{dx}\left(\frac{u}{v}\right) = \frac{1}{v}\frac{du}{dx} - \frac{u}{v^2}\frac{dv}{dx}$$

we obtain

$$\frac{d}{dm}(PCR) = 1/v - m(2bcm + ac + bd)/v^2 \qquad (5.29)$$

where $u = m$ and $v = bcm^2 + (ac + bd)m + ad$. On equating (5.29) to zero, we get $v = m(2acm + ad + bc)$. Substituting for v and solving for m yields the value m_{opt} of m that maximizes PCR, namely,

$$m_{opt} = \sqrt{\frac{ad}{bc}} \qquad (5.30)$$

The optimum number of stages is the integer closest to m_{opt}. Figure 5.61 plots PCR against m according to (5.28) for $a = d = 5$ and $b = c = 1$. The optimum value of m is five, as predicted by (5.30). Hence in this instance, the maximum throughput per unit of hardware cost or, equivalently, the minimum cost per instruction processed, occurs when the pipeline has five stages.

Collisions. As discussed in section 4.3.2 pipelines can have feedback paths that enable a stage to be used repeatedly while processing a single instruction. In Figure 5.60, for example, each stage is used many times while processing the instruction I (vector summation). A new instruction of the same kind cannot be started until clock cycle 17, after I uses stage S_1 for the last time. If a second instruction is initiated at the wrong time—at $t = 9$, for instance—then both instructions will attempt to use stage S_1 at $t = 10$, a situation termed a *collision*. However, a simple add instruction of the kind in Figure 5.57 could be initiated at $t = 9, 11, 13, 14,$ or 15 without colliding with the sum instruction I. Thus up to five add instructions, if available for execution at the right times, could be interleaved with the eight-element sum operation, thereby increasing the pipeline's overall efficiency.

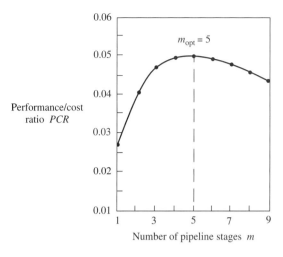

Figure 5.61
Performance/cost ratio PCR for an m-stage pipeline.

In general, pipeline collisions of the foregoing type are avoided by carefully scheduling the times at which new pipeline operations are initiated. We present a pipeline control strategy to avoid collisions and maximize performance in a pipeline with feedback or feedforward connections [Kogge 1981; Stone 1993]. Let P be such a pipeline that consists of m stages $S_1, S_2, \ldots, S_m$ and executes an instruction of type I. (Later we will consider the problem of scheduling different types of instructions in the same pipeline.) We can represent I's usage of the pipeline with a space-time diagram (refer to Figure 5.60), which indicates stage usage in every clock cycle while I is being executed. We will also represent the same information in a slightly different form R called a *reservation table*. The m rows of R represent the stages of P, while the columns represent the sequence of clock cycles required for one complete execution of I by P. An $\times$ is placed at the intersection of row S_i and column C_j if stage S_i is used by I in clock cycle $t = j$. Figure 5.62a shows the reservation table corresponding to Figures 4.52 and 5.60. If the method of Figure 4.52 is used to sum the pair of numbers b_1, b_2, then the small reservation table of Figure 5.62b results.

Two operations of type I that are initiated k clock cycles apart collide at stage S_i of P, if row i of the corresponding reservation table R contains two $\times$s that are separated by a horizontal distance of k. In the case of Figure 5.62b, a collision occurs at every stage if $k = 1, 4$, or 5, as is easily verified. For example, if the first instruction is initiated at $t = 1$ and the second at $t = 5$, in which case $k = 4$, then both instructions will attempt to use all four stages and collide at $t = 6$. Let F be the set of numbers, called the *forbidden list* of R, whose entries are the distances, that is, the numbers of clock cycles between all distinct pairs of $\times$s in every row of R. The collision conditions for R are characterized by the following easily proven result: Two pipeline instructions initiated k clock cycles apart collide if and only if k is in the forbidden list F of R. Thus we can easily meet the fundamental requirement of avoiding collisions by delaying new instructions by time periods *not* appearing in the forbidden list. Much less obvious is how to schedule initiation times that maximize the pipeline's performance.

The maximum number of collision-free operations that can be initiated per unit time under steady-state conditions corresponds to the pipeline's throughput defined

Time t

Stage	1	2	3	4	5	6	7	8	9	10	11	12	13	14	15	16	17	18	19
S_1	×	×	×	×	×	×	×	×		×		×				×			
S_2		×	×	×	×	×	×	×	×		×		×				×		
S_3			×	×	×	×	×	×	×	×			×		×			×	
S_4				×	×	×	×	×	×	×	×			×		×			×

(a)

Time t

Stage	1	2	3	4	5	6	7	8	9
S_1	×	×				×			
S_2		×	×				×		
S_3			×	×				×	
S_4				×	×				×

(b)

Figure 5.62
Pipeline reservation tables for N-element vector summation: (*a*) $N = 8$ corresponding to Figure 5.60 and (*b*) $N = 2$.

by Equation (5.22). The delay occurring between the start of two successive, collision-free pipeline instructions is called the *initiation latency,* or simply the *latency* L in this context. Under steady-state operating conditions, L corresponds to the pipeline's *CPI* and is measured in clock cycles. We now turn to the problem of devising control strategies that maximize the performance of a basic, single-function pipeline by determining the best values of L to use for collision-free operation.

We denote the minimum value of the initiation latency L, that is, the *minimum average latency* by L_{min}. A simpler goal is to achieve the *minimum constant latency,* defined as the smallest fixed value L_{cmin} of L such that any number of instructions can be initiated L clock cycles apart without causing collisions. Clearly, $L_{min} \leq L_{cmin}$. The number L_{cmin} can be calculated from the forbidden list F using the fact that L_{cmin} is the smallest integer L such that hL is not in F for any integer $h \geq 1$. The forbidden lists for the reservation tables of Figures 5.62*a* and 5.62*b* are {1, 2, 3, 4, 5, 6, 7, 8, 9, 10, 11, 12, 13, 14, 15} and {1, 4, 5}, respectively. Thus, as observed earlier, successive sum instructions with the reservation table of Figure 5.62*a* must be initiated at least 16 clock cycles apart, since the latencies L_{min} and L_{cmin} are both 16. In the case of Figure 5.62*b*, new instructions can be initiated as few as two cycles apart. However, the minimum constant latency $L_{cmin} \neq 2$, because $2 \times 2 = 4$ is in F; in this case $L_{cmin} = 3$. If instructions are initiated at $t = 1$ and 3, a third instruction cannot be initiated until $t = 9$, as demonstrated by the space-time diagram of Figure 5.63*a*. The average initiation latency for the pipeline scheduling scheme defined by Figure 5.63*b* is four, because two new instructions

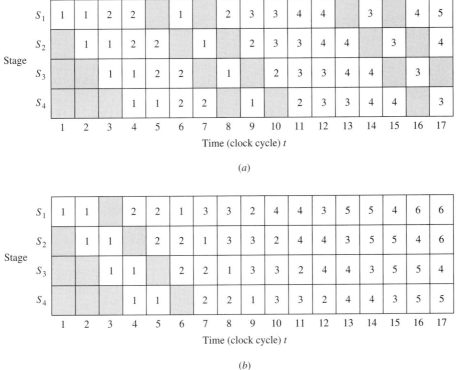

Figure 5.63
Pipeline scheduling strategies for the reservation table of Figure 5.62b: (a) nonoptimal and (b) optimal.

are initiated every eight clock cycles. The minimum average latency is achieved for this example when new operations are initiated $L_{min} = 3$ clock cycles apart, as in Figure 5.63b. Observe that in the latter case the steady-state efficiency of the pipeline is 100 percent.

Control scheme. An elegant way to control a pipeline for collision-free operation is by computing collision vectors. A *collision vector* CV for a reservation table R at time t is a binary vector $c_1 c_2 \cdots c_{M-1} c_M$, where the *ith* bit c_i is 1 if initiating a pipeline instruction at $t + i$ results in a collision; c_i is 0 otherwise. An *initial collision vector* CV_0 is obtained from the forbidden list F of R as follows. Element c_i of CV_0 is set to 1 if i is in F, and c_i is set to 0 otherwise, for $i = 1,2,\ldots,M$, where M is the maximum element in F. A convenient way to store CV is in a shift register CR = $CR_1:CR_M$ called a *collision register*. By inspecting CR_1 at time t, we can determine whether issuing a new instruction in the next clock cycle $t + 1$ will result in a collision. A simple left shift of CR, with the right-most bit CR_M set to 0 prepares CR_1 for inspection in the next clock cycle. If we decide to initiate a new instruction at $t + 1$, then CR is left shifted and its contents are replaced by CR *or* CV_0, where CV_0 is the initial collision vector obtained from F as specified above and *or* denotes the bitwise OR operation. These actions ensure that CR defines all the collision possibilities due either to ongoing pipeline operations or to the newly initiated one.

To illustrate the foregoing concepts, consider again the reservation table in Figure 5.62b. Since $F = \{1, 4, 5\}$, $M = 5$ and the corresponding initial collision vector CV_0 is 10011. The collision register CR is initialized to 00000. When it is decided, say, at $t = 0$, to start the first pipeline instruction at $t = 1$, CR is left shifted and ORed with CV_0, resulting in CR = 00000 *or* 10011 = 10011 = CV_0. At $t = 1$ the new pipeline instruction is initiated, and CR is again inspected. Since $CR_1 = 1$, we conclude that a new instruction must be delayed; CR is merely shifted during this cycle, changing its contents to 00110. At $t = 2$, CR contains 00110 with $CR_1 = 0$, allowing a new instruction to start at $t = 3$. If a second pipeline operation is initiated in the next cycle, CR is shifted and ORed with CV_0, therefore becoming 01100 *or* 10011 = 11111 at $t = 3$. Five subsequent shifts are needed before CR_1 again becomes zero at $t = 8$. A third instruction cannot therefore begin until $t = 9$, as shown by Figure 5.63a. If no new task is started at $t = 3$, CR is 01100, indicating that a new instruction can begin at $t = 4$. If a new instruction is then initiated at $t = 4$, CR becomes successively 11000 and 11000 *or* 10011 = 11011, implying that a third instruction can begin at $t = 7$; Figure 5.63b depicts this situation. Observe that at $t = 6$, CR becomes 01100, repeating the pattern encountered at $t = 3$.

Task-initiation diagram. We can derive an optimal collision-free schedule for initiating pipeline operations from the state behavior of the collision register CR. For this purpose we construct a condensed state-transition graph for CR called a *task-initiation diagram* (TID). The states of the TID are all the collision vectors $\{CV_i\}$ formed by the operation CR *or* CV_0, when new pipeline operations can be initiated. (The other states of CR are formed by shifting these vectors and are excluded from the TID.) An arrow from CV_i to CV_j indicates that there is a sequence of state transitions that changes CR's state from CV_i to CV_j; the arrow is labeled with the minimum number of state transitions n_{ij} required. Thus n_{ij} denotes the minimum latency between the initiations represented by the TID states CV_i and

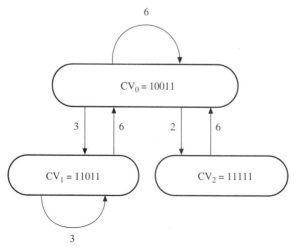

Figure 5.64
Task-initiation diagram (TID)
for Figure 5.63b.

CV_j. A closed path or loop in the TID corresponds to the task initiation schedule for the pipeline that can be sustained indefinitely without collisions. Let s be the sum of the n_{ij} labels along the arrows forming the loop divided by the number of arrows in the loop. Clearly, s is the average latency of the corresponding schedule of pipeline task initiations. Therefore, the average latency of the pipeline is minimized by choosing a task sequence corresponding to a loop of the TID with a minimum value of s, which is then the minimum average initiation latency L_{min} [Kogge 1981].

Figure 5.64 shows the TID derived from the reservation table of Figure 5.62b, where the initial collision vector $CV_0 = 10011$. This TID is obtained in straightforward fashion by examining all the possible states and state transitions of the corresponding CR as described earlier. The states included in the TID are all those loaded into SR when new operations can be initiated, namely, the three states $CV_0 = 10011$, $CV_1 = 11011$, and $CV_2 = 11111$ identified above. For example, the self-loop labeled 3 on state CV_1 is a consequence of the following sequence of state transitions involving CR:

Clock cycle	State of CR	Actions taken
t	$11011 = CV_1$	Initiate new instruction. Left shift CR.
$t+1$	10110	Left shift CR.
$t+2$	01100	Select new instruction to initiate. Left shift CR. CR := CR *or* $CV_0 = 11000$ *or* 10011.
$t+3$	$11011 = CV_1$	Initiate new instruction. Left shift CR.

The TID of Figure 5.64 contains several loops corresponding to pipeline control strategies with different average initiation latencies. For example, the loop formed by the two arrows linking CV_0 and CV_2 has an average initiation latency of $(2 + 6)/2 = 4$ cycles and corresponds to the space-time diagram of Figure 5.63a. The self-loop of state CV_1 has the minimum average latency $L_{min} = 3$ and therefore maximizes pipeline performance; using this loop for pipeline control yields the space-time diagram of Figure 5.63b. The analysis confirms our previous observation that the optimum scheduling strategy for this example is to initiate a new instruction three cycles after the previous instruction. Hence a simple logic circuit based on a modulo-3 counter suffices to control this particular pipeline.

The progress of an instruction stream through a pipeline can be delayed by various unfavorable dependency relationships among instructions and their data operands, which are collectively referred to as *hazards*. We now define the main types of pipeline hazards and discuss some general ways to detect them and reduce their impact on performance.

Control dependencies. Conditional and unconditional jumps, subroutine calls, and other program-control instructions that involve branching can adversely affect the performance of an instruction pipeline. In these cases the address of the next instruction is not known with certainty until after the program-control instruction I has been executed. Hence the question arises: Which instructions should be entered into the pipeline immediately after *I*? If these happen to be the wrong instructions, that is, *I* causes a jump to a distant part of the program, then provision must be made to cancel the effects of the partially executed instructions. This process is sometimes termed *flushing* the pipeline and clearly reduces its throughput. In the case of a two-way branch, it is sometimes worthwhile for the compiler or the pipeline's control logic to "guess" the direction of the branch, that is, to anticipate the outcome of the branch condition test, and enter the instruction at *I*'s more likely target address into the pipeline immediately after *I*. This process is known as *speculative* execution. Pipeline flushing is then needed only when the wrong guess has been made.

We can estimate the influence of branch instructions on the performance of an instruction pipeline as follows. Suppose that the pipeline has *m* stages and that each instruction requires *m* clock cycles, corresponding to one complete pass through the pipeline. If there are no branch instructions in the instruction streams being processed, then an ideal throughput of one instruction per clock cycle is achieved; that is, $CPI = 1$. Let *p* be the probability of encountering a branch instruction, and let *q* be the probability that execution of a branch instruction *I* causes a jump to a nonconsecutive address. Assume that each such jump requires the pipeline to be flushed, destroying all ongoing instruction processing, when *I* emerges from the last stage (a pessimistic assumption).

Now consider an instruction sequence of length *r* that is streaming through the pipeline. The number of instructions causing branches to take place is *pqr*, and these instructions are executed at a rate of $1/m$ instructions per cycle. The remaining $(1 - pq)r$ nonbranching instructions are processed at the maximum rate of one instruction per cycle. Hence the total number of cycles n_c needed to process all *r* instructions is

$$n_c = pqrm + (1 - pq)r$$

This implies that the average *CPI* of the pipeline, which by definition is n_c/r, is given by

$$CPI = 1 + pq(m - 1) \qquad (5.31)$$

with the optimum value $CPI = 1$ occurring when $q = 0$, that is, when no branching occurs during program execution. Note that a comparable nonpipelined instruction processor has $CPI = m$. If $p = 0.2$, $q = 0.4$, and $m = 5$, which are typical values for instruction pipelines, then (5.31) implies that $CPI = 1.32$. Hence, in this case, pipelining reduces the number of cycles per instruction from 5 to 1.32, an improvement by a factor of about four. The improvement is less for longer pipelines, since each branch to a nonconsecutive instruction address causes more partially processed instructions to be discarded. A compiler or programmer can increase throughput by employing fewer branch instructions (to reduce *p*) and by constructing conditional branch instructions so that the more probable results of the condition tests cause no branching (to reduce *q*).

Pipelined computers employ various hardware techniques to minimize the performance degradation due to branching. The Amdahl 470V/7, for example, has special branch-resolution logic to send the result of a branch condition test from the E-unit to the I-unit before the conditional branch instruction has been completely processed. This logic allows the I-unit to initiate processing of the correct next

instruction with a loss of data in only 3 of its 12 pipeline stages. A different
approach is taken by the IBM 3033. Its cache is divided into three separate instruction buffer areas: One holds a normal sequence of consecutive instructions
prefetched under the assumption that no branches will occur; the other two buffers
hold prefetched instruction sequences starting at up to two branch addresses specified by previously decoded branch instructions. Thus when the 3033's CPU
decodes an unconditional branch instruction of the form **go to** A_j, and has an
instruction buffer with available space, it proceeds to prefetch and process instructions starting at location A_j. In the case of a two-way conditional branch instruction
with two target branch addresses A_j and A_k, the CPU selects one branch address for
prefetching. If, when the conditional branch instruction is subsequently executed, it
turns out that the wrong selection was made by the CPU, then time is lost while the
correct instruction is fetched. If the CPU has anticipated the outcome of the condition test correctly, then the required next instruction is either already in the instruction pipeline or is stored in an instruction buffer.

RISC machines rely on instruction pipelines that overlap instruction fetch and
execute to achieve single-cycle execution for most instructions. As we saw in the
case of the MIPS R2/3000 (Example 5.7), special measures are taken to nullify the
delay slots associated with load and branch instructions. A closely related technique
called *delayed branching* is used in some RISCs to reduce the penalty due to pipeline
flushes on program branching. A delayed branch instruction I_1 causes the instruction
I_2 immediately following I_1 to be executed while the instruction I' at the target
address specified by I_1 is still being fetched. The execution of I' then follows that of
I_2 rather than following that of I_1, as would normally be the case. For example, the
IBM 801, the prototype RISC processor, has an alternative *branch-with-execute*
form of every normal branch instruction [Radin 1983]. Thus the instruction
sequence

$$\text{LOAD R1, A}$$
$$\text{BNZ L} \qquad (5.32)$$

for the 801 containing the normal conditional branch instruction BNZ (branch if
nonzero) idles the CPU while the instruction at the branch address L is being
fetched. Suppose that BNZ is replaced by the corresponding branch-and-execute
instruction BNZX and the instruction order is reversed as follows:

$$\text{BNZX L}$$
$$\text{LOAD R1, A} \qquad (5.33)$$

The modified code (5.33) has the same meaning as (5.32), but now the LOAD
instruction is executed while the instruction specified by BNZX is being fetched.
The compiler of the 801 is able to translate about 60 percent of program branches
into the more efficient branch-with-execute form.

Data dependencies. An m-stage pipeline operates at its maximum performance level when it contains m different instructions, each in a different stage of
computation. As we have seen, problems can occur if the decision to execute a particular instruction depends on the outcome of an earlier branch instruction. This
problem is due to the program's flow of control and so is called a *control dependency*. Other, more subtle *data dependencies* can exist among the operands being

processed by different instructions and can also reduce the pipeline's throughput. For example, suppose that instruction I_1 changes the contents of register R and that R is read by a subsequent instruction I_2 in the generic instruction pipeline of Figure 5.55. If I_2 is in stage S_2 (operand read) while I_1 is in stage S_3 (execute), then I_2 will read an old, and possibly erroneous value of R, since I_1 does not write its result to R until it reaches stage S_4. Thus although the instructions have been dispatched in the proper order required by the program, their read and write steps can be processed in a logically incorrect order within the pipeline. This data dependency problem is known as a *read-after-write* (RAW) *hazard*. It is solved by requiring I_1 to complete its execution before I_2 enters the operand read stage, which may mean reducing the throughput of the pipeline.

To identify hazards of the foregoing type, we consider the sets of input and output operands (registers or memory locations) associated with each instruction I_j entering the pipeline. The set of input operands of I_j is defined as the *domain* of I_j and is denoted by $D(I_j)$; the set of output operands of I_j is its *range* and is denoted by $R(I_j)$. For example, the instruction I for the MIPS R2/3000

$$\text{ADD} \quad \text{R1,R2,R3}$$

which denotes the 32-bit addition R1 := R2 + R3, has the domain $D(I) = \{R2,R3\}$ and the range $R(I) = \{R1\}$. If I_2 follows I_1 in program order, then a RAW hazard indicating a potential error situation exists if $R(I_1)$ and $D(I_2)$ contain a common operand. This condition is expressed formally as

$$R(I_1) \cap D(I_2) \neq \emptyset \qquad \text{(RAW hazard)} \qquad (5.34)$$

where $\cap$ denotes set intersection and $\emptyset$ denotes the empty set.

A similar problem called a *write-after-read* (WAR) *hazard* is present if the condition

$$D(I_1) \cap R(I_2) \neq \emptyset \qquad \text{(WAR hazard)} \qquad (5.35)$$

holds. In this case an error occurs if the second instruction I_2 modifies an operand before it can be read by the first instruction I_1. Unlike the RAW hazard, a WAR hazard cannot occur in a pipeline such as that of the R2/3000 (Figure 5.56) because of the relative positions of the read and the write stages. The only stage that reads from registers is S_2 (RD), which precedes the only stage S_5 (WB) that writes to registers, so by the time I_2 reaches the write stage, I_1 has left the pipeline. Only one stage S_4 (MA) controls memory reads and writes, and I_1 always reaches this stage before I_2.

A third type of data-dependency hazard is defined by

$$W(I_1) \cap W(I_2) \neq \emptyset \qquad \text{(WAW hazard)} \qquad (5.36)$$

and is known as a *write-after-write* (WAW) *hazard*. It is present if the pipeline allows I_2 to modify an operand before the same operand is modified by I_1. The RAW, WAR, and WAW hazards are also known as *true, anti,* and *output* data dependencies, respectively. Clearly, data-dependent hazards depend on both the structure of the instruction pipeline and the order of the instructions that access common registers or memory locations.

A pipeline hazard due to a data dependency can be detected by checking for the necessary conditions given by (5.34), (5.35), and (5.36), either during compilation (*static hazard detection*) or at run time (*dynamic hazard detection*). Such a hazard can be avoided by preventing the second member I_2 of a hazardous instruction pair (I_1,I_2) from entering a read or write stage until the first instruction I_1 has exited from the subsequent read or write stage associated with the hazard. As in the case of the control (branch instruction) hazards discussed earlier, we can avoid the hazard by delaying I_2 either by stalling it, preceding it by one or more NOPs, or—most efficiently—reordering the instruction stream so that useful instructions, which neither slow down the instruction stream nor alter program behavior, are placed between I_1 and I_2.

Another way to reduce the delays due to hazards is to build into the pipeline extra operand-transfer paths that permit faster exchange of shared information among interacting instructions. Consider, for example, a five-stage pipeline like that of the MIPS R2/3000. A result R computed by the ALU in stage S_3 (EX) is not written into the register file until stage S_5 (WB) two cycles later. By adding an operand-transfer "forwarding" path P_a from the output S_4 to the input of S_2 (RD), the result X computed by I_1 can be made available to I_2 one cycle earlier than before. As shown in Figure 5.65, we can even forward X from the output of S_3 to the input of the same stage via another path P_b so that X is supplied with no delay penalty to an ALU instruction I_2 that immediately follows I_1. While forwarding paths of this type reduce the delay penalties associated with hazard avoidance, they also add considerable complexity to the pipeline's control logic.

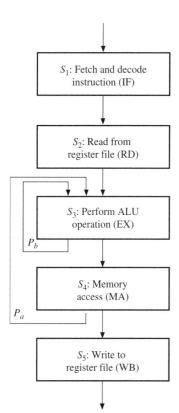

Figure 5.65
Pipeline with forwarding paths to reduce hazard-caused delays.

5.3.3 Superscalar Processing

Microprocessors such as the PowerPC (Figure 5.59) reach performance levels greater than one instruction per cycle—that is, a *CPI* figure less than one—by fetching, decoding, and executing several instructions concurrently. This mode of operation is called *superscalar*. A superscalar computer has a single CPU that attempts to exploit the parallelism that is implicit in ordinary (sequential) computer programs. It is contrasted with a *parallel* computer, which can have more than one CPU and is designed to execute programs whose parallelism is explicit at a high, application level; we discuss parallel computers in section 7.3.

Characteristics. Superscalar operation requires a processor to detect and exploit instruction-level parallelism hidden in the programs it executes. A superscalar CPU has multiple execution units (E-units), each of which is usually pipelined, so that they constitute a set of independent instruction pipelines. The CPU's program control unit PCU is designed to fetch and decode several instructions concurrently. It can *issue* or *dispatch* up to k instructions simultaneously to the various E-units where k, the *instruction-issue degree*, can be six or more using current technology. The need to process so many instructions simultaneously without performance-degrading conflicts greatly complicates the design of the PCU. Figure 5.66 shows in idealized form the differences in instruction-processing abilities between three CPU organizations: a sequential (nonpipelined) processor, a basic pipelined processor, and a superscalar processor, all of which are executing the same instruction stream $I_1, I_2, I_3, \ldots$ Assuming that each instruction requires a total of five cycles, we see that a single five-stage instruction pipeline ($k = 1$) offers a speedup of 5, while the two-issue ($k = 2$) superscalar design has a potential speedup of 10. Observe that at the start of cycle 15, the sequential CPU has completed only two instructions, whereas the pipelined and superscalar machines have completed 10 and 20 instructions, respectively; moreover, the superscalar CPU has already started processing instructions I_{21} through I_{30}.

As Figure 5.66 illustrates, the presence of k independent m-stage pipelined E-units enables a superscalar CPU to achieve speedup factors approaching $k \times m$, compared to a CPU that has no instruction-level parallelism. Keeping k pipelines busy requires the CPU to fetch at least k instructions per clock cycle; hence superscalar designs place heavy demands on the instruction-fetch logic. The resulting high volume of instruction traffic from the program memory to the CPU requires the system to have a large, fast cache, often in the form of an instruction-only cache (I-cache) for program storage, complemented by a data-only D-cache for operand storage. Instruction fetching is supported by an *instruction buffer* or *queue,* a storage unit within the CPU that serves as a staging area for prefetched and (partially) decoded instructions. The PCU dispatches the instructions from its instruction buffer to the various E-units for execution.

The PCU of a superscalar machine is responsible for determining when each instruction can be executed and for providing it with access to the resources it needs, such as memory operands, E-units, and CPU registers, in a prompt and efficient manner. To do so, it must take the following factors into account:

- *Instruction type:* For example, a floating-point add instruction has to be issued to a floating-point E-unit and not to an integer E-unit.

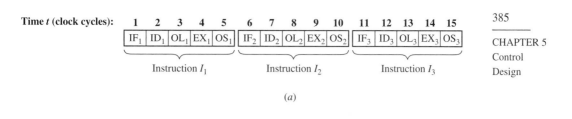

Figure 5.66
Maximum parallelism in (*a*) a sequential CPU; (*b*) a CPU with a five-stage instruction pipeline; (*c*) a superscalar CPU with two five-stage instruction pipelines.

- *E-unit availability:* An instruction can be issued to a pipelined E-unit only if no collisions will result, as determined by the pipeline's reservation table.
- *Data dependencies:* To avoid conflicting use of registers, data-dependency constraints among the operands of the active instructions must be satisfied.
- *Control dependencies:* To maintain high performance levels, techniques are needed to reduce the impact of branch instructions on pipeline efficiency.
- *Program order:* Instructions must eventually produce results in the order specified by the program being executed. The results may, however, be computed out-of-order internally to improve the CPU's performance.

Delaying a problematic instruction before it enters an instruction pipeline can prevent conflicts. Such static scheduling of instructions can occur during program compilation, for example, by implementing the collision-avoidance technique discussed in section 5.3.1. We can improve throughput, however, by issuing all instructions as rapidly as possible and resolving any subsequent conflicts on the fly. We next discuss two control techniques that address these issues: dynamic instruction scheduling and the branch prediction.

Dynamic instruction scheduling. Sophisticated resource scheduling techniques were implemented in some high-performance computers of the 1960s, notably Control Data Corp.'s CDC 6600 and IBM's System/360 Model 91 [Smith 1989]. We outline a method known as *Tomasulo's algorithm,* after its inventor R. M. Tomasulo, who developed it to schedule floating-point instructions in the Model 91 [Tomasulo 1967]. This method is used in several variations for dynamic instruction scheduling in recent superscalar microprocessors.

Tomasulo's approach provides each shared E-unit F_i with a set of *reservation stations* whose purpose is to receive instructions that use F_i, keep track of these instructions' operands, and when all the operand values needed by a waiting instruction I_j become available, initiate execution of I_j by F_i. A reservation station can thus be seen as implementing a *virtual* E-unit of type F_i to which an instruction can be sent immediately on decoding it; however, the instruction may not actually be executed until some later time. While one instruction I_j is delayed at a reservation station waiting for operands, another instruction I_k waiting at the same E-unit whose operands become available sooner can be executed first, even if I_k follows I_j in the program order.

To handle data dependencies, operand values can be reassigned to temporary (virtual) registers at the reservation station, a technique referred to as *register renaming.* A large set of temporary registers is typically needed to support the scheduling of many instructions. Several such registers at different reservation stations can be assigned to the same program variable such as a register operand R[i], which allows several values of R[i] to be maintained concurrently without conflicts. A temporary register is marked by a "tag" to indicate whether the operand value it contains is valid (to prevent an instruction from reading an obsolete value) and whether there are uncompleted instructions that need that particular value (to prevent premature overwriting of a valid value). A reservation station keeps count of the number of instructions waiting for a data value to appear in its result register R[j]; it does not mark R[j] as free to be updated until all the instructions waiting for R[j]'s new value have received it. The Model 91 employed a special bus, called the *common data bus,* to automatically route operand values as they became available to the reservation stations of the waiting instructions.

Consider, for example, the following three-instruction sequence:

R[1] := ALPHA   Instruction I_1 (load)

R[2] := R[1] + R[2]   Instruction I_2 (add)

R[3] := R[4] + R[5]   Instruction I_3 (add)

A superscalar CPU can fetch and decode all three instructions simultaneously, or nearly simultaneously. If the current value of the operand ALPHA in the first instruction I_1 is in main memory, but not in the D-cache (a cache miss), the execution of I_1 is delayed by several cycles. In that case I_1 is sent to a reservation station in the memory control logic—which is treated as an E-unit for scheduling purposes—and I_1's R[1] operand is assigned to a temporary register there, say, TR[3].

Execution of I_1 then stalls until ALPHA arrives and TR[3] is tagged as unavailable. (The current value of R[1] is in some temporary register, which can contain a value that is valid for some earlier instructions still in process elsewhere in the CPU.) The second instruction I_2 is sent to an add unit where it is delayed by the fact that its R[1] operand, which the PCU points to as being assigned to TR[3], is unavailable; thus I_2 is placed in a reservation station at the adder. In the meantime, if all the operand values needed by the third instruction I_3 are available, I_3 can be executed—out of order—by the add unit. When ALPHA eventually arrives in the CPU, I_1 is executed by loading ALPHA into TR[3], whose tag is then changed to indicate that a valid result is now available. At that point I_2 can also be executed in the next available cycle of the add unit.

Branch prediction. A two-way conditional branch instruction of the form

$$\textbf{if } C \textbf{ then } I_1 \textbf{ else } I_2 \tag{5.37}$$

can cause control-dependency delays in an instruction pipeline because the branch's target address, which is the address of either I_1 or I_2, is not known until the condition C has been computed and checked. The delayed-branching method described in section 5.3.2 is one way to mask such delays and has been implemented in many RISC microprocessors. Another increasingly popular and more powerful technique is to predict the value of C, which implies branching to I_j, and then proceed to execute the instructions $I_j, I_{j+1}, I_{j+2}, \ldots$ along the expected path before C's value is known. If the prediction is correct, then a performance gain has been made; if the prediction is wrong, then any instructions executed along the mispredicted path are cancelled. Because of its tentative nature, the execution of instructions before the correct path has been identified is termed *speculative*. Branch prediction and speculative execution require extensive instruction-level parallelism in the form of multiple E-units, temporary data registers, and so forth, which, as we have just seen, are also needed for dynamic instruction scheduling. Like dynamic scheduling, branch prediction techniques were not widely used until the 1990s.

Computer programs have certain characteristics that make it possible to predict instruction addresses. The normal fetching of instructions from consecutive memory addresses depends on an implicit prediction that consecutively executed instructions have consecutive addresses. This simple prediction fails in the case of branch instructions. However, branch instructions often contain two-way (true-false) conditions of the following form: If the "usual" condition is present, execute I_1; execute I_2 only when an exceptional condition, for example, the end of a program loop or an erroneous data value, is encountered. In such cases we can reasonably predict that the program will branch to the I_1 path most of the time.

A superscalar machine can benefit from the simple fixed prediction that the first (second) branch address is the usual one; therefore, it always follows the path corresponding to the condition being true (false). This technique has an accuracy of about 50 percent and costs very little to implement; it is used in such processors as Sun Microsystem's SuperSparc. Clearly, a greater improvement in CPU performance is possible if branch addresses are predicted correctly most of the time. Accurate predictions can be made by having the CPU dynamically monitor conditional branches as they are processed and maintain a record of the paths usually followed, for example, paths around a program loop. Such schemes involve trade-offs between prediction accuracy and control-hardware cost [Uht, Sindagi, and Somanathan 1997]. We will now describe the simplest such method, *1-bit dynamic branch prediction*, which is implemented in the Digital Alpha 21064 superscalar microprocessor, where it is reported to produce a branch-prediction accuracy close to 80 percent.

The idea behind 1-bit branch prediction is to assign a control bit p to a branch instruction I like (5.37) when it is first executed; the CPU then uses the value of p to predict I's branching behavior in the future. The prediction rule of this method is that I will branch to the same instruction as it did the last time it was executed. Thus when iterating through a loop controlled by I, once the loop execution path is entered, p predicts that the same loop path will be followed each time I is encountered. Of course, a misprediction eventually results when the loop is exited, but p can be expected to be right most of the time. The two states of p have the following interpretation for (5.37): $p = 1$ predicts that next instruction will be I_1—that is, C will be 1; $p = 0$ predicts that next instruction will be I_2—that is, C will be 0. Figure 5.67 illustrates the state behavior of p. The eventual outcome of each condition test determines p's next state: p remains unchanged if C's value agrees with the latest prediction made by p; otherwise, p is changed.

Methods that record more detailed information about a branch instruction's history can replace the 1-bit prediction scheme; see problem 5.37. It is convenient to store the branching statistics (p in the above case) in a table—the *branch history table*—along with the address of I and that of the instruction to which I currently branches. For rapid access, we can place the branch history table in a cachelike memory in the CPU called a *branch target buffer* (BTB); see Figure 5.68. The BTB is used as follows: Instruction requests are sent simultaneously to the I-cache and the BTB. If a match is found in the BTB, the accompanying, predicted branch target address is read out. Execution proceeds along the instruction path defined by the branch target address, with all results considered speculative until the outcome of the branch condition test becomes available. When execution of the branch instruction is completed, its target address is updated in the BTB, which permits mispredicted targets to be replaced; the branch instruction's prediction statistics are also updated.

We conclude with an example of a microprocessor that implements all the methods discussed so far for exploiting instruction-level parallelism.

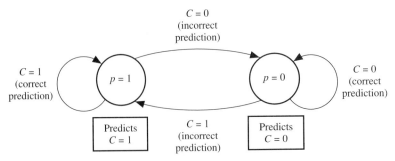

Figure 5.67
State behavior of 1-bit dynamic branch prediction method.

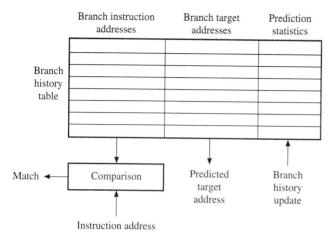

Branch instruction addresses   Branch target addresses   Prediction statistics

Branch history table

Match   Comparison   Predicted target address   Branch history update

Instruction address

Figure 5.68

Organization of a branch target buffer (BTB).

EXAMPLE 5.8 THE MIPS R10000 SUPERSCALAR MICROPROCESSOR [YEA-GER 1996]. This member of the MIPS RX000 microprocessor family was delivered in 1996. It employs the 64-bit MIPS-IV architecture, which is backward compatible with that of the 32-bit R2/3000 (Example 5.7). The R10000 is a single-chip, superscalar microprocessor that can issue four instructions per clock cycle. At a clock frequency of 200 MHz, it can therefore operate at a *CPI* of 0.25 clock cycles per instruction, which is equivalent to a peak *MIPS* throughput of 800 million instructions per second. The initial version of the R10000 contains some 6.8 million transistors.

The R10000's overall organization appears in Figure 5.69. This microprocessor's high performance is due mainly to its fast clock and to the presence of five independent and pipelined E-units: two for executing fixed-point instructions (the integer E-units), two for floating-point instructions (the floating-point E-units), and one for load and store instructions (the load/store unit, which handles address calculations). The length of these execution pipelines varies from three to five stages, and each is preceded by a common two-stage pipeline for fetching and decoding instructions. Consequently, an instruction can pass through as many as seven consecutive pipeline stages; see Figure 5.70. The fixed-point pipelines employ two 64-bit integer ALUs and a 64-word register file. The fixed-point pipelines are designed for 64-bit floating-point numbers using the IEEE 754 format; they are supported by another 64-word register file. To keep the pipelines as full as possible requires an interface to external memory that has very high bandwidth. The R10000 contains a primary (level 1) cache composed of a 32KB I-cache and a 32KB D-cache. The primary cache can be backed up by a much larger secondary (level 2) cache that is off-chip and is linked to the CPU by a dedicated bus.

In searching for parallelism that it can exploit, the CPU prefetches and examines up to 32 consecutive instructions, representing a large block (window) of instructions from the program being executed. Four consecutive instructions are fetched simultaneously from the I-cache. They are usually decoded in the next clock cycle and placed in three queues for execution by the various pipelines. The queues, which combine the functions of instruction buffers and reservation stations, dispatch instructions to E-units where they can be executed out of order. Each queue's control logic performs dynamic scheduling to determine when the operands and execution resources needed by its instructions become available. Various methods, including a register renaming scheme that exploits the R10000's large register files, resolve data

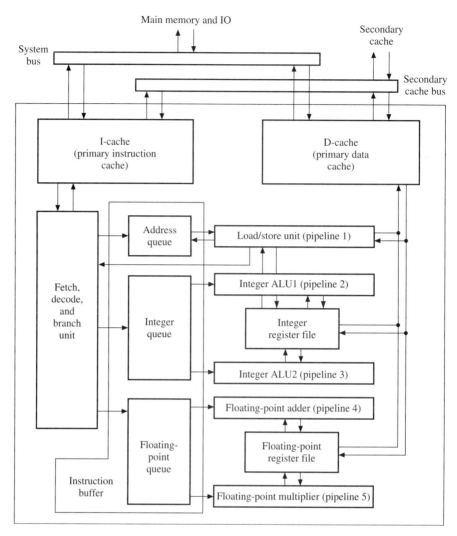

Figure 5.69
Organization of the MIPS R10000 microprocessor.

and control dependencies. Branch prediction is implemented by a 512-entry branch-history table, which permits up to four branch paths to be executed speculatively at the same time.

5.4
SUMMARY

A digital system such as a CPU is usually partitioned into control and data-processing units. The function of the control unit is to issue to the data-processing unit control signals that select and sequence the data-processing operations. There

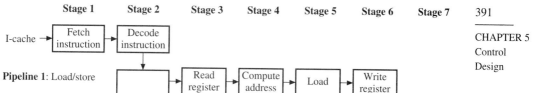

Figure 5.70
Instruction pipelining in the R10000.

are two general types of complex controllers: hardwired and microprogrammed. A hardwired control unit employs fixed logic circuits to generate the control signals. A microprogrammed control unit stores the control signals in sequences of micro-instructions (microprograms) in a control memory. Microprogramming provides a systematic and flexible method for control-unit design, since the control functions can easily be changed by changing the stored microprograms. On the other hand, microprogrammed control units are generally larger and slower than the corresponding hardwired units.

We have considered two general approaches to hardwired control design that are suitable for fairly small control units. The main design steps are state table specification, state code assignment, and design of the combinational logic that implements the next-state and output functions. The so-called classical method minimizes the number of flip-flops used to encode and store the state information, requiring only $\lceil \log_2 n \rceil$ flip-flops for an n-state controller. The one-hot method produces a circuit that contains n flip-flops but is easier to design and debug. Each state is assigned an n-bit binary code containing a single 1. This state-encoding scheme permits the next-state and output functions to be directly specified in a regular and easily implemented form.

A microprogrammed control unit's state information is centered in the control memory CM. The control unit also contains logic to generate microinstruction addresses and to fetch and decode the microinstructions from CM. The methods used for program control at the instruction level, for example, subroutine calls, can also be implemented at the microinstruction level. Microinstruction formats fall into two groups: horizontal and vertical. Horizontal microinstructions are characterized by long formats, little encoding of the control fields, and the ability to control many microoperations in parallel. Vertical microinstructions have short formats, considerable control-field encoding, and limited parallelism. A few processors use two levels of microprogramming for added flexibility: microinstructions are interpreted by nanoinstructions that directly control the hardware.

We can improve the performance of a CPU by structuring its program-control and execution logic in the form of one or more pipelines. An m-stage instruction pipeline overlaps the execution of up to m separate instructions, allowing the performance level of one cycle per instruction (CPI) to be achieved. The simplest two-stage pipeline overlaps (micro) instruction fetching and execution; a typical instruction pipeline has five or more stages. Proper operation of a pipeline requires the avoidance of collisions, which occur when two instructions attempt to use the same stage simultaneously, and hazards due to various data and control dependencies among instructions. Superscalar processors achieve CPI levels less than one by executing several instructions in parallel using multiple instruction pipelines. Complex control methods such as dynamic instruction scheduling and branch prediction are required for efficient superscalar computation.

5.5
PROBLEMS

5.1. Construct a state table corresponding to the state transition graph of Figure 5.71. Is this a Mealy or a Moore machine?

5.2. (*a*) Using the notation of Figure 5.4, devise a general procedure to convert a Mealy state table into an equivalent Moore state table. [*Hint:* Since the Mealy table can have several outputs associated with each current state S_i, consider "splitting" S_i into a set of states, each of which represents S_i for some fixed output combination.] (*b*) Construct the usual two-state Mealy table for a serial adder, and apply your conversion procedure to obtain an equivalent Moore state table.

5.3. Construct a Moore state table that is equivalent to the Mealy state table for the 4-bit-stream serial adder appearing in Figure 2.12.

5.4. Figure 5.72 shows the logic circuit of a DRAM interface controller intended for use with a certain microprocessor. (Some output circuitry has been omitted for simplicity.) This 10-state finite-state machine is implemented with 10 flip-flops and is referred to as "one-hot encoded." However, while 9 of the 10 states have the normal one-hot state

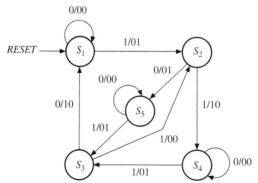

Figure 5.71
State transition graph of a five-state sequential circuit.

encoding (exactly one flip-flop output is 1), the reset state S_0 is encoded as 0000000000, rather than as 1000000000. (*a*) Suggest a reason for using the all-0 code for S_0. (*b*) Construct a complete state diagram (state transition graph) for this controller.

5.5. Modify the procedure given in the text for designing one-hot Moore machines to apply to Mealy machines.

5.6. Use the classical method to design the DMA controller of Example 5.1 with a minimum number of D flip-flops. Use NAND gates to implement the combinational logic.

5.7. A tennis-scoring device *TS* is to be constructed that determines the winner in a two-person game of tennis. *TS* has inputs x_1, x_2 and outputs z_1, z_2. Input x_i is set to 1 whenever player *i* scores a point and is set to 0 otherwise. Input z_i is set to 1 whenever player *i* wins a game; it is 0 otherwise. The rules of tennis can be stated succinctly as follows: To win a game, a player must win at least four points and must be at least two points ahead of the other player. (*a*) Construct a state table that defines the behavior of *TS*. (*b*) Estimate as accurately as you can the minimum number of flip-flops needed to implement *TS* using the classical and one-hot design methods.

5.8. Close scrutiny of the multiplier behavior defined by Figure 5.15 shows that certain states can be merged. Consider states S_2 (load register Q) and S_6 (output register Q). To enter state S_2 requires COUNT = 0 and therefore the control signal COUNT7 = 0, whereas S_6 is entered only after COUNT7 becomes 1. Hence we can merge S_2 and S_6 to form a single state S_{26} if when entering S_{26} with COUNT7 = 0, we match S_2's next-state and output behavior, but when entering S_{26} with COUNT7 = 1, we match S_6's behavior. In the first case the next state is S_3 or S_4 depending on Q[0], and the active output is c_8; in the second case the next state is S_7, and the active output is c_7. Note that since the outputs associated with S_{26} will depend on the primary inputs, we will have Mealy-type behavior. (*a*) Identify a second pair of states from Figure 5.15 that can be merged in this manner and explain their relationship. (*b*) Construct a state table in the style of Figure 5.16 for a reduced, six-state control unit.

5.9. Some early computers had small instruction sets, but did not restrict memory access to load and store instructions (load/store architecture), and so needed fewer CPU registers than a modern RISC. Figure 5.73 shows the instruction set for a CPU of this type

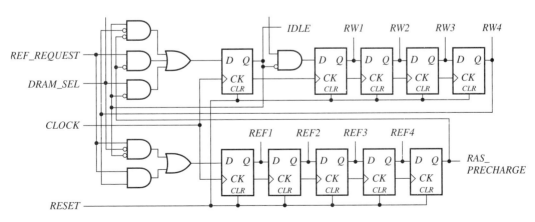

Figure 5.72
A 10-state control unit with modified one-hot state encoding.

Type	HDL format	Assembly format	Comment
Data transfer	AC := M(X)	LD X	Load X from M into AC
	M(X) := AC	ST X	Store contents of AC in M as X
Data processing	AC := AC + M(X)	ADD X	Add X to AC
	AC := AC – M(X)	SUB X	Subtract X from AC
	AC := AC *and* M(X)	AND X	And X to AC
	AC := *not* AC	NOT	Complement contents of AC
Program control	PC := M(*adr*)	BRA adr	Jump to instruction with address *adr*
	if AC = 0 then PC := M(*adr*)	BZ adr	Jump to instruction *adr* if AC = 0

Figure 5.73

Modified instruction set for an accumulator-based CPU.

derived from that of Figure 5.20. The data-processing instructions now reference main memory M, and the data register DR is no longer visible to a program. (It is still used internally for memory access operations, however.) Construct a flowchart in the style of Figure 5.21 for the modified CPU.

5.10. Suppose that the accumulator-based CPU of Figures 5.20 through 5.24 is enlarged to include the following instructions: (1) A left-shift instruction LSH that implements $AC := AC[n-2:0].0$; (2) an add-with-carry instruction ADC that computes $AC + DR + CY$, where CY is a new carry flag that is set (reset) whenever an arithmetic instruction causes (does not cause) AC to overflow; (3) a skip-on-carry instruction SKC that causes the CPU to skip the next consecutive instruction if and only if $CY = 1$. (*a*) Show the changes that need to be made to the flowchart of Figure 5.21 to incorporate the new instructions. (*b*) Specify a minimal set of new control signals that should be added to the list of Figure 5.22*b* to support the three new instructions.

5.11. Consider the design of the control circuit FSM for the accumulator-based CPU defined by Figures 5.20 through 5.24. Assume that it must have the 13 internal states $S_0:S_{12}$ defined by Figure 5.21 and is to be implemented as a Moore machine using the one-hot method with D flip-flops and NAND gates. Assign the hot variable D_i to state S_i and obtain a complete set of next-state and output equations for FSM in sum-of-products form. Estimate the number of NAND gates (including inverters) needed to construct FSM in this way, assuming a D flip-flop is equivalent to five NANDs.

5.12. Answer the following questions concerning the microprogrammed control unit shown in Figure 5.26. (*a*) What control signals are activated by the microinstruction I_5 with address $a_2a_1a_0 = 101$? (*b*) What microinstruction is loaded into CMAR after I_5? (*c*) Suppose that all the control functions performed by the top two microinstructions I_0 and I_1 can be carried out simultaneously. Devise a single microinstruction that can replace both I_0 and I_1.

5.13. A certain processor has a microinstruction format containing 10 separate control fields $C_0:C_9$. Each C_i can activate any one of n_i distinct control lines, where n_i is specified as follows:

$$i = 0 \quad 1 \quad 2 \quad 3 \quad 4 \quad 5 \quad 6 \quad 7 \quad 8 \quad 9$$

$$n_i = 4 \quad 4 \quad 3 \quad 11 \quad 9 \quad 16 \quad 7 \quad 1 \quad 8 \quad 22$$

What is the minimum number of control bits needed to represent the 10 control fields? What is the maximum number of control bits needed if a purely horizontal format is used for all the control information?

5.14. Draw a logic diagram showing how to construct a microprogram sequencer for (*a*) a 64×12-bit control memory and (*b*) a 12×64-bit control memory, using one or more copies of the AMD 2909.

5.15. Using the format of Equation (5.14), specify the control signals needed to perform the following microoperations in a 2909-based microprogram sequencer: (*a*) CALL X, where X is the address on the D bus; (*b*) **go to** 0 if external condition $C_i = 1$; and (*c*) repeat the last microinstruction.

5.16. Describe the changes that must be made to the hardware and the microprogram for the 16-bit twos-complement multiplier described in Example 5.5 in order to do the following: (*a*) 12-bit twos-complement multiplication; (*b*) 16-bit twos-complement multiplication with the following register assignment: R[3] = multiplier, R[2] = multiplicand, and R[1].R[0] = product.

5.17. Design the control logic that is driven by the CONFIG control field appearing in Figure 5.42. In other words, show in detail how the 2901-based processor is dynamically reconfigured while executing the multiplication microprogram of Figure 5.43.

5.18. Use the information in Figure 5.50 and the text to determine the microoperations that implement the call and return microinstructions for the 890 microprogram sequencer. Express each microinstruction in generic HDL format, as in (5.18).

5.19. You are to design a microprogrammed controller for a fixed-point divider that uses the circuit of Figure 4.23 and the nonrestoring division algorithm of Figure 4.24. The divider should handle both positive and negative integers having a 16-bit sign-magnitude format. (*a*) List all the required control signals and the microoperations they control. (*b*) Design a microinstruction format of the type shown in Figure 5.40 in which the control fields are encoded by function in an efficient manner.

5.20. A microprogrammed control unit is to be designed for a floating-point adder with the general structure shown in Figure 4.44. A number of the form $M \times B^E$ is represented by a 32-bit word comprising a 24-bit mantissa, which is a twos-complement fraction, and an 8-bit exponent, which is a biased integer. The base B is two. (*a*) Using our HDL, give a complete listing of a symbolic microprogram to control this adder. (*b*) Derive a suitable microinstruction format that uses unencoded control fields.

5.21. A conventional microprogrammed CPU is being redesigned for implementation as a one-chip microprocessor. At present it has a single 256×80-bit control memory and employs a highly parallel horizontal microinstruction format in which every instruction contains one 8-bit branch address. It is estimated that in a two-level organization of the control unit, only about sixty-four 300-bit nanoinstructions would be needed to implement the current instruction set. If the total size of the control memories is the major cost consideration, should the new microprocessor have one- or two-level control? Show your calculations and state all your assumptions.

5.22. A pipeline P is found to provide a speedup of 6.16 when operating at 100 MHz and an efficiency of 88 percent. (*a*) How many stages does P have? (*b*) What are P's *MIPS* and *CPI* performance levels?

Stage	Time t							
	1	2	3	4	5	6	7	8
S_1	×					×		×
S_2		×		×				×
S_3			×		×	×		

Figure 5.74
Reservation table for a three-stage pipeline.

5.23. The hardware cost of a new m-stage, single-function pipeline is approximated by $22m + 30$. The latency of the function to be executed is 90 ns if pipelining is not used. The pipelined implementation's interstage buffers are expected to add an additional $10m$ ns to this latency. Estimate the number of stages needed to optimize the pipeline's performance/cost ratio.

5.24. (*a*) For the pipeline reservation table appearing in Figure 5.74, calculate the forbidden set F, the minimum constant latency L_{cmin}, and the minimum average latency L_{min}. (*b*) Suppose that the pipeline is to be operated with a constant latency L such that the resulting pipeline efficiency is as close to 0.5 as possible. What is L in this case?

5.25. Construct a task initiation diagram (TID) for the pipeline reservation table appearing in Figure 5.74 and calculate the pipeline's minimum average latency L_{min}.

5.26. For the pipeline reservation table appearing in Figure 5.75, calculate the forbidden set F, the minimum constant latency L_{cmin}, and the minimum average latency L_{min}. Also construct a task initiation diagram for this pipeline.

5.27. Prove informally the following general property of a single-function pipeline. If K is the maximum number of ×'s in any row of the pipeline's reservation table, then $K \le L_{min}$, the minimum average latency. This result provides a useful lower bound on L_{min}.

5.28. Consider the following seven-instruction fragment of assembly language code for the MIPS RX000. Recall that the RX000 has no explicit flag bits and that the general register R0 always stores the constant zero.

```
        SLT    R7,R1,R2    {Set on less than: if R1 < R2, then set R7 to 1, else set
                              R7 to 0}
        BEQ    R7,R0,OUT1  {Branch on equal: if R7 = 0, then PC := OUT1}
        NOP                {No operation}
        ADDU   R3,R2,R0    {Add unsigned: R3 := R2 + R0}
        B      OUT2        {Branch unconditionally: PC := OUT2}
        NOP                {No operation}
OUT1:   ADDU   R3,R1,R0    {Add unsigned: R3 := R1 + R0}
OUT2:   ...
```

(*a*) What is the program's purpose? (*b*) What is the role of its two NOP instructions? (*c*) Redesign this program to reduce the number of instructions from seven to four (or as much as you can).

5.29. The following code fragment is to be executed in the six-stage instruction pipeline of Figure 5.76. Assume that every instruction must pass through all stages, including the three execution stages.

Stage	Time t						
	1	2	3	4	5	6	7
S_1	×			×			
S_2		×					×
S_3			×				
S_4					×		
S_5						×	

Figure 5.75
Reservation table for a five-stage pipeline.

ld	r4, #A	Load constant A into general register r4
ld	r5, #B	Load constant B into general register r5
add	r8, r4, r5	Add r4 and r5 and put the sum in r8
st	m(r1), r8	Store r8 in the memory location addressed by r1
ld	r6, #C	Load constant C into general register r6
add	r9, r5, r6	Add r5 and r6 and put the sum in r9
st	m(r2), r9	Store r9 in the memory location addressed by r2

(*a*) Construct a space-time diagram in the style of Figure 5.57 for this program, and determine how many cycles are needed to completely execute it. (*b*) Determine a valid reordering of the program that will reduce its execution time. Construct the space-time diagram for the reordered program.

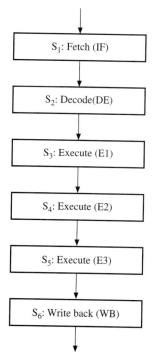

Figure 5.76
Six-stage instruction pipeline.

5.30. (*a*) The three conditions (5.34), (5.35), and (5.36) for RAW, WAR, and WAW data-dependent hazards are considered to be necessary, but not sufficient, for an instruction pipeline to produce invalid results. Show by means of an example why these conditions are not sufficient. (*b*) Conspicuous by its absence from the above set is the *read-after-read* (RAR) condition $D(I_1) \cap D(I_2) \neq \emptyset$. Explain why this condition is not a hazard.

5.31. Consider the following assembly-language program for a hypothetical RISC:

ld	r4, #A	Load constant A into general register r4
ld	r5, #B	Load constant B into general register r5
ld	r6, #C	Load constant C into general register r6
ld	r9, #0	Clear general register r9
beq	r4, r5, adr1	If r4 = r5 then go to adr1
add	r9, r4, r5	Add the sum of r4 and r5 to r9
mul	r9, r9, r9	Square the contents of r9
mul	r9, r9, #1	Increment r9 by one
adr1: st	m(r1), r9	Store r9 in the memory location addressed by r1

Identify all possible RAW, WAR, and WAW hazards that are present if nothing is known about the structure of the RISC's instruction pipeline.

5.32. Suppose the code fragment in problem 5.31 is processed by the four-stage instruction pipeline of Figure 5.55. Assume that data reads (from registers and/or memory) can occur only in stage S_2, while data reads and writes can occur only in stage S_4. Identify all RAW, WAR, and WAW hazards that are present in this case.

5.33. Consider the five-stage instruction pipeline of Figure 5.65. Assume that the program counter can be changed only by program-control instructions in the same manner as a general register. What delay penalty is associated with a branch instruction? By how much can the use of forwarding paths reduce this penalty?

5.34. (*a*) Explain why one is a lower bound on the *CPI* of conventional, nonsuperscalar microprocessors. (*b*) Name and briefly describe two techniques superscalar microprocessors use to make *CPI* less than one.

5.35. Early RISCs such as the IBM 801, which are not superscalar, use a branch-and-execute instruction to eliminate the pipeline delay slots caused by branch-instruction latency, as illustrated by (5.33). (*a*) This feature was deliberately excluded from the later POWER and PowerPC architectures because "it poses a severe handicap for superscalar processors." Explain this statement. (*b*) Suggest a reason why an even later superscalar microprocessor, the MIPS R10000, has the branch-and-execute feature.

5.36. Instead of using conventional instructions and pipelining, we can achieve superscalar performance by employing a *very long instruction word* (VLIW) to control multiple E-units and other CPU resources in much the same way a microinstruction controls multiple resources that execute microoperations. The programmer or compiler determines the control fields of the VLIW instructions and specifies the resources of a VLIW processor to be used in each clock cycle. Like horizontal microinstructions, VLIW instructions aim to maximize the number of operations done in parallel and require simple decoding logic. Superscalar VLIW computers have not been commercially successful. Suggest three reasons for this lack of success.

5.37. One-bit branch prediction can be extended by using 2 bits to record the outcomes of the last two executions of each conditional branch instruction. Devise such a 2-bit prediction method and explain it using a state diagram like that of Figure 5.67. State clearly the rationale for your method's prediction rules.

5.6
REFERENCES

1. Actel Corp. *FPGA Data Book and Design Guide.* Sunnyvale, CA, 1994.
2. Advanced Micro Devices Inc. *Bipolar Microprocessor and Logic Interface (Am2900 Family) Data Book.* Sunnyvale, CA, 1985.
3. Amdahl Corp. *Amdahl 470V/7 Machine Reference Manual,* Publ. G1003 0-01/A. Sunnyvale, CA, 1978.
4. Baranov, S. *Logic Synthesis for Control Automata.* Dordrecht, The Netherlands: Kluwer, 1994.
5. Becker, M. C. et al. "The PowerPC 601 Microprocessor." *IEEE Micro,* vol. 13 (October 1993) pp. 54–68.
6. Cormen, T. H., C. E. Leiserson, and R. L. Rivest. *Introduction to Algorithms.* New York: McGraw-Hill, 1990.
7. Hayes, J. P. *Introduction to Digital Logic Design.* Reading, MA: Addison-Wesley, 1993.
8. Hwang, K. *Advanced Computer Architecture.* New York: McGraw-Hill, 1993.
9. Kane, G. and J. Heinrich. *MIPS RISC Architecture.* Englewood Cliffs, NJ: Prentice-Hall, 1992.
10. Kogge, P. M. *The Architecture of Pipelined Computers.* New York: McGraw-Hill, 1981.
11. Lackzo, F. et al. "32-Bit CPU Design with the 'AS888/'AS890." *ACM Sigmicro Newsletter,* vol. 17 (July 1986) pp. 8–13.
12. Lynch, M. A. *Microprogrammed State Machine Design.* Boca Raton, FL: CRC Press, 1993.
13. Mealy, G. H. "A Method for Synthesizing Sequential Circuits." *Bell System Technical Journal,* vol. 34 (1955) pp. 1045–79.
14. Mick, J. and J. Brick. *Bit-Slice Microprocessor Design.* New York: McGraw-Hill, 1980.
15. Moore, E. F. "Gedanken Experiments on Sequential Machines." *Annals of Mathematics Studies,* no. 34 *(Automata Studies).* Princeton, NJ: Princeton University Press, 1956.
16. Radin, G. "The 801 Minicomputer." *IBM Journal of Research and Development,* vol. 27 (May 1983) pp. 237–46.
17. Smith, J. E. "Dynamic Instruction Scheduling and the Astronautics ZS-1." *IEEE Computer,* vol. 22 (July 1989) pp. 21–35.
18. Stone, H. S. *High-Performance Computer Architecture.* 3rd ed. Reading, MA: Addison-Wesley, 1993.
19. Stritter, S. and N. Tredennick. "Microprogrammed Implementation of a Single-Chip Computer." *Proceedings of the 11th Microprogramming Workshop* (December 1978) pp. 8–16.
20. Texas Instruments Inc. *SN74AS888/SN74AS890 Bit-Slice Processor User's Guide.* Dallas: 1985.
21. Tomasulo, R. M. "An Efficient Algorithm for Exploiting Multiple Arithmetic Units." *IBM Journal of Research and Development,* vol. 11 (January 1967) pp. 25–33.
22. Uht, A. K., V. Sindagi, and S. Somanathan. "Branch Effect Reduction Techniques." *IEEE Computer,* vol. 30 (May 1997) pp. 71–81.
23. Wilkes, M. V. "The Best Way to Design an Automatic Calculating Machine." Report of the Manchester University Computer Inaugural Conference, 1951, pp. 16–18. [Reprinted in E. E. Swartzlander (ed.) *Computer Design Development: Principal Papers.* Rochelle Park, NJ: Hayden, 1976, pp. 266–270.]
24. Yeager, K. C. "The MIPS R10000 Superscalar Microprocessor." *IEEE Micro,* vol. 16 (April 1996) pp. 28–40.

CHAPTER 6

Memory Organization

This chapter is concerned with the design of a computer's memory system and its impact on performance. The characteristics of the most important storage-device technologies are surveyed. The behavior and management of multilevel hierarchical memory systems are discussed, and cache memories are examined in detail.

6.1
MEMORY TECHNOLOGY

Every computer contains several types of devices to store the instructions and data required for its operation. These storage devices plus the algorithms—implemented by hardware and/or software—needed to manage the stored information form the memory system of the computer.

6.1.1 Memory Device Characteristics

A CPU should have rapid, uninterrupted access to the external memories where its programs and the data they process are stored so that the CPU can operate at or near its maximum speed. Unfortunately, memories that operate at speeds comparable to processor speeds are expensive, and generally only very small systems can afford to employ a single memory using just one type of technology. Instead, the stored information is distributed, often in complex fashion, over various memory units that have very different performance and cost.

Memory types. The information-storage components of a computer can be placed in four groups, as illustrated in Figure 6.1.

- *CPU registers.* These high-speed registers in the CPU serve as the working memory for temporary storage of instructions and data. They usually form a general-purpose *register file* for storing data as it is processed. A capacity of 32 data words is typical of a register file, and each register can be accessed, that is, read from or written into, within a single clock cycle (a few nanoseconds).
- *Main (primary) memory.* This large, fairly fast external memory stores programs and data that are in active use. Storage locations in main memory are addressed directly by the CPU's load and store instructions. While an IC technology similar to that of a CPU register file is used, access is slower because of main memory's large capacity and the fact that it is physically separated from the CPU. Main memory capacity is typically between 1 and 2^{10} megabytes, where a *megabyte*, also denoted 1 MB, is 2^{20} bytes, and 2^{10} MB = 2^{30} bytes is referred to as a *gigabyte* (1 GB). Access times of five or more clock cycles are usual.
- *Secondary memory.* This memory type is much larger in capacity but also much slower than main memory. Secondary memory stores system programs, large data files, and the like that are not continually required by the CPU. It also acts as an overflow memory when the capacity of the main memory is exceeded. Information in secondary storage is considered to be on-line but is accessed indirectly via input/output programs that transfer information between main and secondary memory. Representative technologies for secondary memory are magnetic hard disks and CD-ROMs (compact disk read-only memories), both of which have relatively slow electromechanical access mechanisms. Storage capacities of many gigabytes are common, while access times are measured in milliseconds.
- *Cache.* Most computers now have another level of IC memory—sometimes several such levels—called cache memory, which is positioned logically between the CPU registers and main memory. A cache's storage capacity is less than that of main memory, but with an access time of one to three cycles, the cache is much faster than main memory because some or all of it can reside on the same IC as the CPU. Caches are essential components of high-performance computers

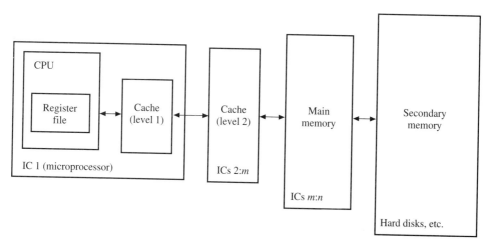

Figure 6.1
Conceptual organization of a multilevel memory system in a computer.

that aim to make $CPI \leq 1$. Unlike the three other memory types, caches are normally transparent to the programmer. Together, a computer's caches and main memory implement the *external memory* M addressed directly by CPU instructions.

The goal of every memory system is to provide adequate storage capacity with an acceptable level of performance and cost. We can achieve these goals by employing several memory types—with different cost/performance ratios—that are organized to provide a high average performance at a low average cost per bit. The individual memory units form a *multilevel hierarchy* of storage devices, as suggested by Figure 6.1. Successful operation of the hierarchy requires automatic storage-control methods that make efficient use of the available memory capacity. These methods should free the user from explicit management of memory space. They should also free programs from the particular memory environment in which they are executed.

Performance and cost. The computer architect can choose from a bewildering variety of memory devices that employ various electronic, magnetic, and optical technologies and offer many cost/performance trade-offs [Cook and White 1994; Prince 1996]. However, all memories are based on just a few physical phenomena and organizational principles. We now examine the features common to the devices used to build cache, main, and secondary memories.

The most meaningful measure of the cost of a memory device is the purchase price to the user of a complete unit. The price should include not only the cost of the information storage medium itself but also the cost of the peripheral equipment (access circuitry) needed to operate the memory. Let C be the price in dollars of a complete memory system with S bits of storage capacity. We define the *cost c* of the memory as follows:

$$c = \frac{C}{S} \text{ dollars/bit}$$

The performance of an individual memory device is primarily determined by the rate at which information can be read from or written into the memory. A basic performance measure is the average time to read a fixed amount of information, for instance, one word, from the memory. This parameter is called the *read access time*, or simply the *access time*, of the memory and is denoted by t_A. The write access time is defined similarly; it is often, but not always, equal to the read access time. The access time depends on the physical nature of the storage medium and on the access mechanisms used. It is calculated from the time the memory receives a read request to the time at which the requested information becomes available at the memory's output terminals.

Clearly, low cost and short access time are desirable memory characteristics; unfortunately, they also tend to be incompatible. Memory units with fast access are expensive, while low-cost memories are slow. Figure 6.2 shows the relationship between cost c and access time t_A for some recent memory technologies. The straight line AB approximates this relationship. If we write $t_A = 10^y$ and $c = 10^x$, then $y \approx mx + k$, where m denotes the slope of AB and k is a constant. Hence $t_A \approx 10^{mx+k'} \approx kc^m + k''$. From the data in Figure 6.2, we can conclude that $m \approx -0.5$. Hence to decrease t_A by a factor of 10, the cost c must increase by about 100.

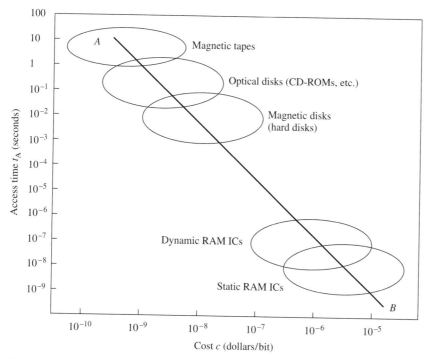

Figure 6.2
Access time versus cost for representative memory technologies.

Manufacturing improvements have steadily reduced the storage cost per bit c for the principal memory technologies. This trend is especially striking in the case of the IC RAMs used to construct main and cache memories, where the storage density per IC has increased steadily while the cost per IC has remained fairly constant. The state of the art in RAM manufacture circa 1975, 1985, and 1995 is represented by single-chip RAMs of capacity 4 Kb, 256 Kb, and 16 Mb, respectively. Here 1 Kb denotes a *kilobit* and equals 2^{10}, or 4096 bits, while 1 Mb denotes a *megabit* and equals 2^{20}, or 1,048,576 bits. At a typical introductory price of $40 for each chip type, the cost per bit c fell from around 0.01 dollars per bit in 1975 to 0.00015 dollars per bit in 1985 and to 0.0000024 dollars per bit a decade later. Similar developments have taken place in other technologies, notably magnetic (hard) disk memories, as storage density has increased steadily with little change in the cost per memory unit.

Although storage density has grown rapidly for the principal memory technologies, access times have decreased at a much slower rate. This disparity has tended to aggravate the speed mismatch—the von Neumann bottleneck—between the CPU and M. Memory speed has increased slowly, but the computing speed of microprocessors has spurted, along with their ability to produce and consume ever-increasing amounts of information. As we will see in this chapter, various design techniques can increase the effective rate at which the CPU can access the information stored in its memory system.

Access modes. A fundamental characteristic of a memory is the order or sequence in which information can be accessed. If storage locations can be accessed in any order and access time is independent of the location being accessed, the memory is termed a *random-access memory* (RAM). IC (semiconductor) memories are generally of this type. Memories whose storage locations can be accessed only in a certain predetermined sequence are called *serial-access memories*. Magnetic disks and tapes, as well as optical memories like CD-ROMs, employ serial-access methods.

Each storage location in a RAM can be accessed independently of the other locations. There is, in effect, a separate access mechanism, or read-write "head," for every location, as suggested in Figure 6.3. In serial memories, on the other hand, the access mechanism is shared by the storage locations and must be assigned to different locations at different times by moving the stored information, the read-write head, or both. Many serial-access memories operate by continually moving the storage locations around a closed path or track, as suggested by Figure 6.4. A particular location can be accessed only when it passes the fixed read-write head. Hence the time to access a particular location depends on its position relative to the read-write head when the memory receives an access request.

Since every location has its own access mechanism, random-access memories tend to be more costly than the serial type. In serial-access memories, however, the time required to bring the desired location into correspondence with a read-write head increases the effective access time, so serial access tends to be slower than random access. Thus the type of access mode contributes significantly to the inverse relationship between cost and access time. In Figure 6.2, for example, the random-access technologies (dynamic and static RAMs based on ICs) and serial-access technologies (magnetic disks, magnetic tapes, and optical disks) are clearly separated into two groups.

Memory devices such as magnetic hard disks and CD-ROMs contain many rotating storage tracks. If each track has its own read-write head, the tracks can be accessed randomly, but access within each track is serial. In such cases the access mode is *semirandom*. Note that the access mode is a function of both memory organization and the inherent characteristics of the storage technology. The IC technologies used for RAMs can also be used to construct serial-access memories; the converse is not true, however.

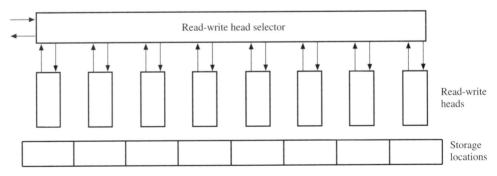

Figure 6.3
Conceptual model of a random-access memory.

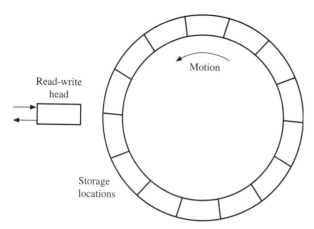

Figure 6.4
Conceptual model of a
serial-access memory.

Read-write
head

Motion

Storage
locations

Memory retention. The method of writing information into a memory can be permanent or irreversible in that once information has been written, it cannot be altered while the memory is in use or on-line. Printing on paper is an example of a permanent storage technique. Memories whose contents cannot be altered on-line—if they can be altered at all—are *read-only memories* (ROMs). A ROM is therefore a nonerasable storage device. ROMs are widely used to store control programs such as microprograms. Compact disk (CD) ROMs are a class of nonerasable secondary memory devices developed in the 1980s that employ an optical (laser) read-write mechanism. A standard (12 cm diameter) CD-ROM has a capacity of about 600 MB and is used to store large program and data files. Semiconductor ROMs whose contents can be changed off-line—and with some difficulty—are called *programmable read-only memories* (PROMs). Programmable CDs are referred to as *CD-recordable* (CD-R) disks.

Memories in which reading or writing can be done with impunity on-line are called *read-write memories* to differentiate them from ROMs. All memories used for temporary storage purposes are read-write memories. Unless otherwise specified, we will use the terms *memory* and *RAM* to mean read-write memories.

In some technologies the stored information is lost over a period of time unless corrective action is taken. Three characteristics of memories that destroy information in this way are destructive readout, dynamic storage, and volatility. In some memories the method of reading the memory destroys the stored information; this phenomenon is called *destructive readout* (DRO). Memories in which reading does not affect the stored data have *nondestructive readout* (NDRO). In DRO memories each read operation must be followed by a write operation that restores the memory's original state. This restoration is carried out automatically using a buffer register, as shown in Figure 6.5. The read transfers the word at the addressed (shaded) location to the buffer register where it is available to external devices. The contents of the buffer are automatically written back into the original location.

Certain memory devices have the property that a stored 1 tends to become a 0, or vice versa, due to some physical decay process. For example, in some IC memories, an electric charge in a capacitor represents a stored 1; the absence of a stored charge represents a 0. Over time, a stored charge tends to leak away, causing a loss

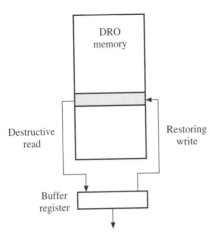

Figure 6.5
Memory restoration in a destructive readout (DRO) memory.

of information unless the charge is restored by a process called *refreshing*. Memories that require periodic refreshing are called *dynamic* memories, as opposed to *static* memories, which require no refreshing. (Note that in this context *dynamic* and *static* do not refer to the presence or absence of mechanical motion in the storage device.) Most memories that employ magnetic or optical storage techniques are static. Main memories are usually built from dynamic ICs referred to as *dynamic RAMS* (DRAMs). ICs can also implement static memories referred to as *static RAMS* (SRAMs). As Figure 6.2 indicates, SRAMs tend to be faster, that is, have lower access time, than DRAMs, but the cost per bit of SRAMs is higher. SRAMs are often used to build caches. A dynamic memory is refreshed in much the same way that data is restored in a DRO memory. The contents of every location are sent periodically to buffer registers and then returned in amplified form to their original locations.

Another physical process that can destroy the contents of a memory is the removal or failure of its power supply. A memory is *volatile* if the loss of power destroys the stored information. Information can be stored indefinitely in a volatile memory by providing battery backup or other means to maintain a continuous supply of power. Most IC memories are volatile, while most magnetic and optical memories are nonvolatile.

Figure 6.6 summarizes these characteristics for some important contemporary memory technologies.

Other characteristics. We defined the access time t_A as the time between the receipt of a read request signal by a memory and the delivery of the requested information to its output terminals. Some DRO and dynamic memories cannot initiate a new access until a restore or refresh operation has been carried out. Therefore, the minimum time that must elapse between the start of two consecutive access operations can be greater than t_A. This elapsed time is called the *cycle time* t_M of the memory and represents the time needed to complete a read or write operation.

The maximum amount of information that can be transferred to or from the memory per unit time is the *data-transfer rate* or *bandwidth* b_M and is measured in

Technology	Primary storage medium	Access mode	Alterability	Permanence	Typical access time t_A
Bipolar semiconductor	Electronic	Random	Read/write	NDRO, volatile	10 ns
Metal oxide semiconductor (MOS)	Electronic	Random	Read/write	DRO or NDRO, volatile	50 ns
Magnetic (hard) disk	Magnetic	Semirandom	Read/write	NDRO, nonvolatile	10 ms
Magneto-optical disk	Optical	Semirandom	Read/write	NDRO, nonvolatile	50 ms
Compact disk ROM	Optical	Semirandom	Read only	NDRO, nonvolatile	100 ms
Magnetic tape cartridge	Magnetic	Serial	Read/write	NDRO, nonvolatile	1 s

Figure 6.6

Characteristics of some common memory technologies.

bits or words per second. If w is the number of bits that can be transferred simultaneously to or from the memory, then $b_M = w/t_M$ bits/s. If $t_M = t_A$, then $b_M = w/t_A$. Some memory types, particularly serial memories, require a long access time t_A to initiate a new access operation; once the operation is initiated, however, data transfer can proceed at a rate b_M much greater than w/t_A. In such cases the manufacturer provides independent specifications for t_A, t_M, b_M, and related performance parameters.

Finally, we mention *reliability,* which is measured by the mean time before failure (MTBF). In general, memories with no moving parts have much higher reliability than memories such as magnetic disks, which involve considerable mechanical motion. Even in memories without moving parts, reliability problems arise, particularly when very high storage densities or data-transfer rates are used. Error-detecting and error-correcting codes can increase the reliability of any memory.

6.1.2 Random-Access Memories

RAMs are distinguished by the fact that each storage location can be accessed independently with fixed access and cycle times that are independent of the position of the accessed location.

Organization. Figure 6.7 shows the main components of a RAM device such as a DRAM IC. At its heart is a storage unit composed of a large number (2^m) of addressable locations, each of which stores a w-bit word. Individual bits are not directly addressable unless $w = 1$. A RAM of this sort is referred to as a $2^m \times w$-bit or 2^m-word memory. The RAM operates as follows: First the address of the target location to be accessed is transferred via the address bus to the RAM's address

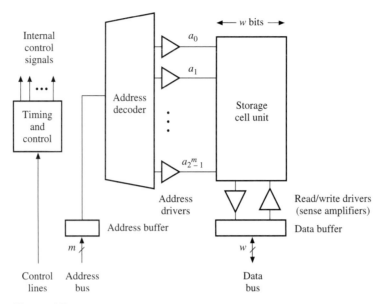

Figure 6.7
One-dimensional (1-D) random-access memory unit.

buffer. The address is then processed by the address decoder, which selects the required location in the storage cell unit. A control line indicates the type of access to be performed. If a read operation (load) is requested, the contents of the addressed location are transferred from the storage cell unit to the data buffer and from there to the data bus. If a write (store) is requested, the word to be stored is transferred from the data bus to the selected location in the storage unit. Since it is not usually necessary or desirable to permit simultaneous reading and writing, the input and output data buses are often combined into a single, bidirectional data bus.

The storage unit is made up of many identical 1-bit memory cells and their interconnections. The actual number of lines connected to the cell and their functions depend on the memory technology and the addressing scheme in use. Each cell is connected to a set of data, address, and control signals. One physical line often has several logical functions; for example, it can serve as both an address and data line. In each line connected to the storage cell unit, we can expect to find a driver that acts as either an amplifier or a transducer of physical signals. Thus we see in Figure 6.7 several sets of drivers for the address and data lines. The drivers, decoders, and control circuits form the *access circuitry* of the RAM and can have a significant impact on the total size and cost of the memory.

A RAM's storage cells are physically arranged into regular arrays to reduce the cost of the connections between the cells and the access circuitry. The memory address is partitioned into d components so that the address A_i of cell C_i becomes a d-dimensional vector $(A_{i,1}, A_{i,2}, \ldots, A_{i,d}) = A_i$. Each of the d parts of the address word goes to a separate address decoder and a separate set of address drivers. A cell is selected by simultaneously activating all d of its address lines. A memory unit with this kind of addressing is said to be *d-dimensional*. Thus the basic RAM of Figure 6.7 is *one-dimensional* (1-D).

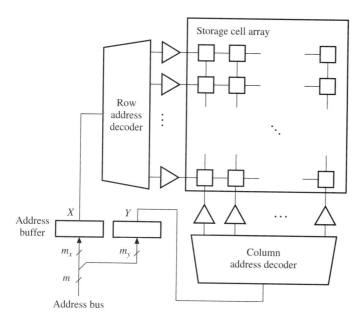

Figure 6.8
Two-dimensional (2-D) RAM addressing scheme.

The most common RAM organization is the *two-dimensional* (2-D) or *row-column* scheme shown in Figure 6.8, where, for simplicity, the data and control circuits are omitted. Here the m-bit address word is divided into two parts, X and Y, consisting of m_x and m_y bits, respectively. The cells are arranged in a rectangular array of $N_x \le 2^{m_x}$ rows and $N_y \le 2^{m_y}$ columns, so the total number of cells is $N = N_x N_y$. A cell is selected by the coincidence of signals applied to its X and Y address lines. The 2-D organization requires much less access circuitry than a 1-D organization for the same storage capacity. For example, if $N_x = N_y = \sqrt{N}$, the number of address drivers needed is $2\sqrt{N}$, whereas the 1-D RAM of Figure 6.7 has $N = N_x N_y$ address drivers. Instead of a single one-out-of-N address decoder, two one-out-of-$\sqrt{N}$ address decoders suffice. In addition, the 2-D organization is a good match for the inherently two-dimensional layout structures allowed by VLSI technology.

Semiconductor RAMs. Semiconductor memories in which the storage cells are small transistor circuits have been used for high-speed CPU registers since the 1950s. It was not until the development of VLSI in the 1970s that producing large RAM ICs suitable for main-memory and cache applications became economical. Single-chip RAMs can be manufactured in sizes ranging from a few hundred bits to 1 Gb or more. Both bipolar and MOS transistor circuits are used in RAMs, but MOS is the dominant circuit technology for large RAMs. Current IC manufacturing limitations make it impossible to manufacture, say, a terabit (2^{40}-bit) RAM on a single IC chip. Consequently, very large semiconductor RAMs must be constructed from a set of smaller RAM ICs.

As observed earlier, semiconductor memories fall into two categories—SRAMs and DRAMs—whose data-retention methods are static and dynamic, respectively. SRAMs consist of memory cells that resemble the flip-flops used in processor design. SRAM cells differ from flip-flops primarily in the methods used to address the cells and transfer data to and from them. Multifunction lines minimize storage-cell complexity and the number of cell connections, thereby facilitating the manufacture of very large 2-D arrays of storage cells.

In a DRAM cell the 1 and 0 states correspond to the presence or absence of a stored charge in a capacitor controlled by a transistor switching circuit. Since a DRAM cell can be constructed around a single transistor, whereas a static cell requires up to six transistors, higher storage density is achieved with DRAMs. Indeed, DRAMs are among the densest VLSI circuits in terms of transistors per chip. The charge stored in a DRAM cell tends to decay with time, and the cell must be periodically refreshed. Hence a DRAM must contain refreshing circuitry and interleave refreshing operations with normal memory accesses. Both SRAMs and DRAMs are volatile, that is, the stored information is lost when the power source is removed.

Figure 6.9 shows examples of MOS RAM cells of both the static and dynamic varieties. The six-transistor SRAM cell (Figure 6.9a) superficially resembles a flip-flop. A signal applied to the address line (also called the *word line*) by the address decoder selects the cell for either the read or write operation. The two data lines (also called *bit lines*) are used in a complex way [Weste and Eshraghian 1992] to transfer the stored data and its complement between the cell and the data drivers.

Figure 6.9b shows a particularly simple and useful memory cell based on dynamic charge storage. This one-transistor DRAM cell comprises an MOS transistor T, which acts as a switch, and a capacitor C, which stores a data bit. Apart from power and ground, the cell has only two external connections: a data (bit) line and an address (word) line. To write information into the cell, a voltage signal (either high or low, representing 1 and 0, respectively) is placed on the data line. A signal is then applied to the address line to switch on T. This action transfers a charge to C if the data line is 1; no charge is transferred otherwise. To read the cell, the address line is again activated, transferring any charge stored in C to the data

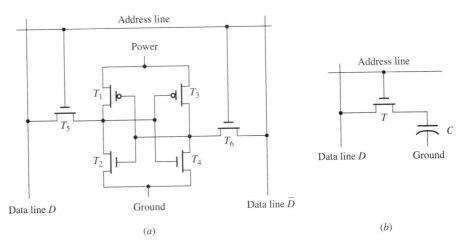

(a)

(b)

Figure 6.9
(a) Static and (b) dynamic RAM cells in MOS technology.

line where it is detected. Since the readout process is destructive, the data being read out is amplified and subsequently written back to the cell; this process may be combined with the periodic refreshing operation required by dynamic memories. The advantages of this DRAM cell are its small size, which means that ICs with very high cell density can be manufactured, and its low power consumption.

RAM design. A RAM IC typically contains all required access circuitry, including address decoders, drivers, and control circuits. Figure 6.10 shows a generic $2^m \times w$-bit RAM IC and identifies its control lines. *WE* is the write-enable line; a memory write (read) operation takes place if $WE = 1\ (0)$. A second control line, the chip-select line *CS*, triggers a memory operation. A word is accessed for either reading or writing only when *CS* is activated. This line signals that the data bus has a word ready to be written into the RAM or, in the case of a read operation, that the data bus is ready to receive a data word. The RAM of Figure 6.10 has a bidirectional data bus *D*, which is directly wired to all addressable storage locations, and so it requires a third control line, output enable *OE*. In write (input) operations this line is deactivated ($OE = 0$), allowing *D* to act as an input bus to all storage locations. Of course, only the addressed location actually stores the word received on *D*. In read (output) operations, *OE* must be activated ($OE = 1$) so that only the addressed memory location transfers its data to *D*.

A memory-design problem that the computer architect may encounter is the following: given that $N \times w$-bit RAM ICs denoted $M_{N,w}$ are available, design an $N' \times w'$-bit RAM, where $N' > N$ and/or $w' > w$. A general approach is to construct a $p \times q$ array of the $M_{N,w}$ ICs, where $p = \lceil N'/N \rceil$, $q = \lceil w'/w \rceil$, and $\lceil x \rceil$ denotes the smallest integer greater than or equal to x. In this IC array each row stores N words (except possibly the last row), while each column stores a fixed set of w bits from every word (except possibly the last column). For example, to construct a 1GB RAM using $64M \times 1$-bit RAM ICs requires $p = 16$, $q = 8$, and a total of $pq = 128$ copies of the 64Mb RAM. When $N' > N$, additional external-address-decoding circuitry is usually required.

Consider the task of designing an $N \times 4w$-bit RAM using $N \times w$-bit ICs of the type appearing in Figure 6.10. Clearly, four ICs are needed to quadruple the word size in this way, since $p = 1$ and $q = 4$. The four are arranged in the 1×4 array configuration of Figure 6.11. Each RAM IC contains a w-bit slice of every stored word. Note how all the address and control lines are connected in exactly the same

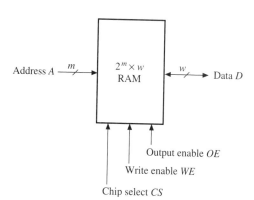

Address A m $2^m \times w$ RAM w Data D

Output enable *OE*
Write enable *WE*
Chip select *CS*

Figure 6.10
A RAM IC showing its major external connections.

way to each IC. Their w-bit data buses are concatenated to form a single $4w$-bit bus, as indicated.

Now suppose we want to increase the number of stored words by a factor of four. This time $p = 4$ and $q = 1$, and again we need four RAM ICs. The number of addresses has quadrupled, hence two lines are added to the address bus. Furthermore, a one-out-of-four address decoder must be introduced, as shown in Figure 6.12, to decode the extra address bits. The original m address lines are connected to the m-bit address bus of every RAM IC; the new lines are the main inputs to the decoder. Each decoder output line is connected to the CS inputs of the RAMs in the same row, ensuring that the row has a unique address. The output buses of all RAM ICs in the same column are designed so they can be wired together without additional logic. (This *tristate* busing technique is explained in section 7.1.1.) The remaining control lines WE and OE are attached to every RAM IC as before. The external CS line is connected to an enable input of the decoder. Making this line 0 forces all CS lines to the individual RAM ICs to 0 so that they are all deactivated and no memory operation takes place.

EXAMPLE 6.1 A COMMERCIAL 64Mb DRAM CHIP [MICRON TECHNOLOGY 1997]. The Micron Technology MT4LC8M8E1, which we will call the 8E1 for short, is a commercial DRAM chip introduced in 1996. It stores 64 Mb, that is, 2^{26} bits of data, in single-transistor storage cells of the kind shown in Figure 6.9b. The stored information is organized as 2^{23} 8-bit bytes, so the 8E1 is also referred to as an 8M × 8-bit DRAM. The memory address size $m = 23$, and the data word size $w = 8$.

The internal structure of the 8E1 appears in Figure 6.13. Two-dimensional addressing is employed, with the 23-bit address broken into two parts: a 13-bit row address and a 10-bit column address. Only 13 external address lines are used, allowing the 8E1 to be housed in a small, 32-pin package, which implies that row and column addresses must be multiplexed over the address bus, a common tactic in large RAM chips. This multiplexing is controlled by two lines: $\overline{RAS}$ (row address select) and $\overline{CAS}$ (column address select), which replace the generic CS control line of Figures 6.10,

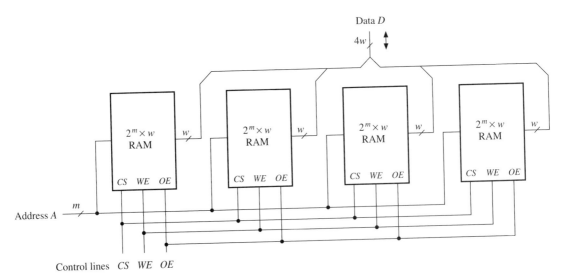

Figure 6.11
Increasing the word size of a RAM by a factor of four.

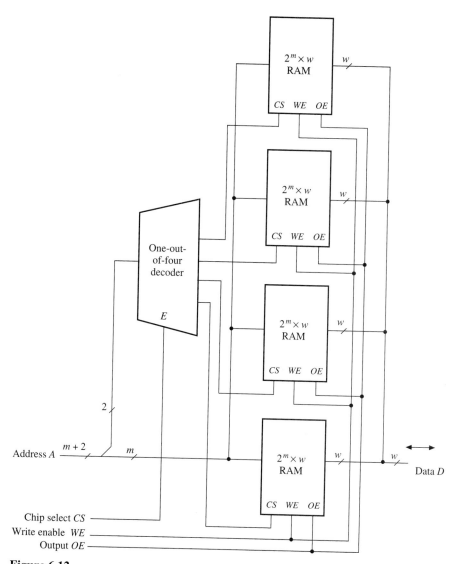

Figure 6.12

Increasing the number of words stored in a RAM by a factor of four.

6.11, and 6.12. First the row address is transferred to the DRAM by the external (master) device, which places the row address on the 8E1's address bus and activates $\overline{RAS}$. The master then places the column address on the address bus, and activates $\overline{CAS}$. $\overline{CAS}$ also serves to indicate that a data word is ready on the data bus (write operation) or that the external bus is ready to receive a data word (read operation). $\overline{WE}$ and $\overline{OE}$ are the write-enable and output-enable lines, respectively. As the overbars in their names indicate, all the control lines are active in the 0 state.

The read access time t_A, which is 50 ns in faster versions of the 8E1, includes the time needed to transfer the row and column addresses to the DRAM and the time to read out a data word. The read cycle time t_M with respect to a "random" address stream is 90 ns, since every such access is followed by an internal restoring write, as depicted

Data bus $DQ1{:}DQ8$

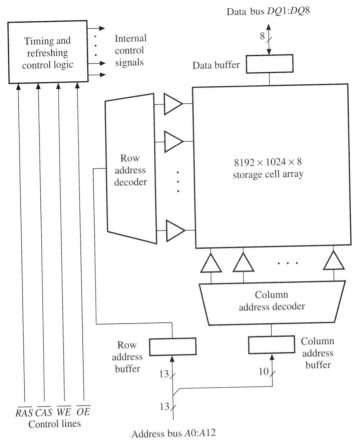

Figure 6.13
Structure of a commercial 8M $\times$ 8-bit DRAM chip.

in Figure 6.5. If a sequence of memory accesses share the same row address, then it is sufficient to transfer the row address to the DRAM once at the start of the sequence. This transfer causes an entire row of data, referred to as a *page*, to be read out and held in an internal buffer. A subsequent memory access to the same page needs to transfer only a column address, thus reducing the effective memory cycle time t_M. This time is further reduced by the fact that there is no need to write back and restore the page data every time a word from it is accessed. A fast access method of this type is called *page mode*, and in the 8E1 case it reduces t_M to 30 ns. The memory address space of the 8E1consists of 8192 rows or pages, each containing 1024 locations. Both $\overline{RAS}$ and $\overline{CAS}$ are normally deactivated before the start of a new read or write cycle. Page mode is established by activating $\overline{RAS}$ to load the row address and then maintaining it active for the duration of a sequence of column-address transfers in which $\overline{CAS}$ is toggled in the normal way.

To ensure that the stored data does not decay, every cell in the memory must be read to refresh it at least once every 64 ms, which is the specified refresh period t_{REF}. An internal restoring write that performs the refreshing accompanies each such read, as in Figure 6.5. The 2-D addressing structure makes it possible to read and restore the contents of an entire row of storage locations in a single read cycle. Hence the refresh controller need only sweep through all the row addresses in a sequence of internal read cycles to implement the refreshing. If a one-row read operation takes 90 ns, then the total time needed to refresh the DRAM once is 90×8192 ns = 0.737 ms. Thus the fraction of time devoted to refreshing is $0.737/64 = 1.15$ percent—a negligible amount.

Other semiconductor memories. Techniques similar to those employed in DRAM technology are also used to build several other types of high-density semiconductor memories for computer applications. Read-only memories (ROMs), as their name implies, cannot have their contents rewritten once they are installed in a system, that is, on-line. They are read using random-addressing methods like those in RAM chips. A ROM has essentially the same internal organization and external interface as a RAM, but without the latter's writing ability. However, ROMs have the advantage of being nonvolatile, so they are widely used to store permanent code at the instruction and microinstruction levels. Various ROM types are distinguished by the methods used to program them. Some types can be programmed only once. Others, known as programmable ROMS (PROMs), can be programmed repeatedly, which requires their contents to be erased in bulk off-line and then replaced via a special writing process referred to as "programming." This programming step resembles that of programmable logic devices such as FPGAs (section 2.2.2).

A recent semiconductor technology called *flash memory* offers the same nonvolatility as a PROM, but it can be programmed and erased on-line. The programming can be done a bit at a time, but erasure is done in large blocks—a "flash erase" process from which this memory gets its name. Thus individual bits can be read randomly, but writing must be done in blocks. The storage densities and read-access times of flash memories are comparable to those of DRAMs, but a simpler single-transistor storage cell makes a flash memory potentially cheaper to produce than a DRAM. Flash memories are suitable for writable control stores and as replacements for secondary memories in some applications.

Fast RAM interfaces. The gap between microprocessor and RAM data-transfer rates (bandwidth), especially those of cheap but slow DRAMs, has given rise to novel methods for enabling RAM units to communicate at higher-than-normal speeds. The use of multiple memory types, serial as well as random access, in a memory hierarchy is a separate speedup issue that we examine later. Here we are just concerned with one level in the hierarchy—main memory, for example.

Suppose a particular RAM technology must supply a faster external processor with individually addressable n-bit words. There are two basic ways we can increase the data-transfer rate across its external interface by a factor of S:

- *Use a bigger memory word.* We can design the RAM with an internal memory word size of $w = Sn$ bits. This size permits Sn bits to be accessed as a unit in one memory cycle time T_M. We then need fast circuits inside the RAM that, in the case of a read operation, can access an Sn-bit word, break it into S parts, and output them to the processor, all within the period T_M. During write operations, these circuits must accept up to S n-bit words from the processor, assemble them into an nS-bit word, and store the result, again within the period T_M.
- *Access more than one word at a time.* We can partition the RAM into S separate banks $M_0, M_1, ..., M_{S-1}$, each covering part of the memory address space and each

provided with its own addressing circuitry. Then it is possible to carry out S independent accesses simultaneously in one memory clock period T_M. Once more, we need fast circuits inside the RAM unit to assemble and disassemble the words being accessed.

Both approaches increase the memory bandwidth by increasing the amount of parallelism in memory accesses, and both require fast parallel-to-serial and serial-to-parallel circuits at the processor-memory interface. Hence an interface technology different from that of the RAM itself may be necessary; therefore, these approaches may not be suitable for single-chip RAM designs. The special interface circuits also add substantially to the overall cost of the memory system.

The S words produced or consumed by the processor in each memory cycle normally have consecutive memory addresses, so we must consider how these addresses are implemented inside the RAM, particularly when S independent memory banks are used. Let $X_h, X_{h+1}, X_{h+2}, \ldots$ be words that are expected to be accessed in sequence by the processor, for example, consecutive instruction words in a program. They will normally be mapped to consecutive physical addresses $A_i, A_{i+1}, A_{i+2}, \ldots$ in the RAM. The following rule is employed to distribute these addresses among S memory banks:

Interleaving rule: Assign address A_i to bank M_j if $j = i$ (modulo S).

Thus $A_0, A_S, A_{2S}, \ldots$ are assigned to M_0; $A_1, A_{S+1}, A_{2S+1}, \ldots$ are assigned to M_1; and so on. This way of distributing addresses among memory banks is *address interleaving*. The interleaving of addresses among S banks according to the above rule is *S-way interleaving*. It is convenient to make S, the number of banks, a power of two, say, $S = 2^p$. Then the least significant p bits of a memory address immediately identify the bank to which the address belongs.

The appropriate number of memory banks S is determined by comparing the cycle time of the RAM technology to the data requirements of its host processor. Consider the case of the Cray-1, an influential supercomputer of the mid-1970s, which uses address interleaving in its main memory M. The CPU cycle time is 12.5 ns, and the semiconductor main memory has a cycle time of $t_M = 50$ ns and a word size of $w = 64$ bits. (The Cray-1 has no cache, however.) Although the number of memory accesses associated with each CPU cycle varies from cycle to cycle, a reasonable estimate is that when operating at maximum speed, one instruction word and two input operand words are read from M and one result word is written into M. Hence a memory bandwidth of four 64-bit words per CPU cycle, or 16 words per memory cycle, is required. Consequently, the Cray-1 has 16 memory banks and uses 16-way address interleaving.

The efficiency of an interleaved memory system is highly dependent on the order in which memory addresses are generated; this order is determined by the programs being executed. If two or more addresses require simultaneous access to the same module, then memory *interference* or *contention* occurs. The memory accesses in question cannot be executed simultaneously. In the worst case, if all addresses refer to the same module, the advantages of interleaving are entirely lost.

Various high-performance interfacing techniques have been devised for RAMs [Kumanoya, Ogaywa, and Inoue 1995]. As discussed in Example 6.1, a 2-D RAM organization with multiplexed row and column addresses facilitates *page addressing*, in which the row or page address remains fixed while the processor supplies a stream of column addresses. This technique, which exists in several variations, has the effect of approximately doubling the data-transfer rate compared with pure "random" addressing. Another DRAM design style called *synchronous DRAM* (SDRAM) achieves a speed doubling by pipelining its internal operations and by implementing two-way address interleaving. To facilitate this internal architecture, the timing relationships among the SDRAM's control signals (*WE, CS,* and so on) are streamlined so that the SDRAM presents a synchronous (clocked) interface to the outside world. The so-called *cached DRAMs* (CDRAMs) feature an on-chip cache realized by a small, fast SRAM that acts as a high-speed buffer or front-end memory for the main DRAM. A common characteristic of the preceding RAM styles is that they can have a fast *burst mode* of operation, where an initial slow access is followed by a sequence or burst of much faster accesses.

EXAMPLE 6.2 THE RAMBUS DRAM AND INTERFACE [PRINCE 1996]. First announced in 1992, this is a proprietary DRAM design with a supporting processor-memory interface that aims to transfer memory data at very high rates over a narrow processor-memory link. It employs several speedup techniques, including a synchronous interface, address interleaving and caching inside the DRAM units, very fast signal timing, and stringent electrical design rules. The Rambus data bus is 8 or 9 bits wide, with the 9th bit typically serving as a parity check. The peak data transfer rate is 500 MB/s which, however, is achievable only in burst mode.

Figure 6.14 depicts the overall Rambus organization. As we will see in Chapter 7, it is closer in style to that of a typical IO interface than a traditional memory interface. Rambus DRAM units are attached to this shared interface—the Rambus channel—which consists of a nine-line data bus D and a small set of control lines. Access is controlled either by the host CPU or a special Rambus controller chip acting as the master control unit. Each Rambus DRAM unit covers part of the memory-address space and acts as an independent slave device that communicates with the master via the Rambus channel. The S_{in}/S_{out} lines that link the DRAM units in daisy-chain fashion are used for initialization. They enable the master to visit each DRAM unit in turn to load a configuration register that determines the range of addresses to which that unit responds.

Normal Rambus operation is as follows. The master transmits an initial "packet" of information on the Rambus channel; this packet contains a target memory address

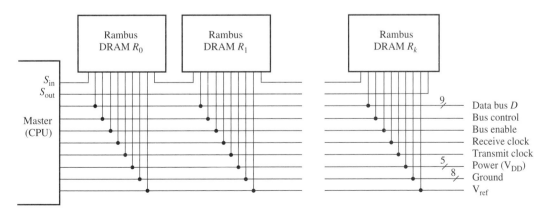

Figure 6.14
The Rambus DRAM interface.

and the desired access (read or write) operation. Each Rambus DRAM chip examines the address, and the DRAM unit R_i containing that address returns either a "ready" or a "busy" control signal to the master. If R_i is ready, the master then proceeds to transfer to R_i a data packet of up to 256 bytes (write case) or R_i sends the master a data packet (read case). This data transmission takes place in burst mode at speeds up to 500 MB/s, which implies accessing and transferring up to 1 byte every 2 ns. If R_i is busy with an earlier operation when an access request arrives, the master must try again later and a significant delay in response time occurs.

6.1.3 Serial-Access Memories

The data in a serial-access memory must be accessed in a predetermined order via read-write circuitry that is shared by different storage locations. Large serial memories typically store information in a fixed set of *tracks*, each consisting of a sequence of 1-bit storage cells. A track has one or more access points at which a read-write "head" can transfer information to or from the track. A stored item is accessed by moving either the stored information or the read-write heads or both. Functionally, a storage track in a serial memory resembles a shift register, so data transfer to and from a track is essentially serial.

Serial-access memories find their main application as secondary computer memories because of their low cost per bit and relatively long access times. Low cost is achieved by using very simple and small storage cells. Long access time is due to several factors:

- The read-write head positioning time.
- The relatively slow speed at which the tracks move.
- The fact that data transfer to and from the memory is serial rather than parallel.

Because access speed is so important, we now consider this factor in detail.

Access methods. Serial memories such as magnetic hard disks can be divided into those where each track has one or more fixed read-write heads and those whose read-write heads are shared among different tracks. In memories that share read-write heads, the need to move the heads between tracks introduces a delay. The average time to move a head from one track to another is the *seek time* t_S of the memory. Once the head is in position, the desired cell may be in the wrong part of the moving storage track. Some time is required for this cell to reach the read-write head so that data transfer can begin. The average time for this movement to take place is the *latency* t_L of the memory. In memories where information rotates around a closed track, t_L is called the *rotational latency*.

Each storage cell in a track stores a single bit. A w-bit word may be stored in two different ways. It can consist of w consecutive bits along a single track. Alternatively, w tracks may be used to store the word, with each track storing a different bit. By synchronizing the w tracks and providing a separate read-write head for each track, all w bits can be accessed simultaneously. In either case it is inefficient to read or write just one word per serial access, since the seek time and the rotational latency consume so much time. Words are therefore grouped into larger units called *blocks*. All the words in a block are stored in consecutive locations so that the time to access an entire block includes only one seek and one latency time.

Once the read-write head is positioned at the start of the requested word or block, data is transferred at a rate that depends on two factors: the speed of the stored information relative to the read-write head and the storage density along the track. The speed at which data can be transferred continuously to or from the track under these circumstances is the *data-transfer rate*. If a track has a storage density of T bits/cm and moves at a velocity of V cm/s past the read-write head, then the data-transfer rate is TV bits/s.

The time t_B needed to access a block of data in a serial-access memory can be estimated as follows. Assume that the memory has closed, rotating storage tracks of the type shown in Figure 6.4. Let each track have a fixed (average) capacity of N words and rotate at r revolutions per second. Let n be the number of words per block. The data-transfer rate of the memory is then rN words/s. Once the read-write head is positioned at the start of the desired block, its data can be transferred in approximately $n/(rN)$ seconds. The average latency is $1/(2r)$ seconds, which is the time needed for half a revolution. If t_S is the average seek time, then an appropriate formula for t_B is

$$t_B = t_S + \frac{1}{2r} + \frac{n}{rN} \qquad (6.1)$$

Memory organization. Figure 6.15 shows the overall organization of a serial-memory unit. Assume that each word is stored along a single track and that each access results in the transfer of a block of words. The address of the data to be accessed is applied to the address decoder, whose output determines the track to be

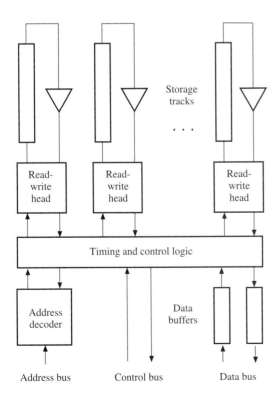

Figure 6.15
Organization of a serial-access memory unit.

used (the track address) and the location of the desired block of information within the track (the block address). The track address determines the particular read-write head to be selected. Then, if necessary, the selected head is moved into position to transfer data to or from the target track. The desired block cannot be accessed until it coincides with the selected head. To determine when this condition occurs, a track-position indicator generates the address of the block that is currently passing the read-write head. The generated address is compared with the block address produced by the address decoder. When they match, the selected head is enabled and data transfer between the storage track and the memory data buffer registers begins. The read-write head is disabled when a complete block of information has been transferred.

The number of different types of storage media and access mechanisms used to construct serial memories is quite large. In many such memories the read-write heads or the storage locations are moved through space by electromechanical devices, such as electric motors, in order to perform an access. The most widely used group of secondary memory devices, magnetic-disk and -tape units, fall into this category, as do many optical memories. Some optical memories—CD-ROMs are an example—employ laser beams with electromechanical focusing as their read-write heads. Only a few serial memories have no moving parts, for example, the so-called solid-state disks, which use semiconductor RAM technology to simulate the behavior of disk memories in applications that need unusually fast (and therefore expensive) secondary memory. Magnetic memories with electromechanical access have had many years of development. The storage media (magnetic disks and tape cartridges) are inexpensive and portable. Electromechanical equipment is less reliable than electronic equipment, however, and is a common source of computer system failure.

Magnetic-surface recording. Magnetic-disk and -tape memories store information on the surface of tracks coated with a magnetic medium such as ferric oxide. Each cell of a track has two stable magnetic states that represent logical 0 and 1. These magnetic states are defined by the direction or magnitude of the cell's magnetic flux in the cell. Electric currents alter and sense the magnetic states, for example, via an inductive read-write head of the type shown in Figure 6.16. The read and write signals pass through coils around a ring of soft magnetic material. A very narrow gap separates the ring from a cell on the storage track so that their respective magnetic fields can interact. This interaction permits information transfer between the read-write head and the storage medium.

To write data, the addressed cell is moved under the read-write gap. A pulse of current is then transmitted through the write coil, which alters the magnetic field at the ring gap; this in turn alters the magnetization state of the cell under the gap. The direction or magnitude of the write current determines the resulting state. To read a cell, it is moved past the read-write head, causing the magnetic field of the cell to induce a magnetic field in the core material of the read-write head. Since the cell is in motion, this magnetic field varies and so induces an electric voltage pulse in the read coil. This voltage pulse, which is then fed to a sense amplifier, identifies the state of the cell. The readout process is nondestructive; in addition, magnetic-surface storage is nonvolatile.

Electromechanically accessed magnetic memories are distinguished by the shapes of the surfaces in which the storage tracks are embedded. In disk memories the tracks form concentric circles on the surface of a plastic or metal disk. In tape memories the tracks form parallel lines on the surface of a long, narrow plastic tape.

Magnetic-disk memories. A magnetic-disk unit employs storage media consisting of thin disks with a coating of magnetic material on which data can be recorded. One or both surfaces of a disk contain thousands of recording tracks arranged in concentric circles as shown in Figure 6.17a. Several disks can be attached to a common spindle; the four disks in Figure 6.17b provide up to eight recording surfaces.

During operation of the memory, the disks are rotated at a constant speed by a *disk drive unit*. Each recording surface is supplied with at least one read-write head. The read-write heads can be connected to form a read-write arm, as shown in Figure 6.17b, so that all heads move in unison. This arm moves back and forth to

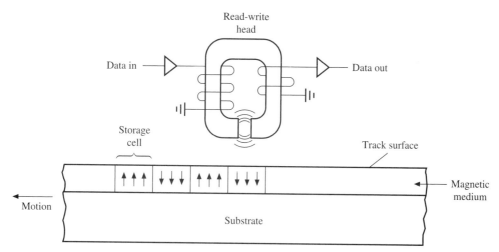

Figure 6.16
Magnetic-surface recording mechanism.

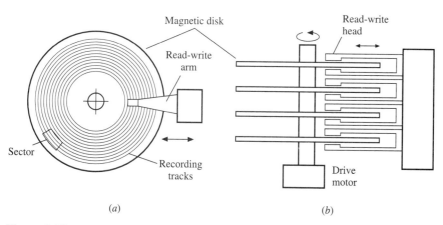

Figure 6.17
(*a*) Top view and (*b*) side view of a magnetic-disk drive unit.

select a particular set of tracks for reading or writing. The recording surface is divided into *sectors* so that the part of a track within a sector stores a fixed amount of information corresponding to the memory unit's block size. Memory control is simplified if all tracks store the same amount of data, in which case the track density (bits stored per cm) on the outer tracks is less than the maximum possible.

Since their introduction in the 1950s by IBM, magnetic-disk memories have undergone steady evolution characterized by decreasing physical size and increasing storage density. Small flexible magnetic disks referred to as *floppy* disks form a compact, inexpensive, and portable medium for off-line storage of small amounts of data, for instance, 1.4 MB. They are contrasted with *hard* disks, which are often sealed into their drive units and have much higher storage capacity and reliability.

EXAMPLE 6.3 A COMMERCIAL MAGNETIC HARD-DISK MEMORY UNIT [QUANTUM CORP. 1996]. The XP39100 is a 9.3 GB hard-disk memory in the Atlas II series manufactured by Quantum Corp. and introduced in the mid-1990s. It is housed in a rectangular box whose dimensions are approximately $14.6 \times 10.2 \times 4.14$ cm. It contains ten 3.5 in (8.89 cm) diameter disks, supplying a total of 20 recording surfaces, each with its own read-write head. Figure 6.18 summarizes the main features of this device. The cited capacity of 9.1 GB is for a *formatted* disk, which stores a directory and other control information needed to make the disk drive ready for use. The number of sectors along a track varies from 108 to 180, and each sector within a track accommodates a 512-byte block. While the sector size is fixed, the number of sectors per track varies due to the fact that the inner tracks are smaller and can therefore store less information at the maximum recording density of the magnetic medium. The average block access time given by Equation (6.1) with the data from Figure 6.18 is

$$t_B = 7.9 + 4.2 + 0.6 = 12.7 \text{ ms}$$

where $t_S = 7.9$ ms, $r = 0.120$ revs/ms, $n = 8$, and we take $(108 + 180)/2 = 144$ to be the average number of sectors per track, implying that $N = 144 \times 512 = 73,728$ bytes/track. Observe that the seek time is the major factor in t_B. The data-transfer rate $rN = 120 \times$

Parameter	Size
Disk diameter (form factor)	3.5 in (8.89 cm)
Number of disks	10
Number of recording surfaces	20
Number of read-write heads per recording surface	1
Number of tracks per recording surface	5964
Number of sectors per track	108 to 180
Storage capacity per track sector (block size)	512 bytes
Track-recording density	110,000 bits/in
Storage capacity per recording surface (formatted)	445 MB
Storage capacity of disk drive (formatted)	9.1 GB
Disk-rotation speed	7200 rev/min
Average seek time	7.9 ms
Average rotational latency	4.2 ms
Internal data-transfer rate	8.7 to 13.8 MB/s
External (buffered) data-transfer rate	20 to 40 MB/s

Figure 6.18
Characteristics of the Quantum Atlas II model XP391000 magnetic hard-disk memory unit.

73,728 = 8.85 MB/s, which is consistent with Figure 6.18. Because of factors such as data buffering in the hard-disk unit and the format of its external interface, the user may see a different and higher effective data-transfer rate.

Other noteworthy features of the XP39100 hard disk are a built-in 1 MB cache to buffer data transfers and an error-correcting code that is applied on the fly to data being stored in the XP39100. The system's reliability is measured by its MTBF, which the manufacturer projects to be 1 million hours.

Magnetic-tape memories. The magnetic-tape unit is one of the oldest and cheapest forms of mass memory. Its main use today is to provide backup storage for a computer system in the event of failure of its hard disk subsystem. Magnetic-tape memories resemble domestic tape recorders, but instead of storing analog sound, they store binary digital information. The storage medium has as its substrate a flexible plastic tape, usually packaged in a small cassette or cartridge. Figure 6.19 shows a standard memory of the data-cartridge type containing a magnetic tape, which is 0.25 in (6.35 mm) wide and about 200 m long.

Data is stored on a tape in parallel, longitudinal tracks. Older tapes employed nine such tracks designed to store one data byte and a parity bit across the tape; newer tapes have as many as several hundred tracks. A read-write head can simultaneously access all tracks. Data transfer takes place when the tape is moving at constant velocity relative to a read-write head; hence the maximum data-transfer rate depends largely on the storage density along the tape and the tape's speed. For example, if an 80-track tape has a per-track storage density of 110 Kb/in and the

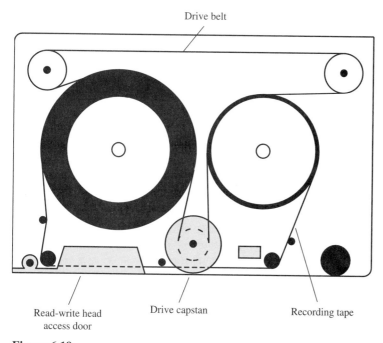

Figure 6.19
A magnetic tape cartridge.

tape speed is 50 in/s, the maximum data-transfer rate d is $110,000 \times 80/8 \times 50 = 55$ MB/s. A 200 m tape of this type can store about $55/50 \times 200/0.0254 = 8.661$ GB, a number that is reduced by formatting requirements. The time to scan or rewind an entire tape is about a minute.

Information stored on magnetic tapes is organized into blocks, usually of fixed length. A relatively large gap is inserted at the end of each block to permit the tape to start and stop between blocks. If the block length is bl and the interblock gap length is gl, then the tape's (space) utilization u is measured by

$$u = \frac{bl}{bl + gl} \tag{6.2}$$

For example, if $gl = 0.6$ in, the storage density $s = 3200$ b/in, and a block stores $bs = 4KB$ of data, then $bl = 4096/3200 = 1.28$ in. Equation (6.2) implies that $u = 1.28/1.88 = 0.68$.

Because of the interblock gaps and the time needed to start and stop the tape between accesses, the effective data-transfer rate d_{eff} seen by the user is less than the quoted, maximum rate d. Let t_D denote the time to scan a data block, let t_G be the time to scan an interblock gap, and let t_{SS} be the time to start and stop the tape. Then

$$d_{\text{eff}} = \frac{t_D d}{t_D + t_G + t_{SS}}$$

If the block and gap sizes in bytes are bs and gs, respectively, then $t_D = bs/d$, and $t_G = gs/d$, so this equation becomes

$$d_{\text{eff}} = \frac{bs \cdot d}{bs + gs + t_{SS} \cdot d} \tag{6.3}$$

and the effective block access time t_B is $1/d_{\text{eff}}$. For example, with $bs = 4096$ bytes; $gl = 0.6$ in, corresponding to $gs = 1.92$ bytes; $d = 100,000$ bytes/s; and $t_{SS} = 2$ ms, Equation (6.3) yields $d_{\text{eff}} = 65,894$ bytes/s, a reduction of 34 percent from the maximum data-transfer rate.

Optical memories. Optical or light-based techniques for data storage have been the subject of intensive research for many years. Such memories usually employ optical disks, which resemble magnetic disks in that they store binary information in concentric tracks (or a spiral track in the CD-ROM case) on an electromechanically rotated disk. The information is read or written optically, however, with a laser replacing the read-write arm of a magnetic-disk drive. Optical memories offer extremely high storage capacities, but their access rates are generally less than those of magnetic disks. Read-only optical memories are well developed, but low-cost read-write memories have proven difficult to build.

The CD-ROM is a well-established read-only optical memory. CD-ROMs are an offshoot of the audio compact disks (CDs) introduced in the 1980s. They are manufactured in the same 12 cm format and can be mass-produced at very low cost per disk by injection molding. Binary data is stored in the form of 0.1 μm wide *pits* and *lands* (nonpitted areas) in circular tracks on a plastic substrate; see Figure 6.20. A laser beam scans the tracks and is reflected differently by the pits and lands. A mirror-and-lens system forms a read arm that can move back and forth across the tracks. The mirror can also be tilted slightly to provide fine tracking adjustments.

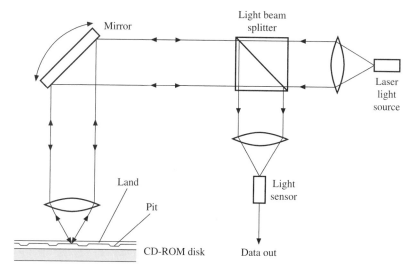

Figure 6.20
Optical readout mechanism for a CD-ROM.

The reflected light from the laser is picked up by a sensor and decoded to extract the stored information, which is then converted to electronic form for further processing. A standard 12 cm CD-ROM has a capacity of around 600 MB, which is enough to store some 240,000 pages of printed text—a large encyclopedia, for instance. Access time is about 100 ms, and data is transferred from the disk at a rate of 3.6 MB/s (in so-called 24-speed CD-ROM drives). Low-cost CD drives are available that allow computer users to create their own CD ROMs under such names as CD-recordable (CD-R) and CD-rewritable (CD-RW). They employ a laser to create (burn) pits on the surface of blank disks. A much denser type of CD called a *digital video disk* (DVD) has recently been introduced in both read-only and read-write forms. With two recording surfaces and one or two storage layers per surface, a DVD can have a capacity as high as 16 GB.

A few types of secondary memory devices combine magnetic and optical recording methods. A *magneto-optical disk* memory uses rotating disks that store information in magnetic form but are accessed by a laser beam similar to that in a CD-ROM drive. Like a magnetic disk, a magneto-optical disk has a magnetizable surface coating whose direction of magnetization can be polarized (up or down corresponding to 0 or 1) as depicted in Figure 6.16. A cell is read by bouncing a laser beam off it. The beam's angle of polarization is affected by the cell's magnetization direction, a phenomenon known as the *Kerr effect*. The slight change in the polarization angle of the reflected laser beam is sensed and decoded by the read mechanism. Writing is accomplished by using the laser beam to briefly heat a chosen cell above a specific temperature (the *Curie temperature* of the magnetic medium), at which point the cell's magnetic coercivity becomes zero, making the cell sensitive to external magnetic fields. An electromagnetic coil placed below the rotating disk then supplies a magnetic field of the required direction. The heated cell captures the magnetic field's direction which is retained after the cell cools below its Curie temperature.

6.2
MEMORY SYSTEMS

This section examines the general characteristics of memory systems that have a multilevel, hierarchical organization. Two key design issues are considered in detail: automatic translation of addresses and dynamic relocation of data.

6.2.1 Multilevel Memories

A computer's memory units form a hierarchy of different memory types in which each member is in some sense subordinate to the next-highest member of the hierarchy. The object of this organization is to achieve a good trade-off between cost, storage capacity, and performance for the memory system as a whole.

General characteristics. Consider a general n-level system of n memory types $(M_1, M_2, ..., M_n)$. Figure 6.21 shows some examples with $n = 2$, 3, and 4. Typical technologies used in these hierarchies are semiconductor SRAMs for cache memory, semiconductor DRAMs for main memory, and magnetic-disk units for secondary memory. The two-level hierarchy of Figure 6.21a is typical of early computers. Figure 6.21b adds a cache of a type called a *split* cache, since it has separate areas for storing instructions (the I-cache) and data (the D-cache). The third example (Figure 6.21c) has two cache levels, both of the nonsplit or *unified* type. Embedded microcontrollers also use the various hierarchical organizations depicted in the figure, but often lack the secondary or the cache levels.

The following relations normally hold between adjacent memory levels M_i and M_{i+1} in a memory hierarchy:

Cost per bit $\qquad c_i > c_{i+1}$

Access time $\qquad t_{A_i} < t_{A_{i+1}}$

Storage capacity $\qquad S_i < S_{i+1}$

The differences in cost, access time, and capacity between M_i and M_{i+1} can be several orders of magnitude. Considerable system resources are devoted to shielding the CPU from these differences, so it almost always sees a very large and inexpensive memory space and rarely sees an access time greater than that of M_1, the first (highest) level of the memory hierarchy.

The CPU and other processors can communicate directly with M_1 only, M_1 can communicate with M_2, and so on. Consequently, for the CPU to read information held in some memory level M_i requires a sequence of i data transfers of the form

$$M_{i-1} := M_i; \quad M_{i-2} := M_{i-1}; \quad M_{i-3} := M_{i-2}; \quad ... \quad M_1 := M_2; \quad \text{CPU} := M_1.$$

An exception is allowed in the case of caches; the CPU is designed to bypass the cache level(s) and go directly to main memory, as we will see later. In general, all the information stored in M_i at any time is also stored in M_{i+1}, but not vice versa.

During program execution the CPU produces a steady stream of memory addresses. At any time these addresses are distributed in some fashion throughout the memory hierarchy. If an address is generated that is currently assigned only to

I: Instruction flow
D: Data flow

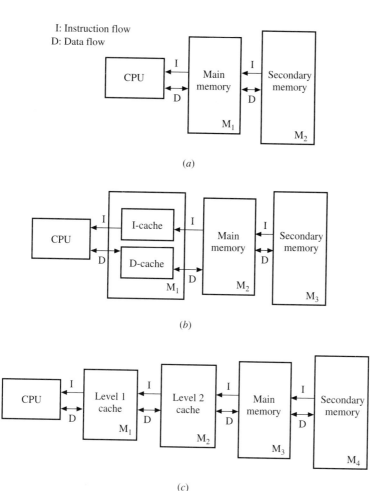

Figure 6.21
Common memory hierarchies with (*a*) two, (*b*) three, and (*c*) four levels.

M_i where $i \neq 1$, the address must be reassigned to M_1, the level of the memory hierarchy that the CPU can access directly. This relocation of addresses involves the transfer of data between levels M_i and M_1—a relatively slow process. For a memory hierarchy to work efficiently, the addresses generated by the CPU should be found in M_1 as often as possible. This approach requires that future addresses be to some extent predictable so that information can be transferred to M_1 before it is actually referenced by the CPU. If the desired data cannot be found in M_1, then the program originating the memory request must be suspended until an appropriate reallocation of storage is made.

Cache and virtual memory. The various parts of a memory hierarchy are controlled in very different fashions. Cache and main memory form a distinct subhierarchy whose design objective is to support CPU accesses with a minimum of delay. Hence hardware controllers that are transparent to both user and system programs usually manage this subhierarchy. Much more than the rest of the memory system, the cache and main memory resemble a single memory M to the software being executed.

Main and secondary memory form another distinct two-level subhierarchy. This interaction is managed by the operating system, however, and so is not transparent to system software, although it is somewhat transparent to user code. The term *virtual memory* is applied when the main and secondary memories appear to a user program like a single, large, and directly addressable memory. Traditionally, there are three reasons for using virtual memory:

- To free user programs from the need to carry out storage allocation and to permit efficient sharing of the available memory space among different users.
- To make programs independent of the configuration and capacity of the physical memory present for their execution; for example, to allow seamless overflow into secondary memory when the capacity of main memory is exceeded.
- To achieve the very low access time and cost per bit that are possible with a memory hierarchy.

A memory system is addressed by a set V of *logical* or *virtual* addresses derived from identifiers explicitly or implicitly specified in an object program. A set of *physical* or *real* addresses R identifies the fixed physical storage locations in each memory unit M_i. An efficient and flexible mechanism to implement address mappings of the form $f: V \rightarrow R$ is the key to successful design of a multilevel memory.

Locality of reference. The predictability of memory addresses depends on a characteristic of computer programs called *locality of reference*, which says that over the short term, the addresses generated by a program tend to be localized and are therefore predictable.

One reason for locality of reference is that instructions and, to a lesser extent, data are specified and subsequently stored in a memory unit in approximately the order in which they are accessed during program execution. Suppose a request is made for a one-word instruction I stored at address A, but this address is currently assigned to $M_i \neq M_1$. The instruction most likely to be required next by the CPU is the one immediately following I whose address is $A + 1$. Figure 6.22, which shows part of the 680X0 program for vector addition discussed in Example 3.8 (section

Machine Language		Assembly Language		
Location	Instruction	; 680X0 program for vector addition		
0100	2078 07D1		MOVE.L A+1000,A0	;Set pointer beyond end of A
0104	2278 0BB9		MOVE.L B+1000,A1	;Set pointer beyond end of B
0108	2478 0FA1		MOVE.L C+1000,A2	;Set pointer beyond end of C
010C	C308	START	ABCD –(A0),–(A1)	;Decrement pointers and add
010E	1511		MOVE.B (A1),–(A2)	;Store result in C
0110	B0F8 03E9		CMPA A,A0	;Test for termination
0114	66F6		BNE START	;Branch to START if Z ≠ 1

Figure 6.22
Code fragment illustrating locality of reference.

3.3.3), illustrates this tendency. The first (4 byte) instruction fetched has address 0100_{16}, the next has address 0104_{16}, the next 0108_{16}, and so on. This type of locality is called *spatial* because it implies that consecutive memory references are to addresses that are close to one another in the memory-address space.

Instead of simply transferring I to M_1 when it is referenced, it is more efficient to transfer a block of consecutive words containing I. A common way to automate this process is to subdivide the information stored in M_i into *pages*, each containing a fixed number S_{P_i} of consecutive words. Information is then transferred one page or S_{P_i} words at a time between levels M_i and M_{i-1}. Thus if the CPU requests word I in level M_i, the page of the length $S_{P_{i-1}}$ in M_i containing I is transferred to M_{i-1}, then the page of length $S_{P_{i-2}}$ containing I is transferred to M_{i-2}, and so on. Finally, the page P of length S_{P_1} containing I reaches M_1, where the CPU can directly access it. Subsequent memory references are likely to refer to other addresses in P, so the single transfer to M_1 anticipates future memory requests by the CPU.

A second factor in locality of reference is the presence of loops in programs. Instructions in a loop, even when they are far apart in spatial terms, are executed repeatedly, resulting in a high frequency of reference to their addresses. This characteristic is referred to as *temporal locality*. When a loop is being executed, it is desirable to store the entire loop in M_1 if possible. For example, in the small, four-instruction program loop shown in boldface in Figure 6.22, the BNE branch instruction with address 0114_{16} is usually followed by the instruction with the nonconsecutive address $010C_{16}$ (START).

The items of information whose addresses are referenced during the time interval from $t - T$ to t, denoted $(t - T, t)$, constitute the current *working set* $W(t, T)$ of a program. $W(t, T)$ tends to change rather slowly; hence by maintaining all of $W(t, T)$ in the fastest level of memory M_1, the number of references to M_1 can be made far greater than the number of references to other levels of the memory hierarchy.

Cost and performance. The overall goal in memory-hierarchy design is to achieve a performance close to that of the fastest device M_1 and a cost per bit close to that of the cheapest device M_n. The performance of a memory system depends on various related factors, the more important of which are the following:

- The address-reference statistics, that is, the order and frequency of the logical addresses generated by programs that use the memory hierarchy.
- The access time t_{A_i} of each level M_i relative to the CPU.
- The storage capacity S_i of each level.
- The size S_{P_i} of the blocks (pages) transferred between adjacent levels.
- The allocation algorithm used to determine the regions of memory to which blocks are transferred by the block-swapping process.

These factors interact in complex ways, which are by no means fully understood. Simulation of a multilevel memory using realistic address traces is often the best way to determine suitable values for t_{A_i}, S_i, S_{P_i}, and other important design parameters. A few analytic models indicate how these factors are related. Some useful models of this kind are discussed next.

For simplicity we restrict our attention to a generic two-level memory hierarchy denoted by (M_1, M_2), which can be interpreted as (cache, main memory) or (main memory, secondary memory). It is not difficult to generalize our analysis from two-level to n-level hierarchies. The average cost per bit of memory is given by

$$c = \frac{c_1 S_1 + c_2 S_2}{S_1 + S_2} \tag{6.4}$$

where c_i denotes the cost per bit of M_i and S_i denotes the storage capacity in bits of M_i. To reach the goal of making c approach c_2, S_1 must be much smaller than S_2.

The performance of a two-level memory is often measured in terms of the *hit ratio H*, which is defined as the probability that a virtual address generated by the CPU refers to information currently stored in the faster memory M_1. Since references to M_1 (*hits*) can be satisfied much more quickly than references to M_2 (*misses*), it is desirable to make H as close to one as possible. Hit ratios are generally determined experimentally as follows. A set of representative programs is executed or simulated. The number of address references satisfied by M_1 and M_2, denoted by N_1 and N_2, respectively, are recorded. H is calculated from the equation

$$H = \frac{N_1}{N_1 + N_2} \tag{6.5}$$

and is highly program dependent. The quantity $1 - H$ is called the *miss ratio*.

Let t_{A_1} and t_{A_2} be the access times of M_1 and M_2, respectively, relative to the CPU. The average time t_A for the CPU to access a word in the two-level memory is given by

$$t_A = H t_{A_1} + (1 - H) t_{A_2} \tag{6.6}$$

In most two-level hierarchies, a request for a word not in the fast level M_1 causes a block of information containing the requested word to be transferred to M_1 from M_2. When the block transfer has been completed, the requested word is available in M_1. The time t_B required for the block transfer is called the *block-access* or *block-transfer* time. Hence we can write $t_{A_2} = t_B + t_{A_1}$. Substituting into Equation (6.6) yields

$$t_A = t_{A_1} + (1 - H) t_B \tag{6.7}$$

In many cases $t_{A_2} \gg t_{A_1}$; therefore, $t_{A_2} \approx t_B$. For example, a block transfer from secondary to main memory requires a relatively slow IO operation, making t_{A_2} and t_B much greater than t_{A_1}.

Let $r = t_{A_2}/t_{A_1}$ denote the access-time ratio of the two levels of memory. Let $e = t_{A_1}/t_A$, which is the factor by which t_A differs from its minimum possible value; e is called the *access efficiency* of the two-level memory. From Equation (6.6) we obtain

$$e = \frac{1}{r + (1 - r)H}$$

Figure 6.23 plots e as a function of H for various values of r. This graph shows the importance of achieving high values of H in order to make $e \approx 1$; that is, $t_A \approx t_{A_1}$. For example, suppose that $r = 100$. In order to make $e > 0.9$, we must have $H > 0.998$.

Memory capacity is limited by cost considerations; therefore, we do not want to waste memory space. The efficiency with which space is being used at any time can be defined as the ratio of the memory space S_u occupied by "active" or "useful"

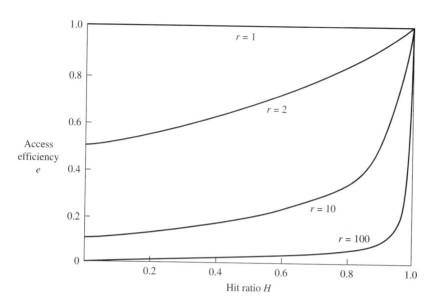

Figure 6.23

Access efficiency $e = t_{A_1}/t_A$ of a two-level memory as a function of hit ratio H for various values of $r = t_{A_2}/t_{A_1}$.

user programs and data to the total amount of memory space available S. We call this the *space utilization u* and write

$$u = \frac{S_u}{S}$$

Since memory space is more valuable in M_1 than in M_2, it is useful to restrict u to measuring M_1's space utilization. In that case the $S - S_u$ words of M_1 that represent "wasted" space can be attributed to several sources.

- *Empty regions.* The blocks of instructions and data occupying M_1 at any time are generally of different lengths. As the contents of M_1 are changed, unoccupied regions or holes of various sizes tend to appear between successive blocks. This phenomenon is called *fragmentation.*
- *Inactive regions.* Data may be transferred to M_1, for example, as part of a page, and may be subsequently transferred back to M_2 without ever being referenced by a processor. Some superfluous transfers of this kind are unavoidable, since address references are not fully predictable.
- *System regions.* These regions are occupied by the memory-management software.

A central issue in managing (M_1, M_2), or any multilevel memory, is to make it appear to its users like a single, fast memory of high capacity. This goal can be achieved in a way that is largely transparent to the users by providing a memory management system that automatically performs the following tasks:

- Translation of memory addresses from the *virtual* addresses encountered in program execution to the *real* addresses that identify physical storage locations.

- Dynamic (re)allocation or swapping of information among the different memory levels so that stored items reside in the fastest level before they are needed.

These issues are explored individually in the following sections.

6.2.2 Address Translation

The set of abstract locations that a program Q can reference is Q's *virtual address space V*. Such addresses can be explicitly or implicitly named by identifiers that a programmer assigns to data variables, instruction labels, and so forth. The addresses can also be constructed or modified by the system software that controls Q. To execute Q on a particular computer, its virtual addresses must be mapped onto the *real address space R*, defined by the addressable (external) memory M that is physically present in the computer. This process is called *address translation* or *address mapping*. The real address space R is a linear sequence of numbers $0, 1, 2, ..., n-1$ corresponding to the addressable word locations in M. It is convenient to identify M with main memory, while noting that R is usually distributed over several levels of the memory hierarchy, including the cache and the level labeled "main" memory. V is a loose collection of lists, multidimensional arrays, and other nonlinear structures, so it is much more complex than R.

Address translation can be viewed abstractly as a function $f: V \rightarrow R$. This function is not easily characterized, since address assignment and translation is carried out at various stages in the life of a program, specifically:

1. By the programmer while writing the program.
2. By the compiler during program compilation.
3. By the loader at initial program-load time.
4. By run-time memory management hardware and/or software.

Explicit specification of real addresses by the programmer was necessary in early computers, which had neither hardware nor software support for memory management. With modern computers, however, programmers normally deal only with virtual addresses. Specialized hardware and software within the computer automatically determine the real addresses required for program execution.

A compiler transforms the symbolic identifiers of a program into binary addresses. If the program is sufficiently simple, the compiler can completely map virtual addresses to real addresses. Address translation can also be completed when the program is first loaded for execution. This process is called *static* translation, since the real address space of the program is fixed for the duration of its execution. It is often desirable to vary the virtual space of a program dynamically during execution; this process is *dynamic* translation. For example, a recursive procedure—one that calls itself—is typically controlled by a stack containing the linkage between successive calls. The size of this stack cannot be predicted in advance because it depends on the number of times the procedure is called; therefore, it is desirable to allocate stack addresses on the fly. Hardware-implemented *memory management units* (MMUs) have come into widespread use for run-time address translation.

Base addressing. An executable program comprises a set of instruction and data blocks each of which is a sequence of words to be stored in consecutive mem-

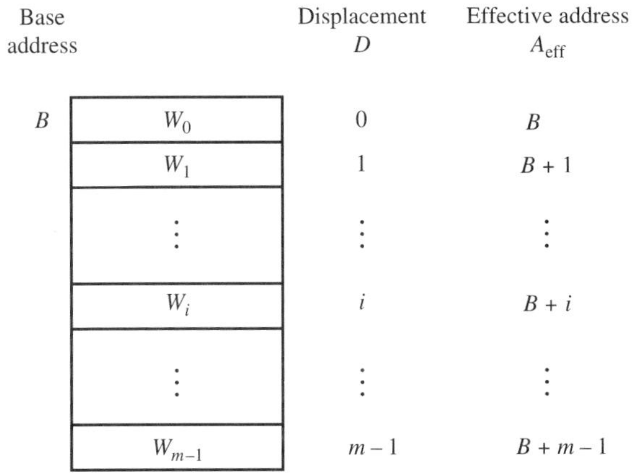

Base address		Displacement D	Effective address A_{eff}
B	W_0	0	B
	W_1	1	$B + 1$
	$\vdots$	$\vdots$	$\vdots$
	W_i	i	$B + i$
	$\vdots$	$\vdots$	$\vdots$
	W_{m-1}	$m - 1$	$B + m - 1$

Figure 6.24
Block of m words with (base) address B.

ory locations during execution. A word W within a block has its own *effective address* A_{eff}, which the CPU must know to access W. (For the moment, we will ignore the distinction between the real and virtual address spaces.) W is also specified by the address B, called the *base address*, of the block that contains it, along with W's relative address or *displacement D* (also called an offset or index) within the block, as shown in Figure 6.24. Clearly,

$$A_{eff} = B + D \qquad (6.8)$$

Often the address is designed so that B supplies the high-order bits of A_{eff} while D supplies the low-order bits thus:

$$A_{eff} = B.D \qquad (6.9)$$

Now A_{eff} is formed simply by concatenating B and D, a process that does not significantly increase the time for address generation.

A simple way to implement static and dynamic address mapping is to put base addresses in a *memory map* or *memory address table* controlled by the memory management system. The table can be stored in memory, in CPU registers, or in both. The address-generation logic of the CPU computes an effective address A_{eff} by combining the displacement D with the corresponding base address B_i according to (6.8) or (6.9).

Blocks are easily relocated in memory by manipulating their base addresses. Figure 6.25 illustrates block relocation using base-address modification. Suppose that two blocks are allocated to main memory M as shown in Figure 6.25a. It is desired to load a third block K_3 into M; however, a contiguous empty space, or "hole," of sufficient size is unavailable. A solution to this problem is to move block K_2, as shown in Figure 6.25b, by assigning it a new base address B_2' and reloading it into memory. This creates a gap into which block K_3 can be loaded by assigning to it an appropriate base address.

With dynamic memory allocation, we must control the references made by a block to locations outside the memory area currently assigned to it. The block can be permitted to read from certain locations, but writing outside its assigned area must be prevented. A common way of doing this is by specifying the highest address L_i, called the *limit address,* that the block can access. Equivalently, the size of the block may be specified. The base address B_i and the limit address L_i are

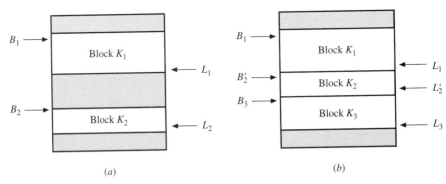

Figure 6.25
Relocation of blocks in memory using base and limit addresses.

stored in the memory map. Every real address A_r generated by the block is compared to B_i and L_i; the memory access is completed if and only if the condition

$$B_i \leq A_r \leq L_i$$

is satisfied.

Translation look-aside buffer. Figure 6.26 shows how various parts of a multilevel memory management typically realize the address-translation ideas just discussed. The input address A_V is a virtual address consisting of a (virtual) base address B_V concatenated with a displacement D. A_V contains an effective address computed in accordance with some program-defined addressing mode (direct, indirect, indexed, and so on) for the memory item being accessed. It also can contain

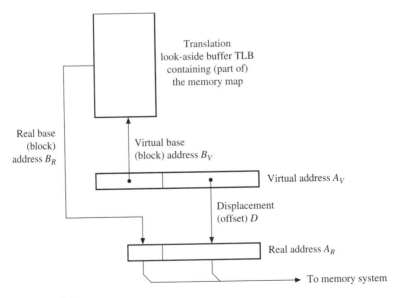

Figure 6.26
Structure of a dynamic address-translation system.

system-specific control information—a segment address, for example—as we will see later. The real address $B_R = f(B_V)$ assigned to B_V is stored in a memory map somewhere in the memory system; this map can be quite large. To speed up the mapping process, part (or occasionally all) of the memory map is placed in a small high-speed memory in the CPU called a *translation look-aside buffer (TLB)*. The TLB's input is thus the base-address part B_V of A_V; its output is the corresponding real base address B_R. This address is then concatenated with the D part of A_V to obtain the full physical address A_R.

If the virtual address B_V is not currently assigned to the TLB, then the part of the memory map that contains B_V is first transferred from the external memory into the TLB. Hence the TLB itself forms a cachelike level within a multilevel address-storage system for memory maps. For this reason, the TLB is sometimes referred to as an *address cache*.

EXAMPLE 6.4 MEMORY ADDRESS TRANSLATION IN THE MIPS R2/3000 [KANE 1988]. The MIPS R2/3000 microprocessor, whose main features were introduced earlier (Examples 3.5 and 3.7), employs an on-chip MMU. The MMU's primary function is to map 32-bit virtual addresses to 32-bit real addresses. (Later members of the RX000 family like the R10000 support 64-bit addresses.) A 32-bit address allows the R2/3000 to have a virtual address space of 2^{32} bytes, or 4 GB. Both address spaces are composed of 4KB *pages,* which are convenient block sizes for information transfer within a conventional memory hierarchy comprising a cache (of the split kind), main memory, and secondary memory. The 4GB virtual-address space is further partitioned into four parts called *segments,* three of which form the system region (or "kernel region" in MIPS parlance) devoted to operating system functions, while the other is the user region, where application programs, data, and control stacks are stored.

The format of an R2/3000 virtual address appears in Figure 6.27. It consists of a 20-bit virtual page address, referred to as the virtual page name *VPN*, and a 12-bit displacement *D,* which specifies the address of a byte within the virtual page. The high-order 3 bits 31:29 of *VPN* form a type of tag that identifies the segment being addressed. Bit 31 of *VPN* is 0 for a user segment and 1 for a supervisor segment; it thus distinguishes the user and supervisor (privileged) control states of the CPU. The user segment is *kuseg* and occupies half the virtual address space. The supervisor region is divided into three segments, *kseg*0, *kseg*1, and *kseg*2, each of which has different access characteristics.

- *kuseg*: This 2GB segment is designed to store all user code and data. Addresses in this region make full use of the cache and are mapped to real addresses via the TLB.
- *kseg*0: This 512MB system segment is cached and unmapped; that is, virtual addresses within *kseg*0 are mapped directly into the first 512 MB of the real address space, which includes the cache, but no virtual address translation takes place. This segment typically stores active parts of the operating system.
- *kseg*1: This is also a 512MB segment, but is both uncached and unmapped. It is intended for such purposes as storing boot-up code (which cannot be cached) and for other instructions and data—high-speed IO data, for instance—that might seriously slow down cache operation.
- *kseg*2: This is a 1GB segment which, like *kuseg*, is both cached and mapped.

The MMU contains a TLB to provide fast virtual-to-real address translation. The TLB stores a 64-entry portion of the memory map (page table) assigned to each process by the operating system. The current virtual page address *VPN* is used to access a 64-bit entry in the TLB, which, as shown in Figure 6.27, contains among other items, a 20-

bit page frame number *PFN*. This real page address is fetched from the TLB and appended to the displacement *D* to obtain the desired 32-bit real address. An R2/3000-based system often has less than 4 GB of physical memory, in which case not all the available real address combinations are used.

Observe that the *VPN* itself is also part of the TLB entry because a fast access method called *associative addressing* is used; see section 6.3.2. Another major item stored in each TLB entry is a 6-bit process identification field *PID*. This field distinguishes each active program (process); hence up to 64 processes can share the available virtual page numbers without interference. There are also 4 control bits denoted *NDVG*, which define the types of memory accesses permitted for the corresponding TLB entry. For example, *N* denotes noncachable; when set to 1, it causes the CPU to go directly to main memory, instead of first accessing the cache. *D* is a write-protection (read-only) bit; an attempt to write when *D* = 0 causes a CPU interrupt or trap.

The MMU has some features not shown in Figure 6.27, which are designed to trap error conditions that are collectively referred to as *address translation exceptions*. When a trap occurs, relevant information about the exception is stored in MMU registers, which can be examined and modified by certain privileged instructions. A common address translation exception is a *TLB miss*, which occurs when there is no (valid) entry in the TLB that matches the current *VPN*. The operating system responds to a TLB miss by accessing the current process's page table, which is stored in a known location in *kseg*2, and copying the missing entry to the TLB. Another address-translation exception type is an illegal access—for instance, a write operation addressed to a page with *D* = 0 (read only) in its TLB entry.

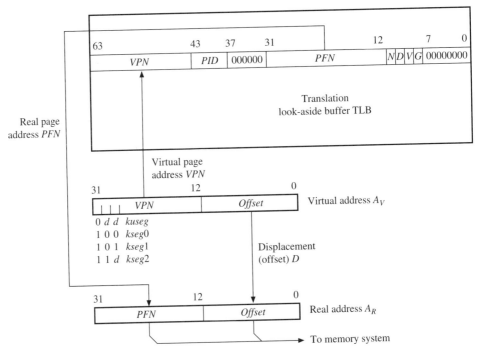

Figure 6.27
Memory address mapping in the MMU of the MIPS R2/3000.

Segments. The basic unit of information for swapping purposes in a multi-level memory is a fixed-size block called a *page*. Pages are allocated to page-sized storage regions (*page frames*), whose fixed size and address formats make paging systems easy to implement. Pages are convenient blocks for the *physical* partitioning and swapping of the information stored in a multilevel memory. It is often desirable to have higher-level information blocks, termed *segments,* that correspond to *logical* entities such as programs or data sets. Segments facilitate the mapping of individual programs, as well as the assignment and checking of different storage properties. For example, write operations may not be permitted into certain regions of the virtual address space in order to protect critical items. It is easier to protect the information in question by making it a read-only segment S, rather than assigning access restrictions to the possibly large number of pages that compose S.

Formally, a *segment* is a set of logically related, contiguous words; it is therefore a special type of block in the sense used in section 6.2.1. A word in a segment is referred to by specifying a base address—the *segment address*—and a displacement within the segment. A program and its data can be viewed as a collection of linked segments. The links arise from the fact that a program segment uses, or calls, other segments. Some computers have a memory management technique that allocates main memory by M_1 segments alone. When a segment not currently resident in M_1 is required, the entire segment is transferred from secondary memory M_2. The physical addresses assigned to the segments are kept in a memory map called a *segment table (*which can itself be a relocatable segment).

Segmentation was implemented in this general form in the Burroughs B6500/7500 series [Hauck and Dent 1968]. Each program has a segment called its program reference table (PRT), which serves as its segment table. All segments associated with the program are defined by special words called *segment descriptors* in the corresponding PRT. As shown in Figure 6.28, a B6500/7500 segment descriptor contains the following information:

- A presence bit P that indicates whether the segment is currently assigned to M_1.
- A copy bit C that specifies whether this is the original (master) copy of the descriptor.
- A 20-bit size field Z that specifies the number of words in the segment.
- A 20-bit address field S that is the segment's real address in M_1 (when $P = 1$) or M_2 (when $P = 0$).

A program refers to a word within a segment by specifying the segment descriptor word W in its PRT and the displacement D. The CPU fetches and examines W. If the presence bit $P = 0$, an interrupt occurs and execution of the requesting program

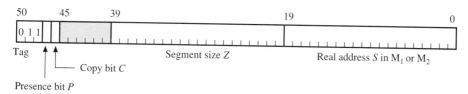

Figure 6.28
Segment descriptor of the Burroughs B6500/7500.

is suspended while the operating system transfers the required segment from M_2 to M_1. When $P = 1$, the CPU compares D to the segment size field Z in the descriptor. If $D \geq Z$, then D is invalid and an interrupt occurs. If $D < Z$, the address field S from the descriptor is added to the displacement D. The result $S + D$ is the real address of the required word in M_1, which can then be accessed.

The main advantage of segmentation is that segment boundaries correspond to natural program and data boundaries. Consequently, information that is shared among different users is often organized into segments. Because of their logical independence, a program segment can be changed or recompiled at any time without affecting other segments. Certain properties of programs such as the scope (range of definition) of a variable and access rights are naturally specified by segment. These properties require that accesses to segments be checked to protect against unauthorized use; this protection is most easily implemented when the units of allocation are segments. Certain segment types—stacks and queues, for instance—vary in length during program execution. Segmentation varies the region assigned to such a segment as it expands and contracts, thus efficiently using the available memory space. On the other hand, the fact that segments can be of different lengths requires a relatively complex allocation method to avoid excessive fragmentation of main-memory space. This problem is alleviated by combining segmentation with paging, as discussed later.

Some computers implement a more specialized form of segmentation. The MIPS R2/3000 divides the virtual address space into four large regions that are treated as segments; see Example 6.4. Just 3 bits of the virtual address define the current segment. Microprocessors in the Intel 80X86 series, including the Pentium, have four 16-bit segment registers forming a segment table that supports a very large number of segments.

Pages. A page is a fixed-length block that can be assigned to fixed regions of physical memory called *page frames*. The chief advantage of paging is that data transfer between memory levels is simplified: an incoming page can be assigned to any available page frame. In a pure paging system, each virtual address consists of two parts: a page address and a displacement. The memory map, now referred to as a *page table,* typically contains the information shown in Figure 6.29. Each (virtual) page address has a corresponding (real) address of a page frame in main or secondary memory. When the presence bit $P = 1$, the page in question is present in main memory, and the page table contains the base address of the page frame to which the page has been assigned. If $P = 0$, a page fault occurs and a page swap ensues. The change bit C indicates whether or not the page has been changed since it was last loaded into main memory. If a change has occurred ($C = 1$), the page

Page address	Page frame	Presence bit P	Change bit C	Access rights
A	0000000	1	0	R, X
C	D6C7F9	0	d	R, W, X
E	0000024	1	1	R, W, X
F	0000016	1	0	R

Figure 6.29
Representative organization of a page table.

must be copied onto secondary memory when it is preempted. The page table can
also contain memory protection data that specifies the access rights of the current
program to read from, write into, or execute the page in question. Page tables differ
from segment tables primarily in the fact that they contain no block size information.

As noted earlier, pages require a simpler memory allocation system than segments, since block size is not a factor in paging. On the other hand, pages have no
logical significance, as they do not represent program elements. Paging and segmentation can also be compared in terms of memory fragmentation. In systems
with segmentation, holes of different sizes tend to proliferate throughout main
memory; they can be eliminated by the time-consuming process of memory compaction. Unusable space between occupied regions is called *external fragmentation.* Since page frames are contiguous, no external fragmentation occurs in paged
systems. However, if a k-word block is divided into p n-word pages, and k is not a
multiple of n, the last page frame to which the block is assigned will not be filled.
Unusable space within a partially filled page frame is called *internal fragmentation.*

Paging and segmentation can be combined in an attempt to gain the advantages
of both. The great advantage of breaking a segment into pages is that it eliminates
the need to store the segment in a contiguous region of main memory. Instead, all
that is required is a number of page frames equal to the number of pages into which
the segment has been broken. Since these page frames need not be contiguous, the
task of placing a large segment in main memory is eased.

When segmentation is used with paging, a virtual address has three components: a segment index SI, a page index PI, and a displacement (offset) D. The
memory map then consists of one or more segment tables and page tables. For fast
address translation, two TLBs can be used as shown in Figure 6.30, one for segment tables and one for page tables. As discussed earlier, the TLBs serve as fast
caches for the memory maps. Every virtual address A_V generated by a program
goes through a two-stage translation process. First, the segment index SI is used to
read the current segment table to obtain the base address PB of the required page
table. This base address is combined with the base index PI (which is just a displacement within the page table) to produce a page address, which is then used to
access a page table. The result is a real page address, that is, a page frame number,
which can be combined with the displacement part D of A_V to give the final (real)
address A_R. This system, as depicted in Figure 6.30, is very flexible. All the various
memory maps can be treated as paged segments and can be relocated anywhere in
the physical memory space.

EXAMPLE 6.5 MEMORY ADDRESS TRANSLATION IN THE INTEL PENTIUM
[INTEL 1994]. The Pentium is a 32-bit microprocessor introduced in 1993 that provides direct hardware support for both segmentation and paging. It is a member of
Intel's 80X86 microprocessor family and maintains some degree of compatibility at the
object-code level with its predecessors back to the original, 1976-vintage 8086 CPU.
Most of the memory-addressing features discussed here originated with the 80386,
introduced in 1985.

Like the MIPS R2/3000 (Example 6.4), the Pentium's real address space can be as
large as 4 GB (2^{32} bytes); however, the virtual address space can be an extremely large
64 TB (64 terabytes = 2^{46} bytes). An on-chip MMU has a segmentation unit that performs address translation for segments ranging in size from 1 to 2^{32} bytes. A separate
paging unit handles address translation for pages of size 4 KB or 4 MB. Any one of the

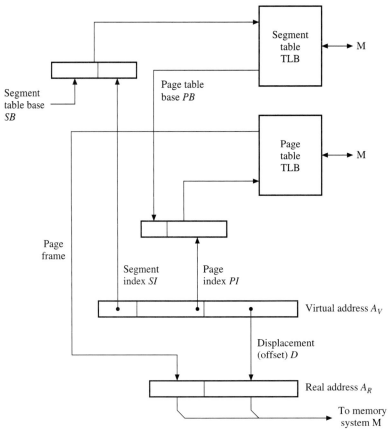

Figure 6.30
Two-stage address translation with segments and pages.

following four memory access methods can be selected under program control: unsegmented and unpaged, segmented and unpaged, unsegmented and paged, and segmented and paged. The output of the paging unit is a 32-bit real address, while that of the segmentation unit is a 32-bit word called a *linear* address. If both segmentation and paging are used, every memory address generated by a program goes through a two-stage translation process

$$\text{Virtual address } A_V \rightarrow \text{linear address } N \rightarrow \text{real address } A_R$$

as depicted in Figure 6.31. Without segmentation $A_V = N$, while without paging $N = A_R$. The segmentation and paging units both contain TLBs to store the active portions of the various memory maps needed for address translation, so the delay of the translation process is small. This delay is further diminished by overlapping (pipelining) the formation of the virtual, linear, and real addresses, as well as by overlapping memory addressing and fetching, so the next real address is ready by the time the current memory cycle is completed.

An active process controlled by the Pentium has several segments associated with it, such as the object program code, a program control stack, and one or more data sets. Each segment can be thought of as a virtual memory of size 4 GB, which has the linear

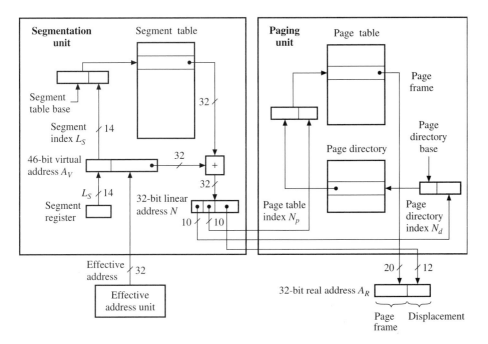

Figure 6.31
Address translation with segmentation and paging in the Intel Pentium.

address organization of main memory. The CPU contains six segment registers that store pointers to the segments in current use. For example, the segment registers CS and SS address a code (program) and stack segment, respectively. These registers are typically used in a manner that is transparent to the application programmer. For instance, when an instruction fetch is initiated, a 32-bit (effective) address obtained from the program counter PC is appended to a 14-bit segment index L_s obtained from the CS register to form a 46-bit virtual address L. As Figure 6.31 indicates, L_s serves as a relative address for an 8-byte segment descriptor stored in one of many possible segment tables. The descriptor specifies the base address and length of the segment S referred to by L_s. It also indicates S's type and access rights, and whether S is present in main memory. The linear address N is constructed by adding the base address obtained from the segment descriptor to the program-derived effective address.

Figure 6.31 also shows how the paging unit processes the linear address N to produce a real address A_R, assuming a page size of 4 KB. A two-step table lookup process is employed to obtain A_R from N. The right-most 12 bits of N form a displacement within the page containing the desired information; they therefore supply the right-most 12 bits of A_R. The remaining 20 bits of N yield a real page address as follows. First a page directory is accessed, which contains entries defining up to 1024 page tables. The left-most 10 bits N_d of N form the relative address of a 32-bit entry E in the page table directory. E contains the 20-bit base address of a page table T, as well as such standard information as a presence bit, a change bit (indicating whether or not the page has been written into), and some protection information. Using the base address derived from E, the page table T is then accessed, and the word E', which is stored at the relative address pointed to by the 10-bit field N_p of the linear address N, is fetched. E', which has the same format as E, provides the 20-bit page address (page frame number) of the desired real address A_R.

Page size. The page size S_p has a big impact on both storage utilization and the effective memory data-transfer rate. Consider first the influence of S_p on the space-utilization factor u defined earlier. If S_p is too large, excessive internal fragmentation results; if it is too small, the page tables become very large and tend to reduce space utilization. A good value of S_p should achieve a balance between these two extremes. Let S_s denote the average segment size in words. If $S_s \gg S_p$, the last page assigned to a segment should contains about $S_p/2$ words. The size of the page table associated with each segment is approximately S_s/S_p words, assuming each entry in the table is a word. Hence the memory space overhead associated with each segment is

$$S = \frac{S_p}{2} + \frac{S_s}{S_p}$$

The space utilization u is

$$u = \frac{S_s}{S_s + S} = \frac{2S_s S_p}{S_p^2 + 2S_s(1 + S_p)} \tag{6.10}$$

The optimum page size S_p^{OPT} can be defined as the value of S_p that maximizes u or, equivalently, that minimizes S. Differentiating S with respect to S_p, we obtain

$$\frac{dS}{dS_p} = \frac{1}{2} - \frac{S_s}{S_p^2}$$

S is a minimum when $dS/dS_p = 0$, from which it follows that

$$S_p^{\text{OPT}} = \sqrt{2S_s} \tag{6.11}$$

The optimum space utilization is

$$u^{\text{OPT}} = \frac{1}{1 + \sqrt{2/S_s}}$$

Figure 6.32 shows the space utilization u defined by Equation (6.10) plotted against S_s for some representative values of S_p.

The influence of page size on hit ratio is complex, depending on the program reference stream and the amount of space available in M_1. Let the virtual address space of a program be a sequence of numbers $A_0, A_1, \ldots, A_{L-1}$. Let A_i be the virtual address referenced at some point in time, and let A_{i+d} be the next address generated, where d is the "distance" between A_i and A_{i+d}. For example, if both addresses point to instructions, A_{i+d} points to the $(d + 1)$st instruction either preceding or following the instruction whose virtual address is A_i. Let S_p be the page size and suppose that an efficient replacement policy such as LRU is being used. The probability of A_{i+d} being in M_1 is high if one of the following conditions is satisfied:

- d is small compared with S_p, so A_i and A_{i+d} are in the same page P. The probability of these addresses both being in P increases with the page size.
- d is large relative to S_p but A_{i+d} is associated with a set of words that are frequently referenced. A_{i+d} is therefore likely to be in a page $P' \neq P$, which is also

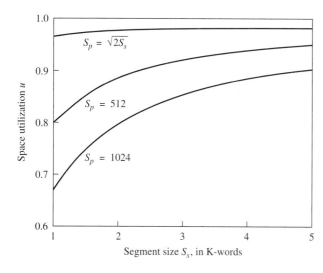

Figure 6.32
Influence of page size S_p and segment size S_s on space utilization u.

in M_1. This likelihood tends to increase with the number of pages stored in M_1; it therefore tends to decrease with the size of S_p.

Thus H is influenced by two opposing forces as S_p is varied. When S_p is small, H increases with S_p. However, when S_p exceeds a certain value, H begins to decrease. Figure 6.33 shows some typical curves relating H and S_p for various main-memory capacities. Simulation studies indicate that in large systems, the values of S_p yielding the maximum hit ratios can be greater than the "optimum" page size given by Equation (6.11). Since high H is important in achieving small t_A (due to the relatively slow rates at which page swapping takes place), values of S_p that maximize H are preferred. The first computer with a paging system (the University of Manchester's Atlas computer) had a 512-word page, while the Pentium discussed in Example 6.5 supports page sizes of 4 KB and 4 MB.

5.6.1 Memory Allocation

As we have seen, the various levels of a memory system are divided into sets of contiguous locations, variously called regions, segments, or pages, which store

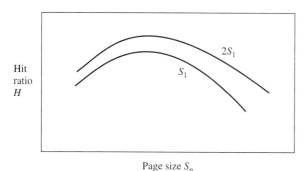

Figure 6.33
Influence of page size S_p on hit ratio H.

blocks of data. Blocks are swapped automatically among the levels in order to minimize the access time seen by the processor. Swapping generally occurs in response to processor requests (*demand swapping*). However, to avoid making a processor wait while a requested item is being moved to the fastest level of memory M_1, some kind of *anticipatory swapping* must be implemented, which implies transferring blocks to M_1 in anticipation that they will be required soon. Good short-range prediction of access-request patterns is possible because of locality of reference.

The placement of blocks of information in a memory system is called *memory allocation* and is the topic of this section. The method of selecting the part of M_1 in which an incoming block K is to be placed is the *replacement policy*. Simple replacement policies assign K to M_1 only when an unoccupied or inactive region of sufficient size is available. More aggressive policies preempt occupied blocks to make room for K. In general, successful memory allocation methods result in a high hit ratio and a low average access time. If the hit ratio is low, an excessive amount of swapping between memory levels occurs, a phenomenon known as *thrashing*. Good memory allocation also minimizes the amount of unused or underused space in M_1.

The information needed for allocation within a two-level hierarchy (M_1, M_2)—unless otherwise stated, we will assume the main–secondary-memory hierarchy—can be held in a memory map that contains the following information:

- *Occupied space list for M_1*. Each entry of this list specifies a block name, the (base) address of the region it occupies, and, if variable, the block size. In systems using preemptive allocation, additional information is associated with each block to determine when and how it can be preempted.
- *Available space list for M_1*. Each entry of this list specifies the address of an unoccupied region and, if necessary, its size.
- *Directory for M_2*. This list specifies the unit(s) that contain the directories for all the blocks associated with the current programs. These directories, in turn, define the regions of the M_2 space to which each block is assigned.

When a block is transferred from M_2 to M_1, the memory management system makes an appropriate entry in the occupied space list. When the block is no longer required in M_1, it is *deallocated* and the region it occupies is transferred from the occupied space list to the available space list. A block is deallocated when a program using it terminates execution or when the block is replaced to make room for one with higher priority.

Many preemptive and nonpreemptive algorithms have been developed for dynamic memory allocation. Accurate analysis of their performance is difficult; as a result, simulation is the most widely used evaluation tool. The performance of an allocation algorithm can be estimated by the various parameters introduced in section 6.2.1, such as the hit ratio H, the access time t_A, and the space utilization u.

Nonpreemptive allocation. Suppose a block K_i of n_i words is to be transferred from M_2 to M_1. If none of the blocks already occupying M_1 can be preempted (overwritten or moved) by K_i, then it is necessary to find or create an "available" region of n_i or more words to accommodate K_i. This process is termed *nonpreemptive* allocation. The problem is more easily solved in a paging system where all blocks (pages) have size S_p words and M_1 is divided into fixed S_p-word regions (page frames). The memory map (page table) is searched for an available page frame; if one is found, it is assigned to the incoming block K_i. This easy allocation method is the principal reason for the widespread use of paging. If memory space is divisible into regions of variable length, however, then it becomes more difficult to allocate incoming blocks efficiently.

Two widely used algorithms for nonpreemptive allocation of variable-sized blocks—unpaged segments, for example—are first fit and best fit. The *first-fit* method scans the memory map sequentially until an available region R_j of n_i or more words is found, where n_i is the size of the incoming block K_i. It then allocates K_i to R_j. The *best-fit* approach requires searching the memory map completely and assigning K_i to a region of $n_j \geq n_i$ words such that $n_j - n_i$ is minimized.

Suppose, for example, that at some point in time M_1 stores three blocks, as in Figure 6.34*a*. There are three available (shaded) regions, and the available space list has the form:

Region address	Size (words)
0	50
300	400
800	200

Further, suppose that two new blocks K_4 and K_5 whose sizes are 100 and 250 words, respectively, are to be assigned to M_1. Figures 6.34*b* and *c* show the results obtained using the first-fit and best-fit methods, respectively, when the memory scan begins at address 0.

The first-fit algorithm has the advantage of needing less time to execute than the best-fit approach. If the best-fitting available region can be found by scanning k

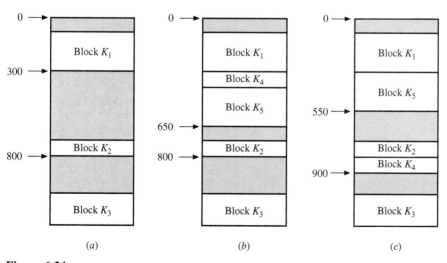

(a)   (b)   (c)

Figure 6.34
(*a*) Initial memory state; (*b*) allocation of K_4 and K_5 by first fit; (*c*) allocation of K_4 and K_5 by best fit.

entries of the available space list, the first fit can always be found by scanning k or fewer entries. The relative efficiency of the two techniques has long been a subject of debate, since both have been implemented with satisfactory results [Knuth 1973; Shore 1975]. The performance obtained in a particular environment depends on the distribution of the block sizes to be allocated. Simulation studies suggest that, in practice, first fit tends to outperform best fit.

Preemptive allocation. Nonpreemptive allocation cannot make efficient use of memory in all situations. *Memory overflow,* that is, rejection of a memory allocation request due to insufficient space, can be expected to occur with M_1 only partially full. Much more efficient use of the available memory space is possible if the occupied space can be reallocated to make room for incoming blocks. Reallocation may be done in two ways:

• The blocks already in M_1 can be relocated within M_1 to create a gap large enough for the incoming block.
• One or more occupied regions can be made available by deallocating the blocks they contain. This method requires a rule—a *replacement policy*—for selecting blocks to be deallocated and replaced.

Deallocation requires that a distinction be made between "dirty" blocks, which have been modified since being loaded into M_1, and "clean" blocks, which have not been modified. Blocks of instructions remain clean, whereas blocks of data can become dirty. To replace a clean block, the memory management system can simply overwrite it with the new block and update its entry in the memory map. Before a dirty block is overwritten, it should be copied to M_2, which involves a slow block transfer.

Relocation of the blocks already occupying M_1 can be done by a method called *compaction,* which is illustrated in Figure 6.35. The blocks currently in memory are compressed into a single contiguous group at one end of the memory. This creates an available region of maximum size. Once the memory is compacted, incoming blocks are assigned to contiguous regions at the unoccupied end. The memory

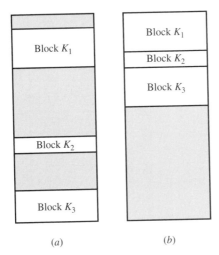

(a)   (b)

Figure 6.35
Memory allocation (*a*) before and (*b*) after compaction.

is viewed as having a single available region; new available regions due to freed blocks are ignored. When the gap at the end of the memory is eventually filled, compaction is carried out again. The advantages of this scheme are its simplicity and the fact that it eliminates the task of selecting an available region; its drawback is the long compaction time.

Organization

Replacement policies. The second major approach to preemptive allocation involves preempting a region R occupied by block K and allocating it to an incoming block K'. The criteria for selecting K as the block to be replaced constitute the replacement policy. The main goal in choosing a replacement policy is to maximize the hit ratio of the faster memory M_1 or, equivalently, minimize the number of times a referenced block is not in M_1, a condition called a *memory fault* or *miss*.

It is generally accepted that the hit ratio tends to a maximum if the time intervals between successive memory faults are maximized. An *optimal replacement strategy* would therefore at time t_i determine the time $t_j > t_i$ at which the next reference to block K is to occur; the K to be replaced is the one for which $t_j - t_i$ has the maximum value t_K. This ideal strategy has been called OPT [Mattson et al. 1970; Stone 1993]. In principle, OPT can be implemented by making two passes through the executing program. The first is a simulation run to determine the sequence S_B of distinct virtual block addresses generated by the program; the sequence is called the *block address trace*. The values of t_K at each point in time can be computed from S_B and used to construct the optimal sequence S_B^{OPT} of blocks to be replaced. The second run is the execution run, which uses S_B^{OPT} to specify the blocks to be replaced. OPT is not a practical replacement policy because of the cost of the simulation runs and the fact that S_B can be extremely long, making S_B^{OPT} too expensive to compute. A practical replacement policy attempts to estimate t_K using statistics it gathers on the past references to all blocks currently in M_1.

Two useful replacement policies are *first-in first-out* (FIFO) and *least recently used* (LRU). FIFO selects for replacement the block least recently loaded into M_1. FIFO has the advantage that it is very easy to implement. A loading-sequence number is associated with each block in the occupied space list. Each time a block is transferred to or from M_1, the loading-sequence numbers are updated. By inspecting these numbers, the memory manager can easily determine the oldest (first-in) block. FIFO has the defect, however, that a frequently used block, for instance, one containing a program loop, may be replaced simply because it is the oldest block.

The LRU policy selects for replacement the block that was least recently accessed by the processor. This policy is based on the reasonable assumption that the least recently used block is the one least likely to be referenced in the future. LRU avoids the replacement of old but frequently used blocks, as occurs with FIFO. LRU is slightly more difficult to implement than FIFO, however, since the memory manager must maintain data on the times of references to all blocks in main memory. LRU is implemented by associating a hardware or software counter, called an *age register,* with every block in M_1. Whenever a block is referenced, its age register is set to a predetermined positive number. At fixed intervals of time, the age registers of all the blocks are decremented by a fixed amount. The least recently used block at any time is the one whose age register contains the smallest number.

The performance of a replacement policy in a given memory organization can be analyzed using the block address stream generated by a set of representative computations. Let N_1^* and N_2^* denote the number of references to M_1 and M_2, respectively, in the block address stream. The *block hit ratio H** is defined by

$$H^* = \frac{N_1^*}{N_1^* + N_2^*}$$

which is analogous to the (word) hit ratio H defined by Equation (6.5). Let n^* denote the average number of consecutive word address references within each block. H can be estimated from H^* using the following relation:

$$H = 1 - \frac{1 - H^*}{n^*}$$

In a paging system, H^* is the page-hit ratio. $1 - H^*$, the page-miss ratio, is also called the *page fault probability.*

EXAMPLE 6.6 COMPARISON OF SEVERAL REPLACEMENT POLICIES. Consider a paging system in which M_1 has a capacity of three pages. The execution of a program Q requires reference to five distinct pages P_i, where $i = 1, 2, 3, 4, 5$, and i is the page address. The page address stream formed by executing Q is

$$2 \quad 3 \quad 2 \quad 1 \quad 5 \quad 2 \quad 4 \quad 5 \quad 3 \quad 2 \quad 5 \quad 2$$

which means that the first page referenced is P_2, the second is P_3, and so on. Figure 6.36 shows the manner in which the pages are assigned to M_1 using FIFO, LRU, and the ideal OPT replacement policies. The next block to be selected for replacement is marked by an asterisk in the FIFO and LRU cases. It will be observed that LRU recognizes that P_2 and P_5 are referenced more frequently than other pages, whereas FIFO

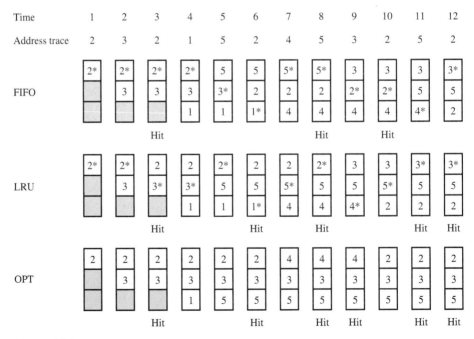

Figure 6.36
Action of three replacement policies on a common address trace.

does not. Thus FIFO replaces P_2 twice, but LRU does so only once. The highest page-hit ratio is achieved by OPT, the lowest by FIFO. The page-hit ratio of LRU is quite close to that of OPT, a property that seems to hold generally.

Stack replacement policies. As discussed in section 6.2.1, the cost and performance of a memory hierarchy can be measured by average cost per bit c and average access time t_A. Equations (6.4) and (6.7) repeated here are convenient expressions for c and t_A:

$$c = \frac{c_1 S_1 + c_2 S_2}{S_1 + S_2}$$

$$t_A = t_{A_1} + (1 - H)t_B$$

The quantities c, t_A, and t_B are determined primarily by the memory technologies used for M_1 and M_2. Once these technologies have been chosen, the hit ratio H can be computed for various possible system configurations. The major variables on which H depends are

- The address streams encountered.
- The average block size.
- The capacity of M_1.
- The replacement policy.

Simulation is perhaps the most practical technique used for evaluating different memory system designs. H is determined for representative address traces, memory technologies, block sizes, memory capacities, and replacement policies. Figure 6.36 shows a sample point in this simulation process. Here the address trace, block size, and memory capacity are fixed, and three different replacement strategies are being tested.

Due to the many alternatives that exist, the amount of simulation required to optimize the design of a multilevel memory system can be huge. A number of analytic models for optimizing memory design have been proposed. Notable among these is a technique called *stack processing,* which is applicable to paging systems that use a class of replacement algorithms called stack algorithms [Stone 1993]. Let AT be any page address trace of length L to be processed using a replacement policy RP. Let t denote the point in time when the first t pages of AT have been processed. Let n be a variable denoting the page capacity of M_1. $B_t(n)$ denotes the set of pages in M_1 at time t, and L_t denotes the number of distinct pages that have been encountered at time t. Policy RP is called a *stack algorithm* if it has the following *inclusion property:*

$$B_t(n) \subset B_t(n + 1) \qquad \text{if } n < L_t$$

$$B_t(n) = B_t(n + 1) \qquad \text{if } n \geq L_t$$

LRU retains in M_1 the n most recently used pages. Since these are always included in the $n + 1$ most recently used pages, it can be seen right away that LRU is a stack algorithm. Some other replacement policies are also of this type. FIFO is a notable exception, however. Consider the following page address stream:

$$1 \quad 2 \quad 3 \quad 4 \quad 1 \quad 2 \quad 5 \quad 1 \quad 2 \quad 3 \quad 4 \quad 5$$

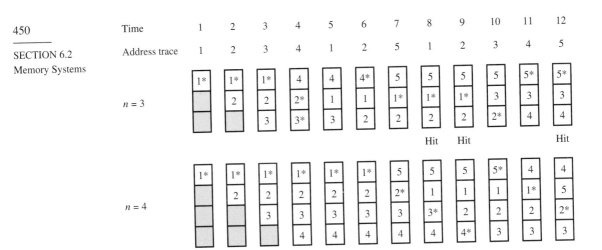

Figure 6.37
FIFO replacement with two different memory capacities.

Figure 6.37 shows how this address stream is processed using FIFO and memory capacities of three and four pages. It can be seen that at various points of time the conditions for the inclusion property are not satisfied. For example, when $t = 7$, $n = 5$, $B_7(3) = \{1, 2, 5\}$, and $B_7(4) = \{2, 3, 4, 5\}$. Hence $B_7(3) \not\subseteq B_7(4)$, so FIFO is not a stack algorithm.

The usefulness of stack replacement algorithms lies in the fact that the hit ratios for different M_1 capacities can be determined by processing the address stream once and by representing M_1 by a list or "stack." The stack S_t at time t is an ordered set of L_t distinct pages $S_t(1)$, $S_t(2)$,..., $S_t(L_t)$, with $S_t(1)$ referred to as the top of the stack at time t. The inclusion property of stack algorithms implies that the stack can always be generated so that

$$B_t(n) = \{S_t(1), S_t(2),..., S_t(n)\} \quad \text{for } n < L_t$$
$$B_t(n) = \{S_t(1), S_t(2),..., S_t(L_t)\} \quad \text{for } n \geq L_t$$

In other words, the behavior of a system in which M_1 has capacity n is determined by the top n entries of the stack. By scanning S_t, we can easily see whether a hit occurs for all possible values of n. This type of analysis permits the simultaneous determination of hit ratios for various capacities of M_1.

The procedures for updating the stack depend on the particular stack algorithm RP being used. There may be little resemblance between the order of the elements in S_t and S_{t+1}; the stack should not be confused with simple LIFO stacks. The following example describes the stack-updating process for LRU replacement.

EXAMPLE 6.7 DETERMINATION OF HIT RATIOS WITH LRU REPLACEMENT. Let $S_t = \{S_t(1), S_t(2),..., S_t(k)\}$ denote the stack contents at time t. Stack processing requires placing the most recently used page addresses in the top of stack so that the least recently used page gets pushed to the bottom. More formally, let x be the new page reference at time t. If $x \notin S_t$, x is pushed into the stack so that x becomes $S_{t+1}(1)$, $S_t(1)$ becomes $S_{t+1}(2)$, and so on. If $x \in S_t$, x is removed from S_t and then

Time t	1	2	3	4	5	6	7	8	9	10	11	12
Address trace	2	3	2	1	5	2	4	5	3	2	5	2
$S_t(1)$	2	3	2	1	5	2	4	5	3	2	5	2
$S_t(2)$		2	3	2	1	5	2	4	5	3	2	5
$S_t(3)$			3	3	2	1	5	2	4	5	3	3
$S_t(4)$					3	3	1	1	2	4	4	4
$S_t(5)$							3	3	1	1	1	1
$n = 1$												
$n = 2$			Hit									Hit
$n = 3$			Hit			Hit		Hit			Hit	Hit
$n = 4$			Hit			Hit		Hit		Hit	Hit	Hit
$n = 5$			Hit			Hit		Hit	Hit	Hit	Hit	Hit

Figure 6.38
Stack processing of a page address trace using LRU.

pushed into the top of the stack to form S_{t+1}. Figure 6.38 illustrates this process for the address stream used in Figure 6.36. To determine whether a hit occurs at time t for memory page capacity n, it is necessary only to check whether the new page reference x is one of the top n entries of S_t; if it is, a hit occurs. The hit occurrences for all values of $n < 5$ also appear in Figure 6.38. The values for the various page-hit ratios H^* are as follows:

$n =$	1	2	3	4	5	> 5
$H^* =$ 0.00		0.17	0.42	0.50	0.58	0.58

It follows from the inclusion property of stack replacement algorithms that the hit ratio increases with the available capacity n. If the next page address x is in $B_t(n)$, it must also be in $B_t(n + 1)$ because $B_t(n) \subseteq B_t(n + 1)$. Hence if a hit occurs with capacity n, a hit also occurs when the capacity is increased to $n + 1$. It might be expected that this inclusion property holds for all replacement policies, but it does not. The example in Figure 6.37 shows that increasing n from three to four pages in a system with FIFO replacement actually reduces the page-hit ratio in this case from 0.25 to 0.17. This phenomenon seems to be relatively rare, not occurring for most address traces.

Other replacement policies. A few other replacement algorithms are used in multilevel memories. As discussed later (in section 6.3), caches often have a low-cost replacement policy called *direct mapping,* where each incoming block from M_2 is assigned to a fixed region of M_1 determined by the block's low-order address bits.

Another interesting and low-cost technique is *random* replacement, where the replaced block is chosen in an apparently random fashion. An example is found in the TLB in the MIPS R2/3000 of Example 6.4—recall that although part of the MMU, the TLB is itself a special type of cache. The block to be replaced (a page entry in the case of the R2/3000's TLB) is selected by a fast process that approximates truly random selection and, unlike LRU, does not use memory-reference data. The R2/3000's MMU contains a 6-bit register called *RANDOM*, which is decremented in each CPU clock cycle. *RANDOM* therefore continually loops through the numbers 8 through 63, each of which can act as an entry point or index to the 64-entry TLB. (*RANDOM* skips the numbers zero though seven so that the first eight entries of the TLB can be reserved for critical parts of the operating system.) When a TLB miss exception is being serviced, the MMU replaces the TLB entry whose index is the current value of *RANDOM*. Hence the randomness of the times at which TLB miss exceptions occur determines the randomness of this register's contents. There is no delay and very little hardware overhead associated with this replacement policy. Although less efficient than LRU, this policy appears to work quite well in practice.

6.3
CACHES

The term *cache* refers to a fast intermediate memory within a larger memory system [Smith 1982; Handy 1993]. Although caches appeared as early as 1968 in the IBM System/360 Model 91, they did not come into wide use until the appearance of low-cost, high-density RAM and microprocessor ICs in the 1980s. Caches directly address the von Neumann bottleneck by providing the CPU with fast, single-cycle access to its external memory. They also provide an efficient way to place a small portion of memory on the same chip as a microprocessor. If an additional off-chip cache is used that employs, say, fast SRAM technology—and the continuing disparity between processor and DRAM speeds makes that desirable—a two-level cache organization results (refer to Figure 6.21c).

A cache serves as a buffer between a CPU and its main memory; in this section we focus on caches used in this way. However, caches appear as buffer memories in several other contexts. We saw in section 6.2 that the translation look-aside buffers (TLBs) used within a memory management system are specialized caches that permit very fast translation of memory addresses. Data buffers built into high-speed secondary memory devices such as hard disk drives are also called caches.

6.3.1 Main Features

The cache and main memory form a two-level subhierarchy (M_1, M_2) that differs in important ways from the main–secondary system (M_2, M_3); Figure 6.39 summarizes these differences. Because it is higher in the memory hierarchy, the pair (M_1, M_2) functions at much higher speed than (M_2, M_3). The access time ratio t_{A_2}/t_{A_1} is around 5/1, while t_{A_3}/t_{A_2} is about 1000/1. These speed differences require (M_1, M_2) to be managed by high-speed hardware circuits rather than by software routines; (M_2, M_3), on the other hand, is controlled mainly by the operating system. Thus while the (M_2, M_3) hierarchy is transparent to the application programmer but visible to the system programmer, (M_1, M_2) is largely transparent to both. Another difference lies in the block size used. Communication within (M_1, M_2) is by pages,

Two-level hierarchy (M_{i-1}, M_i)	Cache–main memory (M_1, M_2)	Main–secondary memory (M_2, M_3)
Typical access time ratios $t_{A_i}/t_{A_{i-1}}$	5/1	1000/1
Memory management system	Mainly implemented by hardware	Mainly implemented by software
Typical page size	8 B	4 KB
Access of processor to second level M_i	Processor has direct access to M_2	All access to M_3 is via M_2

Figure 6.39
Major differences between cache–main and main–secondary-memory hierarchies.

but the page size is much smaller than that used in (M_2, M_3). Finally, we note that the CPU generally has direct access to both M_1 and M_2, whereas it does not have direct access to M_3.

Cache organization. Figure 6.40 shows the principal components of a cache. Memory words are stored in a *cache data memory* and are grouped into small pages called *cache blocks* or *lines*. The contents of the cache's data memory are thus copies of a set of main-memory blocks. Each cache block is marked with its block address, referred to as a *tag*, so the cache knows to what part of the memory space the block belongs. The collection of tag addresses currently assigned to the cache, which can be noncontiguous, is stored in a special memory, the *cache tag memory* or *directory*. For example, if block B_j containing data entries D_j is assigned to M_1, then B_j is in the cache's tag memory and D_j is in the cache's data memory.

Obviously for a cache to improve the performance of a computer, the time required to check tag addresses and access the cache's data memory must be less than the time required to access main memory. Thus if main memory is implemented with a DRAM technology having an access time $t_{A_2} = 50$ ns, the cache's data memory might be implemented with an SRAM technology having an access time of $t_{A_1} = 10$ ns. A basic issue in cache design, which we examine in section 6.3.2, is how to make the matching of tag addresses extremely fast.

Two general ways of introducing a cache into a computer appear in Figure 6.41. In the *look-aside* design of Figure 6.41a, the cache and the main memory are directly connected to the system bus. In this design the CPU initiates a memory access by placing a (real) address A_i on the memory address bus at the start of a

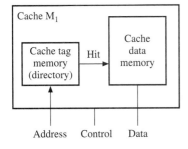

Address   Control   Data

Figure 6.40
Basic structure of a cache.

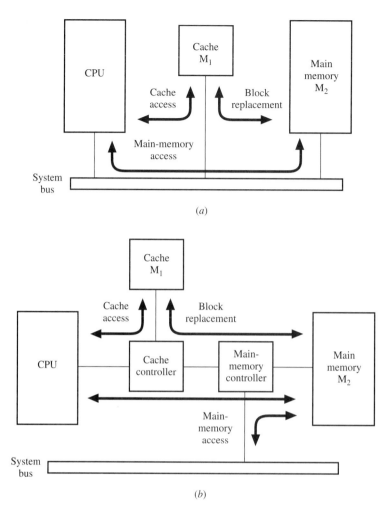

Figure 6.41
Two system organizations for caches: (*a*) look-aside and (*b*) look-through.

read (load) or write (store) cycle. The cache M_1 immediately compares A_i to the tag addresses currently residing in its tag memory. If a match is found in M_1, that is, a cache hit occurs, the access is completed by a read or write operation executed in the cache; main memory M_2 is not involved. If no match with A_i is found in the cache, that is, a cache miss occurs, then the desired access is completed by a read or write operation directed to M_2. In response to a cache miss, a block (line) of data B_j that includes the target address A_i is transferred from M_2 to M_1. This transfer is fast, taking advantage of the small block size and fast RAM access methods, such as page mode (section 6.1.2), which allow the cache block to be filled in a single short burst. The cache implements some replacement policy such as LRU to determine where to place an incoming block. When necessary, the cache block replaced by B_j in M_1 is saved in M_2. Note that cache misses, even though they are infrequent, result in block transfers between M_1 and M_2 that tie up the system bus, making it unavailable for other uses like IO operations.

A faster, but more costly organization called a *look-through* cache appears in Figure 6.41*b*. The CPU communicates with the cache via a separate (local) bus that is isolated from the main system bus. The system bus is available for use by other units, such as IO controllers, to communicate with main memory. Hence cache accesses and main-memory accesses not involving the CPU can proceed concurrently. Unlike the look-aside case, with a look-through cache the CPU does not automatically send all memory requests to main memory; it does so only after a cache miss. A look-through cache allows the local bus linking M_1 and M_2 to be wider than the system bus, thus speeding up cache–main-memory transfers. For example, if the system data bus is 32 bits wide and the cache block size is 128 bits = 16 bytes (a typical value), a 128-bit data bus might be provided to link M_1 and M_2, which would allow a cache block to be replaced in as little as a single clock cycle. The main disadvantage of the look-through design, besides its higher complexity and cost, is that it takes longer for M_2 to respond to the CPU when a miss occurs.

Cache operation. Figure 6.42 shows a small cache system that illustrates the relationship between the data stored in the cache M_1 and the data stored in main memory M_2. Here a cache block (line) size of 4 bytes is assumed. Each memory address is 12 bits long, so the 10 high-order bits form the tag or block address, and the 2 low-order bits define a displacement address within the block. When a block is assigned to M_1's data memory, its tag is also placed in M_1's tag memory. Figure 6.42 shows the contents of two blocks assigned to the cache data memory; note the locations of the same blocks in main memory. To read the shaded word, its address $A_i = 101111000110$ is sent to M_1, which compares A_i's tag part to its stored tags and finds a match (hit). The stored tag pinpoints the corresponding block in M_1's

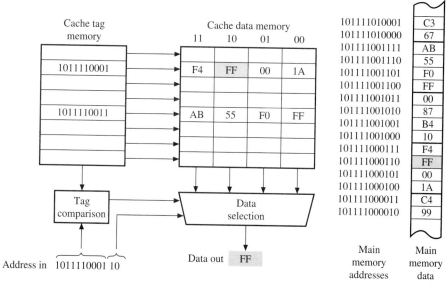

Figure 6.42
Cache execution of a read operation.

data memory, and the 2-bit displacement is used to output the target word to the CPU.

A cache write operation employs the same addressing technique. As shown in Figure 6.43, the tag part of the target address A_i is again presented to M_1, along with the data word to be stored. When a hit occurs, the new data, in this case, 88, is stored at the location pointed to by A_i in the data memory of M_1, thereby overwriting the old data FF. Now a new problem arises: The data in M_1 with address A_i differs from the data in M_2 with the same address. A temporary inconsistency of this sort is acceptable as long as no device—another processor, for instance—attempts to read the old or *stale* data. Preventing the improper use of stale data is the *cache coherence* or *cache consistency* problem. It is a basic design issue in multiprocessors where several CPUs share access to the same main memory but each has its own cache. This issue also arises in single-CPU systems when an IO controller or processor is present that has direct access to main memory, independent of the CPU; see problem 6.38. We can minimize cache-related inconsistencies by implementing a policy that systematically updates the data in M_2 in response to changes made to the corresponding data in M_1. (We will discuss some general solutions to the cache coherence problem in Chapter 7.)

Most of the methods used by virtual memory systems to update secondary memory can be adapted for use with the cache–main-memory subhierarchy. Each cache block in the data memory of M_1 can have a change bit C attached to it, which is set to 0 when the block is first placed in M_1. Any subsequent write operation addressed to that block sets C to 1. When a block with $C = 1$ is replaced, its data contents are then written back to main memory M_2. This technique is referred to as *write-back* or *copy-back*. It has the disadvantage that M_1 and M_2 can be temporarily inconsistent, that is, have different data associated with the same physical

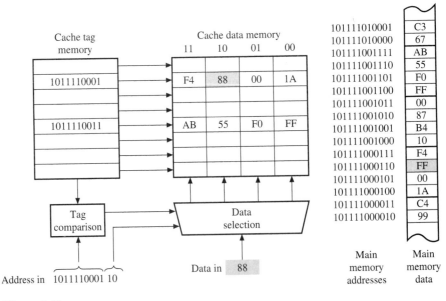

Figure 6.43
Cache execution of a write operation.

address. Difficulties arise if several processors with independent caches are sharing M_2 because their data can become inconsistent. The write-back technique also complicates recovery from system failures.

Direct communication links between the CPU and main memory, which are not present in the virtual-memory case, permit some novel write policies for caches. An alternative to write-back is to transfer the data word to both M_1 and M_2 during *every* memory write cycle, even when the target address is already assigned to the cache. This policy, called *write-through,* is easy to implement, and it guarantees that M_2 never contains stale information. On the other hand, write-through results in more write cycles to M_2 than write-back does. Since the time needed for each write is then the slower (write) access time of M_2, system performance may suffer. However, only a small fraction, perhaps 1/10, of all memory accesses are writes. Some processors support both write-back and write-through so that a user can select the policy that best suits a particular program's memory-access behavior.

6.3.2 Address Mapping

When a tag address is presented to the cache, it must be quickly compared to the stored tags to determine whether a matching tag is currently assigned to the cache. The obvious approach of scanning all the tags in sequence is unacceptably slow. The fastest technique for implementing tag comparison is *associative* or *content addressing*, which permits the input tag to be compared simultaneously to all tags in the cache-tag memory. Pure associative memories are very expensive, however, so it is only feasible to use them in small caches and TLBs (see Example 6.4). Various less costly techniques have been developed to solve this problem, some of which make limited use of associative addressing.

Associative addressing. In an associative memory any stored item can be accessed by using the contents of the item in question, generally some specified subfield, as an address. Associative memories are also commonly known as *content-addressable memories* (CAMs). The subfield chosen to address the memory is called the *key*. Items stored in an associative memory can viewed as having the two-field format

KEY, DATA

where KEY is the stored address and DATA is the information to be accessed. For example, if a page table of the kind shown in Figure 6.29 is placed in an associative memory, the page address can be selected as the key, while the page frame, presence bit, change bit, and access rights form the data. Such a memory can then be accessed with a request such as: Read the page frame number corresponding to page address E. However, we could equally well choose the page frame as the key, which would permit queries such as: Write 1 in the presence-bit field of page frame D6C7F9.

An associative cache employs a tag, that is, a block address, as the key. At the start of a memory access, the incoming tag is compared simultaneously to all the tags stored in the cache's tag memory. If a match (cache hit) occurs, a match-indicating signal triggers the cache to service the requested memory access. A no-match signal identifies a cache miss, and the memory access requested is forwarded to main memory for service. A cache block containing the target address is then sent from main memory to the cache, and at the same time, a data word is sent to the CPU or transferred from the CPU to the cache, in response to the original access request.

Associative memory. Figure 6.44 shows the general structure of an associative memory. Each unit of stored information is a fixed-length word. Any subfield of the word can be chosen as the key. Here the desired key is specified by a *mask register,* whose contents identify the bit positions (which need not be adjacent) that define the key. The current key is compared simultaneously with all stored words; those that match the key output a match signal, which enters a *select circuit,* which enables the data field to be accessed. If several entries have the same key, then the select circuit determines which data field is to be read out. It can, for example, read out all matching entries in some predetermined order. Since all words in the memory are required to compare their keys with the input key simultaneously, each needs its own *match circuit.* The match and select circuits make associative memories much more complex and expensive than conventional memories. Although VLSI techniques have made associative memories economically feasible, cost considerations still limit them to applications in which a relatively small amount of information must be accessed very rapidly, such as address mapping for caches.

The logic circuit for a 1-bit associative memory cell appears in Figure 6.45 [Triebel and Chu 1982]. The cell comprises a D flip-flop for data storage, a match circuit (the EXCLUSIVE-NOR gate) for comparing the flip-flop's contents to an external data bit D, and circuits for reading from and writing into the cell. The results of a comparison appear on the match output M, where $M = 1$ denotes a match and $M = 0$ denotes no match. The cell is selected or addressed for both read and write operations by setting the select line S to 1. New data is written into the cell by setting the write enable line WE to 1, which in turn enables the D flip-flop's

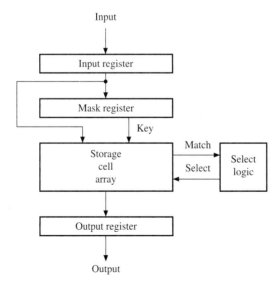

Figure 6.44
Structure of an associative (content addressable) memory.

clock input CK. The stored data is read out via the Q line. The mask control line MK is activated ($MK = 1$) to force the match line M to 0 independently of the data stored in the D flip-flop; MK also disables the input circuits of the flip-flop by forcing CK to 0. A cell like that of Figure 6.45 can be realized with about 10 transistors—far more than the single transistor required for a dynamic RAM cell (refer to Figure 6.9b). This high hardware cost is the main reason that large associative memories are rarely used outside caches.

Associative cells of the preceding type can be combined into word-organized associative memory arrays. Figure 6.46 shows a 16-bit associative memory that stores four words (columns) of 4 bits each. The words are individually addressable via their S lines. All words share a common set of data and mask lines for each bit position. Consequently, an external data bit D_i can be compared simultaneously to the ith stored bit of every word in the memory. The output lines of the cells are designed so that they can be connected to form wired OR or AND gates, as indicated in the figure.

A small associative cache is found in Data General Corp.'s ECLIPSE, a 16-bit computer from the 1970s. This computer has a modular memory design in which each 8K-word main-memory module M_2 is paired with a cache M_1 that stores sixteen 16-bit words forming four 4-word blocks. M_2 is constructed from MOS RAM chips with a 700 ns cycle time, while the cache M_1 uses bipolar RAMs with a cycle time of 200 ns. The memory (tag) addresses of the blocks stored in the cache are placed in an associative memory CAM. When the CPU generates a memory address A, it is sent to the CAM, which compares it to all tags currently in the cache. If the CAM indicates a match, M_1 responds to the memory request directly by either reading or writing the corresponding data $M(A)$. If A is not currently assigned to M_1, then A is processed by the main memory M_2, which responds to the original CPU request by executing a 700 ns read or write cycle. At the same time, M_2 sends a four-word block containing $M(A)$ to M_1, which uses the new block to replace the least recently used cache block. The cache's LRU block replacement policy is implemented by special hardware that constantly monitors cache usage.

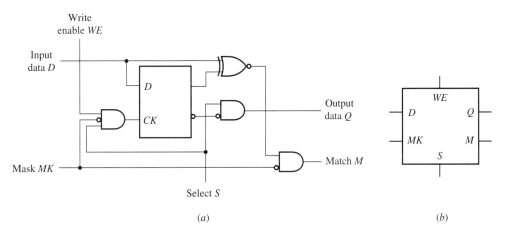

Figure 6.45
Associative memory cell: (a) logic circuit and (b) symbol.

Direct mapping. An alternative, and simpler, address-mapping technique for caches is known as *direct mapping*. Let M_1 be divided into $s_1 = 2^s$ regions $M_1(0)$, $M_1(1),\ldots, M_1(s_1 - 1)$ called *sets*, each of which stores a block of n consecutive words. Main memory M_2 is similarly divided into one-block regions $M_2(0)$, $M_2(1),\ldots, M_2(s_2 - 1)$. With direct mapping, each block $M_2(i)$ in M_2 is mapped into

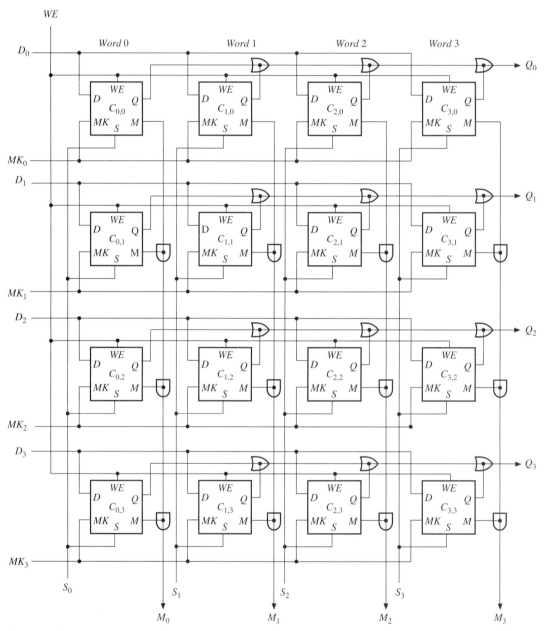

Figure 6.46
A 4×4-bit associative memory array.

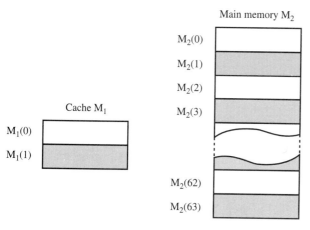

Figure 6.47
Direct-mapped cache with block capacity of two.

one specific set $M_1(j)$ in M_1. The set address j is determined from i by the rule

$$j = i \quad (\text{modulo } s_1)$$

For example, if $s_1 = 2$ as in Figure 6.47, every even-address (unshaded) block in M_2 is mapped into $M_1(0)$ and every odd-address (shaded) block in M_2 is mapped into $M_1(1)$.

The hardware needed to implement direct mapping is fairly simple. The low-order s bits of each block address A form a set address that identifies the unique cache set that can store the block in question. The remaining t high-order bits of A now constitute the tag, and only these bits need be stored in the cache's tag memory. Consequently, the cache tag memory can be an ordinary RAM that is addressed by the s-bit set-address part of an incoming memory address A. If there are 2^d words per set, then the low-order d bits of A form the displacement address of the word in question within its block. Thus an incoming address has three parts: a t-bit tag, an s-bit set address, and a d-bit displacement.

The main drawback of direct mapping is that the cache's hit ratio drops sharply if two or more frequently used blocks happen to map onto the same region in the cache. This possibility is minimized by the fact that such blocks are relatively far apart in the memory-address space. For example, if $s_1 = 2^6 = 64$, then only the blocks with addresses $i, i + 64, i + 128, i + 192,...$ can be mapped into the same cache set $M_1(i)$.

EXAMPLE 6.8 DESIGN OF A DIRECT-MAPPED CACHE [INTEGRATED DEVICE TECHNOLOGY 1994]. In this example we will use off-the-shelf ICs to design an add-on direct-mapped cache memory for a high-end microprocessor, such as the PowerPC. If the CPU has a built-in (level 1) cache, as is frequently the case, this design applies to a level 2 (secondary) cache. The CPU is linked to a byte-addressable external memory via a 32-bit address bus and a 64-bit bidirectional data bus using the the look-aside design style of Figure 6.41a. The desired cache capacity is 256 KB, and the cache block (set) size is assumed to be 32 bytes (32 B). Hence the cache must store $8K = 2^{13}$ blocks, implying that we need a cache tag memory of capacity $8K \times t$ bits to store tags of length t. We also need a cache data memory of capacity $32K \times 64$ bits, where the 64-bit word size is determined by the system data bus. As shown in Figure 6.48, a 32-bit address generated by the CPU contains a 5-bit displacement to address a

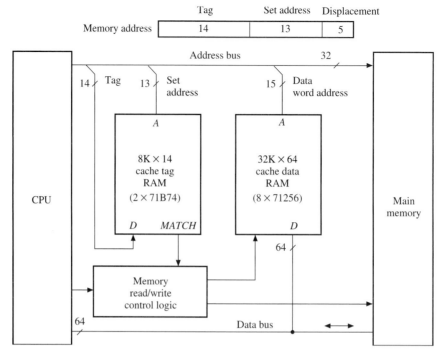

Figure 6.48
A 256KB direct-mapped cache for a microprocessor.

byte within a 32B block and a 13-bit set address to address the 8K blocks in the data memory. Hence the remaining $t = 32 - (13 + 5) = 14$ high-order address bits form the tag. Since the cache's data RAM is accessed one 8-byte word at a time, it requires a 15-bit address consisting of the 13-bit set address plus 2 bits (the two high-order bits of the displacement) to select one-quarter of the current set.

The components selected for this design are the Integrated Device Technology (IDT) 71256, a 32K × 8-bit SRAM chip, which has an access and cycle time of 12 ns, and the IDT 71B74 chip, which is called a *cache-tag RAM*. The 71B74 contains a high-speed 64Kb memory organized as an 8K × 8-bit RAM. The cache-tag RAM is distinguished from an ordinary SRAM by the fact that it has a built-in 8-bit comparator to compare the addressed data (a stored tag) to a word placed on the 71B74's input data bus. A *MATCH* output signal is set to 1 if the stored and applied data words match, and to 0 otherwise; matching can be done by the 71B74 in 8 ns. The *MATCH* signal is supplied to a small control circuit that then issues the memory access control signals (*WE*, *CS*, etc.) either to the cache data RAM (*MATCH* = 1) or to main memory (*MATCH* = 0). To accommodate 14-bit tags, we need two 71B74s. We also need eight 71256s to store the cached data. The final design of this cache unit appears in Figure 6.48.

Set-associative addressing. A more general address mapping method for caches, called *set associative,* includes pure associative and direct mapping as special cases. As in direct mapping, blocks in main memory M_2 are grouped into equivalence classes determined by their addresses. $M_2(i)$ and $M_2(j)$ are in the same equivalence class E if $i = j$ (modulo s_1). The cache is divided into s_1 multiblock

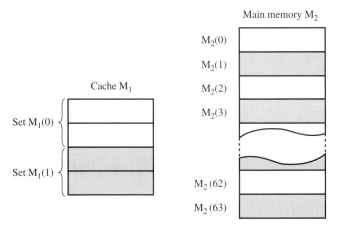

Main memory M$_2$

M$_2$(0)
M$_2$(1)
M$_2$(2)
M$_2$(3)

M$_2$(62)
M$_2$(63)

Cache M$_1$

Set M$_1$(0)
Set M$_1$(1)

Figure 6.49
Cache with two-way set-associative addressing.

regions M$_1$(0), M$_1$(1),..., M$_1$(s$_1$ – 1) called *sets,* each of which accommodates $k = 2^h$ blocks. A block M$_2$(i) in M$_2$ is mapped into the set M$_1$(h), satisfying the condition $i = h$ (modulo s_1).

Each set M$_1$(h) in the cache is effectively a small associative memory, so address mapping within each set is associative. This *k-way set-associative mapping* permits up to k members of the same equivalence class E to be stored in the cache simultaneously, which is not possible with direct mapping. Figure 6.49 illustrates set-associative mapping with cache size $s_1 = 2$ sets and set size $k = 2$. This mapping is therefore two-way set-associative and allows every shaded (unshaded) page in M$_2$ to be mapped into either of the two shaded (unshaded) page frames in M$_1$. Set-associative mapping reduces to direct mapping when $k = 1$; it reduces to fully associative mapping when $s_1 = 1$, implying that k equals the block capacity of the cache. Intermediate values of k lead to address-mapping methods requiring an intermediate amount of associative hardware. Only small values of k, such as $k = 2$ or 4, are used in practice, which makes it feasible to use low-cost RAMs, rather than special associative memories like that of Figure 6.46, to store the tags, as the next example illustrates.

EXAMPLE 6.9 DESIGN OF A TWO-WAY SET-ASSOCIATIVE CACHE. We consider an 8KB cache with two-way set-associative addressing, which is intended for a 32-bit processor. A single 8KB two-way set-associative cache is used by the VAX-11/780, an influential minicomputer introduced by Digital Equipment Corp. in 1978 [Clark 1983]. The on-chip I- and D-caches of the PowerPC model 603 introduced in 1993 are also of the 8KB two-way set-associative type [Burgess et al. 1994; Heath 1994]. The 11/780's cache block (line) contains 8 bytes, whereas the PowerPC 603's caches have 32B blocks. We use the smaller 8B block size here, as in Example 6.8.

The organization of the cache appears in Figure 6.50. The 32-bit address A is interpreted as follows. The low-order 3-bit displacement identifies a byte within an 8B cache block. There are $2^9 = 512$ sets, each containing two 8B blocks, so the next 9 bits of A form the set address. The remaining 20 bits of A constitute the tag. (The number of tag bits needed depends on the size of the real address space actually used; we assume the maximum size.) An incoming tag A_{tag} that matches a stored tag can be associated with either block in the matching set $M_1(i)$. The tag memory is therefore implemented by two 512×20-bit RAMs T_0 and T_1, each of which stores the tag for one block from every set $M_1(i)$. In addition, two 512×64-bit RAMs D_0 and D_1 form the cache's data memory. One of the 64-bit data blocks of $M_1(i)$ is stored at address i in D_0 (tagged by T_0), while the other is at the same address i in D_1 (tagged by T_1). Consequently, the set-address field i of A is used as the address to access both the tag and the data memories.

At the start of a memory access, the 9-bit set part of the address A is used as the address to read T_0 and T_1 simultaneously, and the resulting output data (two stored tags) are compared simultaneously with A_{tag}. If a match occurs, one of two *MATCH* signals, say, from T_i, is asserted and used to initiate a memory access from the corresponding data memory D_i. In a read operation D_i outputs its stored data to the system data bus; in a write operation D_i inputs a data word from the data bus. A 64-bit-wide data bus is assumed in Figure 6.50, which allows a cache block transfer in a single clock cycle. If a smaller data bus is used, then a block must be transferred in several cycles. The data memory can also use the 3-bit displacement field of A to select a part

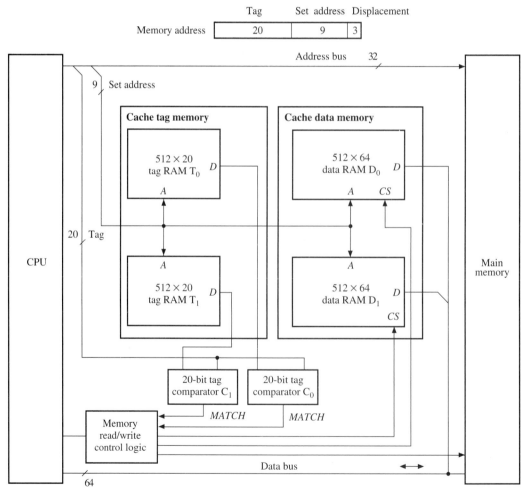

Figure 6.50
An 8 KB two-way set-associative cache for a microprocessor.

of the block, down to a single byte. If a miss occurs, indicated by a no-match outcome from both tag comparisons, the memory controller initiates an 8-byte swap with main memory to bring the desired data into the cache. The block to be replaced is then selected according to some replacement policy from the two available candidates. The VAX-11/780's cache uses a random replacement policy, whereas the PowerPC 603 uses LRU. The 11/780 cache has the write-through memory updating policy, whereas the 603 implements write-back.

6.3.3 Structure versus Performance

We next examine some additional aspects of cache design: the types of information to store in the cache, the cache's dimensions and control methods, and the impact of the cache's design on its performance.

Cache types. Caches are distinguished by the kinds of information they store. An *instruction* or *I-cache* stores instructions only, while a *data* or *D-cache* stores data only. Separating the stored data in this way recognizes the different access behavior patterns of instructions and data. For example, programs tend to involve few write accesses, and they often exhibit more temporal and spatial locality than the data they process. A cache that stores both instructions and data is referred to as *unified.* A *split cache,* on the other hand, consists of two associated but largely independent units: an I-cache for instructions and a D-cache for data. While a unified cache is simpler, a split cache makes it possible to access programs and data concurrently. A split cache can also be designed to manage its I- and D-cache components differently.

Caches are also classified by the level they occupy in the memory hierarchy. Early computers employed a single, multichip cache that occupied one level of the hierarchy between the CPU and main memory. Two developments made it desirable to introduce two or more cache levels in high-performance systems: the feasibility of including part of the real memory space on a microprocessor chip and growth in the size (but not the speed) of main memory in typical computers. A level 1 (L1) or primary cache is an efficient way to implement an on-chip memory. An additional memory level can be introduced via an off-chip, level 2 (L2) or secondary cache. The desirability of an L2 cache increases with the size of main memory, assuming that the size of the on-chip, L1 cache is fixed. As main-memory size increases further, even more cache levels may be desirable.

The PowerPC microprocessor family illustrates some of the diversity of commercial cache types. The caches for the four original members of the series are summarized in Figure 6.51. These models are classified as low end (601), mid-range (603 and 604), and high end (620) in terms of performance. The 601 differs from the others in large part because it is a "bridge" design with architectural features of both the PowerPC and the earlier IBM POWER series; the other listed models are "pure" PowerPC machines. Each model is a single-chip microprocessor with an on-chip level 1 cache. An external level 2 cache is easily added, as discussed in Example 6.8. All PowerPC models have an LRU block (line) replacement policy, and the line size is either 32 or 64 bytes. The normal write policy on cache misses is write-back, but there is software support for write-through. With

Model	General type	Cache size S_1	Associativity k	Line size p_1
601	Unified	32 KB	Eight way	64 B
603	D-cache	8 KB	Two way	32 B
	I-cache	8 KB	Two way	32 B
604	D-cache	16 KB	Four way	32 B
	I-cache	16 KB	Four way	32 B
620	D-cache	32 KB	Eight way	64 B
	I-cache	32 KB	Eight way	64 B

Figure 6.51
Cache features of some members of the PowerPC family.

the exception of the 601, all models have split caches, with identical I-cache and D-cache capacities. As indicated in the figure, the cache size S_1 and the degree of associativity k double as we move from the 603 to each more powerful model.

Performance. The cache is the fastest component in the memory hierarchy, so it is desirable to make the average memory access time t_A seen by the CPU as close as possible to access time t_{A_1} of the cache. To achieve this goal, M_1 should satisfy a very high percentage of all memory references; that is, the cache hit ratio H should be almost one. A high hit ratio is possible because of the locality-of-reference property discussed earlier. From (6.7) we have $t_A = t_{A_1} + (1 - H)t_B$, where t_B is the block-transfer time from M_2 to M_1. The block size is small enough that, with a sufficiently wide M_2-to-M_1 data bus, a block can be loaded into the cache in a single main-memory read operation, making $t_B = t_{A_2}$ the main-memory access time. Hence we can roughly estimate cache performance with the equation

$$t_A = t_{A_1} + (1 - H)t_{A_2} \tag{6.12}$$

A formula similar to (6.12) holds for the average cycle time.

Suppose that M_2 is six times slower than M_1. A reduction in H from 99 percent to 95 percent—approximately a 4 percent drop in the cache-hit rate—changes t_A from $t_{A_1} + (1 - 0.99)6t_{A_1} = 1.06t_{A_1}$ to $t_{A_1} + (1 - 0.95)6t_{A_1} = 1.30t_{A_1}$; that is, the access time increases by about 23 percent. Hence a small decrease in the cache's hit ratio H has a disproportionately large impact on system performance. Consequently, considerable design effort is devoted to making H as close to one as possible. This problem is often restated as that of making the cache-miss ratio $1 - H$ as close to zero as possible.

Consider a k-way set-associative cache M_1 defined by the following parameters: the number of sets s_1, the number of blocks (lines) per set k, and the number of bytes per block (also called the line size) p_1. Recall that the cache is fully associative when $s_1 = 1$ and is direct-mapped when $k = 1$. The number of bytes stored in the cache's data memory, usually referred to as the *cache size* S_1, is given by the following formula:

$$S_1 = k s_1 p_1 \tag{6.13}$$

or, in words,

Cache size = number of blocks (lines) per set × number of sets
× number of bytes per block

Although other factors, such as the tag memory (directory) size, influence the over-all cost C_1 of the cache, it is generally assumed that C_1 is proportional to the data capacity S_1; that is, $C_1 = c_1 S_1$.

Design process. The parameters in Equation (6.13), as well as factors like the block replacement and write policies, influence the cache's hit ratio H in ways that are hard to quantify because they depend on the workloads used with the cache. Such workloads, in turn, are application dependent. As a result, potential cache designs are evaluated by extensive trace-driven simulation experiments with address traces derived from representative programs or benchmarks for the target applications. Experiments involving billions of simulated address references are often carried out in the design of the caches for a new microprocessor.

Increasing k, s_1, p_1, or S_1, individually or collectively, tends to increase H. The size of an on-chip cache is often limited by area considerations. For example, the designers of the PowerPC 604 found that its 16KB caches were adequate for exe-cuting the SPEC benchmarks (see Example 2.8), but not the Transaction-Processing Performance Council (TPC) benchmarks, which consist of programs that manipu-late huge databases in real time and so have large memory requirements. The hit ratios for the TPC benchmarks running on the 604 continued to increase signifi-cantly, when the cache size was increased to 32 KB and beyond, a fact that influ-enced the larger cache size of the 620 [Ewedemi, Todd, and Yen 1994].

A general approach to the design of the cache's main size parameters k, s_1, p_1 follows [Stone 1993].

1. Select a block (line) size p_1. This value is typically the same as the width w of the data path between the CPU and main memory, or it is a small multiple of w.
2. Select the programs for the representative workloads and estimate the number of address references to be simulated. Particular care should be taken to ensure that the cache is initially filled before H is measured.
3. Simulate the possible designs for each set size s_1 and associativity degree k of acceptable cost. Methods similar to stack processing (section 6.2.3) can be used to simulate several cache configurations in a single pass.
4. Plot the resulting data and determine a satisfactory trade-off between perfor-mance and cost.

The cache size S_1 seems to dominate all other design factors affecting both hit rate and overall performance [Przybylski 1990]. S_1 is usually a power of two, hence a basic design question is: How does increasing or decreasing the size by a factor of two affect H? It has been found that, in many cases, doubling the cache size from S_1 to $2S_1$ increases H by about 30 percent [Stone 1993]. This *30 percent rule* is depicted graphically in Figure 6.52, where both the horizontal and vertical scales are normalized quantities. These graphs suggest that beyond a certain point, the improvement in performance measured by the increase in H does not justify the steadily increasing cost.

In general, k-way set-associative caches with values of k limited to two, four, or eight by cost considerations are preferred. However, it can be argued that for a single-level cache of moderate size, set-associative addressing seldom performs better than direct-mapped addressing [Przybylski 1990]. The most popular block replacement policy is LRU, reflecting its tendency to yield lower miss rates than

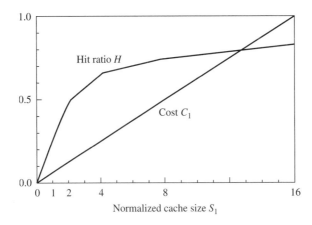

Figure 6.52
Influence of cache size on hit
ratio and cost.

other replacement policies. Write-back and write-through have both been widely implemented in commercial designs. They offer a trade-off between the amount of memory traffic generated (less with write-back) and the amount of temporary inconsistency between the cache and main memory (less with write-through).

EXAMPLE 6.10 CACHE DESIGN FOR THE POWERPC 620 [EWEDEMI, TODD, AND YEN 1994]. Figure 6.53 outlines the organization of a system based on the PowerPC Model 620, which is a 64-bit superscalar microprocessor intended to be of use in high-performance workstations and multiprocessors. As noted earlier (refer to Figure 6.51), the 620 was designed with a split level 1 cache consisting of an I-cache and a D-cache each of size S_1 = 32 KB, set-associative addressing with k = 8, and block (line) size p_1 = 64 bytes. The 620 also has a separate interface with its own 128-bit data bus to support an off-chip level 2 cache of up to 128 MB. The size parameters of the caches are the result of simulations carried out with various standard workloads. Although it was determined that some important workloads such as the TPC benchmarks would have benefited from larger caches, the 32KB values for the on-chip caches were selected because chip-area considerations circa 1993 made larger caches uneconomical.

We now retrace some of the original decisions affecting the design of the 620's level 1 cache [Ewedemi, Todd, and Yen 1994]. The block size p_1 was chosen to be 64 bytes based on the need to balance the time spent loading a block into the cache—it is excessive if p_1 is too large—with the number of such loads—it is excessive if p_1 is too small. Another factor influencing the choice of p_1 was the width of the system data bus, which is 16 bytes. With p_1 = 64 bytes, a cache block can be refilled or written back to the next level of memory in four clock cycles.

The architectural specifications for the PowerPC require a minimum main-memory page size of 4 KB. The low-order 12 bits of the 620's 64-bit memory address word are therefore reserved for a displacement address within a page. From the cache perspective, the high-order half of this 12-bit field forms a convenient set address, while the low-order half can be used to address a byte within a 64B cache block. Six set-address bits imply that each cache can have 2^6 = 64 sets. With S_1 = 32 KB and p_1 = 16 B, a cache can contain a total of 512 blocks (lines). Hence 512/64 = 8 lines can be placed in a set, which suggests the use of eight-way set-associativity—as was eventually decided. This relatively large degree of associativity also gave good performance with the SPEC and TPC benchmark suites. For instance, simulation with the TPC-A benchmark yielded the

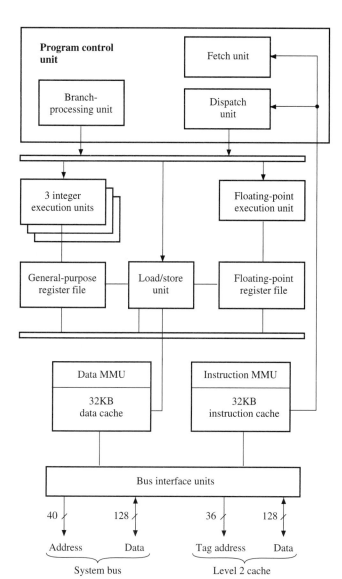

Figure 6.53
Organization of the PowerPC model 620.

following data for D-cache performance:

Cache size S_1	Associativity k	Relative miss rate
8 KB	Four way	1.78
16 KB	Four way	1.36
16 KB	Eight way	1.29
32 KB	Eight way	1.00

Implementation of a k-way cache in the traditional manner illustrated by Figure
6.50 imposes a speed penalty that increases rapidly with k. When $k = 8$, eight tags must

be compared simultaneously; the tag size can be up to 28 bits, depending on the size of the address space. Such comparisons can be quite slow. The 620 has an unusual implementation of eight-way set-associative addressing, which uses several small CAM arrays like that of Figure 6.46 to speed up accesses within a set.

The preceding techniques for designing a single-level cache can be adapted in many ways to add more cache levels to a computer. This task is of particular interest when designing around a single-chip microprocessor that already contains an L1 cache; an off-chip L2 cache is a natural way to increase memory performance. The look-aside design of Figure 6.41a can, in principle, easily accommodate additional cache levels, as Figure 6.54a suggests. Here the system bus carries all the memory traffic due to misses that must be processed by M_2 (the L2 cache) and M_3 (main memory), as well as IO data transfers. Figure 6.54b shows a version of the faster, look-through organization (Figure 6.41b) that is used in the PowerPC 620 (Example 6.10) and the MIPS R10000 (Example 5.8). In each case the processor contains a controller for a two-level cache and a special external bus, separate from the system bus, to which an L2 cache can be connected. Various control methods, some very complex, have been developed to maximize the memory sys-

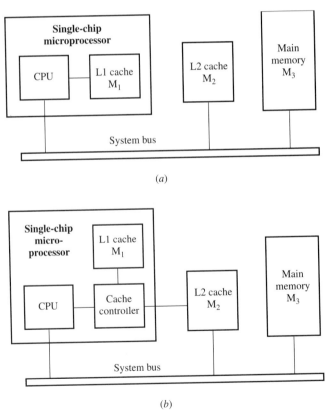

Figure 6.54
Two ways of adding an L2 cache to a microprocessor with an on-chip L1 cache (a) look-aside and (b) look-through.

tem's performance and to ensure the consistency of the information stored in the three memory levels.

6.4 SUMMARY

No one technology can supply all the memory needs of a computer. Fast memories are expensive: cost per bit increases as access time decreases. Consequently, several memory types with very different physical properties can be found in a typical computer system. Besides cost per bit and access time, other important characteristics of memory devices are data-transfer rate, alterability, and compatibility with processor technologies.

Main memory is of the random-access type where the access time of every location is constant. RAMs are organized as two-dimensional arrays to reduce the cost of their access circuitry and facilitate manufacture. The dominant technologies for this application are semiconductor ICs, especially dynamic RAMs (DRAMs) based on single-transistor cells. Secondary memories require a lower cost per bit and a higher storage density. We can achieve these goals by using serial-access memory technologies that share access mechanisms and have access times that vary with location. Serial-access memories store information on tracks that behave somewhat like shift registers. The most widely used technologies in this group are magnetic-surface memories with electromechanical access mechanisms, for example, magnetic-disk and -tape units. Also popular are serial memories that employ optical-recording techniques.

The memory units of a computer are organized as a multilevel hierarchy (M_1, M_2, ..., M_n) in which M_1 is connected to the CPU, M_2 is connected to M_1, and so on. M_i has less capacity, higher cost, but shorter access time than M_{i+1}. The goal of a memory hierarchy is to obtain a cost per bit close to that of the least expensive memory M_n and an access time close to that of the fastest memory M_1. Such a memory system can be managed by hardware (a memory management unit) or software (an operating system) to behave like a single large memory. This behavior is achieved by automatically translating the virtual-memory addresses referenced by programs into real addresses in the physical-address space and by automatically transferring blocks (pages) of information between the various levels of the hierarchy. Locality of reference ensures that data is generally in M_1 when referenced by the CPU. A basic measure of the performance of a hierarchical memory system is the hit ratio H, which is the fraction of all memory references that are satisfied by M_1.

Memory space is a limited resource of a computer and so must be shared by different applications. Dynamic allocation means determining the regions of memory assigned to programs while they are in execution. Nonpreemptive methods assign space to incoming blocks only if an available region of sufficient size exists; best fit and first fit are two possible allocation methods of this type. Preemptive methods assign incoming blocks to occupied regions of M_1 and thereby permit more efficient use of memory space. Blocks to be preempted are selected according to some replacement policy. Least recently used (LRU) is one of the most widely used replacement policies. The block types used to allocate memory space also affect performance. Segments are blocks of variable size that correspond to logical units of a program. Pages are fixed-sized blocks with no logical significance. Memory space can be allocated by segments, pages, or a combination of both (paged segments). The use of fixed-size pages greatly simplifies memory management.

To reduce the speed disparity between CPU and main memory, one or more intermediate memories called caches are used. A cache may be split into an I-cache and a D-cache that store instructions and data, respectively; a unified cache stores both. Information is stored in a cache's data memory in page-style blocks (lines). Each block is marked by a tag address held in a special tag memory (directory). When the CPU outputs a memory address, the cache compares it to the contents of its tag memory. If a match (hit) occurs, the memory access is completed by the cache; otherwise, a block that includes the addressed item is transferred from main memory to the cache. The tag memory of a k-way set-associative cache is divided into k sets, each of which can be searched rapidly via an expensive technique called associative, or content, addressing. A lower-cost direct-mapped cache has only one block per set. The more powerful microprocessor chips incorporate an L1 cache and provide support for attaching a larger but slower L2 cache.

6.5
PROBLEMS

6.1. List the main physical differences between the following memory technologies: SRAMs, flash memories, magnetic floppy disks, optical hard disks, and CD-ROMs.

6.2. When a CPU and its main memory M operate at similar speeds, a one-word load or store can be completed in a single CPU clock cycle. The CPU is often designed to function properly with slower memory technologies. It does so by retaining control of the system bus for two or more clock cycles until a slow load or store is completed; the extra clock cycles, during which the CPU is idle, are known as *wait states*. (*a*) What changes must be made to the memory's external signals given in Figure 6.10 to accommodate wait states? (*b*) Suppose a slow RAM requiring $k > 1$ wait states is used with a fast CPU in a computer that achieves a performance level of p MIPS while executing a fixed workload at a CPU clock frequency of f MHz. Assuming that no other changes are made, describe in qualitative terms what happens to p as f is steadily decreased to zero.

6.3. Consider the generic 1-D RAM organization depicted in Figure 6.7. Assume the storage cell unit is implemented by the DRAM cell of Figure 6.9*b*. Briefly describe three ways in which the RAM can be modified to double its data-transfer rate.

6.4. A 128MB RAM is to be designed from 2M × 4-bit RAM ICs. Assume that 1-out-of-2^k decoder ICs are also available for $k \le 3$, as well as ICs containing standard logic gates. The main design goal is to minimize the total number of ICs used. (*a*) Carry out the design assuming that each RAM chip has a single chip-select line CS and give your answer in the style of Figures 6.11 and 6.12. (*b*) Repeat the design assuming that each RAM IC has two chip-select lines CS_1 and CS_2 and is enabled if and only if $CS_1 = CS_2 = 1$.

6.5. Using the 64Mb DRAM of Example 6.1 as the basic component, design a 256M × 32-bit DRAM. Include in your answer a diagram in the style of Figures 6.11 and 6.12.

6.6. A 16Mb DRAM chip has a word size $w = 8$ bits. Like the 8E1 of Example 6.1, it has a 2-D organization with multiplexed row-column addressing. (*a*) If the column address is 10 bits, what is the size of the row address? (*b*) How many copies of this DRAM are needed to make a $1G \times 32$-bit memory?

6.7. Occasionally, it is desirable to implement a small RAM using a single RAM IC of large capacity. For example, DRAM manufacturers sometimes sell RAMs that are defective but contain sub-RAMs that are fully operational; these units are used in low-cost applications such as toys. Describe how the 64Mb DRAM of Figure 6.13 can be used as a $512K \times 4$-bit DRAM.

6.8. For the 64Mb DRAM described in Example 6.1, calculate the minimum time required to read out the contents of every addressable location in the memory (*a*) if the addresses are generated in a random sequence and (*b*) if page mode is used.

6.9. A RAM is to be designed with a target capacity of 16 MB. Three DRAM ICs of the kind shown in Figure 6.10 are available to serve as components: (*a*) a $4M \times 1$-bit DRAM costing \$22 per IC; (*b*) a $1M \times 2$-bit DRAM costing \$10; and (*c*) a $256K \times 8$-bit DRAM costing \$4.50. Access circuitry, including ICs and wiring, is estimated to cost $\$x + 10y$, where x is the number of RAM ICs used and y is the number of address bits to be decoded externally. Determine which type of DRAM IC would minimize the cost of the memory.

6.10. Consider the three DRAM types a, b, and c defined in the preceding problem. We want to build from one of these DRAM types a memory with a word size $w = 4$ bits. The memory should have the largest possible storage capacity consistent with access circuitry cost of $\$x + 10y$, as before, and a total system cost of at most \$475. Determine the DRAM type to use and the maximum capacity that can be achieved.

6.11. A RAM has N storage cells organized as N_x rows and N_y columns. The number of address drivers needed is $N_x + N_y$. (*a*) If $N = M^2$, where M is an integer—that is, N is a perfect square—show that the number of address drivers needed is a minimum if and only if $N_x = N_y = M$. (*b*) If N is not a perfect square, provide an algorithm for determining values of N_x and N_y that minimize the number of address drivers.

6.12. A certain $1M \times 16$-bit RAM has four-way address interleaving with four memory banks M_0, M_1, M_2, and M_3. (*a*) Identify the bank to which each of the following hex-encoded addresses is assigned: 01234, ABCDE, 91272, and FFFFF. (*b*) If one of the memory banks is busy when a new read request arrives at the memory, what is the probability that the request will be delayed due to memory contention?

6.13. List and discuss briefly three advantages and three disadvantages of the Rambus method (Example 6.2) for interfacing main memory to a very high performance workstation.

6.14. A moving-arm disk-storage device has the following specifications:

Number of tracks per recording surface	200
Disk-rotation speed	2400 rev/min
Track-storage capacity	62,500 bits

Estimate the average latency and the data-transfer rate of this device.

6.15. A certain magnetic hard disk drive has the following specifications in its data sheet:

Number of disks (recording surfaces)	14 (27)
Number of tracks per recording surface	4925
Number of sectors on all recording surfaces	17,755,614

Storage capacity (formatted) of disk drive	9.09 GB
Disk-rotation speed	5400 rev/min
Average seek time	11.5 ms
Internal data-transfer rate	44 to 65 MB/s

Calculate the block size B and the average block access time t_B.

6.16. The seek time of a magnetic-disk memory depends on how fast the read-write head can move between tracks. Suppose there are N tracks numbered 0 through $N - 1$, and the read-write head takes time Dt to move from track i to track $i \pm D$, that is, across D tracks. Hence if an access addressed to read track i is followed by an access to track $j = i \pm D$, the seek time of the second access is Dt. The best-case seek time is 0 and the worst case is Nt. The question then arises: What is the average seek time t_S as a function of N and t? Assuming that the tracks are accessed in a random fashion, demonstrate that $t_S \approx Nt/3$; that is, the average seek time is approximately the time to move the read-write head across one-third of the tracks. [*Hint:* Enumerate the seek times for all the possible (i,j) combinations for a small case such as $N = 8$ and then attempt to derive a general expression for the average seek time.]

6.17. A magnetic-tape system accommodates 2400 ft reels of standard nine-track tape. The tape is moved past the recording head at a rate of 200 in/s. (*a*) What must the linear tape-recording density be in order to achieve a data-transfer rate of 10^7 bits/s? (*b*) Suppose that the data on the tape is organized into blocks each containing 32K bytes. A gap of 0.3 in separates the blocks. How many bytes can be stored on the tape?

6.18. A nine-track magnetic tape has fixed block and interblock gap sizes. The gap length is 0.6 in, and the storage density is 1600 B/in. (*a*) If the space utilization u is 70%, what is the block size in bytes? (*b*) Let the start-stop time be 1 ms and let the measured (effective) data-transfer rate be 55 KB/s to read a single block. What is the maximum possible data-transfer rate?

6.19. The data-transfer rate d_{eff} of a magnetic-tape memory with respect to a single block transfer is given by Equation (6.3). It is possible to increase d_{eff} by accessing more than one block at a time, which spreads the start-stop time t_{SS} over all the accessed blocks. Suppose that $t_{SS} = 1.5$ ms, the block size $bs = 2048$ B, the gap length $gl = 0.25$ in, and the storage density $s = 1600$ B/in. If $d_{eff} = 95,000$ B/s, how many blocks must be accessed simultaneously in order to increase d_{eff} to at least 100,000 B/s?

6.20. Another medium for secondary memories is *digital audio tap*e or *DAT,* which is a small magnetic-tape cartridge adapted from videotape technology. High storage capacity and high data-transfer rates are achieved by storing the data in short, multitrack diagonal strips along the tape and by wrapping the tape (which moves relatively slowly) around a spinning set of one or more read-write heads. This design produces a very high head-to-tape speed. A certain DAT unit has the following specifications: The length of the tape is 90 m. The tape moves at 0.7 in/s (1.79 cm/s), but the head-to-tape speed is 270 in/s (68.58 cm/s). (*a*) If the DAT's storage capacity is 2 GB, estimate the effective normal data-transfer rate in KB/s. (*b*) The DAT drive has a special search and rewind speed, which is 200 times the normal read-write speed. Estimate how long it takes to fully rewind the tape.

6.21. The data sheet of a commercial magneto-optical disk drive includes the following specifications:

Formatted storage capacity of unit with 1024-byte sectors	650 GB
Formatted storage capacity of unit with 512-byte sectors	600 GB
Read data-transfer rate with 1024-byte sectors	0.87 MB/s
Read data-transfer rate with 512-byte sectors	0.79 MB/s

Write data-transfer rate with 1024-byte sectors   0.29 MB/s
Write data-transfer rate with 512-byte sectors   0.26 MB/s

(*a*) The larger (1024 byte) sector provides greater storage capacity and higher data-transfer rates than the smaller (512 byte) sector. Explain why. (*b*) The larger sector size appears to have all the advantages, so why is the smaller size ever used? (*c*) Why is writing slower than reading?

6.22. The storage hierarchy of the IBM System/390 mainframe family of high-performance computers has been described as a pyramid with nine levels, with the internal CPU registers forming the highest level and magnetic-tape storage forming the lowest (ninth) level. Suggest the memory types that define the remaining seven levels and their positions in the hierarchy.

6.23. A computer has a two-level virtual-memory system. The main memory M_1 and the secondary memory M_2 have average access times of 10^{-6} and 10^{-3} s, respectively. We know that the average access time for the memory hierarchy is 10^{-4} s, which is considered unacceptably high. Describe two ways in which this memory access time could be reduced from 10^{-4} to 10^{-5} s and discuss the hardware and software costs involved.

6.24. A two-level memory (M_1, M_2) has the access times $t_{A_1} = 10^{-8}$ s and $t_{A_2} = 10^{-3}$ s. What must the hit ratio H be in order for the access efficiency to be at least 65 percent of its maximum possible value?

6.25. In an n-level memory, the *hit ratio* H_i associated with the memory M_i at level i may be defined as the probability that the information requested by the CPU has been assigned to M_i. Assuming that all information assigned to M_i also appears in M_{i+1}, then $H_1 < H_2 < ... < H_n = 1$. Using this definition of H_i, generalize the expression for t_A given in Equation (6.6) to an n-level memory hierarchy.

6.26. A certain memory configuration has four levels M_1, M_2, M_3, and M_4 with hit ratios of $0.8, 0.95, 0.99,$ and 1.0, respectively. A program Q makes 3000 references to this memory system. Calculate the exact number of references R_i made by Q that are satisfied by an access to level M_i.

6.27. The *residual-hit ratio* RH_i of a level M_i in a hierarchical memory system has been defined as the ratio of the number of access requests that actually reach M_i to the number of such requests that M_i can satisfy. Clearly, $RH_i \le H_i$, the hit ratio, because M_i can satisfy any access request that is satisfied by a higher, faster level of the hierarchy. Calculate RH_i for each level of the four-level memory and the program Q defined in Problem 6.26.

6.28. A high-speed computer has a two-level paged virtual memory. Main memory has a capacity of 64 MB and a cycle time of 50 ns. Secondary memory consists of magnetic-disk units with the following specifications: an average seek time of 7 ms; an average rotational latency of 3 ms; and an internal data rate of 100,000 B/s. Essentially all disk accesses result from page faults, very few of which require a page from main memory to be copied back to disk. We know that main memory has a hit ratio of 0.9999998 and that the average time to access memory as a whole is 60 ns. Estimate the page size P, showing all your calculations.

6.29. Let p_i denote the fraction of memory-access requests that result in an access to level M_i in the three-level memory of Figure 6.55. When a miss occurs in M_i, a page swap always takes place between M_i and M_{i+1}; the average time for this page swap is t_{B_i}. (*a*) Calculate the average time t_A for the processor to read one word from the memory system. (*b*) We want to make $t_A \le 1.1 \times 10^{-7}$ s. In other words, t_A should not exceed the access time of M_1 by more than 10 percent. We can achieve this speedup by replacing M_3 with a faster memory technology that reduces t_{B_2} to a new value t'_{B_2}.

Level i	Access time t_{A_i} (s)	Access probability p_i	Page transfer time t_{B_i} (s)
M_1	10^{-7}	0.999990	0.0005
M_2	10^{-6}	0.000009	0.01
M_3	10^{-4}	0.000001	

Figure 6.55
Data for problem 6.29.

Memory	Capacity	Cost ($/B)	Access time (s)	Hit ratio
Cache 1	16 KB	10^{-3}	10 ns	0.990000
Cache 2	256 KB	10^{-5}	20 ns	0.999900
Main memory	32 MB	10^{-6}	100 ns	0.999999
Disk memory	8 GB	10^{-9}	10 ms	1.000000

Figure 6.56
Data for problem 6.30.

What should t'_{B_2} be? (c) Suggest and justify a more cost-effective way of satisfying the above requirement on t_A than reducing t'_{B_2}.

6.30. (a) What are the average cost per bit and the access time of the four-level memory system specified in Figure 6.56? (b) Suppose that, as a cost-saving measure, the second-level cache is eliminated from the system. Determine the resulting percentage changes in the system's cost and access time, showing all your calculations.

6.31. A memory reference by the PowerPC microprocessor generates a 32-bit effective address A_{eff} that contains a 16-bit virtual address to a page of size 4 KB. Address A_{eff} also contains a pointer to a small set of segment registers that store segment descriptors. (a) How many segment registers does the PowerPC have? (b) Each segment descriptor includes a 24-bit segment address, called the virtual segment identifier VSID. How big is the PowerPC's virtual-address space? (c) As discussed in the text, the Pentium has four memory-address-translation modes, depending on whether or not segmentation or paging are enabled. The PowerPC also has several address-translation modes, one of which, called *real* addressing, is defined as the mode in which the effective and physical addresses are the same. To which Pentium mode does real addressing correspond?

6.32. Assuming page size to be a function of average segment size only, determine the page size 2^k that maximizes memory space utilization when the average segment size is 5000 words and k must be an integer.

6.33. The available space list of a 16KB memory has the following entries at some time t:

Region (base) hex address	Size (bytes)
0000	2 K
1000	1 K
2000	512
31FF	3 K

Time	$t + 1$	$t + 2$	$t + 3$	$t + 4$
Size of block to be allocated	1K	2K		1K
Address of block to be deallocated			2DFF	
Size of block to be deallocated			1K	

Determine the available space list after all these requests have been serviced using (a) best-fit and (b) first-fit allocation. Assume that the memory is searched in ascending address sequence.

6.34. Consider the following page-address trace generated by a two-level cache–main-memory scheme that uses demand paging and has a cache capacity of four pages.

$$1 \ 6 \ 4 \ 5 \ 1 \ 4 \ 3 \ 2 \ 1 \ 2 \ 1 \ 4 \ 6 \ 7 \ 4 \ 1 \ 3 \ 1 \ 7$$

Assume a "hot" start, in which the cache initially has pages 1, 2, 3, and 4 allocated to it. Which of the page-replacement policies FIFO or LRU is more suitable in this case? Show your calculations, and give a short intuitive justification of your answer.

6.35. Computers such as the MIPS R3000 have caches that use a random page-replacement policy that we referred to as RANDOM. The page to be replaced is selected by a fast process that approximates truly random selection and does not use any data on the page's reference history. State whether or not RANDOM is a stack replacement algorithm and justify your answer.

6.36. A variation of the LRU replacement policy, which we call *simplified LRU* (SLRU), has been used in some virtual-memory systems. Every page P_i in an SLRU page table has a reference bit R_i associated with it. Whenever P_i is accessed, its reference bit R_i is set to 1. If the access request for P_i causes a page fault, then R_j is reset to 0 for all $j \neq i$ and P_i is brought into main memory M_1. When a page in M_1 must be selected for replacement, the SLRU algorithm scans all the R_i's in a fixed order. The first page encountered with a reference bit of 0 is replaced. If all the reference bits are 1, then the page with the smallest (logical) address is replaced. (a) For the following page-address trace, determine the page-hit ratio under both SLRU and LRU, assuming that M_1 has a capacity of three pages and is initially empty.

$$2 \ 4 \ 2 \ 3 \ 5 \ 1 \ 3 \ 4 \ 1 \ 2 \ 5 \ 6$$

(b) Is SLRU a stack replacement policy? Justify your answer.

6.37. We want to build a small word-organized associative memory using the 4×4-bit memory circuit of Figure 6.46 as the basic building block. The memory is to store ten 8-bit words having the format shown in Figure 6.57. Any one of the fields A, B, and C may be selected as the key. Assume that all stored keys are unique. When a match occurs, the entire matching word is to be fetched (read operation) or replaced (write operation). Draw a logic diagram for the memory including all access circuitry.

6.38. Suppose an IO processor (IOP) is attached to the system bus of Figure 6.41b. The IOP can transfer data to or from the main memory M_2 without interacting with the CPU,

A	B	C

Figure 6.57
Word format for problem 6.37.

while the CPU transfers data to and from the cache M_1. Assume that a cache write-through policy is implemented, as well as memory-mapped IO. Devise a realistic situation where the IOP's interactions with M_2 can cause the CPU to see stale memory data, resulting in a system crash.

6.39. Suppose that a 2KB cache has set-associative address mapping. There are 16 sets, each containing four cache blocks (lines). The memory-address size is 32 bits, and the smallest addressable unit is the byte. (a) To what set of the cache is the address $000010AF_{16}$ assigned? (b) If the addresses $000010AF_{16}$ and $FFFF7xyz_{16}$ can be simultaneously assigned to the same cache set, what values can the address digits xyz have?

6.40. (a) Suppose the system in Figure 6.48 has its address lines labeled $A_0:A_{31}$, where A_0 is the high-order address bit. Identify the 15 lines used to address the cache's data RAM. (b) Assume that a single-word transfer over the system bus takes 15 ns. Estimate how long it takes the system to fully respond to a memory access when a cache miss occurs.

6.41. (a) Construct a register-level diagram for the IDT 71B74 cache-tag RAM IC used in Example 6.8. (b) Cache-tag RAMs such as the 71B74 have a reset input that clears all the cache-tag RAM's tag-storage locations. Ordinary RAM ICs have no such reset control line. Why?

6.42. An eight-way set-associative cache is used in a computer in which the real memory size is 2^{32} bytes. The line size is 16 bytes, and there are 2^{10} lines per set. Calculate the cache size and tag length.

6.43. Redesign the direct-mapped cache of Example 6.8 with the following changes: the capacity of the cache is to be reduced to 64 KB, and the cache block size and the width of the system data bus are both to be 32 bits.

6.44. Design a four-way set-associative cache in the style of Example 6.9 with the following parameters: the capacity of the cache is 64 KB; the cache block size is 32 B; and the width of the system data bus is 32 bits.

6.45. Discuss in qualitative terms the impact of the following design decisions on cache performance: (a) selection of a cache block (line) size p_1 that is too small; (b) selection of a cache block size that is too big; (c) selection of an associativity level k that is too small.

6.6
REFERENCES

1. Burgess, B. et al. "The PowerPC Microprocessor." *Communications of the ACM*, vol. 37 (June 1994) pp. 34–42.
2. Clark, D. W. "Cache Performance in the VAX-11/780." *ACM Transactions on Computer Systems,* vol. 1 (February 1983) pp. 24–37.
3. Cook, B. M. and N. H. White. *Computer Peripherals.* 3rd ed. London: Edward Arnold, 1994.
4. Ewedemi, S., D. Todd, and J.-T. Yen. "Design Issues of the High Performance PowerPC 620 Microprocessor." unpublished MS, December 1994.
5. Handy, J. *The Cache Memory Book.* Boston: Academic Press, 1993.
6. Hauck, E. A. and B. A. Dent. "Burroughs' B6500/7500 Stack Mechanism." *Proceedings Spring Joint Computer Conference,* pp. 245–51. [Reprinted in Siewiorek, D. P., C. G. Bell, and A. Newell. *Computer Structures: Readings and Examples.* New York: McGraw-Hill, 1982, pp. 244–250.]
7. Heath, S. *PowerPC: A Practical Companion.* Oxford, UK.: Butterworth-Heinemann, 1994.

8. Integrated Device Technology Inc. *PowerPC Secondary Burst Cache Design,* Application Brief AB-02. Santa Clara, CA, 1994.

9. Intel Corp. *Pentium Processor Family User's Manual,* vol. 3, *Architecture and Programming Manual.* Santa Clara, CA, 1994.

10. Kane, G. *MIPS RISC Architecture.* Englewood Cliffs, NJ: Prentice-Hall, 1988.

11. Knuth, D.E. *The Art of Computer Programming,* vol. 1, *Fundamental Algorithms.* 2nd ed. Reading, MA: Addison-Wesley, 1973.

12. Kumanoya, M., T. Ogaywa, and K. Inoue. "Advances in DRAM Interfaces." *IEEE Micro,* vol. 15 (December 1995) pp. 30–36.

13. Mattson, R. L. et al. "Evaluation Techniques for Storage Hierarchies." *IBM System Journal,* vol. 9 (1970) pp. 78–117.

14. Micron Technology Inc. *8 Meg × 8 FPM DRAM,* data sheet. Boise, ID, 1997.

15. Prince, B. *High-Performance Memories.* Chichester, UK: John Wiley & Sons, 1996.

16. Przybylski, S. A. *Cache and Memory Hierarchy Design.* 2nd ed. San Mateo, CA: Morgan Kaufmann, 1990.

17. Quantum Corp. *ATLAS II Hard Disk Drives,* data sheet. Milpitas, CA, 1996.

18. Shore, J. E. "On the External Fragmentation Produced by First-Fit and Best-Fit Allocation Strategies." *Communications of the ACM,* vol. 18 (August 1975), pp. 433–440.

19. Smith, A. J. "Cache Memories." *Computing Surveys,* vol. 14 (September 1982), pp. 473–530.

20. Stone, H. S. *High-Performance Computer Architecture.* 3rd ed. Reading, MA: Addison-Wesley, 1993.

21. Triebel, W. A. and A. E. Chu. *Handbook of Semiconductor and Bubble Memories.* Englewood Cliffs, NJ: Prentice-Hall, 1982.

22. Weste, N. and K. Eshraghian. *Principles of CMOS VLSI Design.* 2nd ed. Reading, MA: Addison-Wesley, 1992.

System Organization

This chapter considers how computers and their major components are interconnected and managed at the processor or system level. It examines the methods used for internal and external communication, as well as the design of input-output (IO) systems. The final topic is the use of multiple processors to achieve high performance, fault tolerance, or both.

7.1
COMMUNICATION METHODS

In recent years computing has become intimately associated with communication. A computer's internal or local communication methods significantly affect its flexibility and performance. External, long-distance communication allows computers to be linked together, for example, via the global Internet network. This section examines the general nature of the local and long-distance communication mechanisms used with computer systems.

7.1.1 Basic Concepts

The difficulty in transferring information among the units of a computer largely depends on the physical distances separating them. We distinguish two cases: *intrasystem* communication, which occurs within a single computer system and involves information transfer over distances of less than a meter; and *intersystem* communication, which can involve communication over much longer distances. Intrasystem communication is primarily implemented by groups of electrical wires called *buses,* which support parallel, that is, word-by-word, data transmission. Intersystem communication, on the other hand, is realized by a variety of physical media, including electrical cables, optical fibers, and wireless (radio) links. Serial (bit by bit) rather than parallel data transmission is preferred for communication over longer distances. Serial links cost less, are more reliable, and are also easier to control than parallel links. A set of computers and other system components that are linked together over relatively long distances constitute a *computer network*.

Buses. The various processor-level components, CPU, caches, main memory, and IO (peripheral) devices within a computer system communicate via buses. The term *bus* in this context covers not only the physical links among the components, but also the mechanisms for controlling the exchange of signals over the bus.

Figure 7.1 depicts the most basic computer bus structure. Here a single bus, the *system bus,* handles all intrasystem communication. All units share the system bus, therefore at any time only two units can communicate with each other. A typical system bus transaction is a memory read (load) operation that involves the transfer of one or more data words over the system bus from the memory (cache or main) M to the CPU. A memory write (store) operation transfers data over the system bus in the opposite direction. Input-output operations normally involve data transfers between an IO device and M. In all the preceding operations M is a passive or *slave* device with respect to system bus transactions, whereas the CPU can actively control the system bus, that is, serve as a bus *master*. IO devices are normally thought of as slave units, but they can be made into bus masters via control units such as specialized IO controllers or general-purpose IO processors.

As Figure 7.1 indicates, the system bus consists of three main groups of lines: address, data, and control. (Not shown are the lines that distribute electrical power to the bus units.) The address lines, typically 8 to 32 in number, transmit the addresses of data items stored in the system's main memory or IO address space. The data lines, typically 16 to 128 in number, transmit data words over the bus. Finally, the control lines perform such functions as identifying the transaction type (memory read, memory write, IO interrupt, and so forth) and synchronizing communication between fast and slow units.

The characteristics of a system bus tend to closely match those of its host CPU and vary widely between different microprocessor families and even between members of the same family. The evolution of CPUs in speed and word size has been matched by a corresponding evolution in their system buses. For example, the first member of Intel's 80X86 family, the 8086 microprocessor, had internal data and (real) address word sizes of 16 and 20 bits, respectively. The CPU data word size became 32 bits, and the address size 24 bits, with the 80286 microprocessor;

System
Organization

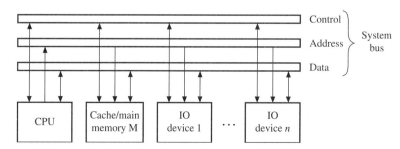

Figure 7.1
Communication within a computer via a single shared bus.

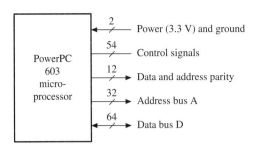

Figure 7.2
System bus of the PowerPC 603
microprocessor.

both became 32 bits with the 80386. The data and address sizes used inside the CPU are often, but not always, the same as those found in the external system bus. The 16-bit 8088, a variant of the 8086 used in the first IBM PC, has an 8-bit external data bus. On the other hand, the Pentium's external data bus is 64 bits wide.

Figure 7.2 outlines the system bus of the PowerPC 603 microprocessor, which is typical of personal computers. It has 64 data-transfer lines D which are bidirectional; that is, they act either as inputs or outputs of the CPU—but not simultaneously. The system bus can transfer from 1 to 8 bytes at a time. Its 32 address lines A allow $2^{32} = 4G$ memory or IO locations to be specified. Twelve parity check lines, one for each byte of D and A, provide error detection. A large set of control lines supports data transfers, exchange of bus control, interrupt processing, and other bus functions.

The principal use of the system bus is high-speed data transfer between the CPU and M. Most IO devices are slower than the CPU or M and present an external interface that is different from that of the system bus. For example, magnetic-disk units and other secondary memories transfer data serially. Therefore, they need to be connected to the system bus via interface circuits called *IO controllers* that perform series-to-parallel and parallel-to-series format conversions and other control functions. A single IO controller can interface many IO devices to the system bus. This leads to the structure shown in Figure 7.3 in which the IO devices are connected to a separate bus called an *IO bus*.

Computer manufacturers and standards organizations have standardized various IO bus types. For example, the Small Computer System Interface known as the *SCSI* (pronounced "scuzzy") *bus* was adopted as a standard by the American

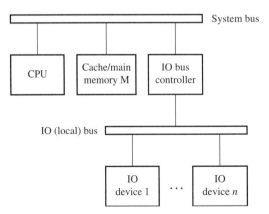

Figure 7.3
Computer with separate system
and IO buses.

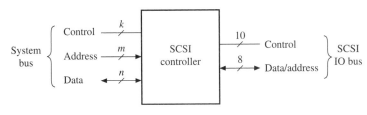

Figure 7.4
The Small Computer System Interface (SCSI) IO bus.

National Standards Institute (ANSI) in 1986. This bus connects IO devices such as hard disk units and printers to personal computers. SCSI was originally designed to transfer data a byte at a time at rates up to 5 MB/s. As can be seen from Figure 7.4, the SCSI bus is smaller and simpler than a system bus like the PowerPC's. Its data subbus is only 8 bits wide and is also used to transfer addresses. Ten additional lines provide all the necessary control functions. Recent extensions to the original SCSI standard have wider data buses (16 and 32 bits), more control features, and higher data-transfer rates.

Another bus with a role similar to SCSI is the so-called Industry Standard Architecture (ISA) bus originally developed by Intel for the IBM PC. Since it allows extra main-memory units as well as IO devices to be added to a computer, it is often referred to as a *local* or *expansion bus,* rather than an IO bus. A more recent bus standard that we examine in detail later is the Peripheral Component Interconnect (PCI) bus, which can transmit 4- or 8-byte words at rates of 500 MB/s or more.

Long-distance communication. There are several important differences between intra- and intersystem communication methods. Whereas intrasystem communication is serial by word, intersystem communication is usually serial by bit because of the difficulty of synchronizing data bits sent in parallel over long distances. Serial transfers also reduce the cost of the communication equipment. Every long-distance data transfer requires a substantial amount of time to establish the communication path to be used, for instance, the time associated with entering a telephone number. To reduce this overhead, a sequence of many bits called a *message,* which corresponds to the concept of block or page in memory systems, is transmitted at one time.

Intrasystem communication is implemented by transmitting digital signals in the form of discrete 0 and 1 pulses over multiline buses. As they are transmitted, the pulses are distorted by variations in the bus's electrical properties, interference between adjacent lines (crosstalk), and similar phenomena collectively known as *noise.* The distortion caused by noise increases with the number of lines in the bus and the signal transmission frequency; it is also affected by the quality of the transmission medium. Beyond some point the pulses become unrecognizable and transmission errors result. Over long distances, therefore, it is more cost-effective to embed the data in analog signals that are transmitted serially, in much the same way as voice traffic has long been sent over telephone lines. Continuous analog signals called *carriers* are generated and varied (modulated) in some manner to produce distinct signal types that denote 0 and 1. A device called a modulator-

Figure 7.5
Long-distance data transmission using frequency-modulated (FM) signals.

demodulator, or *modem*, converts data between the modulated analog form used for long-distance communication and the pulse form used inside the computer.

Figure 7.5 illustrates the modulation method called *frequency modulation* (FM) used by modems that connect a computer to a low-speed, "voice grade" telephone line. The carrier is a sine wave whose frequency f can be shifted slightly to create two distinct frequency levels: f_0 denoting 0 and f_1 denoting 1. Such signals are heard as beeps of different pitch. Since the 1980s, complex signal-processing techniques have been developed to increase the data-transfer rates over telephone lines from 300 bits/s—bits per second is often denoted bps in this context—to 56,000 bits/s, which is close to the maximum possible. These techniques include the assignment of multiple carrier frequencies to the sender and receiver, error-correcting codes that mask noise-induced errors, and data compression that detects and eliminates redundant information in the data being transmitted.

Digital communication networks, that is, networks designed expressly for transmitting information in digital form, can achieve much higher data-transfer rates. An example is the *integrated services digital network* (ISDN), an international standard for transmitting audio, video, and other data in digital form. Although ISDN was originally proposed around 1960, it has only recently been deployed worldwide. ISDN takes advantage of fiber-optic technology and fast communication methods to achieve data-transfer rates of 600 Mb/s or more. Wireless (radio) transmission using orbiting satellites to relay messages can also achieve very high data rates.

Computer networks. Digital communication networks designed to link many independent computers are called computer networks. Their rationale is to permit sharing of computing resources (hardware, software, or data) that are widely dispersed. For communication over distances of a few kilometers or so—within a single office building, for instance—*local-area networks* (LANs) are used. A LAN is a computer network employing data-transmission links that are private to the network in question. Computer networks spread over large geographical areas, that is, *wide-area networks* (WANs), use data-transmission facilities supplied by telecommunications companies, which in many countries are government-owned or -regulated organizations.

Various techniques exist for sharing the links of a computer network that aim at reducing communication costs. One such technique is *message switching,* which uses intermediate switching centers (servers) on long communication paths to store messages and subsequently forward them toward the final destination; this process is called *store and forward*. Messages are collected by each server, where they are organized (grouped into batches) to make efficient use of the data paths connected to that server. Complete message transmission is thus accomplished by a sequence

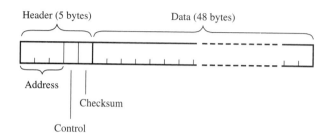

Header (5 bytes)   Data (48 bytes)

Address

Checksum

Control

Figure 7.6

Format of a data packet (cell) used in asynchronous transfer mode (ATM) networks.

of *hops* through a variable number of servers. Message switching utilizes the available communication links far more efficiently than circuit switching.

Messages vary greatly in length so that short messages can be delayed while longer messages are being transmitted. This problem is reduced by dividing messages into *packets* of fixed length and format and then transmitting packets from long messages interspersed with packets from short messages. The store-and-forward servers are then responsible for sorting the packets from the various messages and transmitting them to their proper next destinations. Different packages can be sent by different routes dictated by network traffic conditions. At the final destination a message must be reassembled from its constituent packets. This form of communication is called *packet switching* and is used for fast communication of large amounts of data. A type of packet switching called *asynchronous transfer mode* (ATM) combines voice and data communication using short packets that can be transmitted very fast. An ATM packet called a *cell* consists of a 5-byte header containing the destination address and certain control information, followed by a 48-byte data field, as depicted in Figure 7.6.

Although the goal of a universal or *open* computer network to which any manufacturer's computers can be attached remains elusive, the International Standards Organization (ISO) has developed a set of guidelines that provides a common basis for computer network design. These guidelines are known as the *ISO Reference Model for Open Systems Interconnection* (OSI) and define seven functional levels or *layers* through which users exchange messages in a computer network; see Figure 7.7. Each layer is associated with certain network services—error control, for instance—and different computers in a network can be thought of as exchanging information between corresponding layers. Consequently, a distinct set of communication rules or *protocol* can be defined for each layer. In general, layers 1 to 3 of the OSI Reference Model involve services associated with data communications functions close to the network hardware, while layers 5 to 7 involve software (operating systems) functions close to the network user. The intermediate transport layer (layer 4) serves to interface the network's hardware and software.

EXAMPLE 7.1 THE ETHERNET NETWORK ACCESS METHOD [SIMONDS 1994]. Ethernet is a popular bus-oriented architecture for LANs. Its specification involves only the physical and data-link layers, so it is seen as primarily an access method for LANs. Computer-specific hardware (Ethernet controllers) and software (Ethernet drivers) implement the remaining layers of network control. At the physical level an Ethernet LAN has the structure shown in Figure 7.8. Up to 1024 nodes (computers) can be connected via coaxial cable; their maximum separation is limited to 2.8 km. At the data-link level, communication is by messages or *frames* that contain

Layer	Associated services
1. Physical	Electrical and mechanical hardware interfacing to the physical communication medium.
2. Data link	Message setup, transmission, and error control.
3. Network	Establishing message paths in the network (message routing and flow control).
4. Transport	Interfacing network-independent messages with the specific network being used.
5. Session	Creation and management of communication channels between the communicating applications programs.
6. Presentation	Data-transformation services such as character-code translation or encryption.
7. Application	Providing network support functions such as file-transfer routines to application programs (network users).

Figure 7.7
The protocol layers of the Open Systems Interconnection (OSI) Reference Model.

the address, control, and check bits, as well as a variable-length data field. Total message length can range from 64 to 1518 bytes.

A technique called *carrier sense multiple access with collision detection (CSMA/ CD)* controls access to the Ethernet and some other LAN types. A node wishing to send a message over the Ethernet first senses (listens to) the main coaxial cable via a tap unit and transmits the message only if it detects no carrier signal, in which case the network is not currently in use. Each message is broadcast throughout the network, and its destination address is examined by all nodes as it reaches them. Only the node whose address matches that of the message header actually reads the message. Since all computers on the network have equal access to the main cable, it is possible for two nodes to begin message transmission at the same time. Consequently, as it transmits a message, a node monitors the actual signals on the cable and compares them with the signals that the node itself is transmitting. If the transmitted and detected signals differ,

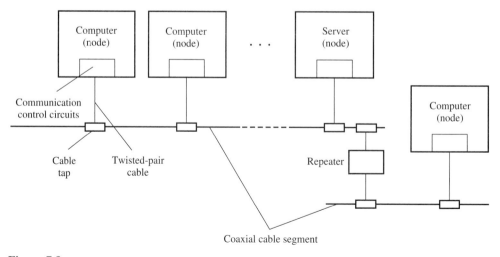

Figure 7.8
Structure of an Ethernet-based LAN.

which will be the case if another computer is transmitting a message at the same time, then a *collision* is said to have occurred. On detecting a collision, an Ethernet node ceases transmission and tries to transmit the same message again later. The time of retransmission is randomly selected so that the chance of another collision is slight, although repeated collisions do occur.

Measurements of Ethernet performance show that the CSMA/CD access scheme is fair in that if n nodes request continuous access to the network over some period of time T, each node gains access to the network for a period very close to T/n. The bandwidth loss due to collisions, even under heavy traffic conditions, is modest—typically less than 10 percent.

Besides the CSMA/CD method used by Ethernet, another common way of controlling access to a LAN is *token passing,* where each node in turn receives and passes on the right to access the network; this right is represented by a special short message called a *token*. The node that possesses the token has exclusive use of the network for transmitting a message, after which it transmits the token to another (fixed) node. Token passing is often used in ring-structured networks (*token rings*), but is also used for bus-structured LANs (*token buses*). When a token ring is not passing normal messages, the token circulates from node to node around the network. A node having a message to transmit waits until the token reaches it. It then holds the token while it transmits its message. In a ring network, a (nontoken) message is usually passed in one direction from node to node until it reaches the destination node; it can then be returned to the source node to confirm its receipt. After transmitting one message, a node puts the token back into circulation so that all nodes get roughly equal access to the network.

The Internet. As discussed in section 1.3.3, the Internet is a huge, worldwide packet-switched computer network descended from the ARPANET, which pioneered the use of packet switching in the 1970s. Each ARPANET site had a computer called an *interface message processor* (IMP), which performed the store-and-forward functions required for packet switching and connected one or more host computers to the ARPANET. Since many types of computers could be hosts, the IMP acted as a standard interface controller between hosts on its local network and a set of remote network servers. To ensure some degree of fault tolerance, the nodes and internode links were chosen so that at least two disjoint communication paths existed between every pair of IMPs.

The *Transmission Control Protocol/Internet Protocol* (TCP/IP) developed for the ARPANET is used by every Internet server. The main function of the IP protocol is to handle the routing of data packets over the Internet; it corresponds to layer 3 (the network layer) of the OSI Reference Model. In particular, IP breaks messages into packets of about 200 bytes each for transmission to remote servers. An Internet address is 4 bytes long, implying a total of more than 4 billion distinct addresses. It is normally represented by a four-part "dotted" symbolic form like *server1.net2.university3.edu.* Because this address format is hierarchical a node needs only limited routing information, for example, the possible paths to all the networks, but not the individual Internet servers, in the domain *edu* assigned to educational institutions.

An Internet packet is transmitted with a header containing its most recent source address and its final destination address H_D, as well as a sequence number indicating its position in the original message. The packets leave the first server S_S with consecutive sequence numbers 1,2,3,4,...; however, they can travel by different routes to the server S_D of the final destination H_D and arrive there at different times, not necessarily in the original order. An Internet server that is not on the local network containing H_D retransmits each packet it receives to another server to which it is directly connected, following a routing algorithm that aims to find the fastest path to the ultimate destination. The actual path can vary with network traffic conditions. For example, having sent a packet to server S_i, the current server may decide to send the same package to a different server S_j to avoid network congestion, faulty links, or the like.

An Internet package can pass through dozens of servers before reaching the target server S_D. The TCP program on S_D, which operates within the OSI transport layer, is responsible for assembling packets in their proper sequence and checking to see if any are missing or contain errors. If necessary, TCP can send a message to a remote server requesting it to resend a missing or erroneous package. When all a message's packages have been received in satisfactory condition, TCP merges them to reconstruct the original message, which it forwards over the local network to H_D. A higher-level protocol called the *hypertext transport protocol* (http) enables the Internet to transfer multimedia files easily and efficiently and is the basis for the World Wide Web.

Interconnection structures. A system's interconnection structure can be defined by a graph whose nodes denote components such as computers, memories, communications controllers, and so forth, and whose edges denote communication paths such as buses. A path designed to link only two devices is said to be *dedicated*. A path used to transfer information between different sets of devices at different times is said to be *(time)shared* or *multiplexed*.

A conceptually simple interconnection method is to place dedicated buses between all pairs of components that need to communicate. The general case in which *n* units must be connected in all possible ways needs $n(n-1)/2$ dedicated buses. Figure 7.9 shows such a system when $n = 4$. Dedicated buses allow very fast information transfer: All *n* devices can send or receive data simultaneously, and there is no delay due to busy connections. Furthermore, systems with dedicated links are inherently reliable because a link failure affects only the two units connected to that link. These units may still be able to communicate if they can send data to each other via other units. For example, if the bus linking U_1 and U_4 in Figure 7.9 fails, U_1 and U_4 can possibly communicate via U_2 or U_3. The main draw-

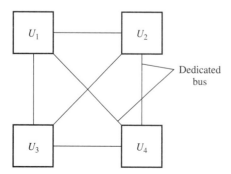

Figure 7.9
System of four units connected by six dedicated buses.

back of dedicated buses is their high cost. The number of buses needed increases as the square of the number of units. Adding a unit to the system is difficult, as the new unit must be physically attached to each existing unit.

At the other end of the spectrum, a single shared bus can provide all communications among n units, as illustrated by Figure 7.1. At any time only two units can communicate with each other via the bus; the remaining units are effectively disconnected from one another. A control method (protocol) is required to supervise sharing of the bus among the n devices. Bus control can be centralized in a special bus-master unit, which can be one of the n communicating units U_i, for example, a CPU. Alternatively, several units can be designed to act as bus masters at different times (decentralized control).

In general, connection to a shared bus is established in two different ways:

- A unit U_i capable of acting as bus master initiates the connection of two units to the bus, perhaps in response to an instruction in a program being executed by U_i.
- A slave unit sends a request to the current bus master for access to the shared bus. The bus master then connects the requesting unit to the link if it is not in use. If the bus is busy, the requesting unit must wait until the bus becomes available. If several conflicting requests are received, the bus master uses some arbitration scheme to decide which request to grant first.

The shared bus is one of the most widely used connection methods in computer systems. Its main advantage is low cost. It is also flexible in that new units can easily be introduced without altering the system's overall structure or the connections to the old units. However, shared buses are relatively slow, since units are forced to wait when the bus is busy. The system is also sensitive to failure of the shared control circuits.

Between the extremes of a set of dedicated buses and a single shared bus lie various interconnection structures that involve some sharing of links, but permit more than one word to be transferred at a time. An example is the *crossbar* network shown in Figure 7.10. A crossbar connects two groups of units $G_1 = \{U_1, U_2, \ldots, U_m\}$ and $G_2 = \{U'_1, U'_2, \ldots, U'_n\}$ so that any unit of G_1 can be connected to any unit of G_2, but two units in the same group need never be connected. For example, G_1 can be a set of memory banks and G_2 a set of processors. Crossbar networks have also been used to connect IO processors to IO devices. As Figure 7.10 shows, each unit in G_1 (G_2) is attached to a shared, horizontal (vertical) bus. The horizontal and vertical buses are in turn connected via a set of $n \times m$ controllers called *crosspoint switches,* which can logically connect any horizontal bus to any vertical bus. At any time only one crosspoint can be active in each row and column. If $k = \min\{m, n\}$, then k units in G_1 can be simultaneously connected to k units in G_2. Hence the crossbar network allows up to k data transfers to take place simultaneously. Access conflicts and delays occur when two units in G_1 attempt to communicate with the same unit in G_2, or vice versa, at the same time.

Many structures employing shared or nonshared buses have been proposed for intra- and intersystem communication in computer systems. More links increase communication speed, but they also increase cost in terms of the buses themselves and their interface circuits. In practice, direct, dedicated connections are provided among only a subset of the communicating units. Units not directly connected must communicate indirectly via intermediate units that relay data in store-and-forward fashion until the final destination is reached. Indirect communication of this type is

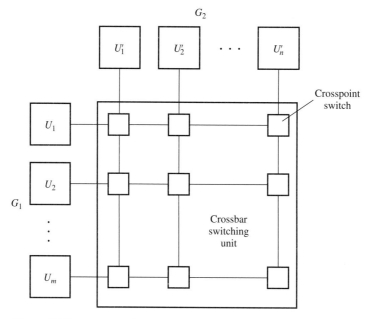

Figure 7.10
Crossbar connection of two groups of units.

slow, and if used extensively, can significantly reduce performance. The amount of such communication occurring depends both on the system's structure and its communication needs. Interconnection structures are therefore selected to balance hardware costs against communication delays for some broad class of applications.

Figure 7.11 shows graphs that abstractly represent some important computer interconnection structures [Feng 1981; Quinn 1994], a few of which we encountered earlier. Here the nodes denote computers or processor-level components such as IO controllers, while the edges denote shared or nonshared buses. The linear or one-dimensional array structure of Figure 7.11a models the basic system-bus based structure of Figure 7.1, provided the buses are shared. The mesh (two-dimensional array) structure (Figure 7.11b) occurs in the systolic multiplier of Figure 4.59. The ring structure of Figure 7.11c adds an extra link to the six-node linear structure, thereby cutting in half the length of the longest path between any two units. It also introduces some tolerance of bus failures by providing two, rather than one, communication paths between each unit pair. The graph of Figure 7.11d is called a star for obvious reasons and has a central or root node connected to all $n - 1$ other nodes. The linear and star graphs are special cases of a tree, which is a graph with no cycles. The three-dimensional hypercube is depicted in Figure 7.11e, while the complete graph for $n = 6$ nodes appears in Figure 7.11f. The ring, hypercube, and complete graphs are considered to be *homogeneous* because all nodes have precisely the same type of connections, making them interchangeable. For instance, each node x has the same number $d(x)$ of neighbors, where $d(x)$ is called the *degree* of x and is a rough indication of the cost of its bus interface. The other examples in Figure 7.11 are not homogeneous, because all nodes do not have the same degree.

Figure 7.12 summarizes some pertinent properties of the preceding interconnection structures. The number of edges and the maximum node degree serve as a measure of the hardware cost of the structure. The *distance* between two nodes is the number of edges along a shortest path in the graph from one node to the other. The maximum of these distances, called the *diameter* of the graph, is an indication of the worst-case communication delays that can occur. In the examples of Figure 7.12, the total number of connecting edges ranges from approximately $n^2/2$ (for large n) in the complete-graph case to the minimum possible value of $n - 1$ for the linear and star graphs. The complete graph and the star share the largest node degrees, while the linear structure has the largest diameter. The other structures exhibit various compromises between hardware cost and delay. Of particular interest is the hypercube, which achieves a reasonable balance between all three parameters. Therefore, it has been used as the interconnection network in several massively parallel computers.

7.1.2 Bus Control

This section examines the methods to establish and control intrasystem communication via a shared bus [Thurber et al. 1972; Gustavson 1984]. Two key issues are the timing of transfers over the bus and the process by which a unit gains access to the bus. We assume the general structure of Figure 7.1, which applies to most system and IO buses. We also assume that one particular unit acts as the bus master

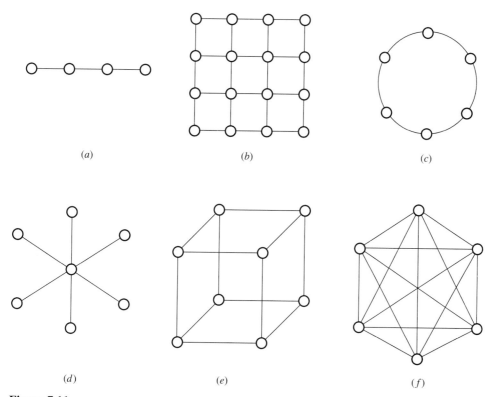

(a)   (b)   (c)

(d)   (e)   (f)

Figure 7.11
Interconnection structures: (*a*) linear; (*b*) mesh; (*c*) ring; (*d*) star; (*e*) hypercube; (*f*) complete.

Interconnection structure	Number of edges (buses)	Maximum node degree	Maximum internode distance
Linear	$n - 1$	2	$n - 1$
Ring	n	2	$n/2$
Mesh ($n^{0.5} \times n^{0.5}$)	$2(n - n^{0.5})$	4	$2(n^{0.5} - 1)$
Star	$n - 1$	$n - 1$	2
Hypercube ($n = 2^k$)	$(n/2) \log_2 n$	$\log_2 n$	$\log_2 n$
Complete	$n(n - 1)/2$	$n - 1$	1

Figure 7.12

Comparison of the interconnection structures of Figure 7.11 assuming each contains n nodes.

and supervises the use of the bus by the other units, the bus slaves. In many cases the CPU is the bus master, while the memory and IO interface circuits are slaves; IO controllers also serve as bus masters, however. Only a master can initiate data transfers, although slaves can request them. Both master and slave participate equally in the data-transfer process after it is initiated.

Basic features. Buses are distinguished by the way in which data transfers over the bus are timed. In *synchronous* buses each item is transferred during a time slot (clock cycle) known to both the source and destination units. Therefore, the bus interface circuits of both units are in step, or synchronized. Synchronization can be achieved by connecting both units to a common clock source, which is feasible only over very short distances. The rising or falling edge of the clock signal, which is one of the bus's control signals, determines when other bus signals attain stable (valid) states. Alternatively, each bus unit can be driven by separate clock signals of approximately the same frequency. Synchronization signals must then be transmitted periodically between the communicating devices in order to keep their clocks in step with each other.

Synchronous communication has the disadvantage that data-transfer rates are largely determined by the slowest units in the system, so some devices may not be able to communicate at their maximum rate. An alternative approach widely used in both local and (especially) long-distance communications is *asynchronous* timing, in which each item being transferred is accompanied by a control signal that indicates its presence to the destination unit. The destination can respond with another control signal to acknowledge receipt of the item. Because each device can generate bus-control signals at its own rate, data-transfer speed varies with the inherent speed of the communicating devices. This flexibility is achieved at the cost of more complex bus-control circuitry. In local communication where a clock signal is present, data transmission can be asynchronous in the sense that the number of clock periods between bus events (signal changes) can be indeterminate, while the events themselves are synchronized by the clock.

A unit is selected for connection to the main bus in two ways. The bus master can initiate the selection of a slave unit U in response to an instruction in a program or a condition occurring in the system that requires the services of U. Alternatively,

U itself can request access to the shared bus by sending a bus-request signal to the bus master. In each case the master unit must perform a specific sequence of actions to establish a logical connection between *U* and the bus. If several units can generate requests for bus access simultaneously, the bus master needs a way to select one of the units; this selection process is called *bus arbitration*. The CSMA/CD collision avoidance technique used by the Ethernet (Example 6.1) is an example of an arbitration process for LANs.

Bus lines fall into three functional groups: data, address, and control lines. The data lines transmit all bits of an *n*-bit word in parallel. They consist of either two sets of *n* unidirectional lines or a single set of *n* bidirectional lines. The data-bus width *n* is usually a multiple of eight, with $n = 8$, 16, 32, or 64 being common values. The address lines identify a unit to participate in a data transfer. Sometimes the same lines transfer addresses as well as data, a method termed *data-address multiplexing*. This method decreases the cost of the bus, along with the number of external connections (pins) of the units attached to the bus. A computer's system bus usually contains separate address and data lines, but its IO buses often do not; see Figure 7.4, for instance. This difference stems from the fact that an address accompanies each data-word transfer over the system bus, whereas data transfers via an IO bus tend to involve long blocks of consecutive words and need only the starting address of the block. That address can be sent at the start of the data transfer. The control lines convey timing signals and status information about the units attached to the bus; they also identify the type of information present on the data-address lines.

Bus interfacing. A significant contributor to the cost of a bus is the number and type of circuits required to transfer signals to and from the bus. A bus line represents a signal path with potentially very large fan-in and fan-out. Consequently, buffer circuits called bus *drivers* and *receivers* are needed to transfer signals to and from the bus, respectively.

A special transistor circuit technology called *tristate* logic is often used in bus design. It is characterized by the presence of three signal values 0, 1, and Z, where the third value Z is the *high-impedance state*. The binary values 0 and 1 have their usual interpretation, and correspond to two specific electrical states of a line, such as 0 volts and 3.3 volts. The high-impedance state Z, on the other hand, denotes the state of a line that is electrically disconnected from all voltage sources, that is, an open-circuited or floating line. Figures 7.13a and *b* define a *tristate buffer,* which serves as a bus-line driver. The inputs *x* and *e* are ordinary binary signals that take the values 0 and 1; the output *z*, however, can take all three values 0, 1, and Z. The tristate buffer (and every other tristate device) has a special input line *e* called *output enable,* which when set to 0 disables the output line *z* by changing it to the high-impedance state Z. When $e = 1$, the circuit becomes an ordinary noninverting buffer with $z = x$. Figures 7.13c and *d* show equivalent circuits corresponding to the buffer in the enabled and disabled states.

Tristate logic circuits have two big advantages in the design of shared buses:

- They greatly increase the fan-in and fan-out limits of bus lines, permitting very large numbers of devices to be attached to the same line.
- They support bidirectional transmission over the bus by allowing the same bus connection to serve as an input port and as an output port at different times.

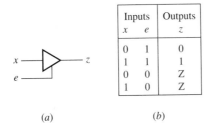

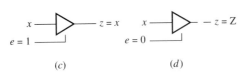

(a)   (b)

(c)   (d)

Figure 7.13
Tristate buffer: (a) logic symbol;
(b) truth table; (c) equivalent circuit
when enabled; (d) equivalent circuit
when disabled.

Figure 7.14 shows how we use tristate logic to interface two units U_1 and U_2 to a set of bidirectional bus lines. If $e_1 = 1$ and $e_2 = 0$, then U_1 controls or *drives* the bus lines in question; information is transferred over the bus from U_1 to U_2, in effect making $x_{2,i} = z_{1,i}$ for all i. Conversely, if $e_1 = 0$ and $e_2 = 1$, then U_2 drives the bus and information is transferred in the opposite direction from U_2 to U_1, making $x_{1,i} = z_{2,i}$ for all i. If $e_1 = e_2 = 0$, then the outputs of both U_1 and U_2 are logically disconnected from the bus and impose only a minuscule electrical load on it. The combination $e_1 = e_2 = 1$ is invalid, because it applies two different signals simultaneously to each bus line making the line's state indeterminate. Proper operation of the bus requires that at most one driver connected to each bus line be enabled at any time.

The bus lines that can be driven by a particular bus unit U, that is, used by U to send data to other units, depend on $U's$ function in the system. Bus masters have the ability to drive most bus lines, including certain lines that slave units cannot

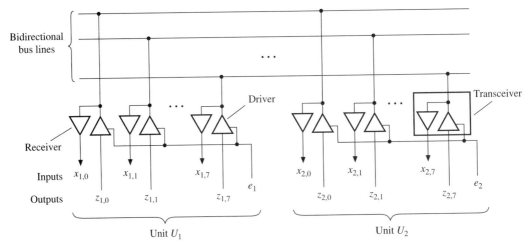

Figure 7.14
Use of tristate logic for bus interfacing.

drive. For example, a CPU can drive all data, address, and most control lines of a system bus. A main-memory unit, which is a bus slave, can drive the data lines but not the address lines, since it only needs to receive information from the address lines.

Timing. The details of some typical data transfers over a bus are shown in Figure 7.15 by means of *timing diagrams*. The *CLOCK* signal of period T serves as a timing reference, making this type of transfer synchronous. In this example, the 0-to-1 transition of *CLOCK*, that is, its rising edge, determines when other bus signals are recognized. All active signals must be set up with their new values before the *CLOCK* signal rises. Signal changes are expected to propagate along the bus to their destinations before the next 0-to-1 transition of *CLOCK*.

Figure 7.15 also illustrates some typical signal exchanges between slave and master units; these exchanges follow certain ordering rules called the *bus protocol*. Consider the read operation depicted in Figure 7.15a. Communication begins when

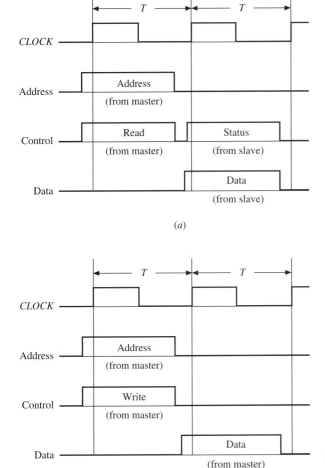

Figure 7.15
Synchronous data transfers:
(*a*) read and (*b*) write.

the bus master places one or more predetermined signals on the control lines specifying the desired bus transaction, for instance, read from memory (load) or read from IO device (input). At the same time, the master places the address of the desired (part of the) slave on the bus's address lines. All potential slave units then examine the active control and address signals. The slave with an address matching that on the bus responds in the next clock cycle by placing the requested data word on the bus's data lines; it can also optionally place status information, for example, (no) error occurred, on certain control lines. A synchronous write operation is similar except that the bus master rather than the slave is the data source; see Figure 7.15b. Note that both edges of *CLOCK* can be used as reference points in a bus transaction, and the read or write transactions of Figure 7.15 can be designed to take place during one clock cycle of period $2T$.

The requirement that the slave respond immediately (in the next clock cycle) to the bus master is lifted by providing a control signal called an *acknowledge* signal *ACK*, as shown in Figure 7.16 for a read bus transaction. *ACK* is controlled by the slave unit and is not activated until the slave has completed its part of the data transfer. The master therefore waits until it has received the *ACK* signal for the current data-word transfer before initiating a new one. Thus an acknowledge signal allows a delay of one or more bus cycles, called *wait states,* to be inserted in a bus transaction to accommodate slow devices. Although *ACK* may be activated in any cycle, its changes are synchronized with those of *CLOCK*. This type of communication is often used between main memory and a CPU. By inserting a variable number of wait states and signaling with *ACK* when it is ready, a memory of essentially any speed can communicate with a faster CPU.

Purely asynchronous timing eliminates the bus's clock signal and replaces it with timing control signals like *ACK*, which are generated by the communicating units. These units are thus self-timed, and units with quite different data-transfer

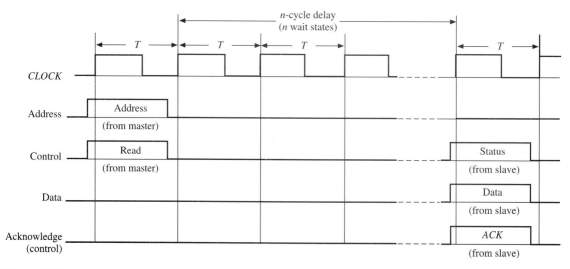

Figure 7.16
Synchronous data transfer (read) with wait states.

rates can communicate asynchronously. We distinguish two cases:

- *One-way* control in which one of the two communicating devices supplies all timing signals.
- *Two-way,* or *interlocked,* control in which both devices generate timing signals.

If one-way control is employed, a single signal controls each address or data transfer. This signal can be activated by the source and destination unit, either one of which can be the bus master. Figure 7.17*a* shows a source-initiated data transfer of this sort. The source places the data word on the data bus. After a brief delay the source activates the control line with the generic name *DATA READY*. The delay is to prevent the *DATA READY* signal from reaching the destination before the data word. Alternatively, the source can activate *DATA READY* and place data on the data bus at the same time. The destination unit must then insert a delay between its receipt of *DATA READY* and its reading of the data bus. The data lines and the *DATA READY* control line must remain in the active state long enough to allow the destination unit to copy the data from the data bus. Figure 7.17*b* shows a data transfer initiated by the destination unit. In this case the destination begins the data transfer by activating the control line *DATA REQUEST*. The source responds by placing the required word on the data lines. Again the data must remain active long enough for the destination unit to read it.

Often the *DATA READY/REQUEST* signals are used to load the data from the source unit to the bus or from the bus to the destination unit. Such control signals are called *strobe* signals and are said to strobe data to or from the bus. For example, the source may generate a data word asynchronously and place it in a buffer register connected to the bus data lines. A signal on *DATA REQUEST* activates the clock input line of the buffer, thereby "strobing" the data onto the bus; Figure 7.18 illustrates this process.

The disadvantage of one-way control is that it does not verify that the data transfer has been successfully completed. For example, in a source-initiated data transfer, the source unit receives no indication that the destination unit has actually received the data transmitted to it. If the destination unit is unexpectedly slow in responding to a *DATA READY* signal, the data may be lost. This problem is eliminated by introducing a second control line that allows the destination unit to send a reply signal to the source when it receives a *DATA READY* signal. This control line has the generic name *DATA ACKNOWLEDGE* or *ACK*. Figure 7.19*a*

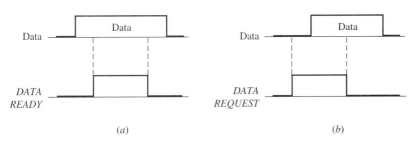

Figure 7.17
One-way asynchronous data-transfer timing: (*a*) source initiated and (*b*) destination initiated.

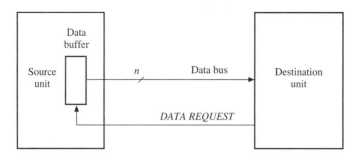

Figure 7.18
Use of a *DATA REQUEST* line to strobe data.

shows the exchange of signals, often called *handshaking,* that accompanies a
source-controlled transfer in this case. The source unit maintains the data on the
bus until it receives the *ACK* signal. The destination activates *ACK* after copying
the data from the bus. This sequence allows delays of arbitrary length to occur
during the data transfer. Figure 7.19*b* depicts a similar technique for destination-
initiated communication. The source unit activates *ACK* to indicate that the
requested data is available on the bus's data lines. The source maintains the data
on the bus until the destination unit deactivates *DATA REQUEST,* an action that
confirms successful receipt of the data at its destination. As Figure 7.19 demonstrates, a pair of control lines can perform the ready, request, and acknowledge
functions for all types of asynchronous bus communications.

Bus arbitration. The possibility exists that several master or slave units connected to a shared bus will request access to the bus at the same time. A selection
mechanism called *bus arbitration* is therefore required to enable the current mas-

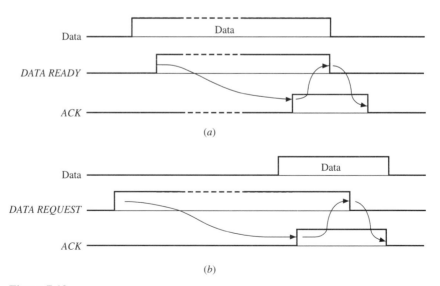

Figure 7.19
Asynchronous data transfer (handshaking): (*a*) source initiated and (*b*) destination initiated.

ter, which we will refer to as the bus controller, to decide among such competing requests. We discuss three representative arbitration schemes: daisy chaining, polling, and independent requesting. These methods differ in the number of control lines they require and in the speed with which the bus controller can respond to bus-access requests of different priorities. Some bus systems combine several distinct arbitration techniques.

Figure 7.20 illustrates *daisy-chaining* arbitration. This method involves three control signals to which we assign the generic names *BUS REQUEST*, *BUS GRANT*, and *BUS BUSY*. All the bus units are connected to the *BUS REQUEST* line. When activated, it merely serves to indicate that one or more units are requesting use of the bus. The bus controller responds to a *BUS REQUEST* signal only if *BUS BUSY* is inactive. This response takes the form of a signal placed on the *BUS GRANT* line. On receiving the *BUS GRANT* signal, a requesting unit enables its physical bus connections and activates *BUS BUSY* for the duration of its new bus activity.

The main distinguishing feature of daisy chaining is the way the *BUS GRANT* signal is distributed; it is connected serially from unit to unit as shown in Figure 7.20. When the first unit requesting access to the bus receives *BUS GRANT*, it blocks further propagation of that signal, activates *BUS BUSY,* and begins to use the bus. When a nonrequesting unit receives the *BUS GRANT* signal, it forwards the signal to the next unit. Thus if two units simultaneously request bus access, the one closer to the bus controller, that is, the one that receives *BUS GRANT* first, gains access to the bus. Selection priority is therefore determined by the order in which the units are linked (chained) by the *BUS GRANT* lines.

Daisy chaining requires very few control lines and embodies a simple, fixed arbitration scheme. It can be used with an essentially unlimited number of bus units. Since priority is wired in, a unit's priority cannot be changed under program control. If it generates bus requests at a sufficiently high rate, a high-priority unit like U_1 can lock out a low-priority device like U_n. A further difficulty with daisy chaining is its susceptibility to failures involving the *BUS GRANT* lines and their associated circuitry. If unit U_i is unable to propagate the *BUS GRANT* signal, then no U_j where $j > i$ can gain access to the bus.

The bus-arbitration scheme called *polling* replaces the *BUS GRANT* line of the daisy-chain method with a set of poll-count lines that are connected directly to all units on the bus, as depicted in Figure 7.21. As before, the units request access to the bus via a common *BUS REQUEST* line. In response to a signal on *BUS*

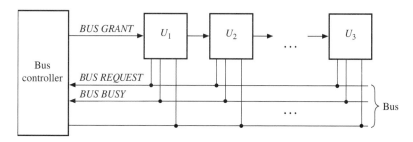

Figure 7.20
Bus arbitration using daisy chaining.

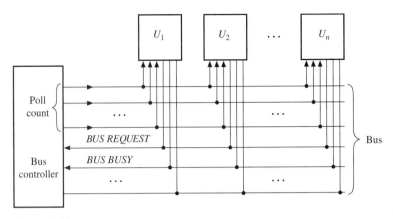

Figure 7.21
Bus arbitration using polling.

REQUEST, the bus controller proceeds to generate a sequence of numbers on the poll-count lines. Each unit compares these numbers, which may be thought of as unit addresses, to a unique address assigned to that unit. When a requesting unit U_i finds that its address matches the number on the poll-count lines, U_i activates *BUS BUSY.* The bus controller responds by terminating the polling process, and U_i connects to the bus.

The priority of a bus unit is determined by the position of its address in the polling sequence. This sequence can be programmed if the poll-count lines are connected to a programmable register; hence selection priority can be altered under software control. A further advantage of polling over daisy chaining is that in polling a failure in one unit need not affect the other units. This flexibility is achieved at the cost of more control lines (k poll-count lines instead of one *BUS GRANT* line). Also, the number of units that can share the bus is limited by the addressing capability of the poll-count lines.

The third arbitration technique, *independent requesting,* has separate *BUS REQUEST* and *BUS GRANT* lines for every unit sharing the bus. This approach,

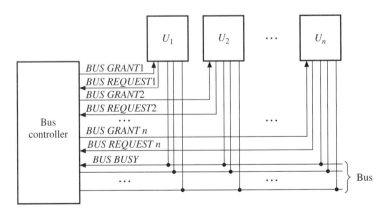

Figure 7.22
Bus arbitration using independent requesting.

which is depicted in Figure 7.22, provides the bus controller with immediate identification of all requesting units and enables it to respond rapidly to requests for bus
access. The bus-control unit determines priority, which is programmable. The main
drawback of bus control by independent requesting is the fact that $2n$ *BUS
REQUEST* and *BUS GRANT* lines must be connected to the bus controller in order
to control n devices. In contrast, daisy chaining requires two such lines, while polling requires approximately $\log_2 n$ lines.

EXAMPLE 7.2 THE PERIPHERAL COMPONENT INTERCONNECT (PCI) BUS
[SHANLEY AND ANDERSON 1995]. The PCI bus, often referred to as a "local" bus,
was developed by Intel in the early 1990s and has since become a widely adopted standard for microprocessor-based computer products such as single-board microcomputers. Unlike some earlier standard buses, the PCI bus is designed to be easily interfaced
with different microprocessor families, main memory, and a very wide range of IO
devices. Many of the PCI bus's lines are optional, so it can be attached to bus units with
as few as 47 pins and as many as 100. It can support either 32-bit or 64-bit data transfers. In version 2.1, the maximum clock rate is 66 MHz, which allows a data-transfer
rate of up to 524 MB/s.

   The PCI bus is basically intended for attaching IO devices to a computer, but it has
many of the characteristics of a high-performance system bus. It can be configured as
an IO bus as in Figure 7.3 so that the microprocessor can communicate with memory
via its system bus while the PCI bus controller communicates independently with IO
devices via the PCI bus. Figure 7.23 shows a different configuration in which the PCI
bus has a more central role. Here the PCI bus is linked to the host CPU's "system" bus
via a memory controller referred to as a *bridge*, which gives it direct access to the
host's main memory. This arrangement, unlike that of Figure 7.3, allows CPU-cache

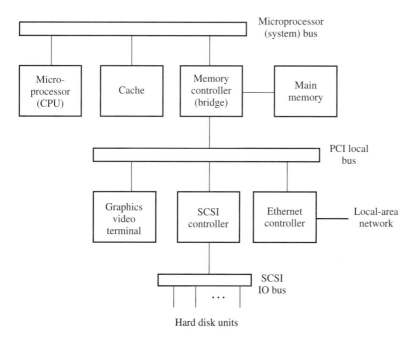

Figure 7.23
Computer system organized around a PCI bus.

and IO-memory transfers to take place simultaneously. High-speed devices such as video terminals and fast network controllers that have little need of the CPU are connected directly to the PCI bus. IO devices intended to conform with other bus standards such as SCSI or ISA can also be interfaced to the PCI bus via appropriate IO controllers, such as the SCSI bus controller in Figure 7.23.

Each PCI device is required to implement a set of registers called its configuration registers, whose format is defined in the PCI bus specification. When the system is first powered up, all such registers are accessed by the system control software to determine which IO devices are currently attached to the PCI bus and their basic communication requirements.

Figure 7.24 summarizes the 100 lines that make up the PCI bus. On the left are the signals required to support basic data transfers using 32-bit or smaller words. On the right are optional lines that support 64-bit data transfers, interrupt control, and other, less-common functions. To reduce pin counts and the size of the connectors needed by PCI-compatible units, addresses and data are multiplexed over a common set of lines denoted AD. A typical bus transaction involves two phases: In the first phase, an address is sent over AD; in the second phase, one or more data words are sent over AD. The remaining lines of the bus perform various control functions, which are outlined below. All bus operations are timed by a clock signal, so the PCI bus is considered to be synchronous; however, ready and acknowledge signals are provided to allow slow devices to insert wait states. Most lines are tristate and are considered inactive in the Z and 0 states, unless they have an overbar, in which case they are inactive in the Z and 1 states.

The command/byte-enable lines perform different functions at different times. During the address-transmission phase, C/BE defines a bus command that the bus master uses to tell the bus slave the type of transaction required. The possible commands include memory read, memory write, IO read, IO write, interrupt acknowledge, and a few others. During the data-transmission phase, C/BE indicates which bytes of AD carry valid data. PAR specifies the parity of the 36 bits $AD[31:0]$ and $\overline{C/BE}$ $[3:0]$; it serves the usual function of single-bit error detection. The lines designated basic interface control include $\overline{FRAME}$, which delimits a data-transfer transaction and therefore

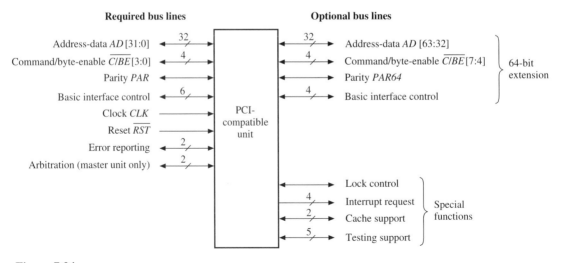

Figure 7.24
Signals of the PCI standard bus.

is active for the duration of the entire transaction; a pair of data-ready/acknowledge lines, $\overline{IRDY}$ (initiator ready) and $\overline{TRDY}$ (target ready), for use by the master and slave, respectively; and a $\overline{STOP}$ line that the slave uses to ask the master to halt the current transaction. The system clock signal CLK is responsible for synchronizing all bus transactions, while $\overline{RST}$ resets all bus-control registers attached to the PCI bus. The two error-reporting lines indicate parity errors and related problems.

A pair of lines $\overline{REQ}$ (bus request) and $\overline{GNT}$ (bus grant) control bus arbitration. The bus-arbitration method is not part of the PCI bus's specification, which requires only that the central bus controller receive a single request at a time on the $\overline{REQ}$ line and that all attached bus masters receive their fair share of access to the bus. The daisy-chaining method discussed earlier is easily implemented. Independent requesting can also be implemented without difficulty by means of priority-encoding logic that selects one of several active requests to forward to the PCI bus's $\overline{REQ}$ line.

Figure 7.25 shows a representative three-word data transfer from slave to master via the PCI bus; for example, an IO read operation. The transaction begins when the initiating master unit (which is assumed to already be in control of the bus) activates $\overline{FRAME}$ by setting it to 0 in clock cycle 1; as its name suggests, $\overline{FRAME}$ frames the entire data transfer sequence. The master then places an address and command word (IO read in our example) on the AD and C/BE lines, respectively; this information should be valid when clock cycle 2 begins. During cycle 2 all the units attached to the bus try to decode the address and command. In this instance an IO unit containing the current address will be successful and will prepare to communicate with the master. In the next cycle the master relinquishes control of AD and places valid byte-enable information on the C/BE lines for the remainder of the transaction. To avoid conflicts when the master stops driving the AD bus (and certain control lines) and the slave begins to do so, an idle, *turnaround* cycle—cycle 3 in Figure 7.25—must follow the address phase. The slave can transmit a sequence of data words via AD, beginning in cycle 4 at the maximum rate of one word per clock cycle. The two communicating units control the actual transfer rate via the $\overline{IRDY}$ and $\overline{TRDY}$ lines, which permit any number of wait states to be inserted after each data-transfer cycle.

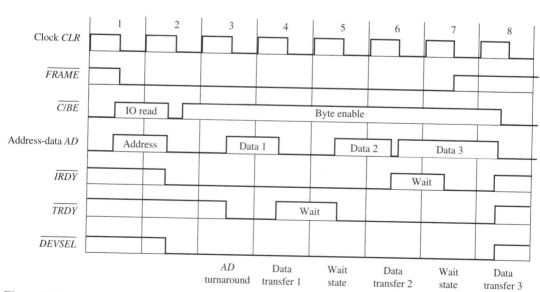

Figure 7.25
Data-transfer transaction (memory read) via the PCI bus.

Data transfer cannot begin until the master activates $\overline{IRDY}$ to indicate that it is ready to receive data; this occurs in cycle 2. The slave makes the data word 1 available and signals this fact by making $\overline{TRDY} = 0$ in cycle 3; the data transfer takes place in cycle 4. In this example the slave immediately deactivates its ready line ($\overline{TRDY} = 1$) making cycle 5 into a wait state; it then reactivates $\overline{TRDY}$ and places data word 2 on AD for transmission in cycle 6. The slave places data word 3 on AD for transmission in cycle 7. This time, however, the master decides to insert a wait state by making $\overline{IRDY} = 1$ for one clock cycle. Consequently, data word 3's transfer is delayed until cycle 8. The master deactivates $\overline{FRAME}$ in cycle 7 to signal that the following cycle marks the end of the bus transaction. The last control line $\overline{DEVSEL}$ (device select) shown in the figure is activated by the slave device in cycle 2 to indicate that the slave has successfully decoded the address and is the target of the current bus transaction. No data transfer can occur until $\overline{DEVSEL}$ is active, so this line serves to tell the master when a bus transaction cannot be completed due to a missing or faulty slave unit.

A write transaction (where the master is the data source rather than the slave) is very similar to that of Figure 7.25. No turnaround cycle is needed after the address-transfer phase, because the master continues to drive AD throughout the transaction.

7.2
IO AND SYSTEM CONTROL

The main data-processing functions of a computer involve its CPU and external (cache-main) memory M. The CPU fetches instructions and data from M, processes them, and eventually stores the results back in M. The other system components—secondary memory, user interface devices, and so on—constitute the input-output (IO) system. In this section we discuss the hardware and software needed to implement IO operations. We also discuss operating systems—the supervisory programs that manage a system's major resources including the CPU, main memory, and IO subsystems.

IO control methods. Input-output operations are distinguished by the extent to which the CPU is involved in their execution. (Unless otherwise stated, *IO operation* refers to a data transfer between an IO device and M, or between an IO device and the CPU.) If such operations are completely controlled by the CPU, that is, the CPU executes programs that initiate, direct, and terminate the IO operations, the computer is said to be using *programmed IO*. This type of IO control can be implemented with little or no special hardware, but causes the CPU to spend a lot of time performing relatively trivial IO-related functions. One such function is testing the status of IO devices to determine if they require servicing by the CPU.

A modest increase in hardware enables an IO device to transfer a block of information to or from M without CPU intervention. This task requires the IO device to generate memory addresses and transfer data to or from the bus (system or local) connecting it to M via its interface controller; in other words, the IO device must be able to act as a bus master. The CPU is still responsible for initiating each block transfer. The IO device interface controller can then carry out the transfer without further program execution by the CPU. The CPU and IO controller interact only when the CPU must yield control of the memory bus to the IO controller in response to requests from the latter. This level of IO control is called *direct memory access* (DMA), and the IO device interface control circuit is called a *DMA controller.*

The DMA controller can also be provided with circuits enabling it to request service from the CPU, that is, execution of a specific program to service an IO device. This type of request is called an *interrupt*, and it frees the CPU from the task of periodically testing the status of IO devices. Unlike a DMA request, which merely requests temporary access to the system bus, an interrupt request causes the CPU to switch programs by saving its previous program state and transferring control to a new interrupt-handling program. After the interrupt has been serviced, the CPU can resume execution of the interrupted program. Most computers have DMA and interrupt facilities, which are supported by special DMA and interrupt control units.

A DMA controller has partial control of IO operations. Essentially complete control of IO operations can be relinquished by the CPU if an IO *processor* (IOP) is introduced. Like a DMA controller, an IOP has direct access to main memory and can interrupt the CPU; however, an IOP can also execute programs directly. These programs, called *IO programs*, may employ an instruction set different from the CPU's—one that is oriented toward IO operations. It is common for larger systems to use general-purpose microprocessors as IOPs. An IOP can perform several independent data transfers between main memory and one or more IO devices without recourse to the CPU. Usually the IOP is connected to the devices it controls by a separate bus system, the IO bus, as illustrated in Figure 7.3.

7.2.1 Programmed IO

First we examine programmed IO, a method included in every computer for controlling IO operations. It is most useful in small, low-speed systems where hardware costs must be minimized. Programmed IO requires that all IO operations be executed under the direct control of the CPU; in other words, every data-transfer operation involving an IO device requires the execution of an instruction by the CPU. Typically the transfer is between two programmable registers: one a CPU register and the other attached to the IO device. The IO device does not have direct access to main memory M. A data transfer from an IO device to M requires the CPU to execute several instructions, including an input instruction to transfer a word from the IO device to the CPU and a store instruction to transfer the word from the CPU to M. One or two additional instructions may be needed for address computation and data-word counting.

IO addressing. In systems employing programmed IO, the CPU, M, and IO devices usually communicate via the system bus. The address lines of the system bus that are used to select memory locations can also be used to select IO devices. An IO device is connected to the bus via an *IO port,* which, from the CPU's perspective, is an addressable data register, thus making it little different from a main-memory location.

A technique used in many machines, such as the Motorola 680X0 series, is to assign a part of the main-memory address space to IO ports. This technique is called *memory-mapped IO*. A memory-referencing instruction that causes data to

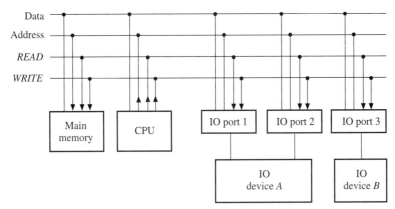

Figure 7.26
Programmed IO with shared memory and IO address space (memory-mapped IO).

be fetched from or stored at address X automatically becomes an IO instruction if X is made the address of an IO port. The usual memory load and store instructions are used to transfer data words to or from IO ports; no special IO instructions are needed. Figure 7.26 shows the essential structure of a computer with this type of IO addressing. The control lines *READ* and *WRITE*, which are activated by the CPU when processing a memory reference instruction, are used to initiate either a memory access cycle or an IO transfer.

In the organization shown in Figure 7.27, sometimes called *IO-mapped IO*, the memory and IO address spaces are separate. This scheme is used, for example, in the Intel 80X86 microprocessor series. A memory-referencing instruction activates the *READ M* or *WRITE M* control line which does not affect the IO devices. The CPU must execute separate IO instructions to activate the *READ IO* and *WRITE IO* lines, which cause a word to be transferred between the addressed IO port and the CPU. An IO device and a memory location can have the same address bit pattern without conflict. A minor modification of the circuit of Figure 7.27 can merge the memory and IO address spaces, if desired.

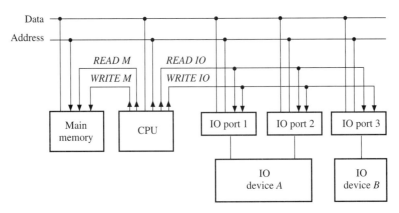

Figure 7.27
Programmed IO with separate memory and IO address spaces (IO-mapped IO).

IO instructions. As few as two IO instructions can implement programmed IO. For example, members of the Intel 80X86 series have two IO instructions called IN and OUT. The instruction IN X causes a word to be transferred from IO port X to the 80X86's accumulator register A. The instruction OUT X transfers a word from the A register to IO port X. The CPU assigns no special meaning to the words transferred to IO devices, but the programmer can do so. Some words may indicate IO device status and others may be control information (commands) for the IO device.

When the CPU executes an IO instruction such as IN or OUT, the addressed IO port is expected to be ready to respond to the instruction. Therefore, the IO device must transfer data to or from the CPU–IO data bus within a specified period. To prevent loss of information or an indefinitely long IO instruction execution time, the CPU must know the IO device's status so that the transfer is carried out only when the device is ready. With programmed IO the CPU can be programmed to test the IO device's status before initiating an IO data transfer. Often the status is specified by a single bit of information that the IO device makes available on a continuous basis, for example, by setting a flip-flop connected to the data lines at some IO port.

The CPU must perform the following steps to determine the status of an IO device:

1. Read the IO device's status bit.
2. Test the status bit to determine if the device is ready to begin transferring data.
3. If not ready, return to step 1; otherwise, proceed with the data transfer.

Figure 7.28 shows an 80X86-style program to transfer a data word from an IO device to the CPU's A register. It is assumed that the device is connected to ports 1 and 2 like device A in Figure 7.27. The IO device's status is assumed to be continuously available at port 1, while the required data is available at port 2 when the status word has the value READY.

If programmed IO is the primary method of input-output control in a computer, additional IO instructions can be provided to augment the IN and OUT instructions discussed so far. For example, the Digital PDP-8, an early minicomputer, has an IO instruction called TSK that tests the status of the IO device and modifies the CPU program counter based on the test outcome. TSK, which means "test IO device status flag and skip the next instruction if the status flag is set," can be implemented by two control lines linking the CPU and the IO device, as shown in Figure 7.29. On executing TSK, the CPU sends a signal called TEST STATUS

Instruction			Comment
WAIT:	IN	1	Read IO device status into A register
	CPI	READY	Compare immediate word READY to A; if equal, set flag Z = 1, otherwise set Z = 0
	JNZ	WAIT	If Z ≠ 1 (IO device not ready), jump to WAIT
	IN	2	Read data word into A register

Figure 7.28
Program to read one word from an IO device.

to the IO device. If the device status flag is set, a return pulse is sent on the SKIP line, which increments the program counter, thereby skipping the next instruction. Given an instruction of this type, the IO program of Figure 7.28 can be reduced to the following:

$$
\begin{array}{lll}
\text{WAIT:} & \text{TSK} & 1 \\
& \text{JMP} & \text{WAIT} \\
& \text{IN} & 2 \\
\end{array}
$$

A common IO programming task is the transfer of a block of words between an IO device and a contiguous region of memory. Figure 7.30 shows an input block-transfer program written in assembly code for the Intel 8085 microprocessor. (The 8085 is described in problems 1.31 and 1.32.) We assume here that the input device generates data at the rate required by the CPU, so no status testing is needed. The Zilog Z80, another early microprocessor that is software compatible with the 8085, has a single instruction INIR (input, index, and repeat) that performs all the functions specified by the last five instructions in Figure 7.30. INIR inputs a word from the IO port addressed by the C register and transfers it to the memory location addressed by the HL address register. INIR then increments HL; decrements B (which is used as a word-count register); and repeats the transfer, increment, and decrement steps until B = 0. Thus, ignoring minor differences between the 8085 and Z80 instruction names, the program of Figure 7.30 reduces

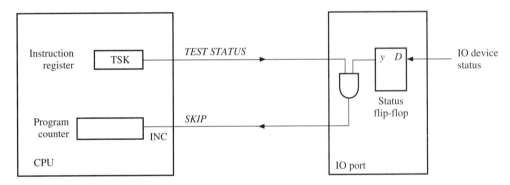

Figure 7.29
Implementation of the test status and skip (TSK) IO instruction.

Instruction			Comment
	LXI	H,10	Load memory address register H.L with 10
	MVI	B,100	Load (move immediate) register B with 100
LOOP:	IN	7	Read word from input port 7 into register A
	MOV	M,A	Store contents of A in memory location M(H.L)
	INX	H	Increment memory address register H.L
	DCR	B	Decrement register B (used as a byte counter)
	JNZ	LOOP	If B ≠ 0, jump to LOOP

Figure 7.30
Program to input a block of data from an IO device.

to the following Z80 program:

```
LXI    H, 10
MVI    B, 100
MVI    C, 7
INIR
```

It is interesting to compare these instructions to the INPUT and OUTPUT instructions of the IAS computer mentioned in section 1.2.2.

IO interface circuits. The task of connecting an IO device to a computer system is greatly eased by the use of standard ICs variously known as IO interface circuits, peripheral interface adapters, and the like. These circuits allow IO devices of widely different characteristics to be connected to a standard bus with a minimum of special-purpose hardware or software. The simplest interface circuit is a one-word, addressable register that serves as an IO port. The major microprocessor families contain various general-purpose and special-purpose IO interface circuits. They are called programmable if they can be modified under program control to match the characteristics of different IO devices.

Among the most basic IO interface circuits are programmable circuits intended to act as serial or parallel ports. Serial ports accommodate many types of slow peripheral devices ranging from secondary memory units to network connections. Parallel ports are designed to interface with IO devices employing multibit, bidirectional data paths. A small interface circuit of the parallel type is discussed in the next example.

EXAMPLE 7.3 THE INTEL 8255 PROGRAMMABLE PERIPHERAL INTERFACE CIRCUIT [INTEL 1993]. This IC, whose structure is shown in Figure 7.31, was designed for interfacing IO devices with the Intel 8085 and other small microprocessors. It is housed in a 40-pin package: 8 pins connect the 8255 to an 8-bit bidirectional CPU data bus; 24 IO pins can be attached to several IO devices. These IO pins are programmable in that the functions they perform are determined by a control word issued by a CPU instruction and stored internally in the 8255. This control word can specify a variety of operating modes involving either synchronous or asynchronous data transfers.

The 24 pins on the IO side of the 8255 are divided into 8-bit groups designated A, B, and C, each of which can act as an independent IO port. The C lines are further subdivided into two 4-bit groups C_A and C_B. They are commonly used as status or handshaking lines in conjunction with the A and B ports. Two address lines A_0 and A_1 select one of the three ports A, B, and C for use in an IO operation. The fourth address combination is used in conjunction with an output instruction of the form OUT CW to store an 8-bit user-specified control word CW in the 8255's internal control. This control word has two principal functions:

- It specifies whether the A, B, and C ports are to act as input, as output or, in the case of A and B only, as bidirectional IO ports.
- It programs certain C lines to generate handshaking and interrupt signals automatically in response to actions by an IO device.

Figure 7.32*a* shows one of the many possible configurations in which the A, B, and C lines are programmed as simple IO ports with no handshaking or interrupt capability. Figure 7.32*b* shows another configuration in which the A port is programmed to

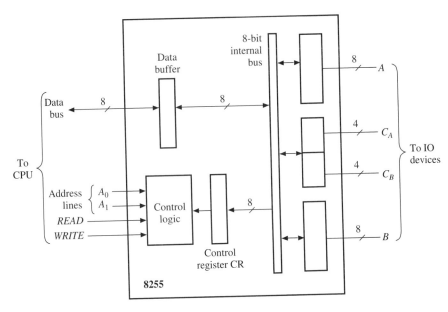

Figure 7.31
The 8255 programmable peripheral interface circuit.

be an input port with asynchronous timing signals generated by the *C* lines. The line called *DATA READY* is used by the IO device to strobe a word into the buffer register at port *A*. The 8255 then automatically generates a response signal on another *C* line, which can be sent to the IO device as an *ACK* signal if the IO device requires two-way control. A third *C* line generates an interrupt signal, which is sent to the CPU to indicate the presence of data at IO port *A*.

The Intel 8256 IC, defined as a multifunction microprocessor support controller, combines a number of useful IO interfacing functions in a single IC [Intel 1993]. As Figure 7.33 shows, the 8256 contains two parallel 8-bit IO ports 1 and 2, which we can program for synchronous or asynchronous data transfers in the same

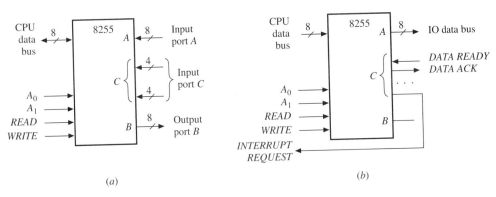

Figure 7.32
Two possible configurations of the 8255 programmable peripheral interface circuit.

way as we program ports *A* and *C*, respectively, of the 8255. The *universal asynchronous receiver-transmitter* (UART) module controls a communications port that supports serially transmitted data with various character lengths and transmission speeds, such as a modem might need. An interrupt controller handles up to eight interrupt requests. We can program a set of five 8-bit counters called *timers* to realize some useful timing functions. For example, timer 5 is designed to operate as a *watchdog timer,* which means that we can program it to generate an interrupt to the CPU if a particular IO event fails to occur within a specified time T. This timer is (re)loaded with value T whenever a specific input line on the 8256's IO interface is activated. The system clock then decrements the timer automatically until it reaches zero, at which point the timer automatically sends an interrupt request to the CPU. Hence as long as the IO device in question triggers the reloading of timer 5 within the specified period T, no interrupt is generated.

7.2.2 DMA and Interrupts

The programmed IO method discussed in the preceding section has two limitations:

- The speed with which the CPU can test and service IO devices limits IO data-transfer rates.

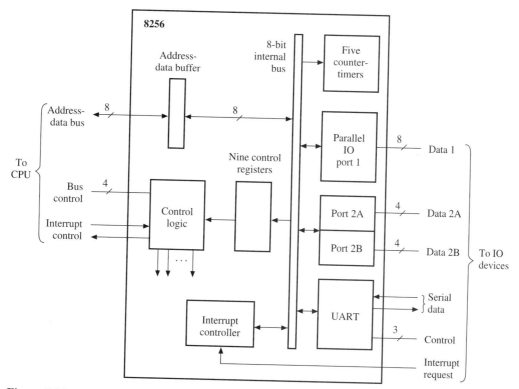

Figure 7.33
The Intel 8256 multifunction IO interface circuit.

• The time that the CPU spends testing IO device status and executing IO data transfers can often be better spent on other tasks.

The influence of the CPU on IO transfer rates is twofold. First, a delay occurs while an IO device needing service waits to be tested by the CPU. If there are many IO devices in the system, each device may be tested infrequently. Second, programmed IO transmits data through the CPU rather than allowing it to be passed directly from main memory to the IO device, and vice versa.

DMA and interrupt circuits increase the speed of IO operations by eliminating most of the role played by the CPU in such operations. In each case special control lines, to which we assign the generic names *DMA REQUEST* and *INTERRUPT REQUEST,* connect the IO devices to the CPU. Signals on these lines cause the CPU to suspend its current activities at appropriate breakpoints and attend to the DMA or interrupt request. Thus these special request lines eliminate the need for the CPU to execute routines that determine IO device status. DMA further allows IO data transfers to take place without the execution of IO instructions by the CPU.

A DMA request by an IO device only requires the CPU to grant control of the memory (system) bus to the requesting device. The CPU can yield control at the end of any transactions involving the use of this bus. Figure 7.34 shows a typical sequence of CPU actions during execution of a single instruction. The instruction cycle is composed of a number of CPU cycles, several of which require use of the system bus. A common technique is to allow the machine to respond to a DMA request at the end of any CPU clock cycle. Thus during the instruction cycle of Figure 7.34 there are five points in time (breakpoints) when the CPU can respond to a DMA request. When such a request is received by the CPU, it waits until the next breakpoint, releases the system bus, and signals the requesting IO device by activating a *DMA ACKNOWLEDGE* control line.

Interrupts are requested and acknowledged in much the same way as DMA requests. However, an interrupt is not a request for bus control; rather, it asks the CPU to begin executing an interrupt service program. The interrupt program performs tasks such as initiating an IO operation or responding to an error encountered by the IO device. The CPU transfers control to this program in essentially the same way it transfers control to a subroutine. The CPU responds to interrupts only between instruction cycles, as indicated in Figure 7.34.

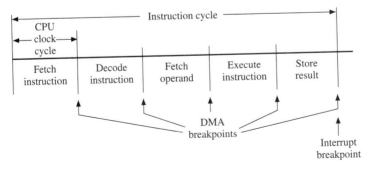

Figure 7.34
DMA and interrupt breakpoints during instruction processing.

Direct memory access. The hardware needed to implement DMA is shown in Figure 7.35, assuming that all access to main memory is via a shared system bus. The IO device is connected to the system bus via a special interface circuit, a *DMA controller,* which contains a data buffer register IODR, as in the programmed IO case; it also controls an address register IOAR and a data count register DC. These registers enable the DMA controller to transfer data to or from a contiguous region of memory. IOAR stores the address of the next word to be transferred. It is automatically incremented or decremented after each word transfer. The data counter DC stores the number of words that remain to be transferred. It is automatically decremented after each transfer and tested for zero. When the data count reaches zero, the DMA transfer halts. The DMA controller is normally provided with an interrupt capability, in which case it sends an interrupt to the CPU to signal the end of the IO data transfer. The logic necessary to control DMA can easily be placed in a single IC with other IO control circuits. A DMA controller can be designed to supervise DMA transfers involving several IO devices, each with a different priority of access to the system bus.

Data can be transferred in several different ways under DMA control. In a *DMA block transfer* a data-word sequence of arbitrary length is transferred in a single burst while the DMA controller is master of the memory bus. This DMA mode is needed by secondary memories like disk drives, where data transmission cannot be stopped or slowed without loss of data, and block transfers are the norm. Block DMA transfer supports the fastest IO data-transfer rates, but it can make the CPU inactive for relatively long periods by tying up the system bus. An alternative technique called *cycle stealing* allows the DMA controller to use the system bus to

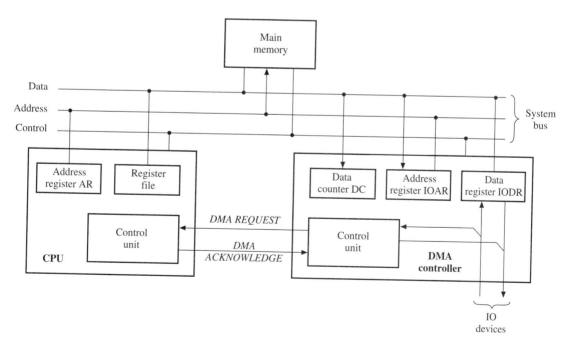

Figure 7.35
Circuitry required for direct memory access (DMA).

transfer one data word, after which it must return control of the bus to the CPU. Consequently, long blocks of IO data are transferred by a sequence of DMA bus transactions interspersed with CPU bus transactions. Cycle stealing reduces the maximum IO transfer rate, but it also reduces the interference by the DMA controller in the CPU's memory access. It is possible to eliminate this interference completely by designing the DMA interface so that bus cycles are stolen only when the CPU is not actually using the system bus; this is *transparent DMA*. Thus varying degrees of overlap between CPU and DMA operations are possible to accommodate the many different data-transfer characteristics of IO devices.

DMA transfers proceed as follows for the system depicted in Figure 7.35.

1. The CPU executes two IO instructions, which load the DMA registers IOAR and DC with their initial values. IOAR should contain the base address of the memory region to be used in the data transfer. DC should contain the number of words to be transferred to or from that region.
2. When the DMA controller is ready to transmit or receive data, it activates the *DMA REQUEST* line to the CPU. The CPU waits for the next DMA breakpoint. It then relinquishes control of the data and address lines and activates *DMA ACKNOWLEDGE*. Note that *DMA REQUEST* and *DMA ACKNOWLEDGE* are essentially *BUS REQUEST* and *BUS GRANT* lines for control of the system bus. Simultaneous DMA requests from several DMA controllers are resolved by one of the bus-priority control techniques discussed earlier.
3. The DMA controller now transfers data directly to or from main memory. After a word is transferred, IOAR and DC are updated.
4. If DC has not yet reached zero but the IO device is not ready to send or receive the next batch of data, the DMA controller releases the system bus to the CPU by deactivating the *DMA REQUEST* line. The CPU responds by deactivating *DMA ACKNOWLEDGE* and resuming control of the system bus.
5. If DC is decremented to zero, the DMA controller again relinquishes control of the system bus; it may also send an interrupt request signal to the CPU. The CPU responds by halting the IO device or by initiating a new DMA transfer.

DMA can be subsumed under a general method for system-bus arbitration. In Motorola 680X0-series computers, for example, the system bus accommodates various types of bus masters including DMA controllers and certain coprocessors designated DMA coprocessors. Three control lines are provided for bus arbitration: bus request $\overline{BR}$, bus grant $\overline{BG}$, and bus grant acknowledge $\overline{BGACK}$. The $\overline{BR}$ line is an input control line to the CPU and is wire-ORed to all other potential bus masters. It is activated ($\overline{BR} = 0$) when one of those devices U—a DMA controller, for instance—requires control of the system bus. The CPU responds by activating $\overline{BG}$ and relinquishing control of the system bus at the end of its current bus cycle, which it does by driving the data, address, and certain control lines to the high-impedance state Z. The requesting unit U detects the end of the bus cycle by monitoring these control lines, at which point U activates $\overline{BGACK}$ and deactivates its $\overline{BR}$ signal. The CPU responds to $\overline{BGACK}$ by deactivating $\overline{BG}$. This step completes bus arbitration. U is the new bus master and can carry out any number of DMA read or write operations. It returns the system bus to the CPU by deactivating $\overline{BGACK}$.

CPUs such as the 680X0 have no internal mechanisms for resolving multiple DMA requests; this must be done by external logic. Passing the DMA (bus) grant signal from the CPU through appropriate priority logic to the potential bus masters controls bus-access priority. External logic may also be needed to implement cycle stealing by forcing the requesting device to deactivate its DMA request signal after some number of bus cycles. In 680X0-based computers these and other DMA control functions are implemented by the Motorola 68450 DMA controller IC, which supports up to four independent and concurrent DMA operations via the 68000 system bus. The 68450 contains four copies of the basic DMA controller logic of Figure 7.35, each constituting a separate *DMA channel.* Other registers in each DMA channel store the priority assigned to the channel and the data-transfer modes to be used. A "chaining" mode of operation is supported that allows a channel to reinitialize its address register IOAR and data-count register DC automatically at the end of the current block transfer. This approach enables the 68450 to carry out a sequence of DMA block transfers without reference to the CPU. When its current data count reaches zero, a DMA channel that has been programmed for chained DMA fetches new values of DC and IOAR from a memory region MR that stores a set of DC-IOAR pairs. An address register in each DMA channel holds the base address of MR.

By reducing the CPU's need to access main memory, a cache can greatly reduce conflicts between CPU and IO data transfers. High-performance microprocessors often have separate cache–CPU and IO–main-memory access paths, which means that a DMA transfer involving main memory can proceed in parallel with CPU-cache operations. In the system of Figure 7.23, for instance, DMA operations use the PCI local bus, while the CPU communicates with the cache via the system bus. Only when the CPU needs access to main memory—in response to a cache miss, for example—does it come into conflict with DMA controllers; such conflicts are resolved by the PCI bridge unit.

Interrupts. The word *interrupt* is used in a broad sense for any infrequent or exceptional event that causes a CPU to temporarily transfer control from its current program to another program—an *interrupt handler*—that services the event in question. Interrupts are the primary means by which IO devices obtain the services of the CPU. They significantly improve a computer's IO performance by giving IO devices direct and rapid access to the CPU and by freeing the CPU from the need to check the status of its IO devices.

Various sources internal and external to the CPU can generate interrupts. IO interrupts are external requests to the CPU to initiate or terminate an IO operation, such as a data transfer with a hard disk. We include in this category interrupts caused by a main-memory miss in a virtual memory system, which requires a main–secondary memory page swap involving one or more IO operations. Interrupts are also produced by hardware or software error-detection circuits that invoke error-handling routines within the operating system. A power-supply failure, for instance, can generate an interrupt that requests execution of an interrupt handler designed to save critical data about the system's state. An attempt by an instruction to divide by zero, or to execute a privileged instruction when not in the privileged state, are examples of software-generated interrupts. An operating system will also deliberately interrupt a user program that has exceeded its allotted time.

The basic method of interrupting the CPU is by activating a control line with the generic name *INTERRUPT REQUEST* that connects the interrupt source to the CPU. An interrupt indicator is then stored in a CPU register that the CPU tests periodically, usually at the end of every instruction cycle. On recognizing the presence of the interrupt, the CPU executes a specific interrupt-handling program. Normally, each interrupt source requires execution of a different program, so the CPU must determine or be given the address of the interrupt program to be used. The presence of two or more interrupt requests at the same time causes a further problem. Priorities must be assigned to the interrupts, and the one with the highest priority selected for handling.

The CPU responds to an interrupt request by a transfer of control to an interrupt handler in a manner similar to a subroutine call. The following steps are taken:

1. The CPU identifies the source of the interrupt, for example, by polling IO devices.
2. The CPU obtains the memory address of the required interrupt handler. This address can be provided by the interrupting device along with its interrupt request.
3. The program counter PC and other CPU status information are saved as in a subroutine call.
4. The PC is loaded with the address of the interrupt handler. Execution proceeds until a return instruction is encountered, which transfers control back to the interrupted program.

Instruction sets usually include instructions to selectively disable or mask interrupt requests, thereby causing the CPU to ignore certain interrupts. Without such control, an IO device that generates interrupts rapidly might require too much of the CPU's time and interfere with the CPU's other tasks. When a high-priority interrupt is being serviced, it is desirable that all interrupts of lower priority be disabled. An interrupt enable instruction must subsequently be executed to give the lower-priority interrupts access to the CPU.

Interrupt selection. The problem of selecting one IO device to service from several that have generated interrupts strongly resembles the arbitration process for bus control discussed in section 7.1.2. Indeed, some interrupt methods require that the interrupting device be given control of the system bus. The techniques employed for bus arbitration—daisy chaining, polling, and independent requesting—can all be readily adapted to interrupt handling and can be realized by software, hardware, or a combination of both.

The interrupt selection method requiring the least hardware is the *single-line* method that appears in Figure 7.36. All IO ports share a single *INTERRUPT*

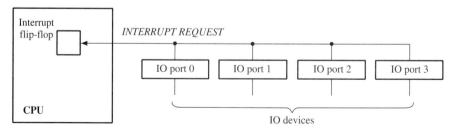

Figure 7.36
Single-line interrupt system.

REQUEST line. On responding to an interrupt request, the CPU must scan all the IO devices to determine the source of the interrupt. This procedure requires activating an *INTERRUPT ACKNOWLEDGE* line (corresponding to *BUS GRANT*) that is connected in daisy-chain fashion to all IO devices. The connection sequence of this line determines the interrupt priority of each device. Alternatively, the CPU can execute a program that polls each IO device in turn requesting interrupt status information. Polling has the advantage of allowing the interrupt priority to be programmed.

Figure 7.37 depicts another common interrupt selection method called *multiple-line* or *multilevel* interrupts, which amounts to independent requesting of interrupt service. Each interrupt request line is assigned a unique priority. The source of the interrupt is immediately known to the CPU, thus eliminating the need for a hardware or software scan of the IO ports. Unless further measures are taken, the CPU may still have to execute a program that fetches the address of the interrupt-service program to be used. This step can be eliminated by another technique called *vectoring of interrupts.*

Vectored interrupts. The most flexible response to interrupts is obtained when an interrupt request from a particular device causes a direct, hardware-implemented transition to the correct interrupt-handling program. The interrupting device must then supply the CPU with the starting address or *interrupt vector* of that program.

Figure 7.38 shows a basic way to derive interrupt vectors from multiple interrupt request lines. Each interrupt request line generates a unique fixed address, which is used to modify the CPU's program counter PC. Interrupt requests are stored on receipt in an interrupt register. The interrupt mask register can disable any or all of the interrupt request lines under program control. By setting bit i of this register to 1 (0), interrupt request line i is disabled (enabled). The k masked interrupt signals are fed into a priority encoder that produces a $\lceil \log_2 k \rceil$-bit address, which is then inserted into PC.

To see how program control is transferred using this type of vectored interrupt, suppose that three devices are connected to four IO ports as shown in Figure 7.39a. Assume that when an interrupt request from IO port i is accepted, the 2-bit address i is generated by the priority encoder and inserted into the program counter

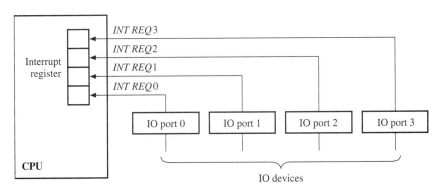

Figure 7.37
Multiple-line interrupt system.

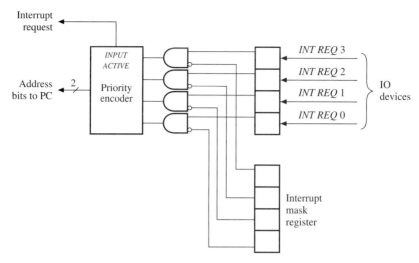

Figure 7.38
A vectored interrupt scheme.

PC. For example, if memory M is addressed by byte and addresses are 4 bytes (one word) long, then *i* might be placed in bits 3:2 of PC and the remaining 30 bits of PC (bits 31:4 and 1:0) can be set to 0. This results in assigning the first four word-storage locations of M to interrupt vectors, as shown in Figure 7.39*b*. The contents of these locations are the user-assigned start addresses of the interrupt-handling

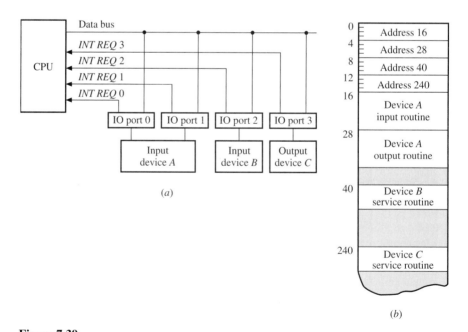

Figure 7.39
(*a*) A system with vectored IO interrupts and (*b*) location of the interrupt handlers in memory.

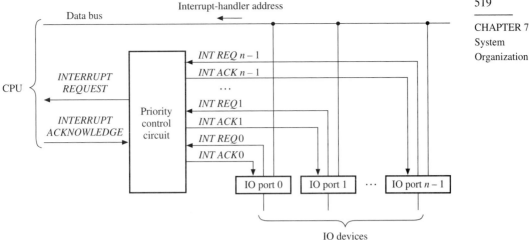

Figure 7.40
Another implementation of vectored interrupts.

routines. The routines themselves are of arbitrary length and can be located any-where in M.

The foregoing scheme has a one-to-one correspondence between interrupt request lines and interrupt handlers. Hence if an IO device requires the services of k distinct programs, it needs k distinct interrupt request lines. Figure 7.40 shows another, more general, vectored interrupt scheme that does not have this restriction: Each IO port can request the services of many different programs. Again multiple interrupt request lines are used, but each IO port now has its own interrupt acknowledge line. When the CPU activates an acknowledge line in response to an interrupt request, the IO port in question places the address of the desired interrupt handler on the main data bus, which transfers the address to the CPU, where it modifies the program counter. This approach requires the interrupting IO port to be able to generate at least partial memory addresses and to act as a bus master.

Another possibility is for an IO device to send the CPU an interrupt vector in the form of a CPU instruction. The CPU removes this instruction from the data bus and executes it in the normal manner. Thus if the IO device sends the instruction CALL PROG to the CPU, execution of this instruction saves essential CPU infor-mation, such as the program counter, and transfers control to an interrupt-handling routine named PROG. 8085-based microcomputers use this technique to imple-ment vectored interrupts.

To reduce the number of external connections to the CPU—an important con-sideration in the case of microcontrollers—the interrupt-priority control logic can be external to the CPU as in Figure 7.40. An interrupt request's priority is deter-mined by the priority circuit input line to which it is connected. An interrupt acknowledge signal from the CPU is transmitted to the highest-priority IO port with an active interrupt request.

PCI interrupts. The PCI local bus discussed in Example 7.1 provides general support for interrupt handling; details such as the vectoring method used are archi-tecture specific and depend on the particular devices using the bus. The PCI bus has four interrupt request lines named $\overline{INTA:D}$ among its optional lines (refer to Figure 7.24). A single-function IO device with interrupt capability must use $\overline{INTA}$ as its interrupt request line; multifunction IO devices can use all four lines. A particular pattern on the PCI bus's command lines denotes interrupt acknowledge. Together, the $\overline{INTx}$ interrupt request lines and the interrupt acknowledge command can implement the request-acknowledge signal exchange needed during an interrupt transaction over the PCI bus.

Every PCI-compatible device must have a standard set of addressable configuration registers CR that identify the device and its communication needs. When the system is powered up, the system controller (operating system) reads the CR registers to determine, among other things, the device's interrupt connections. Its 8-bit "interrupt pin" register in CR tells the system controller which interrupt request line $\overline{INTx}$ the IO device is using. A second 8-bit register in CR called the "interrupt line" register specifies the system controller's input line that is connected to $\overline{INTx}$ so that the routing of the interrupt request lines is programmable. The system controller can use this fact to determine the IO device's interrupt-request priority and to access its interrupt vectors. The CR registers form a small address space that is separate from the main-memory and IO address spaces, as indicated by the existence of configuration read and configuration write in the command set specified for the PCI bus.

EXAMPLE 7.4 INTERRUPT CONTROL IN THE MOTOROLA 680X0 [TRIEBEL AND SINGH 1991]. Interrupts in 680X0-series computers are referred to as *exceptions* and include program-generated traps and hardware-induced errors, as well as external IO interrupts. Each exception has an associated 8-bit vector N, which points to a main-memory location M(4N) that stores the address (the exception vector) of a service program for that exception. Memory locations 0:1023 form an interrupt vector table storing 256 thirty-two-bit addresses used for interrupt processing. (Figure 7.39b has a four-member vector table of this type.) Most of the 680X0's vector table (addresses 256:1023) is reserved for up to 192 user-supplied interrupt vectors; the remaining locations are preassigned by Motorola to specific interrupt types. For example, on encountering a divide-by-zero instruction, the 680X0 executes a trap sequence that transfers control to the program whose start address is stored in locations M(20:23), corresponding to exception vector $N = 5$. Two types (modes) of vectored interrupts are supported: a general mode in which the interrupting device supplies an 8-bit vector number referring to an entry in the exception vector table and a simpler "autovector" mode that allows the IO device to request any of seven fixed exception vectors whose addresses are generated internally by the CPU.

Interrupts are processed in the following way in 680X0-based computers: At the end of each instruction cycle the CPU checks to see whether any interrupt request is pending and tests its priority as described below. If the CPU accepts the request, it suspends normal instruction processing and enters an interrupt-response sequence. The CPU first saves the old contents of the status register SR in a temporary register and then sets the system state to the supervisor mode. It then either reads a vector N provided by the interrupt source (general interrupt mode) or generates N internally (autovector mode), as specified by control signals from the interrupt source. The CPU proceeds to save the contents (return address) of the program counter PC, the old contents of SR, and certain internal information by pushing them into the supervisor stack, one of two stacks maintained by 680X0 CPUs in main memory. Next, using 4N as the address, the CPU executes a memory read to fetch the exception vector M(4N) which it loads into PC; normal instruction processing is then resumed.

Figure 7.41 shows a representative hardware interface used for 680X0 IO interrupts. Three control lines called $\overline{IPL}$ (interrupt priority level) serve both for making interrupt requests and indicating their priority level. $\overline{IPL} = 0$ means that there is no interrupt request, while $\overline{IPL} = i$, where i ranges from one to seven, means that an interrupt of priority level i is being requested. On receiving an interrupt request ($\overline{IPL} \neq 0$), the CPU compares the number $\overline{IPL}$ with three interrupt mask bits I stored in its status register SR. If $\overline{IPL} \geq I$, the CPU responds to the interrupt request at the end of its current instruction cycle; if $\overline{IPL} < I$, the interrupt request is ignored. Since SR can be altered by certain privileged instructions, whether or not the CPU responds to interrupts is under software control. Setting the interrupt mask I to zero enables all interrupt requests. If I is set to seven, all interrupts are rejected except those of highest priority ($\overline{IPL} = 7$), which are nonmaskable. Interrupt sources can thus use up to 192 vectors, each of which can be assigned to any of seven priority levels.

The CPU acknowledges an interrupt request by setting each of its FC (function code) output lines to one to form a 3-bit signal denoting interrupt acknowledgment. It also places the priority level of the interrupt being acknowledged on address lines A1:3. In the general interrupt mode, the interrupt controller responds by placing an interrupt vector number N on data lines D0:7. In the circuit of Figure 7.41 with the

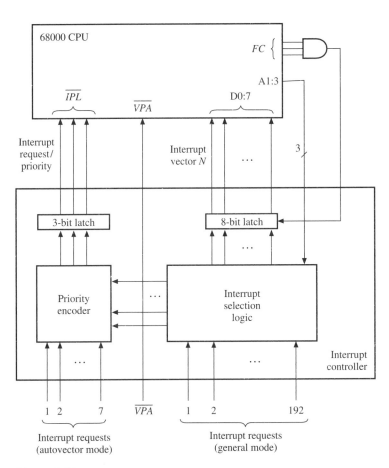

Figure 7.41
Interfacing interrupts to the Motorola 68000 CPU.

68000 CPU, the *FC* signals are used directly to strobe the interrupt vector *N* onto the data bus. To indicate the autovector mode, the interrupt controller responds to $FC = 7$ by activating a special control line ($\overline{VPA}$ for the 68000 and $\overline{AVEC}$ for the 68020), causing the CPU to generate *N* internally according to the formula $N = 24 + IPL$.

Pipeline interrupts. After an interrupt occurs, the controlling CPU must be able to identify the interrupting instruction and the register contents needed for any corrective actions. This is not a problem when instructions are executed in sequence and only one is active at any time. However in a pipelined processor with several instructions in process concurrently, it is possible for instructions to finish out of sequence; that is, an instruction can finish sooner than another instruction that was issued earlier. This condition is illustrated in Figure 7.42, where three floating-point instructions, a 7-cycle multiply and two 4-cycle adds, are being processed by one or more pipelined units. Figure 7.42*a* shows a situation that corresponds to maximum throughput and where the first add instruction add1 is completed before the multiply instruction, even though the latter was issued one cycle earlier. Assuming no hazards occur due to data dependencies, this completion order is acceptable as far as the main computation is concerned.

Suppose, however, that add1 generates an interrupt due to, say, a result (sum) that overflows in its execution stage EX corresponding to cycle 4. Control must then be transferred to an interrupt handler designed to service adder overflow. It is possible that the ongoing multiply instruction will generate another interrupt, say, in cycle 6. This second interrupt can change the CPU's state in ways that prevent proper processing of the first interrupt. In particular, registers affected by add1 can be further modified by the multiply interrupt so that proper recovery from the add1 interrupt may not be possible. In this situation the CPU state is said to have become *imprecise.*

We define a *precise interrupt* to be one where the system state information or context needed both for correct transfer of control to the interrupt handler and for correct return to the interrupting program is always preserved. A more restricted definition requires the system state when the interrupt occurs to be the same as that in a nonpipelined CPU that executes instructions in sequential order. In that case an interrupt occurring during the execution of an instruction *I* is precise if the follow-

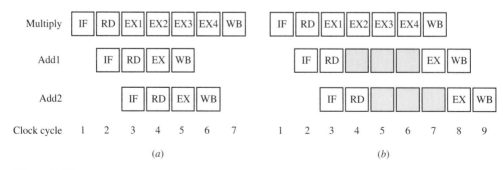

Figure 7.42
Instruction processing in a pipeline with (*a*) out-of-order completion and (*b*) in-order completion.

ing conditions are met [Moudgill and Vassilliadis 1996]:

- All instructions issued prior to *I* have completed their execution.
- No instruction has been issued after *I*.
- The program counter PC contains *I*'s address.

We can solve the imprecise-interrupt problem illustrated by Figure 7.42*a* in several ways. The most direct is to make all interrupts precise by forcing all instructions to complete in the order in which they are issued. This approach is illustrated in Figure 7.42*b*, where the add instructions are delayed so that they complete after the multiply instruction. The undesirable result of this forced, in-order execution method is that the combined processing time for the three instructions increases from seven to nine cycles, so some of the performance benefit of pipelining is lost.

An alternative solution is to allow the state to become imprecise as in Figure 7.42*a*, that is, allow out-of-order completion but provide a mechanism to recover the precise state or context of the processor at the time of the interrupt. A small register set, sometimes known as a *history buffer HB*, is introduced to store temporarily the initial state of every register that is overwritten by each executing instruction *I*. Hence if an interrupt occurs during *I*'s execution, the corresponding precise CPU state can be recovered from the values stored in *HB*, even if a second, conflicting interrupt is generated by a still-completing instruction.

7.2.3 IO Processors

The IO processor (IOP) is a logical extension of the IO control methods considered so far. In systems with programmed IO, peripheral devices are controlled directly by the CPU. The DMA concept extends limited control over data transfers to IO devices. An IOP has the ability to execute instructions, which gives it fairly complete control over IO operations. Like a CPU, an IOP is an instruction-set processor, but it has a more restricted instruction set. IOPs are primarily communication control units designed to link IO devices to a computer. They have also been called peripheral processing units (PPUs) to emphasize their subsidiary role with respect to the central processing unit (CPU).

IO instruction types. In a computer with an IOP, the CPU does not normally execute IO data-transfer instructions. Such instructions are contained in IO programs that are stored in M and are fetched and executed by the IOP. The CPU does execute a few IO instructions that allow it to initiate and terminate the execution of IO programs via the IOP and also to test the status of the IO system. The IO instructions executed by the IOP are primarily associated with data-transfer operations. A typical IOP instruction has the form: READ (WRITE) a block of *n* words from (to) device *X* to (from) memory region *Y*. The IOP is provided with direct access to M (DMA) and so can control the memory bus when the CPU does not require that bus. Like the more sophisticated DMA controllers examined in the preceding section, an IOP can execute a sequence of data-transfer operations involving different regions of M and different IO devices without CPU intervention. Other instruction types such as arithmetic, logical, and branch are included in the

IOP's instruction set to facilitate the calculation of addresses, IO device priorities, and so on. A third category of IO instructions are those executed by IO devices. These instructions control functions such as REWIND (for a magnetic-tape unit), SEEK ADDRESS (for a hard disk unit), or PRINT PAGE (for a printer). Instructions of this type are fetched by the IOP as data and passed on to the appropriate IO device for execution.

Figure 7.43 shows the formats used for IO instructions in the IBM System/360 series and its successors, which have IOPs that are referred to as *channels* [IBM 1974]. The CPU supervises IO operations by means of a small set of privileged instructions with the format of Figure 7.43a. The address field (bits 16:31) specifies a base register B and a displacement (offset) D, which identify both the IO device to be used and the IOP to which it is attached. There are three major instructions of this type: START IO, HALT IO, and TEST IO. The START IO instruction initiates an IO operation. It provides the IOP it names with the memory address of the IO program to be executed by the IOP. The instruction HALT IO causes the IOP to terminate IO program execution, while TEST IO allows the CPU to determine the status of the named IO device and IOP. Status conditions of interest include available, busy, not operational, and (masked) interrupt pending.

The instructions executed by the IOP are called *channel command words* (CCWs) and have the format shown in Figure 7.43b. They are of three types:

- *Data-transfer instructions.* These include input (read), output (write), and sense (read status). They cause the number of bytes in the data count field to be transferred between the specified memory region and the previously selected IO device.
- *Branch instructions.* These cause the IOP to fetch the next CCW from the specified memory address rather than from the next sequential location.
- *IO device control instructions.* These are transmitted to the IO device and specify functions peculiar to that device.

The opcode of a data-transfer instruction can be transmitted directly to the IO device as the "command" byte while the IO operation is being set up. If the IO device requires more control information, it is supplied via an output data transfer.

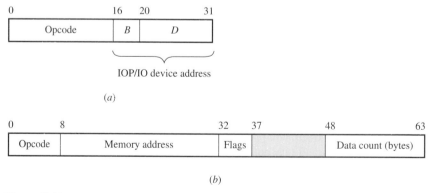

(a)

(b)

Figure 7.43
Formats of System/360 IO instructions executed (*a*) by a CPU and (*b*) by an IOP (channel).

Instruction			Comments
CCW	X'07',	, X'40',	Rewind tape
CCW	X'37',	, X'40',	Skip first record
CCW	X'01',	BUFFER1 , X'40', 100	Write second record from BUFFER1
CCW	X'1F',	, X'40',	Write tape mark
CCW	X'07',	, X'00',	Rewind tape and stop

Figure 7.44

A System/360 IO program to write a record on a magnetic tape.

The flags field of the CCW modifies the operation specified by the opcode. For example, a program control flag PCI can be set to instruct the IOP to generate an IO interrupt and make the current IOP status available to the CPU. Another flag specifies *command chaining,* which means that the current CCW is followed by another CCW that is to be executed immediately. If this flag is not set, the IOP ceases IO program execution after executing the current CCW.

Figure 7.44 lists a small IO program written in System/360 assembly language that writes a 100-byte record on a magnetic tape. The tape is assumed to already contain two records, the second of which is being replaced. Every CCW contains four fields separated by commas, which correspond to the opcode, memory address, flags, and data count fields of Figure 7.43b. This program contains only one data-transfer instruction, which transfers 100 bytes to the tape from the memory region called BUFFER1. The other CCWs control operations that are peculiar to magnetic tapes and do not use the memory address or data count fields. In all CCWs the opcode and flags have been defined by hexadecimal numbers indicated by the prefix X. The flag field X'40' causes the command chaining flag to be set. In the last CCW no flags are set, so the IOP stops after execution of this CCW.

IOP organization. The essential structure of a system containing an IOP appears in Figure 7.45a. The IOP and CPU share access to a common memory M via the system bus. M stores separate programs for execution by the CPU and the IOP; it also contains a communication region *IOCR* for passing information in the form of messages between the two processors. The CPU can place there the parameters of an IO task, for example, the addresses of the IO programs to be executed, and the identity of the IO devices to be used. The CPU and IOP also communicate with each other directly via control lines. Standard DMA or bus grant/acknowledge lines are used for arbitration of the system bus between the two processors, as discussed earlier. The CPU can attract the IOP's attention, for instance, when executing an IO instruction like START IO, by activating the *ATTENTION* line. In response the IOP begins execution of an IOP program whose specifications have been placed in the *IOCR* communication area. Similarly the IOP attracts the CPU's attention by activating an *INTERRUPT REQUEST* line, causing the CPU to execute an interrupt handler that typically responds to the IOP by identifying a new IO program for the IOP to execute. Figure 7.45b summarizes the overall behavior of the IOP and its interaction with the CPU.

EXAMPLE 7.5 THE INTEL 8089 IO PROCESSOR [EL-AYAT 1979]. The 8089 is a one-chip IOP for use in systems based on the Intel 8086 microprocessor. As shown

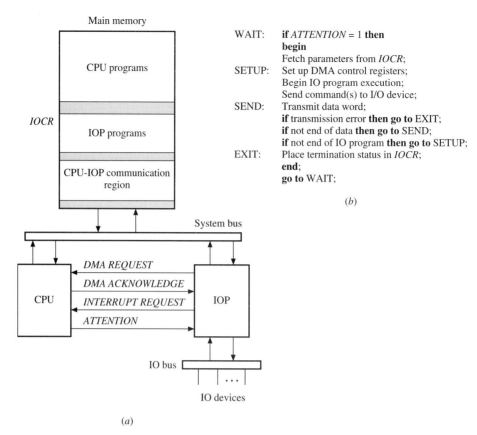

WAIT: **if** *ATTENTION* = 1 **then**
        begin
        Fetch parameters from *IOCR*;
SETUP: Set up DMA control registers;
        Begin IO program execution;
        Send command(s) to I/O device;
SEND: Transmit data word;
        if transmission error **then go to** EXIT;
        if not end of data **then go to** SEND;
        if not end of IO program **then go to** SETUP;
EXIT: Place termination status in *IOCR*;
        end;
        go to WAIT;

(*b*)

(*a*)

Figure 7.45
Computer containing an IOP: (*a*) system organization and (*b*) CPU–IOP interaction.

in Figure 7.46, it has two "DMA channels," each of which can control an independent IO operation. In addition to the usual address and data-count registers found in DMA controllers, the 8089's DMA channels have their own program counters and other circuits necessary to execute an instruction set that is specialized toward IO operations. Thus the 8089 can execute two unrelated IO programs concurrently and logically appears to the CPU like two independent IOPs. The DMA channels share a 20-bit ALU intended mainly for processing memory addresses. They also share bus interface circuits for communication with memory and IO devices. Partly because of pin constraints—the 8089 is packaged in a 40-pin package—the channels also share a 20-bit bidirectional external bus that is used to multiplex data and address transfers to or from IO devices; the same lines also transfer addresses and data between the IOP and memory. Both 8- and 16-bit data words can be transmitted and received by the 8089, which contains the necessary assembly-disassembly circuits for conversion between these two data formats. If desired, external circuits can be used to create separate system and IO buses, as in Figure 7.45. If the 8089 is configured with a local IO bus, then its IO programs can be placed in a private memory attached to that bus, thus reducing the instruction traffic on the shared system bus.

The CPU and IOP communicate via several message regions in memory, which are illustrated in Figure 7.47. Each DMA channel has an associated parameter block *PB* containing a pointer to the channel's current IO program, that is, a channel address word. PB also contains application-specific input parameters for the IO program, as

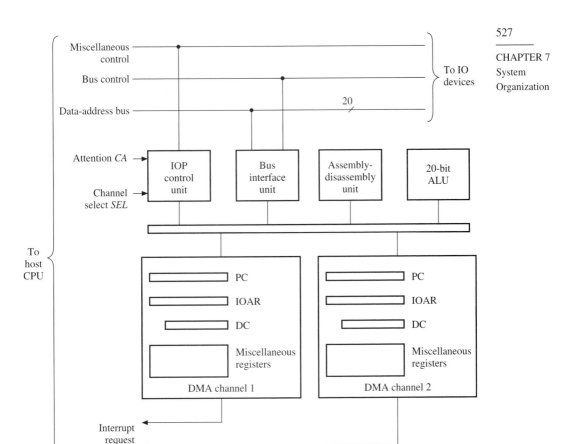

Figure 7.46
Structure of the Intel 8089 IOP.

well as output parameters for variables that the channel is to return to the CPU. These parameters identify IO buffer regions in main memory, IO device names, data addresses in secondary memory devices, and so on. The locations of the two PBs are stored in a channel control block CB, which is created by the CPU when the system is powered up or reset. CB stores status information and a command from the CPU for each channel. These 1-byte commands fill essentially the same role as the START, TEST, and HALT IO instructions of the System/360-370 series. The CPU also uses them to enable, disable, or deactivate the channel's interrupt request line. Thus the CPU supervises each IOP channel by writing into its PB region and into its portion of CB. Once it has set up the necessary control information in main memory, the CPU dispatches a DMA channel, that is, it initiates an IO operation, by executing a data-transfer instruction such as OUT or MOVE that activates the 8089's channel-attention line *CA* and a second line *SEL* that indicates which of the two channels is to be dispatched. The selected channel then proceeds to read its command word from CB, for example, "start IO program execution," which makes the channel load the IO program pointer from PB into its program counter, thereby launching execution of the IO program. The channel then executes the program in much the same way as a CPU. The 8089 uses DMA to fetch IO instructions from main memory and, of course, for memory data transfers. Each DMA channel has a programmable *channel control (CC)* register that defines the type of DMA transfer to be used.

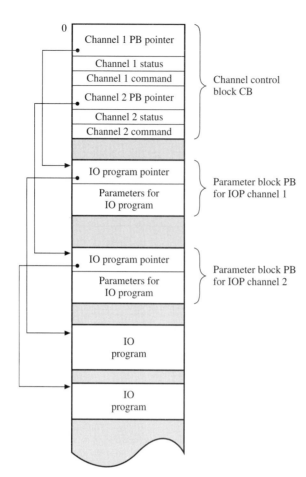

0

Channel 1 PB pointer
Channel 1 status
Channel 1 command
Channel 2 PB pointer
Channel 2 status
Channel 2 command

Channel control block CB

IO program pointer
Parameters for IO program

Parameter block PB for IOP channel 1

IO program pointer
Parameters for IO program

Parameter block PB for IOP channel 2

IO
program

IO
program

Figure 7.47
Memory organization
for the 8089 IOP.

The 8089's instruction set and the corresponding assembly language (which are quite different from those of the host CPU) contain about 50 different instruction types. The instructions are broadly similar to those of a general-purpose CPU but have only a few simple data and address types and limited data-processing and program-control capabilities. For example, the arithmetic instructions consist only of add, increment, and decrement with unsigned or twos-complement fixed-point operands. No provision is made for overflow detection in signed arithmetic operations. The major instruction types are data-transfer instructions that move data or address words between the 8089's internal registers and its external memory-IO bus. Note that in addition to IO operations, the 8089 can execute memory-to-memory block transfers very efficiently. The 8089's specialized IO control instructions include WID (set bus width), which defines the word size for data transfers as either 8 or 16 bits; XFER (transfer), which prepares a channel for a DMA transfer; and SINTR (set interrupt), which activates the channel's interrupt request line, thus enabling an IO program to interrupt the CPU.

Microcontrollers as IOPs. Developments in IC technology in recent years have made it attractive to use general-purpose microprocessors as IOPs by equipping them with specialized IO interface circuits and support software. An example is the Intel i960 RP input-output processor introduced in 1995 as a single-chip "intelligent IO subsystem" [Intel 1996]. Figure 7.48 indicates the complexity of this IC. The IOP is built around the 80960 microprocessor, a member of the i960 family of pipelined 32-bit RISCs. The 80960's instruction set is noteworthy for its fast implementation of call and return instructions, its high-performance integer ALU, and its large register file. The core processor also contains a 4KB two-way set-associative I-cache and a 2KB direct-mapped D-cache. To provide quick response to interrupts, the i960 RP allows the programmer to permanently lock critical IO routines such as interrupt handlers in its I-cache.

The i960 RP IOP supports a pair of 32-bit PCI buses: a primary bus for connection to the host CPU and a secondary bus for IO devices. It also has a 32-bit internal "local" bus—the 80960's system bus—to which IO devices can be attached, as well as some specialized IO buses such as the I^2C (inter-integrated circuit) bus, a serial IO bus developed by Philips Semiconductor. Not surprisingly, this single-chip device has a very large number of IO pins—352 in all. The i960 RP IOP has controllers for three independent DMA channels, two dedicated to the primary PCI bus and one to the secondary PCI bus. It also has flexible controllers to support vectored interrupts, including the advanced programmable interrupt control (APIC) interface used by the Pentium and other Intel microprocessors.

7.2.4 Operating Systems

Except when it is dedicated to a single task, a computer is usually managed by a supervisory program called an operating system, which provides a uniform software interface for other system programs and for applications programs. In multiuser environments the operating system controls such shared resources as CPU time, memory space, IO devices, utility programs, and databases [Silberschatz 1994].

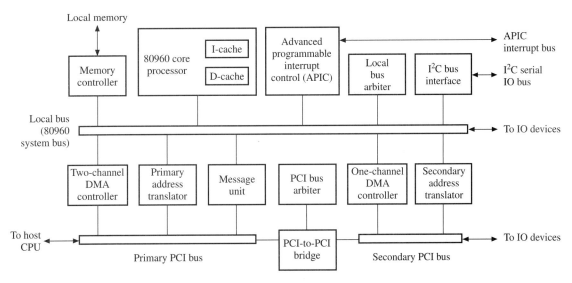

Figure 7.48
Structure of the Intel i960 RP input-output processor.

Introduction. Programs use a computer's resources in various, and often unpredictable, ways. Resource requirements also change dynamically during the execution of a single program. For example, programs often alternate between computations that use the CPU and IO operations that use IOPs and peripheral devices but do not require the CPU. If several programs are available for execution at the same time, then the computer's performance as measured by overall through-put can be improved by assigning one program to the CPU while others are assigned for execution by IOPs. The scheduling of CPU and IO processing is a typical function of an operating system. Another important shared resource is memory, both main and secondary, whose management is also typically an operating system task.

Several types of operating systems have evolved over the years. The earliest system control programs (batch monitors and spooling systems) were mainly concerned with reducing the time required for IO operations involving user programs. Modern operating systems attempt to manage a wide range of computer resources efficiently—not just IO devices. They provide textual or graphical interfaces that allow users to interact directly with the operating system by specifying the resources needed for a particular job. Current operating systems have their origins in several influential systems developed in the 1960s, such as IBM's OS/360, which became a de facto standard for mainframe computers. Early work at Manchester University (Atlas), MIT (Multics), and elsewhere led to the UNIX operating system, which was developed at Bell Laboratories in the mid-1970s and is now in wide use, especially in workstations.

Processes. The basic unit of computing managed by an operating system is a *process,* which is loosely defined as a program module in the course of execution. The resources needed by a process, including processors and memory space, are allocated to it dynamically during execution. Examples of processes are a procedure executed by a CPU and an IO program executed by an IOP. A process can be created in response to a user command to the operating system. Processes can also be created by other processes, for example, in response to interrupts. When no longer needed, a process (but not the underlying program) is deleted by the operating system, and the resources currently allocated to the process are released. While in existence, a process has three major states: ready, running, and blocked, as depicted in Figure 7.49a. In the ready state a process is waiting, perhaps in a queue with other processes, for the resources that it needs to enter the running or active state. A blocked process is waiting for some event to occur, such as completion of another process that provides it with input data. A transition from one process state to another is triggered by conditions such as interrupts and user instructions to the operating system.

Figure 7.49b shows the state behavior of a typical user process P in a system with an independent IOP. It is assumed that P runs on the CPU until an IO instruction is encountered, at which point the operating system intervenes and changes P from running to blocked. P can also be terminated by a timer-generated interrupt, which the operating system uses to limit the amount of time that any one process is assigned to the IOP. In this case P is returned to the ready state, where it remains until rescheduled for execution by the operating system via the CPU. A new process P' can now be created to run on an IOP and carry out the required IO operation. Completion of P' results in an IO interrupt that causes the CPU to transfer P from blocked to ready. At this point P' can be deleted if it is no longer needed by P or other active processes. As soon as the CPU is available to execute P, that is, when there are no CPU processes of higher priority ready for execution, P is transferred once more to the running state. It continues running until it encounters another IO instruction, exceeds its allocated time, or completes execution. In the last case a call is made to the operating system, which can then delete P.

Kernel. An operating system comprises many resource management programs, including processor scheduling routines, virtual memory management routines, and IO device control programs (device drivers). Common utility programs, such as compilers, text editors, and the like, often form part of the operating system. Thus operating systems tend to contain more software than can fit comfortably in main memory. The part of an operating system that resides more or less continuously in main memory and consists of its most frequently used parts is termed the *kernel* or *nucleus*. The other, less frequently used parts, such as file management routines, reside in secondary (disk) memory and are transferred to main memory when needed.

The kernel of an operating system is responsible for the creation, deletion, and state switching of the many processes that define a computer's behavior. The kernel performs its tasks by quickly responding to a steady flow of interrupt requests. These requests have many sources such as user-generated requests for operating system services; CPU-generated process time-outs; memory faults; IO operations; and hardware or software errors. The kernel achieves rapid response by briefly disabling other interrupts while responding to the current one and then dispatching or, if necessary, creating a system process to execute the appropriate interrupt-handling routine. The performance and reliability of the kernel can be improved by implementing its more basic functions in hardware or firmware.

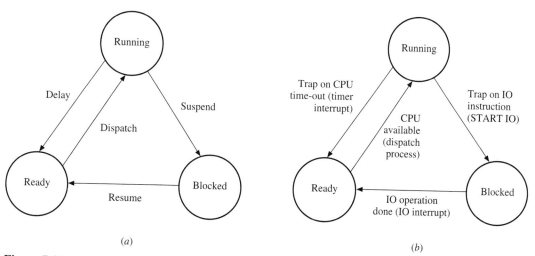

Figure 7.49
Process behavior: (*a*) general case and (*b*) CPU process in system with IOP.

The kernel keeps track of each process by means of a data segment called a *process control block* PCB, which defines the most recent execution state or context of the process. The PCB typically contains all the programmable registers associated with a process, including its program counter, stack pointers, status register, and general-purpose data and address registers. The PCB normally resides in main memory. When the process is about to be executed, its PCB is transferred to the corresponding processor registers. The transfer of control from one process to another (*context switching*) is implemented by saving the context of the old process in its PCB in memory and loading the PCB of the new process into the processor in its place.

Figure 7.50 shows the PCB used by the VMS operating system for the Digital VAX computer series. This PCB contains several stack pointers used by the operating system, the CPU's general registers, the program counter PC, and the program status word PSW. The latter stores CPU status (flag) bits and the interrupt priority level of the process. The last entries in the PCB specify the base address and length of two page tables: one for the user program and one for the user stack. Page tables play an essential role in the firmware-implemented address mapping that manages the VAX's virtual memory. Two VAX instructions SVPCTX (save process context) and LDPCTX (load process context) support context switching by transferring the complete PCB to and from memory, respectively.

An operating system supervises a potentially large set of processes that function asynchronously and concurrently. Many of the more subtle problems in designing an operating system are due to attempts by concurrent processes to use shared resources in undesirable or improperly synchronized ways. Next we consider two basic problems in concurrency control—mutual exclusion and deadlock—and their solutions.

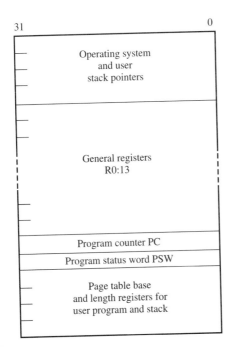

Figure 7.50
Process control block PCB for the VMS operating system.

Mutual exclusion. Suppose that two concurrent processes P_1 and P_2 share read and write access to a data region R in main memory. It is generally necessary to prevent one process from writing into R while the other process is reading from it. Unless precautions are taken, P_2 can modify a variable X of R immediately after P_1 has read its old value; in this case subsequent processing decisions will be based on a wrong value of X. This problem is solved by enforcing certain rules for *mutual exclusion* so that, in the present instance, P_1 has exclusive access to R for as long as it needs it, without interference from other processes. Shared resources like R that require mutual exclusion are termed *critical*.

A software solution to the mutual exclusion problem is to associate with each critical resource R a control variable S called a *flag* that indicates when R is busy. Before attempting to take control of R, a process P first reads R's flag S. If $S = 1$ (busy), indicating that R is already in use, P does not attempt to use it. If, on the other hand, P finds that $S = 0$, implying that R is available, P immediately sets S to 1 (busy) and proceeds to access R. When it has finished with R, the process P resets S to 0 so that other processes can use R.

For the foregoing control mechanism to work, mutual exclusion must be enforced for accessing the flag S to determine the state of R. Some processors provide a test-and-set instruction to implement flag control in the kernel of the operating system. To guarantee mutual exclusion, this instruction is designed to be indivisible in the sense that all the steps of its instruction cycle must be completed without interference by other instructions. The 8089 IOP (Example 7.5) has such an instruction called TSL (test and set while locked). In the following 8089 assembly-language code fragment TSL causes the flag S to be read from memory and compared with 0.

$$\text{TSL} \quad \text{S, 1, WAIT}$$

$$\text{R:} \qquad \ldots \qquad\qquad\qquad\qquad\qquad\qquad (7.1)$$

$$\ldots \qquad\qquad\qquad \text{; END R}$$

$$\text{MOV} \quad \text{S, 0}$$

If $S = 0$, TSL writes the specified 1 value into S and control is transferred to the routine R, which uses the resource protected by S. If TSL finds that $S \neq 0$, then it transfers control to the branch address WAIT. To ensure mutual exclusion, TSL activates a special output signal called *LOCK* on the 8089 chip. This signal drives a bus-lock line of the bus to which the memory storing S is attached; the PCI bus (Example 7.1) has such a line called $\overline{LOCK}$. Activating the lock signal prevents other instruction from using the bus while the TSL instruction is being executed; consequently, TSL has the required exclusive access to S. The final move instruction in the preceding 8089 code implements $S := 0$ to reset the flag. The routine R is an example of a critical section of an assembly-language program, which is protected by the flag S. If the initial TSL statement is replaced by

$$\text{WAIT:} \quad \text{TSL S, 1, WAIT} \qquad\qquad\qquad (7.2)$$

then the test-and-set operation is executed repeatedly until S becomes available. In effect, the process requesting R waits until S changes from busy to not busy.

The preceding flag-control mechanism has several deficiencies. It uses a busy form of waiting in which a processor spends a great deal of time simply testing the flag S. Moreover, a particular process P may never find $S = 0$ and gain access to R because of competition from other processes. These problems are addressed by a special resource control variable S called a *semaphore,* which is a nonnegative integer serving as the control flag for a resource R. It has two indivisible procedures, WAIT(S) and SIGNAL(S), which can be defined as follows, where P is the process calling WAIT or SIGNAL:

WAIT(S):   **if** $S > 0$ **then** $S := S - 1$
                else suspend P and place it in queue Q for R;   (7.3)

SIGNAL(S):   **if** Q is nonempty then dispatch one process from Q
                else $S := S + 1$;   (7.4)

The semaphore S is used to encapsulate the code R for a critical resource with WAIT(S) and SIGNAL(S) operations thus:

$$
\begin{array}{l}
\text{WAIT}(S) \\
\text{R} \\
\text{SIGNAL}(S)
\end{array} \qquad (7.5)
$$

and initializing S to 1. The first requesting process gains access to R and sets S to 0. Subsequent processes attempting to enter R are queued. Hence only one process can use the critical region R, thereby ensuring that mutual exclusion is preserved. By initializing S to a larger value $k > 1$, the number of processes in the critical region can be limited to k. Although (7.1) and (7.5) are superficially similar, the semaphore in (7.5) avoids busy waiting; the queueing by WAIT and releasing by SIGNAL of requests for R ensure that all requesting processes eventually get to use R in some sequence—for instance, FIFO—determined by the queueing discipline for blocked processes.

Deadlock. Another common synchronization problem in system management is *deadlock;* that is, a process is waiting for an event such as the release of a shared resource, but the event in question never occurs. Suppose that processes P_1 and P_2 both require the use of two resources R_1 and R_2 that can only be controlled by one process at a time. Let R_1 be allocated to P_1, which then requests R_2 while still retaining control of R_1. At the same time, let P_2 control R_2 and be requesting control of R_1. If neither process can continue until it obtains control of both processes, then a deadlock results in which each process ends up waiting for the other to release a resource, a circular waiting situation that is characteristic of deadlocks. A single process can also become deadlocked while waiting for an external event such as an acknowledgment signal that fails to appear in an IO bus transaction. Deadlocks can result from hardware faults as well as from hardware or software design errors.

Three basic ways to deal with deadlock are prevention, avoidance, and fault tolerance. The prevention approach tries to eliminate the possibility of a deadlock occurring. Less stringent approaches do not completely eliminate the possibility of a deadlock, but try to ensure that all potential deadlock situations are avoided. The third approach allows deadlocks to take place but provides mechanisms for detecting them and recovering from their effects. In practice, all these techniques are used in various parts of a typical operating system, with deadlock prevention techniques playing the major role.

For deadlock to exist, the processes and resources involved must meet several conditions:

1. *Mutual exclusion.* Each process must have exclusive access to the resources it controls.
2. *Resource waiting.* A process can hold the resources already allocated to it while waiting for access to another.
3. *Nonpreemption.* A process cannot be preempted; it never releases its resources until it has completely finished with them.
4. *Circularity.* A circular chain of processes must exist; each process controls a resource that is being requested by the next process in the chain.

Deadlocks are avoided by designing the relevant parts of an operating system so that one or more of the above conditions cannot occur. Condition 1 usually can't be eliminated without severely restricting resource sharing; however, the other deadlock conditions can be avoided in various ways. For example, no deadlock can occur if a process P is blocked until all the resources it needs become available. Blocking circumvents condition 2 (resource waiting), but it leads to inefficient use of available resources. The partial set of resources tied up by P can be freed by requiring P to release them and rerequest them later along with the other resources not yet available. This latter step preempts P's resources, therefore denying condition 3 (nonpreemption). Eliminating conditions 2 or 3 in this way can cause some process requests to be blocked indefinitely. The circularity condition can be removed by assigning a unique number $p(R)$ to each resource R and enforcing the rule that if P holds R, it can only request additional resources with numbers higher than $p(R)$. This technique works well if the normal order in which the processes request the resources closely matches the order in which they are numbered; otherwise, P may need to acquire and hold low-numbered resources long before it actually uses them.

The detection of deadlock situations, either to avoid them or to eliminate them after they occur, implies the ability to check for the circular wait condition defined above. To do so, the system manager must maintain a list of all the resources held by each process and, for each resource, the names of the processes waiting to use it. These resource assignments and requests can be represented by a *resource allocation graph,* an example of which appears in Figure 7.51. Here the circles denote processes $\{P_i\}$, and the squares denote resources $\{R_j\}$. An edge or arrow from resource R_j to process P_i implies that R_j has been allocated to P_i, while an arrow from P_i to R_j means that P_i is requesting R_j. The existence of a closed loop in which all arrows go in the same direction, in this case, $P_2 \rightarrow R_4 \rightarrow P_5 \rightarrow R_6 \rightarrow P_4 \rightarrow R_1 \rightarrow P_2$, indicates that the given allocation satisfies the circularity condition for a deadlock. Note that the mutual exclusion condition is satisfied by requiring that only one arrow leave each resource in the resource allocation graph.

Figure 7.52 gives a recursive procedure $CHECK(P,R)$ to test for the circularity conditions that lead to deadlock; in effect, it finds closed loops in a resource allocation graph. $CHECK(P,R)$ is intended to be executed whenever a process P makes a request for resource R; it reports a deadlock if the requested allocation results in a closed loop. Suppose that the procedure is applied to the system of Figure 7.51 when P_2 makes a new request for control of R_5. Assume that processes and resources are scanned in ascending numerical order determined by the P and R subscripts. On entering $CHECK(P_2,R_5)$, the resources allocated to P_2, namely,

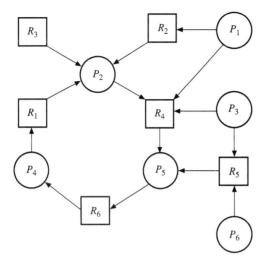

Figure 7.51
Example of a resource allocation
graph.

```
procedure CHECK (P: process; R: resource);
begin
for all resources {Rᵢ} allocated to P do
    begin
    for all processes {Pᵢⱼ} waiting for Rᵢ do
        if Pᵢⱼ holds R then REPORT (deadlock) else CHECK (Pᵢⱼ, R);
    end;
end;
```

Figure 7.52
Procedure for deadlock detection.

$\{R_1, R_2, R_3\}$, are scanned. Then the processes waiting for R_1, namely, $\{P_4\}$, are identified. Since P_4 does not have R_5 allocated to it, $CHECK(P_4, R_5)$ is now invoked. On reentering the $CHECK$ procedure with $P = P_4$ and $R = R_5$, the resources $\{R_6\}$ held by P_4 are identified. Then the processes $\{P_5\}$ waiting for R_6 are considered. It is found immediately that P_5 holds R_5, leading to the conclusion that a deadlock exists. This deadlock corresponds to the loop $P_2 \rightarrow R_4 \rightarrow P_5 \rightarrow R_6 \rightarrow P_4 \rightarrow R_1 \rightarrow P_2$.

EXAMPLE 7.6 THE UNIX OPERATING SYSTEM [SOUTHERTON 1993]. The goal of UNIX is to provide a relatively simple, interactive operating system aimed at a general-purpose time-shared environment. Simplicity is achieved by keeping the operating system quite small so that it can easily be installed in small computers, especially workstations. The kernel of UNIX consists of about 10,000 lines of source code written mainly in C, a programming language developed specifically to implement UNIX. The use of C as the source language, and the general availability of its source code, gives UNIX a high degree of portability among different computer types. The functions provided by UNIX for managing processes, IO, and so on, are quite general, which keeps its kernel small and enables UNIX to address a wide range of operating system tasks. UNIX has associated with it a large set of general-purpose programs (*utilities*), including compilers, debuggers, and text editors. These utilities, most of which are also written in C, are considered an integral part of UNIX and have done much to enhance its popularity. UNIX has a textual user interface called the *shell,* which provides a command language for process management, as well as access to the UNIX utilities.

UNIX recognizes two main types of processes: system (supervisor) and user. Each active program or user-created task is treated as a user process. When such a process requires an operating system function because of an interrupt, a system process is invoked and then becomes the running process. System processes execute in the host processor's supervisor or privileged state, while user processes execute in the nonprivileged user state. (Note that these two processor states have hardware support in many computers ranging from the System/360 to the 680X0.) The information associated with a process, termed an *image* in UNIX parlance, consists of the contents of the memory locations used by the process along with the processor status and register information constituting a process control block. The process image is constructed from several dynamic segments for instruction, data, and control stack storage. A process's image resides in main memory while it is being executed, but can—except for the process control block—be swapped out of memory when the process is inactive or another process needs the space. UNIX employs a FIFO algorithm to allocate both main and secondary memory space.

UNIX makes extensive use of the process concept and has many mechanisms for manipulating processes. The kernel deals with each new task by creating a process to handle it so that at any time many processes are being executed concurrently. Various UNIX operations invoked by shell commands exist for managing processes. Figure 7.53 lists some representative commands available to the user for process control. Processes communicate and synchronize their activities by means of events, which typically are control flags set by the occurrence of some specified condition. A process is suspended by instructing it to wait for an event to occur; it is subsequently dispatched by signaling the occurrence of the event in question.

In a uniprocessing UNIX environment only one process can be executed at a time. Processes are executed in time-shared fashion with each process receiving a slice of CPU time of no more than a second or so before it is suspended and a new process dispatched. UNIX assigns a priority number to every process; the number determines the process to run next. System processes receive execution priorities based on their expected response needs. For example, processes to control disk transfers receive high priority, while processes that service user terminals receive low priority. User processes have lower priority than the lowest system-process priority. To ensure reasonably rapid response, user processes that have received relatively little processor time are given higher priority than processes that have received a lot of processor time. Processes with the same priority are run in round-robin fashion. If a suspended process of higher priority wakes up, it preempts a running process of lower priority. To prevent some processes from being indefinitely suspended, UNIX increases the priority of processes that have been ignored for a long time.

A UNIX file is a one-dimensional array of characters (bytes) and is the basic unit for information storage on secondary memory. Unlike the records found in other file

Command	Function performed
fork	Create a new (child) process
kill	Destroy process
pause	Suspend process until a specified event occurs
ps	Print status information on active processes
sleep	Suspend process execution for a specified time
wait	Wait for a child process to terminate
wake	Resume a suspended process

Figure 7.53
Some UNIX commands for process management.

systems, UNIX files do not have internal structures. There are no restrictions on the length or contents of a file as seen by the user. Files are stored physically in pages (blocks) of a fixed size, initially 512 bytes, but larger block sizes are used in later UNIX versions. UNIX maintains a set of internal tables to keep track of the disk-file usage.

The logical organization of UNIX files as seen by a user is that of a tree-structured hierarchy. This structure facilitates both file management and the protection of files from unauthorized access. Special files called *directories* store related files; a user accesses a file by naming the directory that contains it. A directory can contain other directories, leading to the file organization depicted in Figure 7.54. The directory at the highest level of the tree is known as the *root* and is denoted by the special name "/". The nondirectory files are at the lowest levels of the tree. The level below the root contains major system directories such as *bin,* which stores the UNIX utilities; *dev,* which contains files used to access IO devices; and *usr,* which contains users' files. A file or directory is identified by specifying the sequence of directories that contain it, with directory names separated by a slash. For example, the file "mail" in Figure 7.54 is referred to by */usr/tom/mail,* which is the file's *path name.* UNIX provides many operations to manipulate files, for example, **create, close, copy, open, read,** and **write.**

An unusual feature of UNIX is its extension of the file concept to IO management. IO devices are treated as special types of files, with device-specific IO driver routines serving to create a filelike interface to UNIX. Hence all IO operations can be manipulated by file management operations such as **open, close, read,** and **write,** which implement START IO, HALT IO, INPUT, and OUTPUT, respectively. This approach makes UNIX unusually independent of the characteristics of the IO devices attached to the host system and enhances this operating system's hardware independence. File concepts are also used for more general interprocess communication. A process can send (**write**) information to one end of the special queuelike file called a *pipe,* and the information can be received (**read**) from the other end by a second process.

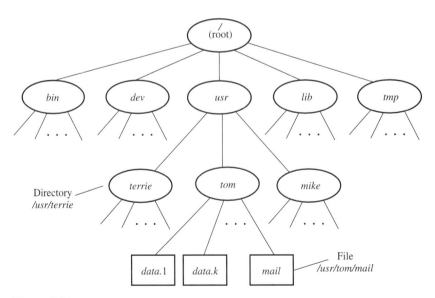

Figure 7.54
Organization of the UNIX file system.

7.3
PARALLEL PROCESSING

539

CHAPTER 7
System
Organization

Computer performance can be increased by executing many instructions simultaneously or in parallel. This section examines processor-level parallelism in computers, focusing on the use of multiple CPUs to achieve very high throughput and fault tolerance.

7.3.1 Processor-Level Parallelism

Although computer performance has increased steadily thanks to faster hardware technologies and processor designs, many important computational problems remain beyond the capabilities of the fastest current machines [Hwang 1993]. Some computer designers believe that processor and memory technologies are approaching physical limits on their size and speed. Size reductions and speed increases well beyond present levels are feasible, but their cost may not be acceptable. One way to address these issues is to exploit *processor-level parallelism,* for example, by building computers containing large numbers—perhaps hundreds or thousands—of low-cost processors that can work in parallel on common tasks. Suppose that such a computer $P(n)$ is constructed by combining n copies of a single (sequential) computer $P(1)$. If a task T can be partitioned into n subtasks of similar complexity and $P(n)$ can be programmed so that its n processors execute the n subtasks in parallel, then we would expect P_n to process T about n times faster than $P(1)$ can process it. In contrast, *instruction-level parallelism* (section 6.3) aims at speeding up the single processor $P(1)$ and can increase performance only by a factor of 10 or so.

A further advantage of processor-level parallelism is tolerance of hardware and software faults. While failure of its CPU is almost always fatal to a sequential computer, a parallel computer can be designed to continue functioning, perhaps at a reduced performance level, in the presence of defective CPUs.

Illustration. Consider the application of parallel processing to the small numerical problem of computing the sum SUM of N numbers (constants) b_1, $b_2,\dots,b_N$. A straightforward algorithm for solving this problem can be expressed as follows:

$$\text{SUM} := 0;$$

$$\textbf{for } i = 1 \textbf{ to } N \textbf{ do } \text{SUM} := \text{SUM} + b[i]; \tag{7.6}$$

If this summation algorithm is implemented on a conventional computer, N consecutive add operations, each taking time T_{add}, are required. Certain other bookkeeping operations are necessary, such as initializing SUM to zero, and the indexing operations implied by the **for-do** loop. These operations depend on implementation details and so are often omitted when estimating the overall complexity of the computation. Thus $N \times T_{add}$ serves as a rough indication of the time a sequential computer needs to execute (7.6). We now consider in detail a parallel processing approach to this problem.

EXAMPLE 7.7 SUMMATION BY A ONE-DIMENSIONAL ARRAY MULTIPROCESSOR. Consider a hypothetical computer containing n identical processors P_i, each

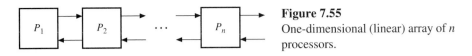

Figure 7.55
One-dimensional (linear) array of n processors.

of which is a small sequential computer with its own CPU and memory, for example, a network of n workstations. The n processors are assumed to be interconnected in the linear (one dimensional) array configuration depicted in Figure 7.55. Each P_i is connected by dedicated buses to its left and right neighbors, P_{i-1} and P_{i+1} (where they exist), and communicates with them by means of two IO operations called **send** and **receive**. The command **send**(NEIGHBOR, MESSAGE) causes P_i to output some data called *MESSAGE,* typically the result of a computational step, either to P_{i-1} (when NEIGHBOR = LEFT) or else to P_{i+1} (when NEIGHBOR = RIGHT). When P_i executes **receive**(NEIGHBOR, MESSAGE), it waits for *MESSAGE* to be sent to it from the designated neighbor; then P_i inputs *MESSAGE* into its local memory. **send** and **receive** can be programmed by message-handling procedures whose implementation details are not of concern here. We assume that the processor array also has IO facilities connecting it to the outside world via the right-most processor P_n, as suggested in Figure 7.55. By repeated execution of **send** and **receive**, data can be transferred between any processor in the array and external devices.

The summation (7.6) can be solved in parallel on this computer as follows: Suppose that $N = kn$, where k is an integer. The N input numbers to be summed are divided into n sets of k numbers, and each set is loaded into the local memory of one of the n available processors. Every processor is provided with a copy of a summation program, which it executes on its k numbers. Since all processors can operate in parallel, nk additions resulting in n partial sums can be performed in the time required to do k add operations. The partial sums must then be summed to give the final result. We assume that each processor P_i transmits its result to its right neighbor P_{i+1}, which then adds the received sum to its own sum and transmits the new result to P_{i+2}. Thus after $n - 1$ sequential summation and data-transfer operations, the final result is stored in P_n.

A program to implement the foregoing parallel summation scheme appears in Figure 7.56. It is placed in the local memory of each processor P_i and is executed using that processor's particular data set (k of the nk numbers to be summed). Processor P_i

```
{Each processor Pᵢ computes the sum of its local numbers b[1:k]}
   SUM := 0
   for i = 1 to k do SUM := SUM + b[i];
{Processor P₁ sends its local result SUM to P₂}
   if INDEX = 1 then
      begin
      if n > 1 then send(RIGHT, SUM);
      end else
{Every remaining Pᵢ waits to receive an external result from Pᵢ₋₁}
      begin
      receive(LEFT, LEFTSUM);
      SUM := SUM + LEFTSUM;
      {Each Pᵢ except Pₙ sends its new value of SUM to Pᵢ₊₁}
      if INDEX < n then send(RIGHT, SUM);
      end;
```

Figure 7.56
Parallel summation code for the machine of Figure 7.55.

also stores a variable INDEX, which is P_i's own address i; in other words, each P_i "knows" its location within the array of processors. Similarly, the processor P_n at the end of the array knows that it has only one neighboring processor, and it interprets the program of Figure 7.56 accordingly. The communication between the processors is such that, on encountering **receive**, P_i waits until P_{i-1} has completed transmission of its result SUM, which P_i then stores internally as LEFTSUM.

The time $T(n)$ needed to execute the parallel summation algorithm on n processors has two main components. There is a local computation time T_L due primarily to the $k = N/n$ sequential additions performed in parallel by each of the n processors. This time can be written $K_1 N/n$, where K_1 is some constant depending on the time needed by the add instructions and any associated bookkeeping operations. The second component T_C of $T(n)$ is the communication time to send $n - 1$ intermediate results from left to right and the time needed to perform the final $n - 1$ additions. T_C can be written as $K_2(n - 1)$, where K_2 is a constant representing interprocessor communication delays. Thus, ignoring minor constant terms, the n-processor execution time is approximated by

$$T(n) = T_L + T_C = K_1 N/n + K_2(n - 1) \qquad (7.7)$$

Since K_2 measures the time for a slow message-passing IO operation, K_2 is much larger than K_1. Thus the reduction in computation time T_L due to increasing the number of processors n is offset by the increase in communication time T_C. Trade-offs of this kind between computation and communication times are common to parallel processing tasks. The time for a comparable sequential computer to solve the summation is obtained by setting n to one in Equation (7.7), yielding

$$T(1) = T_L = K_1 N \qquad (7.8)$$

As expected, the local processing time T_L increases by a factor of n, and the interprocessor communication time T_C reduces to zero.

A problem closely related to the foregoing one is to compute all N partial sums defined by the recurrence relation

$$x_i = x_{i-1} + b_i \quad \text{for } i = 1, 2, \ldots, N \qquad (7.9)$$

Comparing this to (7.6), we see that the latter is designed to compute only one number SUM $= x_N$. However, with a small modification, (7.6) and the program of Figure 7.56 can compute and store the ordered set or *vector* of N values denoted $(x_1, x_2, \ldots, x_N)$ in place of the single, or *scalar*, value x_N. The relation (7.9) can be rewritten as a set of N equations thus:

$$
\begin{aligned}
x_1 &= b_1 \\
-x_1 + x_2 &= b_2 \\
-x_2 + x_3 &= b_3 \\
&\cdots\cdots \\
-x_{N-1} + x_N &= b_N
\end{aligned}
\qquad (7.10)
$$

The solution of these equations is the required vector of N partial sums.

Now (7.10) is a special case of a set of linear equations, which have the following general form:

$$a_{1,1}x_1 + a_{1,2}x_2 + \ldots + a_{1,m}x_m = b_1$$

$$a_{2,1}x_1 + a_{2,2}x_2 + \ldots + a_{2,m}x_m = b_2 \qquad (7.11)$$

$$\ldots\ldots\ldots\ldots\ldots\ldots\ldots\ldots\ldots\ldots\ldots\ldots\ldots$$

$$a_{n,1}x_1 + a_{n,2}x_2 + \ldots + a_{n,m}x_m = b_n$$

Here the $a_{i,j}$'s and b_i's can denote either integer (fixed-point) or real (floating-point) numbers, and the x_j's are integer or real variables whose values are to be computed. Equations (7.11) can be expressed more concisely as

$$A \times X = B$$

where A denotes the two-dimensional matrix, the operator $\times$ denotes matrix multiplication, and X and B denote (column) vectors. The matrix A can be decomposed into a set of n row vectors or m column vectors so that the solution of sets of equations like (7.10) and (7.11) is essentially a vector-processing task. Problems of the foregoing type occur frequently in scientific computation, and their regular structure makes them well suited to solution by parallel processing.

Dependencies. The main benefit of parallel processing is faster computation. A price is paid, however, in the need for a significant amount of extra hardware. Roughly speaking, increasing the number of processors by a factor of n makes an n-fold increase in computing performance possible. In practice, this maximum speedup is rarely achieved because it is difficult to keep all members of a set of parallel processors continually working at their maximum rates. Dependencies among subtasks can force a processor to wait until other processors supply results that it needs. In the parallel summation algorithm for the linear processor array (Figure 7.56), for instance, the processors must wait for data from their left neighbors. The processors in a parallel computer often share resources such as memory banks, IO devices, or operating system routines, which can be used by only one processor at a time. A major issue, therefore, in designing and programming parallel systems is to avoid conflicts in the use of shared resources. The extent to which all processors can be kept busy depends on the computer architecture, the tasks being performed, and the way in which the tasks are programmed.

Parallel computers are far more difficult to program than sequential ones. As illustrated by Figure 7.56, the parallel machines require special programming constructs that allow processors to communicate with one another and to specify complex actions like vector operations. Because parallel programming is still poorly developed, achieving an acceptable level of performance requires a costly software development effort, especially when programming for tasks that, unlike Example 7.7, have little overt parallelism. Ordinary programs tend to contain significant numbers of inherently sequential operations that cannot be processed in parallel. As discussed later, even a small percentage of sequential operations can have a large negative effect on the performance of a parallel computer. Removal of these sequential features is a major challenge in the design of algorithms, programming languages, and compilers for parallel processing.

Classification methods. A processor such as a CPU operates by fetching instructions and operands from memory M (main memory or cache), executing the

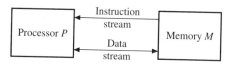

Figure 7.57

Instruction and data streams in a sequential computer.

instructions, and placing the final results in M. The instructions form an *instruction stream* flowing from M to the processor, while the operands form another stream, the *data stream,* flowing to and from the processor, as suggested in Figure 7.57. Michael J. Flynn has proposed a broad classification of processor-level parallelism based on the number of simultaneous instruction and data streams seen by the processor during program execution [Flynn 1966]. Suppose that processor P is operating at maximum capacity so that its full degree of parallelism is being exercised. Let m_I and m_D denote the minimum number of instruction and data streams, respectively, that are active. m_I and m_D are termed the *instruction-* and *data-stream multiplicities* of P and measure its degree of parallelism. Note that m_I and m_D are defined by the minimum, instead of by the maximum, number of streams flowing at any point, since the most limiting components of the system—its bottlenecks—determine the overall parallel processing abilities.

Flynn's classification divides computers into four broad groups based on the values of m_I and m_D associated with their CPUs.

- *Single instruction stream single data stream (SISD):* $m_I = m_D = 1$. Conventional machines with a single CPU capable only of scalar arithmetic fall into this category. SISD computers and sequential computers are synonymous.
- *Single instruction stream multiple data stream (SIMD):* $m_I = 1$, $m_D > 1$. This category includes such early parallel computers as ILLIAC IV that have a single program-control unit and many independent execution units.
- *Multiple instruction stream single data stream (MISD):* $m_I > 1$, $m_D = 1$. Few parallel computers fit well in this class. Fault-tolerant computers where several CPUs process the same data using different programs are MISD.
- *Multiple instruction stream multiple data stream (MIMD):* $m_I > 1$, $m_D > 1$. This category covers multiprocessors, which are computers with more than one CPU and the ability to execute several programs simultaneously. An example examined later in this chapter is the Symmetry multiprocessor from Sequent Computer Systems Inc.

The foregoing classification depends on a somewhat subjective distinction between control (instructions) and data. It is also essentially behavioral in that it says nothing about a computer's structure. We turn next to some ways of classifying parallel computers based on their interconnection structure. Every computer consists of a set of $n \geq 1$ processors (CPUs) $P_1, P_2, \ldots, P_n$ and $m \geq 0$ shared (main) memory units $M_1, M_2, \ldots, M_m$ communicating via an interconnection network N, as illustrated in Figure 7.58. For simplicity, we do not consider IOPs or IO devices in the classification process. In a conventional SISD computer $n = m = 1$, and N is the system bus over which processor-memory communication takes place. The memory units then constitute a global main memory that provides a convenient message depository for processor-to-processor communication. A system with this organization is called a *shared-memory* computer.

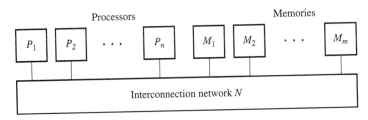

Figure 7.58
General structure of a computer with n processors and m
memory units.

A global shared memory can be a serious bottleneck, particularly when the processors share large amounts of information, since normally only one processor can access a given memory module at a time. If the processors have their own local memories, then the global memory can be reduced in size, or even eliminated completely. To separate the functions of processing (computation) and memory, we will refer to a CPU or IOP with no associated main memory, but with other temporary storage units such as register files and caches, as a *processing element* or PE. A *processor* is then the combination of a PE and a local memory; it can also include IO facilities forming, in effect, a self-contained computer. In a system with little or no global memory, the processors communicate via messages transmitted between their local memories, as in the system of Figure 7.55. In this case the main memory is the sum of the local memories, and the system is referred to as a *distributed-memory* computer. The term *message-passing* computer is also used for such machines. Figure 7.59 illustrates the main structural differences between shared-memory and distributed-memory computers.

The internal structure of the interconnection network N is also used to classify parallel computers. A selection of interconnection topologies appears in Figure 7.60. Because of the ease with which it can be designed and controlled, the single shared bus (Figure 7.60a) is widely used in parallel as well as sequential computers. When n, the number of PEs, and m, the number of memory units, are large, very fast buses are required, and special design precautions must be taken to minimize contention for access to the bus. Bus contention can be relieved (but not eliminated completely) by providing several independent buses. The *crossbar* interconnection network of Figure 7.60b is a special kind of multiple-bus system in which each PE has a (horizontal) bus linking it to all memories, or equivalently, each memory has a (vertical) bus linking it to all PEs. An $n \times m$ crossbar allows up to $\min\{n,m\}$ bus transactions to take place simultaneously. However, in the worst case where all the processors attempt to access the same memory unit M_i simultaneously, the number of bus transactions drops to one. Although crossbar networks have often been employed in computer systems, their hardware complexity quickly becomes very high as m and n increase.

Figures 7.60c and 7.60d illustrate networks that use high-speed, dedicated connections (uni- or bidirectional buses) to link the system components, each of which is an independent processor with its own memory and a small group of neighbors. The neighboring processors are physically close and cooperate in the processing of common tasks. They communicate with one another via **send** and **receive** IO operations of the type discussed in Example 7.7. While neighboring processors can

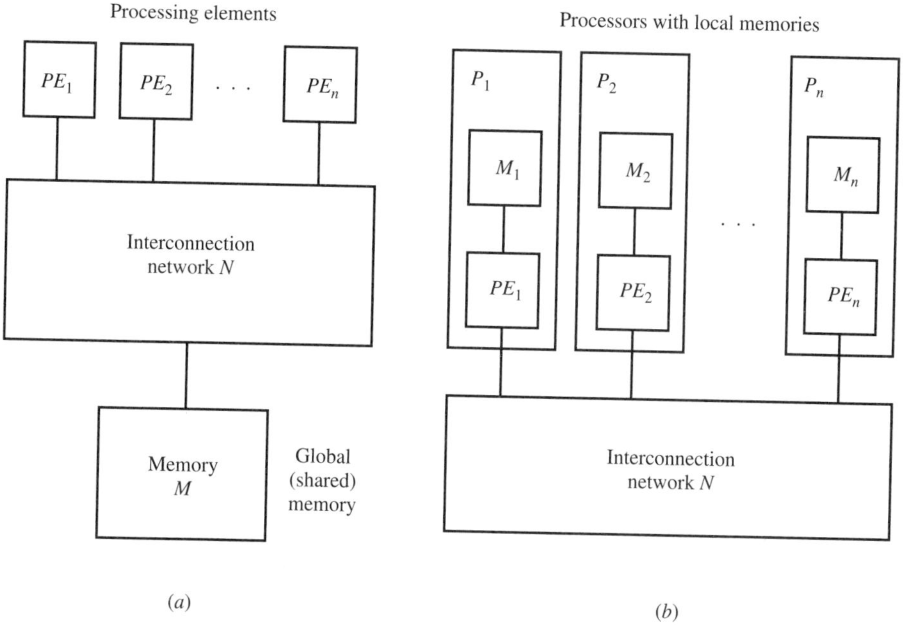

Figure 7.59

(a) Shared-memory and (b) distributed-memory computers.

communicate rapidly via their dedicated bus links, communication between non-neighboring processors is slower and requires intermediate processors to act as store-and-forward message-transfer stations. For example, to transmit data D from P_{000} to P_{011} in Figure 7.60c requires the following two steps: First send D from P_{000} to a neighbor processor such as P_{001} and store D there temporarily. Then send D from P_{001} to its neighbor P_{011}. Various interconnection structures other than those of Figure 7.60 have been proposed for parallel computers, but few have been implemented commercially.

The computer structure in Figure 7.60c is an n-dimensional *hypercube*, also called a (*binary*) *n-cube*. It contains 2^n processors, each of which is connected to n immediately adjacent (neighboring) processors. In the example $n = 3$, so eight processors are used, and the cubelike interconnection structure is clear. If each processor is indexed by an n-bit binary address as shown in Figure 7.60c, then P_i is a neighbor of P_j if and only if their addresses i and j differ by one bit. The interconnection structure of Figure 7.60d is that of a *tree*, in this case a binary tree, because each processor (except those in the bottom row) is connected to two processors—its "children"—in the row beneath. The name tree derives from the fanciful resemblance of Figure 7.60d to an upside-down tree in which processor $P_{1,1}$ is the "root," and processors $P_{p,1}:P_{p,2^{p-1}}$ are the "leaves." This binary tree computer contains $n = 2^p - 1$ processors, so the number p of levels of the tree is approximately $\log_2 n$. As in the hypercube case, communication between neighboring processors (a parent and a child) is fast, while communication between nonneighboring processors is much slower.

Like most multiprocessors with specialized interconnection structures, tree computers are well suited to certain kinds of parallel processing. Consider again

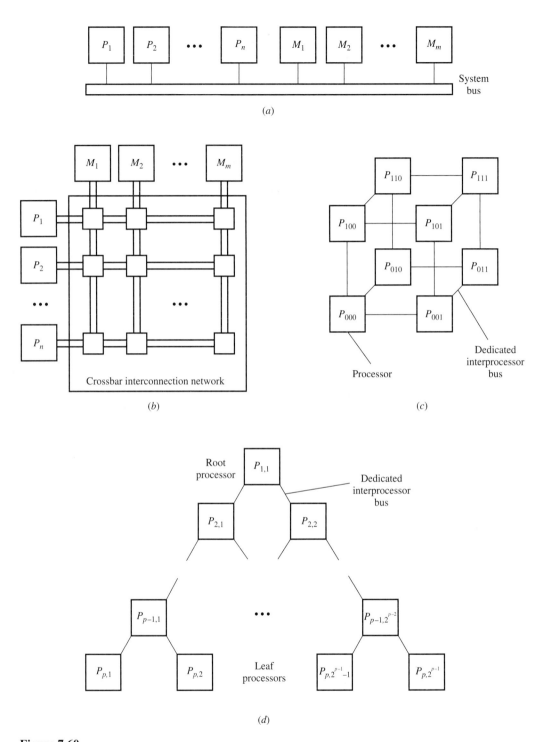

Figure 7.60
Interconnection network structures: (*a*) single bus; (*b*) crossbar; (*c*) hypercube (3-cube); (*d*) tree.

546

$$SUM = b_1 + b_2 + \ldots + b_N$$

where $N = 2^{p-1}$. It can be solved by the following tree-oriented parallel algorithm: Load the input operands $b_1, b_2, \ldots, b_N$ into the 2^{p-1} leaf processors of the binary tree (Figure 7.60d). Then for each pair b_j and b_{j+1} stored in the children of some level-$(p-1)$ processor $P_{p-1,i}$, transfer b_j and b_{j+1} to $P_{p-1,i}$, compute the sum $y_j = b_j + b_{j+1}$, and store it in the parent processor $P_{p-1,i}$. This reduces the number of operands to be added in half, and all are now stored in level-$(p-1)$ processors. These $N/2$ operands are then added in parallel by the processors in level $p-2$, and so on. Eventually, the final result SUM is computed by, and stored in, the root node $P_{1,1}$. The entire summation process requires $p - 1 \approx \log_2 N$ addition times.

We can further distinguish computers on the basis of the unit-to-unit connection paths provided by their interconnection networks. These paths can be *static,* that is, fixed and unchangeable, or *dynamic,* that is, reconfigurable under system control. The single-bus and crossbar interconnections of Figure 7.60 are examples of dynamic interconnection networks, whereas the hypercube and tree have static interconnections. The system bus (Figure 7.60a) allows any of the n processors to connect to any of the m memories for one or more bus cycles, for example, to fetch an instruction. In a subsequent cycle some other processor-memory pair can use the bus, so the communicating bus units vary dynamically. In contrast, each processor in the binary tree (Figure 7.60d) has dedicated buses to its nearest neighbors and must communicate with other processors indirectly.

It is clear from the preceding discussion that the same computer can often be classified in several ways, depending on the aspects of its parallelism that are singled out for attention. A computer in the nCUBE series, for example, can be called a (distributed memory) multiprocessor, an MIMD computer, a hypercube computer, or a (massively) parallel computer.

Performance. The performance of a parallel computer depends—often in complex and hard-to-define ways—on the parallelism inherent in its architecture and the programs it executes. Several basic performance measures encountered earlier in the context of pipelining (section 5.3.2) also apply to processor-level parallelism. An example is the *speedup* $S(n)$ defined by the ratio of total execution time $T(1)$ on a sequential computer to the corresponding execution time $T(n)$ on the computer whose degree of parallelism is n.

$$S(n) = \frac{T(1)}{T(n)} \qquad (7.12)$$

In Example 7.7, where N numbers are summed by an n-processor array, $T(n)$ and $T(1)$ are defined by Equations (7.7) and (7.8), respectively, yielding the speedup formula:

$$S(n) = \frac{K_1 N}{K_1 N/n + K_2(n-1)} \approx \frac{n}{1 + Kn/k}$$

Here $K = K_2/K_1$ is a system constant, and $k = N/n$. If the interprocessor communication delays are ignored by setting K_2 to zero, then $S(n)$ becomes n, which is obviously the maximum speedup achievable with n processors. On the other hand, if K_2

is large relative to n, it is possible for $S(n)$ to become less than one, in which case a single sequential processor with no interprocessor communication requirements is faster than an n-processor system!

A related performance measure expressed as a single number (a fraction or a percentage) is the *efficiency* $E(n)$, which is the speedup per degree of parallelism, and is defined as follows:

$$E(n) = \frac{S(n)}{n} \tag{7.13}$$

$E(n)$ is also an indication of processor utilization and may be so named. In general, speedup and efficiency provide rough estimates of the performance changes that can be expected in a parallel processing system by increasing the parallelism degree n—by adding more processors, for instance. These measures should be used with caution, however, since they depend on the programs being run and can change dramatically from program to program, or from one part of a program to another.

The influence of program parallelism—or the lack thereof—on performance can be seen from the following analysis. Suppose that all computations of interest on a parallel processor are divided into two groups involving arithmetic operations only: vector operations employing vector operands of some fixed length N and scalar operations where all operands are scalars ($N = 1$). Let F be the fraction of all floating-point operations that are executed as scalar operations, and let $1 - F$ be the fraction executed as vector operations. Hence $1 - F$ is a measure of the degree of parallelism in the programs being executed and varies from one, corresponding to all-vector operations, to zero (all-scalar operations). Suppose that vector and scalar operations are performed at throughput rates of b_v and b_s, respectively. Let the average system throughput be b in suitable units such as MFLOPS (millions of floating-point operations per second). Then b, b_v, and b_s are related by the following useful formula:

$$\frac{1}{b} = \frac{F}{b_s} + \frac{1 - F}{b_v} \tag{7.14}$$

The execution time for a single N-element vector operation is $T_v = N/b_v$, while that of a single scalar operation is $T_s = 1/b_s$. These parameters are related by

$$T_v = T_0 + \frac{NT_s}{n}$$

where T_0 is some fixed *setup time* that is independent of vector length and n is the computer's parallelism degree. When N is large, T_0 can be ignored so that this equation reduces to $T_v = N T_s/n$. Substitution into Equation (7.14) yields

$$b = \frac{nb_s}{1 + (n - 1)F} \tag{7.15}$$

Since b_s, the scalar throughput, and n, the processor parallelism, can be taken to be constants, Equation (7.15) defines b as a function of F.

Suppose for example that $b_s = 10$ MFLOPS and $n = 100$. Equation (7.15) then becomes $b = 1000/(1 + 99F)$. The maximum performance of 1000 MFLOPS occurs when $F = 0$, that is, when there are no scalar operations. When $F = 0.01$, in other

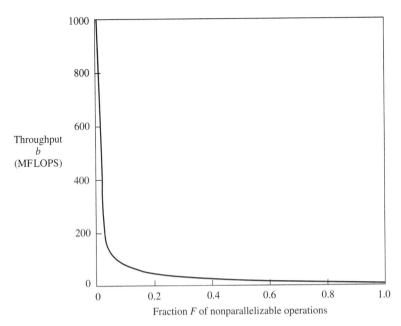

Figure 7.61
Illustration of Amdahl's law for $n = 100$.

words, when 1 percent of the computations are scalar, b drops from 1000 to approximately 500 MFLOPS, thus cutting the throughput in half. Increasing F to 0.1 or 10 percent reduces b to less than 100 MFLOPS, an order of magnitude drop in performance; see Figure 7.61.

This analysis suggests that the performance of a highly parallel computer is very sensitive even to small numbers of nonparallel (sequential) operations, a conclusion that has been verified experimentally for many types of parallel machines. Hence it is often worthwhile to devote considerable effort to "parallelize" programs for such machines to eliminate sequential operations. If we take the speedup $S(n)$ to be b/b_s, then (7.15) can be rewritten as

$$S(n) = \frac{n}{1 + (n-1)F} \qquad (7.16)$$

With F interpreted broadly as the fraction of nonparallelizable operations or instructions, then Equation (7.16) is often referred to as *Amdahl's law,* after Gene M. Amdahl, one of the architects of the IBM System/360.

Besides the presence of nonparallelizable code, there are several other reasons why a computer with n independent processors rarely achieves a speedup of n. These reasons include inefficiencies in task distribution (load balancing) among the available processors and contention for access to shared system resources, especially memory and interconnection networks. It has been conjectured that the speedup typically achievable with n processors in a multiprocessor system ranges from $\log_2 n$ to $n/\log_e n$ (see problem 7.30).

An indication of the influence of contention for shared memory on performance can be obtained by considering a system containing n processors P_1, $P_2,...,P_n$ connected to m shared memory units $M_1, M_2,...,M_m$ via a crossbar or

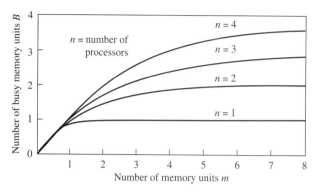

Figure 7.62
Performance of a shared-memory multiprocessor.

similar interconnection network, as in Figure 7.60b. All programs and data used by the processors are stored in the m-unit global memory and are accessed via the crossbar network. It is reasonable to assume that the instruction or data bandwidth b of a processor P_j is proportional to the rate at which P_j accesses memory. The latter is, in turn, proportional to the average number of busy memory units B. Suppose further that the probability of any processor P_j generating a request to M_i is $1/m$; in other words, the memory requests are distributed uniformly. Hence the probability that M_i is idle, and therefore free to respond to memory requests, is $(1 - 1/m)^n$; the probability p_i that M_i is busy is $1 - (1 - 1/m)^n$. If M_i is busy when a new request for access to it is received, that request is not serviced until M_i becomes free again. The average number of busy memory units B is therefore given by

$$B = \sum_{i=1}^{m} p_i = m\left[1 - \left(1 - \frac{1}{m}\right)^n\right] \tag{7.17}$$

As might be expected, if m is fixed and n approaches infinity ($n \to \infty$), then $B \to m$. Similarly, if n is fixed and $m \to \infty$, then Equation (7.17) implies $B \to n$; that is, all processors become busy. Figure 7.62 plots B against m for some small values of n. From this analysis we see that we can improve the performance of a multiprocessor by placing information that is frequently accessed by P_j in a local memory assigned to P_j while limiting the use of global memory to the storage of infrequently shared programs and data.

7.3.2 Multiprocessors

A *multiprocessor* is an MIMD computer containing two or more CPUs that cooperate on common computational tasks. Multiprocessors are distinguished from multicomputers and computer networks, which are systems with multiple CPUs operating largely independently on separate tasks. The various processors making up a multiprocessor typically share resources such as communication facilities, IO devices, program libraries and databases and are controlled by a common operating system.

Motivation. The main reasons for including multiple CPUs in a computer system are to improve performance and reliability. Performance is improved either by distributing the computation of a large task among several CPUs or by performing many small tasks in parallel using separate CPUs. A multiprocessor with n identical processors can, in principle, provide n times the performance of a comparable SISD system or *uniprocessor.* A major goal, therefore, in designing an n-CPU multiprocessor is to achieve a speedup $S(n)$ as close to n as possible. By enabling such resources as secondary memory to be shared, a multiprocessor can reduce overall system costs. Many multiprocessors also have the advantage of *scalability;* that is, the system size can be increased incrementally by adding processors to meet growing computation needs. Scalability is facilitated by making all CPUs identical and allowing each to execute either operating system (kernel) or user code; multiprocessors with these properties are said to be *symmetric.* Finally, system reliability is improved by the fact that the failure of one CPU need not cause the entire system to fail. The functions of the faulty CPU can be taken over by the other CPUs; consequently, multiprocessors enable fault tolerance to be incorporated into the system.

As discussed earlier, multiprocessors are classified by the organization of their memory systems (distributed memory and shared memory) and by their interconnection networks (dynamic or static). Shared-memory and distributed-memory multiprocessors are sometimes referred to as *tightly coupled* and *loosely coupled,* respectively, reflecting the speed and ease with which they can interact on common tasks. Multiprocessors are also classified by the number of processors they contain: *Massively parallel* machines can contain thousands of processors. Most multiprocessors, however, are *modestly parallel,* containing from 2 to about 30 processors; such multiprocessors have existed since the 1960s. The relative success of multiprocessors with a few CPUs stems from the difficulty of programming large numbers of CPUs to cooperate efficiently. The lack of standard, widely used languages and application packages for parallel programming has been a major obstacle to wider use of multiprocessors.

Shared-bus systems. Most commercial multiprocessors have been built around a single shared system bus B because of B's relative simplicity and low cost. The CPUs, memory, and IO units are attached directly to B and time-share its communication facilities. Only one pair of units can use B at a time, either for CPU-memory or IO-memory communication. The memory units and IO devices on B are global to all the processors; hence single-bus multiprocessors are of the shared-memory class. If the access time to the shared memory is the same for each processor, the multiprocessor is said to be of the *uniform-memory access (UMA)* type.

The global bus B is clearly a communication bottleneck in shared-bus multiprocessors, leading to contention and delay whenever two or more units request access to main memory. In practice, memory contention limits to about 30 the number of CPUs that can be included in the system without an unacceptable degradation in performance. Figure 7.63 shows that a single-bus multiprocessor's performance can be improved by supplying each CPU with a local bus. The local bus is connected to a local memory unit that contains part of the shared address space; it can also support a local IO subsystem, as illustrated in Figure 7.63. This system configuration removes most of the routine memory traffic from B so that it can be

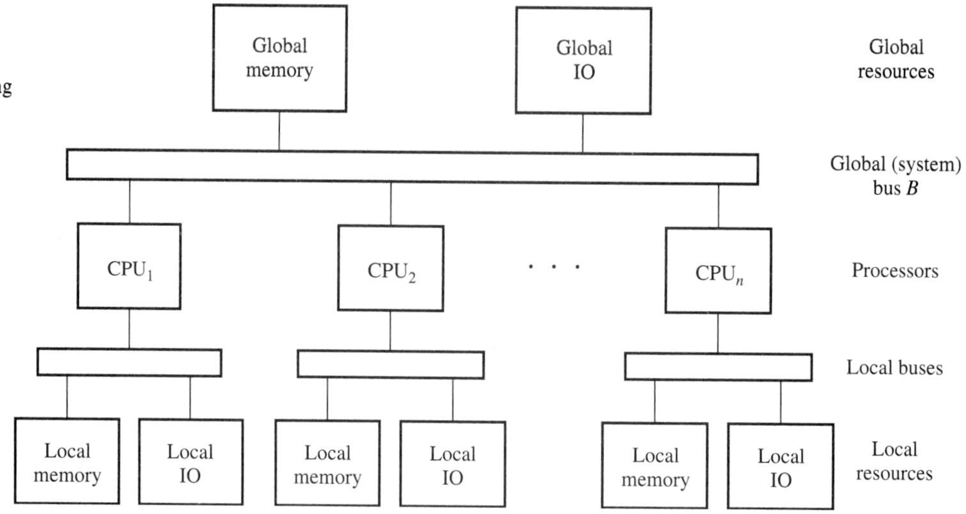

Figure 7.63
Shared-bus multiprocessor with global and local resources.

reserved primarily for interprocessor communication. Many microprocessor families can be configured as multiprocessors in this way. The Intel Pentium, for example, was designed for use in shared-bus multiprocessors, with standard buses like the PCI bus serving as local buses.

Despite its relative simplicity, the shared-bus architecture exhibits some of the basic synchronization problems common to all multiprocessors. Consider the situation in which two CPUs share a region R of global memory where mutual exclusion (section 7.2.3) applies; that is, only one processor should have access to the shared region at a time. Access to R is conveniently controlled by a semaphore (flag) F that indicates whether R is currently being used by some other process ($F = 1$) or is available for use by a new process ($F = 0$). Before it attempts to access R, a CPU first reads F, which must be stored in global memory. If $F = 0$, the CPU then changes F to 1 and proceeds to use R. If it finds that F is already 1, then it does not attempt to use R. The mutual exclusion requirement can be violated if it is possible for two CPUs to independently access the semaphore at the same time and find $F = 0$. This violation can occur if a second processor CPU_2 can read F after the first processor CPU_1 has read it, but before CPU_1 has changed F to 1. The problem lies in the fact that semaphore flag test-and-set instructions issued by the CPUs can be broken down into interleaved bus cycles as follows:

Global bus cycle	Action
i	CPU_1 fetches semaphore $F = 0$.
$i + 1$	CPU_2 fetches semaphore $F = 0$.
$i + 2$	CPU_1 sets F to 1.
$i + 3$	CPU_2 sets F to 1.

At time $i + 4$, both CPU_1 and CPU_2 assume they have exclusive control over the critical region R, with potentially catastrophic consequences. A solution to this problem, which is discussed in section 7.3.1, is to allow semaphore test-and-set instructions to have exclusive control of the system bus while they are being executed. Such instructions lock the bus until their execution is complete, thereby delaying any test-and-set instructions awaiting execution by other CPUs until the first CPU has safely set the semaphore to busy.

EXAMPLE 7.8 THE SEQUENT SYMMETRY SHARED-BUS MULTIPROCESSOR [SEQUENT 1996]. The Symmetry multiprocessor series is built around a high-speed shared bus, multiple CPUs from the Intel 80X86/Pentium series, and the UNIX operating system. Symmetry multiprocessors can be variously characterized as MIMD, shared memory, tightly coupled, scalable, symmetric, and UMA. They are typically used in applications such as on-line transaction processing characterized by heavy computation requirements and a need for high reliability.

The Symmetry 5000 system introduced in 1995 has the general organization depicted in Figure 7.64. It contains from 2 to 30 Pentium CPUs each with a 2MB cache; there are no other local memories. The CPUs are packaged two per circuit board; the system can be expanded to the maximum allowed by adding CPU boards. The main-memory system is also packaged in circuit boards that facilitate modular expansion. The memory is interleaved (section 6.1.2) to increase performance, and an error-correcting code improves reliability. The IO subsystem includes one or more high-speed IO processors designed to communicate with magnetic disk and tape memories via high-speed SCSI buses. Additional, slower IO controllers support other IO devices, as well as various standard external interfaces and communication protocols such as Ethernet.

A key component of the Symmetry 5000 is its proprietary system bus that links all processors, memory units, and IO controllers. This Highly Scalable Bus (HSB) contains a 64-bit data-address bus designed to transmit (in multiplexed mode) 64-bit

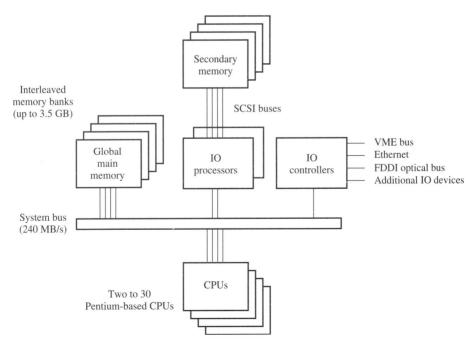

Figure 7.64
Organization of the Sequent Symmetry 5000 multiprocessor.

data words and 32-bit addresses. It has an unusual "pipelined" data transmission mode that supports a simplified form of package switching, which allows memory and IO data to be transmitted in bursts whose transmission can be overlapped. The HSB was designed for a maximum data bandwidth of 240 MB/s.

The Symmetry's operating system, DYNIX, is a version of UNIX with enhancements to support multiprocessing. Each CPU acts like a uniprocessor that is executing independently under UNIX supervision; it executes processes from a list that all the CPUs share. Interrupt signals are generated at periodic intervals to force the CPUs to examine the list of waiting processes and schedule a high-priority process for execution. This approach forces all CPUs to share the system's workload. To avoid conflicts among CPUs when executing kernel routines stored in the shared memory, a semaphore mechanism of the kind discussed earlier enforces mutual exclusion.

Cache coherence. In shared-bus multiprocessors like the Symmetry, caches play a vital role in reducing the contention for the shared system bus. Without caches, connecting more than two or three CPUs to the same bus might be impractical. Typically, each CPU has a private one- or two-level cache, which forms a local memory and allows the CPU to access data and instructions without using the system bus. With an independent cache in each CPU, the possibility exists for two or more caches to contain different (inconsistent) versions of the same information at the same time; this is the *cache-coherence problem*. This problem is alleviated, but not solved, by using write-through, which, as discussed in section 6.3, causes both the cache and main (global) memory to be updated whenever a memory write operation occurs. Suppose, for example, that one CPU updates variable X in both its cache and the global memory. If another CPU then changes X, the new value of X will be written into main memory, but the two caches will contain different values for X. Subsequent reads from these caches can lead to inconsistent results. Thus to ensure coherence we need a mechanism that informs each cache about changes to shared information stored in other caches.

We can solve the cache-coherence problem with either hardware or software. One software-based solution is to mark (tag) information during program compilation as either cacheable or noncacheable. All writable shared items are marked as noncacheable, meaning they can be accessed directly only from main memory. A write-through policy that requires a processor to mark a shared cache item X as invalid, or to be deallocated, whenever the processor writes into X can then ensure cache coherence. When the processor references X again, it is forced to bypass the cache and access main memory, thereby always acquiring the most recent version of X. This approach can significantly degrade system performance, however. Invalidation also forces the removal of needed data from the cache, thus increasing its miss ratio, which, in turn, increases the main-memory traffic.

Hardware-based methods of maintaining cache coherence offer the advantages of higher speed and program transparency, but they tend to be expensive. One possible approach is for a processor to broadcast its write operations to all caches and the global memory via the shared bus. Every cache controller in the system then examines its assigned addresses to see if the broadcast item is presently allocated to it. If it is, the cache block (line) in question is either updated or marked as dirty (modified). The drawback of this technique is that every cache write forces all caches to check the broadcast data, making the caches unavailable for normal processing.

A related, but less costly, hardware-based method known as *cache snooping* equips each CPU with circuitry to continuously monitor or "snoop" on system-bus activity in order to detect references by other processors to memory addresses currently in its cache. The CPU can also signal other CPUs that it has a copy of the referenced item and, when necessary, modify or delay the other CPUs' main-memory accesses. If CPU_2 attempts to read (write) memory data with an address that is currently assigned to CPU_1's cache, CPU_1 detects this attempt in what is called a *snoop read* (*write*) *hit* by CPU_1. On making a snoop hit, CPU_1 determines whether actual or potential incoherence exists and then takes appropriate steps to eliminate it. The following courses of action are typical:

- Suppose that CPU_1 makes a snoop read hit when its cache copy of the requested item is dirty and it has not yet updated main memory—this situation can occur only when the write-back policy is used. CPU_1 signals CPU_2 to suspend its read request while CPU_1 updates main memory by writing back the block containing the requested word. Then CPU_1 signals CPU_2 to complete its memory read operation.
- If CPU_1 makes a snoop write hit, it knows that its own cache copy of the requested item is about to become dirty. It therefore marks that copy as dirty. Hence the next time CPU_1 tries to read the item in question, a cache miss occurs that forces CPU_1 to read a valid copy from main memory.

An alternative response to a snoop write hit by CPU_1 is for CPU_1 to capture the new data on the system bus as CPU_2 writes it to global memory. CPU_1 can then use the captured data to update its cache.

EXAMPLE 7.9 THE MESI CACHE COHERENCY PROTOCOL [MOTOROLA 1994; ANDERSON AND SHANLEY 1995]. To maintain consistency in a multiprocessor, or in a uniprocessor with independent IO processors, a cache controller must keep careful track of the state of each cache block (line) under its control. It does so by attaching a few state bits to every block stored in the cache data memory and processing the states according to some coherence algorithm or *protocol*, as it is often called. Microprocessors such as the Pentium and some PowerPC models employ a standard cache coherence protocol based on the following four states:

- *M* (*modified*): The block has been modified or "dirtied" by a recent write hit to the cache.
- *E* (*exclusive*): The block is "clean," that is, the same as the copy in main memory, and no other processor has a copy.
- *S* (*shared*): The block is clean, but other processors may have a copy.
- *I* (*invalid*): The data in the block is not valid.

A cache-control algorithm using these states is known as the *MESI coherence protocol* for obvious reasons. Figure 7.65 gives a slightly simplified version of the MESI protocol, which shows how the states of a cache block change in response to various read and write conditions, assuming that a write-back policy and a cache-snooping mechanism are used. We also assume a one-level cache, although this protocol works equally well with multiple cache levels.

First consider the effect of read operations on the state of a cache block. Read hits to the block leave its state unchanged. Read misses, however, are not so simple. When a processor P_1 first tries to read the (empty) cache, the cache controller changes all block states to *I* (invalid) and forwards the read request to main memory. Thus *I* acts like a reset state that triggers a block transfer to the cache; the incoming block's state is

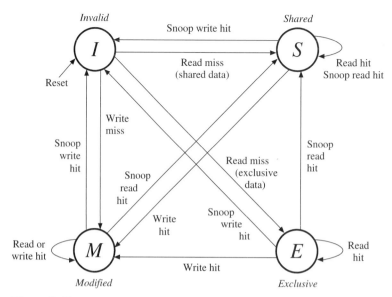

Figure 7.65
State-transition graph (simplified) for a cache block using the MESI coherence protocol.

set to E (exclusive) if no other processor has a copy of the same block. (An initial write also brings into the cache a block whose state is marked E.) If during P_1's read operation, a snooping processor P_2 signals via the shared bus that its cache has a clean copy of the same block, in which case no incoherence exists, the state of the block in P_1's cache is set to S (shared) instead of E. If, on the other hand, P_2 signals that its cache has a dirty (modified) copy of the same block, the caches are no longer coherent. To resolve this incoherence, the signal from P_2 causes P_1 to postpone its memory read and to relinquish the system bus. P_2 then assumes the role of bus master and writes its modified block back to main memory. P_2 also changes the state of its copy of the cache block from E to S because it now knows that the block in question is shared. This state change is specified by the transition from E to S marked "snoop read hit" on the right side of Figure 7.65. Finally, the first processor P_1 repeats its main-memory read request and obtains a clean copy of the block, which it marks as S.

Now consider the cache block's state when P_1 addresses a write hit to it. If the target block is in either of the clean states S or E, the block's state changes to M (modified or dirty). In the S case P_1 signals the other processors that it is writing to a shared block; they respond by marking their copies of the shared block I (invalid). The modified cache block remains in the M state in P_1 during subsequent reads and writes to it, unless P_1's own snooping detects read or write hits addressed to the same block in other caches.

A write miss by P_1 triggers a memory read operation that replaces the target block in the cache, where it is eventually marked M. If some other processor P_2 has a clean (S or E) copy of the same block, P_2 changes the state of its copy to I. If P_2 has a dirty (M) copy of the block in question, P_2 sends a signal to this effect to P_1, causing the latter to delay its memory read. P_2 then takes control of the system bus and writes its modified block to main memory; P_2 also changes the state of its cache copy from I, since it knows that the copy of the shared block in main memory is about to be changed by P_1. Control of the bus is then returned to P_1, which completes its block transfer.

As developments in VLSI technology during the 1980s ushered in powerful one-chip microprocessors and memory (RAM) chips with capacities in the multimegabit range, it has become feasible to build massively parallel multiprocessors, with hundreds or thousands of processors. Multiprocessor architectures with distributed memory systems, where interprocessor communication is by message-passing, avoid most of the contention problems inherent in the use of single shared memories and buses. Such computers can provide extremely high performance, but they also pose problems in algorithm and program design that are far from being satisfactorily solved.

Various static and dynamic interconnection structures have been proposed for massively parallel multiprocessors. Static structures like hypercubes and trees are easier to build and control when many processors are involved. Dedicated buses or IO communication lines typically serve as interprocessor links. Neighboring processors can then interact at the maximum possible rate, with little interference from other processors. Interconnection networks are selected to trade hardware cost for communication speed in some class of applications. The hypercube structure achieves a good balance between these parameters. Consequently, it has been used in several commercial computers of the massively parallel type [Hayes and Mudge 1989].

An n-dimensional hypercube computer is characterized by the presence of 2^n nodes, each consisting of a processor and its local memory. Each processor P_i has direct links to n other processors (its *neighbors*); these links form the edges of the hypercube. A set of 2^n distinct n-bit binary addresses can be assigned to the processors in such a way that P_i's address differs from each of its neighbors in exactly 1 bit; Figure 7.60c illustrates hypercube addressing for $n = 3$. Hypercubes have several attractive features:

- A hypercube can be expanded or scaled up while maintaining a good balance between the number of nodes and the cost of internode communication. As n is incremented by one, the number of nodes doubles, but the node degree and the maximum internode distance both increase only by one (from n to $n + 1$).
- A hypercube is homogeneous in that the system appears the same when viewed from any of its nodes. This feature simplifies programming because all nodes can execute the same programs on different data when collaborating on a common task.
- We can embed other useful interconnection structures, such as rings and meshes, efficiently in the hypercube. We say that (graph) G is *embeddable* in H if and only if every node in G can be mapped into a distinct node in H such that all nodes that are neighbors in G are also neighbors in H. In other words, G is embeddable in H if we can find an exact (isomorphic) copy of G inside H.
- A large hypercube can support multiple concurrent users with each user program assigned to a private embedded hypercube or *subcube* that is disjoint from other users' subcubes. For example, in a four-dimensional hypercube (Figure 7.66b), four-node subcubes can be assigned to two users, and an eight-node subcube can be assigned to a third user.

Embeddability can be used to compare different interconnection structures for multiprocessors. Let C_1 with (static) interconnection network N_1 and C_2 with interconnection network N_2 be computers employing similar processors. If N_1 is

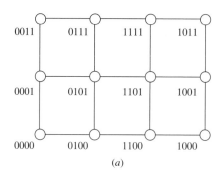

(a)

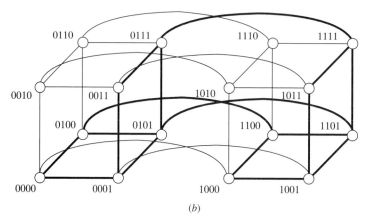

(b)

Figure 7.66
(a) A 3×4 mesh and (b) embedding the mesh in a four-dimensional
hypercube.

embeddable in a sufficiently large version of N_2, then C_2 will be able to *embed* C_1.
Therefore, any structure embeddable in C_1 is also embeddable in C_2, and C_2 is at
least as powerful as C_1 from a static structural viewpoint. Referring to Figure 7.11,
it is obvious that any k-node system can be embedded in a system of k or more
nodes with the structure of a complete graph (Figure 7.11f). A sufficiently big
mesh-structured system can embed any path or ring. It cannot, however, embed a
hypercube, since for $n > 4$, every node of an n-dimensional hypercube has greater
degree than every node of the mesh. A hypercube can embed both the ring and the
star structures. Less obvious is the fact that a mesh can be embedded in a hypercube. An embedding of the 12-node 3×4 mesh into the 16-node four-dimensional
hypercube appears in Figure 7.66. Heavy lines show the nodes and edges of the
hypercube that correspond to those of the mesh.

EXAMPLE 7.10 THE nCUBE HYPERCUBE MULTIPROCESSOR [HAYES AND
MUDGE 1989; nCUBE 1990]. Hypercube multiprocessors were proposed as early as
1962 at the University of Michigan, but the first working machine was not demonstrated until the completion of the six-dimensional (64-node) Cosmic Cube computer at
Caltech in 1983. Influenced by this work, several commercial hypercube computers

were introduced in the mid-1980s, including Intel's iPSC series and the nCUBE (then written NCUBE) series developed by nCUBE Corp. The original nCUBE 1 family included hypercubes of various sizes up to a 10-dimensional (1024 node) machine. Subsequent nCUBE computers increased the number of nodes to $8192 = 2^{13}$.

An nCUBE processor node is equipped with a set of high-speed IO channels, each consisting of a serial input line and a serial output line. One channel connects to a host or front-end computer; the remaining channels connect the node to its neighbors in the hypercube. Processor-to-processor communication is implemented by transmitting messages between buffer areas in the local memories of communicating nodes. Each interprocessor link has both an address register pointing to its message buffer area and a count register indicating the number of bytes to be sent or received. Once a processor initiates a message transfer, the processor can continue with other tasks while the interprocessor message transfer proceeds as a DMA operation between the memories of the communicating nodes. A broadcasting instruction is also supported that allows the same data to be transmitted to all processors in the hypercube; see problem 7.38.

First we consider interprocessor communication in an nCUBE 1 system. Assume that an n-dimensional subcube is assigned to the user and that the message source and destination nodes have the binary addresses $S = s_{n-1}...s_1s_0$ and $D = d_{n-1}...d_1d_0$, respectively. The EXCLUSIVE-OR function $R = S \oplus D = r_{n-1}...r_1r_0$, where $r_i = s_i \oplus d_i$ for $i = 0,1,...,n - 1$, controls the routing process. The values of i for which $r_i = 1$ indicate the dimensions of the hypercube to be traversed by a message en route from source to destination. The operating system kernel residing in each node that receives the message reads the destination address D (a field in the message header); computes $R = P \oplus D$, where P is the address of the current node; and scans R from left to right until it encounters some $r_j = 1$. Node P then forwards the message to the neighboring node P' whose address differs from P's in the jth bit. If $R = 0$, then $P = D$ and P recognizes itself as the destination node and proceeds to process the message. Thus in a six-node subcube of the nCUBE 1, a message being sent from node 7 to node 45 passes through nodes with the following sequence of addresses:

$$S = 000111 \to 100111 \to 101111 \to 101101 = D$$

This *store-and-forward* routing method sends each message along a shortest path so that the minimum number of intermediate nodes relay messages between the source and destination. In the nCUBE 2 computer, each node P contains a high-speed message-routing unit that allows messages for other units to pass though P without affecting P's ongoing operations; this approach largely eliminates the need to temporarily store messages in intermediate nodes.

A node of the nCUBE 2 consists of a full-custom 64-bit CPU on a single IC, plus a six-chip local memory. The CPU's architecture resembles that of the Digital VAX family; it has a CISC-style instruction set with fixed-point and floating-point arithmetic instructions and all the logic necessary for memory management and IO control. Its speedup features include a four-stage instruction pipeline, an I-cache and a D-cache, as well as the special message router noted already. The local memory size can range up to 64 MB per node, so an 8192-node system can have a distributed memory of 256 GB. With a modest clock rate of 20 MHz, each processor delivers about 2.4 MFLOPS (assuming 64-bit operations), implying a peak performance of around $2.4 \times 8192 = 19.7$ GFLOPS, so the nCUBE 2 was classed as a massively parallel "supercomputer."

The structure of an nCUBE 2 system is outlined in Figure 7.67. The hypercube array of processors H is packaged into printed-circuit boards, each of which contains a 64-node hypercube forming a subcube of H. Each processor has 14 communication channels, one of which connects to an IO subsystem, such as a "farm" of IO disks forming the system's secondary memory. Many IO channels to the hypercube array enable a large number of peripherals to operate in parallel to satisfy the nCUBE's

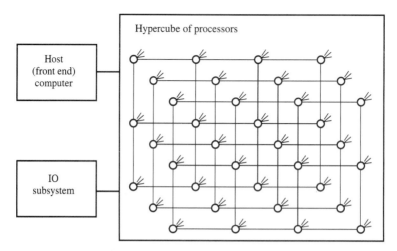

Figure 7.67
Organization of the nCUBE 2 hypercube multiprocessor.

massive computation ability. Each channel is controlled by the nCUBE processor used in the hypercube array. Disk storage capacity can exceed a terabyte (2^{40} bytes), making the nCUBE well suited to the management of very large databases.

The nCUBE operating system provides all the usual UNIX system management and programmer support functions (see Example 7.8). It treats a hypercube of processors as a device, which in the UNIX philosophy is a special type of file. Consequently, a hypercube of any size can be opened, closed, written into, and read from like any other UNIX file. This feature permits the operating system to allocate independent subcubes to different users so that one or two large applications or many small applications can share the processor hypercube concurrently.

Multistage interconnection networks. Dynamic interconnection networks for multiprocessors can be constructed from two-state switching elements of the kind depicted in Figure 7.68. Each switch S has a pair of input data buses X_1, X_2; a pair of output data buses Z_1, Z_2; and some control logic (not shown). All four buses are identical and can function as processor-processor or processor-memory links. S has two states determined by the control line c: a *through* or *direct* state T, as illustrated in Figure 7.68b where $Z_1 = X_1$ (Z_1 is connected to X_1) and $Z_2 = X_2$, and a *cross* state X where $Z_1 = X_2$ and $Z_2 = X_1$ (Figure 7.68c).

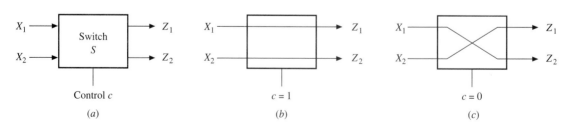

Figure 7.68
(*a*) Switching element; (*b*) through state T; (*c*) cross state X.

By using S as a building block, *multistage interconnection networks (MINs)* can be constructed for use in massively parallel computers [Siegel 1990]. Figure 7.69 shows a small MIN that has 12 switching elements arranged into three stages (columns) and is intended to provide dynamic connections among eight processors denoted P_{000}:P_{111}. By setting the control signals of the switching elements in various ways, many different interconnection patterns are possible. The processor-to-processor connections that are possible depend on the number of stages, the fixed connections linking the stages, and the settings of the switching elements. The particular MIN in Figure 7.69 is called an 8×8 *omega* network. A large version of this MIN was used in the experimental Cedar multiprocessor designed at the University of Illinois in the 1980s. We now examine the major characteristics of some typical MINs, concentrating on those designed for processor-to-processor communication.

An $N \times N$ MIN *SN* provides a flexible set of communication links between N processors, which are the sources and destinations of *SN*. Since the processors are identified by n-bit binary addresses, it is convenient to make $N = 2^n$. The processor-pairs that are connected to each other at any time by *SN* are determined by the states of the switching elements, each of which can be in either the through (T) or cross (X) state. Control logic associated with the MIN sets the switch states dynamically to satisfy interconnection requests from the processors. A particular MIN state is retained long enough to allow at least one package to be transferred through the network. The state then changes to match the source-destination requirements of the next set of packages, and so on. We assume that a processor can buffer or queue its outgoing packages until the MIN is ready to transfer them. The processors accept incoming packages as soon as they arrive.

A fundamental requirement of a MIN is that it be possible to connect every processor P_i to every other processor P_j using at least one configuration of the network; this feature is termed the *full-access* property. It is easy to show that the omega network of Figure 7.69 is a full-access network. Figure 7.70 shows the

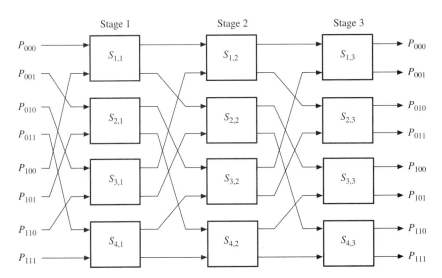

Figure 7.69
Three-stage 8×8 omega multistage interconnection network (MIN).

Destination	Stage 1	Stage 2	Stage 3
P_{001}	$S_{1,1} = T$	$S_{1,2} = T$	$S_{1,3} = X$
P_{010}	$S_{1,1} = T$	$S_{1,2} = X$	$S_{2,3} = T$
P_{011}	$S_{1,1} = T$	$S_{1,2} = X$	$S_{2,3} = X$
P_{100}	$S_{1,1} = X$	$S_{2,2} = T$	$S_{3,3} = T$
P_{101}	$S_{1,1} = X$	$S_{2,2} = T$	$S_{3,3} = X$
P_{110}	$S_{1,1} = X$	$S_{2,2} = X$	$S_{4,3} = T$
P_{111}	$S_{1,1} = X$	$S_{2,2} = X$	$S_{4,3} = X$

Figure 7.70
Switch settings of the three-stage omega network of Figure 7.69 to connect P_{000} to each of the other processors.

seven unique switch configurations needed to connect P_{000} to each of the other processors; here $S_{i,j} = T$ (X) indicates that switch i of stage j is set to the through (cross) state. A complete network configuration in which P_{000} is connected to P_{001} appears in Figure 7.71. In this state the network also connects P_{010}, P_{100}, and P_{110} to P_{011}, P_{101}, and P_{111}, respectively, thus providing simultaneous communication among four processor-pairs. Reducing the number of stages from three to two eliminates the full-access property.

Another useful property of a MIN is the ability to establish a connection between any pair of processors that are not using the network, without altering the switch settings already established to link other processors; this is the *nonblocking* property. The three-stage omega MIN of Figure 7.69 does not have this property and is therefore a *blocking* network. For example, suppose that P_{000} is already connected to P_{001}; this condition requires the top row of switches to be set to T T X, as specified in Figures 7.70 and 7.71. It is now impossible to connect P_{100} either to P_{010} or to P_{011}. The preexisting setting of $S_{1,1}$ creates a path from P_{100} through stage

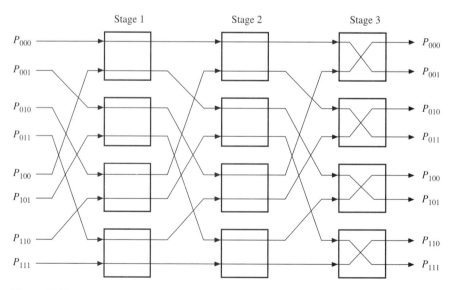

Figure 7.71
One state of the three-stage omega network.

1 to $S_{2,2}$. No links exist from $S_{2,2}$ to $S_{2,3}$, the third-stage switching element connected to P_{010} and P_{011}; hence $S_{2,2}$ cannot be set to forward data to P_{010} or P_{011}. This type of blocking causes communication delays similar to those occurring in a single-bus system when several processors attempt to use the system bus simultaneously. Nonblocking MINs require an excessive number of switches for most computer applications. An $N \times N$ crossbar switch is an example of a nonblocking network because it allows any idle row to be connected to any idle column. However, it contains N^2 complex crosspoint switches, whereas an $N \times N$ omega network contains only $(N/2) \log_2 N$ simpler 2×2 switches.

A few basic interstage wiring patterns characterize the most common MIN types proposed for multiprocessors. Each such pattern is a mapping ψ from a set of sources $\{S_i\}$ to a set of destinations $\{D_{\psi(i)}\}$ for $i = 0, 1, \ldots, N-1$. Here S_i is the address of an output port of a processor or switching element, and $D_{\psi(i)}$ is the address of the input port to which S_i is wired. The *shuffle* pattern is defined by the following mapping:

$$\sigma(i) = 2i + \lfloor (2i)/N \rfloor \quad (\text{modulo } N) \tag{7.18}$$

Here σ is the shuffle function illustrated by Figure 7.72a for $N = 8$. The name *shuffle* comes from the fact that the destination addresses 0, 1, 2, 3, 4, 5, 6, 7 can be mapped into (connected to) the source addresses 0, 4, 1, 5, 2, 6, 3, 7 by interleaving the first half 0, 1, 2, 3 of the address sequence with the second half 4, 5, 6, 7 in the manner of a perfectly shuffled deck of cards. Let each address i be represented by the corresponding n-bit binary number $b_{n-1}b_{n-2}\ldots b_0$. An equivalent definition to (7.18) is

$$\sigma(i) = b_{n-2}b_{n-3} \cdots b_0 b_{n-1} \tag{7.19}$$

indicating that the shuffle function corresponds to rotating the source address 1 bit to the left to determine the destination address. By following a shuffle connection with $N/2$ switching elements, each of which can exchange (cross) a pair of buses, we obtain the single-stage *shuffle-exchange* network, shown in Figure 7.72b for the case $N = 8$. The omega network of Figure 7.69 is built from $n = \log_2 N$ shuffle-exchange stages.

Another useful class of MINs is based on the *butterfly* connection depicted in Figure 7.73a. The 4×4 single-stage butterfly network appears in Figure 7.73b; note that the butterfly connection is placed after, rather than before, the $N/2$ switching elements. Consider an $N \times N$ multistage network with n stages 1, 2, ..., n and N port addresses $i = 0, 1, \ldots, N-1$, where, as before, $i = b_{n-1}b_{n-2}\cdots b_0$. The kth *butterfly function* β_k is defined as follows for $k = 1, 2, \ldots, n-1$:

$$\beta_k(b_{n-1} \cdots b_{k+1}b_k b_{k-1} \cdots b_1 b_0) = b_{n-1} \cdots b_{k+1}b_0 b_{k-1} \cdots b_1 b_k$$

Thus β_k interchanges bits 0 and k of the source address to obtain the destination address. For example, when $k = 1$ and $N = 4$, we obtain

$$\beta_1(00) = 00$$
$$\beta_1(01) = 10$$
$$\beta_1(10) = 01$$
$$\beta_1(11) = 11$$

corresponding to the interconnection pattern on Figure 7.73a.

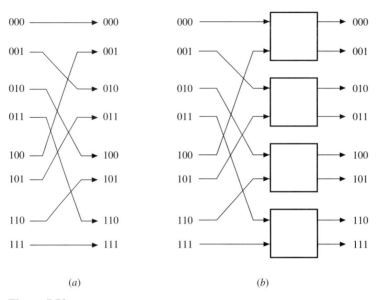

(a)   (b)

Figure 7.72
(a) Shuffle connection for $N = 8$ and (b) single-stage shuffle-exchange network.

The connection pattern defined by

$$\sigma^{-1}(i) = b_0 b_{n-2} b_{n-3} \cdots b_1 \tag{7.20}$$

is called the *inverse shuffle function* σ^{-1}. Equation (7.20) is the same as Equation (7.19), defining the shuffle function σ with the direction of the address bit rotation reversed. Figure 7.74 shows a 16×16 version of a MIN called the *indirect hypercube network*, which in the $N \times N$ case consists of $\log_2 N$ stages of $N/2$ switching elements; the wiring patterns following the stages are defined by β_1, β_2, ..., β_{n-1}, σ^{-1}. This MIN's name comes from the fact that it can easily simulate the connections of a static hypercube interconnection network; see problem 7.39.

Indirect hypercube and shuffle-exchange MINs have similar properties. Suppose that the directions of all the arrows in an $N \times N$ shuffle-exchange network are reversed, implying that the shuffle connection σ in each stage is replaced by σ^{-1}. The resulting $N \times N$ *inverse omega network* and the $N \times N$ indirect hypercube network are essentially the same MIN drawn in different ways. Consequently, for

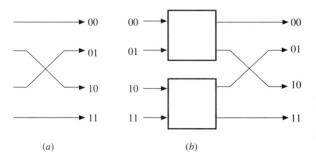

(a)   (b)

Figure 7.73
(a) Butterfly connection for $N = 4$ and (b) single-stage butterfly network.

each state of the indirect hypercube network, there is a state of the inverse omega
network that connects the N processors in exactly the same way, and vice versa. This equivalence is not obvious and explains the many names under which this class of MINs appears in the literature (inverse omega, indirect binary n-cube, butterfly, and so forth).

Since an address contains $n = \log_2 N$ bits, at least $n = \log_2 N$ stages must be present for an $N \times N$ MIN to have the full-access property. With this number of stages, it is also easy to determine the switch settings needed to connect an arbitrary pair of processors, since each stage controls 1 bit (dimension) of the address space. We illustrate this for the indirect hypercube MIN of Figure 7.74. Suppose that a source processor with binary address $S = s_{n-1}s_{n-2}\cdots s_0$ is to be connected to a destination processor with address $D = d_{n-1}d_{n-2}\cdots d_0$. As in the static hypercube

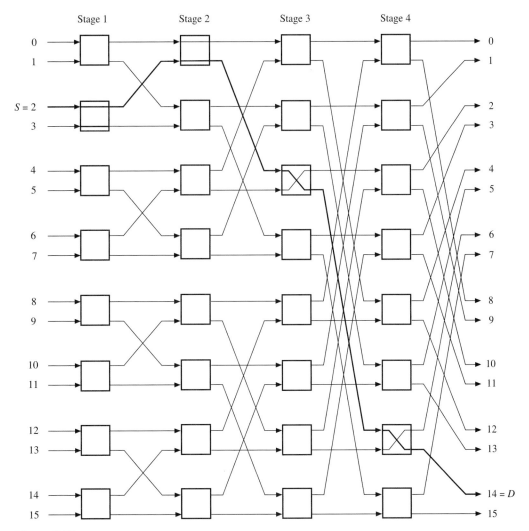

Figure 7.74
16×16 indirect hypercube network.

routing algorithm (Example 7.10), we compute $R = S \oplus D = r_{n-1}r_{n-2}\cdots r_0$, and use R to control the MIN's switch settings. If $r_i = 0$, then all the switches in stage $i + 1$ (assuming again that the stages are numbered 1, 2, ..., n) are set to the through (T) state; these switches are set to the cross (X) state if $r_i = 1$. For example, Figure 7.74 shows the switch settings to connect source $S = 2$ to destination $D = 14$. In this case $R = 0010 \oplus 1110 = 1100$, requiring two T and two X switch settings as indicated. The heavy lines in Figure 7.74 mark the path along which packages travel from S to D. If all switches are set to T, then $S = D$, so each processor is connected to itself via a path through $\log_2 N$ switches. Changing the state of the switch in stage $i + 1$ along this path from T to X connects the source processor to the destination processor that differs from it in the ith address bit. It follows that there is only one path through each of the foregoing ($\log_2 N$)-stage networks linking every source-destination pair.

The routing of packages through a MIN can be managed by a centralized controller attached to the network that examines all source-destination address pairs S, D generated by processors and sets the appropriate switching elements to the states specified by $R = S \oplus D$. An alternative is to attach R as a *routing tag* to each package to be transmitted from S to D and to use R to set the switching element states as the package passes through the MIN. When the package enters a switch $S_{j,i+1}$ in stage $i + 1$, $S_{j,i+1}$ examines the routing tag R using control logic built into the switch for this purpose. $S_{j,i+1}$ then sets its own state to T if $r_i = 0$, and to X if $r_i = 1$. Thus the centralized controller can be replaced by decentralized control logic distributed throughout the MIN. Each package determines its own path through the MIN and so can be viewed as *self-routing*. For example, to transmit a package from $S = 2$ to $D = 14$ in the four-stage MIN of Figure 7.74, the routing tag $R = r_3r_2r_1r_0 = 1100$ is appended to the package generated by the source processor P_2. The switch $S_{2,1}$ attached to P_2 in stage 1 inspects bit r_0 of R. Since $r_0 = 0$, switch $S_{2,1}$ sets itself to the through state T. This setting causes the package to be sent to the topmost switch $S_{1,2}$ in stage 2, which also sets its state to T, since $r_1 = 0$. The package proceeds to the final two stages, which set themselves to the cross state X, since $r_2 = r_3 = 1$.

The Butterfly computer developed by Bolt, Beranek and Newman Inc. around 1980 [Crowther et al. 1985] and its successor the TC2000 introduced in 1989 are examples of commercial multiprocessors based on MINs. They are shared-memory MIMD computers in which the MIN connects N processors to N memory units that form the shared memory. In the original Butterfly multiprocessor, the processors are based on the Motorola 680X0 series, and N ranges from 1 to 256. Every processor contains a microprogrammed coprocessor to handle virtual memory management, package transfer to and from the MIN, and related functions.

The Butterfly's MIN has single-chip 4×4 switching elements, each of which is obtained by cascading two copies of the basic butterfly network of Figure 7.72. Consequently, the processor-memory interconnection network is an $N \times N$ butterfly MIN composed of $\log_2 N$ stages of 2×2 switching elements. Data transmission through the network is by bit-serial packages, which can be transmitted at a rate of 32 Mb/s along any processor-memory path. Each package contains its destination address and is made self-routing in the manner described earlier by employing 2 bits of the destination address to determine the setting of each 4×4 switch through which the package passes. Should two packages attempt to use the same link in the MIN simultaneously, one is allowed to proceed and the other is retransmitted after a short delay. This type of application-dependent contention increases the execution time of a typical program by only a few percent.

7.3.3 Fault Tolerance

Fault tolerance has been defined as "the ability of a system to execute specified algorithms correctly regardless of hardware failures and program errors" [Avizienis 1971]. It is of some concern in all computer systems, while in applications such as spacecraft control and telephone switching, fault tolerance is a major design goal [Siewiorek and Swarz 1992]. Most hardware failures have physical causes such as component wear or electromagnetic interference. The nature and frequency of these failures can be determined experimentally, which makes it possible to study the faults and their consequences using analytic or simulation models. Software faults are primarily due to algorithm or programming mistakes (design errors) and so are more difficult to deal with.

Redundancy. Fault tolerance is intimately associated with the concept of redundancy. When a component fails, its duties must be taken over by other, fault-free components of the system. If those components are intended to improve only the reliability of the system and do not significantly affect its computing performance, they are termed *redundant*. Redundancy can be introduced in several overlapping ways:

- *Hardware redundancy*: Multiple copies of critical hardware units.
- *Software redundancy*: Multiple versions of programs for critical operations.
- *Information redundancy:* Error-correcting or error-detecting codes.
- *Time redundancy:* Repeating or retrying critical operations.

The goal of these redundant design features is to prevent failures due to physical faults or design mistakes from producing *errors*, that is, data values or operating modes that lead to system failure. Information redundancy via coding methods is discussed in section 3.2.1. In this section, we examine the use of redundant hardware to achieve fault tolerance.

Two broad approaches, static and dynamic redundancy, have been identified for designing fault-tolerant systems. *Static redundancy* refers to the use of redundant hardware or software components, which form a permanent part of the system, to mask the error signals generated by faults. One form of static redundancy replaces a critical unit that generates a word X with $n \geq 3$ copies of that unit, configured to generate n independent copies of X in parallel. If the unit in question is a processor, then the resulting system is a type of multiprocessor. The n versions of X are applied to a circuit called a *voter*, which is designed to output the value of X appearing on the majority of its n input buses. Thus errors produced by any of the replicated units are masked by the voter, provided more than half of the units produce the correct X values at all times. A system of this type with n identical units and a voter is said to employ *n-modular redundancy* (*nMR*).

A frequently implemented version of nMR is *triple modular redundancy* (*TMR*), in which $n = 3$, as shown in Figure 7.75. In this case the behavior of the voter is defined by the logic equation

$$X = X_1X_2 + X_1X_3 + X_2X_3$$

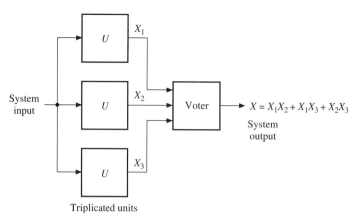

Figure 7.75
Example of triple modular redundancy (TMR).

where $+$ denotes the (word) OR operation; this is the well-known majority function. The voter's output X always has the correct value, assuming that no more than one of X_1, X_2, X_3 is incorrect and that the voter itself does not fail in a way that produces an erroneous output. Thus a TMR system can tolerate faulty behavior by any one of its triplicated units. Although static redundancy can be implemented at any complexity level, it is normally implemented at the processor level where the replicated units are CPUs, memory units, switching networks, or entire computers.

Dynamic redundancy tolerates faults by actively reorganizing the system so that the functions of the faulty unit are transferred to one or more fault-free units. The reorganization is usually achieved in three steps:

1. *Fault diagnosis*: Diagnostic procedures are carried out to detect the fault and isolate it to a replaceable or repairable unit.
2. *Fault elimination*: The fault is removed from the system either by repairing the faulty unit, replacing it by a spare, or logically reconfiguring the system around the fault.
3. *Recovery*: Procedures are executed to restore the system to a state that existed before the fault occurred. Normal operation is resumed from that point.

Although more complex to manage than static redundancy, dynamic redundancy has the advantage that faulty units can be rapidly eliminated from the system. In the static case faults can accumulate undetected until a total system failure occurs.

Figure 7.76 shows an example of a fault-tolerant system employing dynamic redundancy. It is called a *duplex* system because it contains two identical (duplicated) copies of the basic nonredundant or *simplex* unit. The two units operate in tandem, performing the same operations on the same (or duplicated) data at the same time. A circuit called a *match detector* or *equality checker* does a continuous comparison of the results generated by the duplicated units. When the match detector finds a mismatch indicating the occurrence of a fault, normal operation is suspended and a testing procedure is initiated to identify the faulty unit. Once identified, the faulty unit is disconnected from the system, logically if not physically. The system can then be restarted in simplex mode using only the fault-free unit. The failed unit can be repaired off-line and eventually restored to the system.

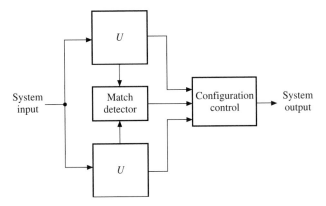

Figure 7.76
Example of a duplex system.

Redundant disk arrays. Magnetic hard disks (section 6.1.3) are the principal technology employed for secondary memory systems in computers. While providing large amounts of storage at low cost per bit, disk memories—both magnetic and optical—have several drawbacks.

- They have relatively slow data-transfer rates.
- Their electromechanical construction makes them prone to both transient and catastrophic failures.

A way to increase the data-transfer rate is to build a disk memory from an array of small disk units, all capable of operating in parallel. With n such parallel units, the effective data-transfer rate is n times that of a single unit. Furthermore, including redundant disk units in the array can improve fault tolerance. In the late 1980s these considerations led to a general approach to disk-memory design known as *redundant array of inexpensive disks* (RAID), which has since been widely adopted by manufacturers of disk memories [Chen et al. 1994].

The idea behind RAID is to distribute the stored data over a set of disks configured to appear like a single large disk. The data can be distributed in various ways referred to as RAID levels 0:6, or simply as RAID-0:6. The different RAID levels, all of which are illustrated in Figure 7.77, provide different performance-cost trade-offs. In RAID-0, the n disk units are intended to increase performance only. There is no redundancy for fault tolerance, and so the system is vulnerable to the failure of a single disk. RAID-1 is a duplex design with $2n$ instead of n units, where all data written onto one disk is duplicated on another. This high-cost approach has long been used under the name *disk mirroring* in applications that must recover instantly from a fault.

The remaining five RAID organizations have less redundancy and rely on various coding schemes to implement fault tolerance. RAID-2 employs error-correcting codes of the type found in RAMs and has extra disks to store check (parity) bits for all data words stored in the main disks. As discussed in section 3.2.1, to achieve single-error correction, we need c check bits for every n data bits, where $2^c \geq n + c + 1$. Therefore, $c \approx \log_2 n$ redundant disk units are required to tolerate single errors. The $n + c$ disks of RAID 2 can be thought of as storing $(n + c)$-bit words, with one particular bit position assigned to each disk in interleaved fashion. (Other

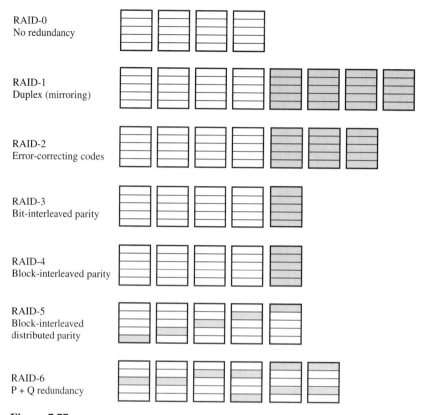

RAID-0
No redundancy

RAID-1
Duplex (mirroring)

RAID-2
Error-correcting codes

RAID-3
Bit-interleaved parity

RAID-4
Block-interleaved parity

RAID-5
Block-interleaved
distributed parity

RAID-6
P + Q redundancy

Figure 7.77
Redundant arrays of inexpensive disks (RAID); shaded blocks denote redundant data.

noninterleaved storage patterns are also allowed.) When an inconsistent check bit is detected during a read operation, the erroneous codeword identifies the erroneous bit and hence the faulty disk that contains it.

It is not necessary to have RAID in order to *detect* an error in a disk unit, since the unit's controller can easily do so via its internal, conventional mechanisms for error detection. Hence it is enough to store a single parity bit in order to correct, and therefore tolerate, a single error in any word. This approach is the basis of RAID-3, where each $(n + 1)$-bit data word $b_{i,n-1}b_{i,n-2}\cdots b_{i,0}p_i$ is spread over an $(n + 1)$-unit disk array. One (redundant) disk stores all the parity bits $\{p_i\}$, and its contents are computed on the fly via a parity equation of the form:

$$p_i = b_{i,n-1} \oplus b_{i,n-2} \oplus \cdots \oplus b_{i,j} \oplus \cdots \oplus b_{i,0} \qquad (7.21)$$

If an error is detected in disk j, then the lost or damaged $b_{i,j}$s in disk j can be recovered from the remaining n disks according to the following equation implied by (7.21).

$$b_{i,j} = b_{i,n-1} \oplus b_{i,n-2} \oplus \cdots \oplus b_{i,j-1} \oplus b_{i,j+1} \oplus \cdots \oplus b_{i,0} \oplus p_i$$

Intuitively, the parity disk stores the "sum" of the data on the other disks. On a disk failure the lost data is obtained by "subtracting" the data on the $n - 1$ good disks from the contents of the parity disk. (Recall that the EXCLUSIVE-OR operation $\oplus$ corresponds to sum or difference modulo 2).

The RAID-4 scheme is similar to RAID-3 except that blocks of arbitrary size are interleaved, rather than individual bits. Because the single parity disk tends to act as a bottleneck—it does not participate in read operations, for example—RAID-5, which distributes the parity bits evenly over all available disks, is preferred to RAID-4. In RAID-4 and 5, write operations, especially short writes, are complicated and performance is reduced by the fact that it is necessary to read all the disk units, including units not being written into, in order to compute the new parity bits. The final scheme, RAID-6, uses two redundant disk units and multibit error-correcting codes to tolerate the failure of up to two disk units.

Reliability. The ability of a system to tolerate faults can be measured in several ways. One useful fault-tolerance measure is *availability,* defined as the fraction of its operating lifetime during which the system is not disabled by faults. The availability of the AT&T No. 1 Electronic Switching System (ESS), one of the earliest computer-controlled telephone exchanges (first deployed in the 1960s), was specified at two hours of downtime over an expected operating life of 40 years. This value is equivalent to an availability of 99.9994 percent.

A more common fault-tolerance measure is *reliability $R(t)$,* defined as the probability of a unit or system surviving (functioning correctly) for a period of duration t. The reliability of a unit can be estimated from the failure statistics for a large number of samples of the unit. The *failure rate* is the fraction of the samples that fail per unit time. For most physical devices, the failure rate varies with time in the manner shown in Figure 7.78. During the early life of the unit (the *burn-in* period), a high failure rate is experienced that reflects faults occurring during manufacture or installation. A high failure rate is again encountered toward the end of the unit's life (the *wear-out* period). During most of the unit's working life, however, failures can be expected to occur randomly at a fairly constant rate; this period corresponds to the flat central part of the "bathtub" curve of Figure 7.78.

Analytic approaches based on probability theory have long been successfully used to study the reliability of computer systems. Suppose that $N(0)$ copies of a unit such as a CPU begin their operating life (after the burn-in period) at time $t = 0$. Let $N(t)$ be the number of units surviving after time t so that the number of failed units $N_f(t)$ is $N(0) - N(t)$. The reliability $R(t)$ of the unit is given by the fraction of

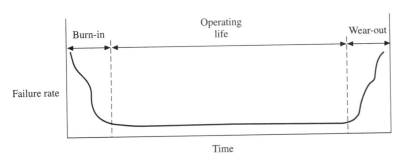

Figure 7.78
Typical variation of failure rate with time.

surviving units at time t; that is

$$R(t) = \frac{N(t)}{N(0)} \tag{7.22}$$

which can be interpreted as the probability of any unit surviving to time t. Let λ denote the unit's failure rate, which, in accordance with Figure 7.78, is assumed to be constant. Therefore, the number of units dN_f that fail during the small interval of time from t to $t + dt$ is given by

$$dN_f = \lambda N(t)\, dt \tag{7.23}$$

Now $N(t) = N(0) - N_f(t)$ and $N(0)$ is independent of t; hence $dN = -dN_f$. Substituting into Equation (7.23), we obtain

$$dN = -\lambda N(t)\, dt$$

Now (7.23) implies that $dR = dN/dN(0)$; hence $dR = -\lambda N(t)\, dt/N(0)$. Using (7.23) again to replace $N(t)/N(0)$ by $R(t)$, we obtain

$$\frac{dR}{dt} = -\lambda R(t)$$

Integration with the boundary value $R(0) = 1$ yields

$$R(t) = e^{-\lambda t} \tag{7.24}$$

This classical *exponential law* of failure is very often used to model the reliability of the components in a computer system.

From the reliability $R(t)$ we can obtain a single number MTTF called the *mean time to failure,* which is a useful measure of the expected working life of a unit. Letting $F(t)$ denote the *unreliability* $1 - R(t)$, MTTF can be defined as follows:

$$\text{MTTF} = \int_0^\infty tf(t)dt \text{ where } f(t) = \frac{dF(t)}{dt} \tag{7.25}$$

The MTTF corresponding to the exponential reliability function (7.24) is

$$\text{MTTF} = \int_0^\infty t\lambda e^{-\lambda t}dt = \frac{1}{\lambda}$$

so the expected working life of a unit with an exponentially distributed reliability is the reciprocal of its failure rate.

System reliability. Once the failure rates of its individual units are known or can be estimated, it becomes possible to calculate the reliability of the entire system. Two basic circuit system structures from a reliability point of view are the series and parallel configurations appearing in Figure 7.79. In a *series* system (Figure 7.79a), it is assumed that if any component fails, the entire system fails. Hence the system reliability which, for brevity, we denote by R instead of $R(t)$, is a product of the component reliabilities.

$$R = \prod_{i=1}^n R_i$$

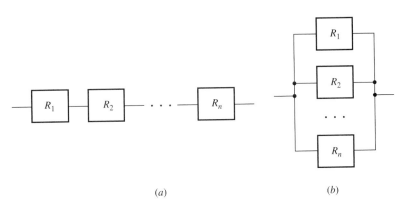

(a)   (b)

Figure 7.79
Two basic reliability structures: (a) series and (b) parallel.

In a *parallel* system (Figure 7.79b), on the other hand, all components must fail in order for the system to fail. Hence the system's unreliability $F = 1 - R$ is the product of the component unreliabilities $1 - R_i$, from which it follows that

$$R = 1 - \prod_{i=1}^{n} (1 - R_i) \tag{7.26}$$

As these equations show, putting units in series decreases reliability, while putting units in parallel increases reliability. A parallel connection of n units is a basic fault-tolerant structure; we find it, for example, in duplex and TMR systems, where $n = 2$ and 3, respectively.

Systems can sometimes be decomposed into series and parallel subsystems, and their reliability can be calculated by repeated application of the preceding equations. For example, the series-parallel system S in Figure 7.80 consists of two subsystems S_1 and S_2, which are connected in series; S_1 and S_2 are themselves parallel systems. Assuming that each individual unit has reliability R, the system reliability $R(S)$ is given by

$$R(S) = [1 - (1 - R)^3][1 - (1 - R)^2]$$
$$= 6R^2 - 9R^3 + 5R^4 - R^5$$

Let us now apply the preceding equations to a TMR system like Figure 7.75. We can view it as three parallel copies of U in series with a voter V. Assume that

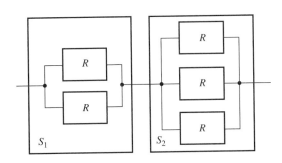

Figure 7.80
Example of a series-parallel system.

each of the triplicated units has reliability $R_1(t) = e^{-\lambda t}$ and that the voter has reliability $R_v(t) = e^{-\lambda_v t}$. Let $P_i(t)$ be the probability of any i of the triplicated units surviving to time t. The system reliability $R_3(t)$ is then given by

$$R_3(t) = [P_2(t) + P_3(t)]R_v(t)$$

Now $P_2(t) = \binom{3}{2}(e^{-\lambda t})^2(1 - e^{-\lambda t})$, while $P_3(t) = (e^{-\lambda t})^3$; hence

$$R_3(t) = (3e^{-2\lambda t} - 2e^{-3\lambda t})e^{-\lambda_v t} \tag{7.27}$$

The voter is usually much simpler than the functional units; consequently, its reliability is very high. If we assume $R_v(t) = 1$, that is, if we ignore the possibility of voter failure, then Equation (7.27) reduces to

$$R_3(t) = 3e^{-2\lambda t} - 2e^{-3\lambda t} \tag{7.28}$$

Figure 7.81 plots this equation for $\lambda = 0.01$. The reliability of a single unit $R_1(t) = e^{-\lambda t}$ is shown for comparison. For values of R less than about $0.7/\lambda$, the reliability of the TMR system is greater than that of the simplex system; beyond this point its reliability is less. In practice, TMR reliability can be higher than the foregoing analysis suggests, since the system may continue to function correctly even if two units fail. For example, if the two failed units never generate incorrect output signals at the same time, then the voter still produces the correct output.

The unreliability density function $f(t)$ corresponding to (7.28) is

$$f(t) = \frac{d}{dt}[1 - R_3(t)] = 6e^{-2\lambda t} - 6e^{-3\lambda t}$$

Substituting into (7.25) yields the mean time to failure $MTTF_3$ for a TMR system.

$$MTTF_3 = \int_0^\infty t(6e^{-2\lambda t} - 6e^{-3\lambda t})dt \tag{7.29}$$

Integrating (7.29) by parts, we obtain

$$MTTF_3 = [t(-3e^{-2\lambda t} + 2e^{-3\lambda t})]_0^\infty - \int_0^\infty (-3e^{-2\lambda t} + 2e^{-3\lambda t})dt = \frac{5}{6\lambda}$$

Since the MTTF of the corresponding simplex system is $1/\lambda$, the MTTF of the TMR system is the smaller of the two. These values are consistent with Figure 7.81, which shows that while the TMR system's initial reliability is high, it falls off more rapidly than the simplex reliability as the two systems age.

The foregoing reliability analysis considered only static systems in which there are no maintenance or repair activities. No matter how fault tolerant we make such a system, it can be expected that its reliability $R(t) \rightarrow 0$ as $t \rightarrow \infty$. With repair, however, it is possible to increase the chances of the system functioning correctly at time t beyond $R(t)$ to a value termed the (instantaneous) availability $A(t)$. In general, $A(t)$ is the sum of $R(t)$, the probability that no faults occurred up to time t, and the probability that the system failed before t but was repaired and continues to survive. With regular repair we can make $A(t)$ approach a nonzero steady-state value as t increases. The working life of a dynamic system that is always repaired after a failure occurs consists of an alternating sequence of periods of fault-free normal operation and periods during which the system is down for repairs. The system's

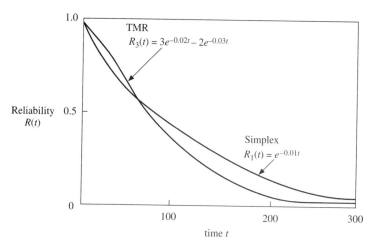

Figure 7.81
Reliability comparison between TMR and simplex systems.

actual availability, therefore, over its entire lifetime L is the ratio of its total fault-free working life to L. If the repair process makes the system "as good as new," then the expected (average) duration between the completion of a repair and the occurrence of the next fault is the system's MTTF. Similarly, we may characterize the duration of the repair process by the *mean time to repair* (MTTR), which is the expected time between system failure and the completion of repair. The expected availability A of the system, which is usually what is meant by the term *availability*, is therefore given by the following useful formula:

$$A = \frac{\text{MTTF}}{\text{MTTF} + \text{MTTR}} \tag{7.30}$$

The denominator MTTF + MTTR is referred to as the *mean time between failures* (MTBF) and is approximately the same as MTTF when MTTR is very small. Equation (7.30) indicates that availability can be increased either by increasing the system's inherent reliability, as indicated by MTTF, or by reducing the time needed for repair after a fault occurs.

We conclude with an example of a commercial fault-tolerant multiprocessor series, the Tandem NonStop, whose technology evolution reflects that of the computer industry in general [Kong 1994]. This series began in 1976 with the NonStop I, a small-scale multiprocessor based on bipolar (TTL) MSI integrated circuit technology. Its CPU was a custom-designed 16-bit processor of the CISC type, with a hardwired, stack-oriented organization. Operating at a clock frequency of 10 MHz, CPU performance was about 0.7 MIP. The NonStop I had no cache, a virtual memory of 512 KB, and each system contained from 2 to 16 processors. A decade and several models later, the Tandem VLX (1986) employed bipolar (ECL) gate-array ICs and a 32-bit microprogrammed architecture incorporating such speedup techniques as pipelining and a 64KB unified cache. The CPU performance had increased to 3.0 MIPS at 12 MHz, and virtual memory had expanded to 1 GB. The Tandem Himalaya series, introduced in 1993, employs the MIPS R4400 64-bit microprocessor, an off-the-shelf CMOS RISC. This superscalar microprocessor supports a two-level cache and a virtual memory of 2^{64} B; its performance is in the 100 MIPS range at 200 MHz. Tandem's Himalaya systems are designed in two- or four-processor clusters built around a high-speed shared bus. Massively parallel systems containing hundreds of processors can be constructed by linking clusters together via a large-scale interconnection network with a meshlike structure. Tandem's goal of high performance coupled with high hardware and software integrity has increasingly become the concern of the entire computer industry.

EXAMPLE 7.11 THE TANDEM NONSTOP HIMALAYA MULTIPROCESSOR [KONG 1994]. Starting in the mid-1970s, Tandem Computers Inc. was the first computer maker to focus on commercial applications with high availability as the principal design goal. An important example is on-line transaction processing (OLTP), such as securities trading or on-line ticket reservation, where even a brief system shutdown can entail huge economic losses. Applications of this sort also tend to have very high performance requirements. Tandem's "NonStop" architectural approach was developed with the following specific objectives:

- A system organization that prevents any one hardware fault—a *single-point failure*—from causing a crash or compromising the integrity of the system or applications software
- Dynamic on-line detection of faults, removal of faulty units for repair, and return of repaired units to service while redundant components keep the system in operation
- Scalability that allows processor, memory, and IO capacity to be increased without affecting the application's software.

To meet these objectives and remain cost competitive with mainstream computer manufacturers, Tandem opted for a modular multiprocessor architecture in which the multiple processors provide much of the redundancy needed both for fault tolerance and for high performance. Components that are not naturally redundant such as the power supply, system bus, and IO controllers are duplicated to ensure that all their single-point failures can be masked. For example, disk mirroring (RAID-1) is used to automatically create backup copies for all data in secondary memory. Standard coding techniques check for errors occurring in the major data paths and main memory. The NonStop operating system kernel is built around duplex, distributed processes that exchange messages for interprocess communication. Hard disks and other IO devices are connected to two IO controllers, one of which "owns" each device. IO device ownership can be switched by the operating system at any time. Software control of each IO device resides in a redundant primary/backup pair of processes. The primary process manages the device but also sends "checkpoint" information to the backup process to keep it up-to-date in case it must take control of the IO device. User processes are handled in a similar way; when a user process starts on one processor, a backup copy of the same process is automatically started on another processor.

Figure 7.82 shows the structure of a four-processor cluster or "section," which is the basic hardware building block of every NonStop system. Each processor contains a CPU, a portion of main memory, and an IO processor. The processors in a section communicate with one another via a high-speed interprocessor bus, the Dynabus, which is duplicated. A set of IO buses (channels) links each processor to a set of IO controllers so that every IO controller is connected to two processors. The processors in a section are tightly linked via the Dynabus. The sections, in turn, can communicate via a LAN-style network to form a loosely coupled system containing tens or hundreds of clusters. Such configurations are well suited to OLTP servers, which typically deal with huge numbers of largely independent tasks.

Although, as noted above, the Tandem family has evolved steadily to embrace advances in hardware technology, the overall design philosophy depicted in Figure 7.82 has remained remarkably intact from one generation to the next. The original Nonstop I (1976) was based on a custom-designed 16-bit CISC processor; recent products like the Himalaya series (1993) use off-the-shelf 64-bit RISC microprocessors. Each Himalaya CPU actually contains two R4400s operating in lockstep, with one processor (the slave) serving as a check on the other (the master). The Himalaya also introduces a novel type of interconnection network, referred to as TorusNet, which uses fiber-optic cables to connect the clusters. Clusters (sections) can be linked together in a ring network, and each cluster participates in separate H (horizontal) and V (vertical) rings. The TorusNet H and V rings accommodate up to 4 and 14 clusters, respectively, so 56 clusters or 224 processors can be connected in this way. As illustrated by Figure 7.83, the interconnection network has a toroidal structure in which every cluster is directly linked to four others, and indirectly to all the clusters in the system. By providing many alternative paths among its processors, a large Himalaya system can tolerate the simultaneous failure of several of its clusters and their interconnections.

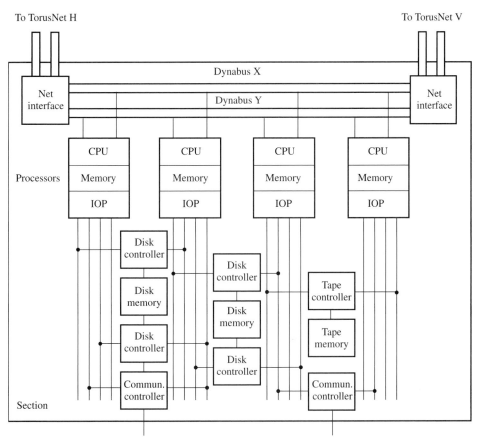

Figure 7.82
Processor cluster (section) in Tandem NonStop computers.

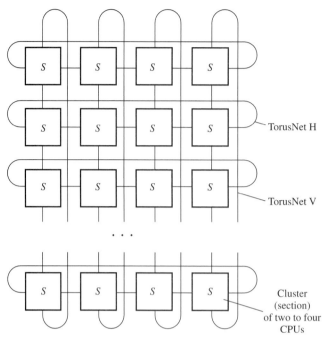

Figure 7.83
Toroidal interconnection network of the Tandem Himalaya
computer.

7.4
SUMMARY

The communication methods used in a computer system depend on the physical
distances involved. Intrasystem communication uses shared buses that transmit
binary signals a word at a time over short distances. Intersystem communication,
on the other hand, is implemented using serial-by-bit data transmission. Many
interconnection structures and transmission media are possible, and they offer various trade-offs between bandwidth and cost. Data transfer over a shared bus can be
synchronous with clock control or asynchronous with handshaking control signals.
At any time only two units can be logically connected to the bus: a bus master,
such as a CPU, an IO processor (IOP), or a direct memory access (DMA) controller, and a bus slave such as a memory unit or an IO port. Arbitration techniques
such as daisy chaining or polling determine which of several requesting units gains
access to the bus. Buses are characterized by the numbers and types of data,
address, and control lines they contain and by the conventions (protocols) they use
for signal selection, synchronization, and arbitration. Standard buses such as the
PCI bus are widely used as system or IO (local) buses.

 A computer network is a connected set of computers and other system components separated by large physical distances. Various standards exist for computer
networks, with the seven-layer OSI Reference Model providing general guidelines
for standardization. A representative standard architecture for local-area network
(LANs) is Ethernet, which employs a shared cable link and CSMA/CD arbitration.

Input-output systems are distinguished by the extent of CPU involvement in IO operations. The use of CPU programs to control all phases of an IO operation is called programmed IO. By providing IO devices with DMA and IO interrupt control, data transfers can be implemented independently of the CPU. Maximum speed and independence are achieved by providing IOPs capable of executing their own programs to manage IO operations. Overall management of a computer is handled by an operating system, which is responsible for efficient sharing of a computer's central processing, memory, and IO resources, both hardware and software. The operating system supervises a set of concurrent processes, which implement system and user tasks. Among the more widely used operating systems are UNIX, used primarily in workstations, and Windows, used in personal computers.

The motivations for introducing parallelism into computer systems are higher performance and reliability. Many methods have been proposed for classifying computer parallelism. A distinction is made between shared-memory and distributed-memory (message-passing) computers; parallel processors are also classified by their interconnection structures. Examples of static interconnections are meshes and hypercubes, while dynamic interconnections are exemplified by shared buses and multistage interconnection networks (MINs). The performance of a parallel processor depends on its architecture and the programs it executes. A basic performance measure is the speedup $S(n)$, defined as the ratio of execution time on a sequential computer to execution time on a comparable computer of parallelism n. The speedups achieved in practice are less than n due to such effects as memory contention and the presence of nonparallelizable code.

A computer containing more than one CPU is a multiprocessor. The CPUs can be tightly coupled via shared memory or loosely coupled via messages transmitted between the processors' local memories. Multiprocessors have been designed around various interconnection networks of which the shared bus is the most common. Advances in VLSI technology have made it feasible to construct massively parallel distributed-memory machines using such interconnection structures as hypercubes. Some large multiprocessors rely on MINs like the omega network for processor-memory or processor-processor communication. A few multiprocessors have fault tolerance as a primary design goal, which they achieve via various forms of static or dynamic redundancy; for example, n-modular redundancy (nMR). Fault tolerance is measured by reliability, availability, and the mean times to failure (MTTF) and repair (MTTR).

7.5
PROBLEMS

7.1. Explain why the single shared bus is so widely used as an interconnection medium in both sequential and parallel computers. What are its main disadvantages?

7.2. A useful characteristic of an interconnection network represented by an n-node graph G is its *bisection width,* defined as the minimum number of edges that must be removed to divide G into two parts, such that each part contains $n/2$ edges (if n is even) or one part contains one more edge than the other (if n is odd). A small bisection width can correspond to a dataflow bottleneck and so is undesirable. Calculate the bisection widths of the six graphs in Figure 7.11.

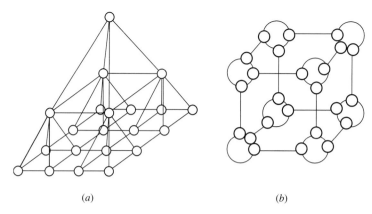

(a)   (b)

Figure 7.84
Two proposed interconnection structures for computers: (a) pyramid
and (b) cube-connected-cycles network.

7.3. A *pyramid* graph consists of a complete, quaternary (degree 4) rooted tree of k levels,
with extra links to make every level into a two-dimensional mesh. With the apex
(root) as level 1, each level k contains 4^{k-1} processors forming a $2^{k-1} \times 2^{k-1}$ mesh. A
three-level pyramid appears in Figure 7.84a. (a) Calculate the number of nodes, the
maximum node degree, and the maximum internode distance (diameter) in a k-level
pyramid. (b) A pyramid tries to combine the advantages of mesh and tree networks.
To what extent is it successful?

7.4. A *cube-connected-cycles* (CCC) graph is formed from a k-dimensional hypercube by
replacing each node x_i (which is of degree k) of the hypercube with a k-node ring or
cycle C_i. Each node of C_i is connected to a distinct edge of the d-member set originally
connected to x_i. A three-dimensional CCC graph appears in Figure 7.84b. (a) Calculate
the number of nodes, the maximum node degree, and the diameter of a k-dimensional
CCC graph. (b) To what extent is the CCC graph an improvement over the hypercube
as a computer interconnection structure?

7.5. Define each of the following terms in the context of bus design: handshaking, lock signal, master unit, skew, tristate, wait state.

7.6. Analyze the three bus-arbitration methods—daisy chaining, polling, and independent
requesting—with respect to communication reliability in the event of hardware failures.

7.7. Consider the timing diagram for a read operation over the PCI bus shown in Figure
7.25. (a) Draw a similar timing diagram to show a four-word read transfer occurring at
the maximum possible rate (burst mode). (b) Repeat this problem for a four-word
burst-mode write operation.

7.8. Intel designed the Multibus (IEEE Standard 796) as a standard system bus for microprocessor-based computers. It supports a heterogeneous set of 8- and 16-bit microprocessors in multiprocessing configurations. Figure 7.85 summarizes the 86 lines
(excluding 20 for power and ground) that make up the Multibus. (a) How large a memory address space is supported (without special logic)? (b) What types of IO addressing
are supported?

Signal type	Bus lines	Functions
Data and address	$\overline{DAT0{:}15}$	Data bus (16 lines)
	$\overline{ADR0{:}23}$	Address bus (24 lines)
Data-transfer control	$\overline{MRDC}$	Memory read enable
and handshaking	$\overline{IORC}$	IO read enable
	$\overline{MWTC}$	Memory write enable
	$\overline{IOWC}$	IO write enable
	$\overline{XACK}$	Acknowledge
Bus arbitration and	$\overline{BREQ}$	Bus request
timing	$\overline{CBRQ}$	Common bus request
	$\overline{BUSY}$	Bus busy
	$\overline{BCLK}$	Bus clock
	$\overline{BPRN}$	Bus priority in
	$\overline{BPRO}$	Bus priority out
Interrupt control	$\overline{INT0{:}7}$	Interrupt request (8 lines)
	$\overline{INTA}$	Interrupt acknowledge
Miscellaneous control	$\overline{CCLK}$	Master clock
	$\overline{INIT}$	System initialization
	$\overline{BHEN}$	Byte high enable
	$\overline{INH1{:}2}$	Inhibit memory (2 lines)
	$\overline{LOCK}$	Lock bus

Figure 7.85
Structure of the Multibus (IEEE 796) standard bus.

7.9. The Multibus (Figure 7.85) has a set of arbitration lines for transferring bus control among a set of potential master units. $\overline{BUSY}$ is activated ($\overline{BUSY} = 0$) by the current bus master, and this line prevents any other unit from becoming master until it is deactivated. When $\overline{BUSY} = 1$, a unit can gain control of the Multibus via the bus priority lines $\overline{BPRN}$ and $\overline{BPRO}$, which can be daisy-chained as shown in Figure 7.86. A potential master then requests control of the Multibus by deactivating its $\overline{BPRO}$ line, which prevents all lower-priority units from accessing the bus. The requesting unit takes control of the bus if its own $\overline{BPRN}$ line has not been deactivated by a higher-priority unit. Design a faster, parallel method for arbitration of the Multibus that uses

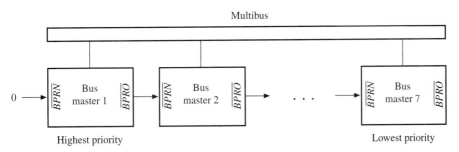

Figure 7.86
Some of the bus-arbitration logic in the Multibus.

only the existing control lines and a small amount of extra logic. Assume that up to eight potential bus masters can be present.

7.10. Compare and contrast the CSMA/CD and token-passing network-arbitration techniques from the viewpoints of response time, fairness, and fault tolerance.

7.11. A computer network's reliability is sometimes measured by its connectivity. The *node connectivity* $c_N(G)$ of network G is defined as the smallest number of nodes whose removal disconnects G, that is, eliminates all paths between at least two nodes, or else reduces G to the trivial 1-node 0-edge graph G_T. (*a*) What is the node connectivity of the ARPANET as it appears in Figure 1.31? (*b*) What is $c_N(G)$ when $G = K_n$, the complete graph of n nodes?

7.12. Another measure of the reliability of a network G (see the preceding problem) is its *edge connectivity* $c_E(G)$, defined as the smallest number of edges whose removal disconnects G or reduces it to G_T. If G has n nodes and m edges, then prove that $c_E(G) \leq \lfloor (2m)/n \rfloor$.

7.13. Define each of the following IO control methods: programmed IO, DMA controllers, IOPs. List the advantages and disadvantages of each method with respect to program-design complexity, IO bandwidth, and interface hardware costs.

7.14. Consider a 32-bit microprocessor with 32-bit data and address buses. The CPU clock frequency is 50 MHz, and a memory load or store instruction cycle takes two clock cycles. Memory-mapped IO is used, and the CPU supports both vectored interrupts and DMA block transfers with arbitrary block length. Typical interrupt response time is 15 CPU clock cycles. It is desired to add to the system a hard disk drive with a data-transfer rate of N bits/s. Estimate the maximum value that N can have for each of the following ways of controlling the disk drive: programmed IO and DMA. Show your calculations, and state all your assumptions.

7.15. (*a*) A typical CPU allows most interrupt requests to be enabled and disabled under software control. In contrast, no CPU provides facilities to disable DMA request signals. Explain why this is so. (*b*) Suppose you want to be able to occasionally delay a CPU's response to a DMA request until the end of the current instruction cycle. Design the necessary add-on logic to implement this type of delayed DMA request, assuming that a conventional one-chip CPU is being used whose internal hardware or instruction set cannot be modified. A pair of existing instructions should serve to turn on (enable) and turn off (disable) the DMA delay. State clearly all the assumptions underlying your design.

7.16. A CISC computer consists of a CPU and an IO device D connected to main memory M via a one-word shared bus. The CPU can execute a maximum of 10^6 instructions per second. An average instruction requires five machine cycles, three of which use the memory bus. A memory read or write operation uses one machine cycle. Suppose that the CPU is continuously executing "background" programs that require 90 percent of its instruction execution rate but no IO instructions. Now D is to be used to transfer very large blocks of data to and from M. (*a*) If programmed IO is used and each one-word IO transfer requires the CPU to execute two instructions, estimate the maximum IO data-transfer rate r_{MAX} possible through D. (*b*) Estimate r_{MAX} if DMA is used.

7.17. In addition to supporting memory-IO communication, some DMA controllers and IOPs also support block transfers from one region of main memory to another; that is, they perform memory-to-memory communication via DMA block transfers. (*a*) Explain how a main-memory block transfer can be implemented by an IOP such as the Intel 8089. Describe also the IO instructions needed to set up this type of operation. (*b*) What are the advantages and disadvantages of this type of main-memory block transfer compared with implementing the same data transfer by means of a BLOCK MOVE instruction, such as is found in some CPU instruction sets?

7.18. Often a new model of a microprocessor has instructions not found in older members of the same microprocessor family. The older microprocessors can, however, be updated by providing them with programs that implement the new instructions in software, a process called *emulation*. (Note the resemblance to emulation of instructions via microprograms.) Explain how an old microprocessor can use an interrupt mechanism to determine when a particular instruction should be emulated in this way, rather than be executed directly.

7.19. Consider the pipelined multiply and add instructions appearing in Figure 7.42. Suppose that the number of execution stages of multiply is increased from four to six (EX1:6) and the number of execution stages of add is increased from one to two (EX1:2). Consider execution of the following three-instruction code segment.

$$r1 := r4 \times r0;$$
$$r2 := r4 + r6; \qquad\qquad (7.31)$$
$$r3 := r2 \times r5;$$

(*a*) What is the minimum number of cycles to process this code with out-of-order completion allowed? (*b*) What is the minimum number of cycles to process this code with in-order completion? Include in your answers timing diagrams in the style of Figure 7.42.

7.20. Imprecise interrupts can be avoided without the performance penalty of in-order completion if a check is made in advance for interrupt-causing conditions. For example, floating-point multiply instructions only generate interrupts due to overflow or underflow. Overflow occurs only if the sum of the multiplier and multiplicand's exponents plus one exceeds the largest valid exponent value; a similar condition holds for underflow. The Pentium's floating-point logic contains special hardware to test for conditions of this sort. If the potential interrupt conditions are not present, fast, out-of-order execution is permitted in situations like that of Figure 7.42; otherwise, in-order execution is enforced. Suppose that in the preceding problem, the multiplier completes a test for potential interrupts in two clock cycles. What is the minimum number of cycles needed to process the code (7.31) when no potential interrupts are detected for multiply? Give a timing diagram for this case in the style of Figure 7.42.

7.21. Instructions such as store instructions that modify memory make it difficult to support precise interrupts in pipelined CPUs. Why is this so? Outline a design method to solve this problem.

7.22. What are the advantages of defining two distinct classes of software processes for system management: system (supervisor) processes and user processes? Describe the hardware features typically provided in a CPU to support this process dichotomy.

7.23. The following three-instruction program written in 80X86 assembly language is proposed for implementing the wait or test-and-set function for a binary semaphore S; all major actions of the instructions are specified by the comments. The CPU is connected via the Multibus (refer to Figure 7.85) to a global memory storing S. The Multibus $\overline{LOCK}$ signal is not activated unless the prefix LOCK precedes an instruction to which the signal is applicable.

WAIT: TEST S, 0   Fetch the variable S and compare to zero. Set the Z flag to 1 if S = 0 (not busy); otherwise, set the Z flag to 0.

        JNE WAIT   Jump to WAIT if Z = 1; otherwise, continue to next instruction.

        MOV S, 1   Set S to 1 (busy)

(a) Explain why this code fails to meet the mutual exclusion requirement for semaphore access. (b) Design a replacement program that solves this problem, using comments to explain your instructions. Indicate how exclusive access to S is ensured.

7.24. Consider the operating system state described by the resource allocation graph G of Figure 7.51. Let resource R_6 and the edges connected to it be removed from G to form a new graph G'. (a) Does G' contain a deadlock? (b) Suppose that P_3 and P_5 request access to R_3 in G'. Can these new requests lead to deadlock? (c) Suppose that P_1 and P_2 request access to a new resource R_7 added to G'. Can this lead to deadlock?

7.25. (a) Identify and briefly compare the mechanisms available for interprocess communication in the UNIX operating system. (b) What are the advantages and disadvantages of treating all IO devices as logical files in the manner of UNIX?

7.26. Redesign the parallel summation program of Figure 7.56 for execution by the binary tree computer whose structure appears in Figure 7.60d. Assume that $N = 2^{p-1}$ and that the N numbers to be added are stored in the leaf nodes initially. The final sum is to be stored in the topmost (root) node.

7.27. Classify under the headings (i) shared/distributed memory, and (ii) SIMD/MIMD/MISD, the following computers mentioned in this chapter: nCUBE 2, Sequent Symmetry, Tandem Himalaya. Identify each computer's interconnection structure type.

7.28. Let 30 be the degree of parallelism of a certain parallel computer C. Let f be the fraction of the operations performed by C that are strictly scalar (cannot be processed in parallel). Assume that all other operations are processed at the maximum possible (vector) rate. Let 20 be the speedup achieved by C for the tasks under consideration. (a) What is f? (b) By how much must f be changed to increase the speedup to 90 percent of the maximum possible?

7.29. Consider a vector supercomputer that processes vectors whose average length is N. The average setup time for vector operations is T_0, and the CPU (and pipeline) clock period is T_{clock}. Derive an expression for the efficiency E of the computer in terms of N, T_0, and T_{clock}.

7.30. It has been conjectured from observing real multiprocessors, that because of memory and bus conflicts, algorithm inefficiencies, and so on, the actual speedup $S(n)$ obtained when n identical processors are used to execute a single large program Q lies between $\log_2 n$ and $n/\log_e n$. Show that if we assume the probability of being able to assign Q to i processors is $1/i$, for $i = 1, 2, \ldots, n$, we obtain the upper bound $n/\log_e n$ on $S(n)$.

7.31. (a) Let s denote the fraction of time that must be spent on the serial parts of a program Q, and let p denote the fraction spent on the parallelizable parts of Q. Assuming that $s + p = 1$, show that Amdahl's law for the speedup $S(n)$ achievable by an n-processor computer executing Q can be reformulated as follows:

$$S(n) = \frac{1}{s + p/n}$$

(b) Amdahl's law makes the implicit assumption that p is independent of N. In practice, the problem size tends to increase with n; that is, problems expand to use the additional processors. This situation suggests that the time for a serial processor to execute Q should be represented by $s + pn$, given that it runs in time $s + p = 1$ on the parallel processor. With this assumption, derive an alternative expression for $S(n)$. Comment on its implications concerning the performance of massively parallel computers.

7.32. A useful measure of communication delay in static multiprocessor interconnection structures is the average distance d_{av} between all pairs of nodes (processors). Calculate d_{av} as a function of n for any three of the six structures listed in Figure 7.11.

7.33. A multiprocessor with two CPUs P_1 and P_2 employs the shared-bus multiprocessor organization (Figure 7.63) and the MESI cache-coherence protocol (Figure 7.65). Assume each local memory is an L1 cache. List the actions of P_1 and P_2 in response to each of the following situations, giving the final states of all affected cache blocks: (a) P_1 reads a word W_1 that is in its cache (a read hit). P_2 also has a copy of W_1, and both copies are marked S (shared). (b) P_1 writes to W_1 in its cache (a write hit). Again P_2 has a copy of W_1, and both copies are marked S. (c) P_1 writes to W_1, but now W_1 is not assigned to its cache (a write miss). However, P_2 has a cache copy of W_1 that is marked E (exclusive). (d) P_1 reads W_1, but W_1 is not assigned to its cache (a read miss). Once more, P_2 has a cache copy of W_1 that is marked E (exclusive).

7.34. Consider the MESI cache-coherence protocol as defined in Figure 7.65. Some of the indicated state transitions caused by regular or snoop hits and misses force a block transfer from global to local (cache) memory. Identify three such cases and briefly explain why the block transfer is needed.

7.35. The PowerPC Model 603, unlike the Model 601, employs a three-state cache coherence protocol called MEI, which is defined as a "coherent subset" of the MESI protocol that omits the S (shared) state. (a) Since the processors in a multiprocessor configuration of 603s still need to know whether their cache data is shared, suggest how the MEI protocol handles this issue. (b) Construct a state diagram similar to Figure 7.65 for the MEI protocol.

7.36. With Figure 7.66 as a guide, devise a general labeling procedure to embed a two-dimensional mesh of size $n_1 \times n_2$ in an n-dimensional hypercube for some n. Illustrate your method by using it to embed a 4×4 mesh in a four-dimensional hypercube.

7.37. (a) Show by construction that for sufficiently large n, it is possible to embed a k-node cycle (ring), where k is even, in an n-dimensional hypercube graph. (b) Show that no matter how large n is, it is impossible to embed the pyramid graph of Figure 7.84a, or any larger pyramid, in a hypercube.

7.38. A multiprocessor node must sometimes send a message to more than one other processor, a task referred to as *broadcasting*. Suppose that a node P_0 in an n-dimensional hypercube system has to broadcast a message to all $2^n - 1$ other processors. The broadcasting is subject to the constraints that the message can be forwarded (retransmitted) by a node only to a neighboring node and that each node can transmit only one message at a time. Assume that each message transmission between adjacent nodes requires one time unit. In a two-dimensional system, for example, P_0 could broadcast a message MESS as follows: At time $t = 0$, P_0 sends MESS to P_1. At $t = 1$, P_0 sends MESS to P_2 and P_1 sends MESS to P_3, thus completing the broadcast in two time units. Construct a general broadcasting algorithm for the n-dimensional case that allows a message to reach all nodes in n time units. Specify clearly the algorithm used by each node to determine the neighboring nodes to which it should forward an incoming message.

7.39. Figure 7.87 shows a three-stage version N of an indirect hypercube MIN. (a) Suppose the four switching elements $S_{1,2}, S_{2,2}, S_{3,2}, S_{4,2}$ forming stage 2 are set to the X state, while the eight remaining switches are set to the T state. Show that these switch settings simultaneously connect the output of P_{ijk} to the input of $P_{\bar{i}jk}$ for all i,j,k. (b) Determine the switch settings needed to connect P_{ijk} to $P_{i\bar{j}k}$ for all i,j,k, and also the settings needed to connect P_{ijk} to $P_{ij\bar{k}}$ for all i,j,k. (c) Explain why N is called a hypercube network.

7.40. Construct a diagram for a four-stage 16×16 omega network in the same style as Figure 7.74. Show the switch settings required to connect input port 3 to output port 12.

7.41. The through (T) and cross (X) states of the switching element S of Figure 7.68 can be augmented by the two additional states defined in Figure 7.88. These are termed the

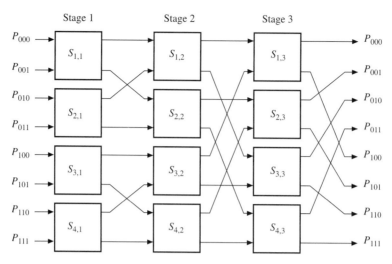

Figure 7.87
Three-stage indirect hypercube network.

upper (U) and lower (L) broadcast states because they allow an incoming message to be sent to both output ports simultaneously. Show that if the two-state switch S of Figure 7.68 is replaced by the four-state switch S', then an $N \times N$ omega network has a state that allows data on any of its input ports to be broadcast directly to any subset of its output ports.

7.42. Show that deleting the final stage of an $N \times N$ omega network with $n = \log_2 N$ stages destroys its full-access property.

7.43. A MIN linking a set of processors is said to provide *dynamic full access* if any processor P_i can be connected to any other processor P_j by a finite number of passes through the MIN, where any intermediate processors visited act as store-and-forward stations. Clearly a full-access network can link any processor-pair in a single pass. (*a*) Show that if stage 3 is deleted from the MIN of Figure 7.87 the resulting two-stage MIN has the dynamic full-access property but not the full-access property. (*b*) Is dynamic full-access retained after deleting two stages from this MIN? Justify your answer.

7.44. Determine whether or not the 4×4 switching element used in the BBN Butterfly computer has the full-access and nonblocking properties.

7.45. A computer series has a mean failure rate of one fault in 5 years; this rate remains fairly constant over a normal 10-year life. If a customer purchases a new computer of this type, what is the probability that at least one fault will occur by the end of the first year?

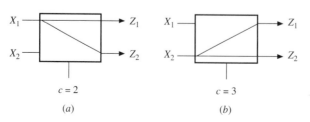

Figure 7.88
Extended switching elements: (*a*) upper broadcast state U; and (*b*) lower broadcast state L.

7.46. A certain computer part is assumed to follow the exponential failure law. The probability that it does not survive more than 50 days is 0.92. How often can one expect to have to replace this particular part?

7.47. Let $F(t)$ be the unreliability function for a certain class of components. The *hazard function* $z(t)$, which is interpreted as the instantaneous failure rate, is defined by

$$z(t) = \frac{f(t)}{1 - F(t)} \text{ where } f(t) = \frac{dF(t)}{dt}$$

Suppose that $f(t) = 0.25 - 0.03125t$, where t is measured in years. Calculate the reliability function $R(t)$, the hazard function $z(t)$, and the mean time to failure (MTTF) for these components.

7.48. (*a*) A system is constructed by connecting n copies of a unit U in parallel. If the reliability of U is 0.8, how many copies of U are needed in order for the system reliability to be (*i*) at least 0.9, and (*ii*) at least 0.999? (*b*) A certain server crashes about once every three days. It takes an average of 3.5 hours to restore normal operation. What are the system's availability and MTTF?

7.49. A variant of TMR called *TMR/Simplex* has triplicated units and a match circuit to identify the failed unit when the first failure occurs. The system begins operation as a TMR configuration. When the first failure is detected, the system structure is changed from TMR to simplex using one of the two correctly working units. Normal operation then continues until the simplex configuration fails. If the reliability of each unit is $e^{-\lambda t}$ and the voter and match circuit are perfectly reliable, calculate the reliability and MTTF of the TMR/Simplex system.

7.50. Consider the 14×4 torus that forms the interconnection network linking nodes (sections) in the Tandem Himalaya computer. Determine each of the following parameters for this network: (*a*) the diameter of the network; (*b*) the minimum number of edges needed to break the network into two disconnected parts; (*c*) the minimum number of edges needed to break it into two disconnected parts, each having the same number of nodes (this is the bisection width).

7.6
REFERENCES

1. Anderson, D. and T. Shanley. *Pentium Processor System Architecture*. 2nd ed. Reading, MA: Addison-Wesley, 1995.

2. Avizienis, A. "Fault Tolerant Computing—An Overview." *IEEE Computer,* vol. 4 (January/February 1971) pp. 5–8.

3. Chen, P. M. et al. "RAID: High-Performance, Reliable Secondary Storage." *ACM Computing Surveys,* vol. 26 (June 1994) pp. 145–85.

4. Crowther, W. et al. "The Butterfly Parallel Processor." *IEEE Computer Architecture Newsletter* (September/December 1985) pp. 18–45.

5. El-Ayat, K. A. "The Intel 8089: An Integrated IO Processor." *IEEE Computer,* vol. 12 (June 1979) pp. 67–78.

6. Feng, T. Y. "A Survey of Interconnection Networks." *IEEE Computer,* vol. 14 (December 1981) pp. 12–27.

7. Flynn, M. J. "Very High-Speed Computing Systems." *Proceedings of the IEEE,* vol. 54 (December 1966) pp. 1901–09.

8. Gustavson, D. B. "Computer Buses—A Tutorial." *IEEE Micro,* vol. 4 (August 1984) pp. 7–22.

9. Hayes, J. P. and T. N. Mudge. "Hypercube Computers." *Proceedings of the IEEE,* vol. 77 (December 1989) pp. 1829–41.

10. Hwang, K. *Advanced Computer Architecture*. New York: McGraw-Hill, 1993.

11. IBM Corp. *IBM System/370 Principles of Operation*. White Plains, NY: IBM, 1974.

12. Intel Corp. *Peripheral Components*. Santa Clara, CA, 1993.

13. Intel Corp. *i960 RP I/O Processor*. Santa Clara, CA, 1996.

14. Kong, C. "A Hardware Overview of the NonStop Himalaya K10000 Server." *Tandem Systems Review,* vol. 10 (January 1994).

15. Motorola Inc. *PowerPC 603 RISC Microprocessor User's Manual*. Phoenix, AZ, 1994. (Also published by IBM Microelectronics, Essex Junction, VT, 1994.)

16. Moudgill, M. and S. Vassilliadis. "Precise Interrupts." *IEEE Micro,* vol. 16 (February 1996) pp. 58–87.

17. nCUBE Corp. *nCUBE 2 Supercomputers*. Beaverton, OR, 1990.

18. Quinn, M. J. *Parallel Computing: Theory and Practice*. 2nd ed. New York: McGraw-Hill, 1994.

19. Sequent Computer Systems Inc. *Symmetry 5000 Series*. Beaverton, OR, 1996.

20. Shanley, T. and D. Anderson. *PCI System Architecture*. 3rd ed. Reading, MA: Addison-Wesley, 1995.

21. Siegel, H. J. *Interconnection Networks for Large-Scale Parallel Processing*. 2nd ed. New York: McGraw-Hill, 1990.

22. Siewiorek, D. P. and R. S. Swarz (eds.). *Reliable Computer Systems*. 2nd ed. Burlington, MA: Digital Press, 1992.

23. Silberschatz, A. and P. B. Galvin. *Operating System Concepts*. 4th ed. Reading, MA: Addison-Wesley, 1994.

24. Simonds, F. *McGraw-Hill LAN Communications Handbook*. New York: McGraw-Hill, 1994.

25. Southerton, A. *Modern UNIX*. New York: John Wiley and Sons, 1993.

26. Stenström, P. "A Survey of Cache Coherence Schemes for Multiprocessors." *IEEE Computer,* vol. 23 (June 1990) pp. 12–24.

27. Thurber, K. J. et al. "A Systematic Approach to the Design of Digital Bussing Structures." *AFIPS Conference Proceedings,* vol. 41 (1972) pp. 719–40.

28. Triebel, W. A. and A. Singh. *The 68000 and 68020 Microprocessors*. Englewood Cliffs, NJ: Prentice-Hall, 1991.

Index